Dwarakanatha

The Lord of Dwaraka

May Lord Ganesha bless and help me to write this book without a hitch

Aum Mahapurushaaya vidmahe,
Vaktratundaaya dimahi,
Tanno Dhanti prajodayaath

The Lord of Dwaraka

Narrated by

Vanamali

DWARAKANATHA: The Lord of Dwaraka

ISBN: 978-81-7305-560-7

Published in **2016** by

Aryan Books International

Pooja Apartments, 4B, Ansari Road, New Delhi-110 002 (India)

Tel.: 23287589, 23255799; Fax: 91-11-23270385

E-mail: aryanbooks@gmail.com

www.aryanbooks.co.in

Designed and Printed in India by

ABI Prints & Publishing Co., New Delhi.

Sri Krishnaaya Paramatmane Namaha!

This book is dedicated to my beloved daughter-in-law,

SUMATI

Whose name is a mirror of her soul.

ॐ

Dwarakanathaya Namaha!

Foreword

For long philosophers, skeptics and devotees are divided on the idea of the 'harikatha' as a genuine source of spiritual commentary and discourse. While some label it as myth, legend or simply a story, others at best hail it as classic literature. The charitable ones among skeptics label the pastimes of Krishna as parables. For the faithful, it is absolute perfect fact and a history that transcends time.

All are, in fact, right within their own field of vision. The Krishna stories have been narrated, retold, sung, painted, enacted and presented by all – the agnostics, the atheists, the literary and creative minded and the devotees alike. The thin line between creative freedom, scriptural sincerity, social correctness and aesthetics of literature remains hazy from a neutral viewpoint but it is always well defined when looked at through viewpoints of each stand individually. From the absolute level, that is, through the eyes of God, it is an equidistant approach. However, any rendition that stirs an understanding or love of God is valid and right.

This book has a mix of them all. It is a dramatized narration of Krishna's kingly pastimes at Dwarka which the author visualizes in a dream world. Despite being a flight of creative liberty, it hovers around the scriptural story line, like a butterfly fluttering over flowers of different hues. It thus leaves the reader to his or her own take on the profound subject.

Everything about Krishna has been narrated and recorded by Vyas Dev, expounded by great sages and all spiritual masters and holy men are agreed on it. About five centuries ago, Chaitanya Mahaprabhu explained that the intricacy of the 'krishnakatha' can be understood not by literary excellence or erudition but by humility and devotion. The pastimes of Krishna are not a material novel, penned by someone expert in wordplay or poetry. However, that doesn't bar a retelling since freedom and choice is the first prerequisite of spiritual life.

Krishna's pastimes in Dwarka form the latter part of his 'leela' when he was known as 'Dwarkadhish' or 'Dwarkanath'. Dwarka is a historical city. It is an important pilgrim centre, it is an archaeologist's playground for research and exploration and it is the site where great stories unveiled. It was a great port and is the subject of much oceanographic research today. Some purists delight in the fact that excavations and explorations beneath the sea point towards a thriving metropolis in ancient times – as if that was the proof of Krishna's existence and presence.

Opinions and agendas of Indologists, historians and lovers of folklore and scriptural purity will always vary. That dilemma should be set aside for once, if only to enjoy the book. The success of a book on fictionalized history or dramatized narrative is a difficult task.

This book is an attempt to walk the narrow path between both though it is based on the 'sahajiya' sentiment of proximity to God. While an assumption of special favour from God is frowned upon, it does not take away the strength of the original story and sentiment. Its appeal will rest in as much and how the reader will relate to the sincerity and the motivation of a retelling of the story of Dwarkanath – the king of Dwarka.

Bhaktiyog Swami
Madhuban Ashram
Hrishkesh

Dwarakanathaya Namaha!

Contents

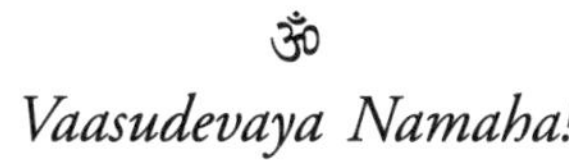

Vaasudevaya Namaha!

List of Illustrations

All Illustrations including jacket cover have been done by Anjali Kamat.

Jacket: The Lord of Dwarka standing in the sea in front of the Golden City of Dwaraka.

Aum Namo Bhagavate Vaasudevaaya

ॐ

Sri Krishnaaya Paramatmane Namaha!

INTRODUCTION

Dwarakanatha
The Lord of Dwaraka

THE HISTORICAL CITY

The famous temple called Dwarakadish, dedicated to Lord Krishna, the king of Dwaraka, is found in the city called Dwaraka on the west coast of India in the state of Gujarat. It is considered to be one of the seven Holy Cities of India. The others are Ayodhya, Mathura, Haridwar, Varanasi, Kanchipuram and Ujjain. According to tradition, the original temple of Dwarakadish was built by Krishna's great-grandson, Vajranabha, over the ruins of Lord Krishna's own palace, which was the only building that was not washed away by the tsunami.

However, the ancient, famed city of Dwaraka existed five thousand years ago during the time of the Krishnavatara. It is no more to be seen now since it lies at the bottom of the sea. Dwaraka's majesty and beauty have been described by many poets and writers, saints and sages of ancient India. It is referred to as Golden City in the Srimad Bhagavatam, Skanda Purana, Vishnu Purana, Harivamsha and the Mahabharata. One of the verses in the Bhagavatam says: "The yellow glitter of the golden fort of the Dwaraka City in the sea, throwing yellow light all round, looked as if the flames of Vadavagni (the fire of eternity) came out, tearing asunder the sea."

It was a bustling port and had an island close by which also served as a harbour. If the number, size and variety of stone anchors are any indication of the size of the port, it can be said that Dwaraka must have been the largest port of the third millennium B.C. on the Indian Coast. As many as 50 stone anchors are still visible. But several hundred must have been buried in the sediment. This was probably one of the reasons why the city got its name. "Dwara" means gate in Sanskrit and the port of Dwaraka was perhaps the gate which enabled the ancient sea-faring cities of the west to enter the great subcontinent of India.

The Sanskrit word 'Ka' also stands for Brahma so perhaps it was a city dedicated to Brahma, the creator in the trinity.

Mathura had been the capital of the Surasenas (one of the clans of the Yadavas), but it was fully exposed and could not defend itself from the continued attacks of King Jarasandha of Magadha. Krishna decided that his clan would have to shift if they wanted a peaceful life without the threat of constant attacks from enemies. By a series of forced marches, he took all his people to the west coast of India to the ancient city of Kushasthali (Gujarat), which had the sea as one of its boundaries, and decided that it was best suited for their needs. He then proceeded to reclaim land from the ocean. There he built a wonderful city called Dwaravati. His kingdom included many of the islands along the shore as well as the Anarta kingdom of the mainland. This is the Dwaraka about which mention has been made in all our Puranas. There are many stories written about Krishna's early life in Gokulam and Vrindavana, but very little about his sojourn in Dwaraka, even though this is the place he spent the major portion of his life.

He had foretold that the part which had been reclaimed would return to the sea seven days after his departure from this planet and that is exactly what happened. The ocean has hidden its secrets well, and for many years the descriptions of the famed Dwaraka were thought to be only a myth and not based on anything real.

However, in the 20th century, archaeological and astronomical studies, as well as many maritime explorations, have established the historicity of the city of Dwaraka and have helped to date many of the events narrated in the epic, Mahabharata. They have also helped to bring to light the history of ancient India. These have led to the conclusion that the Mahabharata War was actually fought in 3126 BCE and that the city of Dwaraka was submerged in the sea 36 years later.

Underwater explorations also unearthed the remains of a city which has been dated to have existed 21000 years ago. Six other cities had been built over this and Lord Krishna's Dwaraka was the last. Archaeological excavations in more than ten thousand sites scattered over major parts of India prove beyond doubt the existence of a flourishing culture now known as the Indus civilization during 3400 BC to 1500 BC. This proves that the cradle of human civilization is not Sumeria in Mesopotamia as western scholars believe, but the Sapta Sindhu, the land of the seven rivers, in northwest India. From the densely populated Sapta Sindhu, our ancestors, the Vedic Aryans travelled from India to various parts of Asia and Europe and spread the knowledge of the Vedic civilization and the Sanskrit language. Sanskrit-speaking people migrated to Iran, Greece, and further west.

The Vedic culture which has come to be known as Hinduism is the oldest religion in the world. The real name of this religion is the Sanatana Dharma (the ancient way of righteousness). It was born and nurtured on the soil of this holy land of Aryavrata or Bharatavarsha. Unfortunately our history books, which have been written by western scholars, say that a tribe of people known as the Aryans came to India from Central Asia in their war chariots in the 15th century BC. According to this fictitious theory, both the Vedas and the Sanskrit language were brought into India by these Aryan invaders. The most influential proponents of this theory were Max Mueller, the famous German Indologist and William Jones who was also a linguist. They arrived at this brilliant conclusion since they were struck by the affinities between Sanskrit and the European languages, not realising that the exodus of Sanskrit as well as so much other mathematical and scientific information went from India to the west and not vice versa. That is how the European languages had their basis in Sanskrit and not the other way round as Max Muller and William Jones would have us believe. The fact is that both these Indologists had a secret desire to undermine the faith of this country and impose Christianity on the so-called heathens! It is a well- known fact that history written by the conquerors always records the view point of the conqueror, and is an attempt to prove the superiority of their own culture and the inferiority of the culture of the country they have subjugated.

Max Muller wrote in a letter to his wife, "My translation of the Vedas will affect the fate of India and the growth of millions of souls in that country. It is the root of their religion and to show them what the root is, I feel, the only way of uprooting all that has sprung from it during the last 3,000 years."

In fabricating a date for the so-called Aryan Invasion, Muller was strongly influenced by the Christian belief that the creation of the world had taken place at 9 am on 23rd October, 4004 BC. Assuming this date to be true for the creation of the world, as Muller did, leads us to the conclusion that the Biblical flood came in the year 2248. If another thousand years are allowed for the waters to subside and the soil to get dry enough for the Aryans to begin their invasion of India, we are left with 1400 BC. Adding another two hundred years before they could begin composing the Rig Veda brings us right up to Muller's date of 1200 BC of the composition of the Rig Veda!! How objective can you get!

David Frawley, truly a great lover of the Veda, says, "Max Muller, with his hidden agenda, lifted metaphorical passages from the Rig Veda to buttress his 'Aryan-invasion-from-Europe' theory. The literary evidence taken in its entirety shows that the Vedic civilization was an indigenous development."

Monier Williams, in a speech given at Oxford to the Missionary Congress on 2nd May, 1877, said, "When the walls of the mighty fortress of Brahmanism are encircled, undermined and finally stormed by the soldiers of the cross, the victory of Christianity must be signal and complete!!" These are the people who were supposed to be objective scholars!

These so-called Indologists also proclaimed that the Aryans defeated the Dravidians who were the original inhabitants of the continent. Modern research has proved that there was neither an Aryan invasion nor a conflict between the Aryans and Dravidians. The term "*arya*" means noble and good. It refers to a quality of behaviour and not of a race. Likewise the word "*dasyu*" which was used to refer to the Dravidians, means misconduct and does not denote a race. The arguments over a separate Dravidian language have also been solved by our own scholars. They have identified some twenty Dravidian words in the Rig Veda and the so-called Dravidian language has borrowed at least fifty percent of its vocabulary from Sanskrit. Many Dravidian scholars credit the creation of Tamil, the oldest Dravidian tongue, to the great sage, Agastya who figures in the Rig Veda as one of the prominent sages of his era. The Dravidian kings have always referred to themselves as Aryans and have traced their descent from Manu. Shiva clearly is the Vedic god, Rudra. Sanskrit has been shown to include some elements from the language of the tribes called Munda. All three languages are indigenous developments. Thus north and south India share a common culture and religion. The whole of India is irrevocably bound together by our common heritage which is the Vedic culture.

When the ruins of the great Indus Valley civilization were discovered, the proponents of the Aryan invasion theory suggested that the invading Aryans had defeated the Dravidian inhabitants of the Indus valley, thus suggesting that the invading Aryans, instead of being the bringers of civilization to the poor barbarians as they had been trying to prove, were instead the destroyers of a great civilisation and culture developed by the native Indians! Moreover, had such an exodus existed it would surely have found mention in the Vedas themselves, which are a vast store-house of information about everything we can think of. They could never have failed to record such an important event. Unfortunately, our history books which are still being used in Indian schools have not yet removed this bit of false information from their texts.

Luckily with modern equipment, the science of Archaeology has been able to prove the truth of the Vedic culture as being totally indigenous, having existed in an unbroken line from the ancient Indus Valley Civilization to the present day. Sri Rajaram records a continuous and original development of the great Vedic civilization going right back to 5000 BC at sites like Mehrgarh and Koldi. He gives a chronological account of this ancient civilization as beginning with the Mehrgarh site in the NW around 6,500 BC. This is the largest urban site of that period known in the world. There is evidence of the domestication of animals, the existence of agriculture, as well as arts and crafts. Mergarh, Harappa and Mohenjadaro bordered the great Saraswati River and made up what is now known as the Indus Valley civilization. The river had more than five hundred sites along its banks. By the time of the Mahabharata, the Saraswati had lost its chief tributary, the Yamuna because of a tectonic plate shift. This was the beginning of the Kali Yuga, 3000 BC. In 1900 BC another tectonic plate shift made the Saraswati lose its next big tributary, the Sutlej. This dried up the river which was the artery of the civilization and caused a massive exodus of the people to the Gangetic plains in the east, whence arose the classical period of Indian civilization. There was another exodus towards the west. These people carried their knowledge of Sanskrit and mathematics and other sciences with them and that is why so many Sanskrit words are found in the European languages. It is said that the first Egyptian king was from India. That is why they worshipped the sun and declared that their kings come from the sun (Surya Vamsa). So much of our history has been buried by the sands of time that even now it is doubtful whether we know even a fraction of our ancient culture. Detailed factual data has been given in our ancient texts and Sanskrit manuscripts, which have been totally ignored by the western scholars. It is only now that the Indian scholars have woken up to the fact that all the proof that they would ever need is to be found in our scriptures themselves. The Mahabharata mentions the names of countless kings and warriors who had come to Kurukshetra to participate in the war. All of them were born and brought up on the soil of India and came from kingdoms that had experienced thousands of years of prosperous and advanced civilisation.

Modern scientific techniques like computers with planetarium software, advancements in archaeological and marine-archaeological techniques, earth-sensing satellite photography and thermo-luminescent dating methods, all have made it possible to establish the authenticity of all that has been said in our Puranas, and also helped in dating many events narrated in the Mahabharata. One of the great advantages of discovering Dwaraka was that the city had not been built upon over and over again as has been done to the temples and cities on land. It still lies in its pristine beauty, as it was when Lord Krishna built it, except for the ravages of the water itself and not through desecration by human hands as we find in Mathura, Vrindavan, and even on the mainland near the present temple of Dwarkadhish.

The on-shore and off-shore explorations carried out in and around Dwaraka during last 50 years have revealed that Dwaraka was a prosperous city in ancient times. The work of great excavators like Sri Z.D. Ansari and Sri M.S. Mate and the chance discovery of temples of the 9th and 1st century AD, which were excavated near the present Dwarkadhish Temple in present day Dwaraka, prompted the Marine Archaeology Centre to work jointly with the National Institute of Oceanography (NIO) and Archaeological Survey of India (ASI) to unearth further material. A project for marine archaeological explorations in Dwaraka was initiated under the dynamic leadership of the great marine archaeologist Dr. S.R. Rao who has the distinction of being awarded "The World Ship Trust Award" for outstanding research done in this field.

Dr. S.R. Rao's team consisted of expert underwater explorers, trained diver-photographers and experienced archaeologists. The technique of geophysical survey was combined with the use of echo-sounders, mud-penetrators, sub-bottom profilers and underwater metal detectors. This team carried out twelve marine archaeological expeditions between the years 1983 to 1992 AD and discovered many articles and antiquities which were sent to the Physical Research Laboratory for dating. By using thermo-luminescence, carbon dating and other modern scientific techniques, these artefacts were found to belong to the period starting from the 15th century to the 18th century BC. In his great work "The Lost City of Dwaraka", Dr. S.R. Rao has given graphic and scientific details of these discoveries and artefacts. He has concluded that the land for building the city of Dwaraka had been reclaimed from the sea between 16th to 15th century BC and a fortified city had been built using the technique known as boulder packing. The city had an outer gateway to the sea and an inner gateway to the Gomati River. This corroborates the references in the Mahabharata that the city of Dwaraka was built by Lord Krishna after reclaiming the land from the sea.

The importance of the discovery of Dwaraka lies not merely in providing archaeological evidence needed for corroborating the traditional account of the submergence of Dwaraka, but also indirectly fixing the date of the life of Lord Krishna and that of the Mahabharata. Pottery found at the archaeological site bears resemblance to pottery found at another site (Bet Dwaraka) off the coast of present day Dwaraka, which dates to around 3500 years BC.

It has been found out that around 2500 BC, the whole Western coast of India disappeared along with Lord Krishna's capital city of Dwaraka. In fact Krishna had prophesied that the sea would reclaim the city seven days after his departure from this planet. Arjuna was a witness to this terrifying tsunami and Vyasa describes this in the Mahabharata, through the mouth of Arjuna: "The sea, which had been beating against the shore, suddenly broke the boundary that was imposed on it by human hands. It rushed into the City of Dwaraka. It coursed through the streets of the beautiful city. The waters covered up everything in the city. I saw the beautiful buildings becoming submerged one by one. In a matter of a few moments it was all over. The sea had now become as placid as a lake. There was no trace of the city. Dwaraka became just a name – a beautiful memory!"

ASTRONOMICAL EVIDENCE

The Mahabharata refers to three sequential solar and lunar eclipses which have been corroborated by modern planetarium software and found to be consistent with their own research. Reference to the first solar eclipse comes in the Sabha Parva (79.29) of the Mahabharata, graphically described by the great sage Vidura. It took place just before the Pandavas started on their journey to the forest after having been banished to twelve years of exile and one year of remaining incognito in a known city. The exile was imposed on them after they had lost everything in the game of dice which had been forced upon them by Duryodhana. After having successfully completed their exile, the Pandavas came back to Hastinapura and demanded their kingdom back, but Duryodhana refused. Several efforts at reconciliation failed and Duryodhana declared war.

The reference to the second solar eclipse is in the Bhisma Parva (3.29) of the Mahabharata, following a lunar eclipse which occurred within the same fortnight. This took place fifteen years after the one mentioned by Vidura, after the Pandavas had returned from their exile. It occurred just before the commencement of the Mahabharata war. The epic also refers to some unfavourable planetary positions between the second solar eclipse and the beginning of the war on Kartika Purnima (Bhisma Parva 3.14 to 3.19).

On Kartika Krishna Ashtami, Saturn was near Rohini and Mars was between Jyesta and Anuradha. Twenty-two days later, on Kartika Purnima, Saturn was near Rohini, Mars was near Jyesta and a rough planet (probably Uranus) was between Chitra and Swati. Another white planet (possibly Jupiter) had moved from Purva-bhadra to Uttara-bhadra. All these pointed to some great calamity which would soon occur, in this case the Mahabharata War.

The final reference to the third solar eclipse comes in the Mausala Parva (2.19 to 2.20) and took place thirty-six years after the great Mahabharata War. This was visible from the city of Dwaraka and was felt to be a premonition of some dire disaster. For these observations to be consistent there should have been three solar eclipses within a period of 50 years. The first one and the second one after a gap of 14-15 years should have been visible from Kurukshetra, whereas the third solar eclipse should have been visible from Dwaraka, 36 years after the second one.

The planetarium software showed that all these predictions were absolutely true and all these eclipses were forebodings of some dreadful disasters which were to take place.

These are the actual words used in the Mahabharata: "Day by day strong winds blew. Earthen pots showed cracks or broke for no apparent cause. Society became corrupt. The day of the new moon coincided with the thirteenth (and the fourteenth) lunation. The fourteenth lunation has been made the fifteenth by the planet Rahu once more. Such a day had happened at the time of the great battle of the Bharatas. (Kurukshetra War). It has once more appeared. After that war 36 years had passed. The messengers proclaimed at the command of Vaasudeva Krishna that the Vrishnis (another tribe of the Yadavas) should make a journey to the seacoast for bathing in the sacred waters of the ocean (16.2)."

KRISHNA! MAN OR GOD?

Now that we have a fairly clear picture of the city of Dwaraka, let us have a look at the personality of the Lord of Dwaraka – Dwarakanatha. For thousands of years, Indians have believed in the divinity of Sri Krishna. But questions have constantly haunted us as to whether Sri Krishna was a historical character or a mythical one and whether the history of India and the story of Krishna and the Pandavas as given in the Mahabharata actually took place or were only figments of Vyasa's fertile imagination. Of course the British took pains to show us that this was indeed so and that the Indians had no history of their own and all our Puranas were only myths. Unfortunately the intelligentsia of our country were happy to believe this and all the history taught in Indian schools even today is meant to put down our ancient culture. The finding of the great city of Dwaraka however is a great break-through and has conclusively proved the historicity of Krishna.

The multi-faceted personality of Krishna Vaasudeva defies all attempts at cutting him down to fit our particular idea of how a human being should look and behave. He is a unique figure and therefore he can never be made to fit into any of the niches in which the human mind loves to categorise people. The wonder is that such a mighty being lived centuries before modern civilization as we know existed. Actually he belongs to the future and not to the past. We still have not reached the heights of his intelligence or powers even though he lived long before us. Of course it is true to say that all those who have made a mark in this world have come ahead of their time, but Krishna was too far ahead. That is why he was not fully understood in his own time and not even in these times. Hopefully there will come a time when he will be fully understood and appreciated.

Krishna is a unique personality. His life accepts no limitations. He was not bound by any rules of conduct. If anyone can be said to have been totally free, it is only Krishna. There was no ground he did not tread, no point where his steps faltered and no limits he did not transcend. This freedom is the ultimate fruit of enlightenment. A truly spiritual person, a *sthitha prajna,* as he calls such a person in the Bhagavat Gita, should unreservedly accept all the dimensions of life. Such a person should be above the dualities of existence and accept all the facets of life, love and hate, sex and abstinence, violence and non-violence, action and meditation as well as asceticism and indulgence. Krishna lived in this world of dualities as the lotus leaf in water, absolutely untouched and unaffected by the environment, like an actor who participates in everything with enthusiasm, but always knows that he is only playing a part. When we look at the life of all the great religious leaders of the world, we find that this type of acceptance is not found in any of them. If you want to ascend to the heights you have to descend to the abyss first. The tallest tree is the one whose roots go deepest into the earth. The entire structure of our lives is held together by the tension of opposites and war is a part of the tension of life. An unbiased examination of the development of our civilization will lead us to admit that war has played the largest share in its growth. All our scientific inventions and technology owe their existence to the fact that we are always preparing for war. We can afford to be lazy and lethargic in times of peace but not so during war. It is an unfortunate fact of life that when confronted with the challenge of war, man's mind begins to function at its highest level. It is only Krishna who accepts all these opposites. He alone can be whole who is prepared to accept the whole which includes all contradictions.

It is not true to say that Krishna supports war, but that he accepts it as part of the game of life. He says it is good to avoid war but if it becomes unavoidable then it is better to accept it bravely and joyfully rather than run away from it. War and peace are two sides of the coin of life. Warmongers like Genghis Khan, Hitler and Alexander accepted only one side of the coin and believed that war was the only way of life. Pacifists like Mahavira, Buddha, Christ and Gandhiji on the other hand chose the other side of the coin of truth. Both these types are easy enough to understand but Krishna is different from either of these. He says that life has to pass through the door of peace as well as through the door of war. If a person wants to maintain peace, he needs to have the strength and ability to fight a war. Whether he wins or loses is immaterial but he should have the strength to face it, if called upon to do so.

Karma Yoga or the technique of action, which he gives to his friend Arjuna in the Bhagavat Gita, tells us how to face every situation in such a way that we are not bound by the effects of the action. Actually this technique is based on the simple law of motion in physics which declares that every action has its equal and opposite reaction. In the human being, it's not the action as such which determines the reaction but the motivation. A thief may cut off the hand of a person in order to steal the bangles or rings that the hand is wearing and a surgeon may amputate a gangrenous hand in order to save the life of the patient. Both are violent actions but we can easily see what reactions will be created by each action. One will release and the other bind!

Goodness suffers from a basic weakness. It wants to avoid any type of conflict regardless of the consequences. This type of personality is portrayed in the Mahabharata by Yudhishtira who was such a good man that he wanted to avoid war at all cost. For the past couple of centuries India has been ruled by such "good men" who were responsible for weakening us to such an extent that we were continuously battered and bruised by powerful enemies who preyed upon our weakness and plundered and looted and tore us apart. Of course it is true that some countries invade others but it is also true that some people invite invasion. You are not only responsible when you hit others, but you are also responsible when others hit you. If you hit someone only fifty percent of the responsibility is yours, the other fifty goes to the person who invited your slap and took it passively by turning the other cheek! Bullies are created by the meek and the mild! It is indeed ironic that the Christian ideals of meekness and mildness have always been practiced by the Hindus. The Christians on the other hand, except for a handful of martyrs, have never practiced it. In fact they have no concept of such a life. The greatest proof of this is that all the world wars starting from the Crusades have been started and fought by the great Christian nations. Actually India is the only country which has never invaded any country or started a provocative war!

The world is facing a situation similar to that which occurred during the Mahabharata War. At that time there were two camps – one which was totally materialistic and did not accept anything beyond the body or matter. They had no idea of *yoga* or spiritual discipline. The scenario now is a bit different. On one side are arrayed the forces which stand for the advance of civilization, taking into account all the known moral standards as given by most religions. On the other side is a force which thinks itself to be totally right and thinks of God as being full of compassion, yet is willing to kill those who do not believe in that God. They will stop at nothing to enforce their beliefs on the whole world. Their beliefs are coloured by some other standard of intellectual integrity totally at variance with modern norms. Krishna is of an entirely different type. Nobody and nothing could get the better of him. He was always the master of every situation and never the victim. History has always shown that if we cannot understand someone who tries to change us, we either kill him or deify him. In Krishna's case it was impossible to kill him and so he was deified even in his lifetime. In the galaxy of spiritual luminaries which the world has produced, Krishna is the only one who fully accepted life in its totality and did not believe that we are living here for the sake of another world. Most religions ask us to abstain from all pleasures, telling us that god and nature are two totally different things and therefore anyone who wants to find god has to shun nature. The Nature that they knew in those times was harsh and cruel. Life used to be very hard in olden days and ridden with fear – fear of Nature and fear of a God whose designs we could not gauge. Religions preyed on this human weakness and made people believe that they would go to a heaven which had all the good things they did not have in this life, if they were good and moral in this life. Otherwise they would be damned to eternal hell! The only way to get to that heaven was to shun this world which was filled with snares for the morally incompetent. In this age of advanced technology, science has already eliminated most of the hardships of life and people have more money than they know what to do with, so the reason to be good has to be something other than the hope of a heaven after death! More and more people are scoffing at religions which promise us heavenly delights if we behave in certain ways which are considered socially and morally good on this earth. We live in a scientific age and one would think that religions believing in renunciation would have no relevance in this age. Unfortunately we find an insidious growth in some sections of our society that have brainwashed their flock into believing that if they die in the propagation of their faith, they will certainly be rewarded in heaven in a most delightful manner. The wonder is that in this day and age there are people who are prepared to sacrifice their very lives for the sake of the uncertain bait of a wonderful hereafter!

Five thousand years ago Krishna had already discarded such a view of life. He insisted that heaven, if there is such a thing, should be here and now. He never offered the uncertain bait of a wonderful life after death in order to entice us to become good and pure in this life. He offers a life, here and now which should be filled with joy. "*Ihaiva tairjita sarga*" is what he says. "Heaven is here and now!" He is the only god who is always laughing, playing the flute and joyously accepting every situation. He looked on life as a drama in which he played every part to perfection. He was a staunch friend, dutiful son, exciting lover and model husband to not just one but to all women who desired him. There was none so poor who called to him with intensity to whom he did not go with speed! There was no one who approached him, whether saint or sinner, in hatred or fear or love who did not attain liberation. The difference between a Kamsa who tried to kill him and a Kuchela who worshipped him may seem enormous. One approached him with hatred and the other with love, but both thought of him constantly and were thus rewarded with *moksha* or liberation. The Pandavas attained him through friendship and Kamsa through fear.

Mortal dread and fear can cause as much absorption of the mind on an object as love can. And if this object of dread happens to be god, concentration on him, even though motivated by antagonism, must purify the person, just as potent medicine consumed even with dislike must necessarily affect a cure. Krishna is indeed a great mystery and everyone has tried to understand him in his own way, according to one's own spiritual light or vision. Yogis consider him to be the absolute truth, the Gopis, the highest object of love, the warriors, an ideal hero, Kamsa, as an object of fear and Shishupala, as an object of hate. But whether one thinks of him as an object of love or hate, one attains him. This is the greatness of Krishna's incarnation.

From 180-165 BCE, the Greek ruler Agathocles issued coins with images of Vaasudeva Krishna holding *a chakra.* The figures of Krishna and Balarama are shown on the coins he made which were found recently in the excavations at Al-Khanuram in Afghanistan.

Megasthenes, the Greek ambassador in the court of Chandragupta Maurya (4th century BC), makes the first reference to the deification of Vaasudeva. He says that Heracles (who is closest to Krishna-Vaasudeva) was held in high regard by the Sourasenoi (Surasenas) who possessed two large cities, namely Methora (Mathura) and Cleisobora (Krishnapura, that is Vraja and Vrindavana). Apart from references by Megasthenes to the deification of Krishna-Vaasudeva, Buddhist texts mention the existence of shrines dedicated to Vaasudeva (Krishna) and Baladeva (Balarama).

Heliodorus, the son of Dia (Dion), a resident of Taxila had come to Besnagar as an envoy of the Greek King Antalikata (Antialkidas) to the court of Kasiputra Bhagabhadra during his 14th regal year. He was the Greek Ambassador to India and became a great devotee of Krishna Vaasudeva. He erected a *stambha* or column at Videsha in BC 113. Heliodorus' Column publicly acknowledged in the most conspicuous way that Vaasudeva, or Krishna, was the "God of gods."

No other single person has influenced the course of India's religion, philosophy, art and literature as much as the life and personality of Krishna.

As a child he was wonderful, as a youth he was physically most perfect and beautiful, as a friend, never failing, as a householder the most ideal, as an intellectual, the very embodiment of Vedic scholarship. As a fighter he was without rival, as a statesman he was extremely shrewd, as a social thinker he was exceptionally liberal, and as a teacher, beyond parallel. His teachings in the Gita embody the immortal message of perfect knowledge, desireless action, and single-pointed devotion. He is the divine charioteer seated in the heart of everyone, the Supreme Guru. In and through the redundant details which have woven themselves round his story through the centuries, it retains its breath taking beauty for it is dominated by the brilliance of his enchanting personality in which the wisdom of the seer is mingled with the charm and simplicity of the child and the glory of God that gushes forth in an inexhaustible fountain of divine love and wisdom.

Needless to say my life from birth has been dominated by his presence, even though I might not have known it at a tender age. Now I know that there was never a second when he was not with me, guiding and leading me through the chequer-board of my life to this pin point of time and space in which I am existing. I am never tired of writing and relating his stories. They have always provided an inexhaustible fount of inspiration for me. Strangely enough there is no complete account of his life in any Purana. His life in Gokula and Vrindavana have been related in the Srimad Bhagavata Purana and the latter part of his life in the Mahabharata, but even that is only in connection with the story of the Pandavas. He has blessed me by allowing me to write a full and complete account of his life in the book "Sri Krishna Lila". I feel truly sanctified, that after all these thousands of years in which he did not choose to reveal his full play, he chose me, poor and ignorant as I was, to write it, in this age and time. Of course I was only an instrument in his divine hands. He chose to reveal himself and he chose me as his divine instrument, "the ordinary pen". Now he has instigated me to write another book about him which is even more intimate than the previous one. Perhaps this is the last story

I will write about him, not because there is nothing more to be said about his infinite incarnations but because I feel I might have exhausted my capacity for storytelling. But I don't really know - everything is left in his hands. This book was a revelation even for me. I had always wondered what role I had played in his life. I was pretty certain that I had been there during his sojourn on earth. In the course of writing this book he chose to tell me who I was and what role I had played in his life. This esoteric secret I have openly declared in this book. Of all the characters I would have chosen to be, this was certainly the strangest and the most unexpected. Yet since I have it from his own mouth, I cannot but believe it to be the truth.

My love affair with him has been a long and turbulent one. It has waxed and waned from life to life but I know that he was always there, always preventing me from giving myself totally to any other human being. My feelings were reflected in Rukmini's dialogue to him, "Which is the woman who has known thee once, who will be able to love an ordinary human being filled with frailties?" When I first read that in the Bhagavatam, my heart skipped a beat and I knew she was only reiterating what I had always felt in the depths of my being. Indeed the Paramatma is the only fitting mate for the *jivatma*. This applies to every one of us either male or female. He is the only Purusha, the supreme male. All the rest of us are females. Through the strange convolutions of my lives from the time of the Krishnavatara, when we both existed at the same time on this planet, I have realised that we have always been inseparably connected with each other, life after life after life until the last moment of this life in which I hope this river will drown itself in the ocean of bliss.

Aum Namo Bhagavate Vaasudevaaya

ॐ

Sri Krishnaaya Namaha!

CHAPTER ONE

Dwarakadish

The setting sun was slowly sinking into the arms of the Arabian Sea. As it neared the horizon it seemed to go down faster and faster. The water was glimmering with shades of red and pink and orange which I knew would slowly turn into mystic lavender. I was sitting on the beach, mesmerised by the glittering rays which were slowly sinking into the eager arms of the horizon. Behind me loomed the huge *shikar* (dome)of the temple of Dwarkadhish, the Lord of Dwaraka. This temple is believed to have been originally built by Lord Krishna's grandson, Vajranabha on the site of the "Hari-griha", which was Lord Krishna's palace. I was brooding over this and watching the rise and fall of the waves in a hypnotic state when a figure rose out of the waters and glided towards me. He was very tall and the setting sun made a halo round his head. I jumped up as he reached me and looked up to be drowned in the most glorious eyes I had ever seen. His compassionate gaze seemed to bore through me. I had to tilt my head right to the back of my neck to look at his face. His face shimmered in tender lavender light and his *kundalas* (earrings) cast a golden shine on his cheeks. His curly locks clustered round his shoulders and were held in place with a simple diadem with three peacock feathers fluttering on the top. He just stood there looking at me. Slowly I tore my gaze away from his mesmerising look in order to look at the rest of his figure. As my look wandered down his face, I saw that his nose was straight, with rosy lips shaped like a bow ending in a determined chin. His upper cloth of yellow silk was worn loosely round his neck which was adorned with a heavy gold chain on which was hanging a deep red, ruby pendent. He wore the same yellow silk *dhoti* round his waist and had a pair of wooden *padukas* (footwear) set in gold on his feet. My gaze came slowly down the whole length of his body from head to toe and went up again to drown in his eyes which were still looking at me with such compassion that tears started to roll down my cheeks. All this time he had stood silently watching me as my eyes travelled up and down his body. Now he lifted the corner of his *uttareeyam* (top garment) and wiped the tears which were rolling down my cheeks. He then placed the tip of his right forefinger under my chin and started to lift me up slowly so that very soon my gaze was parallel to his chest instead of to his stomach as it had been. Now I didn't have to tilt my head so much to look at him. There seemed to be something more than compassion in his eyes now. It was amusement. Was he teasing me? Was he daring me to believe in his reality?

He seemed to answer my unspoken question. "Yes I'm the Lord of Dwaraka – your beloved Vanamali whom you have been worshipping from the beginning of time."

I didn't know whether he had really said the words or was communicating in some other special way. I seemed to be able to answer in the same way without opening my mouth.

'Yes I recognised you even as you came out of the ocean. You are my Vanamali. How can I not recognise you, who have been my constant companion for so many lives?'

He smiled and held out his hand with an unspoken command. I put my palm in his and felt as if my hand was totally engulfed in his. I did not have any questions. How can one question oneself? He led me or shall I say I glided with him into the ocean. We walked along the path gilded with gold by the setting sun. We walked straight into the sunset and there before us I saw golden turrets silhouetted in the sun. Dwaraka was known as the golden city and as we approached the shore, we were bathed in the soft golden glow which emanated from it. Suddenly I realised that we were not walking towards an island as I had imagined, but he was actually taking me back in Time to the coast of Dwaraka which I had just left. But it was not exactly the place I had left. We had left a normal beach, on which I had been sitting in the twilight, but now it was broad daylight and it was a brand new shoreline. I noticed that the whole coast was covered with massive blocks with L-shaped joints to withstand the constant battering of waves and currents. What sort of engineers did the city have who had the skills to build what we call port installations in the sea? They obviously knew the method of modifying the natural rock to serve the needs of a harbour. As we went further we saw a ridge about two metres high running parallel to the shore for a length of five hundred metres. There were several man-made holes on which large ships could be secured to the mooring device with ropes. This was the famous Dwaraka harbour mentioned in the Mahabharata and Harivamsa, which I remembered to have read.

Magnificent ships with many masts were anchored here. They had huge stone anchors which weighed them to the shore. The harbour seemed to be really crowded with people wearing different types of clothes with turbans and beards, some dark, some fair and some brown. As we walked up the beach I saw the huge granite walls which were not only meant as fortifications but also to keep the sea at bay, since obviously this was reclaimed land. There was a massive iron gate which was open at the moment since it was morning, but it had many guards standing at attention. The person at the gate house seemed to be asking for something from everyone who passed it. I passed my question to Krishna who answered in the same way. Every citizen of Dwaraka had to carry a *mudra* (seal) made of conch shell with a 3-headed animal motif. He guessed my interest in it and gave me one. I scrutinised it and was fascinated to note that the three animals were a bull, a sheep and a unicorn!

Strange combination! I wondered why. It was quite big, about 20 mm. The back had a square button with a hole for inserting a ring. I suppose this was a kind of passport. Strangers were stopped from entering until they could provide proper credentials. Everything seemed natural and perfect to me since he was holding my hand. Since nobody seemed to notice us, I realised that he had made us both invisible. Then we came to a magnificent road, about twenty feet wide flanked by *champaka* (sweet smelling flower) trees. The flower had a distinct perfume. I noticed all this only in a superficial way. What I saw distinctly was the chariot which seemed to be waiting for him. It was a small type of racing chariot with just two wheels and two milk white horses with one black ear, who were straining at the bit and were held by a young lad of about twelve, who wore almost the same type of garments as my Vanamali and who on closer glance had very familiar features. He bowed and handed over the reins to Krishna. The boy obviously could not see me. I looked enquiringly at Vanamali. He glanced at me and said with a smile in his voice, "Don't you recognise him?"

I shook my head and enquired with my eyes. He laughed and said, "Not now, later."

He jumped lightly onto the chariot and pulled me up beside him, smiled his thanks to the boy and set off at a brisk trot. I turned back to see the boy running after us. Vanamali slowed down to a canter so that I could take in the sights of the city we were passing. Everything was very beautiful but not strange, as if I had seen it a long time ago and was recognising everything as we passed. There seemed to be some sort of high walls in the distance which we had seen and the city was within these.

To the left I suddenly noticed a kind of caravan with horses and ponies carrying goods. Krishna answered my question. "The city has four gates. We entered by the western gate leading to the harbour, and that is a caravan from Kamboja (Cambodia) and Gandhara (Afghanistan) coming from the eastern gate. These huge horses and small ponies come from Kamboja. The horses which we use for riding and for the chariots are brought by the Cushites (Arabians). The ponies are loaded with all sorts of merchandise: blankets embroidered with gold thread, Kambu silver, zinc, *hing* (asafoetida), walnuts, almonds, saffron, raisins, salt and precious stones like lapis lazuli, green turquoise and emeralds. Some of our sailors go down the coast of Aryavrata (ancient name for India) carrying salt and raisins and trade them for spices like cloves, cinnamon, cardamom and pepper from the tribes who live in the jungles in the south and gather spices from the forest. Some of these tribes are very fierce and blow poisoned darts at the boats, but some are friendly and happy to get whatever small luxury they can afford."

My curiosity satisfied, we rode along the road which was not at all dusty since it had been sprinkled with water (it could even have been rose water since the perfume of roses filled my nostrils). Beyond the line of the *champaka* trees stretched green fields with green sheaths of rice which were still to ripen, waving their heads in the slight breeze as if to welcome their Lord. We passed the fields and came to another ornamental gateway which led right into the city. It was huge and embossed with gold on which mystic *yantras* and *mandalas* were carved on either side. Two caparisoned elephants stood on either side with upraised trunks. At first I thought they were real but then realised they were carvings. A fully grown tusker with all trappings and a *howdah* on top could easily pass through the gates. Guards came out and saluted the Lord as we entered. He tossed them his charming smile and pushed forward. Once inside the city gates, he slowed down so that I could take in everything. Streets criss-crossed each other and there were quadrangles where children were playing and market places filled with people who had brought their merchandise. There seemed to be a lot of selling and buying. A lot of noise and shouting seemed to be going on. What struck me was that none of the streets seemed dusty. They were all sprinkled with water, and strewn with flowers. Ornamented wooden sheds had been erected at cross roads in which weary travellers were resting. Water troughs for horses had been thoughtfully provided as well as mud pots with drinking water for the travellers. A person was always ready to pour a ladle of water into the cupped hands of anyone who wanted to drink. After this came beautifully decorated rest houses in which visitors were accommodated. Another thing I noticed was that there seemed to be many houses with some symbol on them. My charioteer knew my unspoken question and he answered briefly.

"Those are guild halls for different types of traders who come here from all parts of the world, crossing the ocean with difficulty." Next we passed a huge building with many steps leading to the hall or Sabha, known as Sudharma where the cabinet met. Again this was conveyed to me without words. (Later I was told that this had been built for him by the divine architect, Visvakarma at the behest of Indra, king of gods). I really didn't have time to take in the beauty of the architecture of the Sabha. We seemed to have come to the end of the public buildings. Now we passed through shady avenues lined with all types of exotic blooming trees shedding their flowers and perfume on all those who passed. It appeared as if we were entering the residential area. I was to find out later that the city was actually made up of six different sectors with special functions like residential, business, government, agriculture, military and entertainment.

I was suddenly struck by a set of steep steps going down I didn't know where. I asked my Lord about this. He stopped the chariot and took me down the steps. The steps went right down to the bosom of the earth and ended in a lovely pond with crystal clear water. The well was cylindrical in shape like the wells I had seen and built up with bricks but the top was open to the sky and the sun. But unlike the wells I had seen, this one had steps leading down to it. There were also many beautiful sculptures along the sides.

'What is this?' I asked.

"This is called a step well and it never gets dry even during the hottest summer. People go down to drink and collect water and take baths sometimes."

'It is so beautiful!' I exclaimed. 'Are there many like this here?'

"Actually there are about seventy such wells in Dwaraka, enough to supply the people with water even if there is a bad drought."

Peacocks roosted on the walls of the parks and I was high enough on the chariot to peep in and see small deer and some other tame animals roaming about. Lovers twining their arms round each others' necks were also wandering about, oblivious of the surroundings. The sweet cooing of pigeons could be heard and sometimes the raucous call of a peacock. As we came to the residential area, I noticed that all the mansions had small wooden sheds in front of the gates, on which peacocks were strutting and sometimes dancing. These gates were adorned on both sides with pillars inlaid with mother-of-pearl and coral. On top of the pillars were golden pitchers filled with water from which trailed creepers and bunches of leaves. The necks of the pitchers were tied with strips of silk. Banana trunks with bunches of ripe fruit hanging down and areca-nut trees with orange nuts bunched together were also to be seen beside the pillars. Flags were fluttering atop the trees. I could hardly take in everything. It was all so beautiful. I guessed that these houses belonged to the nobles or to ministers.

Next the road widened into a much larger highway in which two or three chariots could easily move without any hindrance. This was no doubt the Raja *vidhi* or the Royal Road. This had not a speck of dust on it and was again obviously sprinkled with jasmine water and scattered with rose petals and barley shoots. We had to pass through another ornamental arch to get into this, and as we passed, guards came out and blew bugles and drummers drummed loudly. Flowers were rained on our heads from above. I was a bit over-awed by everything and clung to my Vanamali's *uttareeyam.* He gave me a reassuring glance as the horses galloped forward. We had to pass through three more such arches before coming to the most beautiful palace I had ever seen. The gateway appeared to be made of crystal encrusted with amethysts. The golden domes of the palace seemed to be stretching towards the heavens. The park in front was laid out in the pattern of a *Sri Yantra* with different coloured flowers filling the different squares and triangles. In the middle was the celestial tree known as the Parijata, which again had been sent by Indra, king of gods. I had heard that anyone who sat beneath this tree would never know the pangs of hunger, thirst, grief, infatuation, old age and death. Many ornamental ponds filled with lotuses and water lilies were scattered about here and there.

We reached the portals of the palace and Krishna jumped down lightly and tossed the reins to the boy who had caught up with us, and helped me to jump down beside him. He climbed up the stairs with me panting behind him since the steps were rather high and I was much shorter than all the people I had seen so far. The steps were made of some white stone, possibly marble and studded with precious stones. As we entered the doorway, a huge man with a crown came to my Lord and said in a booming voice, "Krishna where have you been? We have an important guest. King Kakudmi, son of Revata, King of Anarta (Gujarat) has come here with a proposal of marriage. He has brought his daughter Revati with him. You have to meet them and listen to their proposal. It is a very good alliance for us since his land lies adjacent to ours."

Krishna smiled at his huge brother who literally towered above him and asked teasingly, "How did you find the girl? Is she up to your standards?"

I guessed this to be Balarama, Krishna's brother. He glowered at Krishna and said, "Please be serious. This is a very important matter for us. We are on this piece of land totally unprotected except for the sea, and if the person who owns the land next to us is inimical to us, we will find it very difficult to protect ourselves, so it's imperative that we have King Kakudmi as our ally. It is the grace of the creator Brahma that he has approached us for a marital alliance. We must show all respect to him."

He caught my Lord's hand and pulled him to the assembly hall reserved for kings and special guests. I kept a tight hold of my

Lord's *uttareeyam* and he turned round to smile at me. It was then that I realised that I was quite invisible to everyone else and did not need to be frightened of what people might think of me.

The man who rose to welcome us as we strode in was an overpowering figure. The young girl who stood beside him was statuesque and was a female equivalent of her father. As we reached the couple I saw that Balarama and the girl were actually of the same height. Krishna was much shorter. Balarama bowed before the king and introduced Krishna.

"O King of Anarta, scorcher of foes! Allow me to present my younger brother, Vaasudeva, who has just returned after subduing the forces of Jarasandha, king of Magadha."

Krishna went forward and bowed to the king who held out his arms and embraced him. "Please be seated," he said and led him to the throne kept in the middle. This was flanked by smaller thrones on either side. Krishna led the girl to a throne next to her father and the brothers sat next to them. I sat on the footstool at my Lord's feet. He stroked my head but kept talking to the others.

King Kakudmi turned to Krishna and said, "Has the noble Balarama told you about the purpose of my visit? I find that I am too old and weak to protect my country any more. I would like to make an alliance with you and give my dear daughter, Revati in marriage to you, for I have heard that you are a great hero who has subdued Yavana, the mighty king of the Yakshas. My brothers have already fled from our capital, Kushasthali for fear of the Punyajana *rakshasas.*"

Krishna laughed and said, "O King! I am indeed honoured by your offer, but do you really think I would make a suitable husband for your beautiful daughter? According to our ancient rules of choosing a bride, it is said that one should always choose a woman who is shorter than you. But do not be put out by this. Look at my brother Balarama; he is indeed the fitting mate for your daughter. He is in no way inferior to me as a warrior and is a champion in mace fighting and has been taught by

Parasurama himself. But I am intrigued, O King, to see your stature. How have you both become so tall?"

The king now began his interesting tale. "O Vaasudeva! O Balarama! Listen to my strange story. My daughter and I have just returned from the world of Brahma where we spent a very pleasant evening listening to the celestial musical performance which was going on there. At the end of the recital, I asked my Lord Brahma to tell me who would make a suitable bridegroom for my only daughter.

Brahma laughed and said, 'O King! Time is relative to the speed at which you go. Do you realise how many *yugas* (eons) have passed since you came here? Twenty-seven *Mahayugas* have rolled by. One human year is only one day for gods like Indra and one year of the gods is only a minute for me. You will not find anyone you knew in the world when you return. Peoples' life span has become much less and so has their stature. You will never find anyone to match your daughter's physique. However, I advise you to go to the golden city of Dwaraka made by the great *siddha* – Vaasudeva. He is said to be an incarnation of Vishnu. It is the stronghold of the Yadava clan.'

'When the armies of Jarasandha, king of Magadha kept harassing the Surasenas at their capital of Mathura, Krishna and Balarama fought with them, but after repeated attacks, Krishna realised that the town was totally unprotected, so he made the citizens of Mathura take small portions of all the wealth of the city and proceed towards the west. There was the delightful town of Kushasthali which used to be your capital which is protected by the mountain Raivata. They decided to take over the city which had been left unprotected by your sons. They have made it into an impregnable fortress from which even women will find it easy to fight the foe, what need to speak of the Yadava heroes. It was easy to fortify this place since it had a natural fortification in the form of the sea on one side. Since there was not enough space in the town of Kushasthali, Krishna requested the sea god, Varuna to provide more space. Krishna changed the name of Kushasthali to Dwaraka which means the gateway to Brahma.

"Ka" is actually another of my names. The city is supposed to have been designed by the celestial architect, Visvakarma. Their king is Ugrasena but Vaasudeva and his brother Balarama are the virtual rulers of the place. Go there and you will find that one of the brothers will make a suitable husband for your daughter. The Yadavas have also fortified the mountain called Gomantaka. Twenty-one posts of armed men are left there to ensure that Dwaraka is left unmolested. Many of the younger Yadava heroes belonging to the eighteen tribes are left there to guard the place.'"

King Kakudmi continued, "This is the reason I came straight to this place with my daughter, since I am a king without a land or a city. Brahma had already warned me that I would not find any familiar face when I came back to this land. Even though I don't own it any more, it is my wish to give this land of Anarta (modern Saurashtra) as a bridal gift for my daughter, so one of you should accept her as your wife."

Balarama looked enquiringly at his younger brother and Krishna replied, "Sire, we are deeply honoured that you have chosen us to help you in your quest of a bridegroom for your beautiful daughter. If Revati agrees I'm sure my brother will be only too happy to oblige!"

He turned round and looked at Balarama who smiled his consent. Kakudmi rose up and took his daughter's hand and went forward. All of them stood up and the king placed his daughter's hand in Balarama's and thus plighted the troth.

The brothers requested them to stay on till all arrangements had been made for the marriage. This was quite unusual since normally the groom went to the bride's city and the wedding was conducted there. But since King Kakudmi had no land at this point and he was only king of Anarta in name alone, he had no option but to stay on in Dwaraka till the marriage was solemnised. King Ugrasena and Krishna's parents Devaki and Vasudeva had to be consulted, as well as the priests. Of course this was only a formality since everyone in Dwaraka obeyed Krishna's orders implicitly. Krishna went and consulted the priests who chose the auspicious time and preparations were started for the wedding. Since this was the first wedding in the royal family, everyone was excited. Vasudeva and Devaki had despaired of getting a bride to match their elder son's physique and now Revati not only matched him physically but had also brought a handsome bride price with her. The land of Anarta had been abandoned by Kakudmi's brothers long ago and had been overrun by Kalayavana's hordes. Krishna and Balarama had the arduous task of chasing them away from the land and appropriating it for themselves. But after Krishna had made King Muchukunda pulverise their King Kalayavana by a mere look from his blazing eyes, the Yakshas were without a leader and turned to Kubera to save them from the attack of the two brothers. Kubera was the half-brother of Ravana who had cheated him of his properties and taken away his aerial vehicle called the Pushpaka, and forced him to flee from his own country.

He had come to Kushasthali and pronounced himself as king of the Yakshas. He invited the *devas* to a conclave to determine the ownership of the land. The Yakshas had come fully prepared to fight. They had three hundred *maha-padmas*, carrying various weapons. Krishna did not really want to fight with Kubera. He met Kubera and spoke peacefully to him and told him to go further north and carve out a territory for himself in the Himalayas, where he would not be molested constantly by attacking kings. All the *devas* urged Kubera to this amicable settlement, and the Yakshas agreed to this and left the place to the brothers and went to the Himalayas. After praying to Varuna, Lord of the Sea, the Yadavas under the guidance of Krishna reclaimed a lot of land on which the glorious city of Dwaraka was built. It was situated on the right bank of the River Gomati. The mountain known as Raivata dominated the horizon at the back. (This was the land which had sunk into the sea when the Lord left this planet. What is now known as Dwaraka is actually the ancient city of Kushasthali. Of Krishna's Dwaraka there is not a trace. The sea took back what was taken from it. It had been a gift from Varuna to the Lord, for the duration of his lifetime on this planet and was taken back at the end of that period.)

The Yadavas also took over the island of Bet Dwaraka off the sea coast and the islands known as Antara Dwipa. Bet Dwaraka is also known as Sankhodhara, because of the copious quantities of conch shells found there. It was on this island that Krishna discovered the son of his Guru Sandipany. He had been kidnapped by a trader from the north and taken to the island and forced to work in his shop, making conch bangles. Krishna went to the island to save his *guru's* son. When he saw Krishna, the man took the boy and dived into the sea. Krishna dived in after them and forced him to come up. He was all set to kill him but the man begged for mercy so the Lord freed him. The trader now gave back the son of his *guru* and also presented him with a beautiful "*valampiri*" (right-hand) conch. This was his famous conch known as the Panchajanya. All this was told to me by the Lord when he took me on a visit to the island. I saw that this was actually a well-fortified shipyard where they made all their ships and boats. I also noticed two ramps which were like slipways meant for launching boats. It seemed to have other industries like making shell articles and collecting mother-of-pearl. Obviously Dwaraka was a bustling port. Ships from Arabia and Africa used to come and there was an intermingling of trade from many parts of the world.

I learnt later that Dwaraka was actually a federation of many republics rather than one kingdom under a single king. The population of the city was made up of different tribes known as Andhakas, Vrishnis, Bhojas, Dasarhas and Madhus. The title of king of Yadavas was offered to Krishna since he was the one who had saved them from the threat of Jarasandha and brought them to this beautiful spot. The Lord refused and made Ugrasena, Kamsa's father, who was the king of the Bhojas, as King of the Yadavas.

I spent the night in the Lord's apartment on a couch he had specially made for me at the foot of his bed. His bed was of ebony inlaid with mother-of-pearl. The mattress looked like an ocean with billows of soft white muslin over it. He simply sank into it. He looked like a blue lotus in the middle of an ocean. I was fascinated by a fan which looked like a canopy made of pleated silk, which was waving automatically above the bed. I wondered how it was done. Later I found out that there was a hemp rope attached to it which went through a hole in the wall to the pond below in which there was a water wheel which kept rotating, thus giving momentum to the fan. The room had a warm glow which was emanating from two oil lamps hanging in two corners. I suspected that the oil was scented since the whole room smelt of jasmine.

I was in a state of bliss all the time and never wondered even for a moment as to why I was there and what people would think when they did not see me return. I had come alone to the town of Dwaraka and was staying at a small hotel very close to the exquisite temple of Rukmini. If the hotel management did not see me, no doubt they would start an enquiry and perhaps someone would say that they had seen me go into the ocean and never saw me coming back. I conjectured vaguely about this but the fact was, that my past life up to the moment when I saw the Lord rising from the sea was getting fainter and fainter and what was more important was that I was totally disinterested in it. On the contrary, every moment of this life was like an etching carved on stone and was so clear and so fascinating that I cared not for the past or the future. This glorious "now" was all that I cared about. These golden moments which were slipping through my fingers like pearls from a necklace in the making.

Even though I slept I was always aware of the beloved of my heart at whose feet I had my couch. Sometimes during the night I would get up and lightly caress his feet. These butterfly touches did not seem to bother him. Next morning I woke up before the bards came to wake him up and ran to the gilded balcony overlooking the gardens, and was amazed to see that arrangements were well under way for the wedding. Canopies were being put up and a temple-like structure had been placed at the far end of the garden. Two hours before sunrise the Lord woke up to the tune of the *veena* (lute) and *mridangam* (percussion instrument) with which the musicians had come to wake him. Next came the bards who started to eulogise him and describe his glorious deeds. Then arrived vassals carrying rose scented water in golden basins for the Lord to wash his face and hands and rinse his mouth. Towels of the softest of muslin were then given to him.

After this he sat on a deer skin on the ground facing east and meditated on the Supreme, even though he was by his own nature free of all nescience and was the very form of the Supreme. Not so surprisingly, I found that my Vanamali's room was the only one with an attached bathroom, if one can call it that. A door with a curtain led to another huge room which had a pond as large as a swimming pool. Water seemed to be continually being fed and drained out of it. There were some small plants and creepers around the pool which gave it a very natural look. He was led to this pool into which he plunged and swam about and had a leisurely bath. He came out and donned two pieces of muslin. After this he sat before the fire which had already been lit and poured oblations into it as per the dictates of the Vedas. He then stood before the rising sun and repeated the Gayatri Mantra (I supposed) silently. Next he offered water in his palms to the gods, *rishis* and manes. After this, he gifted silk clothes, deer-skins, sesame seeds and beautifully adorned cows with their calves to many Brahmanas. The cows' horns were capped in gold and hooves in silver and they had pearl necklaces round their necks. He then saluted the cows, Brahmanas, gods, elders, preceptors and all created beings that were all manifestations of his own self.

At this time his personal staff came forward with his clothes made of yellow silk and adorned him with clothes and ornaments. As I looked at his face I thought surely he is so divinely beautiful, he does not need any adornments. Finally the *vanamala* or garland made of five forest flowers (*tulsi*, jasmine, *mandara*, *parijata* and lotuses) which was specially made for him every day was brought on a golden plate. He lifted it and put it over his own head. I was longing to put it for him. From my teens I had been making garlands for my Vanamali and now when I could do it for him personally, I was afraid to go forward and snatch it from his hands. At this point he looked so gorgeous that tears started rolling down from my eyes and I felt like running forward and hugging him. He glanced at me over the tops of the heads of those who were thronging round him as if he understood what was passing through my heart. Just then Daruka, his charioteer came and bowed to him and asked for instructions. Normally he would proceed to the Sudharma or cabinet hall but today he waved him away and said he wanted to inspect the preparations which were being made for the wedding. He next went to his parents' palace. Vasudeva and Devaki had finished their ablutions and were preparing to do their *puja* in their own special temple. A small exquisitely carved temple was in the grounds. Krishna and I went there and I was overjoyed to see the idol which Krishna's parents were worshipping. It was of Vishnu holding the conch, *chakra (*wheel), *gada* (mace) and lotus in his hands, wearing the *vanamala*. I knew that it was made of a special type of black stone called "*anjana*" which had curative properties so that those who drank the water which was ceremoniously poured over it would have immense benefits. I recognised it immediately since it was the same which was now residing in the famous temple of Guruvayoor in Kerala which had been my home town in my previous life.

It is said that when Dwaraka went under the sea, the Lord had instructed Brihaspati, *guru* of the gods, to rescue the idol which was floating on the waters and consecrate it at some auspicious site. Brihaspati had enlisted the help of Vayu, god of wind and scoured the whole land of Aryavrata (India) right to the tip. They came upon a wonderful spot beside a lake near which Shiva and Parvati were dancing. They took Shiva's advice and consecrated the idol, which had been worshipped by the Lord himself as well as by his parents, on this spot which consequently came to be known as Guru-vayur, since it was consecrated by Guru Brihaspati and Vayu the wind god.

Devaki and Vasudeva had just about finished their worship so they turned round to welcome their son. He touched their feet and told them all the details of the wedding which was to take place at the auspicious time at night. The functions preceding the actual wedding were already under way.

"We were just going to see whether Revati had everything she needs. One hundred and one well-trained maids having all auspicious marks have gone to help her. I will take Subhadra and go there now," said Devaki. Just then a tall person with a long grey beard and hair knotted up on top of his head, thus pronouncing that he was a Maharishi, came to the temple. My Lord immediately went and touched his feet as did his parents. Krishna passed the information to me that this was Garga Muni, the *kula guru* (family preceptor) of the Yadavas. All of them sat down and discussed with the sage about the different types of rituals to be performed at the wedding. Of course Garga Muni was in charge of it all since he was a great astrologer. After deciding everything and receiving his blessings, my Vanamali proceeded to the dining hall.

I trotted after him to the dining hall which had tables laden with many types of fruit and pitchers of milk and pomegranate juice as I discovered later. He took a goblet and handed some to me and gestured that I should help myself. I drank the ambrosia he had given me and then waited for him to give me his half-eaten fruits. He smiled and lifted an eyebrow but did not say anything when I first snatched a fruit from his hand before he could take a second bite. Just one bite from that glorious fruit (something like a mango) was enough to send me into another state of consciousness.

As we came out of the door, vassals were standing with auspicious articles in their hands, which he looked at and touched before proceeding to the grounds to inspect all the preparations that had been made for the wedding. Bejewelled ornamental arches were placed at special places, flags were fluttering from all the turrets, floral wreaths and tapestries adorned the place. The gates and entrance arches were flanked by tall plantain and areca nut trees bending with huge bunches of fruit almost touching the ground. He went from place to place, personally inspecting everything himself, giving a word of praise here and some advice there.

The princess Revati and her father had been accommodated in another beautiful palace adjoining Balarama's palace. The bride was already being given her auspicious bath with turmeric and sandal paste to the accompaniment of *mantras*, while the bridegroom had the same rituals done to him in his own palace.

In the distance I could see smoke rising into the air and the Lord as if sensing my curiosity took me there. It was a huge *yajnashala* in which many priests were muttering incantations and reading from the Vedas and pouring libations into the fire. A subtle smell of frankincense, loban, musk and maybe amber filled the air. The sonorous sounds of Vedic *mantras* being chanted fell gently on our ears. The *yajnashalas* were actually the Vedic laboratories. Many experiments were conducted there, on health, agriculture, architecture, weaponry, making of ships called *naus* and even the making of flying machines called *vimanas*. The English word nautical is derived from the word *nau*. The scientific knowledge imbedded in the Vedas and especially the Atharva Veda is enormous. The making of medicines and machines was all taken from this. Knowledgeable Brahmanas who knew the Vedic chants by heart and who were masters in making many things were working in shifts night and day in this huge *yajnashala*. The Vedas dealt with both *jnana* (spiritual wisdom) and *vijnana* (scientific knowledge).

Vanamali took me beyond this into another room which had seemed to be a sort of laboratory. These two rooms were quite devoid of ornamentation. But the little room looked rather pretty with dried plants hanging from the rafters. There was a strong smell of herbs which I found very pleasant but which might not have been liked by many people. All round the walls were jars containing medicinal plants and herbs of all kinds brought from the Himalayas and even from the ocean as I was told later. My Lord went forward and bowed to a rather stern-looking sage who was sitting in the far corner scrutinising a piece of parchment in his hand.

He looked up and I noticed that he had the most piercing eyes I had ever seen. They just bored into you but my Vanamali of course was totally unaffected by this and asked him, "Sire, have you heard of Balarama's approaching nuptials? The bride is the daughter of King Kakudmi of Anarta". He whispered to me, "This is the great sage Chyavana, noted for his vast knowledge of Ayurveda. He married a princess called Sukanya who served him faithfully even though he looked old and ugly. To bless her, he made the herbal concoction known as "Chyavanaprasha" by eating which he got back his youth and was able to give her all that a woman expects from a husband. I think he is working on some other formula now. The person who is helping him is Agniveshya, the foremost disciple of the great physician Atri-Angiras."

Chyavana replied, "Indeed I have heard. The news was brought to me yesterday night by Balarama himself. It is a good choice for him. You may continue with the wedding preparations." He gave a pleasant nod as if to dismiss him but my Vanamali stood his ground and looked curiously at the parchment he was scrutinising. Chyavana said, "This is an ancient recipe to make '*kaya kalpa*' which makes one immortal and gives you a golden complexion. This is a secret which the *siddhas* of old had discovered but the knowledge had been lost".

"Are you going to reveal the secret now?" asked Krishna.

"The time has not come," Chyavana said shortly and turned away to his own devices.

A little further we came to a small copse. It was quite dark and looked a bit fearsome. My Lord pointed to a figure sitting under a tree and meditating. "That is my *guru*, Durvasa," he said. "He is noted for his temper and unbelievable austerity. He is very short-tempered and it is best not to thwart him in any way. He is an *amsa* (spark) of Mahadeva (Shiva). He is not a master of rhetoric like Yajnavalkya or a seer of the Vedic hymns like Viswamitra. His realm lies beyond the word, in the fury that lies behind the curtain of *Maya*. Curses and boons are the only ways in which he chooses to reveal himself. He has reduced life into two segments – retribution and reward. No one is sure what exactly might spark his retaliation. Even the gods are frightened of him. In his emaciated and ragged figure, the gods have learnt to recognise the Supreme Spirit in its most wilful and uncontrollable form. He always shows himself when some devastation is about to occur. But for some reason he often comes and stays here, maybe because he is my *guru* and is fond of me and maybe because I have something of him in me. Sometimes the Spirit manifests itself in me also in its irrepressible and uncontrollable form." He gave me a sidelong glance.

'Why did you choose him as your *guru*?' I asked curiously.

Krishna laughed and said, "He is a totally enlightened soul who has never had a fall like so many other sages. But he is a difficult guest to please. If you don't attend to every single whim of his, he will most certainly curse you, but if you do manage to please him, he is capable of blessing you with anything you choose. As I told you he is able to command the gods. He is the one who gave a *mantra* to Kunti, the mother of the Pandavas, by which she was able to summon any god she wished in order to get a child".

'How did that happen?' I asked.

"Once he had gone to visit her father, Kuntibhoja and was not at all pleased with the way he was being treated but Kunti though very young, tried her best to placate him. Obviously he was pleased, for before he left he called her and said, 'Child! Repeat this *mantra* which I am giving you and memorise it carefully. One day you will be able to use this and invoke the gods. They, who cannot even be seen by anyone, will come as your lovers. One day you will have need of it and you may use it if you wish.' He went off without another word and years later Yudhishtira, Bhima and Arjuna were formed in Kunti's womb, conceived from a divine seed. Kunti taught the *mantra* to Madri, Pandu's second wife, who invoked the twin physicians of the gods known as the Aswini Kumaras and thus got the twins, Nakula and Sahadeva.

"He never stays long at any place. No one knows his goings and comings. Actually no one knows he is here now. By tomorrow he will be gone." I remembered faintly from my past life that I had been shown a tree near the Dwarkadhish temple which I was told was the place where the sage Durvasa used to meditate.

"Do you know why he is called Durvasa?" I shook my head and he continued, "Because his diet for the day is just the amount of water which can be contained inside a *durva* grass. He has unimaginable control over his body and mind. He has no dependence whatsoever on anything or any human being. He is totally above all duality and is indeed a *gunateeta* (one who has gone beyond the three *gunas*). Nothing disturbs him. He is known to have cursed many people but each time he curses, the curse has changed into a blessing for the person. I have learnt many things from him but luckily I have not picked up his bad temper!!" Both of us laughed and I held on to his hand as we came out of the *yajnashala*. Beyond the *yajnashala* there was another fairly big building and I tried to drag my Lord there but he shook his head. "This is not the time to go there."

'What is happening there?' I asked curiously.

"That is Brihaspati's den. All the sacred *mantras* from all the Vedas dealing with special *astras* which can delude and confound and kill people are to be found there. He teaches those *mantras* only to those of his students who are capable of handling them and who would not use them to further their own interests. Many of them are deadly and it is very dangerous for anyone who does not have a controlled mind to possess them. This is an esoteric knowledge which can be imparted to only a very few people, chosen by the *guru*. Knowledge gives power and power in the hands of those who are spiritually weak will lead to untold misery both for themselves and for the whole of humanity."

I thought of the insane misuse of the atom bomb and the possession of nuclear weapons by nations who were morally unfit to possess such knowledge and I realised the truth of what he was saying.

A young man with a large physique followed by another of shorter build came to us.

"Ah Vaasudeva! Where have you been? We have been looking for you everywhere. We just heard about Balarama's wedding. Tell us all about it." Both of them came and stood on either side of my Lord and flung their arms over his shoulder in a familiar way. He communicated their names to me in the same manner as he had been doing. "These are my best friends, Uddhava and Satyaki. Uddhava is also my Prime Minister. We have been friends since childhood."

The three friends went with arms thrown round each others' shoulders to another big building which again was not furbished as the other palaces and buildings which I had seen. They strode in with me hot on their heels. It was the armoury and as we entered we saw the back of another large man who was actually fencing with another man in the open courtyard. This was Kritavarma, general of the Yadava forces. He stopped jousting and turned to bow to my Vanamali. He was rather on the stocky side, not really suited for fencing, but perhaps he was just teaching someone. I was wonder-struck to see the number of weapons hanging on the wall, and took in the number of huge boxes which no doubt contained bows and arrows and other interesting weapons. On the sides of the courtyard where the men had been jousting were interesting looking weapons which resembled modern cannons, except that they had huge iron sticks with a hole at the back. I guessed that they were made to throw stones and fire balls at the enemy. Another courtyard led from this one which was obviously a place for practicing wrestling. Later I got to know that this was a favourite pastime of my Lord who would often come here before his bath and have a joust with someone. There were wooden benches around the arena meant for wrestlers to lie and be oiled before starting.

"Ah! Kritavarma!" said my Lord, "I see that your arms are itching for a fight. This is the time for laughter and romance, not fighting. No doubt you would have heard of my brother's approaching nuptials. So forget your weapons for a while and join us in the merry making."

While the friends were talking I made a round of the armoury and poked my nose inquisitively into each of the huge metal boxes which were placed all round the walls. I gasped to see the number of arrows there. Each box was filled with millions of arrows of iron and steel, wood and silver. All of them had different types of arrowheads – some pointed, some barbed or cleft or shaped like a calf's tooth, or a boar's ear, or a crescent moon or the head of a snake or frog. I turned round to exclaim to my Lord and found him walking off with the others without a backward glance. I ran and caught hold of his *uttareeyam* and he turned round to give me a half smile.

Aum Namo Bhagavate Vaasudevaaya

The Lord made an attractive city in the middle of twelve yojanas of fortified area in the sea. There were properly planned highways, crossed by subsidiary roads, from which proceeded streets, on both sides of which stood houses built according to the rules of town planning and displaying fully the skill of the heavenly architect Viswakarma. There were flower gardens with celestial plants and creepers and parks with various kinds of trees; there were houses and buildings with sky-kissing domes and roofs of gold and crystal. There were halls made of silver and brass, capped with golden domes and houses of gold with tops studded with diamonds and surrounded by courtyards paved with emeralds. There were temples at various places and wooden balconies on tops of the houses for moon baths. There were quarters for all the four *varnas* to stay as well as special houses for the elite of the Yadava clan. Indra had given the celestial tree known as the Parijata and the assembly hall called Sudharma, which had the power of keeping its occupants free from hunger and thirst. Varuna sent fast white horses with one black ear. Kubera presented eight treasures and the guardian deities placed their resources at the Lord's disposal. Krishna who was none other than Sri Hari now transferred all the people from Mathura to his new capital of Dwaraka.

Srimad Bhagavata Mahapurana
10th Skanda. Chapter 51. Verses. 50-56

ॐ

Kamalanaathaya Namaha!

CHAPTER TWO

The Wedding

The four of them with me following, set out on a tour of the city to see the preparations that had been made for the marriage and the feast which was to follow. As usual all the streets were watered and swept. Every gate had a bunch of plantain fruits and other auspicious articles tied to it. The courtyards were embellished with areca nut and banana trees tied with silken cords. Banners, flags and canopies were everywhere. There were festoons of mango leaves and garlands of jasmine and *champaka* flowers.

A huge dais had been built in the middle of the palace garden flanked by artificial lions, elephants and storks. Two huge saffron-coloured elephants with four tusks were kept at the gate as well as two horses with all trappings. All these looked so real that no one could tell whether they were real or artificial. The altar was on top of the dais. Everything was ready for the arrival of the bride and groom.

Next we went to the huge kitchen to supervise the items for the feast which was to follow. Huge mounds of cooked rice, beaten rice, jaggery, sugar candies and salt were heaped in various places. Milk, ghee and curds were brimming in huge pots. Big tanks were filled with sugar cane juice, wine and sweet juices of various fruits and many rice preparations. Different kinds of pickles and side dishes were also kept ready. I marvelled at the speed at which all these preparations had been made. A sweet heady wine known as Maireya was made locally from fruits. This was a favourite of Balarama's. Public houses were forbidden to sell this wine but surreptitiously it was being sold at most places.

We returned to the garden to find that invitees had already started streaming in. Of course all the citizens had been invited and everyone had come dressed in their festive clothes. Old and young, women, children and babies were all brought for the first big event after their arrival at Dwaraka. Invitations had been sent through fast runners, to all the great kingdoms like Matsya, Kekeya, Srinjaya, Kurujangala,Panchala, Sindhu, Anga, Chedi, Madra, Gandhara, Trigarta and many others but since everything was arranged so fast there was no time for all of them to come. The only ones who actually came were Shishupala, prince of Chedi and Uttaran, prince of the kingdom of the Matsyas. Both King Damaghosha of Chedi and Virata, king of the Matsyas, were too old to go at the killing pace which would have been necessary if they were to reach Dwaraka before nightfall. Shishupala's mother was Vasudeva's sister, so he was Krishna's and Balarama's cousin. It is said that when he was born he had four arms. It was also foretold that two of his arms would fall off when he came face to face with the one who would kill him. This happened the first time he met Krishna so he always held a grudge against him. His mother begged Krishna to overlook her son's failings. Krishna promised her that he would tolerate as many as ninety-nine insults from him, but at the hundredth one he would kill him. To this she had agreed and always warned her haughty son to keep his temper in check and recognise the divinity in his cousin, but Shishupala would not listen to anyone's advice and continued to spread lies about his cousin to anyone who might be inclined to listen to him. When he got the invitation for the wedding he was very eager to come and see the fabulous city of Dwaraka which his cousin had reclaimed from the sea. So he set off post-haste and of course became green with envy when he saw the golden city. Both the princes had been accommodated at palaces specially reserved for kings.

The sages had all been invited through telepathic communication so all of them had arrived. First to come was Krishna Dwaipayana Vyasa himself, and with him came Bharadvaja, Sumantu, Gautama, Asita, Vasishta, Chyavana, Kanva, Maitreya, Viswamitra, Vamadeva, Sumati, Jaimini, Kratu, Paila, Parashara, Vaisampayana, Kasyapa, Dhoumya and Shukracharya. Garga of course was already there as well as Durvasa, but the latter never attended any public functions. As for Brihaspati, he was the *guru* of the gods and did not like it to be known that he was on this planet. He had come only to please Krishna and did not want it to be known by anyone else. The sages were all well-versed in the Vedas and proficient in all rituals so they were the ones to officiate as priests.

When Krishna was a baby, he had been taken by his father Vasudeva to the cowherd settlement of Gokula for fear of his uncle Kamsa. His foster father, Nandagopa, chief of the tribe, knew of Krishna's antecedents, and had secretly invited Garga *muni* to come for the naming ceremony of the two boys, Krishna and Balarama, since he was the *Kula Guru* of the Yadavas. He was also asked to cast their horoscopes since he was a famous astrologer. He performed all the rites secretly inside a cow byre since they did not want Kamsa to know the whereabouts of his nephews who he had threatened to kill. It was Garga who gave the name Krishna to my Lord not only because he was dark, but also because he said he was one who would be able to captivate everyone. He gave the name Balarama to his brother since he would grow up to be very strong.

Garga *muni* was famous for his knowledge of astronomy and astrology, so he sat beside the water clock which was an ingenious device for reckoning time. He had calculated the most auspicious time for the ceremony and was waiting for the correct *lagna* or planetary configuration to take place. He had made a special *ghatika* (water clock) only for this purpose. A small copper cup with a hole at the bottom was floated in a golden vessel filled with water. The water would slowly start filling the cup and at the auspicious moment the cup would sink. This was a special device he had made just for this ritual, but he had also made a big clock which was kept in a room at the entrance to the garden which was accessible to anyone who wanted to know the time. Of course there was also a sundial in the garden but since this depended on the sun it would not work on rainy and cloudy days. The *ghatika* however did not depend on the sun. It was made on the same principle as the one he was using for the ceremony. A small copper vessel with a hole floated in a big bowl of water. It was made with such precision that at the stroke of one *muhurta* (little over an hour) the vessel would sink to the bottom. Immediately a gong would strike to denote the time and the person who was in charge for the day would add a small round stone to the line of stones which were kept in a long carved wooden tray like a trough which was kept for the purpose. Anyone who wanted to know the time could come and count the stones and get a fairly accurate idea.

Krishna and his friends quickly went to Balarama's palace. Krishna knew of his brother's weakness for wine and feared that he might be imbibing a bit too much. They found Balarama seated on a golden stool with a jar of wine in one hand from which he quaffed now and again. Priests chanting *mantras* were pouring water, fragrant with herbs and flowers on his head from golden vessels and earthen jars, from elephant tusks and bull horns. His eyes were already red and rolling and he told them to hurry up for he wanted to meet his bride.

They helped him to his feet. He stood towering over all of them, fair and handsome with curly locks falling to his shoulders. He saluted Krishna and said, "My little brother! I see anxiety in your eyes. What is it? What are you frightened of?"

Without speaking a word my Lord forcibly took the jar of liquor from his hand and told him to get dressed fast. Balarama laughed a bit too loudly and told him that he was never a one to succumb to either wine or women! Attendants came quickly and dressed him in blue silk robes. They took out the stone earring he always wore in his left ear-lobe and put one golden *kundala* instead. Many ornaments were also put round his neck and a diadem on his head. Krishna took off his own unfading wildflower garland (*vanamala*) and put it round his neck. He made a magnificent figure but was slightly shaky on his feet. Krishna and Uddhava stood on either side and led him into the garden. Musicians were playing auspicious tunes and dancing girls were dancing before the groom as he slowly went towards the dais. King Kakudmi along with the priests came forward to meet him and led him to the raised dais after washing his feet and offering *arghya* (perfumed water for washing the hands and mouth). Normally the wedding ceremony would have been done at the bride's house and the mother of the bride would welcome her son-in-law to be, with many rites. Since Kakudmi's wife was not present, the Brahmana women, wives of the priests were the ones who performed all the necessary rituals. After doing the *niranjana* (purificatory) rites, they seated him with all due honours on the golden throne and offered him *madhuparka* (a delicious concoction with milk and honey).

In the meantime, I was anxious to see what was happening to Revati. As we came out of the armoury, I suddenly spied Subhadra running as if in haste to go somewhere. I rushed after her and found myself in Revati's boudoir. She was indeed a fitting bride for Balarama. Statuesque was the only word which could describe her. She towered above Subhadra and her attendants. Subhadra of course was quite petite. Revati was fully dressed by the time I arrived. Her ritual bath was over and she had been anointed with sandal oil. Many things had been done to her face, I could see. Her eyes looked large and lustrous with collyrium and her lips were red with the pigment which must have been put on them. Her hair was dressed very fashionably in many knots with the remainder falling down her right shoulder. She wore a blouse studded with gems. Her skirt was of bright red silk with gold embroidery and swirled round her ankles. Ornaments of every type adorned her from head to toe. However she looked a bit downcast. I presumed that this was because she didn't know the man she was marrying and no doubt due to the fact that she was a princess without a fortune and had a father who was king only in name. Moreover she had no mother or any relations to accompany her. Her eyes were full of tears which she tried hard to suppress. I really felt sorry for her. I think Subhadra felt the same. She was a kind-hearted girl and she went up to her and whispered something in her ear which made her smile a little. Her look of sadness departed. Escorted by many Brahmana ladies who were *sumangalis* (married women), carrying golden plates in which were placed small oil lamps, turmeric pieces, *sindoor,* betel leaves and gold ornaments, she proceeded to the temple of the goddess to worship at her shrine before going to the dais. Widows were never allowed to take part in marriage ceremonies. Musicians, dancing girls and bards accompanied the bridal party. Flower girls were throwing jasmine buds over her head and rose petals in front of her on the road. Devaki and Subhadra walked along with her. Her head was covered with a transparent red scarf which she had pulled over her face so that she would be spared the curious looks of the invitees. She walked with long strides with her eyes fixed on the ground. Devaki and Subhadra had to run to keep up with her. Having finished her worship, she came out hanging on to Subhadra's arm as if she felt that she was her only friend.

At this point I left the bridal party and ran to my beloved's side. He cast an enquiring look at me as I panted up. His looks always made my heart turn over and I just gazed at him without being able to say anything.

The air was filled with the sound of the Vedic chants and musical instruments as the bride was led forward by the Brahmin ladies. She was seated next to the groom while the priests repeated chants from the Rig Veda. Garga *muni* now declared that the auspicious time had come and repeating the *mantras* for purification he took a handful of rice grains which had been mixed with curd and *darbha* (kind of grass), added some water and handed it over to Revati and made her shower it over Balarama. Balarama had eyes only for her, but Revati kept her gaze steadily on the ground. The priests made them rise up and started the marriage rites as given in the Rig Veda.

Before the father actually gives away the bride, the names of the ancestors of both parties as well as their lineage – *gotra*, *pravara* and so on are announced loudly so that all the guests would know that both of them came from good families, and had pedigrees which could be traced back to many generations. Then came the actual ceremony in which Kakudmi took his daughter's hand and formally placed it in Balarama's hand. The latter clasped Revati's hand while the appropriate Vedic *mantras* were being chanted. The upper garments of both were tied in a knot at this point. The music rose to a feverish pitch. Cymbals and drums and bugles were all playing at the same time. Flowers were showered on the couple as Revati placed the flower garland round Balarama's neck. They were of the same height, though Revati looked a bit shorter since she was still gazing at the ground. Kakudmi gave many gifts to the groom and Vasudeva and Devaki did the same for the bride.

The sacrificial fire had already been lit and the priests were doing the *homa (*fire ceremony). The loose scarves worn by Balarama and Revati had been tied together and they were forced to sit very close to each other while pouring offerings into the fire with *mantras*. My Lord also offered grains to the bride to be put into the fire. Actually it is the bride's brother who had to do this but since she had no brother, my Vanamali who is the universal brother performed this act for her. Poor girl! I think she was grateful for this and for the first time she glanced sideways at him. My Lord whispered to her that he would always protect her like a brother. After this Balarama took her right hand and they circumambulated the fire seven times. The priests sprinkled the waters of many auspicious rivers like the Sindhu and Saraswati on her head, thus proclaiming her to be fit for married life. The groom then lifted the scarf which was covering her face and applied the *sindoor* or the auspicious red mark on her forehead.

The ceremony was concluded by Kakudmi presenting a golden vessel filled with raw, unbroken rice to the officiating priests as well as gold coins and clothes. Then Balarama gave a cow and one hundred gold coins to each of the priests. Vasudeva distributed many coins and gifts to all the assembled guests and citizens.

It was quite late by now. All the guests were taken to the huge dining hall to partake of the exotic feast which had been specially prepared. My Lord along with his friends took it as his personal duty to supervise and see that every guest was fed sumptuously and was given proper presents. Seeing him thus occupied I hurried after the bridal procession.

The bride and groom were led ceremoniously to Balarama's palace to the bridal chamber which had been delightfully decorated. The bed was set with gems and covered with silk on which jasmine buds had been scattered. Bejewelled lamps were lit in all corners. The couple were placed on the golden swing covered with flowers and made to swing gently. The knot which had been made in their garments was removed and all sorts of delicious things were offered to them to eat. Revati did not eat a morsel despite all the persuasions of her mother-in-law and sister-in-law. At last Balarama laughed and forced her to open her mouth and stuffed a piece of flat rice-cake into it. She swallowed it with difficulty. Balarama signalled to his sister to bring him something to drink. Devaki nudged her and she gave him a glass of milk and honey which he scornfully rejected and gave to Revati. He was getting quite impatient by now and asked his mother to hurry up with the ceremonies and leave them alone. She sprinkled the bride's head with water to make her free from physical troubles and sanctify her for married life. Then they both stood up and Balarama had to touch the heart of the bride by standing behind her and reaching over her right shoulder. This was supposed to allow feelings of love to flow from him to her and thus unite them in a loving bond. Devaki now took them to the veranda and pointed out the pole star (Dhruva) to them to suggest constancy in their married life. The two stars called Vasishta and Arundhati which are to be seen in the formation known as the Great Bear were also shown to them. The sage Vasishta and his wife Arundhati are famous for being the perfect pair; hence these two stars are always pointed out to newly married couples. (It was only recently that western astronomers discovered that this star was actually two stars which was a fact which was known for many centuries by Hindu astronomers.)

Balarama was getting more and more impatient. So Devaki requested the Brahmin ladies to go out. She put out most of the lamps and led Revati to the bridal bed and made her sit down. She blessed her and smelt her forehead. Subhadra came and gave her a hug and whispered something in her ears. Revati said not a word but sat like a statue. Devaki invited her son to come and sit beside her, but Balarama said he would be back in a minute and disappeared from view. Devaki comforted Revati and told her that he would be back soon and told her to take some rest. She then beckoned to Subhadra and both of them left the room, closing the door behind them. Subhadra kept glancing back at her sister-in-law but did not dare to disobey her mother. I hung around hoping I could help her in some way.

In about half an hour, Balarama came reeling back, holding the wine jar in his hand. He seemed to have forgotten his bride but suddenly he spied her. She rose up in fear and tried to run out of the door but he grabbed her hand and forcibly took her to the bed and threw her down. She covered her eyes with her hands and rolled over to the other side. He laughed and lunged at her and dragged her hand away and peered at her face which he was probably seeing for the first time at such close quarters.

"Why are you frightened?" he roared, "I'm your husband. Come it's our first night. We will never have one like this again. Here have a drink and you will feel much better." So saying he thrust the jar to her mouth. She drank a little and threw his hand away with great difficulty and jumped to her feet and tried to run to the door. He laughed and grabbed her hair as she ran and threw her onto the bed and jumped on her. Luckily for her, he seemed to have succumbed to all the wine he had imbibed and rolled off and fell in a stupor on the bed and started to snore. The jar fell from his hand and rolled to the ground. The wine dripped all over the bed and the floor. Revati rose up and sank to the ground and sobbed as if her heart would break. I felt desperately sorry for her but didn't know how I could comfort her. I left her to her fate and slipped out of the door which had been thoughtfully locked by her mother-in-law who knew her son only too well.

Actually Balarama was a good man in his own way and was no doubt good to her when he was in his right senses. But he could never shake off his love for drink and this was something which Revati had to put up with since she really had no choice. In fact I heard later that in the end she succumbed to his persuasions and used to join him in his drinking bouts.

I ran off to find my Vanamali who was still attending to the needs of the guests. Finally the last of the guests had departed and only those who were staying in palaces close by were left. Krishna took special joy in seeing to Shishupala's welfare.

"Ah cousin!" he said, "It was very kind of you to come and I hope you enjoyed yourself. Tell me is there is anything I can do for you?"

Shishupala mumbled something and Krishna told Satyaki to take him to his palace. Uttaran, prince of the Matsyas was a favourite of his so he personally escorted him to his palace and only then did he retire to his own palace.

"Well did you enjoy it?" he asked me without looking at me as he was striding to his room.

'Very much,' I said 'but I'm sorry for Revati. I don't think she is happy.'

"Don't bother your head with such things," he said, "she will have to adjust to my brother's ways. He is a kind man though he drinks a bit too much. That is his only failing."

Aum Namo Bhagavate Vaasudevaaya

Vaasudevaya Namaha!

CHAPTER THREE

Badarikashrama

After staying for a week in Dwaraka, Kakudmi said that he wanted to retire to the place known as Badarikashrama in the Himalayas. Both Balarama and Krishna tried to convince him to remain for some time in Dwaraka to be near his daughter but he could not be persuaded. I don't know what Revati told him, but it is possible that she did not say much to him about her predicament. She seemed to be reconciled to her fate. She had found a lovely family here – mother, father, brother and sister and she was cared for in all ways, so being a sensible girl she decided to adjust to the circumstances. Moreover, she had no relations to go to, even if she wanted to.

All arrangements were being made for Kakudmi's departure and I wished that I could also make the trip to the Himalayas. The Lord who could read the hearts of all asked me if I wanted to make a trip to the mountains. I just looked at him and he said, "Whom are you going to see there? When I am with you, whom else would you want to see?"

I said nothing so he smiled and said, "OK! Let's go!"

I skipped and jumped beside him. Since we would be going through strange territories with very few roads, all of us rode horseback. That is to say he rode a horse and I sat at the back. I didn't find it at all strange that I was riding a horse even though I had never gone on one before. The king had his own retinue given by the Yadava princes. There were pack horses carrying food and all sorts of military equipment in case of attack or being stranded in the desert etc. As far as possible we followed the river – first the Sindhu/Saraswati and then the Ganga. The first part of the journey through the northern part of Aryavrata was fairly easy. We passed through the Anarta region and followed the Sindhu River, passing north through Matsya and Madra and continued till we reached Kurujangala. We by-passed Hastinapura since Krishna said the time had not come for him to meet his cousins, and continued north up the holy river Ganga till we came to the ancient city of Mayapuri or Gangadwara (Haridwar). We stayed the night at the *ashrama* of the great sage Kapila, the founder of the Samkhya system of philosophy. My Lord talked with him through a good part of the night while I sat fascinated by their discussion.

We then proceeded to a place at the foothills of the Himalayas where Raibya Rishi was doing intense *tapas*. In fact he had not moved from the spot where he had started *tapasya* many years ago and his locks had spread all over the place, giving rise to the name of the place which later came to be called Rishikesha (hair of the *rishi*). He had been meditating on Lord Vishnu and when Krishna went and stood before him, he suddenly opened his eyes and found the object of his meditation standing before him in flesh and blood. The Lord gave him *darshana* in the form of Vishnu on whom he had been meditating for centuries. He saw standing before him the beauteous figure of Vishnu holding the conch, discus, mace and lotus in his four hands with all the other accoutrements. I thought to myself that he had agreed to take me to Badarikashrama only to give this great sage his beatific vision. Due to his heavy locks pulling him down, the sage could not rise up and prostrate so he simply bowed to him. My Lord in the form of Vishnu blessed him and released him from his earthly coils.

From there we went to the *ashrama* of sage Vasishta. It was a series of caves on the banks of the Alagananda in a most beautiful spot. The sage was delighted to see my Lord and invited him to stay there for some time. It was so beautiful that we stayed for more than a week. One day the Lord took me into the largest of the caves and showed me a small tunnel leading out of it. He held my hand and took me through the tunnel which led to another smaller cave. There was a *rishi* sitting and meditating with just a small lighted mud lamp beside him. Krishna took me still further into the mountain and showed me any number of *rishis* meditating in the rabbit warren of caves which seemed to extend far into the heart of the mountain. All of them were oblivious of us walking past them through the caves. How did they live? I wondered and Krishna smiled and shook his head.

We returned to the main cave and sitting on the banks of the river he told me, "These are true Sannyasis. They want nothing and ask for nothing. They have total faith in God. If he wants them to live, he will see to it that they get something to eat. Otherwise they fast. They have no dependence on man or beast. Hence they have no duty to perform in the world. If we depend on something for our existence then we have a duty to return the debt by doing something for the society which supports us. But if we have no demands on the world, we have no duties either. They have surrendered all their *dharmas* to God and thus God alone protects them. They live only to promote auspiciousness in the world. Vibrations flow from them to the world outside so that those whose lives are filled with care and toil, fighting and killing, will be benefited by them."

I was amazed to hear this. I had never heard of such people. I thought of a *sannyasi* as someone who had renounced the world and wore ochre robes and was dependent on society for his daily needs. Never had I come across people who asked for no rights and therefore had no duties!

Our entourage proceeded with difficulty up the mountain following the Alagananda. At many places the servants who had been sent with Kakudmi had to hack their way across the forest entwined with lianas and branches of trees. At night if we did not reach an *ashrama* we would have to stay in some cave or make a clearing and a fire and lie beneath the stars near the fire. The fire was a necessity to keep wild animals at bay. Often we could hear the roar of a tiger in the distance and bears would come fairly close. Of course there were plenty of deer in the clearings.

The next place of interest was the *prayaga* (confluence) of the Alagananda with the River Bhagirathi, which was coming from the source of the Ganga from the place called Gomukha. Ages ago, the great King Bhagiratha had performed intense *tapas* at Gomukha to bring down the divine Ganga from the heavens to the earth in order to give salvation to his ancestors. The Ganga agreed to come but told him that if she fell with all force on the earth the whole planet would be washed away, so Bhagiratha did another series of intense *tapas* and begged Lord Shiva to check her fall. Shiva agreed and when the Ganga fell, he caught her in his locks and went back to his own *tapasya*. Poor Bhagiratha went back and did many more years of *tapas* and begged Shiva to release the waters. He did so and the Ganga followed the king as he rode towards the ocean where his ancestors had perished. All the places she flowed through were blessed by the touch of her purifying waters. She is known as Bhagirathi when she comes from Gomukha, in honour of King Bhagiratha who was instrumental in bringing her down.

The Ganga has many names and is known as Alagananda when she comes down from Badarikashrama. The confluence of two or more rivers is considered to be filled with divine energy and bathing at these places is a must for all pilgrims. So we stopped at a small Shiva temple next to the confluence. The two rivers met with a mighty clash below a cliff where the clear waters of the Alagananda mingled with the dark waters of the Bhagirathi. All of us went down the precarious rock cut steps leading to the confluence. The men jumped in without any hesitation, but the current was so strong that a couple of them swirled away and had to be caught and brought back by the others. I had no idea as to what sort of creature I was – flesh and blood or a dream substance. However I was taking no chances and clung on to my Lord's *uttareeyam* when he dipped. I gasped as the icy waters closed over my head. I was totally free from fear. Was I not holding on to him?

We spent the night there and pushed on to our next stop which we reached after a week or so. But of course time had ceased to have any meaning for me. I lived totally in the blissful moment when I was tagging behind my Lord. Krishna told me the story of the place that night while we sat round the fire. "This place is known as Shree-Nagar (the town of the goddess) and this was the place which the goddess Lalithambika chose as her residence. This esoteric secret had been revealed to the sage Agastya by me in my incarnation as Hayagriva (having the neck of a horse). The temple itself is in the shape of a Meru and the mystic *Yantra* known as Sri Chakra has been installed here. Sit down on this rock near the river and meditate." The place was charged with the vibrant energy of the Divine Mother and I cannot describe the feeling of exaltation which came over me as I felt her energy coursing through me like an electric current.

Our next stop was at another famous confluence where the Alagananda met the Mandakini coming down from the place known as Kedar Kanda. The confluence here was also filled with energy and all of us took our dips in the swirling waters. My Vanamali of course never had to take baths or get energised, but in this incarnation he chose to act the part of a human being and follow all the customs of humans in order to set an example.

I've no idea how far we walked and how many miles but slowly the whole terrain started to change. We passed above the tree line. The landscape had only rocks and shrubs with the glittering, cascading Alagananda leaping over rocks and boulders, leading us up and up, showing us the way. The chief difference was that she was going down and we were going up. The only tree growing here was the divine *devataru*, tree of the gods. At one point Krishna told Kakudmi's retinue to carry on and wafted me off to an enchanted place deep in the mountains. I gasped with joy when I saw the place. It was a huge garden, stretching as far as the eye could see, covered with all sorts of tiny, magical flowers. My Vanamali lifted me in his arms and gave me an aerial view of the place. It looked like a huge carpet of mixed design and colours all made of real flowers of every shape, design and hue.

'What is this?' I gasped, inaudibly as usual.

"This is the playground of the *apsaras* (celestial dancers) and *gandharvas* (celestial musicians). Listen carefully and you will be able to hear them." I listened and the most extraordinary melody filled my whole being and a wonderful perfume wafted in the breeze.

"You cannot see them" he said, answering my question, "but you can hear and feel them. Come we will go. As human beings we are not allowed to stay long in this place. If we stay too long they will desert it and go to places which are beyond the reach of humans."

Of course this did come to pass. I remembered hearing about the "Valley of Flowers" in my previous life and how it was crowded with tourists. From there he took me to another place with a glacial lake in which he said the *apsaras* bathed.

"This lake never freezes over," he said. "This is the place where Rama's brother Lakshmana did *tapasya* in order to expiate for the sin of having killed Indrajit."

The lake looked like a mirror since it was absolutely still and the reflection of the snow peaks was perfectly mirrored.

I had always suspected that he was a master of all the eight *siddhis* of which levitation was one but all these days since we had been travelling with others, he had chosen to travel as they did, but now that we were alone he lifted me in his arms and we soon reached the party we had left just a few hours ago. Now we were on our last lap. It was getting colder and colder and soon we got our first sight of the snow peaks. I gave a gasp of pure delight. There, standing stark and white against the bright blue sky, were the great peaks of the Himalayas. From a height, we could see the valley stretching out before us – the valley known as Badarikashrama or Badri Vishal. It was so named because the place abounded with the small thorny berries known as *badari*. This was the place of the divine sages called Narayana and Nara, who were partial incarnations of Vishnu. However, they were not visible to all even though they would certainly have been visible to my Lord. But he chose not to show himself to them and took us to the modest *ashrama* of the great sage known as Markandeya.

The Ganga's name here is Puspabhadra. The *ashrama* was concealed behind a huge rock known as Chitra. The sage was sitting with eyes closed in meditation. Krishna went forward and touched his feet. He jumped up from the tiger skin seat he had been occupying and fell at the Lord's feet. Krishna clasped him in his arms and told him that he had brought Kakudmi, the King of Anarta, who was anxious to spend the rest of his days in the Himalayas. The sage had matted locks and his robes of bark were held in place with a girdle of *munja* grass. The upper portion of his body was covered with the skin of a black buck and a *mala* made of the seeds of the *rudraksha* tree. He made a striking figure and carried a staff, a bunch of *kusa* grass and a *kamandalu* (water pot made of a double coconut shell) in his hands. He promised to help Kakudmi to build a hermitage close to him.

There was a lovely hot spring just below the hermitage and below that roared the Alagananda filled with foam and fury as she forced her way through huge boulders. While we were there my Lord told me the story of the sage Markandeya.

"There was once a poor Brahmana of Avanti who was childless. He and his wife prayed to Lord Shiva who appeared to them and told them that they could have either a brilliant son who would live only for sixteen years or a fool who would live for a long period of time. After thinking it over, the couple opted for the noble child. Very soon the woman conceived and gave birth to a lovely boy who grew up to be intelligent, graceful and devoted to Shiva. When his sixteenth birthday approached, the child saw his parents to be deeply troubled and asked them the reason. Reluctantly they told him the truth. The boy was not at all put out by this tale and told them to take heart. 'The Lord who gave me to you will surely be able to prolong my life,' he said. He started a year- long vow of intense austerity. On the morning of the sixteenth year of his life, the boy was proceeding to their temple for his usual worship of his chosen deity when he saw the shadow of Yama, the god of Death who was striding behind him looming in front of him. He ran towards the temple and hugged the *lingam* of Shiva and begged him to save him. Yama was not able to throw his noose round the boy who was hugging the *lingam* so he threw it round both the *lingam* and the boy. Immediately Shiva jumped out of the *lingam* and told Yama. 'You have done your duty. The boy was expected to live only for sixteen years. Now I will take over and you can go.'

My Lord continued, "Shiva took up the boy in his arms and promised him that he would live for the whole of this eon. He told him to go to the Himalayas and practice austerity at this holy spot. After many years, the sages Narayana and Nara came here to give him some boons but Markandeya refused. At last when they pressed him to accept something, the sage came up with a unique request. He told them that he wanted to experience Vishnu's *Maya*!! The divine sages blessed him and left the place. Very soon Markandeya felt as if a huge deluge had come and covered his *ashrama* and all the places around. He was drowning in the water and coming up for air many times. This was the *samsara sagara* or the ocean of mortal existence. At this time he saw a wondrous sight. A divine infant was lying on a delicate heart-shaped *peepul* leaf and sucking his own toe. Seeing this, the sage swam towards the infant and felt himself to be drawn into the stomach of the child through his breath. Within the child he saw the vision of the universe as he remembered it. The galaxies, the worlds, the stars, the earth with forests and mountains and seas were all there. He saw the wondrous infant also and as he swam forward to embrace him, the baby disappeared and the sage found himself back in his own *ashrama,* and he was surprised that only a few moments had passed since he had the dream. Then he realised that the whole of Time as we imagine it is only a moment in the eyes of God who lives in eternity. For him there is neither past nor future. There is nothing but this glorious present. Thus he was given a glimpse of Vishnu's *Maya* which he had wanted to experience."

'Tell me more,' I begged.

My Lord smiled at my eagerness and continued, "Markandeya composed himself in order to take in everything that he had experienced. One day when he was meditating on the glorious infant, who had tantalised him, he found the vision to have been replaced by the forms of Lord Shiva and Parvati. They also wanted to shower him with boons. Markandeya who had not yet recovered from the effects of one boon prostrated before the divine couple and asked for nothing but firm devotion to God at all times.

Lord Shiva said, 'O Great Soul! All that you have asked for will be given to you. You will be freed from the trammels of old age and death. Your life span will extend to the end of this cosmic dissolution. You will have complete renunciation and total illumination. Those who have your vision will be purified. Your fame shall last for all time.' So saying the divine couple disappeared from view."

My Vanamali said, "You are fortunate to have had Markandeya's *darshana*".

I bowed to him and thanked him for the enlightening story and asked, 'Were you not the one who was lying on the peepul leaf?' He laughed and touched the locket round by neck which had the same emblem, which I wore all the time. I caught his hand and pressed it tightly to my cheek. I suddenly felt something hard against my cheek. It was a signet ring which looked like a seal. It was rectangular in shape and made of conch shell and had a strange motif on it – a bull, unicorn and goat were kind of entwined on it.

'What is this?' I asked.

"This is a *mudra* (seal) which every citizen of Dwaraka has to carry. He will be asked to show it when he enters the city."

'Surely you don't have to carry it.'

"Perhaps not, but I like to set an example to everyone. Why should they obey orders if I don't obey them myself?"

While we were living at the *ashrama,* I took this opportunity to do some service for him while he was without too many attendants. Every morning I would bring Ganga water in a copper pot and wash his feet and apply sandal paste on them and place some exotic wild flowers on them. I would then sing some songs which I knew and place my head on his lotus feet and would be thrilled to feel his hand touching my head lightly. Once he had placed one foot on a stone so instead of bowing at his feet I bowed a little further off. This time I was electrified by the heavy contact of his foot which he placed firmly on my head. I had heard that this was a signal honour which *gurus* give to their favourite pupils. I just stayed there on the ground since I was too dazed to move until he lifted me up. My eyes filled with tears and I whispered, 'Make me worthy Lord!'

We spent some glorious days at this divine place. Sometimes I would ask him to play on his flute. 'Play the same *raga* you used to play for the *gopis,*' I said. He would sit on a big mossy stone in front of a *devataru,* way above the river. The river made such a noise that music could not be heard near it. I would sit at his feet and lean back on his leg and look out into the far distance as I listened to the magic flute. I was one of the *gopis* rushing to meet him, leaving everything behind, caring not for the scolding I would get when I returned, tired and sleepy when the harvest moon was about to set and the eastern sky was slowly turning pink. The anger and scandal of the whole village did not thwart the *gopis* or me from rushing to our divine lover on full moon nights when the rest of the world was asleep. At this time the whole forest would wake up, for all the creatures wanted to listen to the Lord's entrancing music. The deer would come closer and closer and nestle up to him as I have often done and the peacocks would start to dance not knowing that it was still night. The song birds were silent and would perch on the branches of the *champaka* tree under which he was standing, and the tree would shed its lovely golden coloured flowers over him. The River Kalindi would rush out of her boundaries to come closer to the Lord's feet. The sky would be brilliantly lit with moonlight and made brighter by the jewels of the gods who clustered above, anxious to hear the Lord's music. The plaintive call of the flute penetrated into the minds of even the most sluggish hearts so that they woke up and wondered what it was that had woken them up. What did it not do to the *gopis* who had been waiting all their lives for that moment, who had observed a forty-one day vow and prayed to the goddess, Karthyayini, the primeval mother divine, begging her to give them the son of Nanda as their lover? They cared not for anything but their beloved waiting for them to come to him. This was the call of the Paramatma to the *jivatma*. "Come, come, come," it said, "I have been waiting for eons for you to wake up and listen to my call and come to me – your eternal self, your eternal beloved. At the time of death so would the *jivatma* rush naked towards its eternal companion, the Paramatma, without a thought or care or desire for the house, family and children that it was leaving behind....I woke up with a start. He had stopped playing and I was only a poor dream girl leaning against him. I turned round and he had a question as well as an answer in his look as if he knew exactly what I had been experiencing. 'Was I there?' I whispered.

"You were always there," he whispered back.

One day I found the Lord having a preoccupied look on his face. 'What is the matter?' I enquired in the usual method of communication. He was sitting on a rock and I sat at his feet as usual and looked enquiringly at him. "Do you know the reason for my present incarnation?" he asked. I shook my head. "I will tell you the story of this holy land from the time of the great flood when I took my second incarnation in the form of a fish."

I settled back to listen. "This world has passed through many ages and seen many things. There have been many Ice Ages when huge blocks of ice have broken off from the poles and joined the waters of the ocean which would start to rise up uncontrollably. In one of the first Ice Ages when the whole world was about to be drowned in the waters, I told the King called Satyavrata that I would send a boat into the waters, into which he should take all species of animals, annual plants and seeds. The seven sages who knew the Vedas would be in the boat and I myself would take on the form of a huge dolphin and come near the boat. I asked him to attach the boat to my snout and I would take him through the waters which were rising alarmingly. Everything happened as I had said and soon the whole land was submerged. At this time I gave him a discourse on the mystery of life which later came to be called "The Matsya Purana". The book deals with the differentiation between Prakriti and Purusha, (Matter and Spirit) and is known as Samkhya Yoga. It was later taught by the sage Kapila whom we met in Mayapuri. At last the flood waters subsided and the land came up and I took the sages and the king back to where they had started. This was my second *avatara* known as Matsyavatara (incarnation as the fish)."

'I thought this was your first,' I said.

"No, my first was the causal boar, Varaha. That was at the time of the start of creation. Only under certain conditions do planets float as weightless balls in space, and as soon as these conditions are disturbed, planets will fall down into the Garbhodaka Ocean, which covers half the universe. The other half of this spherical dome is the place in which the innumerable planetary systems exist and it is presided over by Brahma. The reason why planets float in space is due to the inner constitution of the globes. The *asura* called Hiranyaksha created a disturbance of these conditions and the earth was detached from its weightless condition and fell down into the Garbhodaka Ocean. That was the time I took the incarnation of the boar and lifted her out of the Garbodhaka Ocean where the *asura* had taken her, and placed her in her present position and restored all the conditions which enabled her to float. I also gave her the law of gravity which ensured that such a thing would never happen to her again. This ocean is below the fourteen worlds and the planetary system presided over by Brahma. That is the ocean on which I recline on Shesha, the thousand-hooded serpent of Time. Thousands of years passed and this holy land of Aryavrata into which the seven sages are born again and again, flourished with spiritual effulgence."

'Did the sages bring the Vedas to this land or were they always here?' I asked.

"The Vedas are *anaadi* (without a beginning) and *ananta* (without an end). They are sound vibrations which always exist in etheric space. They can only be heard by ten-sensory people like the *rishis* whose senses are finely tuned to hear extra-terrestrial vibrations. They can even hear the sound emanating from the sun. That sound is aaa-uuu-mmm which we pronounce as Aum. The *rishis* are born in every age in order to recover the Vedas which are sometimes lost due to the passage of time. As I said, they revive them and pass them on to their disciples who hand them over to future generations. The culture of Aryavrata comes from the Vedas.

"When the waters of the deluge subsided, the *rishis* returned to the land and started to make their small *ashramas* along the banks of the Saraswati and Sindhu in the foothills of the Himalayas. Slowly these turned into small villages and the *rishis* taught them the Vedic culture and the Brahmanas used to chant the Vedas and teach them to their disciples so that the Vedas were a living, vibrant force in the lives of all the people. Slowly these villages started to migrate to the plains where they made towns and cities. The rivers Sindhu and Saraswati and its tributaries formed a huge basin known as the Sapta Sindhu. It was a vast, prosperous and fertile plain on which the culture of this land flourished. Many villages and even great civilisations flourished here."

'What has happened to these civilisations?' I asked.

"They perished due to various climatic conditions and others came in their stead, and these also perished and still others took their place. So it will go on till the end of this period of creation." (I realised that he was talking about what is now known as the Indus Valley Civilization.)

He continued, “The great river Saraswati lost her largest tributary the Yamuna due to a tectonic plate shift. Floods in the Sindhu also made a great impact on these cities. The decline of the culture along the river Sindhu saw a gradual decline in moral and social values. *Dharma* suffered heavily. Some of the migrants travelled west and others started to make small settlements in the Ganga and Yamuna basins. Once again the Vedic civilization started to revive. Those who travelled west took our culture along with them and taught the *mlecchas* (barbarians) who lived in those places the basics of cultured living as existed then in this country.”

‘What about this civilization which is existing now?’ I asked.

“This is one of the civilisations that I am talking to you about. These turned into small republics known as ‘janapadas’. Gradually they enlarged to form ‘Mahajanapadas’ like Matsya and Magadha. They were all very good in the beginning but slowly the kings started to degenerate and there was a marked decline in moral values. My uncle Kamsa is a good example. Narakasura in Pragjyotisha (Assam), Jarasandha of Magadha and his ally Kalayavana who helped him to rout us from Madura are all Mahajanapadas. As you know it was because of them that I was forced to take my people to the safety of Dwaraka. So in a way I have to be grateful to them! There are many more like them who are bent on destroying this ancient culture.”

‘Will Dwaraka also fall at some time?’ I asked timidly.

“Yes indeed, Dwaraka will be submerged in the waters from something like a huge tidal wave which will destroy many parts of Aryavrata after I drop my mortal coils.” I couldn’t bear to think of this and caught hold of his hand and held it tightly to my cheek.

‘What will happen to this culture then?’

“I have taken this incarnation to restore the primeval *dharma* as embedded in the Vedas and make Aryavrata a holy land once again. For this I will have to enlist the support of the Pandavas who are actually Kuru princes who should be living in their capital city of Hastinapura in the country known as Kurujangala. However, they have been ousted from their inheritance and are now hiding in a village known as Ekachakra near Panchala. They are noble souls and they are fit to take up this task of cleansing this holy land of all the wicked rulers and establishing the Sanatana Dharma once again in its pristine glory."

My curiosity was fully aroused and I asked, 'Why are these princes living in Ekachakra? Why were they forced to leave Hastinapura?'

Aum Namo Bhagavate Vaasudevaaya

The Bose-Einstein condensate is not physical matter but something just below it. It is a phase of matter that has completely different properties to any other kind of matter known to science.

Atoms in a gas at room temperature move at about 1,000 miles per hour. They slow down to about 1 metre per hour as the temperature approaches absolute zero, but the atoms in a BEC barely move at all. When the atoms stop vibrating they are able to share the same space, since atoms are 99.999999% empty anyway. Bose-Einstein condensate can only exist at absolute zero (-273°C); a temperature so cold that the energy aspect of energy-matter becomes zero. Absolute zero is the baseline that prevents creation from descending any lower – it is quite literally the bottom of the universe.

The Sanskrit word "Avichi" (meaning waveless) describes the lowest possible state of existence and clearly refers to the non-vibrational state of the Bose-Einstein condensate. The ancient Hindu scripture, the Srimad Bhagavatam 5.26.5 states that the "Garbhodaka Ocean" lies at the bottom of the universe – this clearly refers to the "sea" of Bose-Einstein Condensate that exists below the physical plane.

ॐ

Sananthanaaya Namaha!

CHAPTER FOUR

The Kurus

"Let me tell you their story. They belong to the Chandra Vamsa. Hastinapura is the ancient capital of the Kurus. The city was established by one of their ancestors named Hastin. One of the kings in their lineage called Santanu had a son named Bhishma who was born from his marriage to the river goddess, Ganga. She left him for some reason and much later he fell in love with a fisherwoman known as Satyavati. She was the daughter of the chief of the fisher clan. Once when she was but a maid the great sage Parasara saw her and knew that she was destined to become the empress of the land. He also knew that if she got a child by him, he would become a great sage. Thus she became the mother of the sage, Vyasa who is the considered as the first of all *gurus* for this whole land of Aryavrata. The sage blessed her that she would become an empress. Santanu saw her on one of his hunting expeditions and wanted to marry her, but her father made him promise that her son would inherit the kingdom. The king agreed to the condition and married her thus disinheriting his noble, first born son, Bhishma.

"Satyavati gave birth to two sons who were both very weak. The elder prince, Chitrangada was killed by a *gandharva* who had the same name. When it was time for the second son Vichitravirya to marry, Bhishma decided that it would be better for him to go to the *swayamvara* arranged by the king of Kasi for his three beautiful daughters, Amba, Ambika and Ambalika. Though he was not that young, there was no one who could beat Bhishma and he easily defeated all the other kings and captured the three princesses and brought them to Hastinapura. At the time of the wedding Amba told Satyavati that her heart had already been given to Shalya, king of Madra. Bhishma immediately gave her an escort and sent her to Shalya who refused to accept her since she had been captured by Bhishma in front of the eyes of so many people. She returned to Hastinapura and begged Vichitravirya to marry her. He had already married her younger sisters and refused to marry someone who had previously given her heart to another man. At last in despair she appealed to Bhishma to marry her. He gently refused her and said he was sworn to celibacy. Amba was furious and blamed Bhishma for all her troubles. She swore to take revenge on him. She went to the forest and did intense *tapasya* to Kartikeya, general of the gods. He gave her a garland of unfading lotus flowers and told her that the one who agreed to wear the garland would be able to kill Bhishma. Amba went from warrior to warrior, but everyone refused the dubious honour of killing Bhishma. At last she flung the garland over a pillar in the royal courtyard of Drupada, king of Panchala and returned to the forest to do another bout of penance to Shiva. Shiva granted her the boon that she would be able to kill Bhishma in her next life and that she would have a clear memory of all the incidents of her previous life. Impatient to end her unfortunate life, she immolated herself in a fire."

'Then what happened?' I asked in eager anticipation.

"Vichitravirya died of consumption before he could get any children and the line of the Kurus was in danger of extinction. Satyavati called her noble son Vyasa and begged him to beget children on the barren wives of her sons. At his mother's earnest request, Vyasa did so even though he was a sage and begat a boy called Dritarashtra on the daughter-in-law called Ambika, and another son called Pandu on the daughter-in-law, Ambalika. Since Ambika had closed her eyes when the stern looking sage approached her, she had a son called Dritarashtra who was born blind. As for Ambalika, she produced a pale, sickly looking infant since she had turned pale at the sight of Vyasa! Satyavati urged Vyasa to try once more for a good offspring who would carry on the lineage of the Kuru dynasty, but this time both the daughters-in-law refused to go and sent their maid instead. The maid served the sage well and gave birth to a wonderful child known as Vidura. Dritarashtra married the princess of Gandhara (Afghanistan) who gave birth to a hundred sons who are known as the Kauravas. Their eldest is called Duryodhana. Gandhari's brother, Shakuni accompanied his sister to help her since she chose to blindfold herself since her husband was blind.

"Do you want me to continue with the story?" he asked. I nodded vigorously.

'How do you know all this?' I whispered since I already knew the answer. He gave me a long look and I dropped my eyes.

"Since Dritarashtra was blind, his younger brother Pandu became king. He married Kunti, the adopted daughter of Kuntibhoja. Her actual father was Shoora who also had a son called Vasudeva who is my father. Kunti's real name is Pritha. She had a sister who married Damaghosha, king of Chedi, and Shishupala whom you met at the wedding, is her son. So now you know my lineage and why I am known as Vaasudeva." He laughed and lifted my chin a little and looked into my eyes which made me almost swoon with delight.

'I know that you have no lineage or family or *gotra* or name. You are the supreme formless Brahman who has taken on a form to entice the world. You are the master of all illusion. No one knows the reason for your incarnations.'

He smiled at me and asked, "Shall I continue?" I nodded.

"Pandu also married the princess of Madra, known as Madri. Her brother is the great king known as Shalya who has now become very powerful. Pandu was a great king and acquired many lands and established the supremacy of the Kuru dynasty. After this he left for a holiday to the forest with his wives. For some reason which we need not go into now, Pandu decided to stay on in the forest and lead the life of a recluse. Dritarashtra though blind was helped by Bhishma who actually ruled the country. In due time Pandu's wife Kunti gave birth to three sons who were called Yudhishtira, Bhima and Arjuna who are all said to be sons of the gods. Yudhistira's father is Dharma, Bhima's is the wind god Vayu and Arjuna's, Indra, king of the gods. Kunti had been given a *mantra* by my *guru,* Durvasa, which would enable her to invoke any god so that they would bless her with children. The sage with his deep foresight knew that her husband would not be able to give her any children and that is why he taught this *mantra* to her. As I told you before, even the gods are frightened of the sages for they are totally desireless. Kunti taught the *mantra* to Pandu's second wife, Madri, who invoked the twin gods known as the Ashvini Kumaras and gave birth to the twins known as Nakula and Sahadeva.

"The Kauravas starting with Duryodhana were born in Hastinapura soon after Bhima's birth in the forest. So you see that Kunti is my father's sister and the Pandavas are my first cousins. Arjuna and I are about the same age. Born of the gods as they are, the Pandavas have a noble nature and thus they are the ones I have chosen to help me in the task of bringing *dharma* back to this land."

Where are they now I wondered? He knew my thoughts and answered immediately. "Pandu died in the forest and his wife Madri immolated herself on his pyre, so my aunt Kunti was left to look after all the five boys. When Yudhishtira became sixteen years of age, the sages of the forest persuaded her to return to Hastinapura and stake her claim for her sons who were true princes of the realm. Bhishma was very happy to see them and brought them up as his own grandchildren along with the Kauravas. Bhishma appointed the same *gurus* for all the boys – Drona and Kripa who though Brahmanas were well-versed in the art of warfare. From the first the Kauravas did not take kindly to their cousins who they regarded as usurpers. Matters were made worse by the fact that the

Pandavas excelled them in everything. Not only were they experts in all types of weapons but their characters were also exemplary. They were clever, obedient and polite and everybody loved them. Bhishma was particularly fond of Arjuna and used to place him on his lap even though he was a young boy of fourteen when he came to the court. Duryodhana hated the Pandavas and Bhima in particular who was his own age and similar in stature and excelled in mace fighting. In fact aided by his uncle Shakuni who was his mother's brother, he tried many times to kill Bhima by drowning him, throwing him into a serpent ridden pond and giving him poison etc."

'How do you know all this?' I interrupted even though I knew the answer.

He smiled and said, "I know everything. I even know what passes through people's minds. In fact I am the one who shielded Bhima and saved him from all his trials. But of course they have never met me so they know of me only through hearsay."

He gave me one of his piercing looks which said, "Surely you know this! This question hardly becomes one whom I have shielded so many times from so many dangers!" I hung my head in shame and buried my face between his knees which were most accessible since I was sitting at his feet

After a short break I lifted my face and asked 'Where are they now? Will they recognise you?'

"We have never met but they must have heard of me from Bhishma and Drona."

'How do Bhishma and Drona know you?' I asked.

"They are enlightened beings. They know that I have incarnated as the son of Vasudeva. Moreover the tales of the miracles I performed in Gokula and Vrindavana have gone before me. Bards go from town to town singing my tales." He looked at me with a teasing look and asked, "Have you never heard these stories? Don't you believe in them?"

'My Lord there is nothing that I cannot believe about you. You are Vanamali. What is it that you cannot do?' He smiled and continued.

"Now to go back to our story. When the princes had finished their military training, Drona and Kripa held a competition for them in which the Pandavas excelled as usual. Duryodhana was so angry that he decided to enlist the aid of my brother, Balarama who is famous for his ability to handle the mace, to teach him more tricks. He invited Balarama to Hastinapura and both Bhima and he became my brother's pupils. They were both very good, but for some reason my brother seems to like Duryodhana more than Bhima. I could never figure out how Duryodhana managed to ingratiate himself with my brother.

"Some years ago when Yudhishtira became eighteen years of age, he was crowned as Yuvaraja at the insistence of Bhishma and Drona. This was a terrible blow to Duryodhana who had been certain that he could force his father to make him Yuvaraja. Within a couple of years of his becoming Yuvaraja, the Pandavas enlarged the borders of their kingdom by defeating their powerful neighbours. Of course this made them more laudable to everyone. However it only added fuel to the fire of Duryodhana's wrath. One day he went secretly to his father and swore to kill himself if the Pandavas were not removed. Dritarashtra was a weakling and his attachment for his son made him even weaker and he gave in to Duryodhana's wish. He invited the Pandavas to go for a sojourn in the beautiful and holy city of Varanavata (Varanasi). This city is the most ancient city in Aryavrata, older than Mayapuri to which I have taken you and the favourite abode of Lord Shiva, the Pandavas' tutelary deity. Vidura, who was the Pandavas' uncle, was not at all happy about this apparently friendly invitation. He suspected a plot and warned the Pandavas to be on their guard. The citizens also suspected some plot and wanted to go with the Pandavas. Yudhishtira told them to return to their own homes and he would come back soon. Duryodhana had made a palace of *lac* and other inflammable materials and the Pandavas were invited to stay there. The idea was to set fire to the palace at the end of the year, when the

Pandavas had been lulled into a false sense of security. But Vidura knew everything and told the brothers to familiarise themselves with the forest around the palace. He had also ordered a miner to dig a tunnel leading from the palace to the forest. On the appointed day Kunti told Bhima to go to the cremation *Ghats* on the river and collect six corpses which had not been totally burnt. They left these on their beds and all six of them escaped through the tunnel into the forest after setting fire to the palace. The next day there was a hue and cry and the news of the demise of the Pandavas was sent to Hastinapura. The Kauravas and Dritarashtra shed a few crocodile tears and only Vidura and Bhishma knew that they had escaped and bided their time."

'What did the Pandavas do then?'

"Aren't you tired of hearing this story?"

'How can I ever tire of listening to your nectarine voice? Tell me more,' and I snuggled closer to his legs as he sat on the rock with me at his feet.

"They trekked through the forest which was cleared for them by Bhima. Sometimes he even had to carry all of them in turn on his broad shoulders. Of course his mother he carried all the time. It was at this time that a *rakshasi* called Hidimbi fell in love with the muscular Bhima and exhorted him to marry her. Kunti agreed since she thought that this might be a protection for them against further assaults by the *rakshasa* tribes who roamed around the forest."

'Who are these *rakshasas*?' I asked.

My Lord replied, "They are the original inhabitants of the forest and are cannibals and so all the city people fear and avoid them. They also disturb the sages who live in the forest and it is the duty of the king to protect these sages."

'Then what happened?'

"They lived happily in the forest for a year and Hidimbi gave birth to a strong and lovely boy called Ghatotkacha. At that time Vyasa who knows everything went to meet them and told them that the time had come for them to take up their life where they had left it. He told them to go to the village called Ekachakra. Hidimbi was bereft at the thought of the parting, but she knew that Bhima was a king and she could not keep him forever. All of them had become fond of her and the boy by this time so it was a sad parting for everybody. She promised Bhima that she would send the boy to him whenever he needed him."

'Where is Ekachakra and why did they go there?' I asked.

"This village is filled with Brahmanas so the Pandavas had dressed themselves as Brahmanas and stayed with a family for a year. This village was owned by a *rakshasa* who used to come and rampage the village and take off everything he fancied now and again. At last the villagers made a bargain with him that every week they would send him an ox cart filled with eatables driven by someone from the village and he could eat the whole lot. Three nights ago Kunti found the whole family crying because it was their turn to send the cart, and the only one who could drive the cart was their son. Kunti told them not to weep and prepare the cart and she would send her own son Bhima instead. Bhima was extremely happy at the arrangement since he had been on a meagre diet ever since they had left Hidimbi. He had been greedily eyeing some of the dishes prepared for the *rakshasa,* and as soon as he reached the ogre's den he stopped the cart and started on the dishes himself. The *rakshasa* was furious when he saw this and rushed out of his cave. Needless to say Bhima finished him off and then rode happily back to the village. Everyone welcomed him back with great joy and insisted that he stay on in the village and become their king. They stayed for a while and then Vyasa went to them once again and told them that the time had come for them to move on to Kampilya, capital of Panchala, where King Drupada had arranged a *swayamvara* for his daughter Draupadi."

'Who are they,' I asked?

"Actually, Drupada was well known to Arjuna. Drupada had been Drona's friend when they were studying and when he became king, Drona went and asked him to help him since he was very poor and had no money even to buy milk for his son Aswatthama. But Drupada forgot all the promises he had made to him when they were students and refused to help him. At the end of their period of study, Drona asked his students to capture Drupada and bring him back as *guru dakshina* (fee for the tutor). The boys were thrilled to be able to show their gratitude to their *guru*. They jumped onto their chariots and raced towards Kampilya. Drupada's army chased them all off. Arjuna alone stood between the king and the city and fought single-handedly with him. He then swooped on the king's chariot and caught him and threw him into his own chariot. Drupada had no idea who he was, but was full of admiration for his skill. Arjuna assured him that no harm would come to him and that he was only complying with his *guru's* desire to capture him as a fee. Who is your *guru* asked the monarch and was not surprised to hear that it was none other than Drona, his erstwhile friend and present enemy. Drona was delighted with Arjuna but being a Brahmana he was forgiving by nature and freed Drupada."

'Then what happened,' I gasped, hanging on to his every word.

"Unfortunately Drona forgot that Drupada was a Kshatriya and Kshatriyas never forget or forgive. He swore vengeance and prayed to Shiva to give him a son who would kill Drona and a daughter who would marry Arjuna. Shiva told him to do a fire ritual and out of the fire came a handsome young man with a drawn sword whom he called Drishtadyumna and a beautiful dark-haired, dark-hued girl whom he called Draupadi and who he hoped would marry Arjuna, the brave young man who was able to capture him! Of course Drupada was very sad to hear of the death of the Pandavas at Varanavata, but inside himself he felt certain that the Pandavas were not born for a miserable death like this. He had brought up Draupadi like a man and she was skilled in archery so he wanted her to marry only a man who was also an expert in archery. He has decided to hold her *swayamvara* (marriage by consent) in which the contestants will be asked to take part in a competition to find out who is the best archer. He has called a great craftsman to devise a

Yantra (instrument) to test the prowess of her suitors. The target is going to be a toy fish attached by five strings to a revolving wheel which is going to be suspended on a pole in the middle of a pool. Each contestant will be given five arrows with which he has to bring the fish down by looking at its reflection in the pool. As you can imagine this is no mean feat. On top of that he has made a steel bow which is so stiff that only three people in Aryavrata will be able to bend and string it."

'Who are they?' I murmured.

"I can see from your look that you have guessed that one of them is me. The other is of course Arjuna and the third is Karna."

'Do you want to marry Draupadi?' I asked.

"What do you think?" he asked with a teasing look.

'I don't think she is the right one for you,' I said.

"And why not? She is very brave and very beautiful."

'But does she love you? Of course anyone who sees you will immediately fall for your fascinating charm but I thought your principle is to marry only someone who begs you to marry her and I don't think Draupadi has done that!'

"Why do you think that I am incapable of falling in love?" he teased again.

'My Lord, I think you are capable of loving everyone and everything unconditionally and at all times. But you will never "fall" in love. You will only help all those who love you to "rise in love" in order to attain you – the Paramatma. I know this is what you did to the *gopis* of Vrindavana and I feel sure this is what you will do to any woman who loves you.'

"What do you know of the *gopis* of Vrindavana?" He asked.

'I know that they loved you very much and you raised them to the most exalted state of the *avadhutas*.'

"How do you know all this?" He questioned.

'Maybe from the bards who go from village to village? But can I ask you something?' He looked at me. 'Why didn't you marry Radha?'

"You might as well have asked me why I didn't marry any of them!"

'Well, why didn't you?'

"It would have totally spoilt our relationship."

'Why?' I persisted.

"Radha and the *gopis* loved me for myself. They did not love me for what I could give them. They asked for nothing from me - not marriage, not a home, not money or security. They just loved me as I was with no strings attached. No other woman will love me as they did. They will all want something from me." I didn't say anything. I needed time to think this over.

"Well! Shall I continue?" I nodded. "So now at this very moment, the Pandavas are proceeding along the dusty road leading to Kampilya. It is crowded with people all going to see the fun. All Brahmanas will be given many gifts so the five who are disguised as Brahmanas can step in with the rest of the Brahmanas. All the kings of Aryavrata have been invited. The Kauravas are sure to be there. The Pandavas have just found a place to stay in a potter's house. Now come on, I have to be there too. I have already sent word to Dwaraka asking Uddhava and Satyaki to meet me there. We have to go soon. I have to introduce myself to the Pandavas before they go for the *swayamvara*."

'Can I ask you one more question?' He nodded. 'You mentioned that the third person who could perform the feat of shooting the moving fish is Karna. Who is he? You have never mentioned his name so far.'

"This is a long question but I will answer you very shortly. He is actually Kunti's eldest child born in a miraculous way through the grace of Surya, the sun god. As I told you before, she had been given a *mantra* by Durvasa to invoke any god she wanted. She was curious and wanted to test the efficacy of the *mantra* and invoked Surya who blessed her with a baby boy. She was horrified at what had happened since she was unmarried at the time. She dared not keep the baby and floated him down the river where he was rescued by a charioteer who brought him up as his own son. At the time of the contest which had been arranged for the Kuru princes, Karna came up and showed his skill which was equal if not superior to Arjuna's. He then wanted to challenge Arjuna. Since only those who were equal in rank could challenge another, Drona asked for his lineage. Karna was ashamed and could say nothing. Duryodhana seized this opportunity to get someone on his side that would be the equal of Arjuna and declared that he would now anoint Karna as King of Anga. Karna was eternally grateful to Duryodhana for this and swore that he would always be his friend and lay down his life for him if necessity arose. Afterwards he went and studied under the great Parasurama and gained more expertise. He now lives with Duryodhana in Hastinapura. So now are you satisfied and shall we go?" he asked.

I nodded and we went and took leave of Kakudmi and the sage Markandeya, who prostrated to my Lord and thanked him for having graced his *ashrama* for so many days. 'So he also knows your hidden identity,' I murmured. My Lord laughed and lifted me up in his arms as he had done when he took me to the valley of flowers and we reached the house of the potter in no time. It was night and the streets were dark and still dusty from the number of chariots which had gone over them while the light was good and the feet of the number of people who had trudged up the road. I was used to the clean, dust-free streets of Dwaraka, but once we reached the king's way the paths were clean and watered with sandal water and strewed with jasmine. The palaces were all lit and looked fabulous.

My Lord who had wanted to give me an aerial view of the city now took me back to the potter's hut in which the Pandavas lived. We stood outside the door for a few minutes and listened to the talk inside. Kunti was urging her sons to go to the *swayamvara* the next day and try their luck at the competition.

"You are the greatest archer in Aryavrata and you will surely be able to defeat all of them," she told Arjuna. The brothers always looked up to their mother. Her word was law to them and they agreed to go, but still

I sensed a sort of unease in them. They had gone through so many trials and been cheated so badly by their own kin that it was as if they distrusted their fate itself. What was in store for them? Would they ever be able to get back their lost kingdom? What was the use of their prowess and their exemplary characters if fate snatched the prize from them at the last moment? These were the thoughts that flashed through their minds as Krishna knocked at the door.

Always on the alert, all of them reached for their weapons which were hidden behind the pots while Arjuna went and opened the door. It was a momentous meeting. Arjuna and Krishna were twin souls. They had always been connected with each other in every birth. Of course Krishna knew it all but Arjuna didn't. However he sensed something inexplicable and a surge of love and respect coursed through his veins as he looked at the dark stranger dressed in yellow with a single peacock feather in his diadem. For that split second of eternity, Arjuna knew that Krishna's eyes had watched over him all his life, his was the mind at the bottom of his own mind and that he already knew everything that he was seeking to know. He was his eternal companion ever protecting him. A sense of peace, which he had never known before, spread through him. He knew that whatever he did, Krishna would be there to protect him and save him from his own folly if need be. The Lord smiled his charming smile and the magic moment broke like a bubble, and Arjuna stepped back to let the stranger in, which was something he and his brothers normally never did. Krishna stepped in and asked in his mellifluous voice. "Don't you know me?"

The room was crowded with mud pots stacked one on top of the other and the six of them occupied a small place at one side. In fact Bhima had made a little more space for them by the simple expedient of pulling out the pot right at the bottom which made the whole stack fall down, thus giving them more space. What the potter would have to say about this is anybody's guess. All of them jumped up when Krishna entered and courteously asked him to take a seat. His gaze went from face to face and at last rested on Kunti.

"Mother! Surely you must know me?"

Kunti looked into his eyes and to the astonishment of her sons, she fell at his feet and said, "Lord at last you have condescended to come to us. My sons and I are alone and unprotected. Though born to be kings they have been forced to live like slaves. I was waiting and praying that you would come to our aid."

'Aha! Another one who knows my Lord to be only an actor in a play,' I thought to myself!

Turning to her surprised sons she said, "This is Vaasudeva, your cousin, son of my brother Vasudeva. He is Lord Vishnu who has taken on this particular form in order to bless the world. Remember he alone is our saviour. He alone will be able to take us out of this terrible plight we are in and lift us to our original status." Hearing this all of them bowed at the Lord's feet. However he stopped Yudhishtira and Bhima from touching his feet since they were elder to him and with his usual humility touched their feet instead.

Kunti took out her torn upper garment and spread it on the floor for the Lord to sit. The rest of them sat in front of him. "Well, I am very happy to see all of you, who I have wanted to meet for a long time and this is the opportune moment. You have suffered enough and from now on your lives are going to change for the good. We will go to the competition tomorrow and Arjuna will be successful and marry the princess of Panchala. Drupada will prove to be a powerful ally and we can return to Hastinapura and demand your rights."

The Pandavas seemed to get back their lustre after talking to Krishna. They sat and talked till late in the night. The Lord could easily have gone to one of the palaces reserved for the Yadavas but he chose to stay with the Pandavas in their one room lodging. This was his usual mode. He always preferred the faded flower offered with love by his devotees to the golden lotus offered by those with no love in their hearts.

Aum Namo Bhagavate Vaasudevaaya

They went to the Ashrama of Markandeya in a northern valley of the Himalayas where flowed the river Pushpabhadra beside the famous rock Chitra. Lined with shady trees and creepers, and dotted with lakes of crystal clear water that ashrama was a very sacred place inhabited by many holy men. A gentle breeze blew there cooled by the ice-cold water falls and sweetened by the fragrance of flowers.

Srimad Bhagavatam, Skanda 11, verses, 17, 18, 19.

ॐ

Vasudevatmajaaya Namaha!

CHAPTER FIVE

Draupadi Swayamvara

As we stepped out of the hut, we found ourselves pushed forward to join the crowd which was surging towards Drupada's palace where the competition was being held. People were pouring in from every gate of the city. Artists, craftsmen, merchants and traders were all thronging to the hall to watch their captivating princess choose her husband.

Krishna turned to the brothers and said, "I will leave you now. We will meet at the competition hall but I will pretend that I don't recognise you." The brothers nodded their heads in agreement and suddenly I found myself at the door to the hall in which the competition was going to take place. Here we were stopped by the guards and Krishna was asked to announce his name and lineage.

"Krishna Vaasudeva, son of Vasudeva, from the city of Dwaraka in the country of Anarta." The guards bowed and let us in. The hall was pretty crowded but my Lord spied the Yadava contingent and moved towards them. All of them rose to greet him and he took his place between Satyaki and Uddhava. Balarama and Kritavarma were also there. I looked around curiously. It seemed as if the kings from all the kingdoms of Aryavrata had assembled there. Tales of Draupadi's beauty had been spread by the bards all over the country and every one of the kings and princes wanted a chance to win her. My eyes roved round the hall. There were the Kauravas headed by Duryodhana with Karna, Bhishma, Drona, Aswatthama and Shakuni accompanying them. Shishupala of Chedi, who never missed any function, was there. The old king Jarasandha of Magadha was there to try his luck with the young beauty, even though he already had a number of wives in his harem. Shalya of Madra, Jayadratha of Sindhu and many other kings had come, all set to win the beautiful Draupadi.

The auspicious time was announced by the blowing of trumpets and clashing of cymbals. The kings went to the thrones reserved for them while the Brahmanas sat on the ground. Now Drishtadyumna, Draupadi's twin-brother, born out of the same fire, came to the centre leading Draupadi who was holding the wedding garland in her hands. Many *sumangalis* (married women) carrying golden plates filled with auspicious articles accompanied her, as well as musicians. There was a gasp from the audience as Draupadi entered.

She was indeed a flaming beauty. She was dark as collyrium and had faultless features. Her eyes were really like lotus petals with long curly, soft lashes. Her long luscious locks like dark blue rain clouds fell in bunches of curls to her ankles. The tresses were decorated with thick jasmine garlands. Her face shone with an unearthly lustre. She had shiny coppery nails. A *tilaka (*dot in the middle of the forehead) of musk and saffron was on her forehead. Gem set necklaces covered her swelling breasts. Her arms and wrists shone with bracelets and bangles of gems. The exquisite cluster of diamonds on her ear lobes cast a shine on her dark cheeks. Her waist band was set with seven different types of jewels. Her shapely thighs were covered with red silk. A spangled veil covered her head and shoulders. Her slightly parted lips coloured with red *lac* revealed her small pearly teeth. Her body emitted the perfume of sandal oil, musk and saffron. The silver anklets on her feet made a delightful tinkling sound as she walked in with her undulating gait, carrying the beautiful garland of lotus flowers which she would put round the neck of the man who would win the competition. She was truly a warrior princess and her regal personality as she swept into the hall made everybody gaze at her in rapt adulation. As her brilliant look swept over all of them, each of the kings wished that he would be the lucky one to win her. They could hardly take their eyes off her. Her radiant eyes shone out of her dark face as her gaze roved round the hall as if searching for one familiar face. Did it hover for a few moments longer on my Lord, I wondered? Who could blame her? Who was the woman who could look at him without feeling a flutter of sentiments rushing through her? Next I thought her glance lingered a moment longer on Karna who dominated the group of Kauravas. He was fair and tall and handsome, and stood out amongst the hundred Kaurava brothers who were all on the stout side. After escorting her round the hall, Drishtadyumna led her to her seat which had been specially prepared for her. It seemed to be made of blue lotuses and made a perfect background for her rare beauty.

Drishtadyumna announced to the suitors what was expected of them and pointed to the bow which had been brought in by five strong men. Right in the middle of the hall was a small pool, in the middle of which was a revolving pole. On top of the pole was a toy fish attached to the pole by five strings.

Drishtadyumna held up five arrows and said, "I welcome all the noble kings and others who have come here today to take part in the *swayamvara* of my sister, Draupadi. However, there are a few conditions to be observed before she chooses her husband. Here is a bow and here are five arrows. The person who can string the bow and shoot the arrows at the fish and bring it down while looking at its reflection in the pool will be the one who will win the hand of Panchali, the princess of Panchala. Now you may all come forward one by one and try your luck."

Duryodhana was the first to jump up and stride towards Drishtadyumna with a purposeful look as if he was sure he would win the bride. He had been totally smitten by Draupadi as she entered and was determined to get her at all cost. He took up the bow and pulled it down in order to string it. But though he pulled till the muscles burst the bronze armour on his back he could not succeed and the bow snapped back making him fall to the ground. He was furious and vowed to avenge this "insult" as he put it. As each of them came up, Drishtadyumna announced their names and lineage. My Lord had specially told the Yadavas not to take part so none of them came forward. One by one all the kings came up and most of them found that they could not even string the bow, such was its weight. The string seemed to have a life of its own and sometimes bounced out of the hands of the person, throwing him off and making him fall to the ground, much to the amusement of the onlookers. One by one all the Mahajanapadas came and left in anger and disgust. They started murmuring amongst themselves that Drupada had set an impossible task and Draupadi was condemned to remain a maid forever. At last there were no more kings left. Drishtadyumna cast his eyes over the royal guests and turned his back on them. He then turned to the Brahmanas and announced that anyone amongst them who wanted to compete could now come forward.

A young, slender boy rose from the crowd of Brahmanas. For a split second his eye caught Krishna's and a reassuring message was telegraphed. He threw back his head and strode towards the bow with great confidence. The kings jeered at the thought of a Brahmana being able to accomplish what none of them could do. Drupada looked at him with interest since he reminded him of somebody, he could not quite place who it was, and Draupadi looked at him with admiration since he was the only one of all the suitors who had appeared till now whom she felt she could marry. She had not liked any of the kings who had come forward to string the bow. In fact had any of them succeeded she was wondering how she would have been able to get out of an unpleasant situation since she didn't feel she could marry any of them except Krishna and perhaps Karna, and neither of them were participating. As Arjuna walked forward, the kings began to stir angrily and there was the sound of swords being drawn. Arjuna glanced at Drishtadyumna and asked him to keep an eye on them.

Drishtadyumna smiled and said, "Fear not O Brahmana! You will be safe. My men are placed amongst them and they will see that no one molests you when you string the bow."

Arjuna strung the bow and in five winks he had shot the five arrows, bringing the huge fish crashing down into the pool. Before the kings could react, Draupadi glided forward and placed the wedding garland round his neck. Pandemonium broke loose. The Brahmanas cheered wildly and surrounded the couple, waving their deerskins and shaking their *kamandalus* (water pots). Arjuna threw his dusty *uttareeyam* (upper garment) round Draupadi's elegant form and hustled her unceremoniously through the crowd of angry kings who jumped forward to intercept them. Drupada's men closed in from both sides while some made their way through the middle. Duryodhana pushed his way forward to stop the two from escaping. Bhima immediately plucked a tree and stepped in his way, allowing Arjuna to take Draupadi to safety. The other three Pandavas closed in on them and tried to force a way for them. Both Brahmanas and kings took part in the scuffle that followed. The Lord who had been watching with interest now decided that it was time he took a part.

He stepped forward and stopped the scuffle and announced, "O Kings! Why are you fighting? Draupadi was won in a fair competition. Who can you blame but yourselves for having lost the match? Go home therefore and stop this incessant bickering which is not befitting royalty."

They were all slightly pacified by this and decided that there was no point in hanging around when the couple had already fled. No one except my Vanamali knew where they had fled and he kept his own counsel.

Arjuna sped through the dusty streets hurrying his willing prize along. Very soon the other four caught up with them. Drishtadyumna was following at a discreet distance. My Lord and I followed him. Draupadi had no idea where she was being taken but she had faith in the man who had won her. Even though she did not know him, she sensed that he was no ordinary Brahmana who had come in the hope of getting some money. So she did not struggle or protest at the somewhat cavalier treatment she was getting. They reached the potter's hut and knocked at the door.

Yudhishtira called out, "Mother we have brought a special prize for you."

Kunti replied, "My boys should always share whatever they have, so share it between you." There was an embarrassed silence as Yudhishtira opened the door and all of them trooped in. Arjuna took off his *uttareeyam* and Kunti was taken aback to have this vision of a gorgeous beauty standing in the tiny, dingy room, lit with only a small earthen lamp, with pots stacked in the corner and nowhere to sit. Draupadi looked like an exotic orchid which had somehow found its way to a barn!

Kunti knew where her sons had gone and immediately guessed the identity of the girl they had brought. She took only a moment to recover her composure and picking up the lamp she came forward and said, "I have only this lamp to welcome my new daughter-in-law!"

Draupadi touched her feet and kept silent since she had no idea into what sort of family she had been projected. Drishtadyumna listened at the door and heard Kunti say, "My child you must be quite bewildered but have no fear. The man round whose neck you put the garland is none other than Arjuna, the *madhyama* (middle) Pandava. I am Kunti, his mother and these are my other sons, Yudhishtira, Bhima, Nakula and Sahadeva." Both Draupadi and her eves-dropping brother were thrilled to hear this. Drishtadyumna did not wait to hear any more but sped into the night and told his anxious father of the proceedings, and gave him the happy news that he had just procured Arjuna as his son-in-law as he had wished.

The Lord did not go in but watched till all of them lay down to sleep in the little space that was theirs. The five brothers slept at the foot of their mother and Draupadi, princess of Panchala, used to the most fabulous bed and fineries, happily curled up at their feet. My Lord smiled and gave me a meaningful look. "Poor girl," he said, "I'm afraid she will have to go through many such trials."

'Why? Will they not get back their kingdom?'

"You are too impatient," he teased, "wait and see!"

Next morning my Lord accompanied by Balarama went to the potter's hut laden with gifts and sweets for the couple. Draupadi as well as the others were overjoyed to see them. Krishna congratulated Arjuna on his dexterity and told him that Draupadi had been born as a result of her father begging Shiva for a daughter who would marry Arjuna. Partha (another name for Arjuna) gave a sidelong glance at Draupadi and she smiled shyly. Draupadi was never at a loss of words and turning to Krishna she said, "My Lord, I have not had the pleasure of meeting you, though I have heard a lot about you. Had you not intervened yesterday, the *swayamvara* would have changed into a *yuddha*."

Krishna smiled his usual charming smile, guaranteed to melt the heart of any woman and said, "Draupadi, from now on my only job is to safeguard the interests of the Pandavas. Come let us go to your father's court where he is awaiting you."

Just then Drishtadyumna came driving a cart and shouted out, "Place has been made for you at someone's house so be pleased to come with me."

"Why should we go to a strange house?" asked Yudhishtira.

"Go with him," whispered my Lord. "He is no stranger. He is your brother-in-law."

"So be it," said Yudhishtira and all of them including Kunti got into the cart and were driven to the palace of the king. The cart driver turned into the prince and led them to his father's presence. Draupadi escorted Kunti to the women's apartments.

Drupada turned to Arjuna and asked, "Haven't we met somewhere a long time ago? Can I know the name of the one who was garlanded by my daughter?"

"Sire! Your question must surely have been answered when the mighty fish fell down!"

Drupada laughed and said, "Fate has many tricks in her bag. I had dreamt of getting Arjuna as my son-in-law and when I heard of the death of the Pandavas, I thought I had been cheated, but now without my knowing anything, the Pandava has come back as my son-in-law."

My Lord now stepped forward and spoke "Let me introduce all of them to you. This is Yudhishtira the eldest, Bhima, the second and of course Arjuna the middle Pandava and the twins Nakula and Sahadeva. Let me congratulate you, instead of one son-in-law you will be getting five!"

The king looked startled, "What do you mean?"

"My Lord! Let me tell you one thing. Your daughter is a very beautiful woman. Unless the Pandavas stand united as one man, they will have no chance against the hundred Kauravas filled with avarice and cunning. If Panchali married only Arjuna, the others would always be jealous of him and that would be the beginning of their fall. Their mother Kunti is a very wise woman and she is the one who decided that they should all marry her in turn. In this way, none of them need regret that Draupadi does not belong to him. We can make a working arrangement and say that she will be the wife of one brother for one whole year, starting with Yudhishtira."

The king saw the wisdom of this and agreed to the combined wedding. Thus Draupadi married each of the brothers one by one in five days in her father's palace in the presence of Krishna Vaasudeva and Balarama. Of course I was also there – the unseen and uninvited guest. My Lord was so preoccupied with all the things he had to see to that he hardly had time for me. I was truly grateful for the precious time we had had together at the holy spot of Badarikashrama. After the wedding ceremony was over, both the Yadava brothers and Drupada told Drishtadyumna to go to Kurujangala and tell Dritarashtra everything, and ask him to give back the kingdom which rightly belonged to them. Drishtadyumna went like the wind.

I had been noticing another effeminate-looking young man who seemed to belong to the king's inner circle. While Drishtadyumna had gone to Hastinapura, the Lord and I had some time together and I took the opportunity to ask him about this man.

My Vanamali looked a bit pensive and said, "It is a long story. We have to go back to the time when Amba immolated herself in the fire in order to be born again to kill Bhishma. (Refer page 28). Just at that time, long before he had lit the fire out of which were born Drishtadyumna and Draupadi, Drupada had asked Shiva to grant him a son. Shiva told him, 'Your wife already carries your son in her womb.' The king was very happy but when the child was born she was seen to be a girl and was called Shikandini. Remembering Shiva's words, Drupada told everyone that he had a son and treated his daughter like a son. Once when she was wandering in the garden she saw the garland of unfading lotuses. Propelled by fate she took it off and put it over her own neck. Immediately her whole past life as Amba flashed through her mind, and all her hatred of Bhishma returned with full force. Drupada knew of the story of the garland and when he saw it round his daughter's neck, he was frightened that she might want to provoke a battle with Bhishma and sent her away to the forest. She was in a desperate state wondering if she was condemned to end her life again without getting the revenge for which her heart thirsted. Eventually she came across a *yaksha* who was a sort of magician. Seeing her gloomy face, he asked her what was troubling her. She told him her whole story and he asked her what she wanted from him. 'I want you to change me into a man,' she said simply.

The *yaksha* looked closely at her and asked, 'Are you sure about this? Once I change you, there is no reverting to your womanhood.' She agreed and begged him to help her and stayed for many months in his *ashrama* and eventually he changed her sex and she became a man and called herself, Shikandin. He returned to Kampilya and Drupada accepted him as his son, after he promised that he would not go for a battle with Bhishma! This is the story of Shikandin. He is destined to play a great role in a battle which will take place in the future. So now you know everything and we can concentrate on what tidings Drishtadyumna has brought from Hastinapura."

'You already know everything which is to take place, don't you?' I asked. He smiled his usual smile and kept quiet.

Within a few days Drishtadyumna had returned with Vidura, the Pandavas' favourite uncle. They were overjoyed to see him. He hugged them as if they were children. Turning to my Lord he touched his feet. Ah ha, I thought, another one who knows the true nature of my Vanamali.

"My beloved uncle, let me first thank you for having saved our lives. We owe everything to you. If you had not warned us and arranged everything for us we would surely have died in the fire at Varanavata," said Yudhishtira. "Now tell us what the king said."

Vidura was so happy to see them alive and well and happily living in Drupada's palace that he wished they could continue like that. But he knew that their fate was calling them and they had to do their duty. He exchanged looks with my Lord and was grateful that he had taken them under his protection.

"Return with me my children. Dritarashtra has told me that you will be welcome in Hastinapura. Moreover, Gandhari and the rest of the women are anxious to meet Draupadi."

Yudhishtira was always anxious to please his elders, so the Pandavas set out to Hastinapura along with their wife Panchali and Vidura. Kunti begged my Vanamali to come with them and support her sons, for she feared that Duryodhana would not take kindly to giving away the land which for some time he had thought to be his own. I too was happy when my Lord agreed, since I was anxious to see Hastinapura and the Kauravas about whom I had heard so much. The cavalcade set out escorted by the king's guards.

The citizens had heard of the coming of the Pandavas with their bride and were thronging the streets of Hastinapura to have a glimpse of Draupadi. They cheered wildly when the procession appeared and escorted them right up to the palace gates. They hoped with all their hearts that Yudhishtira would be reinstated as the Yuvaraja. The Pandavas and Draupadi were cordially greeted by Dritarashtra, Bhishma and Drona. Duryodhana sulked in a corner but his eyes gleamed with desire when he looked at Draupadi.

For a few days there appeared to be truce on the surface, but my Lord knew that it was only a passing phase. With Shakuni and Karna to fan the flames of his jealousy and greed, Duryodhana persuaded his weak father to send the Pandavas away once again. Yudhishtira of course was always happy to make friends with the Kauravas but even he was beginning to realise that this was only a remote possibility, so when the king called him, he was prepared for anything. Accompanied by my Lord, the Pandavas walked into the assembly hall of the Kurus.

Dritarashtra said, "My dear children, I feel that it is best if I divide the kingdom. We will keep this half and you can go and make a city in Khandavaprastha which was the ancient capital of your ancestors. You will be happier there."

Yudhishtira was debating on what he should say, but my Lord urged him to accept, on condition that a certain amount of craftsmen, farmers, traders and servitors should be given to them. This was gladly agreed to and the Pandavas left for Khandavaprastha, accompanied by many of the citizens who were only too glad to join them.

Though Khandavaprastha had been the ancient capital of the Kurus, the Pandavas were dismayed to find that it had changed into a wilderness infested with wild animals and *rakshasas* over the passage of time. The only person who was not a whit put out was of course my Lord.

"Cheer up cousins!" he said, "I will summon Vishwakarma, the divine architect who designed the city of Dwaraka for me, and tell him to build you something on the same lines."

Under the capable hands of the divine architect, the whole place was transformed into a celestial city within a short time. They named it Indraprastha as a tribute to Arjuna's father, Indra, the king of the gods. Slowly the population grew since many people who came to admire the city decided to stay on. The gardens and parks began to be filled with songbirds and deer and peacocks instead of tigers and leopards and bears. By the very nobility of his nature, Yudhishtira attracted noble souls from all over Aryavrata. Though the city was really very grand, I didn't think it was a patch on Dwaraka. I was fretting to return to Dwaraka where I would have my Lord all to myself, but he stayed with the Pandavas till the construction was over and left only after Yudhishtira was crowned and started ruling. I knew that my Lord had chosen the Pandavas to be the rulers of this land because his policy was to ensure that those who were at the head of the government should also be highly spiritual. In fact if all the countries of the world could follow this rule, what a wonderful world we would have.

No doubt Yudhishtira would make a very good ruler. I could only pray that the Pandavas would be left in peace now that they had broken away from the ancestral home. However, I doubted if Duryodhana would ever be able to tolerate his cousins, especially if he knew of their prosperity. Envy was his chief characteristic and an envious man can never be happy at another's prosperity, especially if they happen to be his own relations. Duryodhana's envy was like a smouldering piece of coal eating into his vitals. No one could say when it would burst into a conflagration, destroying both himself and the Pandavas. It was becoming more and more certain that the world could not contain both sets of cousins at the same time. My Lord knew the future as well as he did the past, but he kept his own counsel and would not reply to any of my unspoken questions.

Aum Namo Bhagavate Vaasudevaaya

ॐ

Punyaaya Namaha!

CHAPTER SIX

The Abduction of Rukmini

I was really happy to get away from Indraprastha. Arjuna escorted us to the gates and bid my Lord a fond farewell. In fact none of the brothers wanted the Lord to go away and begged him to stay on. With his usual charming smile he said he would be back when the time came. We went on swift horses provided by Yudhishtira. We passed through Matsya and came to the Anarta country in no time and reached the golden city within a week. The Yadavas were delighted to welcome their Lord, who had left them for over a year. His parents and sister as well as his sister-in-law, Revati were all overjoyed at his return.

One morning while I was sitting by his side in the hall called Sudharma where he was listening to state matters, an old Brahmana approached him and whispered something in his ear and gave him a letter. The Lord seated him on a special seat and asked him where he was coming from and what he wanted and so on. The Brahmana replied that he was coming from the city of Kundinapura, capital of the country of Vidharbha. The noble king Bhishmaka was the ruler of the country. He had five sons and one daughter. The eldest son was called Rukmi and his youngest daughter was called Rukmini. She had heard tales of the valour of Vaasudeva, of Dwaraka and had set her heart on marrying him. When she came of marriageable age she whispered to her father that she wanted none other than the Lord of Dwaraka. Bhishmaka who had heard of Krishna's exploits and the fame of the Yadavas was very happy to agree to her request. He was about to send a deputation to Dwaraka to ask if Krishna was agreeable to such an alliance when he was stopped by his son Rukmi who had another plan up his sleeve. Shishupala of Chedi was a great favourite of his and he had already arranged for an alliance between him and his sister Rukmini. He forbade his father from approaching the Yadavas for such an alliance. Bhishmaka was king only in name. His sons were virtual rulers of the country and he had no option but to agree. When he gave this news to his beloved daughter, she burst into tears and said she would rather die than marry Shishupala. The poor king was in a dilemma and did not know what to do.

Rukmini was desperate. The wedding day was fast approaching. She prayed and prayed to Krishna to come and rescue her. Though the Lord knew her heart, he did nothing. I suspected that he was waiting for her to forget her maidenly modesty and her pride of being a princess and approach him with only love in her heart as a woman approaches a man whom she loves – as the *gopis* had approached him, without any sense of shame or modesty. Shame comes only when there is duality, when there is "another". No one has shame to face oneself. My Vanamali was not an ordinary man. He was the Supreme cloaked as a man. As such we should approach him without shame, without so-called modesty, stripped bare of all the pretences that make up our life of sophistication. This was what he expected of all his wives. At last, two days before the wedding Rukmini decided that she had to take matters into her own hands, since her brothers would not listen to reason and her father was helpless to help her even though he wanted to. She found a kind Brahmana who agreed to take a letter to my Lord. She exhorted the Brahmana to go as fast as possible and personally deliver the letter into my Vanamali's hands.

After delivering the letter, the Brahmana proceeded to give all the news to my Lord of how her brothers had decided to get her married to Shishupala without asking for her consent. "Please help her," said the Brahmana, "she is desperate and does not know what to do."

Help of the helpless as he was, my Lord assured the Brahmana that he would do whatever the princess asked for in her letter. He then opened the letter and read it so that both the Brahmana and I could hear. "O Thou who art the most handsome in all the three worlds! Tales of your excellences have penetrated deep into my heart so that I can only think about you day and night. I am wedded to you, body, mind and soul. It only needs you to come and take me physically. My cruel brothers have decided to give me to Shishupala. Please don't let him defile this body which is meant for you alone! I don't know how fast the Brahmana will go and how fast you can reach Vidharbha, but let me give you a hint as to the appropriate time for you to come and snatch me from these jackals as a lion does his prey. On the day of the wedding I will be going with my bridesmaids to the temple of the goddess. Do thou come the previous day, incognito and just at the time when I come out of the temple do thou snatch me and take me away fast, fighting with my relations if necessary. I know this is the *rakshasa* mode of marriage, but if you come at the exact time when I come out of the temple you may be able to avoid unnecessary bloodshed. I should also like to declare that if for some reason you are not able to come or unable to take me away, I will lay down my life and continue to be born again and again until I get you as my husband!"

I looked at my Lord's face. Was there a glimmer of a smile? Was he amused that a gentle princess brought up in such a restricted fashion, who had never been allowed to mingle with other men except her father and brothers, would dare to make such a bold declaration of love to a man she had never met! The final line was also intriguing. Was it a kind of threat to force his hand that she would take her life if he did not come and he would be responsible for her death?

He looked at me and I knew this was exactly what he was thinking. He jumped up and called the stable boy to bring the fastest horse in the stables and get everything ready for instant departure. He also told his charioteer, Daruka to follow him as fast as he could with the Brahmana.

He shouted out to Uddhava to inform Balarama that he had gone to Vidharbha. He nodded to me and I jumped up on the saddle behind him as I had done on our trip to the Himalayas. Vidharbha was quite a distance away from Anarta and the Lord was not taking any chances.

I presume Uddhava must have alerted Balarama of the Brahmana's arrival from Vidharbha and some talk of snatching the bride and of Vaasudeva's impetuous departure to Kundinapura. Balarama must have been sorely perturbed when he heard this and decided to follow with a huge contingent of elephants, horses and chariots with horses just in case there was any trouble. I am presuming all this since we were not there to see. In fact we were racing with the wind. I just clung to him and was not at all frightened, even though night had fallen and we were riding in pitch darkness. We had to pass through quite a bit of the Matsya territory, crossing rivers and deserts. The sun was just rising as we entered the gate of the city. No one asked any questions since the city had been prepared to welcome all those who had come to enjoy the wedding.

As we rode down the royal road, some of the citizens suddenly recognised my Lord and shouted "Hail to Vaasudeva! Hail to the son of Devaki and Vasudeva! He alone is the fitting match for our princess. And she alone is a fitting bride for him. O God, if we have done anything worthy of recompense by you please let Krishna Vaasudeva marry our beautiful princess."

The Lord laughed and waved to them when he heard this. The news of his coming had reached Bhishmaka who was really delighted to hear it. He rushed out of the palace to meet him with all due honours and escorted him to the palace which was normally reserved for the bridegroom. I was not sure where he had lodged Shishupala.

"My Lord!" he said, "You have no idea how happy I am to see you. I know my sons have not invited any of the Yadavas, but my daughter has given her heart to you and I hope with all my heart that you will snatch her away and take her to Dwaraka. I know this is an unusual request for a father to make to his future son-in-law, but let me assure you that you have all my blessings if you do this." My Lord laughed his usual infectious laugh which normally made everyone around him also laugh and assured the king that he would do as he wished.

"Which of the kings have already arrived?" he asked.

"King Damaghosha of Chedi with his son Shishupala, who is the one who has been chosen by my son to marry his sister, is already here, and all the rites that have to be done to the groom have started in his palace. Salva, Jarasandha, Dantavaktra, Viduratha, Paundraka and all those who are against you have come to support him. I don't know why, but they seem to fear that you might come and start a fight with them and have brought a part of their army to support Shishupala." Krishna was highly amused when he heard this.

Just then his chariot with the Brahmana came up and the Lord told him to go straight away and assure the princess that he had already reached Kundinapura and would surely rescue her from the clutches of the wolves as she had wished. The Brahmana was only too happy to comply with this request and no doubt Rukmini's heart must have leapt with joy when she heard this happy tiding. Krishna's charioteer, Daruka, now gave him the news that his brother was hot on his heels along with a good part of the Yadava army. My Lord was mighty pleased to hear this and told Bhishmaka to carry on and welcome Balarama and the Yadava host who would be arriving soon!

My Lord now jumped into the chariot which Daruka had brought and took over the reins. He told Daruka to wait and join Balarama's contingent. He then took a small lane which brought us just outside the temple of the goddess to which Rukmini had gone to worship the divine mother and pray to her to give Krishna as her husband. At least I presumed that was what she was doing. By this time the other kings had also realised that the bride had been taken to the temple and all of them had stationed themselves on either side of the road leading to the temple. Some were mounted on elephants, some in chariots and some on horses. Rukmini came out of the temple accompanied by many *sumangalis* (married women) carrying auspicious articles on golden plates as was the custom. She was a small, petite princess not more than sixteen years of age and her charming face was half hidden by her locks and the veil which had been thrown round her head. Her dainty feet tinkled as she stepped out of the temple. For a moment she lifted her veil as if to reveal her beauty to the onlookers, but actually to see if her beloved had arrived. Of course all the kings and Shishupala in particular thought that she was looking for him. They were totally captivated by her entrancing beauty. Her huge dark eyes with long curly lashes were fluttering here and there in the hope of seeing Krishna. Her rose bud mouth was slightly parted in anticipation. She had the innocent look of an untouched rose. Of course she was decked in gold and gems as befitting a bride. A golden girdle set with gems glistened round her slender waist. Seeing her looking here and there as if searching for someone, all the kings were totally captivated and dropped their weapons and preened themselves a little, hoping to catch her attention. Her mouth drooped a little at not seeing my Lord and she was on the verge of getting into her own chariot when my Vanamali swooped down on her and lifted her up by her slender waist and placed her beside him in his own chariot.

"You are getting into the wrong chariot my dear," he said and before she knew what was happening he had set off at a spanking pace before the other kings could recover their wits and realise what had happened. Shishupala was the only one who didn't realise what had happened since he had been so busy adjusting his attire and by the time he looked at the temple door, she had gone. There was a big hue and cry by all the other kings, who set out in hot pursuit. This was exactly what Balarama had feared and he cut off their approach and started fighting with them, allowing the Lord to speed off with his prize.

"Catch him! Hold him! Don't let him escape! How is it that this cowherd has managed to snatch the prize meant for lions like us?" the irate kings shouted and charged forward to try and stop the chariot.

However by the time they fought with Balarama, we had already gone far ahead. At last they decided to give up and return to their homes.

I heard later that Shishupala was totally dejected when he heard that they were unable to catch up with Krishna and rescue his bride-to-be. The rest of the kings were a bit unsympathetic and told him to cheer up and look for another woman since this one was obviously not meant for him!

However Rimini's brother Rukmi was not going to give up the chase so fast. Before he left he vowed that unless he brought Rukmini back, he would not enter the gates of Kundinapura. He avoided Balarama's soldiers and was hot on our heels. He hated my Lord and was determined to kill him and rescue his sister. He dared not shoot arrows for fear of hurting his sister, but he was close enough for us to hear his shouts.

"Stop! Stop! You scoundrel! You are a disgrace to the race of Yadu! You have kidnapped my sister without our permission! Stop the chariot and face me if you dare or I will send you to the abode of Yama this instant." So saying he took up his bow and sent a shower of arrows at my Lord's head. Krishna had already made Rukmini crouch at the bottom of the chariot so that she would not be hurt. He then turned round in the chariot and cut into pieces every bow and club which Rukmi took up to fight with him. After that he smashed the wheels of his chariot so that he was forced to jump out. Rukmi rushed toward us brandishing his sword which was the only weapon left to him. My Lord had stopped the chariot and turned round to face his enemy. He cut down his sword and took up a small dagger in order to make the final kill. At that time Rukmini who was crouched on the floor of the chariot grabbed Krishna's feet and said:

"O mighty armed one! Lord of Yoga! Please spare my brother!" Rukmini was shaking with terror and her hands which were clasping the Lord's feet were also trembling. Krishna's hand which was holding the lethal weapon came down and he helped up his trembling wife and comforted her. Turning to Rukmi who was still seething with rage, Krishna bound him with his own *uttareeyam* and shaved off one half of his hair with the blade of his dagger as well as half his moustache! The strange thing is that the Lord never committed any violent act in anger. I always made it a point to notice that whenever he was engaged in battle or a fight or shouting at someone, his anger was always a mock one as if he was an actor in a drama. All the correct actions and expressions were there, but I was always left with the feeling that it meant nothing to him. Balarama came up with the Yadava contingent at this crucial point and found Rukmi bound and almost dying of shame.

"Krishna! How could you do such a thing to your relation? Shaving off a person's tuft is tantamount to killing him. It is not correct on your part to do such a thing!"

My Lord did not argue with his brother but he knew that one day Balarama would have to eat his words and do the very things that he had denounced him for doing.

The Lord lifted up his wife who was trembling like an aspen leaf and comforted her. He wiped her tears and told her not to be frightened and promised not to kill her brother however much he insulted him.

Balarama turned to Rukmini and tried to comfort her, but she was already pacified by my Vanamali so he might as well have held his tongue. We heard later that Rukmi had picked up the remnants of his pride and the few men who had come with him and proceeded to build a city at the place called Bhojakota since he had sworn not to enter Kundinapura until he had killed Krishna and rescued his sister who wasn't in the least interested in being rescued!!

News of the Lord's abduction of Rukmini, princess of Vidharbha had already reached Dwaraka and the whole city was brilliantly decorated to welcome the couple. This was the Lord's first wedding and the whole city went crazy with joy. Every house was decorated with banana trees and areca nut trees all carrying bunches of fruit. Banners and flags were raised in honour of Indra, king of the gods. Auspicious articles such as fried grains of paddy, sprouts of barley and a profusion of flowers were to be seen everywhere. Picturesque wreaths, tapestries and ornamental arches suddenly sprang up all over the place. If I had thought the decorations for Balarama's wedding were grand then these were ten times grander. Invitations had been sent to all kings. The Pandavas were there with Draupadi and Kunti, the Srinjayas, the Kaikeyas, the Kuntis and of course Rukmini's father Bhishmaka and others from Vidharbha had all come to take part in the nine day festivities which were being conducted in Dwaraka. It was the first time that the Pandavas had come to Krishna's city and they were overwhelmed by the glory of that golden metropolis. They stayed in a special palace reserved for them. Rukmini was staying with Devaki and Vasudeva for the moment, but an exceptional palace had already been built for her with windows overlooking the sea so that she would have a soft breeze all the time. Her father had sent a hundred maids for her so that all her needs would be met with. He and her mother arrived bringing all the jewellery and other things which were normally given to the bride and which they were not able to give due to the fact that their daughter had eloped with my Lord. All the other kings also brought a lot of gifts for the couple.

My Vanamali was everywhere at the same time seeing to so many arrangements which of course he need not have done since there were so many people to do it, but it was always his way to throw himself wholeheartedly into anything that was taking place.

I ran after him hither and thither and that night before the wedding when we had a little time alone together I asked him if he was happy.

"Have you ever seen me unhappy?" he countered.

'O I didn't mean that. I just wanted to know if you are especially happy.'

"Why the doubt? Don't you think she is a lovely girl?" I had to agree that she was a fitting match for him though I did capture a tinge of envy in myself. But what reason did I have for envy? I who was as ephemeral as a dream? I was sitting at his feet and massaging them. He knew of my misgivings and sat up in bed and tilted my chin with his finger and looked into my eyes and asked, "When the whole of Dwaraka is rejoicing, why are you sad?"

'I'm frightened I'll lose you.'

"Even if you lose me, I will not lose you," he said. "How can I lose you, who are an eternal portion of myself?" He tweaked my nose and flicked off a tear which had fallen without my volition. "Now go and sleep, you have a heavy day tomorrow."

The next morning dawned bright and clear and while all the ablutions were taking place for my Lord, I skipped off to see what was happening in Rukmini's palace. She was also having her ritual bath and being anointed with sandal paste and sandal oil. One Hundred maids were there to dress her and both Subhadra and Revati, her sisters-in-law were also there to put on the finishing touches. She was really looking ravishing. She was so cute and petite, just the opposite of Revati, and she was so happy to have two sisters-in-law since she never had any sisters of her own. She really glowed with an inner happiness and everyone was taken aback to see her in this state of exaltation when she climbed on to the stage. She had to stand on her toes in order to put the garland round my Lord's neck and he bent low to help her. The ceremony was exactly like the one I had witnessed for Balarama except that in this case both bride and groom had beaming smiles and were always looking at each other. At one time when the ritual was dragging on, the Lord bent and whispered something in her ear which made her blush and look down. How fortunate she is, I thought, to get the Lord as her husband. No doubt this was the result of all the *pujas*, prayers and the charitable works she had done for countless lifetimes. At last it was over and the couple was led to the new palace which had been made for her. As his mother closed the door on them, he looked at me and smiled and said. "Tonight you can go and sleep alone in our palace." The blow was softened by the fact that he had said, "our palace". This meant that he would still have time for me in our palace!

The year that followed was one of the happiest I ever had with him. Of course every moment spent with him was filled with joy, but what I mean is that there were few upheavals during this first year of marriage with Rukmini. She was so sweet tempered and so loving that it was a pleasure to see them together. They would stroll in the private gardens sometimes and sometimes he would take her for a ride through the city. I was most privileged to go with them on all these expeditions. Once he took her in a boat to the neighbouring island of Bet Dwaraka which belonged to the Yadavas. Some of the finest conch shells could be got there, and this was the place where they made the seals (*mudra*) which every citizen of Dwaraka had to carry, which he had shown me when we were in the mountains. The craftsmen there were very good. He asked one of them to make a bracelet for Rukmini. It was an exquisite piece made of the finest and tiniest conch shells. The Lord took it and tenderly clasped it round his wife's wrist.

"I think this is prettier than all my gold bangles," she exclaimed.

Another time he took her up the mountain called Raivata which was a lovely climb. It was like a mountain retreat and had all types of places to stay as well. So we stayed a couple of days there. We went to the famous temple of Kali who was supposed to be the guardian deity of the Yadavas. It was a small but powerful temple and Rukmini sat for a long time there in meditation. I suspected that she was praying for a child since it was three years since they had been married. The Yadavas used to go to this mountain for a picnic very often, but my Lord wanted to take his wife all by herself so it was extra delightful. Soon after this she started showing signs of pregnancy and he started taking even greater care of her.

One day the sage Narada came to Dwaraka. I was most excited since I had heard so much about him but had never seen him. He did not look like a sage. He was simply dressed wearing a white cotton *dhoti* and a white *uttareeyam*. He carried a small *vina* (lute) in his hands which he used to touch delicately every now and then so that it made a delightful sound. I noticed that he touched it every time he wanted to emphasise anything he said. The Lord of course welcomed him cordially and paid every respect which had to be shown to a saint. Obviously he had come for some reason which clearly my Lord knew, so before Narada could ask him, he said, "I think you have something to tell Rukmini."

The sage looked rather sheepish and nodded his head. Krishna called Rukmini to come and meet him and tactfully left them. For once I stayed back to listen to what Narada had to say. Without any preamble the sage said, "O princess! I know you are pregnant so I came to tell you something about the child. I think you know the story of Kama, the God of Love who tried his wiles with the three-eyed Lord (Shiva) and was burnt to ashes. At that time Rati his wife as well as the gods who felt guilty since they were the ones who encouraged him to send the arrow at Shiva, begged Mahadeva to bring Manmatha (Kama) to life. Shiva said that it was not possible at that time but he promised that when Vishnu took the *avatara* of Krishna, Kama would be born as his son from his first wife and that means you. But let me tell you that there is a demon called Sambara who is a great enemy of the gods. He had many boons from Brahma who also told him that only the son of Krishna born of his wife Rukmini would be able to kill him! I came here to warn you to take extra care of your baby and not to allow anyone to take him away from this room." So saying, the sage moved on to his next destination. Rukmini was in a panic when she heard this and begged Krishna to safeguard the child. The Lord who knew everything comforted his wife and told her that sometimes some things which are meant to happen will happen. However to please her, he agreed to station guards outside her door as soon as she gave birth.

That evening I was taking a walk with him in the garden and I asked him. 'My Lord, surely you can do something to protect the baby?'

"Why should I do that?"

'My Lord it's your son. Don't you have a duty to protect him?'

"I have placed guards at the door. What else do you want me to do?" He looked quizzically at me. "My dear," he said, "My son is the one who is destined to kill Sambara. How can Sambara kill him?"

'But won't you feel sad if your baby is killed?' He laughed his usual infectious laugh.

"How can the one who is going to be killed become the killer? Sambarasura will never be able to kill my son, who has taken a birth only to kill him. Why should I interfere in the workings of *karma*?"

As usual his arguments confused me. How could a father be indifferent to the fate of his son? Was that natural? Was it fair? Seeing my worried look, he took a seat on one of the wooden benches in the park and patted the place beside him. "Let me ask you something. Why do you love me? Why do so many people love me? Sometimes I behave as if I am cruel and hard-hearted, yet they love me. Why?" He looked closely at my face.

'My Lord, though your ways are inscrutable to me and to everyone, yet I feel that you are divinity incarnate and the workings of the divine can never wholly be known by poor mortals like me.'

"Good enough for a start," he said. "Now listen to me. All of your minds are conditioned by hundreds of impressions from the time you were born. Your parents, your friends, your country, your education, all condition you to a certain frame of mind. You can never go beyond these conditionings. You are not free human beings, you are conditioned human beings. You cannot make any free decision or act because your very thoughts are conditioned. These "*vasanas*" (inherent tendencies) are carried on from birth to birth and you are never free from them. I am not conditioned by anything. I act on the spur of the moment and act from the depth of my freedom, which has never been conditioned by anything or anybody. I can love if I have to, I can hate if I want to, I can marry one woman or a thousand women yet remain totally detached from all of them. I can have one child or a hundred children yet be totally separate from all of them. I am a free agent. I don't have to ask anyone nor can anyone question me. I act as I am meant to act at that particular moment in space and time, because that is the only action which can take place. If I were a conditioned person I would start debating on the pros and cons and the rights and wrongs and inevitably come with some decision which has been dictated by my conditioning and not because it is the only possible decision to be made at that particular time. Do you understand?" I looked a bit doubtful, though I was dimly beginning to grasp what he was saying.

"As long as you are under the sway of the three *gunas* of nature you are only a puppet in her hands. You have to break free of these three strands of nature –*sattva*, *rajas* and *tamas*. Only then will you become a free agent. Not now," he said seeing the next question trembling on my lips. "I will tell you about these three later. But now I will tell you a story about Sambarasura. This will make you understand what I have been telling you." I looked at him expectantly.

"This *asura* called Sambara once made a perfect city for himself in which he created living creatures of gold and even celestial beings. In fact his city was as good as heaven. Of course the gods were upset over this and decided to kill him, but Sambara was too strong for them. However they managed to decimate his army when he had gone somewhere else. Nothing daunted he created three demons called Daama, Vyala and Kata. They resembled him in all ways, but they were like robots in as much as they simply did what he wanted them to do without question. They did not think for themselves since they never had a childhood or a previous life in which they could collect any *vasanas* (inherent tendencies). They did their job so well that the gods had to flee. Of course they ran to Brahma for help. This is what the creator told them. 'Sambara's demons cannot be defeated because they do not know the meaning of fear. They act spontaneously without fear, without caring whether you kill them or not. They have no preconceived notions. They don't know the meaning of war, victory or defeat. They are totally unconditioned so they are invincible.'"

'So what should we do?' asked the perplexed gods.

Brahma answered. 'Allow them to keep on defeating you and keep on retreating. After many times of this, their ego sense will slowly be awakened and they will start feeling that they are great people, and then will come the sense of fear and not wanting to lose their lives and hence the fear of death which is a most debilitating emotion. When this happens they will become weak and you can kill them without difficulty!'

My Lord continued, "The gods did as they were told and very soon they defeated the demons and retrieved their heaven! Do you understand the story?" I nodded. "But my case is a little different. Their unconditioned state arose from their ignorance. Mine arises from my omniscience! Now do you understand?" He ruffled the curls on my head and rose up to continue with his walk.

'What is omniscience?' I asked.

He looked penetratingly at me and said, "Believe if you can. Not a single leaf can fall without my knowledge!" That whole night I stayed awake and thought of what he had told me and eventually I began to have an inkling of the enormity of his state of all knowingness. Could any human being be like him, I wondered. All of us are so conditioned from our cradles onwards. There can be only one Vaasudeva (the all-knowing one). There never was one like him before and never will be again. How fortunate I was to have such an intimate connection with him.

In due time Rukmini bore him a lovely baby boy who was named Pradyumna. One could well believe that he was the incarnation of Manmatha, the God of Love who had been burnt to cinders by Lord Shiva for having dared to shoot an arrow at him. How can I describe the beauty of this baby who was indeed the god of love, born of the most handsome and most beautiful woman in the world? Dwaraka went mad with joy. There was a continuous stream of people coming to see this lovely little soul. The Lord, who is indeed like the lotus leaf in water, never having any attachments though living in the midst of the ocean of life, seemed to take some extra pleasure in carrying the baby who resembled him so much except for the fact that he was fair like the God of Love. Revati who did not have a baby of her own so far was always in the lying-in-room. The grandparents, Devaki and Vasudeva were overjoyed. Later on Revati had two sons called Nishastha and Ulmukha and one daughter called Vatsala from her husband Balarama.

Unfortunately everybody's joy was short-lived. On the eighth day after the baby was born, Sambara slipped into the room in the guise of one of the ladies from the city and took the infant in her arms. Before anyone knew what was happening she had carried the baby away. There was a big hue and cry and the guards went running around looking for the woman, but she seemed to have disappeared. No one had ever seen her coming in and no one knew where she had gone. Rukmini fell to the ground in a swoon. Krishna came rushing in. He seemed dreadfully perturbed, but I who knew him so well, realised that he was only acting the part of a frantic parent. He took Rukmini in his arms and tried to comfort her.

"Please get him back for me," she begged. "I know you can do it if you want."

"My Darling," he said, "you will surely get him back but not now, only after some years."

"But I want him now," she sobbed. "I hardly carried him and even when Narada told me, I thought you would be able to save him." The Lord did not reply but simply carried her in his arms and took her to her bedroom and soothed her.

'Why can't you bring him back?' I asked.

"It is not yet time," he said sternly. "He was born to kill Sambara and he has to do it before he comes back."

'Where did Sambara take him?'

"He threw him into the sea!" He replied nonchalantly.

'What!' I gasped in horror. 'Didn't he die?'

"No! Of course not! A fisherman caught him in his net along with a fish as large as the infant and he has just taken him to the kitchen of Sambarasura in the hope of getting a good price. The cook at the *asura's* palace is actually Rati, the consort of Manmatha. Narada has done his job well and has also gone to her and given her all details of the baby which is being brought to her kitchen just at this moment. She has been told that the baby is actually her husband, Manmatha who has been born in Rukmini's womb as has been decreed by Shiva. Have no fear. She will look after the baby very carefully and tenderly."

'And then what will happen?' I asked, anxious to know the end of the story.

"And then we wait till he is old enough to kill Sambasura!" said my playful Lord and laughed.

And with that I had to be content. 'I have another question.'

"Ask away," he said.

'Can I or any human being become totally unconditioned? Or to put it in another way, is it possible to de-condition ourselves?'

"Ah! That is a good question. It is indeed very difficult for the embodied being to be totally unconditioned since the conditioning actually starts from the womb itself, with the suggestions put to the foetus by the mother coupled with its own *karmic* tendencies."

'Then is there no hope for us?'

"Yes indeed there is. If anyone surrenders totally and whole-heartedly to me, the embodied God or any other form of the godhead that they prefer, then I will surely carry them in my capable arms and take them beyond this ever rotating wheel of *samsara*."

'Is this the only way?'

"There are many other ways described in the Vedas but none as easy as this." He smiled his charming smile and tilted my chin which had fallen a little and said, "Don't you believe me? Don't you think I am capable of this?" My eyes filled with tears and I fell at his feet.

'My Lord I have no other recourse but you. I have no belief in anything or anyone but you. But I don't know the meaning of total surrender. Help me surrender.'

"My beloved child!" he said, lifting me up and wiping my abundant tears with his *uttareeyam*. "Your love has totally won me over. The *gopis* gave me this type of love and surrender and thus they are totally de-conditioned. They don't have a single worry in their lives for I always see to it that they lack for nothing. You belong to that category and I give you my solemn promise that those who surrender to me, like you have done, will never want for anything and will be carried in my arms through the intricate web of this life until you reach the eternal abode. Now are you satisfied? Have your doubts been cleared?" I nodded since sobs were still choking my voice and I could not talk. I didn't know why I cried. Was it for myself or, for this poor, ignorant, struggling humanity who thought that they were in full control of their lives and had no idea of the intricate workings of nature and God.

"It's all right," he said, reading my mind as usual, "Everyone will come to know this sooner or later. No one will be condemned. Come, let's go and cheer up Rukmini."

We turned round to go to Rukmini's palace when the sage Durvasa suddenly appeared before us. He was gaunt and unkempt with long thin legs and dark skin burnished in the sun. The rags he wore flapped behind him. I had not noticed all these details when I had that glimpse of him meditating under the tree. "Who is it who will dare to welcome Durvasa to his home?" he questioned with a malevolent chuckle.

My Lord went forward and said, "O Master! You are most welcome to my humble dwelling. I will call Rukmini. She is very anxious to meet you." I suppose he thought this was a good way to keep her mind off her baby. Rukmini was well aware of Durvasa's reputation and came hurrying out and welcomed the sage and requested him to order anything he wanted. He didn't answer. In fact he didn't seem interested in looking at anything.

"I will take my bath in the river and come," he said and disappeared. Rukmini waited anxiously. Now and again she caught hold of her husband's hand and looked appealingly at him. He smiled reassuringly at her. All preparations had been made for the sage. Every conceivable dish that he might ask for had been made. At last he appeared but didn't look as if he had bathed or changed. He was clad in the same old rags. He was seated with all honour and Rukmini brought out all types of delicious food and spread it all before him on a golden platter. He hardly looked at anything but seemed to have a voracious appetite and polished off every bit of food in a matter of minutes and asked for more. He went through enough food to have fed an army. However Rukmini rose to the occasion. She had made so many dishes that there was no dearth of anything.

All of us expected him to bless Rukmini and go away after his meal but he continued to stay on. He refused to eat anything at all for days. I think Rukmini was frightened that he might curse her and bent over backwards to provide him with anything he asked for. Sometimes he wouldn't be seen at all but then he would suddenly appear looking like a cadaver in all sorts of strange places. He refused to sleep on the soft bed prepared for him but would sleep in all sorts of nooks and corners so that people mistook him for a heap of rags. Sometimes he would take all the furniture in the rooms and break it and throw it around. Neither my Lord nor Rukmini dared to say a word in protest and calmly gave in to his every whim. One day he asked for some *payasam* (milk sweet). It was brought immediately and served to him in golden dishes. Instead of eating it he told my Lord to take off his clothes and smear it all over his body. Without a word my Vanamali did as he was told and smeared it everywhere but under his feet. Rukmini looked the other way and so did I. But my Lord was totally unembarrassed. After some time he told him to go and wash it off. The next day Durvasa ordered an ox cart to be brought and asked my Lord and Rukmini to get in. He drove into the forest and then told them to get out. Of course I was clinging on to my Lord's *uttareeyam*.

His eyes gleaming like red hot coals, he spoke to Rukmini, "You may go back to your world now. You will always have the perfume of lotuses about you and your beauty will never fade. You will follow Vaasudeva even after death." She bowed low and touched his feet.

Turning to my Lord, he said, "As for you, you will die like any other human being. The soles of your feet are your weak points since you failed to smear the *payasam* over them. But what does it matter. You have understood everything that is to be understood. As long as the sun rises in the east and there is food in this world you will be loved. As long as there is even one just man on earth you will have undying glory." With these words he jumped out of the cart and slowly melted into the gloom with his rags flapping after him. My Vanamali helped Rukmini to get into the cart and drove back to the city. Later he told me that his *guru* would return to Dwaraka once again and this time he would give a curse instead of a blessing.

Aum Namo Bhagavate Vaasudevaya

Possessing nothing, calm, free from all desires, and deeply attached to me,

These Mahatmas are benefactors of all beings.

They enjoy a bliss which normal people can never understand.

Srimad Bhagavatam

Omkara is the revealer of its own source, the all pervading Paramatman,

It is the subtle essence of the Vedic mantras; It is the seed of the whole Veda.

Its three syllables 'a, u, m' form the support of sattva, rajas and tamas;

Rik, Yajus and Sama; the three worlds of Bhuloka, Bhuvarloka and Swarloka;

And the three states of waking, dreaming and deep sleep

Srimad Bhagavatam. Skanda 11. Chapter 6.

ॐ

Leelamaanushavigrahaaya Namaha!

CHAPTER SEVEN

Satyabhama and Jambavati

Once when my Vanamali and I were taking a walk along the beach at sunrise, we overtook a nobleman called Satraajit, who was the royal treasurer. He was intently watching the rising sun and offering water to the sun god. We went past him without talking. After he had finished his sun salutation he hurried after my Lord and said, "I wish to go for a forty-one day retreat to do intensive prayers to Surya (sun god). May I have your permission?" Krishna was happy to give permission but asked him where he was going. "I wish to go to the island of Bet Dwaraka where it is quiet and peaceful." The Lord agreed.

After forty-one days Satraajit came back. There was a big commotion in the city and Krishna and Uddhava and the other nobles went to investigate what it was all about. They saw a dazzling figure looking like the sun god, Surya, walking down the King's road. My Lord immediately recognised him as Satraajit, but others went close to investigate and found that the splendour came from a jewel he was wearing round his neck. Everyone clustered round him and made him sit down and relate his story.

"At the end of my forty-one day meditation on the sun god, I was sitting on the seashore meditating on the glory of the morning sun, when suddenly I found a fiery form coming out of the orb and approaching me. I jumped up and bowed low, averting my eyes since the form was too bright for me to look at it directly. I begged him to emit a less blinding light so that I could see him clearly. He took something off his neck and I saw his actual figure which was slightly dwarfish with a body like burnished copper and slightly round, reddish eyes. He told me that he was pleased with my devotion and I could ask for a boon. I immediately asked for the jewel which he had been wearing round his neck.

'Do you know what this is?' asked Surya. I shook my head and he said, 'This jewel is called Syamantaka and it has many miraculous properties. The land which keeps this jewel will never encounter any natural calamities like droughts, floods, earthquakes or famines and will always be full of prosperity. Every day this jewel will produce eight *bharas* (eighty kilograms) of gold. (Four rice grains are called one guñjâ; five guñjâs, one paga; eight paGas, one karca; four karcas, one pala; and one hundred palas, one tulâ. Twenty tulâs make up one bhâra.) The person who keeps it will also have the same benefits, but it is a dangerous thing in as much as it will increase your greed and your ego. Are you sure you want it?'

"I nodded my head and promised to take great care of it and do *puja* to it every day. Surya agreed and handed over the jewel to me. Now I have to go and keep it safely in my house."

All the nobles went and looked carefully at the jewel and some touched it, but were thrown back because it emitted certain rays which hurt anyone who touched it. Krishna, as usual, watched the proceedings with his usual interest in everything that took place and then said:

"I think it would be dangerous for a single person to keep such a precious thing in his house. I suggest that you go and present it to our King Ugrasena, so that the gold which comes from it can be utilised for the upkeep of the city and for the citizens." Everybody agreed with this suggestion and urged Satraajit to go and present it to the king. Satraajit was a greedy man and the thought of relinquishing his precious possession was not palatable to him. He refused point- blank and took the jewel to his house, where he called Brahmana priests to officially install the gem in a room specially meant for it.

The crowd dispersed and Krishna and his friends also walked back to their respective palaces. On the way Uddhava asked, "Vaasudeva, why did you ask him to give the jewel to Ugrasena? I think he misunderstood your request and thinks you have an eye on it for yourself?"

Krishna laughed and said, "Uddhava, I just tried to avert the tragedy which is approaching him. Worship which has to be given to the divine is being given by him to a worthless bauble and I'm afraid it will bring only disaster on him." I shuddered and crept closer to him. He gave me a reassuring smile.

Satraajit had a beautiful daughter called Satyabhama who was a superb rider and expert in archery. I used to see her sometimes since she would often ride into the palace grounds and take a canter round it. Her glances would always be towards my Lord's balcony. She rode a spirited horse and the way she handled it told me that she was indeed a spirited girl. She was handsome more than beautiful, and her long black hair was braided and fell down her right shoulder. Having a very rich father, she was a bit haughty and thought she could get anything she wanted. At the moment I suspected she wanted my Vanamali, but did not know how to get her wish.

When I asked my Lord about it he smiled his roguish smile and said, "Don't worry, she will get her wish soon, but at the moment her father has got her engaged to her cousin Shatadanwa and she is in a quandary since she doesn't like to rebel against her father. But she prays to me daily and I won't desert her, so don't worry."

'But what about Rukmini?' I asked.

"What about her?" he queried.

'Won't she feel sad?'

"Sad because I want to take another wife? My child, you are not being realistic. I belong to anyone who loves me. I will go to anyone who loves me. I cannot be tied to one woman or one friend or one country or one family. I belong to everyone. She will never be able to get happiness if she does not know this about me."

I hung my head in shame. 'Yes My Lord,' I whispered.

"You remember what I told you about being conditioned. I am not conditioned to think that I can be true to only one woman. I am the same to everyone and this stands true not just for now but forever. Do you understand?" He looked at me with such love that again I could only fall at his feet and beg his pardon.

Satraajit had no friends since he always suspected that everyone was after his jewel. The only visitors he had were his brother Prasena and Shatadanwa, his son-in-law to be. Krishna was playing *chaturanga* (the forerunner of chess) with Rukmini to keep her mind from brooding when Uddhava came in without announcing and said, "Vaasudeva, you have to come at once. Apparently Satraajit had given the jewel to his brother who wore it when he went hunting. Prasena has been missing for the past three days and Satraajit is spreading the rumour that you have killed him in order to steal the jewel, which you had coveted from the time he brought it here."

"Now what do you want me to do?" asked Krishna. "If he thinks I'm a thief let him think so. I was called a butter thief in Gokula when I was a child, so why not be called a jewel thief now?"

"Krishna be serious for once," said Uddhava. "You have to clear your name. Let us go immediately and search the forest for Prasena. He has to be somewhere. He can't have vanished." Balarama also insisted that Krishna should clear his name.

"Forgive me, my dear," he said to Rukmini and went with Uddhava. All his friends had gathered outside and all of them set out to the forest to find Prasena.

Penetrating deep into the forest surrounding the Raivata hill, we soon came across the decomposing body of Prasena. It had been raining some days ago and the men searched for some clue as to who could have killed him and found the paw marks of a lion. We wondered why the lion hadn't taken off his kill, but realised that he had taken off Prasena's horse and left him behind. Another curious thing was that it had carried off the gem, perhaps mistaking it for some type of delicious flesh. Following the tracks of the lion up the hill, we eventually found the carcass of the lion. Here there was no clue as to who or what had killed the lion, but again there was no trace of the gem. All of us searched the ground and at last found a few pug marks of some creature, perhaps a bear, said Balarama. Of course my Lord knew everything but kept quiet. In fact he had agreed to come on this expedition only to meet his beloved devotee, the mighty bear, Jambavan who had helped him in the war against Ravana in his previous incarnation as Rama. At last we climbed up the steep rock which led to a cave. "This cave is inhabited by a huge bear," said Satyaki. "He is said to be very ferocious and will kill anyone who dares to go near it."

"All of you can stay outside," said my Lord. "I will go in alone and get the gem. If you don't see me after a few days, you can come inside." Despite all their protests he went in by himself. Of course I was most fortunate since I could accompany him. The cave was huge and very dark, but right at the back there was a brilliant light coming from the gem which was lying on the floor. Next to it sat a young girl who seemed to be examining the glittering thing and trying to hang it round her neck. She looked up startled at the sudden intrusion and saw the handsome stranger coming towards her. She had led a cloistered life with her aged father, the bear called Jambavan, and had never seen human beings before. She gave a shriek of fear and ran inside shouting for her father in a strange language. Jambavan was so old he could hardly see and since he had a young girl living with him, his usual method of greeting strangers was to strike first and ask questions later. As usual he ran forward with wide arms as if to hug the stranger to death. I could see that my Lord was really amused at this unusual greeting, but he was always happy to accept any gift given by his devotees so he happily allowed the old bear to hug him to his satisfaction.

The bear was amazed. His hug normally pulverised the bones of his opponent, but in this case nothing happened except that his opponent hugged him back. He then let go of him and gave him a blow with his mighty fist. Since he could hardly see, my Lord could easily dodge his blows, but very often he allowed him to hit him and happily hit him back, blow for blow. This went on for some days and the mighty bear was beginning to tire. He was totally confused. He couldn't believe that an ordinary human being would be able to survive his blows. At last, with his joints dislocated, enfeebled and exhausted, Jambavan began to suspect that in his foolishness he had actually been fighting his Master Rama or the ape Hanuman, who were the only ones who were capable of defeating him. But it wasn't a hairy body that he had hugged so it must be Rama. He prised open the over-hanging lids of his eyes with his gnarled fingers looking like claws, and was amazed at the bright vision before him. My Lord had changed his form to that of Rama and the bear was given the vision of his beloved Master, who had promised to give him liberation when he came in his next incarnation as Krishna. He gave an unhappy howl and prostrated full-length before him and sobbed his heart out.

"Forgive me, Master! I'm only a stupid old bear. I can't think or see properly. I should have known when you clasped me in your arms that you were that All-pervading Being, Lord of all divinities. I felt such a thrill shoot through me that I should have known. Forgive me Lord. Forgive this stupid bear and give me your vision as Krishna, who is to be my saviour in this life."

"I've never had such a good wrestling bout with anyone in Dwaraka," said my playful Lord. "I have to thank you for this. Some people offer me flowers and some blows, but whatever comes with love from my true devotees, I am always happy to accept. Tell me how you have been all these centuries?"

"My Lord! All these years I have been waiting for you to come and redeem your promise made to me in the Treta Yuga. I am now ready to leave this life which has no joy for me anymore. Kindly lay your divine palms on my head and bless me and I can leave this world with joy. But before I leave there is one thing which I must ask you. About fifteen years ago a stranger came into my cave and in my usual impetuous fashion I gave him a big blow and he fell down dead. At that time I heard a baby cry and when I went out I saw a baby girl wrapped in a shawl left in a basket outside. Obviously the stranger was carrying the child to some other place. From the way the baby was dressed and from the quality of the shawl, I guessed that the child came from good parents. I decided to bring up the baby like my own child and named her Jambavati. This girl whom you see here is that baby. It is for her sake that I killed the lion and took away the gem. When I die, this girl will be left alone. I beseech you to take her and marry her."

He called out to the girl who came running and caught his paw. She looked curiously at this beautiful being that stood before her. "Who is this, father?" she asked inquisitively.

"My child, this is Krishna Vaasudeva, the ruler of this land in which we are staying. He is Lord and God of all creatures, humans and animals. He has agreed to marry you so you should go back with him and he will look after you better than your old father has done."

She hugged the bear and said that she did not want to leave him. The Lord turned his brilliant eyes filled with love on her and a transformation came over her. This was a transformation which came over everyone when he looked at them with his lotus eyes. She gazed at him for some moments and shyly put out her hand to him. The bear took her hand and placed it in my Lord's. He took the jewel and hung it round the girl's neck. He then prostrated full length at my Lord's feet. The Lord ran his fingers over his bruised and battered body and made him whole again and gave him final unction by placing both his blessed palms on his head. Jambavan attained liberation then and there.

Before the child could cry, the Lord lifted her in his arms and strode out of the cave. There was a big and anxious crowd waiting for him outside. Not seeing any signs of the group that had gone in search of Prasena, many of the citizens had followed their footsteps and come to the cave. There was a big cry of joy when Krishna appeared carrying the child, who was wearing the gem round her neck. He narrated the whole story and the happy group returned to Dwaraka where Devaki and Vasudeva and Rukmini and Revati and of course Satyabhama were waiting anxiously for some news of him.

The next day he called Satraajit to the Sudharma Sabha and handed over the Syamantaka to him in full view of everyone. He also told him the whole of the strange story of their quest. Satraajit was filled with shame for having doubted him and returned home pondering how he could win the Lord's favour once again. I'm not sure what his daughter told him since I was not there, but the very next day Satraajit appeared at our palace and requested for an audience. My Lord gave me a big wink and said "You will now see how clever Satyabhama is!"

"Hail Vaasudeva! I know you have a forgiving nature. I have done great wrong to you by doubting you. I am anxious to make amends. I would like to give my daughter in marriage to you along with the Syamantaka if you will accept them."

Krishna said, "I am very conscious of the great honour that you do me and am most happy to accept the hand of your daughter, but I will not accept the jewel. You can keep it yourself since you are the one to whom Surya Bhagavan gave it."

Satraajit had to be happy with this and perhaps he was also happy that Krishna had refused the jewel since he had a secret desire to keep it for himself.

My Lord's wedding to both Satyabhama and Jambavati was conducted at the same time in different pavilions. How he appeared in a dual role is a mystery to me. I had to vacillate from dais to dais, not knowing in which one my Vanamali was. He gave me an impish grin at both places so I was in quite a predicament. Jambavati had a small and somewhat rounded figure and was totally innocent about everything.

She did not have much of an idea about marriages since she had never seen any. However, she was a meek and pliable girl and happily followed whatever advice was given to her by Devaki and Subhadra. She had neither clothes nor jewellery, so everything had to be bought for her by Devaki. After being dressed up she looked like a doll. She was so short that Krishna had to bend his head so that she could put the wedding garland round his head. I don't know if she missed her father, but she adjusted to court life without too much trouble.

Satyabhama was a totally different person. She reminded me a little of Draupadi. She was tall and a bit haughty. She had a beautiful carriage and every eye was on her as she was led to the dais by her maids-in-waiting. She was a golden girl, clad in golden coloured clothes and wearing golden jewellery from head to toe. Her long black hair was braided and fell in one long plait over her right shoulder. Even that had a thin gold chain threaded through it. Her father had brought vast amounts of gifts and horses and maids and jewels, as well as huge quantities of gold. She was well aware of her birth and worth and walked with her head in the air and not fixed on the ground as is usual with brides. I must admit that she looked quite ravishing in her attire, which had been specially made for her by the best seamstresses of the town. The veil was spangled with golden stars and her bangles and anklets made tinkling sounds as she stepped on the dais. Without any trace of false modesty she looked straight into my Lord's eyes. What she saw there I don't know but slowly her head bent down before him. He winked at me over the top of her head and passed a message. "She is a high-bred horse and needs special handling!"

All the three queens including Jambavati had separate palaces, though for the first few days after the marriage Jambavati preferred to stay with Devaki and Vasudeva. Being the only child of her doting father, Satyabhama was temperamental and argumentative. My Lord always admired a woman with some spirit, so he used to enjoy her company. She was also skilled in archery and a good rider as I had seen. She was determined to be not merely a wife but also a helpmate, so she used to go with him when he went out to other places. I had heard it said that she was the incarnation of Bhu Devi, the earth goddess who was one of Lord Vishnu's wives. Rukmini of course was the incarnation of Lakshmi Devi, the goddess of auspiciousness who was another of Vishnu's wives.

We were all leading a sort of idyllic life when Yudhishtira sent a message asking my Lord to go and spend a few days with them. The Pandavas always felt happier when Krishna was around. So my Lord set out with Balarama even though Satyabhama remonstrated and insisted on accompanying him, but he refused to take her and said that it was imperative that she stay back at this time but refused to say why. As he must have known, many things took place as soon as we left Dwaraka. We had hardly gone beyond the boundaries of Anarta, and were camping for the night on the banks of the Sindhu when we were shocked to see Satyabhama arrive, hot and dusty and dishevelled after having driven the whole day and night. Her attendants were far behind. "My Lord! My Lord! She cried. "My father has been brutally murdered by someone who has also taken off the Syamantaka. I have preserved his body in oil and come to you to beg you to catch the culprit and bring him to brook."

My Lord knew everything and had also known that someone who set so much store by his wealth would surely come to grief because of it. However he consoled his wife as best as he could and immediately retraced his steps to Dwaraka. He made enquiries as to who had visited Satraajit's house on the night he was murdered, and found that Shatadanwa, Sayabhama's erstwhile suitor was the number one suspect. His suspicions were strengthened by the fact that Shatadanwa was not to be found in his house or at any other place in Dwaraka. Krishna and Balarama decided to chase him and caught up with him at Mithila, capital of Videha. Here Shatadanwa's horse dropped dead and he took to his heels. Krishna ran after him and caught him and exhorted him to tell the truth. He admitted that he had indeed killed Satraajit and the Lord cut off his head without any compunction, since he had promised his wife that he would kill the slayer of her father. Unfortunately he could not find any trace of the jewel on him.

"What shall we do now?" he asked Balarama.

"He must have given the gem for safe keeping to someone in Dwaraka before he left, so perhaps you should go back and find out about it. As for me, King Janaka of Videha is a great friend of mine and I will stay with him for some time before returning."

The Lord returned and told the grief- stricken Satyabhama the whole story and that he had killed the murderer of her father but the gem was not to be found. He then saw to it that all the due obsequies were done for her father and comforted her as best as he could.

But the matter could not be closed until the gem had been found. Of course my Lord knew everything and set enquiries afoot about the whereabouts of his dear kinsman and devotee, Akrura. He was told that soon after the murder of Satraajit, Akrura had left Dwaraka to Varanavata. Krishna sent people to find out what Akrura was doing there and to invite him to Dwaraka, since he was anxious to meet him. The messengers who had gone to meet Akrura returned with the news that he was happily ensconced in the holy city and was seen to be distributing untold wealth to the poor and feeding people and conducting *yagas*. Krishna smiled when he heard this and sent a convoy to bring Akrura back to Dwaraka. Then he invited him to the Sudharma Sabha and told him plainly, "I know that the gem is with you, so I advise you to produce it before this august assembly and tell us how you got it."

Akrura hung his head in shame and said, "My Lord! You are right as usual. Shatadanwa had approached me and Kritavarma and begged us to help him redress his wrongs. He had been cheated out of his wife and wanted to take revenge on Satraajit. Unfortunately, I have to admit that we teased him and encouraged him in his intentions. We certainly did not suspect that he would go and murder him and take the jewel. After he had committed this most horrendous deed, he was very frightened and woke up Kritavarma and asked him to help him. The latter said he would have nothing to do with the affair. He then came to my house and threw the jewel into my compound and ran for his life. You know the rest of the story. Next morning when I saw the jewel lying in my garden, I was shocked and in a fit of madness instead of confessing everything to you, I decided to leave the town altogether and use the wealth given by the gem for charitable purposes only. My Lord, you know everything and that must be why you sent your men to find out what I was doing. You must have heard of the charity that I am giving in Kasi (Varanavata) and guessed that I have the gem. Here is the jewel. You may decide what you want done with it." So saying he placed the jewel in front of the Sabha so that all could see it and decide what was to be done.

Satyabhama was happy that everything had been cleared up. My Lord asked her, "By all rights the jewel belongs to you and your children. Do you want to keep it?"

Satyabhama refused and my Lord gave the jewel back to Akrura. "This gem will bring only unhappiness to those who keep it for their own aggrandisement. However if it is kept with a noble soul like you who uses the wealth solely for the sake of helping the poor, it will have no bad effect. So you may take it and return to Varanavata and continue to do the good work that you have been doing." Thus did my Lord wind up the whole incident of the cursed gem and return to his own duties.

Aum Namo Bhagavate Vaasudevaaya

> The Lord then married that daughter of Satrajit, Satyabhama who was possessed of all qualifications like nobility of character, beauty, generosity and the like.
>
> *Srimad Bhagavatam. Skanda Ten. Chapter 57*

ॐ

Srivatsakausstubhadaraaya Namaha!

CHAPTER EIGHT

The Grand Elopement

Every day spent with my Lord was filled with excitement for me. Once again Yudhishtira sent word inviting my Vanamali to visit them in their new capital. He told me, "Get ready, we are leaving for Indraprastha immediately." The chariot was brought, and accompanied by his friends Satyaki and Uddhava and his wives, we set out for the Pandava capital. When we arrived there we were greeted joyfully by Kunti, Draupadi and the Pandavas. All the friends and relations were very happy to see the Yadavas and their wives and gave us all a royal welcome.

One day, Krishna and Arjuna set out on a hunting expedition to the forest of Khandava. After having finished with the sport, we had a bath in the Yamuna and were relaxing on the banks when we noticed a lovely girl looking rather pale and sad walking along the banks. Her hair was not tied and was hanging like a canopy down her back. My Lord who knew everything sent his friend to find out details about the maiden. I immediately took the opportunity to ask him about the girl.

"She is actually a river goddess – the river Yamuna to be exact, which is also known as Kalindi. See her colour, dark blue which is the colour of the Yamuna. She loved me at the time when I was a young boy and used to play on her banks with the *gopis*. She had a deep desire to marry me but knew that it was impossible. However she decided to do severe *tapasya* to Surya, the sun god. At last he blessed her and told her to come to this place and she would realise her dream. She calls herself the daughter of the sun since all rivers are daughters of the sun. He dries up all waters and makes them into clouds and expels them back to the rivers. So all rivers have their origin in him. As I told you before I can never reject a woman who has surrendered her heart to me."

In the meantime, Arjuna approached her with respect and asked her who she was and all details about her.

She turned her sad face to him and replied, "My name is Kalindi and I am the daughter of the sun god, Surya. I have done the most severe austerities in order to get Lord Vishnu as my husband. I have heard that he has taken an incarnation in this age and so I am searching for him." Arjuna assured her that she had come to the right place and the person for whom she was searching was sitting right beside him!

My Lord gave me a knowing look and said, "Here comes the next one!"

We returned to the palace with Kalindi. Yudhishtira blessed them both.

The Yadavas set out the next morning taking Kalindi with them. Their marriage was conducted with all formalities on an auspicious day. Krishna had invited Arjuna to go to Dwaraka for a holiday so Arjuna followed the party a month later. The Yadavas were delighted to have him in their midst and arranged a big festival on the Raivata hill. Mountain worship was quite common in those days. I was quite excited over the festivities which were going to be conducted on the mountain and skipped with joy by my Lord's side.

Within a few days the festival commenced. All the clans of the Yadavas came for this – the Vrishnis, the Andhakas and the Bhojas. The region around the hill had many mansions studded with gems, and even artificial trees had been put up even though the mountainside abounded with flowers and trees. In the night, golden poles with lighted lamps were kept everywhere so that there was no dearth of light. Even the caves were lighted. Fountains played to the strains of music. Flags with little bells tinkled in the breeze. Shops and stalls selling all sorts of exciting things had suddenly sprung up all over the hill. Merchants spread their wares and mounds of cloth and heaps of garlands could be seen. Food as well as wine was there in plenty. The rich went round giving gifts to the poor, the distressed, the blind and the helpless. Various musicians were playing *vinas*, flutes and *mridangams* in the square and dancers began to dance to the clapping of hands and the beat of the drums. There were many with beautiful voices who were also singing popular songs. The young men arranged some competitions like wrestling and chariot racing. All the citizens had climbed up the hill to participate in the festival. Some came in their gold-decked chariots and some on foot. The entire hill which was normally filled with the songs of birds was now filled with the strains of all types of music. The women of the family had also come. Rukmini, Satyabhama, Jambavati, Kalindi, Revati, Subhadra, Devaki and Rohini had all come, beautifully attired.

It was the first time that Arjuna had witnessed such a splendid scene. He and my Lord laughed and joked with each other and their friends. In the night we sat and watched the performance of the actors and dancers. Everyone was in a merry mood. My Lord seemed to have completely forgotten my existence. But I had eyes only for him. The rest of the merrymakers were shadows as far as I was concerned. Arjuna of course always had an eye for a pretty girl. He had never met Subhadra before but I noticed that his eyes were always on her. He whispered something to my Lord and Krishna called Subhadra to him and introduced her. It was quite obvious that Arjuna was totally smitten by her. He could hardly take his eyes off her and my Lord kept teasing him about it.

The festivities lasted for a week and then everyone returned to their homes, and Arjuna had to leave without having asked for Subhadra's hand. As soon as he had gone, I asked my Lord what he thought of the alliance.

"I'm very happy about it as you can guess, but I don't know what Balarama will have to say. You might not know this but she is actually my step-sister. Balarama and Subhadra are the children of my father's other wife Rohini, so he will have the final say about whom she should marry. She is supposed to be the incarnation of "Yogamaya," who was born on the same day as I was to mother Yashoda and taken back to Kamsa's dungeon by my father, Vasudeva."

'What objection can Balarama have to Arjuna?' I asked.

"No objection but I think he has promised her to Duryodhana."

'But what about her? Whom does she prefer?'

"I think she is very much attracted to Arjuna. Most girls fall for him!" said my Lord with a disarming smile.

'I must say both of you are very similar in this,' I said, for once daring to tease him. He tweaked my nose gently and gave me a naughty smile.

'So what are you going to do about this?' I asked with my usual curiosity.

"Don't worry, everything will get sorted out."

'You mean you know what is going to happen but will not tell me.'

"You will know in good time. Mark my words, Arjuna will be back before the year is out," he said and I couldn't persuade him to tell me anything else. But I did go to Subhadra's palace now again and would find her sighing and looking at the moon and behaving exactly like someone in love and I felt very sure that she was not pining for Duryodhana!

The very next day, Balarama announced his intention of getting Subhadra married to Duryodhana. Devaki, Rohini and Vasudeva protested vehemently. Subhadra burst into tears and ran out of the room. My Lord of course said nothing but pressed my hand and told me not to worry. Nobody could do anything since Balarama had already sent the proposal to Duryodhana who was delighted to accept.

Wandering *Sannyasis* are allowed to take shelter at some house or palace during the four months (*chaturmasya*) of the rainy season and people consider themselves to be most fortunate to be able to give shelter to such holy men. One such holy man now came to Dwaraka. He had a long beard and was clad in soiled and crumpled clothes and went and sat beneath a banyan tree. He also had a triple staff proclaiming him to be a renunciate. My Lord and I happened to be passing by on our two-wheeled chariot just as he was settling down. My Lord immediately jumped off the chariot and came close to the man and peered at him while the recluse hurriedly got up and tried to conceal himself behind a tree.

My Vanamali ran after him and said, "No need to panic. I recognised you immediately!"

Arjuna (for it was he) heaved a sigh of relief and said, "Vaasudeva, you have to help me. I inadvertently went into Yudhistira's bedroom during his one year with Draupadi and so I was bound to go on a pilgrimage even though he didn't insist on it. I was winding my way by the coast thinking of spending the remaining four monsoon months of my pilgrimage with all of you, but when I reached Prabhasa I heard that Subhadra's marriage to Duryodhana had been fixed. I didn't know what to do so I came here hoping that you would have some solution for my problem, since you are the only one who knows about my love for her."

My Lord said, "I have been expecting you any day. Don't worry. I have brought some ochre robes and *rudraksha malas* for you which you can wear and thus make yourself into a proper *sannyasi.* You already have a beard which conceals your face very nicely and your hair is also long. It can be tied into a top-knot as befitting a sage. Now try to put on a serious expression when anyone comes to visit you and we will think of some good plan."

Arjuna immediately did as instructed and I must admit that he made a very handsome *sannyasi* and unless one was suspicious, no one would recognise him. Very soon Balarama came along. He had a weakness for *sannyasis* and he jumped out of his chariot and approached Arjuna who hurriedly closed his eyes and started muttering on his beads, which my Lord had thoughtfully provided.

Balarama bowed low before him and said, "Hail, O Holy One! Blessed is our city to have the sight of noble ones like you."

The sage opened his eyes slightly and blessed him with his hand without speaking.

It had started to rain a bit so Balarama exclaimed, "It is not proper for you to be spending the rainy season under this tree, exposed to the inclement weather. We have a small cottage which is a perfect retreat for a holy man, so you can safely stay four months there." The only time when it was considered proper for a *sannyasi* to stay in a householder's house was during the four months of the monsoons.

My Lord drew his brother to a side and said, "Brother, beware of bringing strange young men into our house even though they may profess to be *sannyasis*. They are not to be trusted. They are not old enough to have renounced the pleasures of life. Think well before inviting him to our palace. Our sister is a young girl of marriageable age." Though he spoke in a low voice, it was pitched at just the correct note to penetrate the ears of the *sannyasi* who was straining to hear the conversation. Balarama glared at his younger brother and told him to mind his manners. The *sannyasi* started chanting "*Aum Namashivaaya*" (*mantra* of Shiva) in a loud voice to impress Balarama.

Balarama bowed to him and left after giving orders that the holy man should be transported immediately to the small cottage which had been made for such people just next to Subhadra's palace. My Lord winked at Arjuna and gave him a small prayer bag to put round his neck and keep his rosary. He advised him to put his right hand continuously into the bag.

I asked my Lord about this order and he said, "This bag is essential to the success of our plan. It is quite obvious even to the most casual observer that Arjuna's hand is not that of a *sannyasi*, who would be expected to have a calloused second finger due to the constant repetition of countless beads being rolled over that finger. Arjuna however has a calloused forefinger as befitting an archer. So it's better he hides it. But of course in Arjuna's case, he has calloused forefingers on both hands since he is ambidextrous and can shoot equally well with both hands. Let us hope nobody notices this. Come on, let's be on our way and see to the preparations!" My Lord was full of fun all the time. I had never seen him sad or at a loss to know what to do or say. I just hugged his hand to show my appreciation and he turned and smiled at me in a way which made my knees turn to jelly so that he had to support me!

Balarama had lost no time in getting everything ready for the *sannyasi* and had instructed Subhadra to look after all his needs. My Vanamali whispered to me, "It is considered very lucky for a young girl to get the blessings of a holy man. She is sure to get a good husband and many sons!! I'm sure Arjuna will be only too happy to provide her with both!!" I laughed and laughed.

'But how will you manage, without Balarama knowing?'

"Wait and see," was the only response I could get from him!

I would sneak into the *sannyasi's* room and watch the two of them together. I was sure that Subhadra suspected right from the start. Her suspicions were confirmed when she spied the calloused forefinger of his left hand. She knew that only Arjuna could have a calloused forefinger on the left hand. I watched fascinated as the courtship advanced. Arjuna would pat her head lovingly when she bowed to him and watch her every movement as she undulated in and out of the room. I used to report all this to my Lord who of course knew everything in any case.

"The four months are coming to a close," he said, "and after that the wedding season starts. Balarama will arrange the marriage at that time so we have to act fast." He told Arjuna to be alert and that he might get an order to move very soon.

One day my Lord ran to find Balarama and excitedly told him that some people had discovered the ruins of a cave temple on top of the Raivata hill and it was his duty to go and investigate. Balarama was always happy to do such things, so off he went with his entourage.

My Vanamali immediately went and announced to Arjuna that his own chariot equipped with some weapons had been stationed at the gate of the palace to take Subhadra to a religious function. Arjuna was never slow on the uptake and lost no time in grabbing the hand of the willing Subhadra who just happened to come into the room at that very moment. I suspected my Lord's hand in this as well. Arjuna hustled her quite unresistingly into the chariot and whipped up the horses.

The news of the *sannyasi's* abduction of his sister was carried to Balarama who returned hot-foot from the mountain. Without waiting to consult his brother, he sent off some of the Yadava warriors after the erring couple. Since the *sannyasi* was not expected to carry any weapons, he thought the capture would be an easy matter. However he had reckoned without his sister. Not for nothing was she the sister of such valiant brothers! She took over the job of driving the chariot and told Arjuna to use the bow and arrows which my Lord had thoughtfully kept in the chariot. Krishna was innocently sitting in Rukmini's palace playing dice with her when Balarama stormed in and demanded an explanation.

"Did I not warn you, dear brother of the dangers of allowing strange young men into our house? But you refused to listen to me. Now why do you blame me?" Asked my Lord with an innocent expression.

Balarama ranted and raved. His quick temper was not improved by this home truth. He was sure the culprits would be brought back in no time and swore to choke the neck of the *sannyasi* with his own bare hands! At last my Lord took pity on him and disclosed the *sannyasi's* identity.

"Why didn't you tell me the truth? Why do you go about everything in this devious fashion?"

"Well brother," Krishna said mildly, "had I told you about Arjuna's liking for Subhadra, you would immediately have asked me to mind my own business as you had already arranged for her marriage with Duryodhana. In this way you are completely clear of all blame since you didn't know anything about it. Duryodhana can find no fault with you for having broken your word."

Balarama's anger was appeased when he heard this. In fact everyone was overjoyed to hear the true identity of the *sannyasi*. Devaki, Rohini and Vasudeva could not have hoped for a better match for their only daughter. The erring couple was brought back to Dwaraka and all of us accompanied them back to Indraprastha loaded with a huge dowry of golden chests filled with bars of gold and silver, white horses, milk cows and many maids. Balarama had brought a thousand elephants with blankets and bells and thrones on their backs. It was such a lovely ending that I hugged my Lord's hand and congratulated him on achieving the impossible. He gave me his usual mischievous smile.

Arjuna was a bit worried about Draupadi's reception of Subhadra. When they reached Yudhistira's Sabha, Arjuna hurriedly made my Lord go ahead of him so that Subhadra was completely hidden by the two of them.

He went forward and said to Yudhishtira, "Brother! We have brought a treasure for you, our only sister who has become Arjuna's bride." He beckoned to Subhadra who came forward and fell at Kunti's feet. Kunti was delighted to see that her son had made such a precious alliance with her beloved Lord's sister.

She took Subhadra in her arms and kissed her forehead and said, "It is indeed our good fortune that you have come to our family. May you both be very happy and be blessed with many brilliant sons!"

Draupadi said nothing but one could see from her expression that she was not too pleased. She always had a soft corner for Arjuna and I suppose it was only natural that she felt upset at his having taken another wife. However she was a bit pacified when Subhadra ran to her and bowed and told her how happy she was to meet the princess of Panchala about whose beauty she had heard so much.

After staying at Indraprastha for a month, the Yadavas returned to Dwaraka leaving Subhadra behind. On the way I remarked to my Lord,

'Duryodhana certainly isn't going to be very pleased when he hears about the way Arjuna has snatched two of the women he wanted to marry from right under his nose.'

My Lord laughed as usual and said, "There are a number of things Duryodhana won't be too pleased about I assure you." Of course when pressed for an answer he refused to say anything.

Aum Namo Bhagavate Vaasudevaaya

The three *gunas* of *sattva, rajas* and *tamas* do not belong to the *atman*. They are the stuff from which the intellect is formed. By making *sattva* into a powerful mode of the mind, the other two can be overcome. After that *sattva* also should be reduced to its modeless state which is peace. When *sattva* becomes powerful it manifests that disposition which generates *bhakti*.

The fire generated by the friction of bamboos in a forest consumes the whole forest and then subsides. So also the fire of knowledge kindled by the disciplines practised by the jiva's body-mind equipment which is a product of the *gunas* ultimately destroys that very body-mind and then subsides.

Srimad Bhagavata; Skanda 11.

ॐ

Yashodavatsalaaya Namaha!

CHAPTER NINE

Krishna's Wives

Seeing my Lord in a pensive mood I asked him what the matter was. "You know the king of Avanti is married to another of my father's sisters called Rajadhidevi. He has a daughter called Mitravinda whom I have met at some weddings. She is a very beautiful girl, but the important fact is that her brothers Vinda and Anuvinda have arranged a *swayamvara* for her. Even though they are my cousins they are in league with Duryodhana and want him to marry her. Now to come to the point. Before she left, my sister Subhadra told me a very interesting fact. She told me that Mitravinda had confided in her that she was very anxious to marry me, but she didn't know how to broach the matter to her brothers who would certainly have refused their consent."

'So what will you do now?'

"I will go to the *swayamvara* and take her away as I did Rukmini. This is a common thing in these parts as you must have seen."

I was all excited at the prospect of another abduction. What exciting lives these princesses had, I thought to myself. Off we went in his chariot to Avanti (Ujjain).

My Lord told me, "This is the place of the *gurukula* of Guru Sandipany where Balarama and I did our studies. In fact Uddhava had also come with us. I wish we had the time to go and visit him. Anyway let us go as fast as possible to the *swayamvara* even though we have not been invited!"

The procedure here was almost exactly like the one in Vidharbha when he had abducted Rukmini. He swooped down on Mitravinda as she came out of the temple and carried her away right under the astounded gaze of all the kings assembled there who had been invited for the *swayamvara*. Of course the Kauravas were there in full force and as predicted by the Lord, Duryodhana found another source for frustration!

The wedding was celebrated after we reached Dwaraka. Every time he got married there was a lot of festivity with food and music and dancing and of course the citizens got presents! This made him really popular and no doubt all of them hoped he would marry many times!

'Would you go and marry someone you liked even if they did not solicit you?' I asked.

"Of course not!" he said. "Why should I go after anyone? I am here for all those who need me and want me, but I won't approach anyone if they don't approach me. I would never interfere with their free will."

I thought for a while. 'If a thousand women ask you to marry them would you do it?'

"Just wait and see," he said with another of his infectious laughs.

'Will this code of yours apply for all times?'

"What do you think? You are a perfect example for your own question. What "Time" do you think you belong to?"

I looked at him gratefully and snuggled up closer to him.

After thinking a while I came up with another question. 'What about Balarama? Why doesn't he marry again?'

"He's already got two wives."

'What do you mean? Does he have a secret wife?'

"No! No! She's pretty public. He's got Revati and he is wedded to his wine bottle. I've still to figure out which of the two he prefers!"

Arjuna returned with Subhadra for a short stay and was welcomed by all the Yadavas with whom he was very popular. He said that a *swayamvara* had been arranged for Lakshmana, the daughter of Brihatsena, king of Madra. She was also known as Madri or princess of Madra. The Lord already knew that she had set her heart on marrying him.

"Shall we go for the *swayamvara*?" Arjuna asked. "King Brihatsena has arranged an archery competition and all the kings have been invited including the Kauravas. I have a keen desire to forestall Duryodhana in this as I have done twice before."

"No doubt this is a noble aim," said my Lord, "but this time I must tell you to miss your aim since she has already given her heart to me, so I am honour bound to marry her."

"By all means," laughed Arjuna. "Always at your service but we will all go together since I have heard of the beauty of her smile. She is known as Charuhasini (one with a beautiful smile) and I want to see that smile."

"You are most welcome," my Lord said giving one of his most charming smiles. "Haven't you heard that her father plays exquisitely on the *veena*, better than Narada? So there is one more reason for us to go."

Thus all of us set out but Subhadra opted to stay back with her parents and the queens.

The country of Madra was well beyond Indraprastha. We had to go along the Sindhu as usual. The Kauravas headed by Duryodhana and Jarasandha the old king of Magadha were already there, as well as many other princes from many states. The king had arranged a shooting competition very similar to the one at the Draupadi Swayamvara. All the kings including Duryodhana and Jarasandha lost as indeed they had lost at Draupadi's *swayamvara*. At that contest my Lord had refrained from taking part and had told Satyaki also not to take part since he wanted Arjuna to win. This time Bhima refused to take part and Arjuna deliberately missed the aim since he knew that Lakshmana had given her heart to his friend. As soon as Lakshmana placed the wedding garland round my Lord's neck, all the Yadavas as well as Arjuna got into their chariots and rode off fast. The Kauravas and the other kings followed in hot pursuit but Arjuna kept them at bay, allowing Krishna to take the bride away.

I found it rather interesting that all these princesses had to be won in this way after a show of prowess by the bridegroom. 'Is this the general rule?' I asked my Lord after we reached home and the wedding was over.

"Not always," he said. "Wait and see. Today someone will come with a proposal for me."

Santardana was the crown prince of the Kekaya kingdom. He had a beautiful sister called Bhadra who was also known as Kaikeyi since she was the princess of Kekaya. He came to Dwaraka in order to offer his sister's hand in marriage to Krishna, since she had set her heart on him since she was a child.

'How is this possible?' I asked. 'Did she know you as a child?'

"I have met her many times. She is the daughter of King Drishtaketu and her mother is Shrutakirti, another of my father's sisters, which makes her Kunti's sister. So she is my first cousin like the Pandavas."

All of us accompanied Santardana back to Kekaya where the wedding was celebrated on a grand scale by her five brothers. So my question as to there being only abductions of princesses was answered. This was my Lord's normal way of answering things. Even though he knew everything, he allowed events to take their course without interference, thus unfolding the sequence of life naturally.

'Where are we going next?' I asked him when we got back from the wedding.

"One more princess is left," he said with a laugh.

'Who is she?'

"She is the daughter of King Nagnajit of Kosala and her name is Satya, even though she is known as Nagnajiti after her father. She is supposed to be brilliant and again I have come to know of her wish to be my wife. I heard her mental request. She said, 'O Lord! If you think that I have constantly cherished you in my heart as the goal of all my vows, then may you come and accept me as your wife!' There will be no fighting or abducting since her father is a very pious man who has great respect for me."

We went to Ayodhya, capital of Kosala and I was surprised at the way the king greeted my Lord. Obviously both he and his daughter knew of his divinity and he was made to sit on a golden throne and all attention was lavished on him. My Lord however was equally indifferent to the adulation as he had been to the harsh treatment which had been meted out to him at the other places. When he heard the reason for my Lord's visit, Nagnajit said, "Alas I have made a foolish vow that only the person who can subdue my seven vicious bulls at the same time will be able to marry my daughter. How can I go against my own vow? Many kings and princes have come and departed with broken legs and arms after entering the arena."

Krishna laughed with great joy when he heard this and said, "Majesty! Have no fear, I will accomplish this feat and win the hand of your precious daughter."

So saying he girded up his golden coloured *pitambaram* (yellow dhoti), and entered the arena like a wrestler. I was anxiously watching from the balcony as indeed was Satya and her father and friends. He had ordered me not to disturb him while he went into the arena. The bulls came charging at him with lowered horns, snorting and digging the ground with their hooves. Suddenly to our surprise, he seemed to have taken on seven forms and in a trice he threw seven nooses round the necks of the bulls and led them easily round the arena to the amazement of all the spectators. Satya nearly swooned with delight. Her father too was extremely happy since all the suitors who had come for her hand had failed miserably, and he had been wondering if his daughter would ever get married at all.

I wondered at the foolish vows made by the fathers of so many princesses. I supposed it just added zest to life! And certainly I knew my Lord was always anxious for a bit of excitement.

This time the wedding was in the bride's country as had been Bhadra's, and the king presented the groom with the bride price of 10,000 cows, 9,000 elephants, 900,000 chariots and double the amount of horses, 3,000 maids-in-waiting and thousands of male servants.

We returned to Dwaraka in the chariot given by the king, accompanied by his army. Some of the kings who had failed to subdue the bulls now decided to pursue the marriage party, but they were easily routed by the king's soldiers.

Each of his queens was given a separate palace. Now there were eight in number. I counted them one by one and spent quite a bit of my spare time going from palace to palace, looking at what they were doing. By now of course Rukmini had six more sons, but I think she still pined for her eldest. The others also had a few sons each. I don't know how my Lord remembered their names. I used to wonder how he kept them all happy. It was only when I made a tour of the palaces that I understood the secret. Every palace I went to had a Krishna sitting and talking to his wife or playing dice with her or playing the flute for her or listening to her singing or lying on her lap on the swing bed or discussing the state of the country (this was only with Satyabhama) or playing with her children and so on. I would run back to our own palace and find him relaxing.

"Well are you satisfied?" he asked. "Have you finished your inspection of all the eight palaces?"

I ran and clutched his feet. 'How can anyone ever understand you, my Lord?'

"I have told you that I am beyond understanding. All you have to do is to love me!"

One day I was resting at my Lord's feet in Satyabhama's palace where she was playing *chaturanga* with him when Indra the king of gods came to meet him. Krishna got up and made him sit on the throne which was normally reserved for him.

"To what do I owe the honour of this visit? What can I do for you, My Lord?" asked Krishna.

"I have come to complain over the inequities of the son of Bhumi Devi called Bhauma or Naraka. Once, long ago, the earth deity (Bhumi Devi) was snatched away by the *asura* Hiranyaksha who took her to his abode in the nether regions. She prayed to Vishnu to save her and Vishnu took the form of a boar (Varaha) and rescued her from the Garbodhaka Ocean. He lifted her on his snout and kept her in her proper place with the power of gravity. She has never fallen since. But she was pregnant at that time and though the child is said to be Vishnu's, it was actually Hiranyaksha's child and was a proper *asura*. He is known as Bhauma (son of *Bhumi*) as well as Naraka. Due to the many boons he procured from Brahma, he has become insufferable and has been harassing us. He stole my mother Aditi's earrings, Varuna's valuable umbrellas and has threatened to kick us out of the Heavens. He has also plundered the capitals of sixteen thousand kings and stolen their daughters and clapped them in jail as a kindly precaution against abductors like you, my Lord! He also has a boon from his mother that he would only die at her hands!"

My Lord was highly delighted to hear all this and assured Indra that he would settle the matter. Satyabhama was a bit peeved that he was going off so fast before they had finished their game. "Please take me with you," she pleaded. "You never take me anywhere and I am sick of the company of these women who have nothing to talk about but their clothes and their children! Moreover don't you know that I am supposed to be the incarnation of Bhumi Devi (earth goddess), and Indra has just told you that Naraka can only be killed by Bhumi Devi! So perhaps I am the one who has to do it. You know that I am quite proficient in archery as well as in driving a chariot and riding a horse, so you need not be afraid that I will be a hindrance."

I always noticed that the Lord really enjoyed Satyabhama's tantrums. Perhaps it was a pleasant change from the subservient attitude of the rest of his wives!

"All right. Let's go. Get ready and I'll bring our vehicle." Turning to me he said, "You have never seen my Garuda *vimana* have you?"

'No! What's that?'

"It's a flying machine with the face of Garuda, the eagle which is Lord Vishnu's vehicle. Come I'll show you."

He took me to a large shed which I had never seen before and I gasped with delight to see the vehicle. It was like a chariot built for two but the front was in the shape of a huge eagle. It had wheels and two wings which I saw only when we took off from the ground. I peered inside to see the mechanism and saw only a huge number of arrows with different heads which I had seen in the artillery a long time ago. It seemed to be well equipped with weapons of all types. 'How does it fly?' I asked.

"Get in and I will show you." He jumped in and so did I. He took it to the front of Satyabhama's palace and I was surprised to see that she was ready and waiting without her numerous maids. In fact she had draped her clothes in a special way by which she would be able to sit astride a horse comfortably.

Krishna smiled at her and said, "We are not riding a horse but a *vimana*." Obviously she had not seen it either, for she looked rather surprised. She jumped in and we were off before she could make any comment.

'What is the motive power for this?' I asked and he answered without words as he does when other people are present.

"It's a mentally driven vehicle. It is programmed to obey my commands."

'You mean it will not obey anyone else's commands?'

"Of course not! I told you it is programmed to obey only the tone of my voice as well as certain secret commands which I have given it."

'Do other people have these things?'

"They are not common but quite a few people have it. The most famous of them is the Pushpaka owned by Kubera, king of the *Yakshas*. Salva, king of Matrikavarta also has one called the Shaubha which is even more extraordinary. I don't use this often but it will be of great use in the fight with Naraka, whose capital Pragjyotisha (Gauhati) is an impregnable fortress and is surrounded by a moat which we will find very difficult to cross, so the *vimana* will come in handy."

'What is his story?'

"You heard a part of his story from Indra. I will try and tell the rest. He established the kingdom known as Kamarupa (Assam) after overthrowing the last of the *asura* kings called Ghatakasura, and has been terrifying all the kingdoms around him ever since."

Since we were flying, we covered the long distance to Kamarupa in a short time. The fortress was surrounded by an impenetrable barrier of magic mountains. The Lord was unperturbed and hurled his mace at the mountain with an incantation which broke the magic and shattered the mountain in one single throw of the mace. As soon as the mountain barricade was broken, there was a downpour of magical weapons on our heads.

"Bhama! Cover your head!" he shouted as he shot multiple arrows from his bow and destroyed all the weapons. Now we came to the actual fortress which was surrounded by a moat as my Lord had told me. The five-headed demon called Mura lived in the moat and would catch anyone who tried to cross with his huge tentacles. In fact he looked like a five-headed octopus. As our *vimana* flew across the moat, the demon stretched out his tentacles and tried to drag us down. Krishna chopped off his five heads with his *chakra* (discus) and penetrated the fortress, which no one had ever been able to do so far. Naraka came charging out on his four-tusked elephant followed by his elephant brigade. He had never seen a *vimana* before so he was a bit flabbergasted. However my Lord flew at him keeping to the same level as the elephant's head so that it was a fair fight. They fought for quite a while and Naraka used all types of magic since he was an expert in this type of warfare, but my Lord countered all his tricks with his own magic.

At last he told Satyabhama, "Bhama! His time has come. Take the arrow and shoot him since only you can do it." She took over but was no match for Naraka. The *asura* now took his famous javelin called the *sataghni* and hurled it at my Lord who feigned a fall and sank to the bottom of the *vimana*. When she saw him fall, Satyabhama was charged with fear and anger and grabbed the bow and arrow from my Lord and shot the fatal arrow with unerring precision and neatly cut off the *asura's* head, which rolled about the ground in a weird fashion. The head now spoke and asked Sathyabhama to see that his name would ever be remembered. The man who had thought he was invincible was now lying dead on the ground – killed by the incarnation of the earth which had given birth to him and which alone had the power to kill him!

Of course my Lord rose up and said, "O Bhama! It was only a trick to energise you!" She was so happy that she hugged him right before the eyes of Naraka's mother and son, who came out of the palace. She begged Krishna to spare her grandson, Bhagadatta and take him under his protection.

The Lord promised to do so and thus got an invaluable ally for the Pandavas. We then went and freed all Narakasura's prisoners. There were sixteen thousand and one hundred princesses who had been incarcerated in his dungeon. Krishna promised to send them all back with escorts to their own countries. When they heard this all of them started to wail and said, "O Lord! Who will acknowledge us if we go back? Not even our parents will accept us, and certainly no man will agree to marry a woman who has been in the palace of a lecherous person like this for so many months. We beg of you therefore to accept us and take us back to your country. We are prepared to do anything for you." My Lord gave me a sidelong glance. What did I tell you, was the meaning of the glance. I will have to marry all sixteen thousand and one hundred of them!! Satyabhama was not at all happy when she heard this. Bad enough that she had to have seven other rivals for his affection but this was too much. She pouted.

"What did Naraka tell you as his head rolled on the ground?" my Lord asked.

Satyabhama replied, "He asked me to see that his name was always remembered. Today is *chathurdasi* (14th day of the dark phase of the moon) and it shall henceforth be known as Naraka *chathurdasi*. Tomorrow will be *amavasya* (new moon) when we reach Dwaraka. It will be a dark night. Let us celebrate this victory in which I have helped you, and the release of these princesses and have lamps lit all over the city."

"So be it," said Krishna. So this is the origin of Deepavali (the festival of lights), I thought to myself.

When we reached Dwaraka, it was midnight and the whole city seemed to be in flames. My Lord spurred his horse forward. The citizens were in a state of panic. Uddhava, Satyaki, Kritavarma and many other nobles were there, and they had made a living river to fight the fire with barrels of water brought in a line of people stretching all the way to the sea. The barrels were filled in the sea and passed on by the people so that there was never a break and very soon the fire was under control. Luckily the cavalcade with the princesses was expected to arrive only by the next evening. We went into the palace and My Lord asked Kritavarma to tell him what had happened.

"My Lord! He said, "That wretch Shishupala knew you were away and like a coward, he took this opportunity to come with an army and set fire to the city. His Majesty, Ugrasena was on Raivata hill for some festival and he took the king's soldiers captive and fled before we knew what was happening. Of course we gave chase but he had already gone far away and it didn't seem worthwhile to go right up to Chedi. When he knew that he was being chased, he released the Yadava soldiers and we have just returned with them. There didn't seem any point in chasing them further. The news of your victory had already reached us and the city had been lit with innumerable oil lamps to welcome you. This made it very easy for that evil prince to set fire to it."

Krishna did not make any comments, but I knew that one more mark had been chalked to Shishupala's credit!

The princesses arrived next evening, and the day after that arrangements were made and my Lord married all sixteen thousand and one hundred princesses in as many halls at the same time! Nobody seemed to be amazed by this extraordinary display of his powers. All of them knew that he was the Supreme incarnate.

All the princesses were given separate palaces so that there would be no cause for rivalry and conflict. I had already experienced how he paid equal attention to all and was not going to test him again!

Satyabhama however insisted that she wanted a private palace all to herself and not next to the others. My Lord made her a beautiful palace in Bet Dwaraka where she was quite happy. Jambavati was a great friend of hers since she was simple and had no relations, so she took her along for company.

I used to love to go with my Vanamali to Bet Dwaraka and bathe in the sea and play on the beach with Satyabhama and Jambavati. Sometimes my Lord would go riding along the beach with Satyabhama. That was really thrilling since the waves would come and beat on the sides of the horses, wetting their clothes. Satyabhama was as wild and uncontrollable as some of the horses and I think my Lord liked verbal jostling with her.

Aum Namo Bhagavate Vaasudevaaya

ॐ

Haraye Namaha!

CHAPTER TEN

Sons of Krishna

Jambavati had no children so she begged Krishna to bless her with a child. My Lord decided to do *tapasya* to Shiva. 'Why do you have to do *tapas* to Shiva' I enquired, 'when you are capable of doing anything you wish?'

"As you know Shiva is the destroyer in the trinity, and this child who will be born to Jambavati will be the cause of the destruction of the entire race of the Yadavas including me!"

'Why do you want them destroyed?' I asked.

"Don't ask too many questions. I have told you that everything will be revealed in the course of time."

He took me to the temple of Shiva which I had not been to before. It was tucked away behind a huge banyan tree and looked almost like a cave. He had to stoop to get inside. It didn't have much light within, but I could make out the shape of a large *lingam* in the centre. My Lord sat there for the whole day totally withdrawn and immersed in himself. I sat behind him and closed my eyes and meditated on the *lingam*. Suddenly I heard a slight noise and opened my eyes and saw a wispy, formless cloud coming out of the *lingam* which slowly began to take the shape of the Lord of the trident. His whole body was smeared with ashes, his matted hair embellished with a glowing crescent moon which seemed to wax and wane. I was quite fascinated by that moon. A snake with ruby eyes was thrown round his neck like a muffler. Its eyes never blinked and were fixed on me. He wore a huge *rudraksha mala* on his chest and *rudraksha malas* on his arms and wrists. His upper cloth was a tiger skin and the lower, an elephant's. He held a trident in one hand and the other had the *abhaya mudra* for blessing. His eyes were glowing with love. I looked for his third eye but saw only the lines made with *vibhuti*. He corresponded in every way to my mental picture of him. I was utterly captivated and prostrated fully since I realised that he could see me very well.

I realised that my Lord was seeing the same figure inside himself. At last he opened his eyes and bowed to Shiva. "Why have you summoned me here?" Shiva asked.

"My Lord! I want the boon of a child from you."

"Whatever you want shall be yours," said Shankara.

"He shall be called after you and he will be the one to put an end to the race of the Yadavas!"

"So it shall be," said the Great Lord.

"And you, what do you want?" he asked me. I was totally unprepared for the question but the answer came easily to my tongue. 'All I want is total and unadulterated devotion to the feet of my Lord Vanamali.'

"*Tadastu*, (so be it)," he said and slowly seemed to disappear from sight in the same way as he had appeared, getting fainter and fainter until at last only the *lingam* was left and the faint perfume of *vibhuti* (sacred ashes).

'Did I really get the vision of Lord Shiva?' I asked my Vanamali.

"What do you think?"

'Was it an illusion?'

"Everything you think of as real in this world is actually an illusion," he said.

'Why do you tease me?' I asked.

"Because I know you like being teased. Anyway take it from me that he was as real as anything else."

Jambavati gave birth to a lovely baby boy who was called Samba. He was so cute that right from the time he was born, he was petted and spoilt by all the wives and the grandparents. He grew up to be very mischievous and no one had the heart to scold him.

I asked my Lord once, 'Isn't he very much like what you used to be in Gokula?'

"How do you know what I was like in Gokula?"

'I have heard many people talk about it.'

"Yes, you are right. He is very much like me."

Samba was the split image of his father and maybe that's one of the reasons that everyone loved him so much. He used to be a real mother's pet and would get into all sorts of scrapes, but everyone forgave him because of which he was rather a spoilt brat!

Years passed without my noticing it. Arjuna would come very often, accompanied by Subhadra and their little boy called Abhimanyu who was the split image of his father. His favourite toy was a bow and arrows and he would practice on them even at the age of five. He was really an expert. Arjuna took great pains to stand beside him and make him take aim at various things in the trees and on the ground and thus perfect himself. Krishna would join and give some advice now and again. Everyone loved him and the whole of Dwaraka rejoiced whenever Arjuna came. All the boys were about the same age and Abhimanyu loved to come to Dwaraka and play with them.

Eighteen years had passed since Rukmini's first born, Pradyumna had been abducted. One day as I was standing on my Lord's balcony and watching all his wives talking and playing games in the garden, I suddenly saw a *vimana* which slowly descended and landed in the garden. The person who came out resembled my Lord in every way, so all the ladies thought it was indeed their husband and became a bit bashful. Rukmini alone went up to him and asked, "Who are you? I feel as if I know you.

I feel that you are my eldest son who was stolen from me when he was only a few days old. Tell me soon who you are for my heart tells me that you are indeed my son Pradyumna."

My Lord accompanied by Devaki and Vasudeva now appeared on the scene and I quickly came down from the balcony and took my position behind him so as to be able to hear everything. As usual my Lord pretended he knew nothing, but he looked at me and said, "Didn't I tell you to have patience and that one day he would return?"

'Who?' I asked, feigning ignorance. He gave me long look which meant 'don't pretend.'

Just at that time, the celestial sage Narada came and told the story to all of us. "As you all know, this Pradyumna is actually Manmada, the god of Love who was turned into ashes by Shiva's wrath. All the gods begged Shiva to bring him back to life and Shiva said that he would be born as the son of Krishna from his wife Rukmini. However, the *asura* Sambara had been told that only the son of Krishna born of his wife Rukmini would be able to kill him. So he took the form of a woman and kidnapped the baby and threw him into the sea. The baby fell into the net of a fisherman who took the baby and the huge fish which had fallen into the net at the same time to the kitchen of the same *asura*, Sambara. Manmada's wife Rati had been born as the cook in Sambara's kitchen and I had already told her that her husband would be brought there and she should look after him till he became old enough to kill Sambara. She did so and now he has killed Sambara and they have both come back here where they belong."

Rukmini was thrilled to hear that her instinct had been right and this was indeed her first born. Everybody was delighted. My Lord also put on the show of a delighted parent. Most of the Lord's children were now old enough for marriage. Rukmini was anxious that Pradyumna should marry her brother Rukmi's daughter, Rukmavati, and broached the subject to my Lord. He said, "Your brother has sworn enmity to me and has chosen to live in another town called Bhojakata. Do you think he will be prepared to give his daughter to your son?"

"My Lord," she said, "I have heard that he is holding a *swayamvara* for his daughter. Please allow Pradyumna to go and abduct her as you abducted me."

The Lord looked at her for a while and then decided that it would be better to humour her so he gave his assent. Pradyumna was an expert car warrior and he went in his chariot and took off Rukmavati exactly as his father had done his mother. He fought all the other kings who followed him and brought her back to Dwaraka where the wedding was conducted. Though he hated Krishna, Rukmi was fond of his only sister so he didn't make a great fuss about the marriage. Within a year Rukmavati gave birth to a lovely baby boy called Aniruddha, who again resembled his grandfather very much.

At about the same time, the marriage of Charumati, Krishna's daughter by Rukmini was formalised with Kritavarma's son Bali. It looked as if the citizens of Dwaraka were always kept busy with some wedding or other since my Lord had so many wives, each having ten sons!

Once I asked him, 'I know you told me the reason why you married so many women, but why do you want so many sons?'

"My Dear, Dwaraka needs to be populated. The Yadavas have very few children. My brother has only two sons and one daughter and the other chieftains all have very few children."

'But didn't you say that your son Samba will be instrumental in putting an end to the race? Then why keep producing more?'

"Come and sit next to me and I will give you a well-needed lesson. Everything that has a beginning at some period in space and time must come to an end at another point in space and time. Do you understand that?" I nodded. "By not producing anything we will not be able to solve that problem. First of all, it is not a problem. It is the law of nature. All these cities and tribes and kings you see now and consider as invincible will be washed away in the flood of time, just as Dwaraka also will be washed away after my body disintegrates. Another set of people will come and continue this civilisation, because this country - this Vedic civilisation can never perish. It will fall into decay and degeneration but it can never be totally destroyed. Another *avatara* will come, sages will come, special manifestations of God will come to see to it that this *dharma* – the Sanatana Dharma will revive and once again flourish in the land of its birth. It is the ancient law of cosmic righteousness and therefore if it perishes the whole earth will perish. So I continue to do what I have to do which is to populate this country. Another point to be considered is that if I give five children to one wife and ten to another, there will be a lot of misunderstanding, so I thought it best to give them ten each and let them be happy. Moreover we will need all the hands we can muster for the Great War which is going to come."

'What Great War?'

"Have patience. Everything will be revealed." And with that I had to be satisfied as always.

Samba had grown up to be a very handsome young man. He was always wilful and used to having his own way in everything. He had formed an attachment for Duryodhana's daughter, Lakshmana, by his wife, Bhanumati. I think he was keen on enacting the same scenario which his father and his half-brother had done. I heard Balarama mention that her *swayamvara* had been fixed. Duryodhana was a great favourite of his and I think he was a bit annoyed that Duryodhana had deliberately chosen not to invite the Yadavas. My Lord said loudly so that Samba could hear, "Brother, I always told you that your love for Duryodhana is misplaced. His only interest is in furthering his own interests and that is why he asked you to teach him mace fighting. But this does not mean that he has become our friend. Any foe of the Pandavas is no friend of mine," so saying the Lord remained silent. Neither Balarama nor Samba was happy to hear this. Anyway Samba had always been a disobedient child and it was never my Lord's way to curb people's natural instincts, so he did not choose to stop Samba from going.

Nothing more was heard of him for a few days, then we got news that he had tried to capture the bride and had been caught and thrown into jail by Duryodhana. Hearing of the ignominious end of his son's romance, my Lord was all set to go and I too was rather excited at the thought of visiting the Kuru capital once again, but Balarama stopped him.

"Vaasudeva! You will never be able to speak politely to Duryodhana. I know him and he will certainly listen to all I have to say and release Samba without any problem." My Lord gave me a knowing look and laughed at this reading of Duryodhana's character, but did not dispute and allowed his brother to go alone. A week passed without any news.

'I wonder what happened.' I asked my Lord, who must have known everything that was taking place at the court.

As usual he laughed and said, "Don't worry; they are already on their way back with the bride!"

Everybody was anxious to know what had taken place and as soon as Balarama returned they plagued him with questions. He was not too happy to narrate the story but when pressed he said, "I did not go immediately to the palace but asked for an audience with Duryodhana in the garden and asked him to free Samba immediately. I was shocked to hear Duryodhana's reply.

'What!' he roared, 'Has the jackal started ordering the lion? I am the king of the Kurus and who are you but upstarts, led by the cow-herd Vaasudeva!' So saying he strode off to his palace. I was so angry that I dug my *hala* (ploughshare) deep into the ramparts of the city of Hastinapura and slowly started to tilt it towards the Yamuna. The whole city started quivering and shaking as if an earthquake had hit it. I think this made Duryodhana realise my power. He rushed back to me and begged me to stop this rash act. He promised to do whatever I wanted. I told him to release Samba and arrange for the marriage immediately. He did this and as you see he sent us back with a very good bride price as befitting a princess of the Kuru dynasty."

The angry giant did not seem too appeased and was still frothing and fuming about the way he had been treated, but Krishna told him to relax and gave him a bottle of freshly made wine which improved his temper considerably.

As I said, the years were slipping away like beads from a broken *mala*. It was the custom in those days to get boys married between the ages of eighteen and twenty, and very soon Pradyumna's son Aniruddha came of marriageable age. Age seemed to have blunted Rukmi's hatred of my Lord or perhaps his love for his only sister overcame his pride. He had never seen her since her elopement and obviously he had a strong regard for her, for he sent a proposal for Aniruddha for an alliance with his granddaughter, Rochana. He also invited parents and grandparents to come since he was anxious to meet Rukmini. Of course she was delighted and the whole family with sons and grandsons and wives and grandparents all left for the city of Bhojakata where Rukmi was residing. It was a crowded place and I was not very happy to be in the midst of such a crowd of haughty kings and kept close to my Lord.

After the festivities were over, some kings encouraged Rukmi to challenge Balarama to a game of dice. The first round was won by Rukmi but the second was won by Balarama. Egged on by the other kings, Rukmi announced that he had won. He taunted Balarama by saying, "What can cow-herds know of a game which is played only by kings!!"

Balarama, whose temper was never quite under control, lost it totally. He who had once given a lecture to my Lord about not having fights with one's relations and asked him to desist from killing Rukmi when he chased him after the elopement with Rukmini, now took up an iron bar and hit Rukmi on the head in the midst of the festive group and killed him instantly. He was so furious that he whirled the bar around and indiscriminately hit all the kings who had been provoking Rukmi and mocking him. All of them fled. Rukmini was in tears. My Lord comforted her and somehow placated the angry giant. Since such things were common at weddings, nothing much was said by anyone and my

Lord hustled his wives and children to the waiting chariots. He had kept a beautiful chariot for Aniruddha and Rochana and immediately whisked them off to Dwaraka before anything more could be said. He did not reproach his brother for his untimely act, but left him to his own remorse. Of course Balarama always drowned his sorrows in his bottle.

A few months after this incident, Rukmini and Rochana both came crying to my Lord telling him that Aniruddha had disappeared. "We retired to bed together but in the morning he was gone!" said Rochana. The Lord ordered a search to be made but there were no signs of the missing prince. No horse or chariot was missing. The only way he could have gone out of the city was by boat, but though Krishna asked everyone in the harbour, they said they had never seen the prince at any time. The rainy season now set in and a search party could not go anywhere at that time. Again and again I asked my Lord as to where his grandson was. Eventually he told me the story of Banasura who had been a great friend of Narakasura.

"This Banasura is a great devotee of Shankara. Actually his father was the great Emperor, Mahabali who once offered me in my *avatara* as Vamana, the whole of this universe. I told him that I wanted only three steps of land. He was so full of pride that he mocked me for being so stupid as to ask for three steps of land when he was capable of giving me all the three worlds! I insisted on my three steps so he agreed. I enlarged my form and with one step I measured the whole of this earth and with the second I measured the whole of the heavens and then there was no place for my third step so he offered his own head for my third step. I reverted to my original size and took my third step on his bowed head and pushed him into the nether regions where he still lives."

'He sounds like a great man. Why did you do this to him?' I asked.

"My child! This entire universe with all the three worlds above and below are all owned by God alone. The human being buys a few acres of land and calls himself the owner of it and fights and squabbles and even kills others for the sake of 'his' land! What does he own? Nothing but his pride. Though Mahabali was a great man, he had to be taught this lesson and through him to all beings, that not even an emperor owns even one square inch of land. God is the only landowner. Human beings are allowed to lease parts of it from him but never to own it. But because he was a great soul, I myself went and became his gate-keeper in the nether regions. In fact even now I stay there in my form as Vamana."

"This Bana is his son, so you see he has good blood in him. Strange thing about him is that he has a thousand arms with which he plays many instruments and accompanies Shankara when he dances the *Thandava.* He had heard how Vishnu had become his father's gate-keeper, so he got a boon from Shiva that he would become his gate-keeper! Of course all these things made him very proud and he told Shiva that his arms were itching for a good fight! Where would he ever get someone who would be a match for a thousand-handed monster? Shiva told him not to worry and he would soon meet his match."

'What has all this got to do with the disappearance of your grandson?'

"I really don't know anything. I just thought you might be interested in hearing the story of Banasura. The person who knows everything is the divine sage, Narada. He will be coming in a day or two and will give you the entire story."

'Why can't you tell me?' He ruffled my hair and told me to be patient.

The next day the sage arrived and told the whole story to a breathless audience. Turning to Rukmini he said, "Your grandson Aniruddha is at present in jail in the city of Sonitapura belonging to the great *asura* – Bana." The ladies gave a great wail of grief at hearing this and begged Narada to tell them the story of how he got there.

"Banasura has a very beautiful daughter called Usha who had a vivid dream one night of a prince who came and made love to her. The dream was so vivid that Usha became quite despondent the next morning when she found that there was no one beside her and that it was only a dream. Seeing her in this sad state, her dear friend Chitralekha, the minister's daughter asked her what the matter was. When Usha described the dream and the clothes worn by the prince, Chitralekha who was a great artist as well as a *siddha* began to paint pictures of many of the princes of the realm. When she came to Krishna's portrait, Usha began to show signs of excitement and when she drew Pradyumna, she became even more animated and eventually when she came to Aniruddha, she blushed and hung her head. When she heard who he was, she was in despair because she knew her father would never agree to such a match since you, my Lord, had killed his friend, Naraka. Chitralekha had *siddhis* and was able to fly. She went to Dwaraka and wafted away Aniruddha and brought him to her friend, Usha. Aniruddha woke up in the arms of a most beautiful woman and was delighted. Usha was so beautiful and so loving that Aniruddha forgot the passage of time and lived in the palace without thinking of the consequences. However, the eunuchs who guarded Usha's palace found some strange happenings going on and went and reported the matter to her father. Banasura immediately rushed to his daughter's palace and found her playing dice with a very handsome stranger. His men were following and Aniruddha fought them off singlehandedly with his sword. At last Bana bound him with serpent *astras* and cast him into jail where he is cooling his ardour. It is now your duty to go and rescue the Yadava prince."

All the Yadavas led by my Lord marched to Sonitapura. Balarama, Kritavarma, Uddhava, Satyaki, Samba, Gada and many others went with him and surrounded the city which was very beautiful with well laid out gardens and fountains and parks. But of course I didn't think it was a patch on my Lord's city. He looked at me as the thought flashed across my mind and I knew that he was aware of everything that went on in my head. It was such a sustaining thought. I felt so protected and cared for.

Since Shiva was protecting Sonitapura, my Lord had to fight with Shiva's *ganas,* made up of ghosts, goblins and a whole array of misshapen creatures. Having scattered them easily, he started to fight with Banasura's army of well-trained soldiers. He soon killed both his generals and the army scattered in all directions. Bana had been fighting with Satyaki but seeing his army take to their heels, he directed his charge against my Lord. Bana's mother now appeared naked in front of my Lord in order to save her son. Krishna averted his face and Bana took the opportunity and ran back to his citadel since his chariot and weapons were shattered.

Now Shiva let loose the dreaded *astra* (missile) which had the power of producing the most acute form of fever in the opponents. The Yadava host fell back shivering and shaking and the Lord immediately sent a counter-missile of a more virulent and deadly fever, which made Shankara's missile turn back and return to its owner. In the meantime Bana returned with another chariot equipped with many weapons and started fighting with my Lord. It was a funny sight to see the *asura* flaying his thousand arms about carrying various weapons. My Lord methodically started chopping off his arms one by one as if chopping branches off a tree! Shankara now appeared and begged Krishna to spare at least four of his arms.

"This *asura* is my devotee and I have promised to protect him, therefore please do not chop off all his arms."

Krishna answered, "Actually I had given a promise to his grandfather that I would not kill anyone in his family. I chopped off his other arms only because I thought they were a bit of a nuisance to him! Ask him to release my son and I will depart with my army."

Bana was very penitent and he released Aniruddha and brought his daughter Usha out of her apartments where she had been crying and refusing to eat. He formally gave his daughter to Aniruddha along with a huge bride price of horses, elephants, gold and soldiers.

All of us now returned in triumph to Dwaraka where the citizens joyfully welcomed their Lord.

Aum Namo Bhagavate Vaasudevaaya

ॐ

Chaturbhujatachakrasigadashankadyuthayuthaaya Namaha!

CHAPTER ELEVEN

Various Episodes

One of the things I noticed about my Lord was that he seldom wasted his own or others' time by giving them unwanted advice. It was only when someone particularly solicited him for advice that he gave it. Of course he was always giving bits of advice to me, but that was because I was always asking for it.

One day there was a strange incident. Samba came running to his father and begged him to come to the garden. When we went there, we saw many of the Lord's sons peering into a disused well. "What's the matter?" asked Krishna.

"There is a huge garden lizard at the bottom of the well and though we tried to take it out with ropes we could not do so. That's why we called you," said Pradyumna.

I peeped in and saw this enormous garden lizard with golden skin, which was staring up at us with a mournful expression. Krishna looked at it with eyes filled with compassion and the creature made a painful effort to climb up the wall of the well. The Lord reached out with his left hand and lifted it right out of the well and placed it on the ground before him. At the touch of my Lord's divine hand, the creature threw off its lizard skin and attained the form of a glowing celestial and stood with bowed hands before him. I was pretty sure that my Lord knew everything about him, but he took this opportunity to give a small lecture to his sons.

"Who might you be O mighty one? I am eager to hear your story."

The celestial being now replied, "My name is Nriga and I am the son of Ikshvaku of the Surya Vamsa (solar dynasty). Actually I was famous in the whole country as a great giver of charity. I have gifted as many milk cows to deserving Brahmanas as there are stars in the sky. All of them had horns and hooves capped in gold and silver and silks thrown across their backs. I have also given bride prices to many poor girls whose fathers were not capable of giving anything, as well as elephants, houses and money to the poor and needy. In fact it would be impossible to enumerate all the charitable acts that I have done."

All of us were intrigued by this account of this man's charitable deeds so my Lord asked him, "Tell us, O venerable Sir, how it is that one as charitable as you could have come to this wretched plight?"

"O Vaasudeva! One day it so happened that a cow belonging to an austere Brahmana who never accepted any alms strayed into my compound in which all the cows to be gifted were kept. Without knowing it, I gave the cow to the next needy Brahmana who came along. As he was leading the cow home, the owner of the cow saw it and told him that it was his cow. This Brahmana was quite affronted and said, "How can that be? This cow was given to me by the King!' There arose a heated argument between the two. I tried to intervene and even told the owner of the cow that I would give him a hundred thousand cows to make up for this one, but he was adamant on getting his own back. The other Brahmana refused to give it back and thus I was left with an unfulfilled promise. When I died, the emissaries of Yama (god of death) came and took me to his abode. He asked me whether I would prefer to be punished for my one evil deed first and then go on to enjoy the fruits of my meritorious acts or enjoy first and be punished later. I opted for the former and immediately I fell into this well in the form of a garden lizard as you saw. But I am happy about this since it has given me a chance to have your holy *darshana* which I would never have had otherwise."

So saying Nriga went round my Lord three times and fell at his feet and said. "Pray give me leave to return to my celestial abode." Krishna blessed him and gave him leave to depart.

I think my Lord was pleased to get this opportunity to give some advice to his sons. They had become quite haughty and thought that there was nobody like them. They were even rude to their elders and did not have humility, which according to the Lord is the greatest of all virtues. Even if you have all other great virtues, if you don't have humility the rest will come to naught. This is something he had always told me.

So now he told his sons. "Children! Remember that human life is very precious. It should not be wasted on trivial pursuits. The aim of human life is to attain liberation from the wheel of *samsara* (transmigratory life). The sages and Brahmanas are the custodians of spiritual wealth and deserve the highest respect. Higher than a king is the holy man, richer than a king! We should always be careful never to incur the displeasure of a holy sage. If he curses you, the curse will be bound to take effect. So always be restrained in your behaviour towards such people." Thus spoke my Lord who obviously knew what was going to happen in the future. He had already hinted to me about Samba bringing about the downfall of his people. Perhaps he hoped that his warning would have some effect.

After the boys had left I asked my Lord, 'What is so particular about the Brahmanas? Why should they be worshipped?'

"The Brahmanas are so called because they are the knowers of the Brahman. They take their authority only from that Infinite source of power and are not beholden to any earthly source of authority. That is why even the kings worship them. They do not possess weapons. Their only weapon is their tongue. The Brahmana has no need of a weapon to defend himself. The word or curse articulated in his mind conceals a blade sharper than a sword. Hence the true Brahmana is not afraid of even an emperor. You know how frightened people are of being cursed.

A curse if delivered by a true Brahmana will always work. It is infallible and cannot be revoked. It is purely a mental act which invokes the forces of nature in order to make it come true. Hence it's only the Brahmanas who are the custodians of the curse, since only they are in direct contact with the source of all truth which is the Brahman. However their blessings are also infallible. Hence it is that everyone tries to please them for if they are pleased, they will bless you and that will also come true. They owe their power to the fact that they are always in contact with the Brahman. For Brahman is "sat" – Truth - so for good or for bad, whatever they speak will come to pass. This is why I always tell my devotees to be kind and considerate to the Brahmanas for it is dangerous to invoke their wrath!"

'But all Brahmanas are not like that,' I protested.

"Maybe not, but it's better not to take risks," he smiled as he said this and I knew he was thinking of all the fallen Brahmanas who we see hanging around. "All the *rishis* are true Brahmanas and that is why their word always comes true, since they are custodians of the Truth!"

My Lord would go to the Sabha known as Sudharma on most days when he was residing in Dwaraka. This is the place where he redressed the grievances of the citizens and met envoys from other countries and generally saw to the well running of the country. I loved to go with him to this place. His Prime Minister, Uddhava and his home minister, Satyaki always accompanied him in the chariot driven by Daruka, his charioteer and his four horses known as Saibya, Sugriva, Meghapushpa and Balahaka. Saibya had a greenish colour, Sugriva had a golden colour and a beautiful neck, Meghapushpa was the colour of a cloud as his name suggests and Balahaka was white. I was told that anyone who entered this hall would be free from the six ailments which assail the human being – hunger, thirst, sorrow, delusion, old age and death.

As he entered the hall, the heralds would proclaim his name and the names of his father and grandfather and of all the great kings of the Chandra Vamsa (the lineage of the moon). Led by his two ministers, the

Lord would take a throne next to the Lion Throne on which sat Ugrasena, the king of the Yadavas. At the very incept of the city, Krishna had refused to accept the title of king and had insisted that it should go to Ugrasena who had been the rightful king of the Bhojas before his son Kamsa deposed him and grabbed the title.

The Lord had told me the story a long time ago. Kamsa had been a tyrant and he had put his father Ugrasena into the dungeon when he dared to remonstrate with him about his inequities. After that when a heavenly voice told him to beware of the eighth child of Vasudeva and Devaki (my Lord's parents), Kamsa became so frightened that he had them both clapped into the dungeon along with his father. Thus my Lord was born in the dungeon and whisked off to the cow-herd settlement of Gokula before Kamsa came to know of his birth. He had grown up as the son of their chieftain Nanda and his wife Yashoda. At the age of twelve he had returned to Mathura, the capital city of the Bhojas. He had killed Kamsa and freed his parents and Ugrasena and made him take up his rightful position as king of the Bhojas. When the Lord brought all the tribes of the Yadavas to Dwaraka, he insisted that Ugrasena alone should be the king and hence the Lion Throne was always reserved for him. As I told him once, 'The King of Kings has no need of a throne.'

After the nobles took their seats, the Brahmanas came and fluently recited the Sama Veda hymns, while others proclaimed my Lord's valorous achievements and narrated the mighty feats of the great kings of the Yadava line. The *sutas* (professional poets, *magadhas* (chroniclers) and *vandinahs* (panegyrists) recited the Lord's glories. Before starting the business of the day, it was the custom to regale the members of the Sabha with the frolics of master comedians and dancing troupes. Court jesters tumbled and rolled about the floor of the hall and enacted many comic scenes which had the whole court in splits. Then came the dancers both male and female who danced and sang to the accompaniment of *mridangams* (drums), *vinas* (stringed instruments), flutes, cymbals and conch shells, followed by the sound of the *murajas* (another type of drum). It was only after having been thus regaled that the assembly took up the main business of the day.

One day while the Lord was holding his morning audience, a messenger came from the king of Karavirapura called Paundraka. The messenger read out his master's proclamation.

"I am Vaasudeva, Narayana, the Primeval Being who has incarnated himself in order to uplift the world. I hear that you have dared to usurp my title and insignia like the '*sreevatsa*' on the chest and the jewel '*kaustubha*' and the appearance of four arms when necessary carrying the discus – '*sudarshana*' the conch '*Panchajanya*', the mace '*kaumodaki*' and the sword '*nandaki*'. I hear that you are posing as the true incarnation of Vishnu, so I order you to surrender yourself to me immediately or else come and fight so that we can prove to the world who is the true incarnation?

The whole court burst into laughter when they heard this piece of folly. My Lord smiled and said sweetly to the messenger. "Please inform your master that his wishes will definitely be complied with and I will come and meet him in a few days' time so that his doubts will be cleared once and for all."

Everyone had a hearty laugh after the messenger had gone. "Who is this man? Are you really going to meet him?" asked Uddhava.

Krishna said, "Paundraka is a simple sort of man and his so-called friends have led him to believe that he is Vaasudeva, the true incarnation of Vishnu. He has proclaimed that he alone is the true God and no one should worship anyone but him in his country. He has jailed all the *rishis* and Brahmanas who insist on reading the Vedas and doing rituals. Every week he sends a man to ask these people if they have come to their right senses and are ready to accept him as their true and only God. If the answer is in the affirmative they are let out, otherwise they are left to rot in jail till they accept him as the only God! Punardatta, the son of my *guru* Sandipany is one of those whom he has jailed. I have received word from him and all the others begging me to free them from this tyrant. The King of Kasi is his great friend and he is now residing with him. I would have gone there in any case to free the Brahmanas, but now I have a good excuse to do so since Paundraka has invited me!" The Lord gave me a small smile since I had been asking him for some time to take me to Kasi, which has the great temple of Visvanatha (Shiva). I had heard that Kasi (Varanasi) is supposed to be the oldest town in Aryavrata and that at the end of this eon when everything would be submerged in the deluge, Shiva would lift up Kasi on his trident and keep it safe till another creation began. This was the reason that I was dying to see Kasi!

My Lord sent Uddhava to Karavirapura to enquire about the whereabouts of Punardatta. He was taken to the court where he saw people worshipping the king as if he was God. Even the Brahmanas were paying him obeisance. When the king heard that he was a messenger from Krishna Vaasudeva, he had him put into a cave in which he found Punardatta as well as some Brahmanas who obviously had refused to accept the king as Vaasudeva, the Supreme Being. Uddhava and Punardatta escaped with the help of another disciple of Guru Sandipany. Of course I learnt of this only later after we returned to Dwaraka. In the meantime my Lord, accompanied by all the Yadava chieftains had started for Kasi. My Vanamali had taken all his accoutrements with him like the *sudarshana (*discus), his bow, *sarnga*, his mace, *Kaumodaki* and his sword, *Nandaki*. I found it strange that the weapons of all great warriors had names, which made them come alive as it were. He told Daruka to take another chariot and drove his own. Satyaki sat beside him and of course I was behind holding on to his *uttareeyam*. The horses flew like the wind and we had only one stop in the kingdom of Matsya before reaching Varanavata (Kasi). As we entered Kasi, I jumped out and joined the cheering crowds who were awaiting his arrival. This way I could see him in all his glory. He was wearing his yellow garments and his diadem was crowned with a bunch of peacock feathers. There appeared to be a halo round him and he shone with a radiance which put the glory of the sun to shame. I know I was biased but obviously the citizens of Kasi felt the same for they said, "Hail to the King of Kings. If there is a God on earth surely it must be Vaasudeva. How lucky we are to be able to get a glimpse of him. Yet how unlucky we are, for instead of paying homage to him we are forced to worship this fool Paundraka!"

As we went forward, we were met by Paundraka's army which consisted of two *akshauhinies* followed by the army of the King of Kasi. Paundraka had imitated every detail of my Vanamali's attire. It was obvious that he had painted his body a deep blue and branded the *sreevatsa* on his chest. He was clad in yellow and was holding a conch shell and discus resembling my Lord's in every way. I think he feared that the flaws in his attire would be obvious at close quarters, so he stopped at quite a distance and shouted:

"I command you to halt. Are you prepared to admit that I am the true Vaasudeva, the supreme incarnation of Vishnu?"

Krishna obediently halted and said, "O King Sringalavala Vaasudeva of Karavirapura, I - Krishna Vaasudeva of Dwaraka, offer you my greetings. I readily admit the truth of your claims. I am Vaasudeva only because my father's name happens to be Vasudeva. I'm quite ready to be friends with you if you release the Brahmanas that you have incarcerated in your dungeon."

Sringalavala proudly replied, "I have no need of friends like you. Be prepared to fight, for there is no place on this earth for two of us." So saying he took an arrow from his golden quiver and shot it at my Lord.

His army now attacked the Yadava host with various weapons like tridents, maces, wooden tipped and iron tipped javelins, spears and arrows. My Vanamali played along with him for some time and then he tired of the game and said, "O Sringalavala! Whatever weapons you had wanted me to give up to you, I will now give you. Here catch them!"

So saying he threw the discus at him. The poor man was unable to do anything but gape as it hurtled towards him and neatly severed his head from his body. His friend the King of Kasi soon followed him to his heavenly abode. Sringalavala who had been mentally identifying himself with Vaasudeva all his life got release from his mortal coils and attained identity of form with the Lord. After this, my Lord released all the Brahmanas who had been enslaved in the dungeon. He then placed Poundraka's son Shakradeva who was a minor, on the throne with his mother, Padmavati as guardian.

After this we returned to Dwaraka. But very soon when my Vanamali and I were playing in the garden with his children, the distraught citizens came rushing up to say that there was a dreadful fiery creature which was advancing into the city. They feared it was a *tantric* force sent by Sudakshina, son of the King of Kasi who had invoked this in order to burn down the city. My Lord Vanamali as usual did not panic but simply invoked the *sudarshana* which immediately came into his hands and sent it after the *Krtya*. The Lord's discus chased off the *Krtya* which turned back the way it had come and returned to Kasi and burnt up the whole city as well as the person who had sent it.

'Why did you have to kill Paundraka? I asked. 'He was only a foolish man. Did he deserve death?'

"Everyone gets what they deserve. Nothing more and nothing less. Whatever Paundraka deserved, he got. Many times we pass judgements on God's doings. We say, 'O that poor man, he is so good. He didn't deserve such a fate.' Or we say, 'What a wicked man. How is it that he is so prosperous and enjoys such a good life? What justice is there in the world?'

"Who are you to pass judgements? What do you know about that man's past life or even his present life before you met him? We are totally ignorant of the workings of the Law of Karma which is infallible. Remember that: 'It is infallible.' It can never make any mistakes. Every thought and deed of every single person is recorded by a celestial called Chitragupta. He has secret pictures of everyone's thoughts and deeds. It is impossible to escape his eyes. So it is not correct on our part to judge anybody or any action, since we are totally ignorant of the precedents which caused the action. Judgement should be left to God alone. The law of the land of course has a right to judge and punish since that will prove a deterrent to other evil doers, but the individual has no such right. He can try to correct the wrong, but he has to do it without passing judgement. So my dear, the reason why I had to kill Paundraka goes way back to his previous births and it is not necessary for you to go into any of them. Just accept the fact that God makes no mistakes and everyone gets what they deserve. Now do you understand?" He lifted my chin and looked into my eyes. My knees started to quiver and I fell in front of him and clasped my arms round his lotus feet.

Once Garga muni came to my Vanamali and told him of the total solar eclipse which would occur soon. He advised all of us to go the holy lake known as the Syamanta-panchaka which is located at Kurukshetra, which belongs to the Kurus and is the place where they usually fight all their wars.

With my usual curiosity I asked my Vanamali about this place. "That is the holy lake created by Parasurama with the blood of the slain Kshatriyas. He performed many *yajnas* there in order to expiate for this sin, so it is considered holy."

'Why should we take baths during an eclipse?' I asked.

My Vanamali was so sweet. He never put off any of my questions. "During the period of time of an eclipse, especially a solar eclipse, the sun's rays which are continuously falling on the earth are totally cut off. At that time you can notice that all creatures and birds will go into their lairs. They won't eat anything since harmful rays are falling on the earth and will poison anything we eat. So we should take a lesson from the animals and never take food during this period. However, this time is to be utilised for saying prayers and chanting *mantras* and so on. Baths should be taken in holy lakes or rivers thrice during the period of the eclipse – once at the commencement, once during the middle and once at the end when the sun is totally released. In this way, all the harmful rays will be washed off and we can take our food. So now we shall all go to Syamanta-panchaka where we will meet our dear friends the Pandavas.

I will send a message to Gokula so that the *gopis* and *gopalas* and my foster parents can also come. So it will be a wonderful event. Do you want to come?" His teasing look made me wriggle with joy.

All the Yadavas with their families and all my Lord's wives and children set out in chariots, palanquins, horses and elephants. Among the nobility, only Aniruddha and Kritavarma were left back to guard the city, and of course a small garrison of soldiers. We reached our destination the day before the eclipse and camped on the lake side for the night. In the morning all of us took the ceremonial bath at the specified time. It was a very long eclipse and during the time no one took even a sip of water. No food was cooked and even dry foods were kept tightly closed.

After the baths there were many rituals to be performed and only then was food served. I looked around and found that camps had been built all round the huge lake by all the kings from the lands of Matsya, Usinara, Kosala, Vidarbha, Kuru, Srinjaya, Kamboja, Kekaya, Madra, Kunti, Anarta and many others. All had assembled there in hundreds. The *gopalas* of Vraja had also come, eager to see their beloved Lord, Krishna. The Pandavas with Draupadi and their other wives as well as Dritarashtra, Gandhari, Bhishma, Vidura and the Kauravas headed by Duryodhana were all there. This was truly a grand reunion of friends and relatives. My Lord whispered to me, "All these kings will meet again on this very field but for a very different reason."

'Will there be another eclipse?' I asked.

"Something worse than an eclipse!" After that he kept silent as usual. After the final bath everyone served the Brahmanas first and gave gifts to all. Only then did people start mingling and meeting with friends and relations.

My Lord first went and touched the feet of his foster parents, Yashoda and Nandagopa. Vasudeva and Devaki also embraced them and said, "How can we ever repay the debt we owe you? When Kamsa was treating us so cruelly, you are the ones who gave a home to our boys, Krishna and Balarama. You are greater than us for you looked after them when they had no home to go to. You are really blessed for you were able to see their delightful childhood exploits which we have never seen, unfortunate parents that we are."

My Vanamali now approached the *gopis* who were standing apart and looking with tremulous eyes at the grand assemblage of people who had gathered there. They could hardly recognise their companion of Vrindavana, who used to be so simply dressed. Now the only thing they could recognise was his peacock feather which still waved merrily over his jewelled crown. He understood their predicament and immediately changed his attire to that of a *gopala* –a simple cow-herd boy with a garland of wild flowers round his neck and a flute stuck into his waist band. Now they were no longer shy and rushed towards him. All of them flung themselves on him and forced him to sit down on the banks of the lake and flocked round him. There was a cluster of shawls, blouses, veils and flower garlands all round him. They all tried to get close enough to colour his chest with the saffron on their breasts. Some pressed his feet, some snatched a kiss and some kept his hand on their cheek, some ruffled his curly locks and all the while they pelted him with questions. "Why did you never come back? Where have you been all these years? Did you ever think of us even once when you were in Madura and in Dwaraka? Had you been in Madura, we could have made the trip and seen you now and again but you have gone far, far away to some place which we have never heard of and which is too far for us to come. Do you still love us?" I was surprised to see how familiarly they treated him. They just pelted him with questions and some pouted and refused to talk and some kissed him and others caressed him. He did not say a word but allowed them to do what they liked with him.

I remembered what he had told me about them. They were totally pure in their love. They expected nothing in return. They had no inhibitions about showing their love. They were not shy or ashamed because to them he was not a stranger, not 'another', but their very selves. Who feels shame before one's own self? Who feels that she is a stranger to herself? His wives were shy and respectful because they saw him as 'another'. Duality existed between them. But with the *gopis* there was only unity. He was their very self - their own beloved. Whatever he did or did not do meant nothing to them. All they wanted was to love him. I was watching this scene with fascination. He looked at me over their heads and I knew that he was asking me to learn from them. He had told me once that long ago Uddhava, the great intellectual, had been sent by him to Vrindavana to comfort the *gopis* after his departure to Madura. However, Uddhava had come under their spell and realised the high quality of the love they bore for Krishna. At the end of his visit instead of the *gopis* falling at his feet, he, the Prime Minister of the Yadavas had fallen at their feet, for he too got a glimpse of their amazing purity. It was only then that he realised that Krishna had sent him there for a specific purpose – to teach him the meaning of unpolluted and unconditional love. No wonder my Vanamali loved them so much, I thought. Such love as theirs was not to be seen on earth. Mentally I asked him to bless me with love like theirs. Of course they were not aware of me. In fact they were not aware of anyone in that crowded conclave of people. Only Krishna existed for them – Govinda! Damodara! Madhava! They laughed and cried and sang and talked – each of them in their own world peopled only by their Shyamasundara (Krishna), totally unaware of each other or any 'other'. HE alone was there, the beloved of their hearts, the keeper of their souls. I felt more purified by this contact with them than with all the baths I had taken in the holy lake! I fell at their feet and took the dust of their feet and put it on my own head reverentially.

Once I asked my Vanamali to ask them if they wanted to return to Dwaraka with him. "I will ask them only to please you," he said. And sure enough they refused point blank when he asked them.

'Why is this?' I asked him. 'Why don't they want to come?'

"Their love is the love of the lover for the beloved. It is not the love of the wife for her husband. It is clandestine love. They know that they can never marry me but that does not stop them from loving me. They want nothing for themselves. They ask only for the freedom to keep on loving me. What gives great poignancy to this love, is separation or '*viraha.*' Their love does not degenerate into an ordinary affair when the lover feels that she totally possesses the beloved! Nobody can ever feel that he or she possesses me totally. This is true of all my relationships. I don't belong to this or that person. I belong to everyone who loves me. This is the essence of everybody's relationship with me. Hence it is always at an acute stage of ecstasy since no one knows when I might withdraw myself. So the love affair never becomes a boring thing like the physical relationships between husband and wife. Another aspect of stolen love is that the lover is prepared to risk everything the world holds dear like position, security, money and approbation of the society in order to go to her beloved. To violate the rules of conjugal bonds is to deny all earthly bonds and abandon oneself into the arms of the beloved. Such love is totally unselfish. It does not seek to gain anything for itself and it never will gain anything. Anyone who seeks for results alone will gain only that, but one who is uncaring of the gain will find the inmost nectar. This is known as '*prema*', pure love, unadulterated by '*kama*' (lust). The one who pursues *kama* has only one goal and that is to get the utmost pleasure from the object of his lust. The one who follows *prema* abandons herself to a call which is beyond all worldly considerations. Her happiness has two edges to it – the constant fear of separation and of discovery. This makes every meeting with the lover a thrilling experience. The anguish of separation and the anticipation of reunion is what keep this illegitimate love in a constant state of suspense and elation. This is the very nature of illegitimate love (*parakiya dharma*). Only those who have experienced this will get an entry into my essential nature which is '*madhurya*' or sweetness. When all the facades of life are stripped off, layer by layer like bits of clothing, then and only then will one experience my ultimate nature. This is the esoteric meaning of the episode when I stole the garments of the *gopis* when they were bathing in the pool and made them strip themselves and come to me naked."

I listened, entranced by this discourse on the aspect of *bhakti* known as *prema*. It was only now that I understood the greatness of the *gopis* and why my Vanamali did not want to disturb them from their habitat which was in the woods and glades of Vrindavana where they continue to play with their divine lover for all eternity.

One day he told me that he would give me a demonstration about the difference between the love of the *gopis* and the love of his wives. He lay down on his bed and told me that he had a terrible headache and I should go away. I had never seen him ill before and I felt quite desperate. What was I to do? There was no way I could communicate with anyone. I just sat beside him and started to fan him and massage his temples. He waved me away. Luckily his mother Devaki came into the tent. She was quite shocked to see her beloved son in this state and ran to get a *vaidya* (physician). She came back with one of the sages called Agniveshya who was a physician. He went away and returned with a paste which he smeared on my Lord's forehead. After some time he asked him how he felt, but my Lord simply moaned and turned his head away.

"What is the matter my child?" cried Devaki. "What can I get for you? I have never seen you like this." By this time quite a crowd of people had pushed their way into the tent.

My Lord replied in a fading voice, "The only thing which will help me is the dust of the feet of my devotees. That should be mixed in sandal oil and applied to my forehead."

"I don't like to put the dust of my feet on your forehead but I will ask Rukmini and the others to do it," said Devaki and hurried away.

She returned soon enough accompanied by all the eight foremost wives of my Lord. All of them ran to his side and started lamenting and crying at his state. "What can we do?" they queried.

Devaki replied, "He will only be cured by the dust of the feet of one of his devotees. So please scrape some dust off your feet and give it to me and I will do the rest."

All of them fell back at this strange request. "We are only fit to take the dust off his feet. How can we ever give him the dust off our feet? We are not worthy of this. Moreover our feet are clean and delicate like rose petals. What dust can we get from them? Mother, is this a joke that you are playing on us?" They asked Devaki.

In the meantime my poor Lord was groaning and moaning. I couldn't bear it any longer. I had no physical feet to give any dust to him or else I would have given it myself. I ran out of the tent to the place where the *gopis* were sitting and singing about their beloved. I dragged on the upper cloth of one of them and somehow got her to follow me. All of them followed her, not knowing what it was all about. I stopped when I came to my Lord's tent and suddenly they heard him groaning. Without stopping to think, all of them burst into the tent and rushed to his side and asked, "What happened? What has happened to our beloved?"

Devaki told them the whole story and how he could be cured only by the dust of the feet of his devotees. She had hardly finished her narrative when all of them sat down and started scraping the dust from their dirty feet. Since they never wore any footwear and were always working in the fields and in the cow byres, their feet were quite dirty so they scraped off lots of dust from them and offered it to Devaki. She quickly mixed it in sandal oil and applied it to her son's forehead. It was obviously a miraculous cure, for he sat up immediately and smiled in his usual charming fashion and declared that he was quite well. Both his wives and the *gopis* crowded round him. He parried all their questions and thanked them for their services and told them to return to their own abodes.

After they left he turned to me and said, "Now do you see the difference in the love of my wives and the *gopis*? My wives think of me as 'another'. Thus they felt uncomfortable at scraping off the dust from their feet and giving it to me, their husband. The *gopis* had no such qualms. All they saw was that I was in pain and even if they had been asked to give their heads they would have done so without a moment's thought. There was no question of their dust being dirty or that it was not the right thing to be done or the thought of what people would think. Their love is so deep that my comfort is all that matters. In their minds there is no thought of right or wrong or not conforming to the dictates of the norm. Nothing and nobody matters to them except me – their beloved. Now do you see the difference?" I nodded my head vigorously. My throat was so choked with tears that I was bereft of speech. I just poured my heart into my eyes and looked at him. He nodded and tilted my head with his little finger under my chin and wiped the tears with his *uttareeyam*.

That evening I sat by myself and thought about my beloved. I realised that my Lord, Krishna is the attracting power of love which alone has the ability to reconcile all opposites and rise above the logic of the material plane. When Krishna touches our heart, there is an end to all confusion and hatred. He is the validation of our unique essence, which is bliss. At this level, the mind becomes a tool for the purest type of enjoyment which makes even the gods envy the devotee who has attained this *bhava* (attitude). This is his *lila* (play). It is this play that makes light of the daily drudge of our harsh lives. It is this *lila* which makes people cling to life even though they are suffering. He flirts with every soul that is ready for enlightenment. His life is always filled with joy even in the midst of a holocaust as I knew very well. That is why I am filled with joy when I am with him, however harsh the external circumstances in which we were placed. The call of his flute is always there beckoning the sluggish heart entrammelled in worldly desires to come to him. Once having come under the spell of his call there is no going back. Life flows in waves of delight in which he alone is the dancer and the dance, the singer and the song, the way and the goal.

Every evening he would sit on a rock outside our camp and play his flute. It is impossible to describe that experience. Slowly everyone from all the camps would gyrate towards him and close their eyes and listen in rapture to the haunting melody. The *gopis* of course were lost in a magic world all the time. When they heard his call they would stand still like statues totally unaware of the world around, mesmerised by the music. In fact I think all those who clustered round him felt the same. All sentient beings forgot their duty-bound existences and listened with rapt attention to his call. Even the horses would prick up their ears and listen. The swans swimming on the lake would come to the shore and stand with closed eyes, in a state of ecstasy like *paramahamsas (*enlightened souls). I thought I could see the forms of the *devas* in the skies listening to his rapturous music. For me it was the best part of the day. I had a grand stand seat for I was sitting next to him! We stayed three months at this place and every day, my Lord allotted a certain amount of time for the *gopis*. However he always found time to spend with each of the others who loved him so much.

I felt exalted by meeting all these simple people of Vrindavana who were a race apart. They lived for him and in him. At the end of the three months when the time came for them to depart, their prayer to him was this: "O thou who carries the lotus of the world in his navel, thy feet are the object of contemplation by great *yogis* with deep understanding. But O Lord! They are the sole support of ignorant people like us and the only means for lifting us out of this dilapidated well of human existence. May those holy feet ever shine forever in our hearts!"

Subhadra and Abhimanyu stayed all the time in our camp and not in the Pandava camp. She was so happy to be with her dear parents and brothers and sisters-in-law who she had missed sorely. Revati and Rukmini especially were very dear to her and she was so happy to be with them. Abhimanyu loved to compete with Krishna's children and it was apparent that he excelled them in all types of mock fights with javelins, arrows and swords. My Lord was very fond of him, especially so because he was the son of Arjuna and Subhadra who were so dear to him.

Draupadi was very curious to know how my Vanamali came to marry so many women and what they thought of him, so one day she called all his wives together and asked them to narrate the wonderful tales of his various marriages. Of course I got my Lord's consent to attend this women's meeting since I was very curious to know about them! All of them delighted in describing the romantic way in which he had carried them off right under the noses of all the other suitors. Draupadi then wanted to know in what light they regarded him - as a man or as god. All of them agreed that as a husband he was everything that any woman could dream of, yet there was something about him, they said which made them feel that he was not just a man but the Supreme himself who had come to take on the role of a husband for each of them. "Fortunate indeed are we," said Rukmini, "to have got this abode of perfection for our husband. But we are well aware that he belongs to everyone and we always take the opportunity to worship him as God incarnate." I was so happy to hear this. I too thought he was God incarnate and lost no opportunity to worship him with flowers. Of course I went and reported the whole conversation to my Vanamali who gave me his mischievous smile.

Many sages had come to the spot to have a glimpse of the Lord who had taken on a human form. My Vanamali always advocated the worship of great saints so before they could prostrate to him, he went forward and touched their feet and made them take their seats and saw to all their comforts. "Human beings resort to all sorts of things in order to acquire spiritual merits like going on pilgrimages, worshipping idols, undergoing severe austerities and so on. All these things take a long time to purify the mind, but the very sight of holy ones like you destroys the sins of a million lifetimes." The sages were totally bewildered by his assumption of an ordinary human being. They had come to have his divine *darshana* and here he was, touching their feet. They extolled him and said, "Even we, who are noted for being knowers of Truth are totally bewildered by your divine play. All the austerities that we have undergone have come to fruit today by getting your blessed vision. Salutations to Thee O Vaasudeva! You alone are the Self of all and the Supreme Being!"

Taking advantage of the sages who had assembled there, Vasudeva, my Lord's father approached them and asked, "Pray instruct me as to what types of *yajnas* I should perform in order to take away the effects of my past *karmas*."

The sages looked at him pityingly and said, "The fruits of all the good *karmas* you have done in your past births have been embodied in the form of your son, Krishna. What need is there for you to perform any other *yajnas*? Worship him therefore and attain liberation."

I thought to myself, how true it is to say that a prophet is never honoured in his own country. Poor Vasudeva could only see Krishna as his son despite the fact that he had showed him his divine form at birth. Despite all the words of the saints, Vasudeva insisted on performing many *yajnas* and the Lord looked on with a smile on his lips, happy to see his father enjoying himself. Thus all of them who were bound to my Vanamali with different strands of love spent an idyllic three months with him and he made them all happy in different ways. I spent my time running after him as he went from camp to camp talking and joking and laughing with all of them in his usual charming manner. Before parting, Arjuna begged him to come to Indraprastha soon and Krishna agreed.

Aum Namo Bhagavate Vaasudevaaya

Devakinandanaaya Namaha!

CHAPTER TWELVE

Indraprastha

We had to make the trip to Indraprastha before the monsoons set in, when all travel came to a standstill, so we set off despite the blazing heat of summer. But for me who lived in my Vanamali's shade there was no summer. By his side it was cool in summer and warm in winter! The Lord took all his wives since they were anxious to go to Indraprastha and meet their friends, even though they had met them four months ago at Syamanta-panchaka. The morning after we reached, I stood on the balcony outside my Lord's room which was on a small hillock, as were all the palaces, and surveyed the city – Indraprastha – The White City as it was known. In the pearly pink of the morning it looked like an enchanted metropolis. White towers of different heights separated by large swards of grass dominated the scene giving it a chequered effect. Huge outer walls surrounded the city and made it into a perfect square. The walls were covered with ivy and other creepers which sort of melted into the moat surrounding the walls and hid the fact that the bottom of the moat was lined with tiny but deadly barbs which would make it impossible for anyone to swim across it.

One morning Draupadi decided to take all the women and go for a picnic on the banks of the Yamuna. It was a colourful procession which set out. Maids and servants and carts laden with exciting foods and beverages led the way. Draupadi and Subhadra followed with Abhimanyu and some of the other children. Then came Rukmini and all my Lord's wives. Arjuna and my Vanamali guarded them from the rear. We were close to the dark forest of Khandava. I went with Krishna and Arjuna towards the forest. When I looked back I saw that the maids had unloaded the delicacies they had brought and there was a trill of the chatter of voices as the ladies talked and laughed. In front of them were the glistening waters of the Yamuna as she danced her way towards the sea, and the ladies decided to swim in the river since it was so hot. I could hear the soft tones of the flutes and *vinas* and small drums floating in the air towards us.

It was blistering hot in the sun and my Lord and Arjuna also decided to have a bath in the cool waters of the river. As we were walking back, we were accosted by an old man dressed in rags. He was tall and thin but his skin glowed like molten gold. He smiled at them showing his shining teeth. His eyes were flaming red like hot coals. Altogether he was a strange sight.

He said, "My Lords! I'm old and hungry. Please give me something to eat."

I thought it rather odd that my Vanamali remained silent. Usually he was always ready to help anyone. But Arjuna spoke, "Of course. What do you want to eat?"

"The forest of Khandava", said the man very simply as if it was the most natural request in the world.

"Who are you?" questioned the Pandava.

The old man opened his closed fist and there was an ember glistening in it. "I am Agni, (god of fire), he said, "only this dry forest will appease my appetite."

"This is a strange request," said Arjuna.

"My digestion has been totally spoilt by eating too much ghee at the *yajnas* of great kings," said Agni. "The only things that can help me are the medicinal trees of this great forest."

"What is stopping you from eating this forest?" asked Arjuna.

"This forest belongs to Indra and every time I try to eat it, he sends torrential rains and puts me out. I have tried seven times and failed miserably."

Arjuna was in a dilemma. He didn't want to displease his father, Indra and he had already given his word to this man, so as usual he looked at his friend for guidance.

"Tell me, O noble sire, who are the ones who live in this desolate forest?" asked Krishna.

"No one," said Agni.

"What about animals?"

"Quite a few but they will run as I start to burn up their forest and will escape. Have no fear on that score."

"What about the birds and the trees?"

"O Vaasudeva! The birds will fly away and the roots of the trees will not be harmed as they have penetrated deep into the soil and will grow again. Don't you know that no one who is under your protection can ever be harmed?"

"Give us the means," said Arjuna, "and we will hold off Indra for you while you have your fill."

"Here I will give you this bow Gandiva with a quiver of inexhaustible arrows which will make you famous. I will also give you a chariot with four white horses of indomitable strength. They are yours to use until I claim them back. They will stand you in good stead for what is going to come."

As Arjuna strung the bow there was a great cracking sound like a tree straining not to break as the wind tore through it. The earth quivered and shook. Arjuna jumped on to the chariot and Krishna took the reins and said to Agni, "We are ready."

Seven tongues of flame shot out of Agni's brow, his hair blazed and the flames from his brow blasted through the forest setting fire to the entire underbrush. The horses sprang back as the flames hit them and the whole forest burst into flames. The old man vanished into the flames. Indra looked down and saw his favourite forest being burnt and thought to himself, 'Ah he is at it again. He is not content with having been vanquished by me seven times! I think he must be having some strong support which has made him dare to attempt this for the eighth time!'

Suddenly the whole sky was covered with dark, menacing rain clouds, hiding the hot sun and pouring down in huge cascades. Smoke rose up and made the sky blacker than ever. There was not a moment to be lost. "O slayer of foes!" shouted my Lord as he started driving the chariot like a lightning bolt round the forest, "Start your work immediately or Agni will be put out."

Arjuna started shooting arrow after arrow in lightning succession so that soon the whole forest was covered with an umbrella of arrows through which not a drop could penetrate. Agni could hardly be seen as he licked up the whole forest with great joy, totally untroubled by the raging storm above. But still the storm raged and my Lord shouted above the crackling of the flames, "Shoot at the heavens and scatter the clouds!"

Arjuna did as told and the clouds scuttled off in various directions unable to drop their rain any more. Indra appeared in the sky accompanied by a host of other gods. Varuna, god of the ocean, riding on a fish, Yama, god of death, sitting on a buffalo, Kartikeya, general of the gods seated on his peacock, Surya, the sun god, holding a bright dart and the Aswins, celestial physicians, holding medicinal herbs, were all there. Only my Vanamali could see them arrayed in the sky looking down at us with unblinking eyes. "Don't shoot anymore," said Vaasudeva, "I will see to this."

Indra threw his thunderbolt down and Krishna hurled his *chakra* and the two met in mid-air with a gigantic explosion. The thunderbolt lay shattered on the ground while the *chakra* came back like a docile child to my Lord's hands. Seeing this, Indra and the other gods bowed low and extolled my Vanamali, "Thou art the Supreme Lord of all gods. In our foolishness we tried to go above you. May you both be blessed and finish the work for which you have been born on earth." So saying Indra and the gods disappeared from view. As long as I touched my Lord's *uttareeyam* I could see the gods and hear their conversation. It was indeed a unique experience. Despite the fact that he was engrossed in the work, my Lord had time to look at me and smile as I gasped with astonishment to see the heavenly host in the sky.

Far away I could see the banners and pavilions of the ladies lying in tatters on the ground, blackened and charred by the fire. The women were looking on with amazement. Slowly they turned back and returned to Indraprastha. I looked at my Vanamali. His face was quite black and not just with the soot. The colour of his face always changed with his moods. When he was with me in a teasing mood, it was a lovely lavender shade. It kept getting darker when he was talking seriously or when he was engaged in something serious. Now I knew that he was having some sombre thoughts. 'What is it?' I asked.

"Look at those innocent women - Arjuna's wives, Draupadi and Subhadra. We will never see them like this again – so happy, so joyful."

'What is it, Lord? What is going to happen to them?'

"This is the prelude to a mighty drama which will not end for the next twenty years. You will have to wait and see."

The forest was totally consumed and Agni appeared in human form filled with strength, his hair was flaming and his eyes shooting tongues of fire as he chased someone. It was the *asura* Mayan, architect of the *asuras*, who ran and took refuge at the feet of the Pandava. Agni raised his fiery arms in a salute and disappeared and Mayan jumped into our chariot. The trio sat for a while on the river banks to cool down and Mayan said to Arjuna, "O Bharatha! I would like to show my gratitude to you. I am the greatest architect in all the worlds. Let me make you a palace which will be a wonder for the entire world."

Arjuna said, "To accept a favour in return for one, is going against the dictates of *dharma*. I want nothing but you can ask Vaasudeva."

Mayan turned to my Lord and asked, "What can I do for the Pandavas to repay my debt to Arjuna?"

Krishna thought for a while and obviously he knew that the time had come to shift another piece in the checker board of their lives so as to complete the pattern. "You can build a Sabha (assembly hall) for them which will be the wonder of the world and be filled with illusions as befits your name."

"I am very good at that," said Mayan and immediately set about building the Sabha.

He approached Arjuna and said, "Near Mount Kailasa there are many jewels which I have hidden. To the east of the mountain is the lake called Bindu into which was thrown a huge mace by the king of the demons. It has the power of a hundred thousand maces and is a fit weapon for Bhima, just as the Gandiva is for you. The lake also holds a large conch named Devadutta which belongs to the king of the oceans - Lord Varuna. One blast from it can send terror to the hearts of the enemies. I shall bring that also as a gift for you."

Mayan went off to the Himalayas and brought back all the things he had promised and started the construction. It took fourteen months to build but it was indeed magnificent. The columns were golden and radiated an effulgence equal to the sun. The walls were embedded with thousands of multi-coloured jewels which illuminated the entire palace. Inside there were ponds lined with highly polished stones and filled with lotuses whose leaves resembled emeralds and whose stalks were made of precious stones. The water was crystal clear and filled with a variety of gold fish and tortoises. Actually it was very difficult to know where the water began and ended. The whole thing was surrounded by a flight of crystal stairs. Exotic flowers bloomed inside and outside the palace in all seasons.

When it was completed Mayan informed the Emperor and a grand celebration was planned. Thousands of Brahmanas came and chanted Vedic hymns. Yudhishtira gifted thousands of cows and food to all who came. People came from all over Aryavrata to admire the Sabha.

Yudhishtira was really happy and he shone like Indra when he was seated on the gem-studded throne inside the Sabha. For the first time in their storm-tossed lives, I think the Pandavas felt happy and secure. But my Lord had already hinted to me that it was only a lull before the storm. They were destined to enjoy their kingdom for only a few months more. Satyaki came and stayed on after we left in order to learn a few more tricks of archery from Arjuna.

People came in droves to see my Lord. His fame had spread far and wide. The sick and the old and the blind and the deaf and the dumb – the lepers and the hunchbacks and the lame, all came to receive his miraculous touch.

He cured them all, sometimes with a glance from his compassionate eyes, sometimes with a touch and sometimes by lifting them up by placing both his hands under their armpits if they couldn't walk. He would run his lotus palms over the lepers who were forced to stand in another part of the ground from where the others stood. He would always go to them first and cure them before coming to the rest. There was no distinction of caste or creed. He loved them all equally. In fact I saw many dogs, horses and cows come to him to be treated. I suspected he spoke to them in their own language because I could see them nodding or shaking their heads and sometimes licking his hands and feet. Even on the roads when we left we would find the sick and the helpless coming to meet him and he would stop the horses and attend to their wants before proceeding.

At this time Subhadra was expecting her first child. Arjuna was a very good father and he used to sit with her and speak to the unborn child since it is said that the foetus can imbibe vibrations through the womb. Once, Arjuna started to describe to his wife the secrets of the *vyuhas* or battle formations. Actually he was hoping that the child in her womb would hear it. He told her about the famous *vyuha* known as the Chakra *vyuha* or Padma *vyuha*, which is a formation in which soldiers are arranged in the shape of a wheel or a lotus with many, many layers so that it would be impossible for anyone to penetrate it. Even if someone managed to penetrate, the soldiers would close in again so that the person who went into the centre would find it impossible to come out of it unless he knew the technique. Arjuna had just finished describing the method of entry, but by then Subhadra was so bored that she fell asleep. My Lord entered the room at that precise moment and took Arjuna away to some other place before he could finish narrating the method of destroying and exiting from the formation. So obviously the child in the womb who would later be called Abhimanyu knew only how to enter the formation but not to exit it.

'Why didn't you allow him to finish the teaching?' I asked.

"Everyone has to work out his or her *karma* according to what they themselves have desired in a previous life. If I allowed Arjuna to finish the teaching I would be interfering with the law which has to take its own course. I played my part by stopping his recital. That is all that I am allowed to do. This is an important thing about me which you have to understand; otherwise you will always be wondering why I did something and why I didn't do something." I looked at him with wonder in my eyes trying to assimilate what he had said.

Aum Namo Bhagavate Vaasudevaaya

ॐ

Srishaaya Namaha!

CHAPTER THIRTEEN

Jarasandha

After the Sabha was built we returned to Dwaraka before the monsoons broke. One day while my Vanamali was holding court in the Sudharma, a messenger came to him and said:

"My noble Lord! I have been sent by the twenty thousand kings who have been captured and incarcerated in the dungeon of Jarasandha, king of Magadha in his capital city of Girivraja. They are begging you to come and release them."

Hardly had the man finished speaking when Narada, the celestial sage arrived on the scene, strumming his lute. "O All-pervading Lord," he said, "I have just come from Indraprastha where I have advised King Yudhishtira to perform the Rajasuya sacrifice which will enable him to assume the title of Emperor. He has requested me to come to you and get your approval."

The Lord looked at his nobles with a small smile and asked them to decide what they should do first – go and rescue the kings or go to Indraprastha to help the Pandavas. The Elders all seemed to prefer to go to Girivraja and release the kings before starting for the Rajasuya. Turning to his Prime Minister Uddhava, Krishna said, "Let us have your opinion, O Uddhava. That shall decide the matter."

Uddhava replied, "My Lord, it is incumbent on you to help both parties, but the very first ceremony of the Rajasuya is known as *digvijaya* (conquering all enemy territories). The subjugation of Jarasandha will be necessary in any case. Let us eliminate Jarasandha first so that Yudhishtira will become qualified to perform the Rajasuya."

"So be it", said my Lord. He told the messenger from the kings to tell them not to worry and that he would come and defeat Jarasandha and release them very soon. The very next day, My Vanamali and I set out once again for Indraprastha with a large retinue. All my Lord's consorts wanted to come to participate in the Rajasuya. So he sent them all before him, and then both of us went in his chariot driven by Daruka with the Garuda waving merrily on his flag. Part of the army came with us, with chariots, elephants, cavalry and footmen. The musicians went ahead beating tom-toms, kettle-drums, tabors, conchs and trumpets. The ladies came in chariots and golden palanquins, guarded by soldiers. Mules and donkeys carried blankets and clothes. The servants and their wives rode on camels and elephants. Flags, umbrellas and banners fluttered in the wind as the party proceeded towards the North. We passed through Anarta, Sauvira and Matsya. We had to cross a desert and climb over small hills and rivers and of course pass through many villages and towns. Everyone flocked to see my Vanamali as we passed through the villages. Everyone had heard of him and longed for a glimpse of this divine personage. I felt so honoured to be sitting beside him in the chariot even though nobody could see me. After crossing the Saraswati River we had to pass through Kurujangala before we reached Indraprastha. This was a problem when we went with a huge army like this. It took us almost a month to reach Indraprastha. Had we gone alone, we would have reached it within a week.

The roads of Indraprastha were sprinkled with rose water and shoots of different types of grains. Banners and flags were flying and Yudhishtira came with his brothers to the gate in order to welcome my darling Vanamali. The drawbridge had been put down for us to cross and flowers kept raining on our heads as we passed through the streets, and everywhere there were shouts of "Hail to Thee, O Vaasudeva! Hail to Thee O Govinda! God of gods!"

When he entered the palace Kunti came running out followed by her daughters-in-law, Draupadi and Subhadra. After worshipping him they turned to his wives Rukmini, Satyabhama, Jambavati, Bhadra, Kalindi, Mitravinda, Lakshmana and Satya and paid them all homage.

The next day my Lord was invited to the glorious Sabha made by Mayan. Yudhishtira bowed before him and extolled him and asked his permission to conduct the Rajasuya *yajna*.

Krishna spoke, "O King! You have conquered me with your virtues. Now you can start conquering the other countries with your power. My devotee can never be conquered by those who have not controlled their minds, so have no fear. Go ahead and start the Rajasuya *yajna* by which you will become emperor of Aryavrata. But first of all we have to subdue Jarasandha. His fortress is supposed to be impregnable. However he is always ready to welcome Brahmanas so I suggest that Bhima, Arjuna and I go there disguised as Brahmanas so that we can get an easy entry. Then Bhima can have a duel with the king since he is an expert in mace fighting and he is the one who is ordained to kill Jarasandha."

"My Lord! Can't Bhima and Arjuna go with an army and defeat him? You know that I had sent Sahadeva with the Srinjaya warriors to conquer the southern regions and Nakula and the Matsyas to the west, Arjuna and the Kekayas to the north and Bhima and the Madras to the east. They have conquered all quarters and have returned and filled our coffers with gold, enough to conduct a mighty *yajna* like the Rajasuya. Now why do we have to resort to this ruse in order to defeat Jarasandha?"

My Vanamali said, "I will tell you the story of Jarasandha and then you will realise the reason for this. King Brihadratha of Magadha was married to the twin daughters of the King of Kasi. Unfortunately he had no sons. He did severe penance in the forest and worshipped the great sage Chandakaushika. He blessed him and very soon a mango fell on his lap as he was meditating and the sage told him to give it to his wife. The king who loved both his wives equally, cut the mango and gave each of his wives one half. Nine months later his wives gave birth to half a child. Seeing this, the king was horrified and told the attendants to throw the pieces on the garbage dump outside the city. A demoness named Jara got the smell of flesh and took the halves home to eat. She placed the halves together and was astounded to see one complete human child. She realised that this must be the king's child and took it to the palace hoping for a good reward. Needless to say the king was overjoyed and named the boy 'Jarasandha' in honour of the woman who had saved him and of course gave many presents to Jara. He grew up to be a most powerful king and subjugated many other kings and is now thinking of declaring himself as Emperor of Aryavrata. He gave both his daughters in marriage to my uncle – Kamsa, king of Mathura and when I killed Kamsa he swore to kill me. He will never allow us entry to his fortress, so it is best we go there dressed as Brahmanas and then proceed with whatever comes next. However, I must warn Bhima to remember that Jarasandha's weak point is that he is made up of two parts which can come apart easily. You can tear him apart but you must take care to see that you throw the parts in opposite directions otherwise the two halves will join again and become stronger than before. This is a boon given by his foster mother, Jara."

Krishna continued, "Jarasandha is a great example to prove that devotion to God has no merit unless coupled with virtue. He is a great devotee of Shiva and has captured many kings in order to offer human sacrifices to Shankara. For devotion to bear fruit it should go hand in hand with kindness to all creatures. *Bhakti* should be accompanied by *Dharma* to become fruitful."

All of us listened enthralled to this story and the next day we set out for Girivraja disguised as Brahmanas. It was a very long and hard journey from Kurujangala to Magadha (Bihar and Jharkand). We passed through a charming lake of lotuses and then had to climb over the Kalakuta hills and cross many rivers like the Gantaki which rose from these mountains.

Then we came to the delightful country of the Kosalas and crossed the Sarayu River and reached Mithila. We proceeded and came to the Ganga and kept going eastwards and reached the hills guarding the city of Magadha which was really very beautiful.

We reached the gates of the fortress at the hour appointed for the entertainment of unexpected guests. We were let in without any trouble and brought into the presence of the king. Had we gone as Kshatriyas we would have had to wait for days before getting an audience. We were offered all refreshments of which we refused to partake. As soon as he saw us the king said, "I feel I have seen you all somewhere. You don't look like Brahmanas to me. Your forearms bear scars caused by the friction of bow-strings, and your bearing also seems to point to your being Kshatriyas and not Brahmanas. However, the fact that you have come here to petition me reveals that you know and respect my power, so you are free to ask whatever you want and I will give it to you even if it be my head!!"

"Your Majesty! You are indeed right in assuming that we are not Brahmanas. We are Kshatriyas and we have not come to ask for alms but to ask you to fight a duel with one of us," said my Lord.

"But who are you that you have dared to come inside this fortress, and are stupid enough to demand a duel with me?"

"We are your enemies. Know me to be Vaasudeva, son of Vasudeva of the Vrishni clan and nephew of Kamsa whom I killed in Madura long ago. This is Arjuna, the *madhyama* Pandava and this is Bhima, his elder brother, destroyer of Hidimba and Baka and invincible in battle. You may choose with whom you would like to fight."

Jarasandha threw back his head and roared with laughter. "O you are Krishna Vaasudeva whom I defeated eighteen times and forced you to run away and take refuge in the city of Dwaraka, where you live in dread of my wrath! I disdain to fight with you. As for this stripling who you say is Arjuna, he is only a mere boy. It is not correct for a veteran like me to come to grips with this youngster. The only one I can consider fighting with is this man who you say is Bhima, for puny though he is when compared to me, yet is he a more worthy opponent than either of you."

My Lord laughed and said, "I think your Majesty has forgotten the episode at the *swayamvara* of the daughter of Panchala when this 'stripling' as you call him, defeated all the assembled kings and snatched the prize from under your nose. However, we shall not waste time in talking of the past but will get ready to meet our future!"

Bhima and Jarasandha immediately prepared themselves. The weapon chosen by both was the mace (*gada*) since both were experts at mace fighting. They came out of the city and selected a level ground as the arena and closed in combat and began to exchange blows with their diamond hard maces. Both were well-matched and Jarasandha proved to be a more formidable adversary than either Hidimba or Bakasura. Jarasandha had never met such a redoubtable opponent before. They started moving to the left and right, manoeuvring for correct positions like actors on a stage. The noise made by the maces when they collided was like claps of thunder discharging sparks of lightning. Sometimes when they charged headlong at each other they looked like tuskers in heat. Both their maces broke with the force with which they hurled them onto each other's shoulders, hips, feet and collar bones. Then the two charged at each other and started fighting with adamantine fists. The sound made by their palms as they slapped each other resembled claps of thunder. They were so equally matched that they fought for twenty-seven days without respite. The strange thing was that though they fought like fiends during the day, the nights were spent in a sort of friendly truce since both admired the other's expertise. On the twenty-eighth day, Bhima knew that his strength was waning and asked my Vanamali to help him.

My Lord ran his divine hands over his bruised and battered body and made him whole again and asked him, "Have you forgotten the story I told you before we left? Some time ago when Duryodhana sent Karna to subdue Jarasandha, Karna remembered the story and tore him in two, but he threw the halves together and they came and joined again. After this Jarasandha declared a truce and since then he and Karna have become friends. He gave him the city called Malini and made him ruler of Champa, as Duryodhana had made him king of Anga. He has also promised to help the Kauravas in any war they might be called upon to fight."

The next day the fight began with renewed vigour. Bhima felt fit again after my Lord's ministrations, but the mighty king of the Magadhas was flagging in both spirits and strength. Bhima watched carefully for his chance and suddenly he caught hold of the king's feet and threw him on the ground. He pressed his foot with his own and took hold of the other leg with both his hands and split him in two from the anus upwards to his head. Unfortunately he had forgotten the instructions to reverse the pieces. He turned jubilantly towards us when he must have seen the look of horror on our faces and swung round to see the victim's two halves reuniting. Jarasandha sprang up with a terrible oath for he realised that his secret was out. With the strength born out of despair he sprang at Bhima with the ferocity of a tiger. All rules of fair play were thrown overboard as the two mighty giants grappled with each other for their lives. At last with a superhuman effort, Bhima managed to pin him down, pressing his knees on his chest and forcing his arms down to the ground. He cast a despairing look at my Vanamali who cast him a bewitching smile which infused new strength into him. My Lord took up a piece of straw lying on the ground and tore it apart and deliberately reversed the sides and threw the pieces in opposite directions. Bhima suddenly remembered the instruction he had been given and in one quick movement which was difficult for such a heavy man, he caught hold of the king's legs and tore them apart once again, and this time he flung the pieces wide in the prescribed manner so that there was no chance of them coming together again. That was the end of the mighty king of Magadha. The citizens rejoiced for though they enjoyed all comforts in the city, the king did not brook any sort of disobedience and offenders against the law were punished with the utmost severity.

Jarasandha's son Sahadeva now came forward and bowed before my Lord. He placed his lotus hands on his head and blessed him. Sahadeva said, "Thou art the Lord of all Lords, O Vaasudeva! It is my great fortune to have been blessed by you. Allow me to give my daughter in marriage to the Pandava prince who has my own name."

All of us were delighted to accept the offer since Sahadeva, the youngest Pandava was the only one who was still unmarried. After this, all of us went to a kind of prison where twenty thousand kings had been kept captive by Jarasandha. The prison was surrounded by mountains so that there was no hope of escape. They were emaciated and unclean with tattered clothes and shattered hopes. By some luck they had managed to send a messenger in secret to Dwaraka. When they saw my Vanamali standing before them, they were so happy that they just fell in front of him and extolled him. He was looking so beautiful that I too fell at his feet and I too started singing his praises along with the kings.

"O Imperishable Lord! We are actually indebted to Jarasandha, for its only because of him that we have come to realise the ephemeral nature of worldly life. Intoxicated by wealth and power we fought with each other and mercilessly brought about the destruction of our own race. Jarasandha deprived us of all our power and brought us here, due to which we have been granted the great good fortune to have your *darshana* (vision). O Vaasudeva! You are the one who removes the sufferings of all those who bow before you. Therefore, O Govinda! We offer our obeisance to you!"

Saying thus they prostrated again and again at my Lord's lotus feet. My Vanamali was always aware of the slightest needs of his devotees, so he asked Sahadeva to see that all of them were handed over to the care of attendants who gave them baths and fresh clothes, so that once again they shone with a glow befitting their stature. He then gave each of them chariots to return to their own kingdoms. Of course all of them promised to come to Yudhistira's Rajasuya and make it a huge success.

After having installed Jarasandha's son, Sahadeva as king of Magadha, the four of us – Krishna, Arjuna, Bhima and I, returned to Indraprastha. The three heroes stood at the gate and blew their respective conch shells, thus announcing to all that they had been victorious in their expedition. Yudhishtira was overjoyed and clasped them all to his bosom and thanked my Lord for having given him victory.

"O unconquerable spirit of Time! Your ways are indeed mysterious. Life is a game for you in which you make us feel that we are great, when actually speaking you are the greatest of all and it is only part of your game to make us feel that we are rulers and kings. O Lord! Give me permission to start the Rajasuya *yajna*."

My Lord agreed that this was the appropriate time for Yudhishtira to start his Rajasuya since all the enemy kings had been subdued and the others had agreed to recognise his overlordship.

Aum Namo Bhagavate Vaasudevaaya

> He, who understands through the instructions and blessings of the Guru, that the one Paramatma has manifested himself through his yogamaya, as the many, understands the true import of the Vedas. The axe of knowledge has to be sharpened through one pointed devotion to the Guru. Cut open the ego which is the prison house of the jivatma with this axe and attain to the Supreme Purusha. After that even this weapon can be discarded.
>
> *Srimad Bhagavatam. Skanda 11; Chapter 12; verses 23, 24.*

ॐ

Nandagopapriyatmajaaya Namaha!

CHAPTER FOURTEEN

Rajasuya

I always felt that Yudhishtira was not meant to be a king. He was fit to be a recluse in a forest rather than a king in a palace. As I was thinking this I found my Vanamali watching me with his knowing smile. 'He doesn't seem to have an opinion of his own. He is always asking you or his brothers or his mother for advice and approbation. Of course I can understand his asking you but why everyone else? He can never make up his own mind.'

"You have made a correct judgement," said my Krishna. "He needs constant support. But mark my words, soon the time will come when he will come into his own. At that time he will tower above his brothers and will not need any other person's support. So it is not correct to judge him now. Everyone is cut out for certain roles. When they are out of that particular orbit they are considered misfits, but when they are in their own course they shine." He pretended to be angry with me and scowled, but I ran to him and fell at his feet and when I looked up he gave me a wink and smiled so I felt happy again.

Yudhishtira now invited all the sages who were well-versed in the Vedas and most proficient in all the Vedic rituals to officiate as priests in the *yajna*. All the great *rishis* like Vyasa, Bharadvaja, Maitreya, Sumantu, Gautama, Vasishta, Viswamitra, Vamadeva, Jaimini, Kasyapa, Garga and

Dhoumya were all there. Of course all the Kauravas came. Bhishma, Dronacharya, Kripacharya, Vidura and of course Dritarashtra accompanied by Gandhari and Sanjaya arrived, decked in their best attire. Citizens of all castes had been invited and all the great princes of the realm. My Lord told me that people had even come from a place called China which was very far away. They looked and dressed and talked in a strange fashion, but all of them were welcomed. Any guest who arrived was supposed to ring a bell and wash their feet before entering the hall. After a while I found that the bell was constantly ringing and they had to direct a small stream of water all the time before the gate.

The first ritual was performed by the priests who ploughed the field in which the *yajna* was to be conducted. They used ploughs of gold. They then initiated Yudhishtira as the head of the *yajna* (*yajamana*). All the utensils to be used in the *yajna* were made of gold. Even the celestials were spread out in the sky to watch this great event. I could see them if I touched my Vanamali. He turned and looked at me and smiled.

Yudhishtira demarked responsible positions for all his family members. His brother Bhima was put in charge of the kitchen since he loved eating, Arjuna was in charge of looking after the needs of all the elderly people since he had such charming manners, Sahadeva was in the reception and Nakula in charge of stores. At my Lord's instigation, Duryodhana was kept in charge of the treasury. His eyes gleamed with green lights when he saw how much wealth had been amassed by the Pandavas. He was determined to bankrupt the treasury as fast as possible so that the Rajasuya would have an ignominious end. In this he was ably assisted by Karna who was kept in charge of gifts and charity (*dana*). Karna loved to give charity and had never refused any gift to anyone so he gave lavishly to all and Duryodhana doled out more than he was asked for.

When I commented on this to my Vanamali, he winked at me and said, "Don't worry, I have kept Rukmini, the incarnation of Lakshmi, the goddess of wealth to see to it that the coffers never get empty, so the more Karna gives, the more will be the fame that accrues to Yudhishtira."

Draupadi was in charge of food distribution since she loved to give food to people. All the Brahmanas who came expecting a small *dakshina* and a little food were surprised to find that they were given more gold than they had ever seen in their lives and fed to the brim three times a day, for the duration of the *yajna* which lasted for three months. They went away after blessing Yudhishtira and the Pandavas instead of reviling them as Duryodhana and Karna had hoped.

My Vanamali now approached Yudhishtira and asked in his usual joking fashion. "Tell me brother, what post have you kept for me?"

Yudhishtira bowed to him and said, "My Lord! It is always part of your game to make yourself small and elevate your devotees. But in this case you must let me have my way. At the end of *yajna*, the greatest and noblest soul in this assembly will be awarded the signal honour of having his feet washed. I have chosen you for that."

My playful Lord deliberately misunderstood his words and immediately started to wash the feet of all the noble souls who came into the *yajnashala*. This is an important custom in all great functions. Nobody is allowed to come in with dirty feet. Yudhishtira was horrified when he saw this and did his best to dissuade him, so my Lord said, "All right I will do something else," and he proceeded to remove the leaves of everyone who had finished their meals. (Meals were generally served on leaves.) I was highly amused to see my Lord's pranks since this is considered to be a menial service which is done only by servants, but perhaps he wanted to prove to the world that he was prepared to do even the most menial task for the sake of his true devotees. Even though I laughed, tears were pouring from my eyes when I thought of his infinite grace. He looked at me and laughed. He knew every thought that flashed through my mind, sometimes even before I knew it. Subhadra's son Abhimanyu was there. He was a very small child and toddled along after his aunt to distribute food. I noticed another five very handsome boys who were going around making themselves useful in all ways. 'Who are they?' I asked my Lord.

"They are the sons of Draupadi, one from each of the Pandavas," said my Lord.

'How handsome they are,' I thought as I looked at them. They all had Draupadi's royal bearing and the features of the Pandavas.

The Rajasuya was a magnificent success. There was no place where my Vanamali's eyes did not reach. At one time he would be found in the music hall entertaining guests with his flute, at others in the kitchen trying out a new dish, at other times in the dining hall serving guests and removing the leaves on which they ate, at others escorting visitors to the apartments specially prepared for them, taking into consideration all their likes and dislikes.

Indraprastha was filled with all sorts of amusement parks, dancing halls, dining halls, drinking halls and so on for the entertainment of those guests who did not like to remain in the *yajnashala* all the time watching the religious ceremonies which were being conducted throughout the day. Money, jewels, horses, elephants and cattle poured into the land from all the kings who had agreed to be his vassals.

I was surprised to see that Shishupala did not attend any of the functions so I asked my Lord about this. He smiled at me and said, "Shishupala did not want to come and has been forced by his parents. He is avoiding me and keeping to his own quarters. Actually while we were away in Pragjyotisha he had gone and set fire to Dwaraka along with his friend. So he is frightened to confront me. Come with me and we'll have some fun. The fact is that though he has so much enmity to me, I have a soft corner for him!"

Taking my hand he walked purposefully towards Shishupala's apartment. Just at that moment, Shishupala, who had had enough of sitting cloistered in his mansion and listening to the strains of music and revelry going on everywhere, had decided to venture forth. There was no way that he could have avoided us. But he pretended not to notice and would have passed us pretending that he had not seen us, but my mischievous Lord accosted him.

"Ha cousin! Where have you been all these days? I met my aunt and your father and enquired after you, but they said you were here. I was rather concerned at not seeing you and was just coming to enquire about your welfare. I do hope you have been getting the best treatment and are not bored by your self-confinement inside your apartment!"

Shishupala gave him a haughty look and not deigning to reply, he moved on quickly before his cousin could make some further remark. My Lord gave me another naughty look and off we went on our other errands.

On the day when the final libations with the Soma juice had been made, Yudhishtira personally honoured the sacrificial priests and gave them rich *dakshinas* and presents. After this, Vyasa made an announcement. "From today, Draupadi will be the Emperor's wife alone. The younger brothers will have to honour them as parents." All of them bowed in agreement.

I watched their faces and saw that Arjuna and Bhima looked rather downcast. I suspected that Bhima loved her more than any of the others, and I was sure she had a decided partiality for Arjuna. I don't know what made me come to this conclusion but I just felt it. I questioned my Vanamali of course about the correctness of this decision and whether he felt as I did. He just gave me a quizzical look and refused to comment.

I was quite excited to watch the actual coronation. Waters from all the holy rivers of the land had been brought and the royal couple were seated on a single throne and the consecrated ablution with the sanctified waters was performed. At the end of the ceremony came the "*Agrapuja*" or the tribute given to the noblest man present. Yudhishtira had already decided on the Lord for this signal honour and had hinted to him about it, but he wanted to consult his brothers so he asked his youngest brother Sahadeva, who was noted for his wisdom, to speak up.

Without hesitation Sahadeva said, "The worshipful Lord Krishna Vaasudeva, the protector of all devotees alone is worthy of this honour. This entire cosmos is his manifestation. This whole universe is his form.

It is only by his grace that we have been able to conduct this magnificent *yajna* which will bring good to all. What doubt is there that he should be worshipped as the foremost amongst the honoured guests? By worshiping him we shall be honouring all beings including ourselves. A tree may be very large, with many branches, spreading in many directions, some filled with flowers, some with fruits and some with leaves. In fact the branches and flowers may be so attractive that our attention may be caught by them alone, but when the time comes to water the tree, does anyone doubt where the water should be poured? Therefore if you wish the fruits of your *yajna* to be endless, offer the *Agrapuja* to Vaasudeva, the soul of all, the perfect, the supremely peaceful, in whose eyes nothing is different from himself."

Yudhishtira as well as all the assembled guests were very pleased with this speech of his wise young brother. I gazed enraptured at my Vanamali and thought to myself, 'He is indeed the root from which the variegated tree of the world has projected itself. What doubt then that his feet should be washed in the final *puja*?'

Bhishma, the grandsire now added, "In this great and glorious assembly, Krishna Vaasudeva shines as the sun in the midst of his own rays. His presence alone has shed lustre on this ceremony. He alone deserves this signal honour!"

Vyasa promptly endorsed this and declared my Vanamali to be god incarnate. He was seated on the specially prepared jewelled throne. Yudhishtira accompanied by Draupadi and his brothers came forward with gem-studded, golden pots containing perfumed water from all the holy rivers. Placing the lotus feet of my Lord tenderly on a golden plate, Yudhishtira washed them with great love. Tears were streaming continuously from his eyes. Draupadi and his brothers followed suit. I stood on one side and I must admit my tears also flowed profusely. I could not tear my gaze from his holy form which seemed to be shrouded in a lavender mist. His feet also looked like twin lotus petals. His eyes met mine and I fell on my knees and worshipped him. This consecrated

Yudhishtira and Draupadi washing the feet of the Lord during the *Argya Puja* of the Rajasuya Yajna.

water was sprinkled reverently on the heads of all those present. Yudhishtira was overcome with emotion and could not speak a word. Everybody felt exalted to have been present at such a unique function. Jubilant shouts of, "Jai Sri Krishna! Jai Vaasudeva! Jai Govinda! Jai Madhava!" rent the air as everyone showered flowers on him.

At this auspicious time, Shishupala, prompted by death itself jumped up and said scornfully, "A bastard (Yudhishtira) has asked the son of a river (Bhishma) for advice. The person chosen is a poor cow-herd, who in his childhood has been accused of eating mud, stealing butter as well as the clothes of the *gopis* and dallying with them. He killed his own uncle and schemed to have the powerful Jarasandha exterminated. In this noble gathering of illustrious kings and saintly *rishis*, could you not have found anyone superior to this basest of the Yadavas? He is not the equal of anyone of us here and should never have been invited in the first place. To choose him in preference to all others is an insult to this august assembly. If honour is to be given to age, then his father Vasudeva can claim it; if it is to the foremost king present, then Drupada should be honoured; if it is to wisdom, Drona is the most worthy; if it's to holiness, Vyasa is the greatest. Drona's son has more knowledge than Krishna, Duryodhana is peerless amongst the younger men, Kripa is the worthiest priest and Karna the greatest archer. For what reason should homage be paid to Krishna, who is neither the holiest nor the wisest nor the greatest warrior nor the foremost chieftain? It is a shame to this assembly that overlooking all these great souls, this cow-herd should be so honoured." Shishupala had been nursing his hatred for my Lord for many years and for many reasons, starting with the abduction of Rukmini!

Turning to Yudhishtira he continued, "O Yudhishtira! Don't think we have submitted to you through fear of your powers, but because we honour your nobility and wisdom. Now that you have shown yourself to be devoid of both, it is better for us to leave before we are insulted any further. Come, O kings!" he shouted to his allies who had come with him, "Let us kill this upstart Yadava immediately and defeat the Pandavas who have subjected us to these intolerable insults!"

I looked at my Vanamali and saw his eyes were bright and had a look of pity in them as he started to speak in a calm voice, "O princes and kings!" he said, "This Shishupala is descended from a daughter of our race and I certainly never wanted to do any injustice to him. But once when I had gone to Pragjyotisha, this Shishupala came to my city of Dwaraka at night and set fire to it and razed the temple to the ground. His inequities are too numerous to relate but I will mention a few. Once he broke his promise to a king and cast him into prison and seized his queen by force. He disguised himself as the husband of a chaste princess and deceived her. He has even tried to force himself on my Rukmini. I have desisted from killing him all these years since I had promised my aunt, his mother, to pardon a hundred insults from her son. I have more than fulfilled my vow and I will now slay him before all of you."

Shishupala said scornfully, "I do not fear this cow-herd and will seek no mercy from him!"

I felt a bit sorry for Shishupala. He had bottled up his hatred for my Lord for so many years that it had festered and become a cancer inside him. The assembly broke up into two factions, some supporting the Emperor and others Shishupala. The Rajasuya seemed in danger of degenerating into a vulgar brawl. I looked at my Vanamali. His colour was slowly getting darker. I knew something momentous was about to happen and that Shishupala's death was imminent. Having exhausted his fund of vituperative accusations, Shishupala sprang towards my Lord brandishing his sword of hatred. Arjuna and the other Pandava brothers immediately surrounded Krishna. I watched fascinated as he gently pushed them aside and rose up in a leisurely manner from the jewelled throne and strode forward to meet Shishupala who had his sword raised like the hood of an angry cobra. With a look of infinite compassion on his face he hurled his discus (*sudarshana*) at him and neatly servered his head from his body. All the guests were amazed when they observed a glow of light emerging from his body and melting into the purple aura surrounding my Lord.

Everyone looked on amazed while thunder rolled in the skies and lightning flashed and the rain poured in torrents. Some of the kings laid hands on their weapons to avenge Shishupala's death, others seemed happy that he had been killed and all the Brahmanas started praising my Lord. Yudhishtira told his brothers to perform all the funeral rites for Shishupala and his body was cremated and oblations poured over it. His son was then proclaimed as King of Chedi.

Later I asked my Vanamali to explain the reason for this and he told me, "Like my uncle Kamsa, this Shishupala has spent so much of his life thinking only of me that he has achieved identity with me! Actually there is a story connected with this. Eons ago there were two attendants of Lord Vishnu known as Jaya and Vijaya. Once when the four boy sages known as the Sanat Kumaras came to see Lord Vishnu, they obstructed them at the gate and prevented them from entering. The sages cursed them that they would have to take birth on earth for many years. The guards begged the Lord to have mercy on them and he said that the curse of a sage could never be revoked but that they could choose to have three births in confrontation with him and thus cut down the stipulated period. They chose to do so. In their first birth they were born as the great titans, Hiranyaksha and Hiranyakashipu, in their next birth as Ravana and Kumbakarna and now in this last birth as Shishupala and Dandavaktra in which Vishnu promised that he would deliver them from their curse in his form as Krishna! So now I have kept that promise. As you will notice their ferocity decreased with every birth."

'I spend all my time thinking of you. Will I also achieve identity?' My Lord gave me one of his old-fashioned looks which meant, 'how silly can you get?'

"Why do you have to wait for your death to achieve identity? Have you not already achieved it? Aren't you a *jivan mukta*?" I could not say a word. My voice was choked. All I could do was gulp my tears back and fall at his feet. "You are doing too much of this," he chided me. "Stop crying and stand erect. I like to see your face!"

The final ceremony of the *yajna* is known as the '*avabhritha snana*,' or the bath of purification and glory. All the kings and exalted guests joined the procession that wound its way to the river Ganga. Yudhishtira and Draupadi led the way on the beautifully caparisoned royal elephant. All the kings were there flying their different flags, with gorgeously decorated elephants, chariots, horses and soldiers. The procession was preceded by musicians playing *mridangams*, conch shells, drums, kettledrums and bugles. Dancers went before them and singers playing *vinas*, flutes and cymbals followed. The Brahmanas who had been performing the *yajna* were chanting the Vedas. Many of the Lords and ladies from Hastinapura had come wearing beautiful garments, decorated with jewellery and emanating the perfume of floral oils. People were throwing saffron water, oil, milk and yogurt on each other. My Lord's queens as well as the wives of the Kauravas were all brought on palanquins. The first to enter the river were the Emperor and Empress. After that, all the other kings and queens took their bath. Then the rest of the citizens, consisting of all the four castes, Brahmanas, Kshatriyas, Vaishyas and Shudras took their baths.

After this, the Emperor who was seated on the banks of the river with his queen Draupadi gave clothing and ornaments to all the priests and all those who had participated in the grand *yajna*. Everybody returned home satisfied beyond all expectations. I mentioned this to my Lord and he smiled and said. "Let the Pandavas bask in their glory while they can. They will soon be deprived of it."

'My Lord!' I pleaded, 'Won't you tell me the nature of the catastrophe about which you keep hinting?' As usual I pleaded in vain.

"You will know when the time comes," was all he said.

'Why can't I know now?' I begged.

"It's dangerous to know too much about the future. Ordinary people will not be able to avoid the temptation to meddle if they know what is to come."

I pondered over this remark and came to the conclusion that as usual he was absolutely right. It is always better to let things take their natural course.

One by one all the guests left but Yudhishtira begged my Vanamali to stay behind and he agreed. The day after the ceremonial bath, Krishna asked Yudhishtira to accompany him for a walk in the garden. The Emperor asked my Lord, "Do you think there has ever been such a wonderful *yajna* as this in this country?"

My Lord didn't say anything, but as they walked towards the place where the food had been served, they saw a strange sight. A small mongoose was rolling about on top of the grains of rice which were left behind. After rolling he would turn his head and look at his body. The fur on half of his body was gold and the other half was brown. He would then go to another spot and repeat the performance. Yudhishtira was intrigued and asked my Lord, "Why is this creature behaving in this extraordinary fashion?"

"Let us ask him," said my Vanamali, casting a knowing look at me. Of course I did not understand what he was implying, but due to my Lord's ability they were able to converse with the mongoose and ask him why he was behaving in this eccentric way.

The mongoose replied, "I used to live outside the hut of a poor man named Saktuprashta who was very wise and noble. He and his family adhered strictly to a life of *dharma* as given in our Puranas. Once the whole family consisting of his wife, son and daughter-in-law were just sitting down for their meal when a hungry Brahmana came to their door. Saktuprashta immediately rose up and gave his share of the food to the guest. The visitor gobbled it up and looked up hungrily. The wife without hesitation also gave her food. This was also devoured in a trice by the man who apparently had not eaten for days. Actually Saktuprashta's family also had not eaten for days. They were on the verge of dying of starvation when some kind soul had come and given them some grains. This was what had been cooked and they were just settling down to a good meal when the hungry mendicant came to their door. Seeing their parents give their food unhesitatingly, the son and his wife also offered their own food. You know that our tradition always tells us to consider the guest as God himself. Thus the whole family were prepared to forfeit their own lives in order to follow the dictates of *dharma*.

"The guest then revealed himself to be none other than Lord Vishnu who wanted to test the poor man. Vishnu washed his hands in the water and blessed the family. I went there to see if any food was left on the ground. I rolled on the food particles and the water in which Vishnu had washed his hands. I was thrilled to find that the part of my body which had touched the water had become golden. From that time onwards I have been going from *yajna* to *yajna* to find another person whose generosity would match that of Saktuprashta. Only if I find such a one will the rest of my body turn golden. O noble king! I had hoped for that same miracle to occur here, but I have been disappointed and I will have to keep on searching for one whose sacrifice is as great as that poor Brahmana in whose garden I used to live."

I looked at my Vanamali's face on which there was a small smile as he looked at Yudhishtira. I realised why my Lord had brought him to this particular place. Yudhishtira was normally a humble man but after the unbelievably brilliant conclusion of the Rajasuya *yajna*, he had started to feel that he was indeed a great soul. It was to stop his ego from increasing that my Lord had brought the mongoose before him. As my eyes locked with his, I came to understand the whole plot!!

Yudhishtira was a weak man. He could not bear to hear that his Rajasuya was not as great as the small offering made by the poor Brahmana. He turned to Vyasa for comfort.

Vyasa said, "O noble king! Great vicissitudes lie before you. You must be courageous enough to meet them. Exercise great patience and self-control and see that you never hurt anyone."

My Lord stayed for a hundred days after everyone else had left. He knew that Yudhishtira did not have much interest in affairs of state. He was quite happy to leave everything in the capable hands of my Lord. I understood many things about the Pandavas and about running the state during the time we stayed there since my Vanamali was a master in the art of king-making as I thought of it, because actually Yudhishtira was not fit to be a king which of course my Lord knew. All he longed for was a life of celibacy and frugality. He believed it was his duty to uphold the divine law –*dharma* and the sacred precepts of the scriptures. He always felt suffocated with all the glory and the machinations which went on in the court. Neither his brothers nor his wife understood or appreciated his agony. The four of them had been taught to obey him implicitly and this they did, but they were incapable of leading. Of course they were exceptional beings in their own ways. Bhima was strong but simple. He was their shield but not their leader. Arjuna was dashing and brave but he was decisive only in matters of the heart and not of government. Nakula was charming but lacked humility. Sahadeva was both humble and wise but tended to avoid confrontations.

Actually the Pandavas owed everything to my Lord who was not only their cousin and friend but their god. I have never been able to find out why the Lord chose the Pandavas as his instruments in making Aryavrata into a united country. He could easily have done it himself and made himself the emperor. But as I had been noticing for so many years with him, he never wanted any great post for himself, but was always instrumental in putting his devotees in high positions. In the hundred days that followed, he made Yudhishtira sign trade treaties with foreign nationals, make alliances with invaders and plant the seeds of an Imperial army which would control the whole of Aryavrata. A road connecting the whole of Yudhishtira's empire from Indraprastha to Kishkinda in the south was planned. Construction work had started by the time we left. My Lord knew that Yudhishtira was not interested in all the multifarious activities which had to go on in the ruling of a country, so before we left he started training the Empress Draupadi for the task of running the whole machinery of the government. She proved to be an excellent statesman with a hard head and a shrewd ability to evaluate any situation. He always called her Panchali – the princess of Panchala.

"Panchali! You have done well indeed. Now I can leave you with an easy mind since I know you can handle everything. If you are in need ask your sons to help you. You will have to take care of the finances, especially the financing of the army, granting of titles, collecting taxes and judging disputes. I have given you a very good set of courtiers, courtesans and spies. They are all utterly loyal to you and you can trust them."

"My Lord! Why do you have to go and when will you return?" she asked, afraid of being left to bear so much responsibility.

"I will stay for a week more and then I will be forced to return," he said. "Even as we are talking, messengers are on their way asking me to return." It was on the tip of my tongue to ask him about the messengers, but he looked at me and I knew that this was not the time for questions.

My Lord had sent off all the other Yadava heroes. We were the only ones to remain. But since Vyasa had told him to be extra kind to everyone, Yudhishtira invited Duryodhana to stay on despite the warnings of his brothers. My Lord said nothing and allowed destiny to play out its intricate pattern. I often felt that he even gave a nudge to destiny if it appeared too tardy!

Seeing the splendour of the Pandavas' palace and the glory that the Rajasuya had brought them, Duryodhana was sick with envy. He longed to possess all this for himself but didn't know how to go about it. His anger was enflamed by a couple of incidents which took place while they were staying in the palace. One day Bhima took the Kaurava brothers on a conducted tour of the famous Maya Sabha or hall of illusions, created by the architect Mayan. Yudhishtira was sitting at the end of the hall with Draupadi on one side and my Vanamali on the other. Of course I was sitting on a cushion at his feet. I think the very sight of Yudhishtira's opulence drove Duryodhana crazy. He hurled abuses at the guards as he went through the grand doors, to show his importance. Bhima tried to stop his impetuous charge into the hall and warn him of the dangers of the place, but he preferred not to listen since he wanted to show that he knew everything. His brothers followed close behind him. He came to a beautiful lotus pond in the middle of the hall and carefully skirted it only to be met with Bhima's mocking laughter and Draupadi's titter. Infuriated by this he strode forward with a determined look. I could almost see what was passing through his mind, 'I'll show these bastards that I am not to be trifled with.'

He strode along till he came to another pool filled with lotuses which he imagined to be another illusion. With a careless smile and a knowing look, meant to convince the onlookers of his superior knowledge of such things, he plunged in to find himself sprawling in an undignified heap in the water. His clothes were drenched, his diadem awry and his necklaces knotted up. Draupadi was unable to contain her mirth this time and was in splits. Bhima's guffaws filled the hall and all the other spectators were convulsed at the sight of the pompous Duryodhana in such a ridiculous predicament. I must admit that I also burst into laughter and turned to look at my master and found him smiling his inscrutable smile.

Yudhishtira alone could not bear anyone to be hurt and ran to comfort him. He offered him the costliest of clothes and jewellery, but Duryodhana would not be appeased and by the look on his face, I'm sure he swore vengeance on the Pandavas. He cast a glare of pure hatred at both Bhima and Draupadi as he took up his fallen crown and set right his jewels.

"In such an open court like this in front of an assembly, I will redress the insults you have heaped on me today," he roared and picking up the tattered remnants of his dignity he strode out of the hall followed by Shakuni and his brothers.

Yudhishtira was cast in gloom at the tragic end of the Rajasuya. His grief increased when my Lord told him that he had received an urgent summons from Dwaraka that it was being besieged by Salva. Yudhishtira offered to send his army with Krishna, but he refused and told him to keep it for he might need it. All the Pandava brothers and Draupadi and

Subhadra as well as their muscular sons came with us to the gate. Just before he left he called Draupadi to a side and said. "Panchali, don't hesitate to call me when you are in need. Think of me and I will come to your aid."

Her lovely eyes were overflowing with tears as she said, "My Lord! I have five heroes as my husbands and five stalwarts for sons, yet I know that you are my only succour and saviour."

I didn't miss the fact that he said 'when you are in need and not if.'

As we were leaving, Yudhishtira said, "We owe everything to you, O Lord! It is only because of your presence that I was able to perform this *yajna*." With these words he touched his feet.

My Lord lifted him up and said, "You are now the Emperor of this holy land. Rule with your father's wisdom. Look after your people like the rain which nourishes the parched fields; be a shade to them in hot weather. Ever be free from pride and passion, and rule with justice and holiness, O Yudhishtira!" With these words he got into the chariot and Yudhishtira turned away with his eyes filled with tears.

Arjuna came with us outside the drawbridge and a long way down the great road which was being constructed. Then reluctantly he took leave of my Vanamali. Taking his hand in his, my Lord told him, "O Bharatha! You will have to face many trials before we meet again, but remember that I will never desert you."

Aum Namo Bhagavate Vaasudevaaya

"Kaunteya prathijannehi,
Na me bhakta pranasyati"
I swear to you O son of Kunti,
My devotee will never perish.

Srimad Bhagavat Gita.

ॐ

Yamunavegasamhaarine Namaha!

CHAPTER FIFTEEN

Salva

My Vanamali's four steeds streaked like lightning towards Dwaraka. I was sitting right behind him and hugging him round the waist and tried to ask him about Salva. Despite his preoccupation he took the trouble to answer me.

"Salva's capital is known as Matrikavarta. We are just passing through his country, which is to the south-west of Madra and to the west of Matsya. There is no point in going to his capital since the whole army must have gone to Dwaraka. He loved Shishupala like his own brother. He is burning with anger at the death of his friend and has sworn to kill me. He has decided that this is the right time to demolish Dwaraka since he knows that both Balarama and I are not there. He has got the blessings of Shiva whom he propitiated with great *tapasya*. He is the proud owner of a *vimana* called Shaubha which has all sorts of contraptions. It is said that he may have got it from some other planet. This *vimana* is an aerial car made of sixteen different types of metals and propels itself by using a metal called mercury. It has remarkable powers as you will see shortly."

'Will Pradyumna and the others be able to hold on till you reach them?'

"Actually we are always prepared for unexpected attacks and in this case I had foreseen such an attack well before I left for Indraprastha. I had made sure that the city's fortifications were in good shape. It has walls on all sides as you might have noticed, and the streets have been barricaded with spiked wood. All the towers at all corners are well-supplied with provisions. We have lances, swords, clubs, forks, plough shares, rockets, balls of stone and battle axes, shields embossed with iron and machines for hurling fire brands, iron balls, bullets and boiling liquids. As soon as any enemy is spotted, the Yadava heroes have orders to station themselves at the commanding posts. Of course they will be aided by elephants, cavalry and foot soldiers. I have also given orders that as soon as there is an alarm, all bridges over rivers have to be destroyed and no boats will be allowed to sail. All dancers and singers who might be spies will be ordered to leave the city. All the land around the city for full two miles has already been made uneven and trenches have been built round the city, spiked with poles. Pits have been dug beyond the trenches, filled with combustibles. Ugrasena has given orders that nobody should drink. The citizens are well aware of the fact that they will be under grave danger unless they remain sober and watchful. They have all been given seals. Nobody who does not carry a seal will be allowed to enter or go out of the city. Of course the soldiers have all been promised to be paid in gold and will be given various other benefits."

I was amazed at this account of the fortifications. 'All this you did before you left which means you must have known about what was to happen.'

"I always know what is to happen but it does not mean that I always take precautions. Sometimes I take and sometimes not. It depends on the circumstances."

'This means that you also know of something dreadful that is going to happen to the Pandavas!'

"Of course I know."

'Then why don't you do something to prevent it?'

"You might as well ask, 'why didn't I do something to prevent Dwaraka being attacked?'"

'So why didn't you?'

"My child this is not the appropriate time for such deep questions. We are approaching Dwaraka. Do you see the devastation which has taken place in the farms and surrounding valleys and houses outside the city? Look! There is Salva's army, surrounding the city. Look how he has stationed his forces on a level ground with a good water supply. The only places they have avoided are cremation grounds, temples, sacred trees and ground covered by ant-hills. They have blocked all the roads leading to the city as well as all the secret entrances. He seems to have a huge army of soldiers, cavalry, elephants and chariots. They have already destroyed all the gardens and forests surrounding the city. But I don't see the Shaubha anywhere, which means he is not here. Anyway let us get inside the city and find out all details before chasing him."

'Is there nobody there to forestall him?' I asked.

"Yes indeed, my sons Pradyumna, Samba and Charudeshna and of course Uddhava, Satyaki, Kritavarma and all the Yadava heroes must have come out of the city to stop his forces from invading the city."

"Come!" He said, yanking me out of the chariot. "There is not a moment to be lost. We have to go inside the city. They have blocked all the secret passages, but they have not found the one which is inside the Vishnu temple here and which leads to the Vishnu temple next to my palace.

"Daruka! You must hide the chariot and horses far away and follow us as fast as possible."

He grabbed my hand and I scurried after him. There was a tunnel leading from the sanctum sanctorum of the temple through which we sailed along. At least that is what it felt like. The only light was the glow that emanated from him. Very soon we reached the temple next to the palace. The tunnel opened into the inner sanctum as in the other temple. We rushed out to find all the streets deserted. There was no sound of Vedic chanting or the usual bustle of a city.

My Lord went and bowed to his father and King Ugrasena. They gave a resume of all that had happened. He also asked Kritavarma for news and was told that Pradyumna had ably resisted the attack, but had succumbed to one of Salva's missiles. Uddhava, Satyaki, Samba and others were still fighting outside.

Just then Pradyumna's charioteer returned carrying his master back since he had been wounded by Salva. He recovered immediately and saw his father and begged him to pardon him for having turned back. The charioteer immediately said that he thought it proper on his part to bring him back since he had been badly wounded. My Lord commended him and presented him with the necklace round his neck. He placed his divine hand on his son and made him whole again.

"What is happening outside?" he asked as if he knew nothing.

Pradyumna said, "As soon as we heard that Salva was attacking the city, all of us went out with an army. He had already devastated the whole place by the time we reached there. When he saw us he started using magic, but I countered with our *astras* and shattered his illusions. The Shaubha would suddenly appear here and there and all of us tried to shoot it down but we did not succeed. None of us abandoned our posts despite the shower of weapons which were being hurled upon us. Using twenty-five arrows with gold shafts and iron heads, I struck down his commander-in-chief, Dyuman and with another hundred shafts I struck Salva himself. At the same time I pierced his officers, his chariot drivers and horses. However just a while ago Salva's minister, Dyuman whom I had wounded a while ago, ran up to me and struck me with a club. My charioteer thought my chest had been shattered and quickly brought me here. I regained consciousness and told my charioteer to take me back immediately, but he insisted on bringing me here since it was his duty to do so. I'm sorry father; I know that no one born in the family of the Yadus has ever been known to abandon the battlefield. My reputation has been stained forever. Please forgive me." My Lord comforted him and told him to rest, but Pradyumna insisted on returning to the battlefield.

By this time Daruka had come and my Lord asked him to go and fill a new chariot with all the *astras* from the artillery room. He then took leave of all the elders and got their blessings, as well as the blessings of the Brahmin priests. "Have no fear!" he told them, "I will not return till Salva is killed." Only two of his horses, Saibya and Sugriva were yoked to the chariot and away we went swiftly out of the city through the south gate.

I was horrified to see the devastation. My Lord stopped some of the survivors who were fleeing from the battleground and asked them what had happened after Pradyumna had left the field.

"We don't know exactly what happened, but it looked as if Salva had sent just one projectile charged with the power of the universe from his *vimana* which rose up in an incandescent column of fire as bright as a thousand suns rising all together. It went up in a perpendicular explosion with billowing smoke clouds. The smoke formed into expanding circles like the opening of giant umbrellas. We have never seen anything like it. It is an unknown weapon like an iron thunderbolt, a gigantic messenger of death which annihilated our entire army."

We looked at the corpses and found that most of them were unrecognisable. The hair and nails seemed to have fallen out. To escape from the fire, the soldiers threw themselves into the sea to wash themselves. I shuddered when I saw this. I was a child when the first atomic explosion took place and this appeared to be very much like what I had heard about it. None of Salva's forces were to be seen.

Obviously they had returned to their city along with their king after having devastated the land of Anarta. My Lord gave instructions to those who were still alive as to what should be done. He did not want to waste any more time since I think he believed that the Shaubha would return after refuelling, to complete the destruction of the city. We rode swiftly towards Salva's city of Matrikavasta. We passed through many of the places we had passed the previous day. Then we got information that the Shaubha was seen hovering over the sea off the coast of Dwaraka. We turned around and drove towards the ocean. Just then I noticed a huge aerial vehicle slowly flying along the coast.

'What is that?' I gasped and clutched my Lord's arm.

"That is the Shaubha. Observe it carefully. It is one of the most sophisticated *vimanas* existing in Aryavrata. People think that he got it from some other planet. It is something like the Tripuras (three cities) which Lord Shiva vanquished a long time ago. That was also said to have come from another planet. Shaubha, is Salva's city, flagship, and battle headquarters. In it, he can fly wherever he chooses. I have heard that it can also land on water." I thought it looked very much like the pictures of an UFO I had seen in my previous life. It was sort of rounded on top and was sparking brilliant lights from the sides.

'Why couldn't you have brought the Garuda *vimana* to combat this?'

"The Garuda is not really meant for warfare. It's only meant for travel. It doesn't have all the complicated instruments of the Shaubha. Of course I did use it to go to Pragjyotisha, but Naraka's army is very poor compared to this. However don't worry. I have enough *astras* to combat him."

The *vimana* was at least a few *yojanas* off the coast when Salva started to rain thousands of arrows at us. My Lord retaliated but unfortunately his arrows didn't reach him. The Yadava troops who had come after us could not see the Shaubha at all. All they could do was to stand on the shore and watch the fight like spectators at a show. At last my Lord's arrows penetrated into the *vimana* and killed the soldiers positioned inside it. The dead started to fall into the waters and huge fish came out of the ocean and devoured them. Seeing this, Salva started to use his power of illusion and began to hurl maces, ploughshares, winged darts, lances, javelins, battle axes, swords and arrows all blazing like meteors and thunderbolts. Night and day seemed to appear alternately. Sometimes it was clear, sometimes gloomy, sometimes very hot and sometimes severely cold. There were frequent showers of hot coals, ashes and weapons from the sky. Then suddenly there was a huge blast and the dome of the sky blazed as if a hundred suns had lit up at the same time. This was what had been described by the survivors of the last battle. This caused devastation amongst our troops. In fact we couldn't even see our soldiers since most of them had perished in the blast. Even Daruka seemed to be wounded. He sank to the ground and said in a faint voice, "My Lord! I don't think I can continue to fight." There was not a spot on his body which was not covered with arrows. Blood was oozing from every pore. My Lord laid his divine hand on his body and he became a little better, but was still too weak to drive the chariot. My Lord took the reins himself.

The Shaubha now appeared to be everywhere at the same time. It came on the water, in the sky and on the mountain peak of Raivata. Sometimes it became totally invisible. It was like a whirling, flaming firebrand, never remaining in one place at any time. When it became invisible my Lord sent a special *astra* which could discover an unseen enemy by seeking him out by sound alone. Salva's soldiers were mown down by arrows which came unerringly towards them hearing the sound of their clashing weapons.

Then Salva started hurling huge boulders which my Lord countered with antiballistic missiles which cut them all to pieces before they reached the ground.

Just at that time a person who was known to Ugrasena came from Dwaraka and gave my Lord the dreadful news that his father Vasudeva had been killed by Salva. "The king wants you to return to Dwaraka immediately," said the messenger. For the first time I saw my Lord looking stunned. "If my father has been killed, this can only mean that my brother and sons are also dead. They would have defended him to the last."

My Lord recovered himself and turned to the Shaubha and saw his father with disordered hair and dress falling from the car of precious metals. He appeared to be like a shot bird. For a second it appeared that my Lord had swooned for he sat down on the floor of the chariot. But this lasted only for a minute. When I questioned him about this later, he told me that it looked as if he had swooned only because for a second he had to transport himself to the Sabha being held at Hastinapura in which Draupadi was being insulted. There was no time to ask him any questions about this.

Within a second I think he realised that the whole thing was a trick by Salva. Now he did not hesitate any longer and hurled the Sudarshana Chakra at the Shaubha. My Lord's discus was like a blazing sun. It whirled towards the Shaubha and cut it in two and set the whole *vimana* ablaze. Somehow Salva escaped from the doomed vehicle which was falling into the sea in blazing pieces and jumped to the ground. He ran with an upraised club to finish off his sworn enemy. My Lord also jumped out of the chariot to meet Salva on equal ground. The Sudarshana had returned like a faithful servant to my Lord's hand, and this time he hurled it with ease and as if in play at the oncoming Salva. The discus cut him in two halves and thus the whole drama came to an end.

Of course I immediately asked him why he had not done this earlier instead of exhausting himself in such a long drawn out battle. Again he laughed and said, "My child! Where is the game if I do that? Have you watched a game of *chaturanga*? Supposing all the players had wonderful dice which always threw the correct numbers, where would be the joy of the game? The joy of any game lies in the suspense - when the chances of your winning or losing are equal. If the dice are heavily loaded against one party, what fun is there in it? Moreover everyone has a fixed time for death as well as birth. I had to wait till his time had come before I could kill him. In fact Pradyumna could have killed him at one time by using his invincible *astra,* but the gods stopped him from doing so since they knew that I was the one ordained to kill him. So now are you satisfied?"

I nodded my head a bit doubtfully and said, 'This needs thinking over.'

Krishna smiled and said, "Look there! It appears that we have another of Shishupala's friends coming to avenge his death."

'Who is this?' I asked.

"His name is Dantavakra and he is the king of Karusha and is a cousin of mine, like Shishupala. He thought Salva would avenge Shishupala's death and now that he has heard that Salva is dead, he is coming to kill me. He is so angry that he has not waited to collect his army or even his chariot. Look at him marching towards me like an angry demon making the earth quake with the strength of his steps!"

My Lord very sweetly got down from his chariot to meet his enemy who was on foot and carried only a club. Krishna also carried only his club - Kaumodaki. When he saw his archenemy in front of him, Dantavakra raised himself to his full towering height and addressed my Lord. "My dear Krishna! Even though you are my cousin, I am forced to kill you to avenge the deaths of my friends Shishupala and Salva. The only way I can clear my debt to Salva is by killing you today."

With these words he swung his mace and roaring like a lion he struck my Lord a heavy blow on the head. I was so pained that I fell to the ground. My beautiful Lord did not say anything but he whirled the Kaumodaki round his head and struck Dantavakra hard on the chest. The blow appeared to have split his chest in two and he started to vomit blood and fell to the ground dead. In the full sight of all those present, again the same phenomenon that had happened at the time of Shishupala's death was repeated and a strange blue light was seen to come out of that body and melt into the aura surrounding my Lord.

Dantavakra had a brother called Viduratha who was filled with grief and anger when he saw his brother slain. He immediately charged at my Lord with upraised sword. This time Krishna hurled his discus at the oncoming man and severed his head.

Once again my Lord lifted his conch to his lips and blew his victory call which was heard in Dwaraka. The gates were opened and all the excited citizens came running out. We were taken back in great triumph.

Whenever I touched my Lord and looked up at the sky I could see all the celestials looking on with delight. Of course Dwaraka was decorated and lighted and all the clans of the Vrishnis and Yadus came to pay their respects to him. The citizens had been under great strain for the past few months. At last the imposed ban on liquor and dancing etc. was lifted and everyone danced and drank with abandon.

My Vanamali went and slept with all his sixteen thousand, one hundred and eight wives that night. Of course he slept with me in our own palace and I liked to think that this was the real Krishna. Though what was real and what unreal was something I could no longer figure out.

That night I repeated the question I had put to him on the battlefield. 'Why don't you stop dreadful things from happening when you are certain they are going to happen?'

He countered with another question. "Do you think God knows what is going to happen everywhere?"

'Of course he knows.'

"Then why doesn't he stop bad things from happening?"

'I don't know,' I said sheepishly.

"My Dear! This world has been made with certain laws. Everything in this cosmos goes by these laws. The sun rises every day in the east. If for some reason God decided to ask him to rise in the west, do you think that would be a good thing? All the planets and the creatures and all the other aspects of creation follow these laws without a question. It is only the human being that questions and also goes against these laws by which the creation was made. This is why we quarrel and fight all the time against other people, against our own relations, against the whole world and even against God and thus make ourselves miserable. If we obeyed this natural law which is called *dharma,* we will not make ourselves or others unhappy. As I told you, the laws of living given to us by our *rishis* are collectively known as the Sanatana Dharma because it is an ancient set of rules for enlightened living. This law is not subject to time and has no beginning and no end. Everything in life comes into creation at a certain point in space and time and has to depart from this sphere at another point in space and time. God does not meddle in this flow of this natural law and impose his will on the natural course of events. He allows them to take place as they are meant to take place. Human beings should not meddle with this law either. This is the reason why I did not go to the dice game which the Pandavas played with the Kauravas. Had I gone, I would have felt that I should interfere and that would be going against natural laws. Of course I have the power to stop dreadful things from happening, just as God has the power. But just as he does not exercise this power, I too do not exercise this power. If I did, I would be going against the divine plan. Do you understand?" He lifted my chin with his finger and looked into my eyes and I felt as if I had understood everything.

"My child! Life is a game – a *lila.* If the game is too simple there would be no joy in it. It has to have some adventure, some difficulties, only then will there be enjoyment. Why do we enjoy playing *chaturanga*? Because it's difficult and makes us use our brain. If God made everything smooth and easy, we would find it very boring. Trust in Him totally. He knows what's best for you. Do you understand?"

I nodded but of course I had a thousand other questions. 'What has happened to the Pandavas? What is the dice game you are talking about? Why did you disappear from the battlefield at a crucial moment and tell me that you had gone to Draupadi's aid?'

Aum Namo Bhagavate Vaasudevaaya

Like fire covered by smoke,
Like a mirror covered by dust,
Like the unborn foetus covered by the membrane,
So is the wisdom of even the wise covered by the invisible fire of desire,
The constant enemy of the Self.

Srimad Bhagavat Gita, Chapter 3.

ॐ

Balabhadrapriyaanujaaya Namaha!

CHAPTER SIXTEEN

Pandavas

My Vanamali did not reply to my questions about the Pandavas since he had so many matters to attend to in the city. But I noticed that he was quite pensive at times and seemed to be thinking of other things. This was very rare with him. However grave the situation he always seemed to be above it. He was always above the ordinary considerations of normal human beings and very seldom had I seen him looking grave or troubled. We were walking in the garden with Satyaki and Uddhava one day and the Lord told them, "I think it is time for us to go to Indraprastha and find out how our friends are faring."

"As you wish O Govinda. We will make all arrangements."

Hardly had he finished talking when there was a big commotion and Subhadra came running with Abhimanyu in her arms and fell at my Lord's feet.

"Brother!" She sobbed. "All is lost. The Pandavas have lost everything and have gone to the forest." She was sobbing so much that nothing much could be got out of her. My Lord lifted her up and carried Abhimanyu in his arms, and all of us went to Vasudeva's palace where she poured out the whole story after she had calmed down a little.

"I don't know where to start," she said. "Everything happened so quickly after you left, brother! As I watched you depart both my sister,

Panchali and I felt a deep foreboding and our right eye started to throb which is not a good omen for ladies. Do you remember how angry Duryodhana was when he left Indraprastha? He swore to get even with my brothers and especially Draupadi for having dared to laugh at his mishaps in the Maya Sabha. Soon after that our dear uncle Vidura came to the court with an invitation from our paternal uncle, Dritarashtra. Of course all of us welcomed him very happily. After all the formalities were over, Yudhishtira asked him the reason for his visit.

Vidura said, 'The Kauravas have constructed a hall called, "The Jayanta Sabha" and they have sent an invitation with me asking you to come for a friendly game of dice with Duryodhana. As you know Duryodhana was filled with jealousy at seeing the magnificence of the Rajasuya. On top of this he felt terribly insulted at all the ignominious incidents that happened to him at the Maya Sabha. When he returned home he could neither sleep nor eat. Karna immediately offered to come here with a force and defeat all of you and bring back everything that Duryodhana desired. Shakuni vetoed this idea and said that they would never be able to defeat you in an open battle at this moment when all the kings of Aryavrata were on your side! Then that wicked prince of Gandhara (Shakuni) offered to win the whole of your kingdom without shedding a drop of blood. He concocted this hateful plan of inviting you all to a game of dice in the new Sabha and has promised Duryodhana to take over all your wealth for him. Duryodhana was delighted by the brilliant plan and persuaded his weak father to write an invitation and also insisted that I should be the one to deliver it to you. At first I totally refused to come and Duryodhana called me an ungrateful wretch who ate his bread but whose sympathy was all with the Pandavas. At last I agreed to come only because I thought I could persuade you to refuse this invitation. The whole thing is a plot by that wretch Shakuni to deprive you of your kingdom. Therefore I urge you not come on any account.'

"So saying uncle Vidura handed the letter to Yudhishtira. He read the letter carefully and in his usual polite fashion he said, 'My dear Uncle!

I value your opinion more than anything else. Had it not been for you we would all have perished at Varanavata. But I am in a dilemma now. Let me ask my brothers what they think about it.'

"He turned to all of them and asked them whether he should accept the invitation. All of them except Bhima vehemently vetoed the idea. Yudhishtira sat for a long time cogitating and at last he said, 'My dear uncle! Please don't be angry with me, but how can I refuse an invitation sent by someone who is like my own father and brought by one who is so dear to me? It would be an insult to both of you if I refused to come. Let it not be said that Yudhishtira has failed to respect his elders.'

"Vidura immediately said, 'I assure you I will not take it as an insult if you refuse to come. As for Dritarashtra he is completely under the thumb of his son. It is your duty to look after your own welfare first without bothering about what others will think.'

Subhadra continued, "However my elder brother was determined to accept the invitation. The next day all of them including my dear sister, Draupadi and mother Kunti set out in five glittering golden chariots with all their royal equipment and servants. I was told to stay at home and keep an eye on all the children even though I was anxious to accompany them. I'm not sure what exactly happened there. But uncle Vidura sent his own chariot and charioteer to bring me here and he told me that there was a terrible scene in which the Emperor was challenged to a game of dice by Duryodhana, but the dice were actually thrown by that wicked uncle of theirs who is a master player and a master cheat.

"Apparently our elder brother wagered all his money and all his jewels, his jewelled chariot with golden bells, and all his cattle; still he played on, and he lost his thousand war elephants, his slaves and beautiful slave girls, and the remainder of his goods; and next, he staked and lost the whole kingdom of the Pandavas, save the lands which he had gifted to the Brahmans. Nor did he cease to play then, despite the advice offered him by the chieftains who were there. One by one he staked and lost his brethren; and then he staked himself and lost." Once again Subhadra burst into tears and had to be comforted by her parents.

Devaki asked, "Then what happened?"

Subhadra continued. "When he had lost even his own brothers, Duryodhana taunted him and asked him to play just one more time and this time he could wager the Empress Draupadi herself!! I don't know how to say this, but apparently it was a terrible scene when my dear sister was dragged into the open assembly by that wicked Dusshasana and thrown on the floor. Duryodhana ordered all the Pandavas to take off their *uttareeyams* and their crowns and jewels and throw them on the floor. Then that horrible wretch ordered Dusshasana to disrobe Panchali since she was also a servant of theirs. He gleefully grabbed her upper garment and started to pull. At first my dear sister cried out to all her husbands to help her, but the charioteer said that all of them hung their heads in shame since they were already slaves and dared not go to her help.

"For the first time my dear courageous sister wept and said, 'Why this silence? Is there no man among you to protect a sinless woman? Fie to the fame of the Kurus, the ancient glory of Bharatha and the prowess of the Kshatriyas! Won't the sons of Pandu protect their outraged queen? Has the grandsire lost his virtue and Drona his power? Has my husband Yudhishtira stopped defending one who is wronged? Why are you all silent when this dastardly crime is being committed before your eyes?'

"As she spoke her gaze roved round her husbands one by one and they hung their heads in shame. Bhima clenched his fists, Bhishma's face became dark, Drona clenched his teeth and Vidura walked out of the assembly."

Subhadra turned to my Vanamali and said, "Then, O brother! She called out to you. She started to shout loudly, "O Krishna! O Yadava! O thou dweller in the city of Dwaraka! O Govinda! Why have you deserted me in this dreadful predicament? You promised to come to my aid when I needed you. I need you desperately now. I have five heroes as husbands yet none of them can save me now. Help of the helpless, you are my only saviour!'"

Looking at my Lord, Subhadra said, "I'm sure you must have gone there to save her because after her first shocked tears, her voice changed. She looked up and must have seen you because uncle Vidura's charioteer said that her whole expression changed and she raised her arms above her head and started chanting your names in an exalted fashion. Her agony seemed to have changed to ecstasy. The more she sang, the more Dusshasana pulled, but however much he pulled he could never totally disrobe her. In fact the pile of cloth on the side started to reach enormous proportions and Dusshasana became so exhausted that he fell to the ground in a faint!"

I turned to look at my Vanamali and as his eyes locked with mine he answered my question, 'where had you gone when you appeared to have fainted?' He had told me that he had gone to Draupadi's aid, and I also remembered the promise he gave her as we left Indraprastha that he would go to help her when she needed him.

Subhadra was sobbing again and could not talk for a few minutes.

"Then what happened?" asked all of us.

"Did the Elders of the Kuru assembly do nothing to stop this atrocity?" asked my Vanamali.

Subhadra shook her head. "I don't know, I think nobody dared to go against Duryodhana. Then the charioteer told me that Duryodhana bared his thigh and offered my sister Draupadi a seat! Can you imagine such a contemptible act? I can't imagine how that wretch ever dared to do such a thing! But my sister as you know is a very courageous person and her spirits had not been broken as yet. She turned to him and cursed him, 'O Duryodhana hearken to my words, one day you will die on the battlefield with your thighs broken and vultures and wolves hovering around you!'

"Then, O brother! That dreadful Karna, in order to support his dear friend Duryodhana said to her, 'Your husbands are like sesame seeds removed from their kernel so now you can find some other worthy husbands. You already have five husbands. Why don't you take

Duryodhana also? One more will not make a difference to you!' Her husbands jumped up but sat down again in shame and Karna jeeringly said, 'A woman who has five husbands is only a whore and not a wife! She has no shame or honour!'

"Then my husband swore that one day he would kill Karna! All the brothers also took dreadful oaths. My strong brother Bhima is supposed to have said, 'I swear I will not drink water with my hands until I kill this wicked wretch Dusshasana and drink his blood and tie my Panchali's hair with my bloodied hands. I swear I will kill all the hundred Kaurava brothers and kill Duryodhana by breaking his thighs. I swear this by Krishna, by Shiva and by Durga!'

"Sahadeva swore to kill Shakuni and Nakula to kill Shakuni's son Uluka. Once again that poor lady whose hair had been so cruelly pulled by Dusshasana said, 'My hair will remain untied till Bhima ties it with his hands anointed with the blood of Dusshasana. Then the hair of all the Kaurava widows will droop down!'"

All of us who were present were in tears by the end of this recital. "Then what happened?" All of us asked.

Subhadra continued with difficulty. "I'm not sure exactly what happened, but it appears that at last Dritarashtra became terribly alarmed at all the curses that had been heaped on his sons' heads and intervened and offered to give back everything to the Pandavas. Of course Duryodhana was furious and refused.

'Yudhishtira lost everything in a fair play. I will not give back anything. They can be our slaves and live here and eat what we throw them!'

"Apparently Drona intervened and said, 'Let the Pandavas and their wife be banished to the forest for twelve years and after that they can live incognito for one year in some city of their choice . If they are discovered during this year they have to repeat the entire banishment. This is the only way to avoid bloodshed between the cousins.'

"Then Dritarashtra said, 'When they come back I give my word that they will be given back half the kingdom which is theirs by right.'"

"What did Duryodhana say to this?" asked Balarama who always had a soft corner for him.

Subhadra continued, "Brother! Apparently Duryodhana was the first to agree to this. I suppose he thought it would be impossible for the Pandavas to remain incognito in any city and that he would easily be able to discover their whereabouts, and then of course they would have to go through the whole of the twelve years once again!"

"What did the Eldest say to all this?" asked Satyaki.

"My dear brother Yudhishtira is so good and noble that all he said was, 'I shall abide by whatever my Elders say.' But my spirited princess of Panchala said, 'I refuse to go into exile as a slave. Please have a final throw of the dice for our freedom. We don't want the kingdom but we must depart as free people and not as slaves.'

"Duryodhana insultingly asked, 'Your husband is already a slave. What does he have to wager against me, who am the mighty monarch of all of Aryavrata!'

"My noble brother said, 'I place all the *punya* (spiritual merit) I have accumulated in all these years against the riches which Duryodhana boasts of possessing.'"

All those present asked with bated breath, "Then what happened?"

Subhadra said, "Duryodhana was elated of course and said he would give back everything they had lost plus their freedom if they won."

Subhadra turned to Krishna and said, "Just before he threw the dice, Draupadi reminded the Eldest to think of you and repeat your twelve names. Yudhishtira then repeated. 'Ha Keshava! Ha Govinda! Ha Narayana! Ha Madhava! Ha Vishno! Ha Madhusudana! Ha Trivikrama! Ha Vamana! Ha Sridhara! Ha Hrishikesha! Ha Padmanabha! Ha Damodara!' There was utter silence when the dice rattled in the box and everyone except the Kauravas let out a sigh of relief when for the first and only time Yudhishtira won!! There were no cheers or jibes. Everyone remained silent since Duryodhana had promised to give back everything if Yudhishtira won. True to their own natures, Duryodhana sulked and my noble eldest brother accepted only their freedom and disdained to take anything else even though Duryodhana had promised. 'I will claim my share of the kingdom after the successful completion of the stipulated time of thirteen years which has been decided upon by the Elders,' was all he said."

"Where are they now?" asked Uddhava.

"I'm not sure," said Subhadra. "My charioteer says that all of them left Hastinapura along with their priest Dhoumya to go to the forest, clad in bark and deerskin. The Eldest is supposed to have covered his face with his upper cloth, Bhima kept flexing his muscles and thinking of revenge, my husband was scattering sand as if they were arrows of future destruction and the twins had covered their handsome faces with ashes while the princess of Panchala alone walked proudly with her head held high and her long black hair falling like a cloak behind her. The high priest Dhoumya was plucking *kusa* grass and reciting Vedic verses for the dead as a prophecy of what was to come for the Kauravas.

"Apparently many bad omens were seen and heard as the Pandavas left and uncle Vidura told his brother Dritarashtra that all of it boded evil for his sons! The king was sunk in gloom when he heard this, but as usual he was too weak to go against his son. Then uncle told his charioteer to go immediately to Indraprastha and bring me and Abhimanyu here and take the five sons of Draupadi to their grandfather's abode in Kampilya. And that is how we have come here," said Subhadra and sank into her mother's arms and started to cry softly again.

"What happened to my sister Kunti, the heroic mother of the Pandavas?" asked Devaki.

"I think my uncle Vidura took her to his own abode. The charioteer said that he refused to live any more in the place where such *adharma* has been committed and is now living in a small hut outside the city gates."

My Lord had been silent all this time, but I could feel his sorrow at the fate of his dearly beloved cousins. He called some of his men and told them to go immediately to the court of Drupada and bring back the five sons of the Pandavas so that they could be brought up with their cousin Abhimanyu. He sent a letter to King Drupada with the messenger telling him that the boys were very fond of Subhadra and she would be a second mother to them, so it was best that they lived with their dear cousin Abhimanyu and learned all the martial arts from his own sons. I knew of course that Draupadi had had five sons from her five husbands some time before Subhadra had Abhimanyu. She had Prativindhya from Yudhishtira, Sutasoma from Bhima, Srutakirti from Arjuna, Satanika from Nakula, and Srutakarma from Sahadeva. At that time Prativindhya was eleven years old and Srutakarma only seven. Abhimanyu was still only a baby of three.

Turning to Subhadra Krishna said, "My child, it is your duty now to look after all the boys as your own sons. I know you will give them all the love that you give Abhimanyu. My sons Pradyumna, Samba and others will be able to teach them all that they need to learn in the art of warfare and Kritavarma will teach them all military tactics." Subhadra seemed to brighten up when she was given these orders. I think my Vanamali did this not only for the sake of the five brothers, but also for her sake so that she would forget all that had happened and start to take interest in the welfare of the children.

Turning to Satyaki and Uddhava he said, "Prepare to leave for the Kamyaka forest. The Pandavas must have gone there and we must go and comfort them."

Satyaki in his own impetuous way said, "Why don't we take our army and march against Hastinapura and kill Duryodhana? We can give the kingdom as a gift to Yudhishtira. That will put a stop to everything!"

My Lord smiled at the suggestion and said, "I don't think this is the time for such an action. Yudhishtira will not thank us for this! He is used to giving gifts, not receiving them."

Aum Namo Bhagavate Vaasudevaaya

I assume a human form for the sake of my devotees,
In order to drive out the darkness of ignorance,
And to raise the banner of happiness,
Through the righteous,
I take birth age after age.

Srimad Bhagavat Gita, Chapter 4.

ॐ

Putanajeevitaharaaya Namaha!

CHAPTER SEVENTEEN

Kamyaka

The next morning all four of us including me set out to the forest of Kamyaka. On the way we met many sages who had gone with the Pandavas to the forest. Krishna questioned them.

The sages replied, "The Pandavas passed through the north gate of the city after praying to Shiva and Durga and went through the town of Vardhamana and reached Pramanakoti by nightfall. Many of the citizens followed them, but the king persuaded them to return and look after the elders. Pramanakoti is a beautiful spot on the banks of the Ganga. This is where Duryodhana once tried to poison Bhima. But the tribe called the Nagas who live in the forest rescued him, and revived him when he was about to die of the snake venom. The Pandavas pushed on to the Kamyaka forest which is situated on the banks of the river Saraswati to the west of Kurukshetra. There is a lake here called the Kamyaka Lake and this is where the Pandavas have camped."

The sages continued, "Many of the citizens refused to return to Hastinapura and opted to go with the Pandavas and live in the forest rather than be subject to Duryodhana's tyranny. Many sages are also there. Draupadi was in a dilemma as to how she could feed this huge retinue. She asked Dhoumya to help her, and he told Yudhishtira to pray to the sun god to help them. Surya has given them a vessel which is an '*akshaya patra*.' However much food you take out of it, the provisions will never get exhausted. The only condition was that Draupadi should eat only after feeding everybody else, because after she ate the pot would not produce any more food for the rest of the day. So this is how Draupadi is feeding all the people who have accompanied them to the forest.

"The Pandavas had to travel for three days before reaching the forest. At the entrance to the forest, they were stopped by the *rakshasa* called Kirmir who was a friend of Hidimba and wanted to kill Bhima to avenge his friend's death. Bhima fought with him and killed him and only then were they able to reach the forest." My Lord thanked the sages for the information.

We pressed on and finally reached the Pandava camp. Needless to say all of them were overjoyed to see my Lord. My Vanamali said to them, "Had I been there in Hastinapura when this unfair match was held, all this would never have happened. I would certainly have put a stop to it. Now it is too late. You will have to go through the exile. But this is a good opportunity for you to get some extra weapons from the gods. Bhishma, Drona and Karna are the disciples of Parasurama and they have the latest types of *astras*. It would be good for Arjuna to go to the Himalayas and do *tapas* to Shiva and get the famous Pasupatastra from him. When the time comes, Vyasa will come here and tell you what to do."

He turned to Draupadi with eyes filled with pity and said, "Ah Panchali! What has fate done to you?"

She burst into tears and said, "My gracious Lord! Think of my fate had you not come to my rescue in my greatest hour of need! Duryodhana wanted to make me his slave. He and Karna taunted me and spoke many insulting words to me while my five husbands looked on in silence. Is it not the duty of a husband to protect his wife? These valorous husbands of mine who are like lions in battle did not lift a hand to save me! Had you not come to my help, surely I would have died of shame on that very spot." Her lovely eyes filled with tears as she said this and she looked appealingly at my Lord, "O Vaasudeva! You are my only succour, my only saviour!"

My Lord in an unusually harsh tone spoke decisively to her, "Do not grieve, O Panchali! I promise you that you will live to see the wives of these men who persecuted you lament over their fallen husbands with their hair untied and drooping down as yours is now. Don't cry, O princess! I shall never desert the Pandavas and will do for them whatever lies in my power. Once again you shall be the queen of five kings. The heavens may fall and the Himalayas move, the earth may be rent and the oceans dried up, but know for certain, O Panchali that my words will never prove false."

Arjuna added, "Do not weep my lady! What Krishna has said will come to pass. It cannot be otherwise!"

She fell at Krishna's feet and stayed there for some time, overcome with grief. He lifted her up tenderly and said, "Now you must ask your husband Yudhishtira to comfort you with proper words. He is the son of Dharma and will know more about *dharma* than any of us."

I thought to myself, this is always his way - to give honour to his devotees and take a secondary role for himself. I had seen him doing this any number of times.

Draupadi turned to Yudhishtira and said, "O King! I lie on the ground, remembering my soft luxurious bed. I sit on a grass mat but cannot forget my ivory chairs. You, who were once an emperor, are now a beggar. You, who were clad in silken robes, are now clad in bark. What peace can my mind know? My heart is full of grief. Doesn't your wrath blaze up to see me and your brothers like this? Are you totally devoid of anger? How can you call yourself a Kshatriya? This is the time for you to seek vengeance. This is not the time for forgiveness!"

Yudhishtira looked at his wife with compassion and said, "Anger is the root cause of all destruction. In a moment of anger a person may commit many sins. You think I am weak but let me tell you that a weak man will not be able to control his anger. Men of wisdom seek to subdue their passions, not give in to them. Just because Duryodhana has acted in anger and against *dharma*, should I do likewise? If a wrong is righted only by punishment, the whole world would be destroyed. Angry people know only to destroy. My dear wife, it is good to forgive. Forgiveness is the greatest virtue. It is holy. It is a *yajna* in itself. He who is self-controlled will attain sovereignty. The qualities of self- control are forgiveness and gentleness."

"How is it O King that your virtue has not shielded you? It seems as if all creatures are moved like puppets by the great ordainer. They who have wronged me so woefully are now happy and we who have always followed *dharma* are in great distress!"

Yudhishtira replied sadly, "My dear, one should follow the path of *dharma* at all times. I am not a trader in goodness who does noble acts only for the fruits I might gain from it. God is the giver of all fruits and he will give just rewards. Do not turn away from him, O Draupadi. Success depends on time and circumstance. So be patient my dear and accept what fate has given you."

Then Bhima spoke and I was shocked to hear him speak harshly to his brother. Usually he never said a word against him. "O brother! Battle is the highest virtue for a Kshatriya. How can you bear to allow the delicate princess of Panchala to suffer like this? This is the time to strike down your enemies and not wait for them to grow stronger."

"Bhima, when you wound me with your hot words and reproaches, I am silent, because your words are justified. But truth means more to me than all the wealth of the earth. My wife, my brothers and my possessions do not amount to even one-sixteenth part of my *dharma*. One should not do a wrong thing on the impulse of the moment. We will get our chance when the exile is over. At that time, within the bounds of *dharma*, you can do anything you please, but till then you must listen to my words though they may not be so pleasing. No one and nothing can make me swerve from the path of *dharma*. My heart does indeed burn to see the plight of my beloved wife and brothers, but I have given my word to remain in exile for twelve years and I will not violate my word," said the king and remained silent. Of the six of them it was only Yudhishtira who appreciated the charms of forest life. He knew that adversity was as much a part of life as prosperity and I think this is why my Lord did not go to the dice game and allowed them to go through these trials.

The three Yadavas and the four Pandavas sank into silence after this for they knew that they would not be able to shake their brother from his vow.

The one thing which amazed me was the solidarity of the brothers. They always acted as one person. However much they disagreed with him, all of them were totally faithful to Yudhishtira who suddenly seemed to have become a much stronger personality. He seemed to have come to his own. I remembered my Lord's words that one day he would rise to his full stature. Yudhishtira revelled in the fact that he could actually practice the high code of *dharma* he had kept for himself and which he had failed to follow during the dice game. It was as if he was trying to make amends for that lapse which had such tragic consequences. Even when the brothers disagreed with him there was never a talk of splitting up. Actually they were not beholden to follow him since Yudhishtira had only pledged his own life to the forest and not that of his brothers and certainly not of Draupadi. She was another source of amazement to me. She could easily have opted to wait at Panchala with her father and look after her five sons as Subhadra and the wives of the other brothers did. But obviously she did not even consider it. I was astonished by the determination of this princess who had always had the best, yet who chose to leave everything and follow her husbands. I looked at my Lord and of course he knew what was going on in my mind and smiled as if he agreed. He told me what had taken place between Yudhishtira and Draupadi before they left.

"The Eldest called Panchali and made her sit beside him and told her, 'My dear there is no need for you to follow us to the forest. You are not meant for hardship. You should return to Hastinapura and take care of Dritarashtra and Gandhari and our mother – Kunti.'

My Vanamali continued, "This is why I always side with the Pandavas. Even though they have been ill-treated so badly by the Kauravas, Yudhishtira has no hatred for them and is even prepared to let his beloved wife go and take care of the very persons who were responsible for his downfall!"

Just then their uncle Vidura came to see them. All of them were very happy to meet him and everybody sat under the shade of the trees beside the beautiful lake and I think for once even Draupadi felt a bit happier. They were all anxious to know about the state of affairs in Hastinapura. Vidura said, "Soon after you left, Dritarashtra called me aside and asked me what he could do to save his sons from the curses which all of you had made. I told him that the only way he could save his sons would be to give back his country to Yudhishtira, throw Shakuni out of the palace and make Dusshasana apologise to Draupadi before the assembly. I also told him that if Duryodhana could not continue to live in the palace along with the Pandavas, he would have to imprison his son since that was the only way to save the Kuru dynasty. My brother was so angry when I said this that he shouted at me and called me a traitor and asked me to leave the city immediately. I was really happy to hear this since I had already decided to leave the place. I was anxious to see you all so I came here immediately.

"Before I left both Vyasa and Maitreya had come to give some advice to Dritarashtra. They warned him that unless he did as I had advised, in fourteen years' time there would be a colossal war in which all his sons would perish! Dritarashtra was filled with fear for his sons but too frightened of Duryodhana to do anything about it. Maitreya called Duryodhana and advised him to make peace with his cousins but the arrogant prince slapped his thigh in derision. Maitreya added his curse to Draupadi's and swore that he would die with his thigh broken by Bhima on the battlefield."

Draupadi's brother Drishtadyumna and Dristaketu, prince of Chedi had also come to commiserate with the Pandavas. Nakula had married Dristaketu's daughter Karenumati and Drishtaketu promised to take his son Niramitra along with him to his kingdom to be with his mother. Drishtadyumna promised to take Draupadi's children back to Kampilya, but my Lord told him that he had already written to Drupada that it would be better for them to stay in Dwaraka with their cousin Abhimanyu and learn all the martial arts from the Yadava youth. Nakula had married Karunamati who was Drishtaketu's sister and he promised to take his sister back to Chedi. Sahadeva's wife was the princess of Magadha and was sent back to her country. As I said, I was amazed that Draupadi did not take the opportunity to return with her brother and live in comfort for the next twelve years. I think Yudhishtira was also aware of her sacrifice and he looked lovingly at her and asked her if she would like to return with her brother. She looked at him with her large eyes filling with tears and said as I had heard that Sita had told Rama in another age, "A wife's place is with her husband."

Draupadi now started to set out lunch for everybody and hardly had they finished when Sanjaya came to the camp. He had been riding hard for the past three days and was quite exhausted. "What has made you come here? How is my brother Dritarashtra?" asked Vidura.

Sanjaya replied, "The moment you left, the king became most agitated. He could not even sit down. He walked up and down and at last called me and told me that he had a made a big mistake and that he could not live without you. He guessed that you must have come to meet the Pandavas and he begged me to come and get you immediately. Please return with me, otherwise I will not be able to face him."

The Pandavas were unhappy at the thought of their dear uncle going back. "Why should you return to be insulted by the king and his sons for your loyalty to us? We fear for your life. Duryodhana will stoop to anything to save himself. He knows that his father is partial to you and he knows that you will advise him to give back the country to us."

Vidura replied, "My dear children. It is best for me to return. Then I can find out what further plots are being hatched by Duryodhana and his great advisor and then perhaps I can let you know what is happening. May you have a peaceful time in this beautiful forest and may you gain wisdom by meeting with the sages and *rishis* who will be visiting you. But it is my duty to go back and help my poor misguided brother if possible."

Once again the Pandavas were feeling sad after their uncle left, and they felt worse when Krishna said that it was time he returned to Dwaraka. My Lord said, "See who has come to keep you in good cheer." I looked up and saw the great sage Markandeya whom we had met in Badarikashrama coming to us. Having bowed to him and given him all respect, all of us settled down to listen to his talks. He told us the story of the Ramayana as well as of the ancient king called Harischandra who always adhered to truth and *dharma* and how he had to undergo so many trials and tribulations. This was to encourage the younger Pandavas and Draupadi to accept the situation. Yudhishtira of course had no problem in accepting the state of affairs. He revelled in the discourses of the sage which made him realise the transient nature of life and worldly possessions. He saw how little the sages needed to enjoy life and discovered the same source within himself, and began to take pleasure in his life in the forest.

Before leaving my Lord told them, "Perhaps it would be better for you to go further south to the beautiful forest known as Dwaitavana. There is an attractive lake there abounding with flowers and many species of birds. The great river Bhogavati passes through it. Since everybody knows you are here, people will keep coming and troubling you so it's best for you to go to this forest."

The brothers and Draupadi decided to follow my Lord's advice. He bid them a fond farewell and promised to come to their aid any time they wanted him. The Pandavas spent five years in that forest and their spirits were kept up by many sages and *rishis* who went to them and told them stories of the great kings of their dynasty who had to go through similar troubles.

The party which returned to Dwaraka was a sad one. Nobody had the heart to talk much and my Vanamali was immersed in his own thoughts, and I didn't dare to question him even though I was bursting with a thousand doubts.

My Lord's wives, children and parents were anxiously awaiting our return. As soon as we arrived they pestered him with questions, some of which he answered and some of which he parried. All the time that we spent in Dwaraka I felt that my Lord's mind was with the Pandavas and he was helping them to bear their sorrow in some way or other.

One day he said, "Come, I will take you to Dwaitavana where Vyasa has just gone to meet them." So saying he wafted me through the fourth dimension to that beautiful forest where the sage was just coming to meet them. They prostrated before the *rishi* and made him comfortable near the lake. Vyasa said, "Five years of your exile have passed and it is imperative that you make use of the rest of the time to get some divine weapons to guard yourself in the war which is inevitable. Duryodhana hopes that you will die in the forest or else be discovered during the thirteenth year, but all the same he is busy making preparations for war. He is seeking alliances from all the great rulers. Remember that Drona, Bhishma and Karna are all disciples of Parasurama and they all possess very powerful weapons. Of course it is true that as long as you are protected by Vaasudeva, nobody can kill you but even then it is better for one of you to go to the Himalayas and do *tapasya* to Lord Shiva and ask him to give you his famous Pasupatastra."

Vyasa left and we watched while the Pandavas debated on who should go to get the *astra*.

Yudhishtira said, "I think it is best for Arjuna to go since he is the one who is the expert in archery. The Pasupatastra is an arrow potentiated with *mantras*. One who has it will become invincible in war."

Arjuna took permission from the Eldest and bid a fond farewell to the others and set out to the Himalayas. Draupadi was weeping and told Arjuna, "Remember you are taking all our hearts with you. May you be successful in your mission and return soon."

'Are we staying with the four or are we going with Arjuna?' I whispered to my Lord.

"Of course we will go with Arjuna. I want to watch over him and I know you love to go to the Himalayas. In any case the others are not going to stay long in this forest. They miss Arjuna so much that they will return to Kamyaka very soon."

'Where is he going now?' I asked.

"He is going to the mountain called Indrakila in order to get his father's blessings."

'Was Indra his father?'

"I told you that the *rishis* were superior to the gods. Durvasa was the one who gave the *mantra* to Kunti so that the gods were forced to come down. She used the *mantra* when she found that her husband was not able to have any children."

'Ah! I remember you told me this. Does Arjuna know this *mantra*? How will he make Indra come down?'

"Human beings cannot order the gods as the *rishis* can. Arjuna will have to go through the usual steps of intense *tapas* before Indra will come to him."

Arjuna sat down to meditate. After doing severe *tapas,* Indra, the king of the gods appeared before him. He was a striking personality. I had actually seen him once when he appeared in the sky during the time when my Lord and Arjuna had destroyed the forest of Khandava.

Arjuna bowed before him and requested him for all the divine weapons that he could give him.

Indra said, "My son, first of all you will have to propitiate Lord Shiva and get the Pasupatastra from him. I will give you my weapons after that. I will also have to go to Karna and beg for his invincible armour. Only then will you be able to defeat him."

"Will he give it to you?" asked Arjuna.

"Karna is known as the greatest giver of gifts. He will never refuse anything to anyone. I will approach him after he has performed his usual noon-time rituals to Surya since that is the time that he has kept aside for giving gifts. You don't have to worry about that. It is something I will do for you. Now you can proceed to the Himalayas and worship the three-eyed god."

Arjuna went forward through thick forests and eventually came to the pine forest. Beyond that was the snow line where no trees grew. There were only some thorny bushes. There he passed many days practicing severe austerities.

We left him to this and returned some months later when my Lord said that it was time for Shiva to appear.

He was still standing on one leg and obviously had not stirred for many days since an ant hill was slowly starting to grow up his legs. Suddenly there was a snorting sound which disturbed his deep meditation. A wild boar broke out of the bush and charged towards him across the meadow. Immediately Arjuna fitted an arrow to his bow and shot the animal just as it was charging towards him. As he shot the arrow the bowstring snapped with a dreadful sound and the arrow found its mark in the boar's body and it fell with a roar. Arjuna ran forward and knelt beside it and found two arrows side by side buried deep in its body.

"Now watch the fun," whispered my Lord.

At the same time a huge mountain man ran towards the boar and shouted at Arjuna, "Thief! Get away from my dinner!" Startled, Arjuna looked up and saw a tall, fair rustic dressed in a white tiger skin, holding a short bow in his hands.

"What are you doing here, poaching on my land?" asked the rustic.

Arjuna said, "I'm sorry I didn't know it was your land. It looks as if we have both hit him."

"I hit him first," shouted the man and without waiting for a reply he threw a dart at Arjuna which missed his head by half a finger. Arjuna was mad and ran back to get his quiver and arrows and sent a shower of arrows at the hunter, but the arrows broke against the hunter's body and fell in splinters around his feet.

The huntsman then sent an equal shower of arrows at Arjuna which just appeared to miss their mark and shouted, "Use your best arrows."

Arjuna kept shooting down the hunter's arrows until at last he found to his horror that the inexhaustible quiver which Agni had given him was empty!

I looked at my Lord, 'Aren't you going to do something?'

He gave me a wink. "Watch and don't talk so much!"

Arjuna took up his bow and gave a mighty blow to the hunter's head. Even I felt that blow.

The hunter said, "How unfair of you to smite me with your bow. I can easily retaliate but I won't." With these words he jumped at Arjuna's throat and they grappled with each other. It appeared that Arjuna who had been famished and almost on the verge of fainting gained some strength from the hunter's hands and they fought for some time. However he found his strength to be ebbing away. He felt the world spin and fade away and fell in a swoon on the ground. After some time he regained consciousness and for the first time a sense of helplessness overcame him. He took some mud and made a clay *lingam* of Shiva and started worshipping it, begging his favourite deity to come to his aid. He managed to get some flowers from a bush and made a garland and put it round the *lingam* but the garland disappeared. By this time he knew something was really wrong and looked around and saw the hunter sitting on a rock beside the boar wearing the garland he had just put round the *lingam*. Everything fell into place now. He sprang to his feet and ran towards him, "*Aum Namashivaaya*!" he said and prostrated before him.

The perfume of the pine trees filled the air. The moon-crested Lord of all creatures shone with the light of the sun. He smiled and held out his hand and said. "Come and sit by me, O Bharata! You have done well and you will get what you have come for."

The twilight deepened and darkness fell over the mountains. Shiva handed over the celestial weapon to Arjuna. There was a clap as of thunder as the great Lord disappeared and the spirit of the weapon stood beside Arjuna, ready to obey his orders.

With another clap of thunder all the gods appeared on the summit of the mountain – Indra, king of gods, Varuna, god of waters, Yama, king of the dead and Kubera, Lord of the Yakshas. All of them gave Arjuna many celestial weapons. They blessed Arjuna and vanished.

'Where is Arjuna going now?' I asked.

"Indra is taking him to his heaven since he wants him to do some work for him. Come, we will return to Dwaraka where I have some work."

Aum Namo Bhagavate Vaasudevaaya

Men of the earth, brothers in eternity, shake your souls awake,
The hour so long waited for, the promised hour has come.
Over the dark firmament of suffering humanity,
Is rising the morning star,
Heralding the day when you will understand,
Man's sacred duty to be MAN.
That is to manifest life, intelligence, truth and love.
And you who realise this will break the fetters of ignorance and fear
That bind unconscious humanity,
And know yourself to be eternal manifestations of the Unmanifest.
Witnesses of the Absolute,
Sons of the great All whom we call – God.

Inspired by the Vedas. Author Unknown.

ॐ

Shakataasura Bhanjanaaya Namaha!

CHAPTER EIGHTEEN

Dwaitavana

After staying for some months in Dwaraka I asked my Lord, 'What are the Pandavas doing now?'

"Let's see what they are doing," he said, "but I won't be taking my retinue."

'What about me?' I asked anxiously.

"Where would I leave you?" he asked in his usual teasing voice which I hadn't heard for a long time. "Come, let's go." It was only then that I realised that he was going to perform another of his miracles of appearing in different places at the same time which is what he did during the wedding ceremonies with so many princesses. This way he didn't have to offer any explanations to anybody since as far as everyone in Dwaraka was concerned, he was still there.

As usual he took me through the 4th dimension and we looked down at the sorry sight of the five of them looking very gloomy since they didn't have the jovial Arjuna to keep up their spirits with his usual jokes and antics.

'You know, I feel that Yudhishtira is actually coming to love this exile. He is more fitted to be a recluse than a king,' I said.

"No doubt you are right," said my Lord, "but his *karma* has made him a king and he will have to follow the *dharma* of a king if he wants salvation."

'Can we never change our *karma*?' I asked.

"Of course, it is possible to do that to a certain extent but not totally. The environment and order in which you are born are the best suited for you to get out of the trammels of your *prarabdha karma*. Therefore progress on the evolutionary scale is faster if you accept the situation and do your *swadharma* within the confines of the circumstances in which you have been placed."

'What is *prarabdha karma*?'

"Your *prarabdha* is what you have acquired from a previous life or lives, and that is what has propelled you to be born in a certain family and placed you in the situation in which you find yourself now. That can never be changed. You have no control over that. But the future is still in your hands to a certain extent. Yudhishtira has been born a king. For him to refuse to accept his responsibility would be wrong on his part, even though he may dislike the role he has been called upon to play. For example, Lord Rama was also a little like Yudhishtira. He was a peace-loving man and he loved the interlude in the forest like the Eldest. But that did not stop him from doing his duty as a king and protecting the rights of his citizens. By following one's own *swadharma*, even though it may not be quite to his liking, the human being can attain the highest."

'Yudhishtira is a natural contemplative. He would be happier in the forest. Can't he live on in an *ashrama* and ask his brothers to go and fight and get their kingdom if they want to?'

My Vanamali turned me around and looked into my eyes. "Do you really think that is his *dharma*?" he asked. Of course I hung my head in shame.

"Look at him now. He has to combat with the two people he loves most in the world – his wife and Bhima."

'Do you think he loves Bhima most?' I asked.

"Well let's say that he has a decided partiality for him though of course he loves all of them. But it is a strange fact that patient people always have a fascination for the angry and impatient. Just look at them bickering. Bhima is very much of the earth and Draupadi is the daughter of Fire. Bhima's anger is growing not only because he doesn't get enough to eat, but because he has sworn to drink only what he can get by dashing his mace in water and drinking what splashes up! He spends sleepless nights thinking of the time when he can break Duryodhana's thighs and drink Dusshasana's blood!"

Draupadi was always happier when Arjuna was around and now that he was not there to comfort her, she lost no opportunity to taunt Yudhishtira. "I know that anger is not good, but for a Kshatriya continued patience is also not good. There should be a happy blending of the two. What has all this patience and adherence to *dharma* brought you? Only poverty, humiliation and exile!"

Yudhishtira said, "Anger blinds one to truth and kills the soul. I cannot go back on my word."

In sheer exasperation Panchali retorted, "Your love for *dharma* is greater than your love for any of us. Sometimes I find your patience maddening!"

"Patience does not choose everyone. I must prove worthy of her choice," said her husband. "I have given my word to remain in exile for twelve years. Till then you must listen to my words. No one and nothing can make me swerve from *dharma*!"

I noticed that Nakula and Sahadeva hardly ever took part in these arguments even though they did not possess the infinite patience of their eldest brother. Sahadeva actually seemed to be more interested in the stars. He would lie on the ground and watch the passage of the stars and planets for hours. No wonder he is an excellent astrologer, I thought.

"I will send someone to them who will be of great help to them," said my Lord. As he said this I saw an enormous figure going towards them.

'Who is he?' I asked.

"He is Ghatotkacha, Bhima's son by the *rakshasi* called Hidimbi. You remember I told you that story." I nodded my head. Though he looked so huge and ferocious, I thought his face had a peaceful look like that of a child. The Pandavas and Panchali were delighted to see him and made much of him. Apparently he lived with them for five years while they were in that forest.

"Now look who is coming," said my Lord. "That is the sage Brihadwasa who is an expert in the art of dice playing known as Akshatridya. He will teach Yudhishtira all the ramifications of the game so that he will never become a prey to avid dice players again."

'Did you instigate him to go there?' I asked. My Lord gave me a knowing smile.

"Even if I can't thwart their *karma*, I can at least help them in small ways. This art is going to be of help to him in the thirteenth year. See who is coming to them now."

It was the great sage Narada whom I recognised since I had seen him in Dwaraka. He saw how despondent all of them were looking and suggested that they make a pilgrimage around the holy land of Aryavrata. He gave them detailed accounts of all the holy places and descriptions of the various benefits to be got from going to such places. Having said this he left them, for he never stayed more than a couple of hours at any place.

'How will they find their way to all these places where they have never gone?' I asked.

"I will send someone else who will guide them personally. That is sage Lomasa who is also urging them to go for a pilgrimage over the whole of Aryavrata. They are going to the forest called Vishakhayyupa to the north of Kamyaka where they will stay for a year. See, it is on the banks of the Yamuna River which runs through the village of Gokula where I spent my childhood. She is one of my favourite rivers."

'I thought you didn't have favourites.'

"Sometimes I do!" he said with a wink. I hoped that this meant that I was a favourite.

After staying there for a year, the five of them set out to the great pilgrim centres of the country like Prayaga, Pratisthana, Brahmasaras and many others, following the route of the great rivers.

'When will Arjuna return?' I asked

"In another four years. One human year is only one day for the gods, so by the time Arjuna returns, five years would have passed and the Pandavas would be entering their twelfth year of exile."

'What will they do now?' I asked.

My Lord replied, "They will go on this pilgrimage round the holy land and end with the Himalayas where they will meet Arjuna."

I was really curious to know about time and questioned him. 'How can one day of the gods be equal to one human year? Do you mean to say that Arjuna stayed only for five days in heaven?'

My Lord replied, "Time is actually a mental concept but even so we are bound by it. The human mind can only function within the three points known as *desha*, *kaala* and *nimitta* (space, time and causation). When we are children time seems to exist forever. The older we grow the faster time goes. As our consciousness evolves, we automatically seem to know that time is not real. In the case of the gods, time goes even faster since their consciousness is more enlarged. So to them our one day is only a tiny fragment of their day. Their day and night is the equivalent of our one year. Their daytime is what we call Uttarayanam and it lasts for six months according to our human calculations, from January 14th to July 14th when the sun appears to be moving towards the north. This is spring and summer in the northern hemisphere where we are living. Their night is what we call Dakshinayanam when the sun appears to be moving south for six months, from July 14th to January 14th and we experience autumn and winter. So you see that time is cyclical. One Uttarayanam is succeeded by Dakshinayanam and so on. Even a day is cyclical since it's based on the sun's rotation. So there is nothing called the end of time. Even when this universe is finally destroyed, it only portends a period of *laya* when everything seems to be suspended, but this is only the prelude to another creation. So this world is subject to endless cycles of creation, suspension and destruction. As you know the three gods Brahma, Vishnu and Maheswara (Shiva) are in charge of these three."

'How long does one creation exist?'

"It exists for the lifetime of one Brahma. His one day is one thousand Mahayugas." Before I could question he continued. "A Mahayugas consists of four *yugas*. These are called, Satya Yuga, the golden age, Treta Yuga, the silver age, Dwapara Yuga, the copper age and finally Kali Yuga, the Iron Age. We are now at the end of the Dwapara Yuga. We can expect Kali Yuga to start if and when the Pandavas and Kauravas go to war."

'It sounds like an awful lot of time to live.'

My Lord laughed. "The whole of this life which we are living in now happens to be the first day of the fifty-first year of the present Brahma. And it is said that he is already unhappy and fearful of death since it's the beginning of his fifty-first year! So you see my child that everyone is fearful of death."

'Even Brahma?'

"Of course."

'How can we get rid of this fear of something like time which is only a concept?'

"Where does fear reside?"

I thought for a while and replied, 'I think in the mind.'

"You are absolutely right. So it is the mind which is fearful of the passage of something called time which in reality does not exist except in the mind. Isn't there a strange inconsistency about this?"

'Of course! But how do we get rid of this strange fear which is baseless?'

"My child, this fear can only be got rid of when you catch hold of THAT which is changeless and timeless."

'Who or what is THAT?'

"That Brahman alone is the changeless, eternal, ever-present uninvolved witness to all things. That alone is free from fear and we will become fearless only when we experience THAT!"

'Why is our mind conditioned to believe in time and have this fear?'

"This is because it is always living in illusion. For instance we think the sun rises and sets. But actually it neither rises nor sets. When we think it is setting it is only because of the rotation of the earth which makes it appear as if it is sinking into the horizon. When the earth completes its rotation, it appears as if it is coming up from the eastern horizon and heralds the beginning of a new day. This happens every day and yet the mind refuses to believe this fact and continues to delude itself that the sun sets and rises. So the whole of this physical world is composed of such illusions which make us believe in a reality which actually does not exist. But even this illusion has to rest on something, and that is called the Brahman on which everything rests and which is above all the illusions of our mind. Unless we can experience THAT we can never know peace."

'How can we know THAT?' I asked.

"You can never know it, you can only experience It!"

'Well how can we experience That?' I queried.

"What time are you living in now?" he asked with his usual tantalising smile.

Again I thought for a while and came to the conclusion that I knew nothing. 'I don't know.'

"Think again and tell me, why are you not aware of the passage of time?"

I thought again and came up with the brilliant answer. 'I don't know because I am living in you.'

"How fortunate you are that without your knowledge and without undergoing any special *sadhana* (spiritual practice), you have come to that timeless state where there is no fear and no time. How is that possible? Think for yourself and come to a conclusion."

I had no difficulty with this one. 'My Lord! You are that immortal, eternal Brahman who has taken on a human form to help deluded creatures like me. They who have become one with you will never know the meaning of fear and never be bewildered by the concept called Time! I am experiencing you, living in and through you, without really knowing you!' I fell at his lotus feet and stayed there till he lifted me up and wiped the tears of joy which were rolling down my cheeks.

'What have I done to deserve this bliss?' I thought to myself.

Of course he knew my thoughts and spoke, "You have been my devotee for many, many lives. You have loved me and remained faithful to me despite all the lures of a world filled with so-called enjoyments. As I told you before, this is the easiest of all paths - loving me with the clear understanding that I am that non-dual Brahman. Total surrender to me will get you to that fearless state. I will carry you like the mother cat, her kittens. They don't have to do anything except cry and they will be carried to a safe place. Have no fear my child, you are reposing in my arms even though you may not know it. Having once surrendered yourself to me, it is my duty to take you safely to the further shore."

I was speechless with joy and could do nothing except prostrate again and again to this amazing Being who had decided to bless me in this extraordinary fashion. 'This is why you are known as the *purnavatara*! You are indeed the supreme Brahman.'

'Can I ask you one more question?' He nodded.

'How ancient is our culture? When did it start?'

"Why do you think our culture is called the Sanatana Dharma? Sanatana means ancient. It has no beginning and hence no end. It has existed forever from the beginning of this epoch. It will degenerate and go into *laya* (dissolution) and then start again from the beginning as I told you. The concept of time in our culture goes back billions and trillions of years. We measure time from a *truti* which lasts only 1/ 1,000,000 of a second to *mahakalpas* which last for 311 trillion years. *The rishis* of our culture have fathomed the secrets of the universe by being in touch with that cosmic energy of the Brahman. They did not discover anything by themselves. They delved into the fathomless well of cosmic knowledge and thus their findings are indisputable. There will come a race of human beings in the future who will be able to understand their sayings. But even they will not be able to experience what they experienced unless they become THAT, as the *rishis* did. The *rishis* always lived in that Truth and hence they can never tell an untruth. Everything they say as a blessing or as a curse has to come to pass, as I told you before. "

'You have told me already that we get a new birth due to our desires. What is the mechanism of this?'

"As I told you, birth is only half the picture of life. The other half is death. So every construction is followed by destruction. After a cycle of universal dissolution, that Supreme Energy by the force of its own nature recreates another cosmos so that those *jivas* who are waiting for another birth can experience worlds which have shape and solidity. Very subtle atoms begin to combine, eventually generating a cosmic wind that blows heavier and heavier atoms together. Depending on the *karma* they have collected in a previous world system, the *jivas* spontaneously draw to themselves atoms that coalesce into a body which is appropriate for the fulfilment of their *vasanas* (desires). Does that satisfy you?"

'Yes, my Lord. I am satisfied for the moment. Now can we go and see what is happening to the Pandavas?'

"Why don't you want to find out what's happening to the Yadavas? Don't you think I have a duty to them?"

'My Lord! In their case I feel that everything is totally under your control, but in the case of the Pandavas you have to take into consideration their *karma* which is driving them to greater disasters.'

"You think I can't stop these disasters?"

'You can do anything my dearest Master but as you already told me you won't interfere.'

"Good! I'm glad you have understood this much. Let's go and see what's happening to them."

'Are we going with them?' I asked.

"No. But we will see them in a couple of years' time when their journey will bring them to the forest near Dwaraka. So let us go back and see to the affairs of the Yadavas."

The years passed in no time in the blissful company of my Lord and one day he said, "Come, let us call the others and go to the forest which the Pandavas have reached and where they are resting."

We called Satyaki, Uddhava and Kritavarma, Akrura and some of the other Yadavas and all of us went to the forest beyond Raivata and found the brothers sitting under a tree.

All of them were delighted to see Krishna and all their dear friends who were closer to them than their own cousins. "Since we are not supposed to enter a city, we were hoping that you would come here," said Yudhishtira. The Yadavas were appalled to see their condition. They were clothed in bark and grass and all of them, even Bhima seemed to be totally worn out. They could not bear to see them in this state. Satyaki could not control his anger and said, "Why should virtuous people like you suffer when the Kauravas who are steeped in *adharma* are growing sleek and fat? Let us go immediately and attack them. You may be under an oath but we are not. Come let us all march to Hastinapura and kill them immediately and we will install you on the throne."

Everyone looked at my Lord for support. Without saying anything he merely pointed at Yudhishtira and said, "If he agrees, we will go to Hastinapura!"

The Eldest bowed to him and to all the others and said, "I beg of you to understand. Our *dharma* has been decided. I have already made a pact with Duryodhana in front of all the Elders that we will spend twelve years in the forest. It would be *adharmic* to look for loopholes now. I have to follow my *dharma*!"

My Lord gave me a knowing look and said only to me. "See, if any *adharma* has to be committed it will have to be by me and not by them!" I was to remember this cryptic statement during the course of the war.

Satyaki was quiet. Nobody could argue against Yudhistira's infallible logic! They stayed in that forest for a month during which all of us visited them in turn. Subhadra and Abhimanyu also came with Draupadi's children. Yudhishtira and the others were thrilled to see how much their children had grown in five years and felt sorry that Arjuna was not there to see his two sons. Eventually they returned to the Kamyaka forest.

'Only nine years have passed. How will they spend the rest of the time?' I asked my Lord.

"They will go towards the Himalayas and visit many holy shrines, bathe in all the sacred rivers and converse with many pious Brahmanas and sages, all of whom will bless them. Indifferent to heat and cold they will wander in sunshine and rain and snow. Sometimes they will have to face storms and tempests and walk on stones and thorns. Very often Bhima will have to carry Panchali in his arms. In fact he will have to carry his brothers also sometimes on his back since they will also become totally exhausted. Yudhishtira alone will maintain his equilibrium under all circumstances for he is a true *sthitha prajna* (man of steady intellect). They will also pass through beautiful forests filled with flowers and fruit and have some happy times. However, now we have to return to Dwaraka since I'm expecting an important visitor. Come let's go."

Aum Namo Bhagavate Vaasudevaaya

The Stitha prajna (man of steady wisdom) is not bound by selfish attachments,
He neither rejoices in good fortune nor shuns the bad.

Srimad Bhagavat Gita, Chapter 2. Verse 57.

ॐ

Nandasrivrijananadine Namaha!

CHAPTER NINETEEN

Dwaravati

One day my Lord was relaxing on the swing bed in Rukmini's palace. Suddenly he got up and seemed unable to concentrate on anything. I was surprised at this unusual behaviour. He kept going to the balcony and watching the road. At last timidly Rukmini ventured to ask him what the matter was. "I'm expecting a very dear friend," he replied. "Prepare the best room and your very best dishes for him, for he is very dear to me."

All of us watched for the arrival of a fancy chariot or coach, but nothing appeared till evening. Suddenly my Lord jumped out of the swing bed and rushed to the palace gates. Rukmini followed in haste carrying all the auspicious articles she had kept ready to welcome the royal guest. When we reached the gate, Rukmini and I were surprised to see my Lord clasping to his chest an emaciated and wizened morsel of humanity, a mere bundle of skin and bone held together by a few rags. However at a sign from her Lord, Rukmini hurried forward to wash his feet with water perfumed with sandal and offered him *arghya* and other auspicious articles.

Anxiously Krishna asked him, "Did you have any difficulty in passing through the gates?"

The old man shook his head and said, "There were some other Brahmanas along with me, so we were allowed to pass through the three camps of the guards and three walls with gates, and then we reached the mansions occupied by the Vrishni chieftains and at last arrived at the centre of the city to your blessed abode as well as the palaces of all your consorts. It is only through your grace that I have reached you."

My Lord practically carried the man upstairs to Rukmini's audience chamber and seated him on his own favourite swing bed. He sat himself beside the old man and flung his arm round his scraggy neck. Rukmini proceeded to fan them both with the royal yak tail fan. The poor man seemed to shrink into himself and didn't know what to say. But he seemed very happy to cling on to my Lord's arm. In fact he seemed to be in a state of delirious happiness and tears rolled down his cheeks. I whispered to my Vanamali, 'Who is this?'

It was only when he heard my question that he seemed to realise that nobody knew who this was. "This is Sudama who studied with me at Sandipany's *gurukula*. His father was a Brahmana called Matuka and his mother was called Rochana Devi. He was my best friend at the *gurukula*. When we parted we promised to keep in touch with each other, but I'm afraid I was so caught up with the affairs of state that I never found time to visit him and enquire about his welfare."

Turning to Sudama, my Lord enquired solicitously, "How have you been, my dear friend? It looks as if life has not treated you very well. You look tired and old and thin. My dearest friend why didn't you come and tell me about your bad times? I would certainly have helped you." Sudama didn't say a word but simply pressed his skinny frame closer to my Lord's side, much to my disgust and perhaps Rukmini's!

The Lord continued. "Do you remember the day when we went to the forest to collect firewood at the request of the *guru's* wife? There was an unexpected storm and the whole ground was flooded and we could not trace our way back to the *gurukula*. Night had fallen and we decided to spend the night sitting on a tree. We had nothing to eat except a small bundle of rice flakes which the *guru's* wife had thoughtfully given us. The next morning our *guru*, sage Sandipany came with his disciples to search for us. When he found us he blessed us, 'My dear boys you have carried out the commands of your *guru* disregarding your own safety. This is indeed most creditable. May all your desires and ambitions be fulfilled. May the understanding of what you have learnt in the *gurukula* remain in your memory always. May you never have any disappointments in this life or the next.' It is only by the grace of the *guru* that a person can attain the summum bonum of life. We are indeed fortunate that we got the blessings of our *guru*. He from whom we are born into this world is our first *guru*. He who invests the sacred thread and teaches us the Vedas is the next *guru*, but he who imparts the wisdom of the Supreme is the greatest of all *gurus*. So many such incidents flash across my mind about the wonderful time we had at the *gurukula*. So much time has flown by since then. I am sure you have married and have children. Tell me everything that happened to you after we parted. Is there anything I can do for you?"

Sudama looked up adoringly at my Lord and said, "You are the teacher of the whole world. What more fulfilment can I have in life than to have spent some magic moments with you in the *gurukula*? How can I ever forget those days? I have spent the rest of my life in the blissful contemplation of those days. I need nothing more."

I noticed that the Brahmana appeared to have something tucked under his armpit which he was loathe to show and which he hugged to his side all the time he was speaking and even when he nestled close to my Lord. Of course this was not unnoticed by my Lord. He knew everything and at last he asked him playfully, "My dearest friend! What gift have you brought for me? I'm sure your dear wife would not have allowed you to come empty handed!"

The Brahmana shook his head and pressed his arm even closer to the side of his body. I inferred from this that he was overwhelmed by the greatness of my Lord and ashamed to offer him whatever it was that he had brought!

My Lord who always liked to tease his devotees now asked, "My dear friend! Even a trifle, be it a fruit or flower or leaf, offered to me with love is more precious to me than anything great which might be offered without love." With these words he looked pointedly at Sudama's armpit out of which a small piece of cloth was sticking out. Despite these obvious hints the bashful Brahmin looked down and did not present his bundle.

At last tired of teasing, my Lord stretched forward and pulled out the miserable bundle from his armpit. "Ah! What is this?" He asked teasingly with a twinkle in his eyes. "O you sly one! I see you were keeping this as a surprise for me!"

With these words my Lord eagerly untied the rag and looked at the contents. "How clever of you to guess what I would like most! Do you remember the rice flakes our *guru's* wife used to make for us? I have never eaten such delicious stuff since then!" He gave a side-glance at Rukmini and said, "These royal princesses are not used to making such stuff!" Poor Rukmini looked a bit abashed. Perhaps she had never known his passion for this common fare!!

He was just going to eat it when Sudama stopped him and said, "My Lord, this is not worthy enough for you to eat. I had nothing in my house which could be brought for you, so my wife went to some other house and got a handful of unhusked rice and she pounded it herself and gave it to me to present to you. Actually I knew it was not a worthy gift for you, but I took it to please her and also because I thought this was a good excuse to come and see you. Please don't eat it. It is full of stones and husk and is not fit for you to eat. Please forgive me for bringing this poor gift, but the fact is that I am too poor to bring you anything at all." The Brahmana said all this with great difficulty but my Lord hardly listened to him. It appeared as if he was in a great hurry to eat it. He took a fistful and stuffed it into his mouth and chewed it with evident relish.

He was just about to stuff another fistful into his mouth when Rukmini caught his hand and said, "Lord! Be not so hasty. Are you trying to give me away as well?" What did she mean by that? I wondered.

He looked at me and answered, “This rice is potent stuff, charged with the entire love of Sudama’s heart as well as that of his wife. The moment I ate a few grains he became eligible to all the goods of the world. Now Rukmini is afraid that if I accept a few more, she herself may have to go and become the handmaid of his wife!! So perhaps I should not take any more. I certainly don’t want her to go!” He laughed and pinched my cheek.

I wondered how it was that people who offered so much gold and money at temples seldom got what they asked for. Of course he knew what was passing through my mind and said, “Most people do not offer gifts to me. They offer bribes. Theirs is the market place of barter love. I give you something and in return you have to give me something. How little they know me. I am the creator of the whole universe. There is nothing I lack. What is it that they can give me which I don’t already possess? The only thing they can give me is their love, and if they offer anything which is drenched in that love, of course I will accept and bless them. But people like Sudama do not ask for any return. They are not traders and bargainers. They give without expectation of reward and hence they will be showered with all the world’s goods. They will not examine my gifts with a shrewd and calculating mind. They will accept whatever I give with joy. Look at Sudama. His wife has sent him here to request that I give them something since she knows that I am his friend and can help them. The only reason she asked him to go is because she can no longer bear to see her children dying of starvation. Yet did you notice how reluctant he was to give the bundle flakes to me since he did not think it to be a fitting gift for me? And now take notice, he will leave without asking for anything! This is the nature of the true devotee. But don’t be afraid, I shall bless him with everything both material and spiritual.”

The Brahmana spent a blissful evening and night with my Vanamali. I don’t think he even remembered the reason for his visit or the pitiable condition of his wife and children. My Lord kept prompting him many times to test him. "My friend! Is there anything you want? You have only to ask and I shall give you whatever you want. Even if you don't need anything I'm sure your wife and children will have some requirements. Please don't feel shy to ask. You know I'm your friend and will give you anything you ask for."

Sudama shook his head. He was replete. How could he want anything more?

"My Lord!" he said, "You have blessed me with everything. I'm like a vessel which has been filled to the brim! What more can I want?"

The next day after taking his meals, the Lord allowed him to return home. Sudama I think was hoping that he might ask him to stay another day, but my Lord made no such request and wished him a good journey and told him to come and visit him frequently.

I felt a bit sorry for the old man as he fell at my Lord's feet and hugged him again and again. Why didn't he ask for anything, I wondered. My Lord personally escorted him to the gate and bid him a fond farewell. When he returned Rukmini immediately questioned him about this. "My Lord, why didn't you give him anything?"

"Didn't you stop me from eating any more of those delicious flakes of rice? Why did you do that?" he asked her with a raised eyebrow.

"I know you must have given him something. I just wanted to know what you gave him."

"Well if you must know I will tell you. As soon as he left the palace, Sudama realised that I had given him nothing. He had not hoped for anything, but what was he to say to his wife who was waiting expectantly for his return? He knew how anxious she was about the fate of their children. The family had not lit a fire in the hearth for over a week. They had come to the end of their tether and that was when she decided to ask her husband to come and see me. At this moment he has just reached his village and is searching anxiously for his hovel. Listen to me my dear Rukmini. He will never find that hovel. In its place he is seeing a wonderful mansion surrounded with gardens and ponds. He does not know what to do. He thinks that he must be a bit delirious with the joy of having met me and has forgotten the way to his own house. While he is hesitating he sees a vision in silks and gold approaching him. He fears that she must be the lady of the manor who has come to reproach him for hanging around there and is just about to turn away when she greets him.

"Ah husband!" she says, "I see that you have approached the Lord and received his blessings. Don't be afraid. This is your house and I am your wife! These are your children who are looking so charming and so well-dressed."

"What was Sudama's reaction?" asked Rukmini.

"Sudama is looking totally confused but gently she is leading him to the house. She makes him take a bath and dress himself in the costly garments she has laid out for him."

'What effect does all this have on Sudama?' I ask him silently.

He answered me directly, "I know what is going on in my dear friend's mind. He is greatly disturbed by all this wealth and is praying to me. 'The fact that you have showered me with so much wealth is a great trial to me. All I want is to be blessed with undying devotion and servitude to you, life after life. This is my only prayer.'

"Then what did he do?" asked Rukmini.

My Lord answered, "He is a true *bhakta.* He prayed that this change in his material status would not affect his spiritual life. He wanted to renounce all this and take to the forest, but when he saw his wife's joy and his children's delight, he decided that he should sacrifice his own desires for their sake. 'I did not mind it when you gave me only tatters to clothe myself. Why should I mind it now that you give me silks?' So thinking, that noble soul continued to live in that mansion as unaffected by his affluence as he had been by his poverty!"

We left Rukmini to her own devises and returned to our own mansion where I could question him with more freedom.

'You must have known of his straitened circumstances. Why didn't you help him before?'

"I have told you many times that God will not interfere in a person's life unless called upon to do so. He has never asked me for aid so far. He did not ask me now either, but his wife has asked me and it is for her sake that I gave them everything. Listen my child; God has kept certain eternal laws by which the world has to be ruled. This is known as the Law of Karma. It is a very simple law which is only a reflection of the law of nature that decrees that every action must have its equal and opposite reaction."

Newton's 3rd law of motion, I muttered to myself as the thought flashed through my mind.

"Exactly so," he said with a smile. "When we apply this law to our actions, we see that every act of ours is a cause which has to produce some sort of effect in the future which may come today, tomorrow or a hundred years later. This effect has to be experienced by us and only by us. The effect cannot be passed on to anyone else. So now we see that all of us do hundreds and thousands of actions which are actually causes, which will definitely produce effects which have to be experienced by us and not by anyone else. So whatever we are experiencing now is only the effect of our acts at some past time. This past may be the immediate past or even a past life. For God to interfere in the perfect running of this natural law would be totally unacceptable. The person who committed the act will have to enjoy its benefits if it was a good act, or be punished if it was a bad act. How can I interfere in this?"

'You mean Sudama was poor because of some bad action of his in a previous life?'

"Of course! Why do you doubt it? Do you think that I would have deliberately cast my dear friend to a life of utter poverty if I could have helped it?"

'You mean all of us are now either enjoying the benefits or being punished for the acts of a previous birth if not of this birth?'

"Most definitely! God is never unkind. He never deliberately gives one person a life of affluence or thrusts another into a hell of misery. How can you ever believe that? Every human being enjoys or suffers the consequences of his or her past deeds. You have no one to blame but yourself for the state of your life. The remedy is entirely in your hands. You can change your life by changing your attitude. If all your acts are aimed at producing the best for others, then only the best will come to you. If you hate the world, the world will give you back hatred in return. If you love the world you will get love from it."

'How is it that the Pandavas who are such good people got such a bad fate?'

"I have just answered your question. How is it that this Brahmana who appears to be a very good person had to suffer such privation? The same is the case with the Pandavas."

'You mean their sufferings are due to some past actions of theirs!'

"Indeed yes. Their enjoyments in Indraprastha were also due to their good deeds in the past and after the thirteen years are over, once again they will enjoy the benefits of their noble acts."

'Is this the reason for reincarnation?'

"Exactly! Very often our life is not long enough to enjoy the benefits of our good actions or be punished for our wrong doings. Nature cannot tolerate anything which is half-finished. Every cause has to have an effect and if we do not live to enjoy these effects in this life, we will have to take another life in order to enjoy or be punished. This is known as the wheel of *karma*."

'Does this mean that this wheel keeps on revolving for eternity? Is there no way by which we can get off this wheel?'

"Ah! Now you are getting to the crux of the matter. As long as you enjoy going round and round you can keep going for eternity if necessary. If anyone wants to get off he can do so, the ability is in her own hands."

'How is this possible?'

"It is the desire for the fruits of the action that keep you bound to the wheel. Nature will see to it that every desire of the human being is eventually fulfilled. When you perform an action and desire that the fruits should come only to you, obviously you have to live to get those fruits and if you don't live long enough to get those fruits in this life, you have to take another life. Is that clear?"

I nodded. "So you see that it is the selfish desire for the fruits that keep you bound to the wheel. If you cut off the desire, what is left is only the action which you have to perform in any case. Nature abhors a vacuum. It will not allow anyone to remain inactive even for a moment. Even if you are inactive physically, you are still very active mentally and in the human being it is the mental action which binds and not the physical. God gives you only one right and that is the right to perform your action – the right to do your *dharma*. He has not given you the right to demand your wages. Nobody realises this simple fact. Yudhishtira realises this and that is why he said, 'I'm not a tradesman. I do not barter my *dharma* for the sake of anything else. I do my duty regardless of whether I get anything out of it or not.' This is the correct attitude for the evolved soul. God and nature will assist him in every possible way to perform his *dharma* if he has this attitude. Such a person is not worried about the consequences. Results will always follow an action. We do not have to bother about it. Our duty is only to perform our work to the best of our ability. Whether we achieve perfection or not is not our concern. God only looks at the sincerity with which the action is performed and not whether it is done perfectly. An action done with full sincerity is perfect in the eyes of God. A child makes a castle out of sand. He does his best to see that it is as beautiful as he can make it. After it is made he goes off to play some other game. It is not his concern that the sea comes and washes the castle away! However the human being is constantly obsessed with the results of his action. Will they be what he has hoped for? Will they be beneficial to him? Will it bring him profit? All these worries keep revolving in his mind until he gets the results and if these results are what he hoped for, he is happy, if they are not what he wanted he is depressed. If he dies before the fruition of his desires, he has to take another birth. This is what is known as the *samsara chakra* (wheel of life)."

'My Lord! It is not that easy to cut ourselves off from the desire for some sort of results from our actions.'

"OK! Then let me tell you a method by which you can get out of this wheel. I have noticed that you always like to give me something. Every day you make a little garland and bring it to me. Every day you pluck some *tulsi* leaves and lay them at my feet. Obviously you like to bring small gifts to me."

'Of course I do. I would like to give you something all the time, not just in the mornings.'

"Now I will let you into a great secret. Every day, all the time you are doing something or other, if not with your hands and feet, then certainly with your mind. You are constantly thinking and planning and plotting. Don't you have a certain expectation of results or rewards from all these activities?" I nodded.

"The secret of cutting off from the wheel is to get into the habit of presenting me with the results of all these thousands of activities. Let me deal with the results. Let me be the judge of what you should receive for everything you do. Let me decide your wages!"

'My Lord! Aren't you the one who decides this in any case?'

"Ah! Now you have discovered for yourself the secret of action. As I told you in the beginning, God gives you the right to act but actually you have no control over the results. Human beings think they can control the results but this is wishful thinking. Sometimes it appears that the results you get are the ones you were hoping for and that makes you believe that you are the sole agent of the action with the right to control the results. This is a mistake. You cannot control the results since those are controlled by a different law. In fact they are controlled by a cosmic law. God alone is the dispenser of all rewards and punishments. Your duty is only to act in the best possible fashion. God does not expect anything else from you. Act according to your *dharma* and leave everything in his compassionate hands. Then you can lead a peaceful and happy life free from all worries. Present the results to him in a nice packet and live without fear or regrets. Have you understood my dear? Now do you know how to get off the wheel of Karma?"

'Suppose I act hoping only for good results for everyone and not just for myself, is that also wrong?'

"I have just told you not to hope for anything either good or bad. Just act. That is all. If you hope for good results for everyone, that will also be a bond since you have to live to see the effects of that action on others and get pleasure from it. So this is also a bond which will tie you to the wheel. A flower blooms for the sake of others. So become a flower."

'How can I act without thinking of any results?'

"All right that is why I'm telling you, perform your action and give over the results to me, your Lord and God. I will take care of them and see to it that you get your just results. What more do you want?"

I looked at him with tears in my eyes. 'Here I am with you and I'm hoping that this moment will go on forever. Is that wrong?'

"My child! Surrender even that thought to me. Surrender everything to me as you are doing now. You sit when I sit, you stand when I stand, you eat when I eat, and you sleep when I sleep. You are only a body which is being driven by me, your inner self. I am the charioteer in the chariot of your body. Realise this and let yourself be controlled entirely by me. As long as you demand free will, I will give it to you but you must be prepared to take the consequences of a fall or a success or a victory or a defeat, with equilibrium. The safer path is to give me full control over your life, allow me to lead you as I think fit, and allow me to take you over hard and easy times according to my will. Let your will to be totally submerged in mine and then you will be completely safe. This is safest and easiest and the most evolutionary path. In this there is no fear of fall since I will be there to catch you if you fall. Have you understood what I'm trying to say? You are indeed dear to me or else you would not be here with me at this moment."

I just fell at his feet and the hot tears came pouring out and washed his lotus feet and I kissed them again and again and said, 'My Lord! My Master! I understand, though imperfectly since my capacity is poor. I do not ask to understand but only to obey. Help me to act as you have just pointed out to me. Help me to obey implicitly without questioning.'

He helped me to my feet and wiped my tears with the edge of his upper cloth and said, "Come, let's go and see what Draupadi's children are up to."

'I would like to see what Draupadi and the Pandavas are up to.'

"All right I will show you but I will not make my presence felt."

Aum Namo Bhagavate Vaasudevaaya

When Brahma created the world, he created it with the spirit of sacrifice instilled into everything.
He told all creatures, 'Each one of you has your own prescribed duty to perform. This performance will become your wish-fulfilling tree and will never forsake you. By doing your own duty you nourish the gods and in turn they will nourish you. Thus by nourishing each other in this way, the whole of creation will prosper. The one who goes against this natural law of creation will have to suffer.

Srimad Bhagavat Gita. Chapter 3.

ॐ

Satchitanandavigrahaaya Namaha!

CHAPTER TWENTY

The Himalayas

"Come, we will go with them to the Himalayas, your favourite place on earth!"

'My favourite place is at your feet, my Lord!'

"Look, Sage Lomasa and the other sages are accompanying the Pandavas to the Himalayas. For some reason Panchali is very anxious to visit the mountain called Gandhamadana and they are proceeding there. They have to go through extremely treacherous terrain, clutching at creepers and trunks of trees as they climb up."

I clutched my Vanamali's arm as a huge tempest came up out of nowhere. It became pitch dark. Trees were uprooted and rain fell in torrents so that the path which the Pandavas were walking became a river. A howling, rattling wind blew volleys of stones at them, dry leaves whirled and dust covered the sky. Sahadeva clutched the clay jar that held their fire and ran into a cave with Yudhishtira and Dhoumya. Lomasa, Nakula and the Brahmanas hid behind rocks and anthills. Bhima carried Draupadi and ran under an overhanging rock and shielded her with his body as the cold, biting rain lashed at them. A foaming river filled with trees and rocks whirled under their feet. After the tempest had passed all of them crept out of their shelters, but the incident was too much for the delicate princess of Panchala and she swooned in Bhima's arms. He laid her on a large leaf and started to fan her while the twins rubbed her feet.

I think for once even Yudhistira's iron resolve was shaken and he broke down with tears in his eyes. "The King of Panchala hoped that his daughter born out of fire and brought up in palaces would always have a happy life. Alas! I am the sole cause of all her miseries."

Turning to Bhima, he said, "It is obvious that she is in no condition to walk. What shall we do?"

Bhima immediately thought of Ghatotkacha who suddenly manifested himself out of the clouds, looming above everybody. "My son! Your mother is too weak to walk so you will have to carry her. I have also become very weak or else I would have carried her."

"Father, you have only to order me," said the giant. "I will carry all of you and my friends will carry the Brahmanas."

The *rishi* Lomasa said that he had the *yogic* power to travel in the air and would meet them at Badarikashrama, the ancient land blessed by Lord Narayana. The air was like ambrosia and waterfalls and cascades jumped down the rocks to the Ganga below. The Himalayan peaks soared above, glinting gold and silver in the setting sun.

I loved this place where I had spent such a glorious time with my Lord. I wished I could bathe with them in the Alagananda and the Bindusaras. 'I wish we were there in our bodies,' I whispered to my Lord.

"You were never there in your body. You are only an idea in my mind," he smiled.

'I wish I could ever be an idea in your mind,' I said.

"You will always be," he whispered.

'Look, there is Bhima going for a stroll with Panchali. Let's go with them. Do you think Bhima loves her more than the other brothers?'

"It is difficult to judge," said my Lord. "No doubt he is the one who is always alert to her needs, but I think Yudhishtira also loves her deeply even though he is incapable of showing it."

We were following the couple when suddenly Draupadi saw a beautiful flower floating towards them. The whole air was suddenly perfumed. It fell at her feet and she picked it up and said, "I think this is the famed Saugandika flower about which I have heard. I would love to get a few more and perhaps the seeds so that we can grow a tree in our own garden, (when we have one)," she said, under her breath.

Of course Bhima could refuse her nothing. He immediately brought her back to the makeshift camp where they were staying and took his brother's permission and set off armed with his mace and sword to find the flowers.

'Can we follow Bhima? I love flowers,' I looked appealingly at my Lord.

"Of course," he said.

Bhima had to traverse across some terrible territory but he was not deterred. No doubt his love for Panchali gave wings to his feet! He passed forests, lakes and mountains with the silver peak of Mount Kailas looming ever nearer. At last he reached a garden with huge plantain trees from which were hanging bunches of ripe, yellow fruit. He plucked a huge bunch and polished it off. He must be really hungry, I thought, since he hadn't eaten anything for some days. After finishing the repast, he prepared to go forward but found his path blocked by a huge, ancient monkey. It had copper-coloured fur and very broad shoulders and a short, thick neck. His small ears were red and he lay with his eyes closed and head resting on his arms. Bhima gave a lion's roar hoping to scare off the monkey, but the animal did not stir. He gave another roar and this time the monkey raised his hanging eyelids with his gnarled claws and said, "Why do you disturb me? You are a Kshatriya who should show kindness to all animals. Why have you come here? No mortal can pass beyond this point. However, if you insist on going, you can jump over me since I really can't shift myself to another place."

Bhima said, "It is wrong to jump over any creature since the same *atman* is in everyone, so kindly remove yourself since I have promised to get some flowers for my wife."

"If that is the case, you can simply shift my tail with your mace and continue with your mission."

"Watch carefully," said my Lord. "This is going to be fun!"

Bhima obviously thought this would be a simple matter and he gave a light nudge to the monkey's tail. To his surprise it did not budge an inch. He then pushed the tip of his mighty mace under the tail and tried to lift it. It must have been really heavy because he fell back with the effort. He heaved the mace again but with the same effect. He fell back exhausted and asked, "Who are you that can thwart the strength of the son of the wind?"

"Only the son of the wind god can thwart the son of the wind," said the monkey.

Bhima looked up startled. "Are you Hanuman?" The monkey nodded.

"Then you are my brother!"

"You have guessed right, my little brother! I am indeed Hanuman. I was lying here in order to see you. However this is the land of the Yakshas. It is very dangerous for you to proceed in this direction. I advise you to return. The Yakshas may kill you!"

"I cannot return without getting the flowers for Draupadi," said Bhima.

"I see you are determined. However when you meet their king, Kubera, tell him you are under the protection of Krishna Vaasudeva and he will treat you kindly. Now tell me, what I can do for you?" asked Hanuman.

Bhima replied, "I think war is bound to take place between our cousins and us after we return. Perhaps you could help us to win the war."

"Indeed I will help you. I will sit on Arjuna's pennant and frighten everyone. He will be known as Kapidwaja! (one with a monkey on his flag)."

Bhima bowed to him and got his blessings and pushed on into the forbidden territory. From the height of the peak on which he was standing, he looked down on the lake filled with the flowers he had come to collect. The perfume was so intoxicating that he had to stand still for a few moments to get his breath. On the far side of the lake was a huge gate set with jewels which suddenly flashed as it was closed for the night. It was the gate to the palace of Kubera, Lord of wealth and king of the Yakshas. He could see the soaring towers and turrets of silver and gold. There were rows of flags waving in the wind on golden flag posts. Bhima went towards the lake and was stopped by hundreds of Yakshas who flew towards him altogether like a gust of wind and stopped him from advancing.

"You cannot go forward," they said.

"I only want some flowers from the lake," said Bhima.

"The lake belongs to our master, the god of wealth. Without his permission you cannot touch the flowers."

Bhima used his mace to good effect and scattered the Yakshas who flew off to Kubera and gave him the news. Kubera himself came in his aerial vehicle and asked Bhima who he was and why he wanted the flowers. Bhima said, "I'm Bhima, the second Pandava, son of the Wind God, brother of Hanuman whom I just met. We are protected by Krishna Vaasudeva."

When he heard this, a sudden change came over Kubera. He got out of his flying chariot and came to greet Bhima with open arms. "Why didn't you tell me who you were? Are you here with your brothers? You are all welcome to come and stay with me. I know all about the cruel way in which the Kauravas have treated you. As for Krishna Vaasudeva, I'm eternally grateful to him for releasing my two sons from a curse. I'm afraid my sons succumbed to the fate of all those who have too much wealth. They became intoxicated with the power that wealth brings and started to behave in a very haughty manner, thinking that their wealth would save them from everything. They totally forgot that it is only God who has that power. Sage Narada wanted to save them from their own folly and cursed them so that they became two huge trees in the compound of Krishna's father at Gokula. When he was a little boy, Krishna's mother tied him to a pounding mortar for having perpetrated some mischief. Baby Krishna dragged the heavy mortar and took it between the two huge trees. The mortar got stuck between the trees and forced them to come crashing down and thus released my two sons, Nalakubera and Manikooda. I can never forget that. I will do anything for those who are under his protection."

I looked questioningly at my Lord and he smiled and nodded.

Bhima was surprised at the sudden change in Kubera's attitude, but he was always a friendly soul so he said, "My Lord! I thank you for your kind invitation but we have come to this mountain to await the return of my brother and the others will be waiting for me, and Draupadi will also be waiting for me to bring her the flowers from your lake."

Kubera immediately ordered his men to get some flowers and they returned and poured a heap of flowers into Bhima's *uttareeyam*. Bhima was obviously overjoyed to get the flowers for his beloved Panchali. He returned with arms laden with sweet-smelling blossoms and poured them into Draupadi's lap, much to her delight.

According to my Lord, the Pandavas stayed in that holy place for a month. We left them for some time and returned to Dwaraka since my Lord had to check on certain things. Of course no one knew that he had left and life in Dwaraka continued in its usual fashion, but I noticed that more and more of the nobles seemed inclined to imbibe larger quantities of liquor. Even my Lord's sons were involved in this. Samba in particular seemed to be closely following in his uncle's footsteps. I wondered if Balarama was responsible for this. No doubt people thought that if their leaders could have it so freely, why not them? I did not dare to question my Lord about this but as usual he knew my heart and one day he said, "There is a limit to which we can give advice, even if it be to our own children or siblings. Everyone knows it is wrong to drink. It is not lack of knowledge which makes them continue with the bad habit, but due to a certain degree of helplessness. One has to discipline oneself from an early age. The emotions drag us to dangerous places like untrained horses. If we don't take the trouble to curb them at an early age they will become totally uncontrollable. I make it a point never to give advice unless I am asked for it. If someone asks you for advice, it means that they are in a receptive mood and that is the time that you can give it and it is possible that they will listen to you. Unwanted advice is always unacceptable and a waste of time."

My Vanamali always loved to tease Rukmini. She was so sweet and docile that he often tried to get a rise out of her. One day Narada as usual came on his rounds and after being given all honours, the Lord invited him for dinner. As they sat Narada asked, "How do you look upon all your wives?"

Of course Narada also loved a joke so Krishna answered, "Well I look on Satyabhama as this pickle which is tangy and spicy and exciting. Jambavati is this delicious sweet."

"And what about Rukmini?" asked the sage.

"Ah! Rukmini is this salt," replied my playful Lord.

Rukmini's face fell as he said this and she was silent for the rest of the meal. Next day all of us met for dinner and everyone started to complain about the food. "What's happened to this? There is no taste in anything!" said Vasudeva.

They immediately called the cook who told them that he had orders from the Lord himself that he should serve everything without salt!

"So salt is what makes everything tasty," said Narada with a beaming smile since Rukmini was always his favourite.

My Lord turned to look at his wife and Rukmini's forlorn look slowly changed to one of delight and she beamed back at him.

Some days had passed when he said, "Come, we will have another peep at the Pandavas." When we went to Badarikashrama we found the Pandavas in a state of acute anticipation, waiting for Arjuna's arrival. He was a general favourite and had been sorely missed by all. Dhoumya tried to cheer them by pointing to the Himalayan heights.

"This is Mount Meru around which the sun, moon and stars circle. This is the abode of Maheswara where he lives surrounded by sages and celestials. As he was speaking, all of them were struck to see Indra's chariot driven by his charioteer, Matali coming over the snow peaks. It landed softly on the meadow in front of them. Indra came out first followed by the Apsaras and Gandharvas. He came close to Yudhishtira and promised that one day he would reign in splendour. All of them bowed to the king of gods but they were expectantly looking beyond him. Arjuna now appeared shining with a golden aura and wearing a diadem. Yudhishtira threw his arms round him. Arjuna turned to Draupadi and poured heavenly ornaments into her lap. The aerial car disappeared in the flash of light produced by the jewels. He embraced all his brothers one by one.

They pelted him with questions and begged him to tell them in detail all that had happened to him in Indraloka (the world of Indra). They sat down under their usual tree and he started to narrate his adventures.

"After I received the Pasupatastra from my Lord Shiva, I was wondering what to do when suddenly ten grey horses pulling a silver chariot came through the clouds and settled down gently near me. Matali, the charioteer of Indra got out and invited me to go with him. We sped into the sky and soon we left the sun and moon behind, so that there was nothing to guide us in the darkness except the stars which hung like pendants in the sky. We passed through the gates of heaven and entered the capital. We sped through Nandavana which was the abode of the *apsaras* and the Gandharvas and reached the palace of Indra where he was seated on a throne with his queen, Indrani. He welcomed me and made me sit beside him and gave me a starry diadem. Then came the celestial dancers and musicians who could make any man giddy just by looking at them. After that I was allowed to retire to my bedroom. Imagine my surprise when there was a knock at the door and Urvasi, the most beautiful of all the *apsaras* came into my room and literally threw herself at me!"

He glanced in embarrassment at Draupadi as he said this and she asked, "And what did you do?" All the brothers looked embarrassed since they all knew of their brother's weakness for the opposite sex, but Arjuna continued without the slightest embarrassment.

"Despite the fact that I have never seen any woman who was so attractive and seductive, I have to admit that I felt no attraction towards her and told her that I could only see her as a mother and never a mistress!"

"Then what did she say?" asked Panchali with wide open eyes and lips.

Arjuna looked a bit embarrassed and said, "In the end when she realised that I would not succumb to her solicitations, she cursed me and said, 'Since you deny me your manhood, I curse you to become a eunuch.' With this curse she departed and I fell into a state of despair as you can imagine. The next day I reported the whole incident to Indra who comforted me and said, 'My son, this curse will prove a blessing for you. I will prevail upon her to mitigate it so that it will last for only one year and you can choose the time when you want to use it. Believe me you will be glad of it very soon.'

"Then I became the pupil of Chitrasena, king of the Gandharvas who was the dancing master of the court from whom I learnt all the fine arts like music and dancing and also the method of using the divine weapons I had been given by the gods. I had hoped to be able to come to you after this, but my father said that he had brought me to heaven mainly to annihilate the *asuras* called the Nivatakavachas and the Kalakeyas who could be killed only with the Pasupatastra. He sent me with Chitrasena and Matali and we fought with the *asuras* for a long time. At last in despair I prayed to Durga to help me and she whispered to me that I would be able to kill them using the Pasupatastra at a time when they would put their hands to their mouths. I didn't know how I could make them do this and used a *mantra* to make myself invisible. The *asuras* thought I had fled and they put their fingers to their mouths to whistle in derision and at that split moment I killed them with the Pasupatastra.

"My father was really pleased with me and gave me more weapons and blessed me and came with me in his chariot as you saw."

The brothers were overjoyed to hear this recital and Draupadi was delighted to hear of his rejection of the celestial nymph. Now it was Arjuna's turn to ask them what had happened to them while he was away and they each took turns to describe all their trials.

'It is really sweet to see them so happy altogether, isn't it?' I asked my Lord.

He nodded. He was also looking happy. 'Where will they go now?' I whispered.

"Watch and see," he said.

The Pandavas descended the mountain which they had grown to love, leaving behind the crags and the cascades, the *devataru* trees and the pines, the waterfalls and the animals. Yudhishtira was perhaps wondering if he would ever return to this perfect spot again. He left with many lingering looks back.

They made their way back to the forest of Kamyaka, but all of them were in a much more cheerful mood since Arjuna was back with them.

"They are now in their twelfth year," said my Lord, "and I'm afraid they will have to face a few more trials."

'What more trials do they have to face?'

"Wait and see. Even on their way back they will have some trials." he said.

Aum Namo Bhagavate Vaasudevaaya

ॐ

Navaneetha Nataaya Namaha!

CHAPTER TWENTY-ONE

Duryodhana

My Lord knew that I was loathe to leave the Himalayas so we followed the Pandavas and their entourage of *rishis* as they started on their long journey back to the forest of Kamyaka. One day Bhima went to the forest to hunt. He had hardly gone a few miles when he suddenly found himself in the grip of the largest python he had ever seen.

'Surely it must be child's play to Bhima to release himself from the grip of a python,' I said.

"Wait and see. This is no ordinary python."

Luckily for Bhima instead of squeezing him to death and swallowing him which is the normal procedure of a python when it catches its prey, the snake started to speak to him, much to his surprise.

"I will tell you my story before I eat you," said the snake. "My name is Nahusha and during the time when Indra, king of the gods was in hiding, the celestials asked me to rule the heavens. I agreed but as is usual with human beings, I became very haughty and started to order the gods about. Once I even ordered them to bring Indra's wife, Indrani to me since he was not there. They were very unhappy and consulted their Guru, Brihaspati. He told him to ask Indrani to request me to come in a palanquin carried by the *saptarishis*! She did so and I ordered the *rishis* to do my bidding and sat inside the palanquin. As you know the great sage

Agastya is small in stature and he could not keep up with the rest of them. Caught in the coils of rage, I shouted at him, and said, '*Sarpa*! *Sarpa*!' which means, 'Faster! Faster!' in Sanskrit. It also means "snake." In my arrogance I even gave him a kick. The sage did not stay to hear any more. He immediately cursed me to become a snake. I am that unfortunate king who was cursed by the sage Agastya. I thought I should give you the sorry tale of my life before eating you since I am forced to eat you to keep up my own life."

"Is there no reparation for this?" asked Bhima who did not relish the thought of turning into the snake's breakfast!

"I have been told that I will be freed from this curse when a Kshatriya can answer my questions."

'You are a Kshatriya. You can answer his question,' I whispered to my Lord.

"Have patience. Yudhishtira will come soon and put him out of his misery."

Yudhishtira in the meanwhile had seen many bad omens and went in search of Bhima. He was surprised to see him in the grip of a python and guessed it was no ordinary snake since Bhima could have easily freed himself from the grip of an ordinary snake.

Bhima said, "Brother, this is no common snake. He is a celestial who has been cursed. He says he will release me only if you answer some questions."

My Lord whispered to me, "The Eldest loves to answer questions on *dharma*, ethics and philosophy so he will be only too happy to oblige."

The snake started to question him on just these things. The snake and Yudhishtira seemed to be getting on very well indeed. It was only poor Bhima who was suffering inside the snake's stranglehold which did not seem to lessen, even though he was asking questions which Yudhishtira seemed to be answering very well. I didn't pay much attention until he asked a question which was interesting to me.

'I had been planning to ask you about the castes,' I said to my Vanamali.

"I know and that is why I brought you here to listen to Yudhishtira's explanation," he said. It was amazing how he could read my mind constantly and also amazing how he always tried to get other people to take credit for what he could easily have done himself. I just looked at him with eyes filled with love.

"Who is a Brahmin?" asked the python.

Yudhishtira answered, "It is said by Brighu that in the beginning of the world there was no distinction between the different orders. Only Brahmanas existed since everyone was created equally by the Creator. That was the *Yuga* known as Satya and everyone spoke only the truth. As time passed there was an intermingling of character traits due to the different *gunas* that existed in them and thus they came to be distributed into four different orders. True Brahmanas are those whose chief attribute is goodness or *sattva*. Those Brahmanas whose chief attribute is passion or *rajas* came to be known as Kshatriyas, and those Brahmanas who had an admixture of goodness and passion – *sattva* and *rajas* - took up the professions of cattle-rearing, agriculture and trade and came to be known as Vaishyas, and those Brahmanas that were fond of untruth and injuring other creatures and engaged in all types of prohibited acts in order to gain a living became Shudras. All four orders have the right to perform all pious acts and sacrifices. The other three castes were created when the Brahmanas fell from their high values."

The snake asked, "So who is the real Brahmana?"

Yudhishtira said, "The true Brahmana is one who has been sanctified by rites, who is pure in behaviour, engaged in the study of the Vedas and in whom truth, charity, abstaining from injury to others, compassion, benevolence and penance predominate. The indications of a Brahmana are purity, good behaviour and compassion to all creatures. A Brahmana is not a Brahmana by birth alone or a Shudra, a Shudra by birth alone. His natural-born qualities decide his caste. He who engages in the profession of battle and rulership, who studies the Vedas, who gives charity and takes wealth from those who he protects, is called a Kshatriya. He who makes a living from the keeping of cattle, who is employed in agriculture as a means of acquiring wealth, who is pure in behaviour and studies the Vedas is called a Vaishya. He who takes pleasure in eating all types of food, who is engaged in doing all types of work, who is impure in behaviour, who does not study the Vedas and whose conduct is unclean is said to be a Shudra. A Brahmana who does not have the qualities which have been enumerated here should not be called a Brahmana, and a Shudra who does not have the qualities given here should not be called a Shudra. Therefore the orders should be recognised by their qualities and not by their birth. Everyone, regardless of their caste should practice self-restraint and resist from avarice and wrath. One should protect penance from pride and knowledge from dishonour and disgrace. One who does all acts without desire for fruit, whose whole wealth is kept for charity and who performs his daily rituals is a true *karma-sannyasi.* A person should be a friend to all creatures, abstain from all acts of injury, reject all gifts and master his passions. Thus, O intelligent serpent! Character is the essential requisite for every caste. As long as a person has not been initiated into the Vedas he is to be considered a Shudra even if he is born in a Brahmin womb. Whoever conforms to the rules of pure and virtuous conduct, him I consider to be the true Brahmana!"

The snake was greatly pleased by Yudhishtira's answers and released Bhima. My Lord told me that Bhima had actually been blessed for he had been given part of Nahusha's strength. Nahusha now cast off his snake skin and assumed the resplendent form of a celestial. He blessed the Pandavas and ascended to his celestial abode.

After this episode the Pandavas descended the mountain and returned to the forest of Kamyaka once again. 'Now what's going to happen to them?' I asked.

"I'm afraid Duryodhana is not going to leave them in peace in the forest even though he has forced this banishment on them. He has invited my *guru* to Hastinapura and given him royal treatment and slyly suggested to him that he should also make a visit to his dear cousins in the forest who would be extremely happy to see him. Of course the sage knows everything, but he decided to pretend ignorance and asked Duryodhana with feigned innocence what would be a good time to visit them. Duryodhana knew all about the *akshaya patra* which Draupadi was using to give food to everyone and also knew that after she ate, nothing more would be got out of it for the day. So he suggested a time when he was sure she would have finished eating. He was hoping that Durvasa would curse the Pandavas for not giving him food. Now I have been informed by my *guru* that he is on his way to the Kamyaka forest to meet the Pandavas. I know very well what is going to happen so I want to be there to help Draupadi."

'How did your *guru* tell you all this?' I asked.

"My dear, he knows the hearts of everyone. He knew of Duryodhana's evil intentions but decided to play along with him since he has decided to bless the Pandavas. For this he needs my help and he has sent me a telepathic message."

'What did he say?' I asked breathlessly since I was being whisked by my Lord through the air. At least I suppose it was through the air. I never did find out which dimension he used for such types of transport.

"He says that he has just gone for his bath in the river along with his ten thousand disciples and will be returning soon for his meals. He suspects that Draupadi must have finished her meal and must have cleaned the vessel and kept it ready for the next day."

By this time, we had reached Kamyaka forest and sure enough there was Draupadi looking desperate. As it was, their plight was terrible and all it needed to make it worse was to have an irate Durvasa curse them. Her husbands as usual were totally incapable of helping her even though Arjuna made a small effort to say that he could go and kill a deer and bring it to her, but of course Durvasa being a Brahmana would not eat meat. Bhima said he would go and try and get some fruits and roots and he was sure that the sage would not expect anything more from those who were staying in the forest. Draupadi shook her head and as usual in her hour of need she must have thought of Krishna. Now I realised why my Lord was anxious to go to her aid. I felt a bit jealous of Draupadi. What *bhakti* she had for my Lord. Obviously there was never a doubt in her mind that he would go to her help whenever she called to him. Such a deep bond existed between them that neither time nor distance could break it.

"Such a bond exists between me and all my true devotees," he told me in answer to the unasked doubt in my mind. I felt a bit abashed.

The Lord made himself visible and approached Draupadi in his leisurely fashion and said, "Panchali! I'm dreadfully hungry. Give me something to eat."

"Govinda!" she said, "I have finished eating for the day and the pot is empty and Durvasa and his ten thousand disciples have gone to the river for their bath and will be back any minute wanting to be fed! What am I to do?"

"Never mind about them," said my playful Lord. "Give me something to eat first."

"My Lord!" she said, "I just told you the pot has been washed and kept. What can I give you?"

"You are a princess and you have never been taught to wash pots. I'm sure you have not washed it properly. Bring that pot here. Let me examine it."

Sadly Draupadi went to get the bowl which she had scoured and put away an hour ago. Krishna examined it carefully and found a microscopic bit of leaf and a small grain of rice sticking to one side which perhaps she had overlooked. Placing his precious find in his right palm he asked Panchali to pour a little Ganga water into it and drank the concoction with evident relish.

"Ah! Now I am replete," he said. Turning to Bhima he told him to go and escort the sage for his meals. Draupadi was horrified.

"But Lord, what shall I feed them with?" Draupadi pleaded. Yudhishtira looked troubled but Bhima did as he was told.

Very soon he returned and told us that the sage and his disciples were not hungry anymore and did not want to come to the *ashrama* for their meals!

"What is the reason for this strange behaviour?" asked Yudhishtira.

"I have no idea," said Bhima. "When I went to the river bank, I found that the sage and his disciples had finished their ablutions and were burping as if they had just had a full meal. In fact they had been on the verge of creeping off without returning to the hermitage for they feared that they would not be able to do justice to the hearty meal which must have been prepared for them."

I suddenly realised that I too felt very full as if I had just enjoyed a good meal. In fact all the brothers were also burping.

"Was Durvasa angry with us?" asked a worried Yudhishtira.

"He did appear angry but I think his anger was directed at Duryodhana who he said had sent him here. I fear he cursed the Kauravas with a speedy end!"

Yudhishtira looked a bit sad but the other brothers were quite happy at the way things had turned out.

Of course Draupadi knew that the whole miracle was my Lord's doing and fell at his feet. He blessed her and said, "All of you are blessed souls. You always adhere to *dharma* and *dharma* will not desert you. You will have the blessings of the sage."

After this we returned to Dwaraka. Of course no one knew that he had gone anywhere since he appeared to be still in Dwaraka. On the way I asked him the reason for this miracle.

He said, "You know that a person who is in a state of cosmic consciousness can expand his consciousness to touch everything else. When I ate that little grain with the *bhavana* (concept) that I was the soul of the universe, the entire universe with all its beings was simultaneously satisfied and replete. Didn't you feel full?" he asked with a twinkle of his eyes.

I nodded my head but wanted to have the last word. 'My Lord, I always feel replete when I am with you!' He smiled and chucked me under the cheek.

'What are the other trials which are going to happen to them?' I asked.

"Whenever the Pandavas go hunting they leave Draupadi in the care of their priest Dhoumya in the hermitage of the sage Trinabindu. You know that the Kauravas have a sister called Dusshala and she is married to Jayadratha, the king of Sindhu and Sauvira. Well, he is on his way to the kingdom of Salva and he has just seen Panchali standing in the doorway of their hermitage. Now let us watch."

I could see that Jayadratha was smitten by her beauty. He sent his friend Kotikasya to bring her to him. He approached her and said, "O beautiful maiden! Who are you? Are you a mortal or a goddess? I have been sent by Jayadratha, King of Sindhu to take you to him."

Draupadi replied, "I am Panchali, wife of the *pancha* (five) Pandavas. It is not correct for me to speak with strangers. However I think you are both related to my husbands so please stay and accept our hospitality and they will come soon."

Kotikasya went back to Jayadratha and told him that the lady was none other than Draupadi, wife of the Pandavas. Jayadratha was even more excited when he heard this and thought it was a heaven-sent opportunity for him to appropriate her.

He approached her and said, "O noble lady! I have heard of your beauty and now that I have seen you I see that the stories did not do you justice, for you have made me a prisoner of your beauty. Why do you waste your loveliness in this forest in the company of beggars? I am a king. Come with me and leave the wretched Pandavas to their fate."

'Why don't you go to her aid?' I asked.

"She is capable of taking care of herself. Moreover her husbands are the ones who should defend her at this point," said my Lord.

"Come with me in my chariot for a ride," said the shameless king.

"Beware, O foolish king," said Draupadi, "My husbands will come now and will not spare you," so saying she turned her back on him and the shameless Jayadratha caught hold of her hand and forced her into the chariot with him. She started crying for help. "Fie on you!" she cried. "But beware; my husbands will surely kill you. Even Indra the King of the gods will not be able to abduct one who is under the protection of Janardana of the Vrishni clan." Dhoumya heard her cries and ran after the chariot but couldn't catch up with them.

'Should you not go to her rescue now? She is depending on you.'

"I will see that nothing happens to her but look, the Pandavas have seen the deer running here and there in fear and they know that some people have entered the forest and they are returning fast. I think that this time I should give them a chance to rescue her."

They returned quickly to the *ashrama* and the whole story was told to them by the maid. Yudhishtira told Bhima and Arjuna to go after her. The brothers raced out of the forest and saw Jayadratha far ahead of them on the road. Seeing them catching up on him, Jayadratha dropped Panchali on the road and fled in his chariot. Bhima stopped to help her while Arjuna chased Jayadratha and caught him and brought the culprit before Yudhishtira. He was about to kill him when Panchali stopped him.

"He is my sister Dusshala's husband. I would not want her to be a widow. So please don't kill him, but you can deprive him of his manliness." So Bhima shaved Jayadratha's head and left only five tufts of hair and forced him to kneel before Yudhishtira and profess that he was his slave. After that he set him free!

"A wounded cobra is deadlier than a live one," murmured my Lord. "He has been humiliated and disgraced and has become the bitter enemy of the Pandavas."

'What can he do to them?' I asked.

"He is going to do rigorous penance to Lord Shiva and will ask for the boon of being able to kill the Pandavas."

'Will Shiva give this to him?'

"No! Shiva will say that no one who is under my protection can be killed by him, but has granted him the boon that he will be able to do some great harm to all of them except Arjuna for one day. His father is also aware of the danger and has received another boon from Shiva that if Jayadratha's head falls on the ground, the head of the one who cuts it off will also burst into pieces. So now father and son think that they are fully protected."

'I think they have underestimated your powers!'

"My child I will always protect those who follow their *dharma*. Anyone who commits *adharma* will have to face the consequences. No amount of penances can overcome the effects of his *adharmic* actions."

'What is the latest that Duryodhana has thought of?'

"Shakuni is just telling Duryodhana that the Pandavas have returned and are just starting their twelfth year. 'Go and see how they live. It will give you great pleasure to see them living like animals in the jungle!' Duryodhana was delighted at the prospect of spying on his cousins.

"Once in three years, it is the custom of the Kuru kings to inspect their cattle which were left free to roam about in the forest and to brand the new calves. So Duryodhana has a very good excuse for going to the forest. Of course many people accompanied him, chief of them being Shakuni, Dusshasana and Karna and many of the ladies of the royal household. Karna is also delighted at the prospect of spying on the misery of the Pandavas. "

'Karna is really an enigma to me', I said. 'At times he seems such a noble soul and at times he behaves in this mean and inexplicable manner. Why is that?'

"My child! Every human being has a mean streak in him. Every one of us has a *deva* and an *asura* lodged in our minds. If our companions are *asuric*, the *asura* in us comes to the forefront. If we keep the company of noble souls, our *daivic* qualities will come to the fore. Unfortunately for Karna, he is always in the company of the *asuric* Kauravas and thus his true nature has become distorted. Our *Shastras* always insist on the necessity for *satsang* or the company of the holy."

'Suppose we live in a place where it is impossible to meet anyone holy, what should one do?'

"My Dear! The holiest of holy ones is God himself and he is ever present with you. Have recourse to him therefore, and you can be sure that you will be guided aright."

My eyes filled with tears. He had told me this so many times and yet I kept questioning. Would there be no end to my questions, I wondered?

The Kauravas went with eighty war chariots and thirty elephants. They set up tents and were making merry. Some of the men went to the lake where Duryodhana and his entourage normally bathed and indulged in water sports. Unfortunately this was a favourite spot of the *gandharvas* (celestial musicians) and *apsaras* (celestial dancers) and the lake was filled with them. There was a guard before the lake who told the men that the lake was closed by order of the Gandharva king and no one had the right to enter. Duryodhana in his usual arrogant fashion set forth on his elephant and said, "Dritarashtra's son, the mighty Duryodhana will go where he chooses. Stand aside!"

Of course the celestial beings refused to accede to the haughty command of a human being and told him to take himself off since the lake belonged to them. Duryodhana ordered his men to disperse them by force and he himself charged on them on his elephant. The Gandharvas flew off and reported the matter to their king. Karna and Duryodhana were exultant since they thought they had defeated them. But the Gandharvas multiplied themselves by hundreds and attacked Duryodhana's men from every side so that they scattered in terror. Only Duryodhana and Karna stood their ground. Karna covered himself and Duryodhana with blinding shields, but Chitrasena, the king of the Gandharvas captured Duryodhana and threw him into an iron net. His elephant trumpeted in fear and ran towards the lake while Karna was pinned under his chariot. The other Gandharvas threw Dusshasana,

Shakuni and all the Kauravas they could catch into the net along with Duryodhana, but they left the unconscious Karna behind.

Of course I was highly amused to watch the scene.

"Look over there at what is happening," said my Lord. I turned round to see that some of the courtiers who had fled had gone to the other side of the lake where the Pandavas had made their hermitage. They were very happy to see them and recounted the whole story to Yudhishtira. He immediately ordered Bhima, Arjuna and the twins to go and fight the Gandharvas and release their cousins.

Bhima said, "I think Duryodhana has come here to do us some harm so we should be glad that the *gandharvas* have helped us. Let them take him off. He deserves it."

Yudhishtira as usual was full of sympathy and said, "He is our cousin. Whatever quarrel we have with him should not stand in the way of our helping him if an outsider tries to harm him. You must go immediately and rescue him."

Of course Yudhistira's word was law and Bhima and Arjuna went towards the net and told the Gandharvas to release the Kauravas. When they refused Arjuna made a cage of arrows and imprisoned them inside it. Arjuna kept his bow drawn and was scanning the sky for their king. Their king, Chitrasena now appeared and turning towards Arjuna he said, "I am your dear friend Chitrasena. Why are you fighting with me?"

Arjuna immediately put down his bow and asked him to release their cousins.

Chitrasena said, "Duryodhana came to mock at you. He is always planning some evil against you, which is why I came to protect you."

Bhima said, "You are welcome to keep him if you want!" But Arjuna requested his friend to release them since Yudhishtira had ordered this.

So the king released them and disappeared in a flash of brilliant light. Bhima and Arjuna returned with a shame-faced Duryodhana who refused even to look at Yudhishtira. Panchali seemed very happy to see the ladies and started to chatter with them about all that went on in the court and how many children they had and so on, but Duryodhana was far from being happy at being rescued by the Pandavas.

"He who had come with the intention of mocking at the fate of his cousins is now in the sorry position of being mocked at by them," said my Lord. "See how the law of *karma* works. One has to reap the consequences of one's intentions! Now watch the fun."

Panchali immediately laid out a feast for all of them.

"My dear brother!" said Yudhishtira to Duryodhana, "It is indeed very kind of you to have thought of making a visit to us when we are in this forest. I am so happy that now we can at least enjoy a meal even though it may not be as grand as the fare you get at the palace."

This was indeed rubbing salt in the wound even though I'm sure Yudhishtira meant everything he said. Duryodhana made pretence of being happy and hurriedly left the place as soon as the meal was over.

'What will he do now?' I asked.

"Watch! This is going to be great fun." My Lord had a great sense of humour and I think he enjoyed seeing the arrogant Duryodhana humbled.

"I have nothing more to live for," said the mighty king of the Kurus. "I will sit here and fast to death. You may all return to Hastinapura and wait on those who are greater than me."

His friends tried to remonstrate with him but he would not listen and spread a grass mat and sat on it, apparently absorbed in mediation.

'I wonder what he is meditating upon,' I thought to myself.

In the meantime Karna came to meet him and thought that he had conquered the Gandharvas. "I'm sorry I fell unconscious and was not able to help you, but I'm glad you were able to do it yourself!"

Duryodhana looked disgusted, "I have been disgraced. They captured us in a net and the Pandavas had to rescue us. I have decided to end my life here. You may return in the morning to Hastinapura and Dusshasana can take over my kingdom."

Karna did his best to dissuade him and when he refused Karna said, "I shall also die with you." So saying he walked off into the jungle.

'Will he die?' I asked my Lord.

Krishna laughed heartily at the idea. "Duryodhana is not meant to die like this. His bad *karmas* are so much that he will have to pay for it on the battlefield and bleed to death with his thighs broken since that is the curse Panchali gave him when he bared his thigh to her and made highly improper suggestions."

'So what's going to happen now?' I asked.

"You know that the *devas* and *asuras* are constantly at war. They represent the positive and negative poles of creation. The conflict goes on in the heavens and on earth as well as in the hearts of all human beings. Duryodhana was born in order to fight on the side of the *asuras*. In fact many *asuras* have been born as kings on this earth and of course their *asuric* counterparts will help them. Duryodhana is the king-pin in their plot to create anarchy in this country and they will certainly not let him die. They have taken his astral body to their realm and they have promised to help him in the war with the Pandavas. No, that is one place you cannot go to," he told me, seeing my questioning look. "They have just made a promise to him that they would enter the hearts of noble souls like Bhishma, Drona and Kripa so that they would fight without showing any mercy even on women and children. They are urging Duryodhana to return and have no fear of any of the Pandavas. Of course Duryodhana is very happy to hear all this. They have now returned his astral body to his physical body. Very soon he will open his eyes and wonder if it was a dream or whether these things really happened. He has decided that it had really taken place and that the demonic hordes have indeed agreed to help him."

Duryodhana looked as if he had just woken up from a dream. However his depression was gone and he got up to return to Hastinapura. He went out of the tent and saw Karna sitting at the entrance his face stained with tears and dust. He knelt beside his friend and said, "Come, my friend. Let us forget all this and return to Hastinapura."

My Vanamali and I also decided to follow him. When he reached the court he found his father and elders were all full of praise for the Pandavas, for the tale of his rescue had already reached the court. Bhishma strongly advised Duryodhana to make friends with them so that they could live together in peace. Duryodhana's face darkened and an ugly scowl marred his features. Without a word he strode out of the assembly.

'Now what is he going to do?' I asked.

"He has decided to hold a *yajna* called the Vaishnava, almost like a Rajasuya so as to rival Yudhishtira. Look he is sending messengers to invite the Pandavas for it."

'What will Yudhishtira say?' I wondered aloud.

"Do you doubt what he will say? Look he has sent back a message that though he knows this will bring great glory to the race of the Kurus yet he and his brothers cannot attend since they don't want to break the pact of the twelve years of exile."

My Lord laughed and I asked him why he laughed. He said, "I'm laughing at the reply which Bhima has sent. 'Tell your master that when the exile is over we will conduct a mighty sacrifice with weapons and offer the whole of Dritarashtra's family into the fire!'

"Duryodhana scowled at the message and Karna to console him said, 'When you have killed the Pandavas you can hold the Rajasuya and I will be there to extol you! I swear to you that I will not eat meat or wash my feet till I have killed Arjuna!'

I trembled when I heard this and crept closer to my Vanamali. He put his arms round me and told me not to be afraid. "See how Yudhishtira trembles like you when his spies reported this matter to him. He fears for the day when Karna and Arjuna will have to face each other in a deadly combat!

"We will return to Dwaraka now," said my Lord. "I have to find out what my people are doing."

'Are you trying to convince me that you don't know what's going on there?'

He laughed and before I knew it we were back in our own palace in Dwaraka.

This was a good place for me to question my Lord so I asked him, 'My Lord! Why do you love the Pandavas so much?'

"My child! I love them not only for their nobility but also for the fact that they have put their entire trust in me and have surrendered to me completely. I consider Yudhishtira as my head, Arjuna as my shoulders, Bhima as my trunk and the twins as my feet. I myself am the heart and head of this body of the Pandavas. Actually I am seated in the hearts of all human beings but they don't realise this, but the Pandavas do realise this. Arjuna has utter faith in me and thinks all his powers are only due to my grace. Once when we were going for a walk we saw a bird flying in sky and I asked him, 'Is that a dove?' He immediately replied, 'Yes it is a dove.'

"Then I asked him, 'Is it an eagle?' and he promptly replied, 'Yes it is an eagle.'

"I laughed and asked him again, 'No, no! It looks like a crow to me. And Arjuna replied, 'It is undoubtedly a crow!' So I scolded him and said, 'Why do you keep agreeing with whatever I say?' He replied, 'Vaasudeva! To me your words carry more weight than the evidence of my senses. You can make night into day and day into night so when you say it's a crow, it must be a crow!'

"It is because of this utter faith in my words that I can never desert them and will even commit *adharmic* acts for them if necessary for I'm above the Law of Karma and they are not. Such strength of character and forbearance cannot be seen in any other people. Because they have always obeyed me implicitly they have imbibed my strength! Now are you satisfied?"

Aum Namo Bhagavate Vaasudevaaya

People do not realise that life has been given to us so that we can serve creation and not just for the purpose of increasing our own enjoyment. People have forgotten this and become slaves to their selfish desires and anger.

Srimad Bhagavat Gita. Chapter 3.

ॐ

Anaghaaya Namaha!

CHAPTER TWENTY-TWO

Trials

'Are their trials over now?' I asked my Lord since there were only a couple of months to go.

He looked a bit pensive and said, "No, they have to undergo a few more trials. Let us watch them and see what happens."

One day Draupadi happened to be walking in the woods. After all her terrible adventures, her husbands seldom allowed her to go walking alone, but somehow she had wandered off and she came upon a strange tree from which was hanging a delicious looking fruit. She had never seen such a fruit before so she called out to Arjuna to get it for her. Both Arjuna and Bhima were always keen on doing anything for her, so he came as soon as she called, thinking that something terrible had happened to her. She pointed to the fruit and begged him to get it for her. He immediately brought it down with an arrow. Hardly had she picked it up to eat it when some of the ascetics living in the forest came upon the scene and exclaimed in great anxiety.

"What have you done? This tree belongs to the great Amrita Muni who lives only on this fruit. He will surely curse you if he sees this."

Arjuna said, "It's my fault. I will take the blame. Let him curse me if he wills."

Yudhishtira immediately said that their mother had told them to share everything whether good or evil and the result of this act would be shared by all. Of course Draupadi felt wretched since the entire fault was hers. She knew that the only one who could save her was her beloved Krishna so she thought of him and begged him to come, little knowing that he was already there. He made his presence felt and asked them what the problem was.

Draupadi narrated the whole tale and begged him to put the fruit back on the tree. My Lord smiled and said, "It's not that easy, Panchali. You will all have to do it as a combined effort."

"What can we do?" she asked in surprise.

"All six of you should open out your hearts and reveal the truth of what lies in your innermost hearts. Then the fruit will go up little by little. The Eldest can start." His eyes roved over all of them and except for Yudhishtira, all of them looked a bit perturbed.

Yudhishtira began. "I treasure *satya* (truth), *dharma* (righteousness), patience and self-control in my mind always." As he said this the fruit slowly started to go up to one sixth of its original height.

Bhima continued, "I treat all women as my sisters. I always honour them. I never covet the property of another. I treat the miseries of all as my own." As he finished speaking the fruit went up another one sixth.

Arjuna spoke, "Life is short but during this span one should live with courage, valour and honesty." The fruit ascended another one sixth. It was now half way to its original height. Everyone started feeling rather optimistic.

Nakula said, "Beauty, wealth, prosperity and fame are useless without learning, wisdom and knowledge." The fruit meekly went up another few inches.

Sahadeva announced, "Truth is my father, knowledge my mother, *dharma* my brother and compassion my wife." The fruit was now only one sixth away from its original place.

It was Draupadi's turn. She said, "I have never thought of anyone except my husbands and prayed that they should always be blessed with prosperity." Much to everyone's surprise the fruit did not budge an inch!

My Lord spoke softly, "Panchali, if you don't speak the truth all of you are doomed. The sage may return any minute." She looked desperately at him and he nodded and gave her a reassuring smile.

"My five husbands always have priority in my mind, but sometimes for a fraction of a second I must admit that I have thought of someone else." The fruit immediately ascended to its original position. The brothers looked surprised but did not question her further. She hung her head and looked at my Lord who again gave her a comforting nod. Seeing that none of them were in a mood to enquire either from him or from her about this stranger who had crept into her mind, my Lord said, "Well, I will leave you to your life and will return when you need me."

'Who does she think about apart from her husbands?' I asked.

"Can't you guess? Who is the one who has a striking resemblance to them and is in fact most closely related to them?"

'Karna!' I exclaimed. 'Does she know who he is and does she really have a soft spot for him?'

"She doesn't know but she instinctively sees the resemblance and is no doubt attracted to him due to that. I wanted to give a hint to the brothers about Karna, but it looks as if they are not fated to know anything till the bitter end. What can one do?"

'Why don't you openly reveal the secret to them?' I asked.

"My dear, certain things are not to be revealed suddenly. They have to be discovered by the people concerned. My duty is only to give hints and not to tell everything."

'Do you think if they knew who Karna was, Yudhishtira would go to him and ask him to join them? This would mean that he wouldn't become king since Karna is older.'

"Yudhishtira will always adhere to his *dharma* but the question is whether Karna would agree. I doubt if he would. We can only wait and see. Each one will have to reap the consequences of his actions."

'But Karna didn't have a chance.'

"Chances are always given to everyone to amend their mode of conduct, but very few make use of these chances. Chances will certainly be given to him, but it is doubtful if he will take them!"

'When will we see the Pandavas again?' I asked.

"Very soon," said my Lord. "They are going to call me very soon."

'On what pretext?' I asked. He smiled at my use of the word.

"You know that they are as attached to me as I am to them, so they don't need much of an excuse to call me. This time it is an interesting wager they have taken. Each of them thinks that they have more influence over me since they are greater devotees. Bhima and Arjuna especially pride themselves on being my greatest devotees, so look what they are going to do! They are like children playing games."

One day the six of them decided to invite my Lord for lunch. Arjuna was sure that he was my Lord's favourite and said that he could make him come in a moment. So he sat down and meditated on Krishna, but we were watching the fun from above and my Lord winked at me and said, "Let him wait. He is getting a bit too proud of his friendship with me. I never allow anyone to take me for granted!"

'Am I taking you for granted?' I asked anxiously.

"If you were I would disappear in a minute," he said, "just like I did with Radha."

'What happened with Radha?' I asked.

"Well, she thought she was the only one I really loved. One day she became even more proud when I took her alone with me to the forest. I had made a garland for her and was just going to put it on her hair when the thought darted into her mind that she possessed me completely and was the sole owner of my heart. Of course she had to learn the lesson that I am the same to all my devotees and everyone who loves me is loved in return. I just disappeared and she was left alone in the dark forest and started to cry until the other *gopis* found her and comforted her."

'Sometimes I think you are a bit heartless.' I whispered.

"Do I appear heartless to you?" he asked.

'No.'

"Why is that?"

'I don't know,' I whispered.

"I'll tell you. It's because you have never taken me for granted. Never, ever do that. Even though I am always with you and everyone who worships me, the fact is that once they start taking me for granted I will not be as close to you as you imagine. God does not like being taken for granted. Constant communion should be there between the devotee and the deity – sleeping, waking, eating, talking, working – whatever you are doing, you should be in constant communion with me. That is the only way to ensure that I am with you always."

'Do you mean to say that if I don't think of you, you won't think of me?'

"My child! The Ganga is constantly flowing, rain or sun, but only the one who has a pot will be able to fill it for herself! Do you understand?"

'Yes, My Lord,' I said and hung my head in shame for having doubted him. 'Please bless me that the pot of my heart is always kept open for you and if you suspect that it has been closed with a lid, please break open the lid and force an entrance. That is my only prayer.' He just gave me one of his long looks with his radiant eyes and my own filled and overflowed.

"Come let's see, who is the next Pandava who thinks I will run to his bidding?"

It was Bhima's turn. He always used forceful methods. He flung up his huge mace into the air and standing directly beneath it, he shouted, "Vaasudeva! If you don't appear this very minute, I will die, crushed by my mace!"

My Lord caught my arm and jumped into their midst and Bhima dodged the deadly mace just in time. Everyone had a hearty laugh and all of us sat down to a delicious lunch produced by Panchali from her *akshayapatra*.

We returned to Dwaraka after this episode but soon after we reached there, Satyabhama came to my Lord and begged him to take her to the forest to meet the Pandavas.

"You seem to be going there all the time and you never take me anywhere. Please let me come with you when you make your next visit," said Satyabhama in her usual petulant fashion.

"Of course I'll take you my dear," he said. "You have never asked me. I always thought you may not like life in the forest."

"If Draupadi can bear it for so many years, surely I can go and stay for a couple of days," was her retort.

"You have much to learn from Panchali," was his cryptic retort.

The very next day we set off in a chariot with all the usual retinue. I much preferred our usual mode of transport. However I squeezed in, between them.

The sage Markandeya and some others were at the hermitage so my Lord and the Pandavas took their seats beneath the trees to listen to the words of the sages. Satyabhama took this opportunity to meet Draupadi and walked into the hermitage to find her. With a nod in the direction of the hermitage, my Vanamali directed me to go with her. I went reluctantly since I was not really interested in women's talk and much preferred to listen to philosophical discourses. However my master's word was law.

Draupadi was delighted to have some compatible feminine company and pelted Satyabhama with questions about life in Dwaraka. Satyabhama had come with a definite purpose so she answered her briefly and then started the topic closest to her heart.

"Tell me, O Panchali! How do you manage to keep the Pandavas who are all intelligent and valiant, so obedient to your every wish and whim? I have heard that they never get angry with you but are always alert to do your every bidding. Do you use some spells or incantations or is it due to the practice of your vows and asceticism? If so tell me soon what these are so that I can make use of the same in order to keep Vaasudeva obedient and submissive to me."

I was shocked to hear this. Can anyone hope to tame the wild wind and keep it under her control, I thought to myself. Obviously Panchali was also shocked by Satyabhama's questions for she answered rather forcefully.

"My dear sister," she said, "How can you believe even for a moment that I would resort to spells and incantations to keep my husbands under control? Such things are the weapons of evil women who want to subjugate their husbands. I do not want to subjugate them. I only want them to love me."

Satyabhama looked a bit abashed. "Tell me how you would describe them to someone who had never seen them. Of course I have seen them all fleetingly except for Arjuna, whom I saw at close quarters when he was courting Subhadra. I have never seen any of the others and I'm anxious to see them through your eyes."

Draupadi looked a bit shy and said, "I will do my best to describe them to you. The Eldest has a complexion like pure gold. He has a prominent nose and large eyes. Like all of them with the exception of Bhima, he has a small physique. He is always just, never swerves from *dharma* and is ever merciful. I am his only wife and I know he loves me very much. He has never had eyes for any other woman. Bhima is just the opposite. He is huge, tall and has an enormous physique with long arms and beetling eyebrows which come together in a ferocious frown when he is angry. He never forgets an enemy and of course he is master of the mace."

"What about the middle Pandava?" asked Satyabhama.

"He is dark and slight of build which is the reason why he is an excellent archer. He is most intelligent and though he is capable of withstanding any foe, he will never deliberately commit an act of cruelty. But I think you told me that you know him best since you saw him in Dwaraka when he stayed during the four months of the monsoons."

Satyabhama nodded and said, "Please continue."

"Nakula is the handsomest man I have ever seen. He is also slight of build and a master swordsman and is unflinchingly devoted to his brothers. He is always kind and considerate to me. Sahadeva is of course the youngest and like the others he is formidable in war and in the observance of *dharma*. He is highly intelligent and eloquent, yet humble and devoted to his elder brothers. He is an excellent astrologer."

Satyabhama asked with a knowing look, "Now that you have described them so well, tell me, are you not partial to any of them?"

Draupadi continued. "I don't have partiality to any of them. I treat them all in the way which suits their personality. I mould my personality to suit theirs. I am serious with Yudhishtira and Bhima, flirtatious with Arjuna and loving in almost a maternal way to the twins, who lost their mother soon after their birth. My heart has never been attracted to anyone else. I'm always conscious of their needs and never eat till they have finished their meals and never sleep until they have slept. I honour them when they return after a tiring day in the forest or from their assembly. I am kind and courteous to their friends and guests. I keep the house and precincts clean and neat and beautiful. I love them all very much and can never be separated from them for long. I have trained myself to like only what they like and dislike what they dislike. Depending on the likes of the person I am with, I see to it that my dressing and jewellery is to his liking. They are attached to me because I never flaunt the fact that I am a princess born in an illustrious family who had everything she desired. I show them that I consider them to be the greatest and that the happiness I get from them is greater than what I got in my country as a young girl. A husband should be a wife's god and refuge. I always show them that I have no other refuge but them, but I will tell you a secret. In my heart of hearts I know that my only refuge is Vaasudeva, but of course I would never dream of telling them this. I never show any jealousy of their other wives. In fact I always treat them with great respect.

When they were in Indraprastha, the illustrious sons of Kunti had a hundred serving maids, all beautiful and adorned with jewellery, but I never showed any jealousy of any of them. In fact I always took an interest in their welfare and dressing. I have heard that Vaasudeva has sixteen thousand one hundred and eight wives. I advise you never to show jealousy towards any of them. But of course he is a totally different personality. It would be impossible for anyone to understand him. To me he is God incarnate. I love him above everything else, even above my husbands, but of course not in the way I love them. But remember I am telling you this in secret. He is the cosmic beloved and I know he is the same to everyone. Many times when my husbands have found it impossible to come to my aid, Krishna has never deserted me. O Satyabhama, you don't realise how fortunate you are to have him as your husband. He is the *purnavatara* (supreme incarnation) of Vishnu. Defer to him therefore in all things for he is indeed omnipotent and omniscient. He can never go wrong. Worship him in all ways and not just with your body. Do not treat him as an ordinary man because he is no ordinary person. He is the Infinite clothed in a human body. There is no one else like him in all the worlds."

I mentally applauded Draupadi's description of my Lord which tallied exactly with mine. Satyabhama did not look too pleased with this, but she nodded her head and said, "I know he is different, impossible to label or gauge. I was madly in love with him from the time I was a young girl and actually got him to propose by resorting to a trick. Of course I realised that he had seen through my stratagem but he gave in to my wishes, because he knew how much I loved him. I cannot wish for a better husband, but I do wish to have the ability to control him as you seem to control your five husbands."

"Dear Bhama," said Panchali, "Reconcile yourself to the fact that you will never be able to control him. He cannot be controlled by anyone. He is the wild wind, the raging storm; he is also the tender southern breeze and the autumn sky. Be grateful to him for having agreed to marry you and do not strive to control him."

Satyabhama nodded her head and made up her mind to control her temper and her tongue and be submissive to her Lord's wishes.

The ladies parted on this note and went to meet the men who had finished their discourse on *dharma* which was a topic which never failed to grip them all. Krishna looked questioningly at his wife and told her to get into the chariot. He smiled at Draupadi and once again told her, "Panchali, remember if you ever want me you have only to think of me and I'll come."

We returned to Dwaraka and found that the five princes, the Upa Pandavas or sons of the Pandavas by Draupadi had become teenagers and were being trained in all types of warfare by Pradyumna, Samba and the other sons of my Lord. Subhadra's son Abhimanyu had become a handsome young man who looked very much like his father. He looked and behaved as if he were much older than his fifteen years. My Lord went to see his sister for he knew that something was worrying her.

"What is it?" he asked turning her round to face him. "I know something is troubling you. Tell me."

Tears were welling up in her eyes. "Brother, I have something to tell you. Abhimanyu has fallen in love with Vatsala, brother Balarama's daughter. She is actually a little older than he, but he is quite infatuated with her and she with him. I told Revati about this and she talked to brother Balarama. At first he agreed but then he changed his mind. Apparently he told Revati that he wanted his daughter to marry someone with property and not a gambler's son! You know his partiality for Duryodhana and now it appears that he wants Vatsala to marry his son Lakshman. Abhimanyu is heartbroken. He and I had made up our minds to run away to the forest to meet his father, but now that you have come I know you will find some solution."

She called Abhimanyu who fell at my Lord's feet and begged him to help him as he had helped his father to marry his mother. Krishna raised him up and said, "My child! This is a very delicate situation. I don't know if your mother has told you but even in their case, I had to resort to a trick since Balarama was keen that Subhadra should marry Duryodhana who was his favourite pupil. It seems as if history is repeating itself. If I help you, my brother will surely be very angry with me. However I have a solution. We will call Bhima's son Ghatotkacha to come to our aid. His mother is a *rakshasi* called Hidimbi. He is very strong and intelligent so we will invoke him."

My Lord has his own ways of summoning people and Ghatotkacha came as soon as he was summoned. My Lord explained the whole situation to him. He was a huge fellow and had to bend down to hear what my Lord had to say. I was really intrigued by his face which looked so much like Bhima's. His nature also was very much like his father. He had the innocence of a small child. As soon as he heard the story he told Abhimanyu and Subhadra not to worry. That very night, he transported both Abhimanyu and Vatsala to the forest and got them married and made them stay with his mother in a lovely forest glade. He then returned in time for the wedding of Duryodhana's son Lakshman with Vatsala, which was going to take place the next morning. Marriage preparations were going on at a spanking pace and my Lord joined the arrangements most enthusiastically. In the hustle and bustle nobody noticed the absence of the bride. Duryodhana and the Kauravas had arrived and were given a royal welcome by Balarama. Just at that moment, my Lord disappeared from the scene since he didn't want to have any sort of friendly banter with someone who had treated the Pandavas so shamefully. Balarama obviously had no such qualms and both he and Revati were very happy that their daughter was going to make such a fortunate alliance.

My Lord kept out of the way but he knew what Ghatotkacha had planned. The time came for the bride to be brought to the dais. I was sure that the secret would be out now since I knew that Vatsala was not in her room. She was enjoying her honeymoon with Abhimanyu in the forest. But Ghatotkacha was not as simple as he appeared. *Rakshasas* have the ability to change their form at will and he took the form of the bride and came on the dais where the marriage was to take place. The main part of the function is when the father of the bride takes his daughter's hand and places it in the hand of the bridegroom and exhorts him to take good care of his daughter who is being given as a gift to him. Balarama took Vatsala's hand as he thought, and placed it in Lakshman's hand, but Ghatotkacha squeezed his hand so hard that the poor bridegroom fainted. Duryodhana jumped up and fanned his son and everyone rallied round to try and revive him. Only my Lord stood at a side and did nothing to help. Balarama looked round to see what happened to his daughter and was shocked to see Ghatotkacha standing there. He had never seen him before and did not know who he was and how he came to be there. There was a big hue and cry and a search was started for Vatsala. Just then Revati came and said that Abhimanyu had also disappeared. Balarama looked round and saw my Lord.

"Krishna!" he thundered, "Do you know anything about this?"

"Brother! All I know is that Abhimanyu and Vatsala loved each other but this was known by you also and you had even consented to their alliance, but when Duryodhana suggested marriage with his daughter you went back on your word since you thought this was a better alliance! Obviously the children took matters into their own hands!"

Duryodhana was furious. He remembered a similar scene many years ago when Balarama had promised to give Subhadra to him and Arjuna came along and eloped with her and now the same thing was happening and Arjuna's son had eloped with the bride meant for his son! The more he thought about this the more his hatred for the Pandavas grew and he swore he would hound and kill them while they were in the forest. Balarama was apologising profusely but he couldn't quell Duryodhana's anger.

I looked at my Lord whose eyes were dancing with mirth. 'You look so innocent yet there is nothing you don't know, is there?' I asked. He just looked at me and I was silent.

'Why do you have to let someone else always do the things that you can so easily do?'

"My dear, I have told you often enough that I cannot act on the information I know of the future. Things have to be worked out in their own fashion by the people who are meant to do it. If I do everything for others, where would be the fun in life? I am only a witness as God is a witness. I will not directly participate unless called upon to do so. But I can and will give advice if necessary."

We dallied there for a few more days to try and comfort Balarama who refused to be comforted since he suspected that his brother had a hand in this. Abhimanyu and Vatsala now returned and of course there was no other course but to welcome them back. Subhadra was most grateful to my Lord who told her to keep his part in this a secret.

'Now can we go to see the Pandavas?' I begged and he agreed.

'How are they doing?' I enquired.

"They are doing well and even Bhima and Panchali are happy since they are coming to the end of their tenure, but the Kauravas are getting more and more anxious. They were hoping that their cousins would be killed by wild animals in the forest or die of some natural disasters, but they have overcome everything and the time is fast approaching for their stay in some town, incognito. Duryodhana is even more furious at what happened at his son's wedding. He is determined to kill the Pandavas at all costs and has just approached his dear uncle and they have concocted a diabolical plan. They have approached a black magician called Kalamamuni. He is performing an *abhicharya* (black magic) rite in which an evil spirit has just emerged. The spirit has been told to go and discover the whereabouts of the Pandavas and drink their blood. However, the magician has warned Duryodhana that there was every possibility of evil plans failing when dealing with virtuous people who were protected by me!"

'So what happened?' I asked. Life was such a thrill when living with my Lord.

"Yudhishtira's father, Dharmaraja is going to take a hand to protect them. We will go and see," he said.

We went to the forest where the Pandavas were resting after their meal. The fire used in *yajnas* is normally made by rubbing two special sticks. Dharmaraja, in the form of a magnificent deer caught one of the sticks in its antlers and ran away into the forest. The Brahmanas ran to the Pandavas to help them since that stick was crucial for them in their fire ceremonies. The brothers were ever ready to do a good deed and all of them set out after the stag which ran off leading them deeper and deeper into the heart of the forest where it appeared as if the sun had set. It was very dark and gloomy and the Pandavas were feeling very thirsty. The Eldest asked the youngest to climb a tree and see if he could spot any water. Sahadeva saw water-loving trees growing a little further off and set off to find the source of water. When he didn't return, Yudhishtira sent Nakula, then Arjuna and finally Bhima. When none of them returned he began to feel really alarmed and followed them. By this time, he was totally dehydrated. The sight of all his four brothers lying dead on the banks of the lake was too much for him and he lost consciousness and fell to the ground.

Just at this moment the spirit sent by Kalamamuni traced the Pandavas and found their bodies. It had no desire to eat corpses so he darted back, his hunger unappeased and his anger at its peak and devoured his creator Kalamamuni!

My Lord and I looked at each other and started to laugh. Yudhishtira however had only lost consciousness and had not died. When he regained consciousness he was bereft when he saw his brothers lying on the ground like fallen trees and decided to give up his own life by drinking the water which he guessed was poisoned. As he approached the water an eerie voice said, "Stop! This is my lake and if you want to drink the water you will have to answer my questions first. Your brothers refused to obey me and have paid the price of their folly."

Yudhishtira said, "Ask and I will answer."

The voice now shot a quiver full of questions which the Eldest answered without faltering and without conceit. Of course I was avidly listening to this exchange.

"Hopefully this will stop you from pestering me with questions," said my Lord with his usual twinkling smile.

"What makes the sun rise and set?"

"Dharma" said Yudhishtira.

"Who is one's best companion?"

"A steady intelligence (sthitha prajna)."

"Why are Brahmanas ranked with celestials?"

"Because they are the knowers of the Brahman."

"What is weightier than the earth?"

"The mother."

"What is fleeter than the wind?"

"The mind."

"What is more numerous than grass?"

"Thoughts."

"Where does happiness lie?"

"In good behaviour and contentment."

"Who is taller than the sky?"

"The father."

"Who is the friend given by god to man?"

"The wife."

"How can one become wealthy?"

"By renouncing desire."

"What disease is incurable?"

"Avarice."

"What is grief?"

"Ignorance."

"What is man's enemy? Who is holy and who unholy?"

"His enemy is anger and his disease is covetousness. He who seeks the good of all is holy and he who is selfish and cold is unholy."

"Who is worthy of eternal torment?"

"He who denies food to a hungry Brahmana who has come to his house; he who declares the Vedas to be false; he who is rich and does not give to the poor."

"What is charity?"

"Protecting all creatures."

"What makes a Brahmana?"

"Virtue and good behaviour. Not birth or education."

"What is the most surprising thing in the world?"

"The fact that day after day we see people dying everywhere, yet no one thinks that they will also die one day."

"Who possesses every kind of wealth?"

"One who is above the dualities of happiness and sorrow, pain and pleasure, gain and loss, past and future."

Many such questions were asked which I can't fully remember, but I do recall that Yudhishtira answered all with great humility and due consideration for he knew that the lives of his beloved brothers depended on him.

At last the voice said, "I am very pleased with your answers and shall bring one of your brothers to life. You can choose which one."

Without hesitation Yudhishtira replied, "Let it be Nakula."

The voice enquired in surprise, "Why not Bhima, whom you love so much or Arjuna who will get your kingdom back for you?"

Yudhishtira replied calmly, "I cannot swerve from *dharma* to pander to my emotions. Among Kunti's sons, I am alive so let one of Madri's sons also live."

The voice now materialised and said, "I am your father, Dharmaraja. I am truly proud of you, my son. You have answered all my questions with great intelligence. You have indeed conquered the kingdom of righteousness. Now you can ask for a boon."

Again Yudhishtira surpassed himself and said, "Having had your *darshana* I do not need anything more but if it pleases you, do grant me victory over the six deadly enemies of lust, anger, avarice, covetousness, arrogance and envy."

Dharmaraja answered, "My son you have already conquered these six in your mind so you don't need this boon. But I will give you some boons on my own behalf. I assure you that no one will recognise you during your 13th year of exile. I took this form to save you all from the monster who had been sent to devour you. Remember this, victory will always be where Vaasudeva is and *dharma* will also be there. So go in peace. I am proud of you."

I felt exalted after this discourse and clung to my beloved Vanamali's arm. He looked at me and smiled. "Yudhishtira has at last come to his own," he murmured, "and you have learnt a lot, haven't you?" I nodded gratefully.

The brothers woke up as if from a deep sleep and all of them hugged each other and pelted the Eldest with questions as to what had exactly transpired. He explained everything to them and they were all amazed at Duryodhana's perfidy and the manner in which the Lord protected them all the time. They then wended their way back to the hermitage and told the whole story to Draupadi who was anxiously awaiting their return.

"Do you realise," said Arjuna, "that our exile ends in three days' time?"

Aum Namo Bhagavate Vaasudevaaya

There is one sure way to act without attachment O Arjuna!
That is to remember Me at all times and dedicate your actions to Me.

Srimad Bhagavat Gita, Chapter 3.

ॐ

Anaghaaya Namaha!

CHAPTER TWENTY-THREE

Matsya

'Where will they go now?' I asked my Lord.

"They are discussing their future plans. In a way, all of them have got used to their life in the forest and even Bhima and Draupadi have learnt to accept it if not to enjoy it. As for Yudhishtira, you know that he was totally uninterested in the intrigues of court life and has now blossomed into the perfect picture of a man who stands by his *dharma,* come what might. Of course this is a critical year for them. Duryodhana will try his utmost to discover their whereabouts so they have to be very careful."

'You will be keeping a watchful eye on them, I'm sure,' I murmured.

"Of course we will not leave them even for a minute," he said smiling at me, for he well knew how anxious I was to know how they fared.

"This year is going to be a crucial one for us," said the Eldest. If we are discovered in this year, we will have to repeat the whole thing all over again. What is the use of getting the kingdom after that? I'm already forty-seven years old now. Bhima is forty-five, Arjuna forty-three and the twins three months younger. If we have to get the kingdom it has to be now. We have to be very careful in selecting a place which will not be discovered by Duryodhana's spies."

'How is it that the twins are only three months younger than Arjuna?' I asked.

My Lord replied, "Soon after she conceived Arjuna, Kunti gave the *mantra* to Madri who used it and conceived almost immediately. So her twins were born three months after Arjuna and I were born!"

'O, so you and Arjuna are the same age?' I exclaimed. He nodded.

The Pandavas thought of many places and at last Vyasa came and told them to go to the country known as Matsya whose ruler was King Virata who was unfriendly with the Kauravas. Before leaving the forest they prayed to Durga. "O thou slayer of Mahishasura! Help us in our distress and confer victory upon us. Let us not be discovered during our last year of exile."

The goddess blessed them and added her boon to the one given by Dharmaraja that they would not be discovered during their 13th year. They took leave of all their friends who had accompanied them to the forest since they would surely be discovered if they went to the city with their retinue. They were especially sorry to part from their priest Dhoumya. He continued to live in the forest since he didn't want to be caught by the Kauravas who might torture him and force him to tell them the destination to which the Pandavas had gone. They returned the *akshayapatra* to the sun god since that was the pact he had made with them that it would be returned at the end of their stay in the forest.

Now that they had decided on the city, they had to think about what work they would engage themselves in when they reached the place. Yudhishtira decided to offer his services to the king as an adviser and an expert in dice playing. He had learnt the art from the sage. He would pose as a Brahmana called Kankabhatta. Bhima who was an authority on cooking said he would offer his services in the kitchen. This was a neat way of ensuring that he would never run out of good food which he had been deprived of for twelve years. The *akshayapatra* served good solid food, but it was always the same. There was no variety. Arjuna suddenly recalled that he had been cursed by the celestial nymph Urvashi that he would become a eunuch and his father had made her cut down this curse to one year. He opted to accept this curse during this year and call himself

Brihannala, a master of music and dance which he had learnt from Chitrasena. Nakula was remarkable with horses and he said he would take the name Granthika and apply for a job in the royal stables. Sahadeva was an expert in everything to do with cattle and milking, so he would accept a post in the cattle sheds under the name Tantripala.

Yudhishtira started to worry about Draupadi. How could she ever do menial work – she who was a princess and a queen? Draupadi knew what was passing through his mind and said that she was a specialist in hair dressing and would apply for a job as ladies' maid to Virata's queen and just go by the name Sairandhri or maid. She was going to tell the queen that she had been Satyabhama's maid. Having decided on their respective occupations and names, they slipped past Duryodhana's spies in the night, crossed the Yamuna and went towards the city. Of course they couldn't enter the city carrying their weapons, so they cogitated on how best to hide them. Arjuna pointed out a giant Sami tree with lots of foliage, which was difficult to climb and which was growing right next to the cremation grounds littered with charred corpses. Since it was next to the burning grounds, hardly anyone went near it and no one would see them hiding their weapons in it. They took out all their weapons and wrapped them securely in a piece of leather. Nakula climbed up the tree and hid them all in a hollow in the tree and tied them securely with ropes and made sure that no one could see the bundle from below. He also brought a half-burnt corpse from the cemetery and tied it on the branches so that people would not dare to come anywhere near the tree.

Sahadeva was the most inconspicuous of them all, so they sent him to the city to get suitable clothes for all of them to wear since obviously they could not offer their services in a palace clad in bark and deer skin. They entered the city one by one since it would have been disastrous had they entered all together. Yudhishtira went first and approached the king who asked him, "Who are you and why have you come to this country? You look like a stranger. I haven't seen you around."

Yudhishtira replied, "I'm a Brahmana called Kankabhatta. I have lived many years in the forest and learnt the art of dice. If you will appoint me in your household, I will teach you the game of dice playing and how to move ivory chessmen with skill." He took out his blue cloth bag and showed the king his golden dice set with turquoise. "I can teach you all the tricks of the game so that you will never lose. But remember, I don't want to be involved in any dispute over dice."

The king was most impressed by Kanka and said, "Kanka! You're welcome. All my doors are open to you and if anyone who is pressed with misfortune or one who is seeking work comes to you, then I shall employ him at your word!"

During the night, Arjuna sat in the fields and called up the power within him and invoked Urvashi's curse upon him. "May my manliness be gone for a year," he said. "May my hair come to my knees and may the scars on my wrists be hidden by bracelets, and earrings adorn my ears, and ornaments, my neck." Next morning Virata observed him coming. He was dark and slight with long wavy hair and large eyes.

"Who are you?" asked the king. "You are dressed as a woman but something tells me that you are not one."

Arjuna replied, "My name is Brihannala and I have no sex, but I am an expert in singing and dancing and playing the flute. I can teach all this to your daughter Uttara."

The king told him to play something on his flute and as soon as he heard the heavenly music that Arjuna had learnt from the celestial musician, he was enchanted and ordered his servants to take him away and make sure that he was not a man. It was only after the physical examination was over that he was allowed to enter the women's apartments where he became dance teacher to the Princess Uttara. He moved about freely with the other maids and friends of the princess. He was also able to converse with Draupadi since she was maid to the queen.

That afternoon when Kanka and Virata were playing dice, the king glanced out of the window and saw a tall, heavy man dressed in black passing by. He was fair, with prominent eyes, dark as a bull's. He had a bull neck with three creases; his shoulders were broad and his arms long and thick. He walked like an elephant and wore his hair bound in a cloth and carried a large brass ladle as if he was carrying a mace.

"Look!" said Virata, "there goes another stranger."

Kanka said, "I met him on the road when I came here. His name is Vallala and apparently he was King Yudhistira's cook."

"Call him and let me talk to him," said the king, "we are in need of a good cook."

Bhima came and told Virata, "I have come here from the Kuru kingdom. I used to be cook in the kitchen of the great king Yudhishtira, but now he has vanished and I have no work."

Virata said, "Vallala, you served an unfortunate king and now you are unemployed due to no fault of your own. I will be happy to employ you in my kitchen provided your dishes are tasty. If I don't find them palatable, you will be out of a job!"

Bhima said, "Majesty, just give me a chance and I assure you that you will not be disappointed."

One day in the evening, Kanka called the king outside and told him that there was another stranger called Tantripala who was a cow-herd by birth who was seeking employment. The king asked for a lamp and saw a bearded man dressed in deerskin who spoke in the rough dialect of the cow-herds.

"Majesty, I am Tantripala. I am an expert in reading the signs in any cattle. Just by looking at them I can know their past and future. When I care for them they will never get ill. They multiply under my care and the cows give more milk."

"This man seems to be honest. Perhaps you should employ him," said Kanka.

Another day, another stranger approached the king when he went to inspect the stables. The man was dark and handsome with a broad chest. His hair was bleached by the sun. Nakula said, "I am Grantika, a horseman from the land of Sindh. Put your horses in my care and they will run faster and live longer. I will feed them carefully and make iron plates for their feet. I worked for a while with Jaydratha, king of Sindh, brother-in-law of the Kauravas."

The king looked at Kanka for approbation and when he nodded he said, "You are welcome to stay. I was looking for an expert for the horses."

In the evening, Draupadi walked fast through the streets amidst the admiring looks of the onlookers and went to the queen's apartments dressed as a serving maid. Her long black hair was bound into a single braid and fell forward over her shoulder. She wore a cloth over her head and was dressed in a single piece of silk which looked soiled and worn. A maid saw her and took her to the queen. Draupadi said, "I seek work in your majesty's service."

"Who are you and what is your name?" asked the queen.

Draupadi replied, "Satyabhama, the wife of Vaasudeva for whom I used to work, used to call me Malini but now I have no name except Sairandhri, the serving maid. I am skilled in dressing ladies' hair and making sweet-scented perfumes and garlands of jasmine and lotuses. I left Dwaraka to see the world but now I have no money to return, so please let me work for you so I can earn some money and return to my home in Dwaraka."

Virata's queen's name was Sudheshna and seeing Panchali's enchanting form she was most reluctant to appoint her despite her recommendations.

"You say you are only a serving maid but you can pass off as a queen if you were properly dressed and there are many men here. It will not be safe for you."

Draupadi knew what was passing through her mind and said, "I am married to five Gandharvas who have gone somewhere and have kept me here for safety. They will return in a year's time. I will only stay in the inner apartments where no men come and it is your duty to protect my chastity. If anyone accosts me, my Gandharva husbands will kill them without compunction. However I have a few requests which you should grant me. I shall not eat leftover food and I will not massage anyone's feet." The queen agreed to all the conditions after hearing about the Gandharva husbands and accepted her as her chief maid.

I was extremely happy to hear of all these plans and how all of them had successfully entered the service of the king. 'Isn't it wonderful how they have all managed to get jobs in the same place so that they can at least see each other now and again?' I whispered to my Lord.

"Actually I am only worried about Bhima. His stature is unmistakable and I'm afraid he might go in for his favourite pastime of wrestling which might give the game away," said my Lord.

Four months passed quickly while the six of them attended to their own work without any problem. At that time a great festival to Brahma was held in the city to which many wrestlers came to participate in the wrestling bouts, which were a normal part of the festivities, and perhaps gain name and fame and money. Among them was a huge man called Jimutan who proudly declared that he had defeated every known wrestler in the country.

"Do you have anyone here who can give some exercise to my muscles?" he asked arrogantly.

At the bouts that followed, he kept his word and defeated every single wrestler who was put up by the king. Virata was at his wit's end. The prestige of his country was at stake. Just then his new friend Kanka came to him and said, "Your majesty, please do not grieve. A new cook has been appointed in your kitchen. I hear that he is an extraordinary wrestler so allow him into the arena tomorrow and see what happens."

There was a huge crowd at the arena the next day when the citizens heard that a new person was going to represent their state against the famous Jimutan. Valala came on the scene clad in simple wrestling attire and went and bowed before the king and Kanka who whispered to him not to display his usual techniques. The match started amidst cheers and shouts. Jimutan thought he could easily subdue his opponent, but was amazed to see that the other parried his every move. Soon he began to tire and his breath came in gasps. Valala suddenly jumped and caught Jimutan's neck in a vice-like grip which slowly tightened till he went limp and fell to the ground. The citizens of Matsya went crazy with joy. At a signal from Kanka, Valala quietly left the arena after saluting the king so as to avoid unpleasant publicity. However his reputation as a wrestler began to grow within the country, much to the anxiety of the brothers.

'Will Duryodhana's spies come to hear of this?' I asked my Lord.

"Not yet but another incident is to happen before they leave which might give the game away. However we can't avoid it. Come, we will return to Dwaraka," he said, "and leave them to their work." In Dwaraka my Lord had to attend to a hundred matters. He took a keen interest in the military training of the Upa Pandavas and Abhimanyu.

'Were they born with a gap of a year between them?' I asked.

"No," he answered. "Prativindhya or Shrutavindhya as he is also called is the eldest and is Yudhishtira's son. The second eldest is Nakula's son called Satanika. The third is Bhima's son called Sutasoma. The fourth is Sahadeva's son called Srutasena and the last is Srutakarma, who is Arjuna's son. Sahadeva's son, Suhotra by his other wife Vijaya, is also there. Prativindhya is the heir apparent and will have to be taught how to administer a state and not just how to fight."

'I thought Draupadi liked Arjuna the most. How is it that his son is the youngest?'

"Don't you know that Arjuna was away on a long pilgrimage and he came to Dwaraka and fell in love with Subhadra and so on? Obviously she conceived his child only after his return."

Ten months passed before we went to check on the Pandavas.

My Vanamali told me something about the military situation in Matsya. "As you can see, Virata is quite old and the actual power is invested in the commander-in-chief of his army who is a man called Kichaka who is a military genius and is also his brother-in-law. He has been away on various military expeditions and has just returned, bringing many spoils of war. He has also brought various gifts for his dear sister, Sudeshna and is just going to her apartments to give them to her personally. Come we will go there and see what's happening."

As soon as she saw a man approaching, Draupadi went into the queen's private gardens as was her custom. Kichaka was just about to leave when some fragrance from the garden prompted him to go there. The moment he set eyes on her he was totally infatuated. He had seen many beautiful women before but never had he set eyes on someone as bewitching. He tried to cajole her but for the first time in his life he was given a cold shoulder by a woman and one who was only a maid! He returned to his sister and told her that he must have this woman at all costs. The queen tried her best to dissuade him but at his insistence she promised to send Sairandhri to his palace the next day.

Next day the queen told Draupadi to go and fetch some exotic wines for her from her brother's palace. Draupadi refused at first but was forced to go at Sudheshna's insistence. She didn't want to offend the queen who had given her protection and treated her so well for ten months.

Kichaka was awaiting her with great anticipation. He had spread a banquet for her and rose up to greet her. He was perfumed and ornamented and dressed in the finest silks. He tried to win her with winning words. "You are not meant to be a maid servant. Stay here in my palace. I have kept clothes and ornaments for you. I am the real Lord of Matsya and you shall be my queen," so saying he made a grab at her hand.

I gasped and clutched my Lord's arm. 'Please go to her aid,' I begged.

"She is quite capable. Let her be."

Sairandhri broke free and fled with Kichaka pursuing her like a lion after a fawn. She ran straight to the court where Virata was sitting with Kanka and fell at his feet. Kichaka ran after her and caught her by her hair and smiled at the king and Kanka who was watching with burning copper eyes. Valala heard the commotion and burst on to the scene. Seeing Draupadi in distress he tried to uproot a tree in the courtyard to smash

Kichaka's head. With great presence of mind Kanka said, "That moist tree is not good for firewood. Go find some dry tinder somewhere else." Bhima glowered angrily at his brother and left the scene. Kichaka also left, glaring at Draupadi.

"Is there no justice in this kingdom?" Draupadi demanded. "Is there no one to punish this wicked man who had molested me?"

The spineless king replied, "I will have to find out exactly what happened. I will have to investigate further before proceeding."

To add fuel to the fire Kanka said, "It is unbecoming for a woman to shed tears in public. Please return to the queen's chamber and wait for your Gandharva husbands to come to your aid."

Draupadi glared at him and ran out of the court room mentally calling my Vanamali to help her. He immediately materialised before her and comforted her and wiped her tears with his *uttareeyam*. Of course I felt a bit jealous because this was something he always did for me. However I felt so sad for her that I didn't really mind. "Go to Bhima in the night" he said. "He is the one who will help you now."

In the middle of the night, she crept into Bhima's room who was overjoyed to see her and took her in his arms. She was weeping and showed him her hands which were rough and worn with the menial work she was doing. "I do not mind all this," she said, "but you saw what that vile wretch did to me in the presence of the king and your brother. You have to do something or else that Kichaka will force me." She started weeping on his breast. Bhima's thick black brows came together in a dark frown and smoke shot out of his smouldering eyes as he took her hand and kissed it and said. "I have a plan. Pretend to be won over by him and invite him to the dancing hall at midnight, where Arjuna teaches the princess and promise to meet him there!"

Draupadi wiped her eyes for she was sure that her Bhima would protect her. Next morning she went to Kichaka's apartment and promised to meet him at midnight. Kichaka could hardly believe his ears. "Ah! She has fallen for me," he thought and promised to meet her at the chosen place.

Three people were anxiously awaiting the stroke of midnight. Kichaka who had dressed with great care, perfuming and anointing himself and wearing fabulous silks and jewels. Bhima who had also dressed with care covering himself with the long flowing robes of a woman and Draupadi who had concealed herself behind a pillar. There was a bed at one end of the dancing hall and he lay there waiting for the lovelorn Kichaka to come. Sairandhri was behind the pillar, confident that her dear Bhima would not fail her.

My Lord and I were watching with amusement. It was like a play enacted before our eyes. I had to stifle my laugh when Bhima entered and lay on the bed. He looked so ludicrous. If there was anyone who was most ill-fitted for a female role it was Bhima!

It was a dark night and the dancing girls had all left the hall when the lover came in, impatient for the climax of his ardent love. He placed a lamp on the table, by the light of which he was just about able to make out the form of a woman on the bed.

"My darling one," he said, "You don't know how impatiently I have been waiting for this hour when I can take you in my arms!" So saying he went up to the bed and put his hand on the person lying there and was shocked to find a hard, muscular body rather than the soft, yielding one he had expected.

My Lord and I were in splits of laughter which we managed to hush.

Bhima threw off the blanket which was covering him and jumped to his feet with an oath. Kichaka realised he had been deceived and sprang at Bhima with raised sword. Bhima dodged but Kichaka kicked him while he was off balance and he fell to his knees. Kichaka carefully aimed his sword to strike off his head, but just then a fierce and wild wind seized the building and shook it like a leaf. The sword cut into the floor and Bhima jumped to his feet with a roar. He caught hold of Kichaka and cracked his bones as if they were bamboo sticks. Draupadi's piteous face flashed before his face and Bhima broke every bone in Kichaka's body and rolled him up into a shapeless ball of flesh. Sairandhri now came out of her hiding place and shuddered when she saw the condition of her would-be lover. Bhima gave her a quick hug and jumped out of the window.

I too shuddered at the sight of that mangled body and asked my Lord if he had sent the wind which made Kichaka's sword miss its mark. As usual he refused to answer and took me away from the gory scene.

The next morning there was a big hue and cry since the commander-in-chief was not to be seen in his palace. At last one of the dancing girls found the lump of flesh in the dancing hall and reported the matter immediately. Kichaka's brothers were known as the Upakichakas and they immediately came to the spot and were horrified to see the state of their brother's body. "No human being could have done this to him," they said and decided to question Sairandhiri for they knew about their brother's partiality for her.

She immediately said, "He tried to molest me even though I told him that I was married to five Gandharvas and now I think they must have done this deed."

They were furious with her and when they took their brother's body to be cremated, they forced her to go with them. "You are responsible for our brother's death and you shall be burnt along with him to give him in the next life what you denied him in this!"

As usual she thought of Krishna and my Lord obviously prompted Bhima for he came on the scene on the pretext of getting some firewood and massacred all the brothers in quick succession! The rest of the party was too terrified to interfere.

Sairandhri ran back to the queen's apartments. Sudheshna was weeping at the fate of her brave brother and realised that her maid must have called her Gandharva husbands to help her. She was most alarmed at the turn of events and told Sairandhri to leave the country immediately. Draupadi begged to be allowed to stay for one more month since her husbands had promised to come and take her away then. The queen relented more out of fear than love.

Aum Namo Bhagavate Vaasudevaaya

In whatsoever way people approach me,
In that same way will I receive them.
For all paths eventually lead to me O Arjuna.

Srimad Bhagavat Gita. Chapter 4.

ॐ

Muchukundaprasaadakaaya Namaha!

CHAPTER TWENTY-FOUR

The Cattle Rustlers

Eleven months had passed and Duryodhana's spies were unable to find a trace of the Pandavas. They returned to Hastinapura and said, "The Pandavas have disappeared without a trace. They have either died or run away in fear."

Duryodhana was overjoyed but Bhishma laughed at him and said, "I certainly don't think the Pandavas have died and even less do I believe that they have run away. Find a country in which nature has been lavish in her gifts with a just king and you will have found the Pandavas!"

'Why is the grandsire trying to help him?' I asked.

My Lord smiled and said, "He has already calculated that one year is over and it is time for the Pandavas to reveal themselves. Now see what I feared has come to pass and Duryodhana will put two and two together and realise that Bhima is the one who has killed Kichaka! See his spies have just given him the news that Kichaka, the powerful commander of the Matsya kingdom, has been killed by a mysterious assailant on account of a woman."

A sudden burst of light came into Duryodhana's mind. "No one except Bhima would have been able to kill Kichaka and he must have done it to save Draupadi, so the Pandavas are hiding in the kingdom of Virata! I have a brilliant idea. Let us ask Susarman to help us and we will go and invade their country and steal their cattle. Now that Kichaka is dead, the old king is helpless and we can easily take away the cattle. Of course we may have to share half with Susarman but it's worth it. In this way we can also smoke out the Pandavas if they are there!"

He sent a message to his friend and told him to draw Virata away from the city while the Kauravas went and rounded up the cattle. "The Pandavas will surely come to help him and thus we will get the cattle as well as expose the brothers," said Duryodhana who felt rather pleased at his brilliant plan.

The next day Susarman led the Trigartas and swooped down on Matsya from the south and seized the cattle. The cowherds ran with the news to Virata who wished with all his heart that his brother-in-law was alive, for he would have made short work of the invaders. In fact they had not had such a raid for many years, not since Kichaka was made commander of his army. Everyone knew of his prowess and never tried any tricks. He did not know what to do. It was many years since he had fought any sort of battle and he didn't think he was up to this. Seeing his worried look his new found friend Kanka came to the rescue and said that he would round up a few of the others and they would help him to chase the invaders. He called Vallala the cook and the cow-herd Tantripala and Grantika the stable-in-charge and told them to collect some chariots and meet them outside the city gates immediately.

My Lord and I watched with great excitement as the motley crew set forth to intercept the cattle thieves. The Trigartas were already fleeing with the cattle when they caught up with them and after a fierce battle Susarman captured the king and made off to his kingdom. Bhima intercepted him and jumped into his chariot and captured and bound him and released the king. Kanka and the twins had by now chased off the Trigarta army. Bhima waited for them to return and presented the trussed up Susarman to Kanka who immediately told him to release him. "Return to your friend and tell him that Matsya is not helpless even though its commander is dead!"

The king was a bit bewildered at the strange way in which a desperate situation had been totally reversed by help from such an unexpected quarter! He didn't know how to express his gratitude to Bhima who had saved him from ignominy!

While this was going on, the Kurus attacked the country from the north and herded the cattle away without any resistance from the cowherds. Some of them ran to the palace with the news, but the king and his strange helpers had not returned and the city was left under the care of his son Uttara Kumara, who was only a very young boy with absolutely no experience of fighting. The news of the new attack was brought to the queen who didn't know what to do.

Her son now remarked, "If only I had a good charioteer I would go and rout the enemy!" Hearing this Sairandhri remarked, "Apparently, Uttara's dancing teacher is an excellent charioteer and if this Brihannala agrees to go with him, your son will be able to defeat the attackers."

The queen was not totally convinced of the ability of the dancing teacher to become a charioteer and questioned Brihannala who made a show of refusing at first but at last agreed to go.

The prince was in good spirits when they set out, but when he saw the Kaurava hordes making off with the cattle he suddenly lost all his courage and shouted, "Brihannala! Stop! Please take me home. I don't care if people laugh at me but I don't want to meet them." He jumped out of the chariot and started running back. Brihannala ran after him, his long hair flowing and his women's robes waving from under the armour which had been put over them. He caught Uttara Kumara and dragged him back to the chariot.

"Brihannala please set me free," begged the prince. "I cannot face those warriors who are all as tall as trees!"

Arjuna laughed and placed Uttara Kumara in the charioteer's place and said, "Don't worry just drive the chariot and I will do the fighting. Take me first to the cremation ground near the Sami tree." Uttara Kumara obeyed Arjuna and turned back.

The sight of the fleeing prince accompanied by what appeared to be a half-man, half-woman had the Kaurava hordes in splits of laughter. I must say that I too found the sight ludicrous and when I looked at my Lord his face was also suffused with mirth.

When they reached the tree, Arjuna told the prince to climb up and bring the bundle down.

"There is a corpse hanging on the tree," said the frightened prince.

"Fear the living and not the dead," was Arjuna's retort.

Reluctantly he climbed and brought the package down and cut it open. He sprang back dazzled by the sight of the contents. There were five bows, five swords, and five conch shells and arrows.

"Whose are these?" asked the prince.

"These belong to the famous Pandavas. That long bow with a hundred golden knobs which has no knots is the Gandiva, the famous bow of Arjuna the middle Pandava. The one with the golden elephants on it is Bhima's. The bow with the sixty gold scarabs belongs to Yudhishtira. The one with the three suns is Nakula's and this one set with diamonds is Sahadeva's."

Uttara Kumara looked totally bewildered and Arjuna continued, "The thousand arrows in two quivers are Arjuna's and this is his sword with a frog on the hilt. The iron arrows are Bhima's as well as the sword in tiger skin with bells. The quiver with five tigers on it and dark blue sword in goatskin are Nakula's. Sahadeva's arrows are painted with different colours and the thick ones with triple heads are Yudhistira's. The curved scimitar belongs to Sahadeva and the flexible sword with flashing steel is Yudhistira's."

"But how are all these here and how can you dare to take the things belonging to the Pandavas?" asked the puzzled prince.

"Know me to be Arjuna. Yudhishtira is Kanka your father's friend and adviser and Bhima is the cook in your palace and Nakula and Sahadeva are working in the stable and cow sheds. We had to take one year in disguise at some city and we chose your kingdom. Now the year is just over so there is no problem in my donning my armour and taking my weapons."

"How did you lose your manhood?" asked the boy.

Arjuna said, "That was my disguise but now it's over." He removed his bracelets and donned his archer's gloves and lizard skin. He tied up his hair, fastened his sword and put his bow and arrows in the chariot. He took his conch shell and said, "Now tie up the rest of the things and put them back on the tree and let's go."

Uttara Kumara did as he was told and got into the chariot and took up the reins. Arjuna jumped in beside him and blew his conch – Devadutta. The leaves on the tree quivered with the terrific sound. He then strung his bow and drew it and let go with a shattering twang.

'Will they not recognise these sounds?' I asked my Lord who nodded comfortingly.

"It is all right. The thirteenth year is finished. In future this day will be celebrated as Vijayadasami – the day of victory."

Duryodhana was jubilant since he thought he had discovered the Pandavas. He rode his bull elephant to Bhishma and said, "That must be Arjuna and they will have to return to the forest for another twelve years!"

Bhishma smiled and said, "Duryodhana beware! The day of reckoning is approaching. The thirteenth year was over the moment you heard the sound of the Devadutta (Arjuna's conch shell) and the twang of the Gandiva."

"I will not give the kingdom to them," shouted Duryodhana.

"Then take half the army and go back to Hastinapura with the cattle and leave Drona and me to deal with Arjuna."

Arjuna shot three arrows which fell at the feet of his teachers Bhishma, Drona and Kripa as a salute to them. "I have only heard their names but I have never seen any of them. Please point them out to me," said Uttara Kumara.

"Watch carefully. In front is Karna waving a white flag with an elephant rope on it. Right at the back is Duryodhana on an elephant flying a golden flag with the elephant sign. Kripa is near Karna, wearing a tiger skin. His chariot is drawn by red horses, his flag is blue and on it is an altar of gold. Just behind him is Drona with a golden flag having a hermit's water bowl and a bow. Beside him is Aswatthama, with a black flag and lion's tail. And that my child is the great Bhishma with a blue banner which has a palm tree and five stars. He is dressed all in silver with a white helmet and white umbrella. Now drive fast towards them for I'm thirsting for a good fight which I have been denied for thirteen years" Arjuna fought with the pent up anger of so many years and so many insults and completely routed all of them including Karna who was always boasting of his ability to defeat Arjuna. Aswatthama taunted him with barbed words which were more hurtful that Arjuna's arrows.

My Lord and I were lost in admiration over Arjuna's tactics.

Once again he launched a second attack on them and finally he used his "*mohanastra*" or the spell of illusion by which all of them fainted for a few minutes. Arjuna told Uttara Kumara to drive towards the main warriors so that he could cut off pieces of silk from their clothes to be presented to the princess, Uttara who had asked him to bring some silks back for her as trophies. The victorious pair drove back to the Sami tree where Uttara Kumara replaced the Gandiva and all the other weapons. Arjuna returned to the women's apartments and the prince to the palace. He refused to say anything to anyone including his mother and sister who were congratulating him on his victory! The prince turned red with shame but did not say anything since Arjuna had told him to keep quiet.

'Now what will they do?' I asked my Lord.

"Let's go to the room where Kanka and the king are playing and watch the fun."

Virata was overjoyed at the supposed victory of his son and told Kanka, "I will give you a beating in dice as my son has given the Kauravas."

Kanka replied in his usual calm fashion. "Your son was lucky to have had Brihannala as his charioteer, without whose help victory would not have been possible!"

The angry king threw the dice at Kanka and drew blood from his head. Sairandhri who happened to be passing ran and collected the blood and told the king, "If this man's blood falls on the ground, your country will not have rain for the next seven years!"

Uttara Kumara came in at that moment and was horrified to see the blood and implored his father to apologise. He looked at Kanka who nodded his head and the prince revealed to his startled father the identity of his charioteer.

"Brihannala is none other than Arjuna the middle Pandava and this person whom you have just hurt is the great Yudhishtira, your cook is Bhima and Nakula and Sahadeva are posing as experts in cattle and horses. Sairandhri is the queen Draupadi. They were hiding here during their stipulated time of remaining incognito for one year."

Virata couldn't believe his ears and felt very happy that he had given shelter to the great Pandavas for a year. He was truly thankful to Arjuna for having saved their cattle and his reputation. "How can I show my gratitude? Please accept my daughter Uttara as your bride."

Krishna smiled to see his friend's discomfiture. "See what Arjuna replies," he said.

"Your majesty!" said Arjuna, "the princess has been my pupil for a year and is in the position of a daughter to me. However in order to strengthen our alliance I would be happy to accept her as a bride for my son Abhimanyu." The king gladly accepted the offer. Invitations were immediately sent to all relations and friends for the wedding which the king wanted to celebrate immediately.

I looked at Draupadi. Her son Prativindhya was twenty four years old and still unmarried. Why had Arjuna chosen Abhimanyu and not him? Moreover I knew that Abhimanyu already had one wife. Subhadra had opted to stay on in Dwaraka and enjoy the sight of seeing her son grow up while Draupadi had faithfully followed her husbands and denied herself the pleasure of seeing her sons grow up. Was she to be deprived of the joy of seeing her son married? I looked at my Lord. He shook his head. "I have told you before that I have to allow things to take their course and not interfere!"

We had to arrive with all due ceremony from Dwaraka with Balarama and Revati and of course Subhadra and Abhimanyu and eight of my Lord's wives and many of their sons and the chiefs of the Yadavas like Uddhava, Satyaki, Kritavarma, Vasudeva and of course Devaki. We came carrying many gifts of horses, elephants, gold and silver. Virata also gave many such gifts to his daughter. Drupada and Drishtadyumna came from Panchala with more gifts. The Kauravas were not invited.

Subhadra was delighted to see her daughter-in-law. She told Draupadi, "Sister! See how beautiful your daughter-in-law is. However she is not a patch on you. Perhaps you will get daughters-in-law who are more beautiful than you for your sons." Draupadi kept silent. Who knew what was passing through her mind!

Uttara was a radiant bride. She was only thirteen years old and Abhimanyu was sixteen and it was his second marriage. They made a handsome pair. Virata and his queen were delighted at the prospect of their daughter marrying the son of the greatest archer in Aryavrata. The wedding of his only daughter was conducted with great pomp. Draupadi was happy that after thirteen years she could dress in fine attire, even though she left her hair loose.

Food and wine were there in plenty. Virata gave away his daughter along with seven hundred thousand horses, two hundred elephants and a million jars of gold. Gifts were given to all and the citizens were fed for a week. After the banquets were over the musicians, magicians, dancers and acrobats and jesters came and entertained the crowd. Thus for a week, the Pandavas dined and wined and were entertained royally by the king. They who had been living like animals in the forest for twelve years and like servants for one year were now treated like the sovereigns that they were in actuality.

Aum Namo Bhagavate Vaasudevaaya

We who are the most noted among the knower of Truth become bewildered by the deluding influence of thy maya when we see thee, the Supreme Being and master of maya, assuming a human form, hiding his divinity and behaving like one subject to ignorance like an ordinary man. Wonderful is this sport of thine.

The earth brings out various forms of nature so thou the one desireless and changeless being, produces, sustains and dissolves this whole universe of forms into thyself. But thy inherent divinity is not the least affected by it.

Srimad Bhagavatam. Skanda 10. Chapter 84. Verse 17.

ॐ

Tribhangi Mathurakritaye Namaha!

CHAPTER TWENTY-FIVE

Upaplavya

Virata was so grateful to them for having saved his kine and accepted his daughter that he gave the Pandavas a village called Upaplavya close to his capital where they could rest and decide on their future. Immediately after shifting to the village, Yudhishtira invited my Lord and many of the Yadava chiefs from Dwaraka for the council meeting which he was going to hold. Draupadi's father and brothers from Kampilya had also come. Yudhishtira welcomed all of them and asked them to express their views on their next best course of action.

My Lord was the first to speak, "The Pandavas and Kauravas are equally related to us and we must decide on something which is favourable to both parties. The Pandavas have successfully completed the terms and conditions of their thirteen year exile, and now it is up to the Kauravas to keep up their part of the bargain and return half the kingdom to them as Dritarashtra had promised and live in peace and friendship forever."

Balarama immediately countered this and said, "The completion of the thirteen years of exile only entitles the Pandavas to their freedom but not to their kingdom! Duryodhana might be cajoled into giving half the kingdom, but he can't be compelled to do so because Yudhishtira knowingly gambled away their share of the kingdom. Moreover," he muttered under his breath, "after having enjoyed the whole kingdom for so long I doubt if Duryodhana will be happy to part with any share!"

Satyaki was furious when he heard this and jumped up, "I don't agree at all. Even before the gambling match, the Pandavas had been wronged many times by their wicked cousins and our dear Yudhishtira was virtually compelled to gamble. The whole game was most unfair, as Shakuni who is an adept in dice played for Duryodhana. Dritarashtra had stated categorically that they would return half the kingdom after the successful completion of the exile and even Duryodhana had agreed to this. Hence the Pandavas have a legitimate claim to it."

The others unanimously agreed with Satyaki and promised their whole-hearted support.

My Lord again wound up the whole topic, "Of course we all know that peace is preferable to war and we should explore every means for a peaceable ending. On the other hand, we should also be prepared for war since I feel that Duryodhana will not be happy to part with any of his land. But first I think we should send an ambassador of good will to the Kurus, who is soft-spoken, patient and polite yet able to speak with clarity. The sage called Uluka in Virata's court has all these qualifications."

Yudhishtira was happy to hear this and was just going to call Uluka when Duryodhana's messengers burst in and said, "The Kaurava monarch regrets that as Arjuna revealed himself before the completion of the thirteenth year, the Pandavas have to spend another thirteen years in exile!"

Yudhishtira and my Lord laughed when he heard this but all the others jumped up with oaths. "Tell Duryodhana to consult his elders," said Yudhishtira. "They will be able to convince him that thirteen years had ended well before Arjuna revealed himself."

Satyaki as usual was furious and said, "Evil people seldom change. This proposed sending of a peace maker is ridiculous. Peace can never be negotiated from a position of weakness. Only the strong have the power and means to destroy their opponent and negotiate for peace. Let us start to amass a strong army before we start negotiations."

Drupada seconded this view and my Lord also gave his support. Duryodhana had already started amassing an army since he had already decided on war. Now on my Lord's advice the Pandavas also started to approach various kings for their support.

Uluka was received at the Kaurava court with all the respect due to an elderly sage. Uluka stood in front of the elite of the Kurus and spoke: "I come here as Yudhistira's ambassador of peace and goodwill. He is truly a great man and always follows the path of *dharma*. Dritarashtra promised to give their share of the kingdom on the successful completion of the exile. So keep your promise and let the Pandavas and the Kauravas live in peace. Do not mistake Yudhistira's love for peace for cowardice. The Pandavas are invincible as you saw during the recent skirmish when Arjuna fought off the whole of the Kuru army single-handedly!"

Bhishma now said, "Uluka has indeed spoken well. It is best for you to keep your promise and return their country to them." Drona, Kripa and Vidura all supported Bhishma and urged Dritarashtra to return their kingdom to them.

Karna jumped up in fury and said. "The Pandavas have no rights at all." Turning to Duryodhana he continued, "Don't worry my friend. We are more than a match for all of them."

Bhishma was really angry and sneered at him, "Enough of your bragging. How many times have you bragged about defeating Arjuna yet every time the two of you meet, you are defeated by him including this last time during the cattle raid. Duryodhana! Let not Karna's boasting spoil your judgement. Apart from their own strength, they have Vaasudeva the great Lord to protect them."

Dritarashtra as usual dithered between greed and fear and told his son weakly to listen to his Elders. Duryodhana defiantly replied, "The Pandavas lost their kingdom through gambling. They will not get it back through negotiation. I certainly never made any promise to return their kingdom when they came back."

Vidura and Drona also tried to instil some sense into him but he walked out insolently without listening to them. At last Dritarashtra told Uluka, "Please tell the Pandavas that I will convey my decision through Sanjaya." Uluka returned and gave the message.

'What will happen now?' I asked my Lord.

"Yudhishtira has realised that war is inevitable and will start canvassing for support from other kings. Emissaries will be sent in all directions. Duryodhana has already started amassing soldiers. In fact he has already got eleven *akshaunis* (divisions). Since both sides are related, the kings will find it difficult to choose which side they should support. So they have decided to join the side that asks them first and in this Duryodhana has scored since he has already decided on war and is least interested in peace negotiations.

"Come we will return to Dwaraka since both parties are soon going to come and ask me for my support!"

'Surely Duryodhana knows that you will support the Pandavas.'

"Of course he knows that, but Shakuni has asked him to make a bid at least for my army so he will be coming soon. So we have to be prepared for his visit."

In Dwaraka my Lord told me that he wanted some rest so he went and relaxed on his swing bed. He told me to put a seat at his feet since he was expecting visitors. I stood next to him and was fanning him when Duryodhana was ushered in. He saw the seat at the foot of the bed and removed it and sat at my Lord's head. 'I suppose he thinks it's below his dignity to sit at the foot of a common cow-herd!' I thought to myself.

Soon after Arjuna came on the same errand and stood patiently at the Lord's feet looking at the ground. He refused to acknowledge Duryodhana's presence. I knew of course that my Lord never slept at that time and the whole tableau was a farce. When he woke up of course he saw Arjuna first. "Ah Arjuna! When did you come? You should have woken me."

Duryodhana coughed from the back and my Lord turned to him and said, "Ah cousin Duryodhana! What a coincidence that both of you have come at the same time! What can I do for you? Is this a casual visit, or do you have a common purpose?"

Duryodhana said, "I have come to seek your assistance in the forthcoming war."

Arjuna immediately said. "My Lord! I have come for the same purpose."

My Lord laughed and said, "This poses a problem. You are both related to me so I am bound to help you both so what can I do? I have an idea. I will go to one side and the other side can have my crack regiment known as the Narayana Sena led by Kritavarma. Many of my sons are in it. Satyaki and Uddhava will definitely decide to side with the Pandavas, but I will give first choice to Arjuna since I saw him first and moreover he is younger."

Duryodhana immediately objected. "That's not fair. You are capable of defeating our entire army if you wish so you have to promise not to take up arms!"

My Lord was highly amused by this, "So this is your idea of fairness that I alone and unarmed should go to one side and my crack regiment to another?"

Duryodhana nodded. "But still I give first choice to Arjuna. Do you want my best regiment or do you want me alone and unarmed?"

Arjuna unhesitatingly chose my Lord. Duryodhana was jubilant. The Pandavas were always fools he thought to himself and hurried off to get Balarama's support. He was disappointed to hear that Balarama was going on a pilgrimage in the event of war. He had presumed that Balarama would positively fight on his side.

"Krishna will definitely take the side of the Pandavas," he said, "and I don't want to fight against him. I hope you will fight according to the rules of *dharma* which I have taught you!"

When Duryodhana left to find Balarama, my Lord asked Arjuna, "Why were you so foolish as to choose me when you knew I would be unarmed?"

Arjuna replied, "My Lord if you agree to become my charioteer, I can fight the whole world. I do not need anyone else!"

Krishna smiled and I smiled with him for these were my sentiments absolutely.

My Lord and I returned with Arjuna since Yudhishtira was anxious for another attempt at peace. When we reached Upaplavya we heard of another deception played by Duryodhana. Yudhishtira said, "When Arjuna went to Dwaraka to ask for your support, I had sent someone to Madri's brother Shalya, our uncle, asking him to join us. While he was marching towards us with a huge army, Shakuni advised Duryodhana to set up camps all along the way in order to entertain and feed the whole army. Shalya thought this had been arranged by us so he was happy to partake of it, but later Duryodhana met him and requested him to join his army. Shalya could not refuse since he had eaten Duryodhana's food and accepted his hospitality. He came here personally to apologise to me and I didn't have the heart to insist on his joining us. But Shalya has promised to demoralise Karna at a decisive moment during the battle. He gave his blessings to us and said that our adherence to *dharma* will give us victory and of course the fact that we are supported by Vaasudeva!"

Dritarashtra had promised Uluka that he would send his final answer through his minister, Sanjaya. Soon after, Sanjaya came to the assembly with his message. Everyone loved Sanjaya so he was received with great warmth and love. He read out the message sent by the wily king.

"War is a terrible thing and both parties will suffer. As you know, my sons are obstinate and will not listen to me but I know that you are all noble souls so why don't you strive to live in peace? Spiritual pursuits are more valuable than material prosperity, so why do you wish to fight for the sake of a kingdom and lose your spiritual merit? Besides, now you are all used to a forest life which is so conducive to meditation and spiritual practices so why not go back to that and not proceed with this insane war? Or else you can ask Krishna Vaasudeva, who is your great friend to help you. Why not go to Dwaraka and live as his guests rather than give cause for a family feud?"

This remarkable speech on the quality of renunciation was heard in silence by all. Even Yudhishtira was shocked by this hypocritical message cloaked in deceitful words. Bhima and Arjuna jumped up with their hands on the hilts of their swords. The twins were taken aback by this blatant attempt on the part of the old king to save the skins of his own sons by depriving them of their rightful patrimony.

Only my Lord smiled as if he expected nothing but deceit from the Kauravas. He addressed Sanjaya, "My dear Sanjaya, I fear the Kurus are coming to the end of their days since they have surpassed themselves in their hypocrisy and deceit. Remember that *adharma* will bring its own punishment as *dharma* brings its own reward! Tell Duryodhana that a thief who steals wealth unseen and one who seizes it in open daylight are both to be condemned. The Pandavas' share is indisputable. Why should they submit meekly and watch while that share is seized by the avaricious Kauravas? Why should they be dependent on my hospitality when they have a kingdom of their own? A paternal kingdom is surely preferable to sovereignty received from friends. When the fair daughter of Drupada was seized by Dusshasana, all the Kurus, young and old, including you, were present. What stopped you from propounding your views on righteousness and morality then? When Karna insultingly asked her to choose one of the Kauravas as her husband, why did you not protest? When the sons of Pandu departed to the forest clad in bark, why did the old king not protest? Now when the time has come to redeem his pledge and return their kingdom, he talks of the quality of mercy and righteousness. He is the root of this tree of evil passions of which his son Duryodhana is the trunk, Shakuni its branches, the other brothers its blossoms and Karna its fruit. He is the one who has watered it. The Pandavas on the other hand make up a mighty tree of righteousness with

Yudhishtira as the trunk, Arjuna and Bhima its mighty branches, the sons of Madri, its flowers and fruit and I myself with all *dharma* at my command, its mighty roots.

"Tell the king that his brother's sons have always been ready to wait on him if he chooses to follow the code of *dharma*. Let him give back their patrimony and thus bring about peace or let him banish them and thus opt for war. In the meantime I shall make a last bid for peace, since I know that Yudhishtira wants it, and come to Hastinapura and try to make the king see reason.

"Brother," he said turning to Yudhishtira, "Now it is your duty to give your opinion on this matter."

Yudhishtira was torn between his desire for peace and his desire to please his brothers and wife who he knew were thirsting for war. He turned to my Lord and said, "My mind is in a dilemma as to where my duty lies. I surrender to you who have always been our one source of succour and inspiration. I take refuge at your lotus feet. I will do whatever you say."

I knew that my Lord admired Yudhishtira for his attempt to stick to his high principles. He knew what was going on in his mind and as usual I felt that he felt it was his duty to take the Pandavas across the murky river of war to a successful completion.

Turning to Sanjaya he said, "Go and tell Dritarashtra of Yudhistira's greatness, but even he is not in a mood to listen to the arrant nonsense which the king has sent through you. I see now that it is my duty to try and avert the catastrophe which is threatening to destroy the race of the Kurus."

Sanjaya bowed and left after taking an affectionate leave of the Pandavas and wishing them all the best.

Yudhishtira now turned to my Lord and said. "Krishna! You are our only hope. You are not only our relation but our friend and guide. I know I do wrong to ask you this, but my heart still craves for peace and if anyone is able to bring this about, I know it's only you. I beg of you to go to Hastinapura as our ambassador. I hope that Suyodhana (another name for Duryodhana) will heed your words."

My Lord replied, "Brother! Tell me what you expect of me and I will do it."

Yudhishtira said sadly, "Krishna, I fear that Dritarashtra expects to make peace with us without giving us the kingdom as he promised. I am not inclined to wage war against them. So please do your best for an amicable settlement. Govinda! They may be our enemies but that does not mean that we should kill them. We have numerous kinsmen, elders, friends and relations on their side. To kill them would be a sin. O Keshava! We may win or lose if we fight but it will be at the cost of many lives. In order to destroy our enemies we will have to resort to cruelty so I am hoping that we can get our kingdom without resorting to war. So please use your persuasive words and if that doesn't work, you can use harsh language and settle the matter. You are the only one who can guide us."

My Lord replied, "I hear your words O brother and will do my best. I know that Duryodhana will never heed my words, but I will seek to put a peaceful proposition to the Elders in the hope that they at least will be willing to see reason. I will enumerate your virtues to them and point out Duryodhana's arrogance and brutal dealings with you. I shall strive for peace without sacrificing your interests. If the peace talks are accepted, well and good and if they fail, at least I will be able to assess their strength and war strategy, so in all ways it is good if I go."

Turning to the other brothers he said, "I would like to hear your opinions on this matter."

Bhima said, "We should try with all our powers to settle for peace as our elder brother wants, but in case this fails we should also mentally prepare ourselves for war!"

Arjuna said, "Krishna! You know everything. But this is the only opportunity we will ever get to fulfil the oaths which we took at the time of that disgraceful scene when they tried to disrobe Draupadi. I know you will do your best but as you said, the omens are unfavourable for peace and Duryodhana will never agree to give us our share."

Nakula spoke, "We seem to have lost all sense of pride. I am for war and I don't think that anyone, even you my Lord can force Duryodhana to keep to his word. You heard what he said during the cattle raid when Bhishma tried to talk sense with him."

Sahadeva now spoke in his usual calm fashion, "O Govinda! You know everything and can stop the war if you wish. But the question is, 'do you wish to do it?' My brothers all have spoken against war but do you really think Duryodhana will be agreeable to this?"

My Lord laughed and said, "How do you think I can stop this war?"

Sahadeva answered, "The solution is simple. Kill Arjuna, bind Bhima with chains, shave off Panchali's hair and install Karna on the throne. Of course in order to do this I will have to tie you up."

My Lord smiled and said, "Most of what you say might be possible but do you really think you can bind me? Only my mother Yashoda has done this and that was when I was a baby. Even she had to take ten ropes before she could tie me round my little waist!"

"I can easily do this," said Sahadeva.

"Come let's go to a secluded spot," said my Lord and led him away. He then took ten thousand identical forms and challenged Sahadeva to tie him up. Sahadeva was quite calm and unruffled and sat down and meditated on the Lord and I supposed begged him to allow himself to be bound as his mother had once done in Gokula. I was mighty pleased to see my Lord standing in front of Sahadeva with hands and feet tied and a mischievous look in his eyes.

My Lord said, "Sahadeva, I am really impressed by the power of your devotion. Now untie me."

"Not till you promise to protect us always,"

"Do you have to beg for this?" asked Krishna.

Just before Krishna left, Yudhishtira made a last attempt. "Vaasudeva, please make some reasonable demands to Duryodhana which he can't possibly refuse. Of course first of all you should ask for the restoration of our lawful rights over the city of Indraprastha as well as half the share of the kingdom. If this is refused you can ask for a small share of the territory. If this is also refused ask for five villages. I don't want just any village. I want Varanavata as a reminder of the attempt to burn us alive, Vikraprastha where they tried to poison Bhima, Jayanta where the gambling match took place, Indraprastha which Duryodhana took away by deceit and one other village which can be of his choice. If he refuses even this, ask for at least five palaces for the five of us. If he refuses even this, then I'm afraid we will have to declare war!"

Satyaki controlled his anger as best as he could and said, "I don't think we should agree for unconditional peace. It is an insult to our Kshatriya blood. Duryodhana will never agree for peace so your journey will be in vain."

Bhima roared, "I'm ashamed to be the brother of this man who stoops to demean himself in this manner. Krishna please don't go to the Kuru court. Your holy feet which even the *rishis* and gods long to see, should not grace the halls of Hastinapura. Let me go instead. My stay will be brief and my mace will do the talking!"

Draupadi now came forward and said, "Ah Aravindaksha! (lotus-eyed one)! I was born from the sacred fire. I am the daughter-in-law of the great Pandu. My husbands are endowed with great valour. I have powerful sons and you yourself regard me as a sister. Despite all this, I would have been disgraced and disrobed in the middle of the Kuru Assembly had it not been for your grace and compassion. My tresses, sanctified at the time of the Rajasuya were caught by that wicked man who dragged me into the open assembly and insulted me in the presence of my husbands. Please remember all this when you go for your peace talks. At that time Bhima swore that he would kill the wicked Dusshasana and tie my hair with his bloody hands. Now what has happened to him? Fie on Partha's bowmanship, fie on Bhima's might since Duryodhana and Dusshasana are still alive. If my noble husbands will not fight, my aged father and his warlike sons will avenge my honour. My sons led by Abhimanyu will fight for my honour! What peace can this bitter heart of mine know until I see Dusshasana's hand severed from his trunk? That arm which pulled my hair so cruelly! That arm which tugged my garments and tried to denude me! Thirteen long years have I spent suffering untold hardships in the expectation of better times, hiding my wrath like a smouldering fire beneath the ashes. But now pierced by my husbands' words, that heart of mine is about to break!" So saying she began to weep.

My Lord took hold of her tresses and wiped her tears with his *pitambaram* and said, "Panchali, do not weep. I assure you that their oaths will come true. As your hair is bound up, so will the tresses of the Kuru widows fall down. If they don't listen to my words, the sons of Dritarashtra will surely lie on the earth and become food for dogs and jackals. Cease your tears, Panchali. I swear to you that you will soon see your husbands crowned with all prosperity and your enemies slain on the battlefield."

Yudhishtira said, "Tomorrow is a very favourable day for your journey so let's make preparations."

My Lord called Satyaki and asked him to put his weapons into the chariot. He asked some of the other Yadavas to follow him to Hastinapura and ordered Daruka to get the chariot ready for travel. The next day my Lord set out on his peace mission.

I asked him, 'My Lord! Both sides have already started collecting armies from various places and you yourself say that Duryodhana will never listen to reason. So why are going through this farce of making a bid for peace?'

My Lord replied, "There are two reasons for this. As Satyaki said, a weak person is not in a position to negotiate for peace. We can only ask for peace if we are in a strong position. Now that we have seven *akshauhinies* at our command we can ask for peace with honour. Otherwise they will think that this is only a coward's way out of an impossible situation. The next point is that I want the world to know the nobility of Yudhistira's character and the fact that the Pandavas tried every possible means to have peace. No blame should accrue to them that they are war-mongers. Moreover there is a one percent chance that Duryodhana may change his mind. We live in a field of all possibilities. Anything can happen and the wheel of *karma* may change at the last minute. It is my duty to try and reverse its course if possible."

Aum Namo Bhagavate Vaasudevaaya

Govindaaya Namaha!

CHAPTER TWENTY-SIX

Ambassador to the Kurus

Just after the rains when dew falls in the morning and the sun is mild and air clear and invigorating, my Lord set out on his peace mission. Conch shells blew and trumpets blared as we got into his gem-studded chariot drawn by his favourite horses, Sugriva, Meghapushpa, Saibya and Valahaka. The two wheels of the chariot resembled the sun and moon. I was terribly excited to be perched beside him. Uddhava and Satyaki rode with us and Arjuna accompanied us as far as the city gates. All along the way from Upaplavya to Hastinapura, the roads were lined with people longing to have a glimpse of that divine presence whose fame had by now spread far and wide. They gazed at that charming face with its enchanting smile and glorious eyes which cast a blessing on all those at whom he glanced. Everyone had heard of his super-human feats and he was already being deified as God incarnate. In Hastinapura not a single soul remained in their houses. The old and blind, lame and sick all came to welcome my Lord. His enchanting look swept over all of them so that they felt blessed and returned home cured of their ailments. I was so proud to be sitting beside him. We made a halt at Kushasthali and I think Duryodhana's spies went and told him of our approach. I learnt later that Dritarashtra had ordered Sanjaya to prepare a grand reception for my Lord. He called Vidura and told him to get the best palace ready which belonged to Dusshasana, for his stay.

I begged my Lord to give me leave to go and listen to the dialogue at Hastinapura. He laughed and sent me there.

Vidura spoke bluntly to the king with the familiarity of a brother. "O King!" he said, "How can we who do not have the capacity to give five villages to the Pandavas afford to give a palace to Vaasudeva? Are you trying to bribe him into leaving the Pandavas and coming to your side? Let me tell you that there is nothing he lacks and he will accept nothing from you. If you want to please him, help him to accomplish what he is coming for, which is for a peaceful settlement with no loss to the Pandavas or to the Kauravas. If you do this he will be more than pleased with you."

"Whether you please him or don't please him, Krishna never becomes angry. Do what he says and bring about peace with the Pandavas," urged Bhishma.

"He will come and tell us to give half the share of my kingdom to them. I will never agree to this. I have a brilliant idea. Let us imprison Krishna and then the Pandavas will be like parrots with broken wings. I will thus conquer both the Yadavas and the Pandavas," boasted Duryodhana.

Everyone was shocked at this suggestion. "He is coming here as an ambassador. We have to respect him. What has he done to deserve imprisonment?" asked Dritarashtra.

Bhishma left the hall in anger. All the others followed suit.

In those days it was the custom for the host to go two *yojanas* (about ten miles) to receive a distinguished guest. Dritarashtra deputed Bhishma, Drona, Vidura and others to go to the outskirts of the city and welcome the Lord. Duryodhana was stopped from going by Shakuni who said that it was not worthy of a monarch of his stature to go to welcome a cow-herd.

As soon as he saw the elders waiting to welcome him, my Lord jumped out of the chariot along with Uddhava and Satyaki and saluted them with great humility. All of them urged him to accept the Kuru hospitality and go with them to the palace reserved for him. He refused all the offers in his charming fashion and chose to go with Vidura to his humble hut. Vidura had left Duryodhana's palace at the time when the Pandavas were exiled, since he said he did not want to eat the salt of such treacherous people. Vidura couldn't believe his ears when Krishna said that he preferred to spend the night in his hut. He danced with delight and said, "What penance have I done that this humble hut of mine is going to be graced by your divine feet?"

As soon as we reached his hut, he shouted out to his wife to come out soon for the Lord had come to their abode. She was in the midst of a bath, but on hearing this she rushed out without putting on all her clothes and prostrated before him. He put his *uttareeyam* over her and covered her. But she was totally in a state in which she was not even aware of her body. All she knew was that the Lord had come to her hut and she had to be there to greet him. The couple preferred to live frugally rather than stay in Duryodhana's palace and receive his grudging patronage.

Kunti, mother of the Pandavas was living in another hut next to theirs. When she heard that her beloved Krishna had come she ran across to meet him. She wept when she saw my Lord. "Vaasudeva, there is nothing unknown to you. My sons were born to rule and they have been wandering like animals in the forest. How are they? Is my Yudhishtira safe? What about Bhima, Arjuna and the twins? Is my daughter-in-law safe? I hear that they have sent you here to beg for their heritage. Why are my sons asking for their portion like beggars? They were born from the seed of the gods and now they live like dependents. Tell them that a Kshatriya woman gives birth to sons only in the hope that they will become valiant heroes. You alone are our God and preceptor. Please advise them."

My Lord comforted her and said, "You know the Eldest is always keen on acting according to *dharma*. He will never budge from his principles. It is my duty to see that his wishes are adhered to as far as possible. The others are ready to do as he wishes even if it goes against theirs. Your daughter-in-law alone has begged me not to agree for peace at the cost of honour. She can never forget or forgive the insults which were heaped on her that day at the gambling match. Her hair waits to be tied by Bhima with hands stained with the blood of her tormentor! Fear not, mother! I will see to it that your sons are not deprived of their patrimony for a second time." Kunti's eyes filled with tears as she bowed low before him.

Vidura's wife, Sulabha was also a great devotee. She was actually my Lord's step-aunt, the daughter of his grand-father Devakan by a Shudra woman. She knew that my Lord loved the green herbs known as *bethua*, which grew wild in their small plot of land and she prepared a delicious dish with these leaves and served him with a heart filled with love. An amusing incident took place after that. Vidura had brought a small bunch of bananas to offer the Lord. His wife sat at Krishna's feet and wanted the honour of feeding him. He agreed. Looking lovingly into his tender eyes, she started peeling the bananas and feeding him with the skin and discarding the fruit. I wanted to warn her of what she was doing but of course I couldn't say anything and as for my darling Vanamali, he didn't want to interrupt her concentration and kept eating the skins without a word of complaint. Satyaki, Uddhava and Kritavarma had gone out to see the sights of the town and Vidura and Kunti were equally engrossed in the Lord's face like *chakora* birds looking at the moon, so no one noticed what was happening. It was only when she came to the end of the bunch that she suddenly noticed that there were a pile of bananas beside her and no signs of the skins.

My eyes met my Lord's and as usual his were full of mischief.

Needless to say Sulabha was abjectly sorry for what she had done, but my Lord comforted her and said, "Don't worry, mother! I have never eaten such delicious banana skins in my life!"

Now Vidura spoke to him, "My Lord, your sanctified feet should not touch the floor of the Kuru Assembly. Duryodhana is headstrong and stubborn and his father a weakling. Having eaten their salt the Elders keep quiet. What purpose will be served by your visit?"

My Lord said, "The learned say that he who knows what *dharma* is and does not strive to save a friend from *adharma* is a wretch. I must do my best to save the foolish Duryodhana from his own folly. If he doesn't listen to my words he will be inviting his own end. If I can bring about peace without sacrificing the interests of the Pandavas, I will have served the purpose of *dharma* and the Kauravas will be liberated from the mesh of death. But if they seek to injure the Pandavas, rest assured, O noble one, that I will not give in to their demands and shall do my best to see that they get their just deserts. I want the world to know of Yudhistira's nobility and Duryodhana's deceit. Future generations should not blame the Pandavas for having fought a war unjustly. It is my duty to make every effort at peace since war is indeed a terrible thing and will result in the death of thousands."

The next morning he sent Satyaki and Uddhava ahead of him to the Assembly hall where all the Elders were awaiting him. Duryodhana was furious that my Lord had spurned his invitation to stay with him the previous day and had gone with Vidura instead. He gave strict orders to everyone that no one should stand up to greet him when he came in and that he would set fire to the homes of anyone who dared disobey him!

Vidura, Satyaki and Uddhava were greeted cordially when they arrived. Then my Lord strode into the hall and looked around at everyone with his usual disarming smile. As if moved by some irresistible impulse, one by one all of them rose up and greeted him by prostrating before him. Only Shakuni did not get up. Karna felt compelled to stand up but he turned his head away to avoid having to prostrate himself. Strangely enough Duryodhana's throne suddenly tilted forward and threw him sprawling on the floor right in front of my Lord's feet. My Lord suppressed his smile which only I saw and said, "I'm really moved by your devotion to me, my dear Suyodhana!"

He then turned to the Elders and saluted them and greeted everyone and was escorted to a jewelled seat. He glowed like a sparkling sapphire mounted in gold in his yellow garments. Duryodhana could not contain his anger and burst out, "It was most unkind of you not to accept my hospitality. I had prepared the best palace for you and a magnificent repast."

Turning his radiant eyes on him, my Lord replied, "One takes food from the house of another only when the offer is made with love or if one is starving and has no other recourse. At present O King, you have not inspired love in me by any act of yours nor has your invitation been given with love, neither am I on the verge of starvation. You are also well aware of the code of conduct by which one cannot become the adversary of someone whose hospitality he has enjoyed. You know well how you tricked Shalya into joining your side! However if my mission is successful I shall be happy to accept your offer and be your guest!"

The blind king now courteously requested my Lord to declare his mission. A deep silence fell over the hall as my Lord rose up and started to speak in his mesmerising voice which thrilled the audience. "As you know, the Pandavas have successfully completed their thirteen years of exile. They have suffered greatly from the injustice which has been meted out to them by your sons but they are prepared to forget and forgive. The terrible danger which threatens to overwhelm the entire clan of the Kurus, O King, has its origin in the conduct of your sons. Therefore the establishment of peace depends entirely on you. Having lost their father at an early age, the Pandavas look upon you as their father. Treat them therefore as your sons and behave towards them as a father. Remember that they are your brother's children. It is your duty to protect their interests. For the sake of virtue (*dharma*), profit (*artha*) and happiness (*kama*), make peace with the Pandavas and give them back their portion of the kingdom which you promised to give as soon as they returned from their exile."

Turning to Duryodhana he continued, "I work for the sake of universal good, O Duryodhana! I desire your good as much as I desire theirs. You hail from an illustrious race which has always adhered to *dharma*. You will attain great fame if you restore to the Pandavas half their kingdom which was promised to them thirteen years ago."

Duryodhana who had been seething with rage during my Lord's talk now burst out, "The Pandavas gambled away their kingdom voluntarily. Completion of their exile only entitles them to live as my subjects and not to any share of the kingdom. Pandu was made king only because my father was blind, but I am the elder brother's son and I am not blind and the kingdom is rightfully mine. They can live as your guests in Dwaraka if they so desire," he added insolently.

Shakuni fanned the flames by adding, "This is the first time that I am hearing of the loser in a gambling match asking for the return of his lost stakes!"

My Lord replied sternly, "The gambling match was forced on Yudhishtira and Duryodhana won by a trick – by making you play in his stead. At that time Dritarashtra made a promise that half the kingdom would be given to them when they returned after the successful completion of their exile. Why should they be forced to accept my hospitality when they have a kingdom of their own? Do not confuse their love for peace for weakness. If you deny them their due, they will surely declare war which will lead to loss of life, poverty, famine and suffering. I ask everyone here to consider the consequences if the Pandavas are not given back their rightful heritage. Parents will lose sons, children will lose fathers and women will become widows. There will be an extermination of the very flower of the Kuru race! Think well before you decide!"

Karna interrupted, "What do you have to say about Yudhistira's disgraceful act in gambling away his wife? Such a person does not deserve a kingdom!"

My Lord answered forcefully, "Yudhishtira was taunted and instigated into staking his wife by Shakuni who capitalised on his weakness as well as his evil times. What about your disgraceful act in taunting her and asking her to choose one of the Kauravas as her husband? Have you forgotten that? What about Duryodhana's disgraceful act in asking his brother to disrobe her in front of the Assembly? Even the lowest of the low will not stoop to such an atrocity!"

Turning to Duryodhana he continued, "Duryodhana! I think you are not aware of the horrors of war nor do you appreciate the value of peace. If war takes place, the cries of the bereaved will rent the air. Every house in Hastinapura will be denuded of its sons and fathers. Everyone will curse the one who caused the war and you alone will have to bear the brunt of their curses. Don't underestimate the strength of the Pandavas. Have you forgotten your recent defeat at their hands in Matsya during the cattle raid and your defeat at Kampilya? Arjuna drove you off single-handed. Their request is most reasonable. They have sent me here to negotiate for peace out of their love for it and not out of their fear of war!"

Bhishma, Drona, Vidura and even Aswatthama now advised Duryodhana to see reason and accept the peace offer. "I don't want to see the end of Kuru dynasty which I have fostered for so many years," said Bhishma.

"There is no question of the Kauravas winning as long as Krishna and Arjuna are in their camp," said Drona.

Karna, Dusshasana and Shakuni said scornfully, "Let the Pandavas get their wishes fulfilled on the battlefield!"

Once again my Lord turned to Dritarashtra and said, "O King! If the Kauravas and the Pandavas live together peacefully, they will have no rival in the world to challenge the house of the Kurus. Your family will become famous throughout the world. But if you choose the path of war and *adharma,* the destruction of your family is certain. You shall be the cause of countless deaths. I see all the kings gathered in this august assembly going into the jaws of death. Only you can save them. You have the opportunity to rectify the mistakes committed by your sons. You can choose the path of truth or the path of unrighteousness! The choice is yours. So I request you again and again to make your sons listen to reason."

No one stirred for a while after my Lord spoke. At last Dritarashtra said, "O Vaasudeva! Can't you see that I'm powerless? My sons will never listen to me. They even refuse to listen to the advice of their mother or Bhishma or Vidura. If you can convince them I would be happy."

My Lord turned to Duryodhana once again and said, "You are the descendent of a very noble family. I can't understand your enmity towards your cousins who have always treated you well. Envy and greed are the qualities of base men. You should choose the path which will bring happiness to everyone and not stick stubbornly to your own opinions."

Duryodhana said, "Why do you utter such harsh words to me alone? All of you hate me. Yet I see no fault in me. I will not bow down to anyone even if it be Indra himself, let alone the sons of Pandu. We are Kshatriyas. If we die in battle, heaven awaits us. That share of the kingdom which was formerly given to them by my father will never again be given to them by me. If they want it, let them fight for it!"

My Lord spoke sternly to him. "You say you have not committed any offence against the Pandavas. From the time they came to Hastinapura as young boys with their mother after the death of their father, you have hated them and tried to harm them in every possible way. You tried to burn them in the house of *lac* in Varanavata. You tried to kill Bhima with poison, poisonous snakes and cords. Conniving with your uncle you wrested their possessions from them in an unfair game of dice. Not content with that, you dragged their wife into the open assembly and insulted her. Even while they were living in the forest you could not leave them alone but sent *rakshasas* to kill them and torment them. And now you are trying to cheat them of their rightful heritage even when they are asking only for their fair share which was promised to them. And yet you declare that you have done them no wrong! But beware, O Suyodhana

(Duryodhana)! You will be forced to give it all to them after you are laid low on the battlefield!"

My Lord continued, "Despite all this, Yudhishtira still hopes for reconciliation. In the interests of peace he is willing to accept even a small portion of land." Duryodhana insolently refused this, then my Lord asked for five villages and when that was also refused he said, "At least give them five houses!"

Duryodhana thundered, "Not even five needle-points of land will I give them. I am against all giving however insignificant."

Aswatthama now butted in and said, "You were so generous in giving Karna a kingdom, surely you can afford to give the Pandavas five houses and settle the issue without going to war?"

Furious at these words, Duryodhana marched out of the Assembly followed by his satellites.

My Lord tried once again to convince the Elders. "Not only Duryodhana but all of you will be guilty of destroying this race if you don't stop him from his folly. The time has come to forcibly seize and bind this depraved Kuru prince as Kamsa, the wicked son of Ugrasena was killed by me in order to save the race of the Yadavas. For the sake of a family an individual may be sacrificed. For the sake of a village, a family may be sacrificed. For the sake of a country, a village may be sacrificed and for the sake of the *atman* a man may sacrifice the whole world! Therefore bind fast this Duryodhana and make peace with the Pandavas!"

Dritarashtra was terrified by what Krishna had said and immediately asked his wife Gandhari to come. He also recalled Duryodhana who came with eyes burning with anger. Gandhari said, "My child, I want to see you happy. It is not easy to rule such a kingdom as this. No one with pride and greed can rule it. You can conquer your enemies only when you have conquered your own mind. You are going to be the cause of a great calamity. You are a fool if you think you can defeat the Pandavas with the help of Bhishma, Drona and Karna. Krishna and Arjuna are Narayana and Nara. When they stand combined no one in the whole world will be capable of defeating them. I am your foremost well-wisher. Listen to me and do what Krishna has advised and live happily."

Duryodhana sullenly refused to listen even to the words of his mother who was one of the few people he loved.

Then my Lord spoke to him sternly, "Since like a miser you deny the Pandavas even five houses, give me your hand and swear by striking this pillar that you are ready for war!"

Duryodhana swung his head back and said impertinently, "I refuse to take the hand of a mere cow-herd pleading the cause of men whom I humiliated and disgraced and who have been living like wild beasts in the forest. I really wonder how food went down their throats after they behaved is such a cowardly fashion thirteen years ago, meekly bearing my taunts as well as the humiliation to their wife." With this parting shot he swaggered out of the assembly before it broke up.

My Lord realised the futility of talking to someone like him anymore. Turning to the Elders he said, "All of you are witness to the fact that I have done my best to drive some sense into Duryodhana's head. A great calamity is going to overtake the house of the Kurus. No one should blame the Pandavas for bringing it about."

So saying he saluted the Elders and walked out of the court accompanied by Uddhava. Vidura and Satyaki stayed behind to find out what was happening in the Assembly. Satyaki returned after some time and gave my Lord an account of what had happened after he left.

"Duryodhana returned soon after your departure my Lord, and vent his fury on Vidura against whom he had been nursing a grudge since childhood, since he never minced his words when giving him advice which was always contrary to that given by his maternal uncle Shakuni. One is the epitome of virtue and the other of vice. All the venom he had been collecting for years was now discharged in a vituperative flow. I feel bad even to repeat it. 'You ungrateful wretch,' he said, 'your belly depends on the royal food of the Kauravas but your heart is beating with love for the Pandavas. You live as my vassal in my kingdom and yet you had the effrontery to play host to that cow-herd after he had rejected my hospitality. But what else can be expected from the son of a maid, who always bestows her favours on the highest bidder?'

Satyaki continued, "Vidura was stung to the quick not just by the insults heaped on him but for the fact that they were uttered on the spot hallowed by your footprints, my Lord. He said, 'You vile wretch! For insulting my mother I should sever your head but being my brother's son, you are in the position of a son to me. I was toying with the idea of helping you in the eventuality of a war but now I have decided against it. My bow will no longer be at your service in the war.' So saying he strung his invincible bow and pointed an arrow straight at Duryodhana's head and to the amazement of everyone he broke his famous bow, known as Govardhana, into two halves and walked out of the court. The bow broke with a thunderous noise accompanied by a flash of lightning.

"Bhishma immediately remarked. 'Whatever doubts I had about the outcome of the war are now resolved. Without Vidura and his bow, the Kauravas are doomed.'

"Duryodhana said in a flattering tone, 'I do not depend on this old man to win the war. I have you, Karna, Drona and Aswatthama on my side.'

"Karna immediately said, 'Don't depend on these old and feeble men, my friend! I shall personally kill Arjuna and the other Pandavas for you.'

"Bhishma laughed scornfully and asked, 'Have you forgotten your defeat at Arjuna's hands a few days ago at Matsya?' Karna was furious and left the hall."

Satyaki said, "I didn't wait to hear any more but came back here, but I fear that evil man is plotting something." My Lord seemed rather pleased by this narration since he knew that despite his age, Vidura would have been a formidable opponent.

"At least one of the Elders has been eliminated," he said to me.

'What is the significance of Vidura's bow?' I asked.

"His bow has been given to him by Lord Vishnu and is known as 'Govardhana'. It cannot be defeated by any weapon, not even by Arjuna's Gandiva."

'Are there any other such celestial bows?' I asked.

"Yes indeed," said my Lord. "Karna has the bow called Vijaya which was made by the celestial carpenter, Vishwakarma for Lord Shiva in order to fight the Tripuras (3 asuras who lived in three flying cities). Later he gave it to Indra who in turn gave it to Parasurama, who gave it to Karna. It is as tall as Parasurama and is so heavy that it can be lifted only by very few people. Arjuna will find it impossible to defeat him while he is wielding the Vijaya. He will of course use it during the war."

'But didn't Arjuna defeat him during the time of the battle when they were trying to take away King Virata's cattle?'

"Yes but Karna didn't have the Vijaya with him at that time."

'What will Arjuna do?' I asked.

"Though the bow is invincible, the arrows have to be potentiated by *mantras* in order to be effective and Karna has been cursed by his *guru* that he will not be able to remember the *mantras* at the time when he needs them. Even then Arjuna will find it very difficult to overcome him as long as he wields the Vijaya."

'Are there any other famous bows?'

"Of course I have the bow called Sarnga as you know, but since I will not fight it is of no consequence."

In the evening Duryodhana came himself accompanied by his cronies to invite my Lord to the court the next day. My Lord raised his eyebrows and agreed. Satyaki was most suspicious of this sudden change of face and returned to the Assembly to find out what the reason was for Duryodhana's spurt of friendliness. I think he suspected foul play and warned my Lord not to proceed. But of course my Lord just laughed and said, "My dear Yuyudhana (another name of Satyaki), have no fear. Even if he gets the help of all the gods he will not be able to capture me."

My Lord strode into the Assembly followed by Uddhava, Satyaki and Vidura. It was my custom to sit at his feet when he sat on any seat. This time he had already warned me not to sit at his feet but to go somewhere in front and watch the fun! It was only later that I discovered his import. Duryodhana and Shakuni led him very cordially to the bejewelled seat reserved for him. Hardly had he sat and made his greetings to all than to the horror of everyone present, the seat suddenly hurtled down into some pit which obviously had been made the previous night. I gasped and ran forward while the Kauravas guffawed and danced with joy proving that this had been a carefully planned ploy. Satyaki rushed forward, with upraised sword but before he could reach the yawning chasm where the seat had been, everyone was struck with wonder to see the Lord rise from the pit and spiral upwards until he assumed a gigantic form which seemed to stretch to infinity.

Turning to Duryodhana he said in a voice that resembled thunder, "O Duryodhana! Thinking me to be a mere mortal you have tried to kill me. But know me for what I am and behold my cosmic form. In me are all the gods – the Adityas, the Rudras, the *siddhas* and the sages. In me are the Pandavas, the Vrishnis and the Yadavas."

Saying this he burst into laughter and as he laughed, from his body that blazed like blue fire, there issued myriads of gods like streaks of lightning coming out of the dark blue sky. On his forehead appeared Brahma and on his breast Rudra, and from his mouth Agni, Indra and the other gods. From his two arms came Balarama with the ploughshare and Arjuna with the Gandiva. Behind were Bhima and the sons of Madri and Pradyumna and all the Yadavas. The form had many hands bearing the discus - Sudarshana, the conch - Panchajanya, the bow - Sarnga and the sword – Nandaki and many other accoutrements of Vishnu. From every pore there issued rays as blinding as a thousand suns.

The entire assembly stood up with folded palms and closed eyes since the effulgence was too much for them to bear. Only Bhishma, Drona, Vidura and the *rishis* had open eyes. They started to extol him with many hymns. It is said that out of his compassion, the Lord gave Dritarashtra, misguided monarch though he was, temporary vision so that he was able to behold this unique sight. Gandhari also removed the bandage from her eyes in order to drink in this remarkable sight. Dritarashtra prayed, "O mighty Lord of the Universe, unworthy though I am you have deigned to show me your Viswaroopa. I am blessed and do not desire to see anything anymore."

I too felt truly blessed because poor and insignificant though I was, in his infinite mercy he allowed me to have a glimpse of this cosmic vision which was given only to the great souls assembled there. Again and again I prayed, 'May this wicked prince come to his senses and realise that neither he nor his friends have a chance against your might. Let him call off this terrible war before it goes any further. Let him realise that he is only a puny human being and cannot pit his might against the gods!'

The Elders prayed silently, "O Janardana! Forgive us for associating with these wicked people and for helping them for we have eaten their salt and cannot help but obey."

Once more the voice thundered, "O Duryodhana! Steeped in *adharma* you planned to kill me an ambassador which none but the basest of people would think of doing. I can kill you and all the Kurus assembled here with a mere look but I shall not do so for you are not meant to die at my hands but at the hands of the Pandavas! This is your last chance to save yourselves. This *avatara* of mine has been taken in order to root out *adharma* in this holy land of Aryavrata and establish the rule of *dharma*. Do you really think that you can fight against the might of the gods? The Kauravas are rushing into the jaws of death like moths into a flame. Listen to me and to the Elders who are your well-wishers and agree to the terms I have put to you and avoid war or else be branded forever as the destroyer of your dynasty. Kurukshetra is waiting for its blood bath and Yama (god of death) is ready to enfold you in his arms!"

The voice died away into silence and as the stunned assembly opened their eyes, they saw him walk out of the hall arm in arm with Satyaki and Uddhava. Duryodhana and his brothers had seen nothing. They had only heard the thunderous voice and they quivered with fright. Yet their arrogance was so much that they did not join the assembly as all of them prostrated. Dritarashtra cried out, "O Keshava! I am innocent of this crime. My sons will not listen to me!"

I felt pity for this poor old man who was swayed now there, now here, unable to make up his mind and take a strong stand once and for all.

I was still in a state of trance after having witnessed that amazing sight. It is one thing to be told that everything has its being in the Lord but to actually witness this was something indescribable.

Aum Namo Bhagavate Vaasudevaaya

ॐ

Yoginampathaye Namaha!

CHAPTER TWENTY-SEVEN

Radheya

Some nameless fear had gripped Duryodhana at the time when the Lord showed his cosmic form, but he had only heard him speak and had not seen that terrifying figure. He brushed his fears aside as being baseless and bolstered up his ego by saying that this was another trick of the wretched cow-herd. I felt that his *karma* was relentlessly driving him to pursue the senseless path of destruction he had chosen. He rushed out after us to see what my Lord was going to do.

My Lord asked Karna to join him in his chariot along with Satyaki and Uddhava. He drove out of the city and then asked Karna to accompany him for a walk, leaving the other two in the chariot. "Karna," he said, "you are embodiment of *dharma,* equal to Yudhishtira. Your knowledge of the Vedas and Shastras is profound. I do not understand why you are siding with this most *adharmic* and sinful Duryodhana."

Karna sat down under the shade of a large banyan tree and replied, "My Lord! I may be the greatest of givers, I may also be well-read in the Vedas but if there is anyone to whom I owe my allegiance, it is Duryodhana. When the world censured me as a Suta Putra, it was Duryodhana alone, who stood by me and made me the king of Anga. When Bhima mocked me that day during the tournament, and when Arjuna's words were filled with contempt, it was Duryodhana alone, who stood up for me and offered his friendship. You know very well that on that day I swore to give my very life to him if need be and in his happiness alone lies mine."

"But what about Dharma? The code that you are supposed to protect?"

"Vaasudeva! From the time I was born the cards were stacked against me. Obviously my mother must have been from a princely family since I was decked in gold and silver when she chose to float me down the river. I was rescued and brought up by the charioteer Athiratha and his wife Radha. Though the gods have given me great prowess, yet society chose to ignore this and only mocked me for being a Suta Putra. Wherever I went I was scorned and taunted for my lowly parentage even though I knew and everyone knew that I was foremost amongst archers, equivalent to Arjuna! When I went to Dronacharya and asked him to teach me, he as well as the rest of the Kuru clan taunted me for not being a Kshatriya. Then I went to the great sage Parasurama who taught me everything yet cursed me when he suspected that I might be a Kshatriya and not a Brahmana as I posed to be! Even though he gave me the knowledge of all the great *astras* with one hand, with the other hand he took it all away from me by cursing me that I would forget all the *mantras* at the time when I needed them most! So what am I? Who am I? What sort of game is fate playing with me? Why give me anything at all if I was not meant to use it? Why was I not left to live as a mere Suta Putra? I would have been happy to have lived the life of a charioteer's son, the beloved of my parents. Why? Why was I given so many talents when I was not meant to use them and constantly taunted about my low birth?

"After my Guru's curse, I was bereft of hope and returned to Hastinapura at the time when a tournament was being held to celebrate the completion of the education of the Kuru princes. When I saw how proud Arjuna was of his prowess in archery, I could not help but challenge him since I knew that I was equally good. However I was asked to provide my family background and when they heard who I was, the Pandavas mocked at me, and Drona said I was not fit to fight with Arjuna, his star pupil whom he loved more than his own son! The only person who befriended me was Duryodhana who made me king of Anga. I asked him what I could do for him in return and he just took my hand and said, 'I want only your friendship.'

"My Lord, many years have passed since then and I am under an eternal debt of gratitude to him. In my whole life I have been given love only from two people, my mother, Radha and my friend, Duryodhana. I will do whatever I can for their happiness. Even though I know he is steeped in *adharma*, I cannot desert him now at a time when he needs me most. You asked me what my *dharma* was and all I can say is that my *dharma* is to my king – Duryodhana, as yours is to the Pandavas. I have promised him that I will slay the Pandavas and make him king of Aryavrata."

"Do you know who your mother and father are?" asked my Lord.

Karna looked at my Lord with fearful eyes as if he was in the grip of some fever. "Do you know who my parents are? Who is my father? Who is my mother?" he whispered, hoping that he would get the answer to the enigma of his birth which had troubled him his entire life.

My Lord's eyes filled with tears of compassion and he said, "Karna, your lineage is impeccable. The time has come for you to hear the most jealously guarded secret of your birth. Lord Surya, the sun god whom you worship daily three times a day is your father. Your mother is the mother of five of the greatest warriors, the like of whom the world has never seen and will never see."

"No! No! Vaasudeva! Please don't tell me anymore. I cannot bear it," he cried in despair as he jumped up. "I am only the son of a humble charioteer."

My Lord shook his head in infinite compassion as he continued, "You are my own cousin. You are not Radheya (son of Radha) but Kaunteya (son of Kunti). It is time for you to know the story behind your divine birth. You are the son of Kunti, mother of the righteous Pandavas. You are her eldest son, born from the sun god Surya. That is why you were born wearing his *kavacha* (armour) and *kundalas* (earrings). Since you were born before her marriage, Kunti was frightened to acknowledge you and floated you down the Ganga in a basket which was found by Athiratha and his wife, Radha who brought you up as their own son. But now that you know who you are, it's your duty to take your rightful place beside your brothers in the coming war."

Karna stood in shocked silence as my Lord continued his narration. Even though he heard everything, his brain refused to process any of it. He didn't know how to react to the fact that his sworn enemies were his own brothers! The weight of what he had just heard felt like a huge burden so that he was forced to sit down.

"*Karma* has come back to kick me again below my groin this time. This surely is its cruellest blow. All my life, I have taken the blows of *karma* and continued to move forward but this time, I don't think I can stand it," he whispered as he sank to the ground.

"My Lord! You knew this all this time and yet you never told me anything. Why are you revealing this to me now?"

"I want to save you from certain death. You are the eldest Pandava. You are like Yudhishtira in righteousness, like Bhima in compassion, equal to Arjuna in archery, as handsome as Nakula and as wise as Sahadeva. Come with me. You will gain five brothers and a mother and enjoy the kingdom of the Kurus for you are the eldest and will be made king. Yudhishtira will not stand in your way. I can assure you of that."

My Lord put his arm around his shoulder and said reassuringly, "It's not too late. Acknowledge your rightful heritage and join the Pandavas. You will be made king and your brothers will worship the ground you trod upon."

Karna replied, "Ah Vaasudeva! Don't mistake my pain for weakness. My loyalty to my king is greater than my loyalty to a set of new-found brothers who have always treated me with great scorn. A man must cling to what he believes in. In my heart I already know the outcome of the war which is inevitable. In fact the moment you decided to side with the Pandavas, I knew that ours was a lost cause. I can see a legion of warriors moving steadily towards Yama, the Lord of Death. I will be assured of a place in heaven only if I fight this war on the side of Duryodhana. Only then will my *karma* stop following me like a rabid dog!

"I thank you for divulging the secrets of my birth to me. But I don't know whether it brings me joy or sorrow. Of course I am proud of the fact that the righteous Pandavas are my brothers. But, my Lord, my real mother abandoned me at a very tender age. My mother Radha means more to me than she. I am even known as Radheya. Her love has supported me and helped me throughout my life. I can never disown my parents now, whatever be the temptations to do so. As for Duryodhana I stand eternally in his debt. I have pledged my word to support him and I cannot back out of it just because of some new-found relations. I have to help him. He depends entirely on me. I shall die with him on the battlefield. What is the use of my life if I gain it by betrayal of my best friend? It has been my long cherished desire to fight Arjuna on the battlefield but after hearing about our relationship my enthusiasm has flagged. Fate has always dogged my footsteps from the time I was born. And now this disclosure from you has put the seal on a life of shame and uncertainty. No doubt you have some reason for having disclosed this to me at this critical juncture of my life. I know you to be the ultimate redeemer and I know you work for universal well-being. The Pandavas are indeed fortunate to have got you as their protector. They will be invincible."

"How can you be so sure of the Pandavas' victory?" asked my Lord.

Karna replied, "O Madhusudana! This war of Kurukshetra is a *yajna* (fire sacrifice). You are the *yajna purusha* (presiding deity), Arjuna is the chief priest. The other Pandavas are the helpers. Bhishma, Drona, Kripa, the Kauravas including me and the soldiers are the offerings in this *yajna*. We will all be offered into the fire of this cosmic *yajna*. I beg of you to bless all those who fall on this battlefield that they will attain heaven."

My Lord took his hands in his and told him to ask a boon for himself since the boon he asked for the others was already granted. Karna spoke with difficulty, "My Lord, apart from my mother, I think you are the only one who knows the secret of my birth. I beg of you not to disclose my identity to the Pandavas or anyone else while I am alive. If the noble Pandavas come to know who I am, they will not be able to fight against me. Yudhishtira is the embodiment of *dharma*. Fate has given him many trials, but in the end I feel that he will be the greatest emperor of Aryavrata under your guidance. If he knows who I am he will offer the kingdom to me and if he offers it to me I shall immediately give it to Duryodhana, so all your efforts at establishing a reign of unprecedented righteousness in this country will be put to naught. So I beseech you not to disclose my secret to anyone. I feel that I will have only a short life but I wish it to be a glorious one. I shall get fame even in death!"

My Lord's eyes glimmered with tears. He was full of admiration for this mighty hero who had the cards stacked against him from the time of his birth. He clasped him in his arms and said, "It shall be as you wish. The battle will commence on the new moon day one month hence and I assure you that all the heroes who fall in battle will attain heaven."

Karna touched the Lord's feet and said, "If we come out of this great battle alive, may we meet here again?" My Lord did not reply and his lotus eyes were filled with sympathy. Karna saw the look and said, "If not O Janardana, we shall surely meet in heaven!" Once more he looked into those compassionate eyes which were full of blessings for him and said sadly, "Perhaps we are fated only to meet in heaven!"

Sadly they returned to the chariot in which Satyaki and Uddhava were waiting and returned to the city. Having dropped Karna they returned to Vidura's hut. My Lord then went to Kunti's house which was just next to Vidura's.

She embraced him with great love and made him sit beside her. Even though she had exhorted her sons to act like Kshatriyas, she was well aware of the ruinous effects of a war and she asked with trepidation, "Have your attempts at peace been successful?"

"Every attempt at a peaceful solution has failed. Duryodhana is determined to bring about his own destruction and the annihilation of the house of the Kurus." He took her hands in his and looked into her eyes and asked, "Do you have any knowledge of your firstborn whom you abandoned so long ago since you were unmarried at the time of his birth?"

She snatched her hands away from his and said in a shocked voice, "How did you come to know of this?" She thought for a while and then said, "Of course you are omniscient. No secrets can be kept from you. Why are you telling me this now?"

My Lord said, "That baby whom you abandoned is Karna, Duryodhana's chief champion and support. Without Karna, Duryodhana is doomed. I have just met him and told him the truth about his lineage and asked him to join the rank of the Pandavas, but he is so deeply in Duryodhana's debt that he refuses to leave him even if it means his own death. I admire him for his fidelity and gratitude. He is a noble soul. Had he not associated with such *adharmic* people like the Kauravas, he would have been greater than Yudhishtira. Now I am going to ask you something. Think well before you speak. Would you prefer your eldest son Karna to live or do you want the Pandavas to live? You have a choice between the two. Karna has sworn to kill Arjuna and if he does that, the other four will also kill themselves since they are like a five-headed cobra. They fight together or die together!"

Kunti was greatly agitated when she heard this and said, "I know what I will do. I will go and reveal myself to Karna and persuade him to join his brothers. Surely he won't refuse his mother!"

Krishna smiled and said, "Yes you can try to do that but I fear he will refuse. He has already refused me so why should he agree to please a mother who abandoned him as a baby? He told me that he has only one mother and that is Radha, the wife of Atiratha, the charioteer. However, even if he refuses to join the Pandavas, you can ask for two boons from him – that he will kill only one of your five sons in battle, be it Arjuna or any of the others and that he will use the Nagastra only once during the battle."

Kunti's heart melted with love for her new-found son and she asked tearfully, "Won't Karna's life be jeopardised if he gives these boons? I don't want him to be harmed."

"Of course it will," said my Lord. "Again you have to choose between the lesser of two evils. That is the only choice that all of us have. Do you want to eradicate *adharma* from this holy land or do you selfishly want the lives of all your six sons? You cannot have both. I know you to be a strong Kshatriya woman who is prepared to sacrifice all her sons for the sake of a righteous war so now why are you hesitating? When you floated him down the river as a baby you made a choice between two evils – whether to save your reputation and the name of your family from disgrace or to take a chance and float him down the river in the hope that someone would save him! At that time you chose the lesser of two evils so the same choice is open to you now. Why do you hesitate?"

"You are god incarnate, omniscient and omnipotent. How can I argue with you?" she asked sadly. "You have incarnated in order to establish *dharma* and it cannot be achieved without the destruction of *adharma*. Creation is your game and destruction your sport! Both go hand in hand with each other." Her eyes filled with tears and she said, "I have never been a mother to Karna and now it seems that I have to be his slayer!"

My Lord felt great pity for her and said, "Mother, you renounced your duties to your firstborn the moment you floated him down the river. Now your duty is to your other sons so proceed to Karna and do as I told you."

My Lord now went out of the house to the forest close by. 'What are you going to do now?' I asked. He looked very serious and replied. "There is one more thing I have to do to safeguard Arjuna."

'Are you concerned only about him?' I asked.

"No, I am concerned about all the Pandavas. I depend solely on them to establish *dharma* in this holy land."

'Can you establish *dharma* by using *adharmic* methods?' I asked.

"My child, as I told Kunti no one has a clear cut choice between good and evil. The two are always inextricably mixed so our choice is always between the greater evil and the lesser evil. I have opted for the lesser evil so that I can avoid the greater evil. I admire and love Karna very much and that is why I tried my best to bring him round to the Pandava side, but since he has refused, I have no other choice but to try to cut his wings so that he will not kill Arjuna and thus destroy the Pandavas. Think of the state of this country if the Kauravas win. They are steeped in *adharma*. They have tried every mean trick to kill their cousins. Even now they will stoop to anything to save their own skins. See how they conspired to kill me! Together they make a veritable colossus of evil. If I sit back and allow things to take their course, there is a possibility that they might win and you know full well the consequences of such a victory. The Kauravas are really *asuras*. They are filled with hate and greed and violence. To subdue them we will have to resort to many tricks, some righteous and some unrighteous. I have used only *dharmic* means up till now and you have seen how futile that has been. They are simply not interested in an amicable settlement which will not violate the law of *dharma*. They are determined to kill indiscriminately in order to achieve their desires. Nothing and no one can stop their mad rush towards self-destruction. Resorting to weak means will only evoke scorn from them. They are incapable of seeing the good in others. They see only goodness in themselves as Duryodhana declared at the Assembly.

"Once I asked Duryodhana to point out to me a good man with noble attributes. He told me that he had looked everywhere and had not found anyone with good attributes other than himself! Another time I asked Yudhishtira to find someone who had the worst qualities of any human being. He searched everywhere and returned and told me that he could not find such a person and if at all anyone had bad qualities it was himself! Thus you see that Duryodhana is steeped in his own conceit and can see no goodness in anyone but himself whereas Yudhishtira is filled with humility and can see nothing bad in anyone. Duryodhana believes that he has been misjudged by everyone including his own father. Nothing can deter him from hurtling down the crazy, heedless path of destruction which he has chosen. My duty is to protect my devotees by whatever means at my disposal. For this I will have to take the help of Arjuna's father."

He sat on a stone and closed his eyes and very soon Indra appeared in front of him. "Your son's life is in great danger," he said. "Karna has sworn to kill him in the forthcoming battle. Proceed straight to him and beg for his *kavacha* (armour) and *kundalas* (ear ornaments). As long as he wears these, he is said to be invincible even though I must admit Arjuna defeated him during the recent cattle raid at Matsya. However it is better not to take any chances. Karna is the most generous man alive and he will not refuse anything to anybody. Usually he gives charity to anyone who asks for anything before noon. At midday he does his worship of his father, Surya and after that he cannot be approached for charity. So please disguise yourself as a mendicant and go immediately before the sun reaches its zenith."

I marvelled at the way my Lord strove to bring out the best points in his devotees so that the world would ever extol them even at the cost of bringing disrepute on himself. I wished I could be present when Indra approached Karna. My Lord knew my mind so he took me to the river where Karna was having his morning ablutions before sitting for his usual practice of giving charity to all who approached him. Even though Indra, disguised as a beggar was a little late, Karna saw him and asked him what he wanted.

"I have come to ask you for a gift," he said.

"Ask and it shall be yours," said Karna.

"Well then give me your *kavacha* and *kundalas*," he said.

Karna was surprised to hear such a strange request from an old beggar. However to his eternal credit, without a word of protest, he went inside the house to tear off the *kavacha* which was attached to his body from birth. Just then he heard the voice of his father, Surya telling him not to give anything to this old man who was actually Indra in disguise who was doing this to save his son Arjuna. Karna had never refused anything to anyone and did not heed this advice. He tore off his accoutrements and went out with bleeding chest and ear lobes from which he had torn the jewels. He held them out to the beggar and said, "My Lord Indra, I know that one of your names is Parjanya or the giver of rain. I am indeed proud that today, you, the great giver is standing before me with upturned palms ready to accept a gift from me. Here are the things you asked from me. You may have them!"

Indra felt ashamed of himself and said, "Karna, you are indeed a noble soul. In future the world will say 'the greatest giver of gifts is Karna and not Parjanya!' However I cannot accept your sacrifice without giving something in return. Ask for whatever you want and it shall be yours."

Karna replied, "A gift loses its charm and merit if I ask for something in return. However to safeguard you from the ill-fame of accepting my prized possessions without giving anything in return, I will ask you for something."

"You can ask for whatever you want," said Indra.

"I would like to have your Shakti weapon if it pleases you."

I think Indra felt like bowing and touching the feet of this most magnanimous being he had ever seen. "Here! Take my Shakti weapon," he said, giving him the invincible dart of that name. "But remember that it will be useless against Arjuna since he is protected by Krishna. However it will enable you to kill one of the most formidable heroes on the Pandava side."

Before Karna could thank him, he had disappeared from sight.

I said to Krishna, 'My Lord, you are hemming him from all sides so that there will be no escape for him!'

"My child," he said, "have I not given him a chance to change sides if he wants to do so but he has refused. As I told Dritarashtra, even a son has to be renounced if he endangers the whole race so also a friend who leads you down the path of *adharma* should be avoided before he leads you to perdition. Remember Duryodhana's friendship was given with a totally selfish motive. He immediately saw in Karna a challenge to Arjuna and took the opportunity to make a friend of him. In his innocence Karna only saw in him someone who befriended him in the face of all the others who denounced him. I assure that I will not hesitate to exterminate my own clan if they prove a threat to *dharma*!"

'Your path is bitter, my Lord. There are very few who will be able to follow it.'

"Karna has made his loyalty to Duryodhana as his highest principle. He has even put it higher than right and wrong. Only God deserves such unflinching loyalty. He aided his friend even when he was doing grossly unjust and shameful deeds. Loyalty is no doubt a great value but when it overrides *dharma*, it can only lead to a tragic end. See how Ravana's brother Vibhishana deserted him when Ravana refused to change his *adharmic* ways. He realised that loyalty to an ignoble soul would lead even a good man to a tragic end and thus he left him and joined Rama.

"I cannot afford the luxury of weak sentimentalism. Everyone cannot be saved at the same time. Each one has his own time for attaining liberation. It may be in this life or in another. At the moment my role is only to remove the obstacles that stand in the way of the Pandavas' victory. That does not mean that I hate those who stand in my path. In fact I love everyone, even Duryodhana, misguided though he is. I am alike to all – friend or foe, but the goal I have chosen in this incarnation is the establishment of *dharma* and to that end I have to work."

I bowed before him and whispered, 'I am only a poor deluded human being with a very partial understanding. Help me to overcome the limitations of my intellect.' He smiled at me and I felt that I understood everything.

'Can I ask you one more question?' He nodded.

'What is the significance of the "*kavacha* and *kundalas*" in Karna's life?'

My Lord looked deeply into my eyes and said, "That story goes back to the previous eon, known as the Treta Yuga where the great *asura* called Dambhodbhava did intense *tapas* to the sun god in order to receive boons from him. He asked for immortality but since this was something no god could give to lesser beings, the *asura* craftily asked that he be given one thousand *kavachas* and one thousand *kundalas* and one thousand lives so that each time the *kavacha* broke he died and got another life and another *kavacha*. Only a person who had done intense *tapas* could break his *kavacha*. So he came to be known as Sahasrakavacha or the one with a thousand armours. Hardly had Surya granted him this boon than he started wreaking havoc on gods and humans alike. At that time Murti, one of the daughters of Daksha, father of Sati, prayed for a son who could kill this cruel *asura*. She gave birth to a couple of twins who were actually incarnations of Vishnu. They were called Nara and Narayana. They were inseparable. When Sahasrakavacha came to the Himalayan regions where Nara and Narayana were doing *tapas* he started to fight with them. While one of them fought with him the other did *tapas*, thus alternately fighting and doing *tapas*, they broke nine hundred and ninety nine *kavachas*. When the *asura* realised that he could never beat the two brothers, he ran and took refuge with Surya. Nara and Narayana approached Surya and asked him to give up the *asura*. Surya refused and Narayana cursed him that he would be born as a human being. In order to fulfil the curse, Surya and Sahasrakavacha were both born in one body as Karna! In order to complete their task of killing the *asura*, Nara and Narayana were born as Arjuna and Krishna!"

Seeing my look of wonder my Lord continued, "Yes I am Narayana and Arjuna is Nara and one of the reasons for our incarnations is to kill Sahasrakavacha. For this, as you know one of us has to do *tapas* while the other fights. In the war which is to come, I will not be taking up arms and Arjuna will do the fighting and will kill Karna. This *kavacha* which he wears is the last of the one thousand which was granted to him by Surya. Arjuna will surely die if he breaks the *kavacha* that is why his father Indra has gone and got it from Karna. Since Indra is an immortal he will not die. Since a part of Karna is actually the *asura*, Sahasrakavacha, he has had to face many problems and even commit many crimes against the Pandavas. But since he has the Sun God also inside him, he is fearless, brave, strong and charitable and will go down in history as a great hero. Since he has both *deva* and *asura* in him, there is a conflict of *daivic* and *asuric* qualities in him. So now are you satisfied?" he asked. I nodded vigorously.

"Tomorrow morning we will set out for Upaplavya where the Pandavas are anxiously awaiting my arrival to know the outcome of the peace talks."

'Can't I eavesdrop on Kunti's conversation with Karna before going?' I asked.

He smiled and gave his consent. "I have something to discuss with Vidura while you go to the river."

Kunti went in the morning to the Ganga where Karna was worshipping the rising sun. She stood looking at him with new eyes as he stood gazing fixedly at the sun. He seemed to be enveloped in a golden glow. How was it that she had never noticed his striking resemblance to Yudhishtira, she wondered. In fact he was taller and more handsome than Yudhishtira and had a golden complexion. She was shocked to see the wound on his chest where his *kavacha* had been torn from him. Who could have done such a thing, she wondered. How am I to approach him, she thought. Does he know that I am his mother?

She went forward but he was deep in meditation on the golden orb and didn't see her. She waited patiently till he had finished. When he saw her he got up from his seat and escorted her to his palace. "What can I do for you?" he asked politely.

"Didn't Krishna tell you who I am?" she asked.

"Yes, he did tell me but many people have approached me and pretended to be my mother to get a share of my kingdom, but I have a shawl which was put over me by my real mother when I was a baby and if this shawl is put over anyone other than my mother it will burn her up. Are you willing to undergo the test?" he asked, hardening his heart against her.

"Of course," she replied.

He brought out a fabulous golden shawl out of the chest in which he had been floated and threw it over her as if hoping that by some miracle she would turn into ashes. He knew that what my Lord had told him must be true but if by some marvel, it was not true then so many issues could be avoided. He could continue to hate the Pandavas and side with Duryodhana without any feeling of guilt. The shawl draped round her shoulders as if it belonged there and she smiled at him with love pouring out of her eyes.

"So you are indeed my mother," he said bitterly, "who abandoned me as a baby and never thought to find out where I might be and who has suddenly appeared at this juncture in my life for some ulterior purpose of her own!"

"Why are you berating me like this?" she asked. "I admit that I did you a grave injury when you were born but please try to understand that I was helpless. If my father or any of the others had found out that I had a child when I was unwed, can you imagine the consequences? My family name would have been tarnished. I would have been branded forever as a woman of low morals and would have had to remain a spinster. I was not strong enough to bear this penalty. Forgive me, my son. I know I have wronged you woefully." Tears started to pour down her cheeks and Karna, ever the compassionate one, could not bear to see this. He ran to her and fell at her feet and said, "So you are indeed my mother. How can a son not forgive his mother? I have longed to see you all these years and now that you have come I wish I never had a mother."

"My child! Please don't say this. You are my firstborn - eldest of the Pandavas. Your rightful place is with them as their leader. Believe me they will gladly serve you and accept you as the Eldest."

"Mother! Please don't say anything more. For a few minutes at least let us forget the reason why you have come. Let me pretend that you have come because you love me and not for any other reason. Let me rest my head on your lap and imagine that I'm only a child."

So saying he laid his head on her lap and Kunti stroked his hair and murmured, "My darling child, how I have wronged you. Let me make it up to you. You are right, for some time at least let us pretend that the shadow of a war is not looming over our heads and that we are just enjoying each other's company." He closed his eyes and she crooned to him some ancient song which he felt that he remembered from a past life. Was it only a memory or had it really happened? Time stood still while mother and son enjoyed this moment snatched out of the river of time, which they had never experienced before and would never experience again.

At last Karna got up with a sigh and said, "Mother, you know that I can never come back to you as your son in this life. Perhaps I might in some other life. My life is already flowing towards the river of war. I cannot swim against the tide. I owe everything to Duryodhana. He has made me what I am today. But for him I would be only a *Suta Putra* – a charioteer's son. Because of him I am Anga Raja – King of Anga. Because of him I was able to marry the princess of my choice. I will never abandon him whatever you might say. To the whole world he might be a devil but to me he is a god."

Just then a voice came from the solar orb advising him to accept Kunti's request but Karna's heart did not waver. He said bitterly, "You abandoned me as a baby. No enemy could have done more. And now, I know that you have come, not for my sake but for the sake of your other sons who might be slain by me. But nothing will make me betray my only friend at this crucial juncture."

"Duryodhana is indeed fortunate to have you as his friend, my child," she said. "Your loyalty to him makes me proud of you. Maybe this is why Krishna sent me to you so that I would discover your greatness. However the law of *karma* is inexorable. Each one must reap the consequences of what he sows. Fight then for Duryodhana if you must but I have two requests to make."

Kunti cast down her eyes and did not know how to make her request. But she knew that she owed it to her other sons to ask this boon even though her heart was breaking for him.

"What is it mother?" he asked. "What is troubling you? Can I help you in any way? You have only to ask and I will be happy to do anything for you other than abandoning my friend. In fact I consider myself truly blessed to be able to give boons to a mother I have hardly met!"

Kunti whispered so that he had to bend his head to hear her, "Promise me that you will not kill your brothers in battle!"

Karna laughed a harsh laugh, "You have asked for the one thing that I cannot give. I have promised Duryodhana that I will kill Arjuna in battle or be killed by him so I cannot go back on that promise. But I can assure you that under no circumstances will I kill the other four. Even if I kill Arjuna, be satisfied O Mother, that the number of your sons will remain the same! Now what is your other request?"

Kunti hung her head in shame. What she was going to ask would probably turn the tide of events in Arjuna's favour. But she comforted herself with the thought that even without this support, Arjuna had conquered Karna quite a few times all by himself.

"Tell me mother, what is it you want?" he urged.

She said softly, "Please don't use the *Nagastra* more than once against Arjuna!"

Karna laughed bitterly, "My suspicions were correct. It is only your love for your other sons that has prompted you to approach me today! Indeed why should you have love for me who am an utter stranger to you. I have not had the good fortune to be dandled on your knees or kept on your lap or be suckled by you so why should you feel sorry for me and why should you not strive to save the life of your beloved son Arjuna? But why are you so worried? Krishna is Arjuna's charioteer and it is ordained that victory will follow wherever Vaasudeva is. He has incarnated to rekindle the ancient path of *dharma* in this land. Even if I refuse your request my efforts will come to naught. But Mother! Surely you know that a heroic archer will not use an arrow more than once so you need not have made this request at all. Krishna also must know this so he has prompted you to request this boon from me in order to test my adherence to *dharma*! However this will not affect my loyalty to Duryodhana in any way. Therefore I grant your request without any problem. Since you have asked two boons from me should you not grant me a favour?"

"I would be more than happy to grant you anything which I am capable of granting my dearest son," she said.

Karna again came out with such noble requests that I could not help but shed tears at the magnanimity of this soul who was being badgered so badly by his past *karma*.

"Promise me that you will not reveal my identity to your other sons for the time being. If Yudhishtira knows who I am, he will offer me the kingdom and I in turn will offer it to Duryodhana who will grab it without any qualms, so it is best to keep quiet about this till the end of the war. Who knows what the outcome will be except Krishna!

"If, however I am killed by Arjuna on the battlefield, you should come to the battlefield and take my body on your lap and mourn for me, thus declaring my birth and lineage and your relationship with me."

Kunti burst into uncontrollable tears. Karna did his best to comfort her. "Mother do not grieve. What has to be will be. We can only hope to play our part perfectly and you have done your best for your sons and that is a mother's duty."

I could feel her agony but I could also realise her utter helplessness. We are all pawns on this checker-board of life, waiting to be pushed into the correct place by the master player. I knew who the master player was, but I also realised that in a way he was also helpless.

She hugged him and kissed him and blessed him over and over again and parted from him with many a lingering look.

As I followed her, I looked back and saw Karna sitting with his head in his hands and musing over his life. Imbued with all noble qualities, evil association alone had brought him to this pass. Generous to a fault, he had never been guilty of refusing a gift to whoever asked him for anything. To Duryodhana he was prepared to give the greatest gift of all – the gift of his life. No doubt my Lord had prompted me to be present at all these interviews with the sole intention of allowing me to witness his greatness.

Aum Namo Bhagavate Vaasudevaaya

My true nature has been paralysed by self pity and
I'm totally confused as to my duty,
I beg of you to tell me exactly what I should do,
I have surrended my ego to you.
Please accept me as your disciple and teach me.

Srimad Bhagavat Gita. Chapter 2.

ॐ

Vatsavaatacharaaya Namaha!

CHAPTER TWENTY-EIGHT

Preparations for War

We returned to Upaplavya the next day and after we had rested, we went to meet the Pandavas who were anxiously awaiting our arrival. Yudhishtira asked my Lord, "O Keshava! What is the outcome of the peace talks? Has Duryodhana agreed to any of the proposals that I had given you?"

My Lord replied, "O son of Pandu! He is not willing to part with even five pin-points of land, much less a kingdom. Dritarashtra is also supporting him or pretending that he is helpless and that his sons do not listen to him. With death awaiting them they will become the cause of a universal destruction! Your mother Kunti told me to tell you that she has been a constant witness to the humiliations that you had to suffer under Duryodhana's hands since childhood and that she realises that war is inevitable. My messengers told me that the moment I left, Duryodhana roared that all the eleven *akshauhinies* he had collected should march straight away to the field of the Kurus."

Yudhishtira kept his head on his hands and sat for a long time ruminating on the consequences of a fratricidal war. Out of all the five, perhaps he was the only one who envisaged the horrors of war. Draupadi as well as the other four brothers were delighted at the turn of events. The injustice and cruelty they had suffered at the hands of the Kauravas from childhood had fostered a bitterness which could never be appeased except in battle. At last Yudhishtira bowed to the will of fate. They had only seven *akshauhinies* to the eleven that the Kauravas had already amassed. Yudhishtira picked out the generals who were to lead these. They were Drupada, Virata, Drishtadyumna, Shikandin, Satyaki, Chekitana and Bhima. He then asked his brothers to choose the commander-in-chief of the entire army from one of these. Sahadeva recommended Virata, Nakula suggested Drupada, Arjuna pointed at his brother-in-law Drishtadyumna and Bhima voted for Shikandin.

Turning to my Lord, Yudhishtira said, "The strength and weakness of everything in the universe as well as the intentions of everyone are already known by you, O Keshava! Old and young, skilled and unskilled, let him be the leader of my forces who is indicated by you, for you are at the root of our success or failure. In you we have invested our lives, our kingdom, our prosperity and adversity, our happiness and our misery. You are indeed the ordainer and the creator. In you alone is established the fruition of our desires. So it is up to you to name the leader of our army. Having selected him and worshipped our weapons, we will under your orders march to the field of battle!"

My Lord immediately chose Sweta, the eldest son of King Virata of Matsya who was an acclaimed warrior. He had been doing intense *tapasya* to Shiva when the Pandavas were staying incognito in his capital city. The battlefield of the Kurus was known as Kurukshetra and this was automatically chosen as the scene of battle. I asked my Lord if there was anything special about this field. He said, "King Kuru, the progenitor of the Kuru dynasty had ploughed the land before the commencement of a *yajna* and had prayed that all those who died there should attain heaven. That is why the Kurus chose this as their battlefield. In the Treta Yuga, Parasurama had slaughtered twenty-one generations of evil Kshatriyas and made a lake of their blood which is now known as the Syamantaka Panchaka Lake. This is the place we went to have a holy dip during the time of the eclipse, don't you remember?" I nodded my head.

Balarama now arrived on the scene and told Yudhishtira that he would not take part in a war against his favourite pupil, Duryodhana. He did not want to fight on the side of the Kauravas, as Duryodhana had expected him to do, since he didn't want to fight with his brother. So he had decided to go on a pilgrimage. Before he left he repeated the rules for *dharmic* warfare for everyone to hear.

"War should only be fought from dawn till dusk. Those who are injured or have lost their weapons should not be attacked. Battles should only be fought between equals. Those riding chariots should not attack foot soldiers who are supposed to fight only amongst themselves. No one should attack the enemy from the back. At sunset everyone should return to their respective camps and they should be allowed to mingle with each other freely. The injured should be treated by physicians who accompany the army." He looked piercingly at Krishna and continued, "But I'm sure that by the end of the war all these rules will go overboard so I don't want to stay and see this. I will meet you once again before I leave. I hear that Vidura has made the same decision so perhaps we might meet each other at some point."

My Lord said, "If you really wished well for Duryodhana and wanted to avoid war, why didn't you come for the peace talks with me and try to instil some reason into him? It is possible that he might have listened to you even though he refused to listen to any of the other Elders!"

I had never heard my Lord argue with his brother or question him in any way so I was rather surprised. I think Balarama was also surprised but of course he had no reply to this pertinent question so he chose not to answer but returned to Dwaraka with Akrura.

Duryodhana's force had eleven *akshauhinies* so there was no space in Hastinapura even to accommodate the chiefs of his main armies. They overran the land known as Kurujangala, and the forest of Rohitaka and Ahichatra, Kalakuta, Varana, Vatadhana and all the hill tracts up to the border of Yamuna as well as the banks of the Ganga.

The Eldest now gave orders for our armies to march towards Kurukshetra. Duryodhana's men were already swarming all over the place. Our troops were on that part of the field which was level, cool and abounding in grass and fuel. Yudhishtira told his men to avoid burning *ghats*, temples and compounds consecrated to the gods as well as the *ashramas* of sages. Drishtadyumna and Satyaki measured the ground for the camp. It was near the banks of the River Hiranwati.

Yudhishtira of course depended solely on my Lord to make all arrangements which of course he did with great precision. When he perceived the sea of well-known faces in the opposite camp, Yudhishtira was once again filled with remorse at what was going to happen. Once again he approached my Lord and asked him, "O Keshava! Can't you put a stop to this extravaganza of death which is going to take place?"

My Lord answered, "My dear brother. If you withdraw at this moment, remember that you will not only be responsible for a Kaurava victory, but you will also be responsible for the victory of *adharma* in this country. A king has a duty to his country. It is not enough to keep one's own hands clean in order to bring about a righteous empire. He has to fight and abolish *adharma* before he can establish an empire of righteousness and prosperity. We have tried our best to avoid war but the Kauravas have refused all attempts at peace. I did not tell you this before since I knew it would upset you, but the fact is that Duryodhana even tried to capture me and laid a trap for me! They will stop at nothing to get their way."

When he heard this, Yudhishtira was struck with remorse and said, "I cannot believe that Duryodhana actually dared to try and injure you. Now all my objections have gone and I am determined to fight till every single one of them is destroyed like cobras in their nest!"

Yudhishtira now asked my Lord to tell him the names of all the kings who were helping the Kauravas. My Lord made a list of the main Kaurava leaders.

"Apart from the one hundred Kaurava brothers, there is Duryodhana's great friend, Susharma the leader of the Trigartas who helped him in the cattle raid against the Matsyas. They are dare-devil warriors and can be conquered only by Arjuna. Sudakshina, the ruler of Khamboja is his brother-in-law, the brother of his wife Bhanumati. Alambhusha is a *rakshasa* warrior who is a great friend of his. The brothers Vinda and Anuvinda, princes of Avanti are the brothers of my wife, Mitravinda and have joined him.

"Bhagadatta, the son of Narakasura who had been defeated by me is the ruler of Pragjyotisha. He possesses both the Vaishnava *astra* as well as the Narayana *astra*. Bhurisravas is the son of Somadatta. He is the uncle of both the Kauravas and the Pandavas. Somadatta is the son of King Valahika from the kingdom of Vahlika. He is Bhishma's cousin and hates the Yadavas. His father has also come and he is the oldest among the Kuru warriors.

Jayadratha is Duryodhana's brother-in-law, husband of his sister Dusshala and ruler of the Sindhu kingdom. After he was routed by you in the forest when he came to try and abduct Panchali, he did *tapas* to Shiva and was granted a boon that he would be able to defeat all the Pandavas other than Arjuna just once.

"Kritavarma is known as the bull of the Yadavas and he is my cousin but since he is also the commander-in-chief of the Narayana Sena which I have given to Duryodhana when he came to ask for my help, he will be fighting on the Kaurava side. His son Matrikavat is also with him as well as many of my own sons and grandsons.

"Kripacharya is the grandson of the great sage Gautama. He is the one who taught the Vedas and martial arts to all the Kuru princes as well as to most of the warriors at Kurukshetra.

"Shalya is the king of Madra, uncle of Nakula and Sahadeva. He is their mother, Madri's brother as you know and Duryodhana has deceitfully forced him join the Kauravas. We all know that the Madraas are well known for being terrible warriors.

"Of course Bhishma, Drona, Karna and Shakuni, the prince of Gandhara who as you know is the mastermind behind Duryodhana's evil policies and his sons are all with Duryodhana."

My Lord had just finished speaking when Yuyutsu, Duryodhana's stepbrother, came to us and begged Yudhishtira to accept him publicly at the start of the war. I was reminded of the Ramayana when Ravana's brother, Visbhishana went to join Rama.

"Even though he is my brother, I will not tolerate Duryodhana's inequities," he said. "I would be happy to help you and inform you of his wicked plans which include poisoning the water which is being kept for the soldiers to drink. So please be on your guard. There is no end to his evil designs. He is also trying his best to kill Bhima is some way or other for he fears Bhima's oath to kill all his brothers."

Yudhishtira was very happy to accept his offer and cordially welcomed him to the Pandava side, but Yuyutsu said he would not join them now but would find out more of their nefarious plans and then come to him at the start of the war. I could see that my Lord was very pleased about this. Later I asked him to tell me the story of Yuyutsu.

My Lord said, "Yuyutsu is Dritarashtra's son by a Vaishya woman called Sauvali, who was one of Gandhari's maids. Gandhari's pregnancy lasted for two years and Dritarashtra feared that she would deliver a dead child and would never be able to conceive again. Yuyutsu was born on the same day as Duryodhana and is older than the other Kauravas. Even though he has been closely associated with the Kauravas, he has chosen the path of righteousness. Duryodhana always taunted him as being a *Suta Putra* even though he is his step brother. Yet Duryodhana championed the cause of Karna who was also a *Suta Putra* and not even his brother. Doesn't that make you think that Duryodhana's motive in befriending Karna was purely selfish? However Karna being a noble soul chooses to believe that he loves him for his own self and not due to his ability to thwart the Pandavas and Arjuna in particular. Yuyutsu is one of the Maharathis of the Kaurava side so we are fortunate to have got him.

Actually Gandhari's third son, Vikarna is equally righteous and totally disgusted with Duryodhana. As you saw during the peace talks, he did his best to persuade his brother to listen to me and the Elders, but unlike Yuyutsu he has decided not to leave the Kauravas. So you see my dear, people are given freedom to choose what they want. If they choose something only out of emotional attachment like Karna or out of a misplaced sense of duty like Vikarna, what can I do?"

The next day Yuyutsu came again and told us about the Kauravas choice of leaders and various other matters.

"Duryodhana has the sense to realise that Bhishma and Drona are helping him not because of their love for him but because they don't want to betray their salt. So he has decided that Bhishma should be the commander of the whole army. The grandfather has graded the kings according to their abilities. Athirathas belong to the first category and are capable of fighting on their own without support from cavalry and foot soldiers. Next come the Maharathas, Samarathas and Artharathas, the lowest category who have to be protected by many soldiers. Karna received an unpleasant shock when he was degraded to the lowest category. The grandfather said that without his armour and earrings, he was totally vulnerable and would need to be protected by many soldiers. Duryodhana did his best to pacify him but Karna swore that he would not enter the battlefield as long as Bhishma was in command. 'As long as Ganga's son is in command, O King, I shall never fight but after he falls, I shall fight and kill the wielder of the Gandiva as I promised.' Duryodhana tried his best to persuade him to change his mind but he refused."

"What other atrocities are the Kauravas planning, O Yuyutsu?" asked my Lord.

"O Vaasudeva! I'm ashamed to tell you this but Duryodhana has decided on having a human sacrifice on an auspicious day in order to ensure a Kaurava victory. He asked the grandfather about this and Bhishma said, 'The person must have all the thirty-two physical attributes of the perfect human being.'

"Where can we find such a being?" asked Duryodhana.

"There are only three such people here and they are all in the Pandava camp. They are Krishna Vaasudeva, Arjuna and his son Iravan, by Ulupi, daughter of the Nagas. Of course you cannot approach Krishna or Arjuna so that leaves you with no other choice but Iravan. As for the choice of an auspicious date, Sahadeva is the greatest of all astrologers and he is also in the Pandava camp."

Yuyutsu continued, "This shameless brother of mine will be coming to your camp tonight to ask Sahadeva and Iravan to help him. So be prepared!"

My Lord feigned annoyance and told Sahadeva and Iravan to be on their guard and not to give in to any persuasion by Duryodhana whose selfishness knew no end. Yudhishtira on the other hand told them both to adhere to *dharma* whatever be the cost.

What surprised me was that Duryodhana had no doubt about the greatness of the Pandavas and their adherence to *dharma*!

The next morning Yudhishtira asked Sahadeva if Duryodhana had come to his tent at night.

Sahadeva replied, "Yes brother. He did come and ask me to give him an auspicious date for the performance of a human sacrifice which would make him victorious."

"And what did you say?" asked the Eldest.

"I consulted my almanac and told him that whoever conducts a human sacrifice to Kali, on the new moon day (*amavasya*) in the month of Margashirsha (November/December) would definitely be victorious in whatever he wanted to do. Actually this month has already had a lunar eclipse on *pournami* day and there will be a total solar eclipse on *amavasya* day which is day after tomorrow. A big comet will also be seen heralding the start of the war."

The fact that Duryodhana believed him implicitly was proof of the fact that he had no doubts about the character of the Pandavas and their inherent nobility.

Yudhishtira now turned to Iravan and asked him if Duryodhana had approached him in the night. Iravan replied, "Duryodhana came to my tent in the night and woke me up to ask if I would be prepared to sacrifice myself on the night of *amavasya* to ensure a Kaurava victory! Of course I was quite surprised at his selfishness in asking me such a thing but since you had already warned me to adhere to *dharma* I promised him that I would come to the Kali temple on the night of the new moon! He seemed very pleased and commended me on my unselfish attitude!"

Yudhishtira embraced both Sahadeva and Iravan and said, "I am indeed proud of you both for not swerving from *dharma* even though your actions may bring about our destruction." He then turned to my Lord and said humbly, "O Keshava! We are in your hands. Do with us as you will."

My Lord pretended to be angry and said, "With your extreme adherence to *dharma* you land yourselves into trouble and then expect me to rescue you. The Kauravas are steeped in *adharma*. There is nothing they will not stoop to, in order to bring your downfall. Surely you realise this. They cannot be fought by following *dharmic* standards alone. We will have to defeat them at their own game and resort to certain tricks in order to overcome them and if you can't do this, I will have to do it for you since you have placed yourself entirely in my hands. I will never desert a devotee of mine."

So this was the secret, I thought to myself. One who placed herself entirely in his hands would always be led to victory.

"I am willing to sacrifice myself for your sake and take Iravan's place, but that won't solve your problem since without me it is not likely that you will win this war."

Of course as soon as he said this all of them jumped up and said that they would not allow him to do such a thing. My Lord laughed and said, "I know you will not so we will have to think of another plan. Day after tomorrow is *amavasya* and there will be a total solar eclipse on that day. You should get one thousand and two hundred Brahmins to worship the sun and moon tomorrow and persuade three hundred sages to observe the rites pertaining to *amavasya*, tomorrow instead of the day after."

Without asking any questions the Pandavas obeyed all his instructions and got the required number of Brahmanas and sages to commence the *amavasya puja* the next day instead of the following day. Since I was always close to the Lord I saw a wonderful sight the next day when the rituals were going on in full force. Loud chants and fire rituals were in full flow since the Brahmanas were prepared to do anything which entailed a good *dakshina* (monetary gift). The sages knew very well who Krishna was and had absolute faith in anything he said. At this time I saw the deities of the sun and moon looking like balls of gold and silver coming to our tent to complain to my Lord.

"My Lord!" They said, "*Amavasya* is tomorrow so why are these people performing all these rites today? Why don't stop them from making this blunder?"

My Lord gave his charming smile and said sweetly, "I'm so happy to see you both together. But you must of course be knowing why and when the *amavasya* occurs."

They looked questioningly at him and he continued, "When the sun and moon come together, the light of the moon is totally eclipsed and that is the new moon or *amavasya* and now that you have both come here together obviously today is *amavasya* and not tomorrow! Now you may both return to your respective abodes."

They were a bit puzzled at this neat definition but had nothing to say. Iravan now came and told my Lord, "I have promised Duryodhana that I shall present myself at the Kali temple on the night of the new moon so I should go today. It is unlikely that he will appear so grant me permission to sacrifice myself on this auspicious night. I would like to do this for my father and uncles. I shall cut my flesh piece by piece and offer it to the goddess to ensure a Pandava victory. But my Lord, please grant me the boon that even though I will be almost like a skeleton I will not die there but will die on the battlefield after I have made my contribution in the battle. I would also like to see the battle till the end." My Lord granted him both these boons.

That night Iravan adorned himself in the accepted manner with a red garland round his neck and went to the Kali temple and offered his flesh, piece by piece to the goddess. She was pleased and granted him his boon. Due to her blessings as well as the promise my Lord had given him, Iravan found that he was still alive even though gaunt and without much flesh but since all his vital organs were still intact, he continued to live. Since he was half a Naga he had mysterious powers and even looked like a *rakshasa*.

Yuyutsu told us the next day that Duryodhana had gone to the temple at midnight the following day and was furious when the priest told him that *amavasya* had come and gone and all the rites had been done and Iravan had come and sacrificed himself for the sake of the Pandavas since Duryodhana had not appeared!

Yuyutsu said, "Duryodhana hoped to get some sympathy from his mother and went straight to her and complained bitterly about what had happened. For once she didn't pamper him but told him quite simply, 'my son, remember that where there is *dharma* there will be victory. You have deviated so far from *dharma* that you were shamelessly prepared to ask Arjuna's son to sacrifice himself so that you might be victorious!'

Yuyutsu continued, "But of course Duryodhana has never repented anything he has ever done and in order to vent his venom he has asked Shakuni's son Uluka to come here with a message for you. Ah! There he comes now. I don't want him to see me here." So saying Yuyutsu left by the back entrance.

Uluka was a fitting son of his wicked father and was delighted to have been chosen to deliver this insulting message. "Duryodhana has sent me here to deliver a message to you. 'The time has come, O cousins to make good your oaths. Shamelessly you stood and watched your wife being insulted and then meekly went away and lived like animals in the forest! Is there no man amongst you? Yudhishtira hides his cowardice under the cloak of righteousness. But beware, Bhima will soon be slaughtered by me, Arjuna by Karna and as for the two little darlings, they are not fit to wield arms! Your wife Draupadi is a common woman and the cow-herd Krishna's sorcery will be of no avail on the field of battle!'

Arjuna spoke forcefully, "Only eunuchs fight with words. When the time comes my Gandiva shall give a fitting answer to your master!" So saying he gave a mighty twang on his bow which could be heard in the Kaurava camp.

Bhima roared, "Tell him that I will break his thighs and drink Dusshasana's blood as I have sworn to do."

Nakula growled, "I will personally tear you limb from limb, O Uluka for what you have dared to say in front of my noble brother!"

Sahadeva said in his usual deliberate manner, "And I will take great pleasure in slitting the throat of your father, Shakuni and letting him bleed to death, for the devious role he has played in bringing about this dreadful war."

Yudhishtira spoke with tears in his eyes, "Remind Duryodhana that I made every effort to obtain my just dues through peaceful means, not out of fear but because I can envisage the horrors of war and I believe in peace!"

My Lord alone gave his hearty laugh and said, "O gambler's son! Tell your cousins that the cow-herd's chariot will move like lightning through the ranks of the Kauravas, leaving death and destruction in its wake!"

After Uluka's departure, Yudhishtira was sunk in gloom once again thinking of the senseless sacrifice of lives which would ensue in the coming battle. My Lord consoled him and said, "You have done your best. Nobody could have done more. But we are Kshatriyas and it is our duty to uphold *dharma* and fight *adharma* at all cost."

Balarama came once again with Akrura before he left for his pilgrimage. He told Yudhishtira, "This fierce and terrible slaughter seems inevitable. It is without doubt a decree of fate. But fear not O Yudhishtira, your victory is certain for it is Krishna's wish. I have equal affection for both

Duryodhana and Bhima so I cannot participate in this battle. I will return at the end of the battle," so saying he departed.

Bhishma and Sweta, the generals of the opposing parties met the next day and decided the rules of warfare which were exactly what Balarama had told the Pandavas with a few additions. Verbal jousts should not be violated with weapons. The battle would consist of indiscriminate fighting between foot soldiers and duels between equals. A single person should never be attacked by many. Many such rules were decided upon by the righteous commanders, but I doubted if the Kauravas would stick to any of these rules. Duryodhana had only one idea in his mind and that was to win by hook or by crook.

The ten days following the new moon on which the human sacrifice was to have been made were spent in *ayudhapuja* (worship of the weapons) by both sides.

'Why do they have to worship their weapons?' I asked my Lord.

He replied. "The weapons which are going to be used in this war are not ordinary weapons. All the great warriors have recourse to *astras*. Do you know what an *astra* is?" I shook my head.

He replied, "An *astra* is a supernatural weapon presided over by a specific deity. It can be an arrow, a mace or a sword. The person who uses the *astra* would have to know the *mantra* which would invoke the deity, who in turn would endow the weapon with celestial power. It would be impossible to counter this weapon by ordinary means. There are many conditions involved in the usage of *astras*, the violation of which could be fatal to the person who uses them. Because they have such power, the knowledge of these *astras* is always given by the teacher to the pupil by word of mouth alone depending on the character of the pupil. For instance Dronacharya gave the deadly *astra* known as Brahmasiras to his brilliant pupil Arjuna and withheld it from his own son Aswatthama."

'Why didn't he give it to Aswatthama?' I asked.

"The Brahmasiras is the most deadly *astra* known to us. It can cause terrible destruction which can last for generations. It causes severe environmental changes. The land will become barren and all life in and around that area will cease to exist and men and women will become infertile. There will be no rainfall and the land will become totally useless for any cultivation. It should never be used during war and it can never be given to anyone who has no control over himself, who might use it in a fit of anger. Drona knew he could rely on Arjuna but did not have the same trust in his own son."

'Are there any other deadly weapons?'

"Yes, the Brahmastra is the weapon of the creator Brahma and it can be used in war. There is no defence against it except something called the Brahmadanda which is a stick created by Brahma. The Brahmastra never misses its mark and has to be used with a very specific intent against an individual or an army. The target would be completely annihilated. It can only be used once by any person. The person would have to have immense powers of concentration. This is the *astra* used by Salva when he came to destroy Dwaraka. If you remember the whole countryside outside the town was devastated. It has not recovered till now. Brahma is said to have created this weapon only for the purpose of upholding *dharma* and *satya*. It is a weapon to be used only as a last resort. Only Bhishma, Drona, Arjuna and Karna have knowledge of the Brahmastra. Aswatthama eavesdropped on his father when he was teaching Arjuna. He learnt the method of summoning it but he was not able to hear the method of retracting it. The Brahmasiras has four times the power of the Brahmastra and should never be used at any time."

'Are there any more of such powerful *astras*?' I enquired.

"Of course there are many more. You know the Pasupatastra which Arjuna acquired from Shiva after great *tapas*. It is a crescent-shaped, irresistible and most destructive weapon used by both Kali and Shiva. It can be discharged mentally or by using a bow and arrow.

"Then there is the Narayana *astra* and Vaishnava *astra* which come from Vishnu. All of these are potent but none as potent as the Brahmastra and the Brahmasiras.

"The presiding deity of both the Narayana *astra* and the Vaishnava *astra* is Lord Vishnu. Both these can be obtained only by doing *tapas* to Vishnu. The Narayana *astra* will create a shower of arrows and discs. Its power will increase with resistance. The Vaishnava *astra* will destroy the target completely irrespective of the nature of the opposing force."

'What *astras* do you use?' I asked timidly, wondering if he would be annoyed at my question.

"Don't you know that I use only one *astra* and that is the Sudarshana Chakra?"

'Is it fatal?'

"Of course it is fatal but I never give it to anyone so I am the only one who uses it and I know when to use it. It will come to me when I need it. In fact this is true of all *astras*. They come to the users of their respective *mantras* as and when they are needed."

'I heard Kunti telling Karna not to use the Nagastra more than once. What sort of *astra* is that?' I asked.

"The presiding deities of the *astra* are the *nagas* and the weapon takes on the form of a deadly snake which can either coil round the opponent and immobilise him or inject him with severe poison which will kill him within minutes."

He smiled his charming smile and told me to watch the warriors carefully to see how they used their weapons by invoking the *mantra* of the *astra*.

"Most of the usual *astras* can be used many times and all of them have their counter *astras*. For instance if someone invokes the Agneyastra, it will discharge flames which are inextinguishable through normal means. These flames can only be extinguished by the use of the Varuna *astra* which will discharge torrential volumes of water. This is the only weapon which can counter the Agneyastra."

Yuyutsu came once again to report that Vyasa had visited the king and told him, "Your sons and the sons of Pandu have arrayed themselves on the field of the Kurus, O king! They are ready for war. It is not too late even now for you to stop them."

Dritarashtra replied, "You know that I have no control over them. What else did you see?"

"I heard ravens cawing ominously. The trees around the field were filled with kites and vultures waiting for their feast. The sun is bright but has a black circle around it and a very rare comet is seen to be hovering over the field foretelling death and destruction."

"What else?"

"The ocean is rising, holy fires turn blue and sacred trees have been struck down by lightning. Outside Hastinapura the wells are dry but inside they overflow and flood the city. The Himalayas are exploding and tumbling down. As I entered my left eye was twitching. Will you sit and do nothing?"

The blind king said, "Who will obey the commands of a blind man? My sons care not for my opinion. I am helpless."

"So be it," said Vyasa, "but do not grieve when you hear of what happens to your sons."

"How can I know of what is happening?" asked the king.

"I will grant cosmic vision to Sanjaya so that he can see the events and hear the conversations which are going on in the battlefield. He will report all these things faithfully to you," said the sage and left for the forest.

Yuyutsu continued, "Last night Duryodhana went to Bhishma's tent and told him that he was depending on him to lead him to victory."

Bhishma said, "I will do my best for you but I will not kill any of the Pandavas who are like my sons and I will not fight with a woman or one who resembles a woman or one who was born a woman and has changed her sex. So if Shikandin, the prince of Panchala, comes before me I will not even look at him because he was born a woman and changed his sex."

"He is not to be feared and we can easily keep him away from you," said Duryodhana.

I went out of our tent and looked at the opposite camp. I saw a great city of silken tents made like coloured houses for the kings and ordinary ones for the soldiers, musicians, mechanics and physicians. Women had separate tents I supposed. Every tent had its own flag merrily flying in the cold wind. Chariots were cleaned and polished and ready to go. Pale towers of mist rose from the river near Duryodhana's camp. I turned round and the scene behind me was pretty much the same. I shivered with the cold as well as with the grief which was gripping me when I thought of what was going to happen.

My Lord had chosen to be Partha's charioteer. I wondered at the menial role he was willing to play in order to help his beloved devotee. 'May I sit at your feet in the chariot?' I asked.

He tweaked my ears in assent.

That evening all the kings met together in Yudhistira's tent and discussed their plan for the next day. I saw the chiefs of the Pandava army for the first time. Purujit was the ruler of Kuntibhoja and the brother of Kunti, mother of the Pandavas. Dhrishtaketu was the ruler of Chedi and the son of Shishupala. Nakula had married his daughter, Karenumati. Vrihadhakshatra was the leader of the five Kekaya brothers of the kingdom of Kekaya. Sahadeva, king of Magadha, son of Jarasandha was with us. Satyaki and Chekitana were the only Yadavas who insisted on fighting on our side. My Lord had sent the others to Duryodhana. King Drupada and his sons, Drishtadyumna, Shikandin, Yudhamanyu, Uttamaujus, Satyajit and their sons were all with us. Yudhamanyu and Uttamaujus were delegated to protect Arjuna's chariot from either side. It was normal to protect their best warriors by having someone to flank them from either side. Apparently ten sons of Dritarashtra had been kept only to protect Bhishma, the star of the Kaurava army.

King Virata of Matsya and his sons, Sweta, Uttara Kumara and Shankha were of course with us. In fact Sweta was our general on the first day. Among the second generation the star was Abhimanyu, son of Arjuna and Subhadra. Though he was the youngest – only sixteen years of age, he would surely excel his father soon I thought. After that came the five sons of Draupadi by the five brothers – Prativindya, Sutasoma, Shrutikirti, Satanika and Shrutakarman. Nakula's son, Niramitra and Sahadeva's son Suhotra were also our star warriors. All of them had been taught by Pradyumna and by my Lord also, at various times so they were all excellent warriors.

Every day both camps would decide on the type of *vyuha* which they would have the next day. My Lord had already told me that a *vyuha* was a special type of battle formation. Yuyutsu told us that the Kauravas were preparing the Krauncha *vyuha* which was in the form of a huge crane with enormous flying wings, so our commander, Sweta declared that we would form the *vyuha* known as the Vajra which was a needle pointed thunderbolt which could pierce the body of the flying crane. Since we had only few men compared to the Kauravas this was our best bet.

Thus everything was set for the war the next day. I watched the night sky in fascination as the huge comet hovered in the sky. It had a fiery tail which was shimmering and shivering in eager anticipation as to what would follow. At least that is what it seemed to me.

Aum Namo Bhagavate Vaasudevaaya

I know what my dharma is yet I am not able to follow it,
I know what adharma is yet I am unable to avoid it,
O Lord! Seated in my heart,
I can only act as you direct me.

Mahabharata.

ॐ

Ananataaya Namaha!

CHAPTER TWENTY-NINE

Mahabharata War

Winter rains had swept the field. Kurukshetra was wet and slushy when the Great War commenced on the eleventh day of the bright fortnight, when the star Krittika was in ascendency in the month of Margashirsha (November-December). It was the auspicious day known as Vaikunt Ekadasi. The great message of my Lord to Arjuna which later came to be known as the Bhagavat Gita or "Song of the Lord" was given on the morn of the first day of battle.

I came out of our tent and looked at the Kaurava army which had already come out. The sun was behind them and had a dark, ominous circle round it. The Kaurava army looked dark and forbidding like thunderclouds about to shed their waters. They were in the Krauncha *vyuha*. I ran back and jumped into my Lord's chariot.

When our army advanced, there was a shout of appreciation from both sides since we were facing the rising sun and the metal shields and armours were shining like gold and the leather ones gleaming and all the flags flying proudly since the wind was blowing from east to west against the Kauravas. Our army seemed to be illuminated by the rising sun whereas the Kaurava army appeared shaded and dark. As planned the day before, Bhima was right in front flourishing his huge iron mace with deadly looking spikes. Right across from him was Bhishma, the ancient knight, dressed all in silver on his silver car above which fluttered his banner bearing the device of a palm tree. He put his conch shell to his lips and blew loud and long inciting the soldiers for battle. At that moment to the amazement of everyone Yudhishtira dismounted and walked up unarmed to Bhishma and Drona. The Kauravas sneered mockingly at what they thought was a last cowardly act on the part of the Pandava king to beg for peace! Fearlessly he walked up to the Elders and bowed low and spoke, "In our desire for the kingdom, we have dared to array ourselves against you both who are worthy of worship! Pray forgive us and bless us and grant us permission to fight against you!"

Bhishma and Drona were full of love and admiration for this great pupil of theirs who had never deviated from the path of *dharma*. Both of them blessed him and gave him permission to fight against them.

My Lord now took Arjuna to get the blessings of the grandsire who welcomed them and said, "Hail, O Madhava! You know the past, present and future. Everything is a divine sport for you. You know full well that as long as I carry weapons I can never be killed by anyone except you, O Keshava! Therefore it is my sincere wish that you should take up arms against me! Let me see if you will grant my wish!"

Then turning to Arjuna, his favourite grandson, the old knight laid his hands lovingly and tenderly on his head and blessed him. Arjuna was unable to speak but with eyes brimming with tears, he touched his feet and saluted him and returned.

Yudhishtira now shouted to the opposing ranks, "Is there anyone amongst you who is desirous to come over to our side? If so you are welcome."

At this Yuyutsu publicly acknowledged his allegiance to the Pandavas and walked over to the Pandava side with Duryodhana scowling at him and muttering imprecations, "Ungrateful bastard! I knew you were not to be trusted!"

Just then my Lord's attention was drawn to a lapwing that had built her nest on the turf in the middle of the field and was flapping her wings and chirping in great distress due to her anxiety for her nestlings. He jumped out of the chariot and moved the nest carefully to one side of the field and placed a large elephant bell over the nest. "Poor little mother," he said tenderly. "Let this be your protection." Through the eighteen days of raging battle that followed, the lapwing and her nestlings were kept in safety by the mercy of the Lord who never failed to give her some food daily and who was the only one who could spare a thought to the smallest of his creations, even at such a crucial time like this.

I noticed that all through the eighteen days that followed, he took similar care of every person on the battlefield even though their limited vision stopped them from appreciating this fact fully. Some deserved death and some life and to each was given his just deserts. But everything was done so unobtrusively that it appeared as it if it was all by chance. Life was a drama to him in which he allowed the actors to play the parts which they were meant to play by their own nature and will. Sometimes he would remove an obstacle or put an obstacle so that the will of the players would have unimpeded scope. In this way he allowed events to work themselves out according to the law of *karma*, striving ever to aid the course of destiny even though this led in the end to the self-destruction of all things. Actually he was guiding the destiny of both sides in an unobtrusive manner, but for the sake of the Pandavas who had surrendered their all to him, he often broke his normal code of conduct and played an active part in order to save them from the consequences of their own folly, even though his role as a charioteer was apparently that of the uninvolved witness. If there was any unrighteous act to be done he always did it himself for he is above his own laws, whereas for the human being to transgress these laws would result in infamy and *karmic* reaction. His devotee might act in a quixotic and sometimes foolhardy fashion, but he would always intervene and save him even at the risk of tarnishing his own reputation. With his wide-angled vision covering all the three states of time - past, present and future, he was able to judge and decide what was best for them. By the sheer power of their love and total surrender of their will to him, the Pandavas compelled him to do everything for them.

As decided the previous day, our army was in the shape of the *Vajra* or needle-pointed thunderbolt. Bhima stood right in front. He was foremost amongst those who fought at close range, skilled in mace-fighting. He could fell any numbers of warriors on foot or on horses. He could bring down a chariot by striking at the weak points which were its yokes, wheels and horses. He could even crush a war-elephant by striking at its vulnerable parts like the trunk and smiting the centre of the head by jumping on top of its head. Not even Duryodhana could equal him in this. Nakula and Sahadeva protected him from either side since both were expert swordsmen. Draupadi's five sons, all expert archers protected his back. Behind them came Abhimanyu, with Yudhishtira in the middle. He was followed by Sweta and Drishtadyumna, both skilled sword fighters. Next was stationed Shikandin and then Arjuna, the greatest archer of all time, who was in charge of sending surprise showers of arrows like lightning bolts which would be followed by thunder which was nothing but the noise made by the charge of those in front who were all equipped with the short-range weapons like maces, battle axes, lances and swords. The swords were forged by master craftsmen and could rip open the heavy helmets worn by the kings. Behind Arjuna was Satyaki, who was also an expert archer and would join Arjuna in the lightning strikes. He was followed by Yudhamanyu and Uttamaujas. Then came the Kekaya brothers and Drishtaketu, king of Chedi and the Yadava chief, Chekitana. The rear of the Vajra was protected by the aged kings of Matsya and Panchala – Virata and Drupada. This was the formation of the Vajra which was supposed to pierce the heart of the Krauncha (crane) formation of the Kauravas.

I had found out from my Lord how the elephants and horses were deployed in the war. The cavalry is the most mobile section of the army and it was placed on either side of the army like its wings so that it could be sent to any part of the field as and when required. Our army was well equipped with both horses and elephants even though the Magadha army on the Kaurava side had ten thousand elephants. An elephant with a few expert archers on its back made a powerful unit on its own. It could protect the foot soldiers or a chariot which would normally have a warrior who could deploy his long range weapons, *astras* and arrows shot in rapid succession, with great precision.

Both armies were in battle formation when Arjuna leaned forward and spoke to my Lord, "O Madhusudana! Please drive our chariot forward and place it in the middle of the ranks so that I can observe our opponents once again before the start of the war."

Obedient to his role as a charioteer Krishna, the Lord of the universe, drove the chariot to the no-man's land between the two armies and stopped it exactly in front of Bhishma and Drona. I figured that he did this with a definite purpose. Had he stationed the chariot in front of Duryodhana there would have been no opportunity for my Lord to sing his song celestial to his friend and through him to all humanity. By placing it in such a strategic position, he brought out a great revulsion in the heart of his friend which he had been bottling up for some time. It was only when he faced his beloved grandsire and revered Guru that the full impact of the terrible destruction which was to take place hit him like a blow in the solar plexus. His whole body trembled with the shock, his mind reeled, his mighty bow, the Gandiva fell from his nerveless grasp and he collapsed in a heap on the floor of the chariot.

"O Madhava!" he said, "War is a terrible thing and war between relations is even worse. They are not my enemies who are standing on the opposite side, but my relations – my grandfather, who dandled me on his knee, my *guru* without whom I would not be standing here today and my uncles and cousins and close relations. I would rather that they killed me, unresisting than kill them and gain a victory. I would not do it even for a bit of heaven much less for a kingdom in the world. Let us turn back, O Krishna! I cannot fight this war. My hands are shaking so much that I cannot even hold the Gandiva let alone string it and shoot arrows. The Kauravas are standing there without a thought of the holocaust which is about to take place. But we who know better should not act in this senseless fashion." At last when he had exhausted all his ethical and logical arguments against war, Arjuna turned to my Lord and said, "I am totally confused as to my duty. I surrender to you. Pray advise me and guide me."

In all the years that they had spent together Arjuna had never asked Krishna for advice. This was the first time, when he felt his human limitations weigh heavy on his heart - his sentimental weakness which differentiated between relations and strangers, friends and enemies, yours and mine with the result that this hero lost all his strength and surrendered his ego to this god-man who happened to be his friend – his sole friend as he was to discover. How can I ever hope to be able to narrate the advice given by my Lord to his dear friend at this crucial stage of his life? The only people who heard this was Arjuna sitting inside the chariot, Sanjaya describing the details to Dritarashtra in Hastinapura, Hanuman who hung over the flag staff and listened with full attention and of course myself curled up next to my Lord when he turned round to answer Arjuna.

"O Partha! First of all you have to understand who you are. You are not the body, you are not the mind and you are not the intellect. You are that immortal, eternal *atman* which never being born, can never die! You think you are the killer and they are the killed. Let me tell you that you can neither kill nor be killed. It is their *karma* which has brought them to this field and if their *karma* is to die here, they will die with or without you. Have no doubts about that. At best you can only be an instrument in bringing about their end. But remember even then you can only destroy their bodies and never the eternal spirit residing in them. That is indestructible because it is a divine energy and that energy can never be destroyed. It can only change its form. Like people throwing away old clothes in order to don new ones the *jivatma* discards its old body and enters into a new one after the death of its body. What is there to grieve in this? Even considering your duty, it is certain that you should fight since it is the duty of a Kshatriya to fight a righteous war. We have given them enough chances to opt for peace but if they insist on war, what option do we have but to fight? You are a king and you have a duty to your citizens to rescue them from the tyranny of this evil king.

"My dear friend! Everyone is under the sway of the three *gunas* of Prakriti – *sattva*, *rajas* and *tamas*. These are the thieves who bind the immortal soul to the mortal body and make it believe that it is also mortal. Therefore go above these three and take your stand in the *yoga* of the supreme intellect which will guide you in the right direction."

He then spoke to him about action. This is something he had already told me about: How to convert *karma* into *karma yoga*. "O Partha! We live in an active world and everyone is forced to do *karma* or action. Even for the maintenance of our own lives we have to do some work. It is said that it is *karma* that binds us to the wheel of *samsara*. How can we get out of this dilemma? We cannot sit back and refuse to act since action is compulsory. Therefore the only way is to transform ordinary *karma* into a *yoga* which will take us towards our goal of liberation and not force us into the labyrinth of further bondage. The binding aspect of *karma* is that it is always done with a selfish motive. There is a natural law that decrees that every action has to have its equal and opposite reaction. We get back from the world what we give to it. If we give love we will receive it, and if we give hate that will also be returned with equal force. It is not the action which binds us, but the selfish desire for results which will be beneficial only to us. The universe gives us only one right and that is to do our duty, but it does not give us the right to demand recompense for the action which is to be done as a duty.

"The secret of action is that every action should be done as a *yajna* or offering to God. This applies to any type of action, even the most menial. The result of every action which is done as a *yajna* should be taken as *prasada* or the leftover of what has been offered to God. In this way we can avoid the binding effect of action.

"Therefore Arjuna it is your duty to fight this righteous war which has been forced on you, without worrying about victory and defeat. All you have to do is to put forth your best and leave the results to God who will decide what your just deserts are."

Arjuna had not been present when my Lord showed his cosmic form at the assembly of the Kurus so now he begged him to show it to him. I realised how much my Vanamali loved him for he was ready to show him this form which could not be seen by ordinary eyes so he gave him divine eyesight. I was indeed fortunate for I could see it for a second time. But this was a bit different from what he had shown at the Kuru court. There he showed that all the gods emanated from him and all of them would come to him if he called them. Here he showed a totally different aspect. He showed his form as Kaalaswarupa or the figure of all-consuming Time. Actually Time is the only destroyer. When one's time is up, nothing and no one can stop us from dying. Everything and every creature in the universe has a time to exit from this world. My Lord showed Arjuna this terrifying form in which the Kaurava host was being consumed by the huge gaping mouth of the Lord of Time. Everyone was being crunched by the huge canines of this terrible figure. There was no escape from this fearful colossus. Neither I nor Arjuna could bear to look at this gigantic figure of destruction.

"Pray show me your original form," he shouted and so did I whimper and pray to be shown his beauteous form as my Vanamali.

He immediately withdrew that form into himself and once again stood before us as my beloved Vanamali. Both of us gave a sigh of relief and prostrated to him.

"Forgive me Lord!" cried Arjuna, "Not knowing your greatness I have often treated you familiarly, calling you, 'Hey Krishna! Hey Yadava!' and so on. I have joked and played tricks on you who are the Lord of Lords! Forgive me! Pray forgive me!"

I too joined Arjuna and begged my Vanamali to forgive my transgressions.

He looked tenderly at me and through me at Arjuna and said, "O Partha! What is there to forgive? You and I are one. We have never been separated. I have been your friend in all the lives you have ever taken. You may not remember or recognise me, but I have been your sole friend and companion for countless lives. In this life I have chosen to reveal myself to you. You are my chosen instrument for fighting the corruption and canker which is eating into this society. Just do your duty to the best of your ability. That is all I ask of you. Be a perfect instrument in my hands and I will see to it that you will be led to the final consummation of life. The instrument can never be blamed for anything. Neither praise nor blame will it incur – neither victory nor defeat or sin and merit. I will take over that part. If anyone has to be blamed it will be me and never you. My dearest friend, I will let you into the greatest of all secrets. Surrender yourself totally to me. Abandon all your worries of what you will do and what you will not do and how you will live and a hundred other things. Leave it all to me and rest in peace. I promise you that I will carry you to the further shore of this ocean of life and lift you to the peak of exaltation and ecstasy!"

My eyes filled with tears and the roots of my hair tingled when I heard these words. He had told me this many times before but I was never satiated by hearing his nectarine words. I fell at his feet and kissed them again and again.

Obviously Arjuna felt the same. Once more he regained his original look of anticipation and readiness and told my Lord, "Let us drive back, O Keshava! I am ready to obey your commands!" I realised that when the *jivatma* and the Paramatma stand united, nothing and no one could defeat them.

Just as we were going to go back to join the Pandava forces, I heard Duryodhana approach Drona and taunt him about how his disciples were the ones whom they had to face now. "You are the one who has taught Arjuna and all the others the method of warfare which they are going to use against us now!"

The Brahmin's face drew into a forbidding frown and he turned away in disgust.

Duryodhana now turned to Bhishma and exhorted him to do his best and not allow his partiality towards the Pandavas affect his capacity for fighting.

Bhishma replied, "Arjuna alone is capable of killing your entire army and I have already told you that I will not kill any of the Pandavas. However I promise to kill ten thousand of their soldiers every day."

Bhishma sparked off the battle with his clarion call to the ranks. "O Kshatriyas! Here is a golden opportunity for you to exhibit your heroism. We are now standing on the threshold of heaven. The portals are open to you. To die of old age and disease on a comfortable bed in his own house is a shame for a Kshatriya. To die on the battlefield fighting for a righteous cause is his supreme good fortune. Dying thus with courage, with your bodies pierced all over with arrows you will go directly to heaven!"

So saying he gave another blast on his conch shell.

Bhima replied by putting his famous conch, the Paundra to his lips and blowing loud and long. I clapped my hands with delight when my Lord blew the Panchajanya and Arjuna the Devadatta. From both sides the other warriors joined by sounding their own conch shells and brass horns so that the air resounded with their clamour. After this there was a positive cacophony of drums, gongs and cymbals. I jumped out of the chariot to watch as my Lord and Arjuna come forward. It was such a wonderful sight. They were in a jewelled chariot with four milky white steeds whose reins were held by my own Vanamali who was shining and resplendent in the morning sun with a halo round his golden crown. His look, filled with compassion roved over the entire host as if to grant liberation to all. The reins of the prancing horses were held lightly yet firmly in his slender fingers and his unfailing smile swept over the entire host as if in benediction. Arjuna stood behind him, dashing and handsome holding the Gandiva in his hands and a smile hovering on his lips.

Hanuman was sitting on our flag making grimaces at the opposing forces as he had promised Bhima some time ago.

The rival forces were all set now and charged forward with blood-curdling shouts and yells aided by the clarion call of the trumpets. The cobra banner on Duryodhana's flag waved in the wind so that it looked as if it was getting ready to strike! His brother Dusshasana was the first to let fly a volley of arrows on the first day of battle.

Maddened by Duryodhana's taunts, Bhishma went through the Pandava army wreaking havoc. When Arjuna hesitated to go forward to resist him, his son Abhimanyu went straight at Bhishma and cut down his banner with the palm tree blowing softly in the wind. He then cut through his bodyguards and attacked Bhishma himself. It was a wonderful sight to see the oldest and the youngest of the Kurus forestalling each other with such expertise! I think Bhishma looked at the boy and saw his dear Arjuna in him and did not want to do much damage to him. I too had a real soft corner for this son of Arjuna. Finally this young boy, the pride of his father, managed to fell Bhishma's horses and then he turned to Shalya and Kritavarma and fought valiantly with both these seasoned warriors.

Another young boy whom I watched with great interest was Uttara, prince of Matsya who had been trained by Arjuna and had now become quite a good warrior. He came up and challenged Bhishma and killed his charioteer and destroyed his chariot. Bhishma was in a dilemma as to what to do with this young boy, but Shalya had no such qualms and aimed a deadly javelin at his heart and killed him instantly. This was the first *adharmic* act of the war. Sweta, his elder brother, commander of our forces was infuriated at this act and turned his fury on Bhishma. He possessed an invincible bow from Lord Shiva and Bhishma found himself helpless against his onslaught. Realising that Sweta was invincible as long as he held the bow, he taunted him, "Were you taught only archery? Can't you fight with a sword?"

The chivalrous Sweta immediately took up his sword. Now Bhishma also tarnished his fair name by cutting off Sweta's right arm with an arrow. Sweta continued to fight with the sword in his left hand, but Bhishma severed his other arm as well and left Sweta to bleed to death. In utter dismay Yudhishtira tried to console King Virata for the loss of both his beloved sons on the very first day of battle.

By this time the sun had set and Arjuna and Krishna withdrew their troops as did the other party with cries of delight at their victory. The Pandavas entered their tents in a very subdued mood thinking of the terrible way their commander had been slaughtered on the very first day of battle. My Lord said, "Even on the very first day the rules of a *dharmic* war have been overthrown. Remember Yudhishtira that they can only be fought using their own methods. They will stick at nothing to achieve their ends. So be prepared."

Yudhishtira called another meeting of all the commanders and Draupadi's brother, Drishtadyumna, was chosen as commander.

I could hear the music and the sound of bells and revelry coming from the Kaurava camp. The streets of the camp were lighted with golden lamps burning fragrant oils. Duryodhana rode on horseback to Bhishma's tent and congratulated him. "Our army is like a shoreless ocean crested with waves of an oncoming storm. Do not spare the Pandavas out of kindness, O Grandfather!"

"Be silent Duryodhana! I will never slay the innocent, or those without weapons, or chariot drivers or women or those who run away or surrender or are fighting with others."

"I know that Sire. All I want is that you should keep on as you did today. It is a happy day for us and a good omen. The air is bright and sparkling. I know we will win."

'How is it that the Kauravas have such a vast army compared with ours?' I asked my Master.

"Vedic civilization is based on the four divisions of society, but there are people in the far south who do not fit into any of these. They belong to the eight non-Vedic *varnas*. For instance, Duryodhana's kitchen is managed by the Chola king who is from the South and who is his vassal.

"Duryodhana has also taken all the lower fighters on to his side. They resort to mean and primitive types of warfare like throwing rocks and sticks. They smear poison on their teeth and go and bite the elephants' legs and make them faint. They go under the legs of the elephants and prick their tails with needles. Duryodhana uses them to go into the elephant division and give something to the animals to make them sick. He is always using them against Bhima who becomes violent when he sees these people throwing stones and sticks at him and his elephants. In fact they are like annoying insects when compared to the Vedic warriors, but they are a definite asset to the Kaurava army."

Aum Namo Bhagavate Vaasudevaaya

Denukaasuramardanaaya Namaha!

CHAPTER THIRTY

Succeeding Days of Battle

The winter morning dawned clear and white. It was the second day of battle and it commenced with a confident Kaurava army facing the Pandavas, sure of their victory.

Drishtadyumna had decided on a Garuda *vyuha* or eagle formation. He placed Arjuna in the van and King Drupada surrounded by a large number of troops at the head. Kuntibhoja and Saibya became the two eyes. Many of the rulers were placed at the neck. Nakula and Sahadeva were placed on the left wing and Yudhishtira with a number of other armies from various places was the right wing. Virata was the tail, aided by the Kekayas, the ruler of Kasi and Drishtaketu, the ruler of Chedi. Elephants were placed at the joints of the wings and chariots were along the back and neck.

Arjuna stood apart and told my Lord to drive his chariot towards Bhishma since something needed to be done immediately to restore confidence in the Pandava army. He tried to engage the grandsire in a battle, but the Kaurava brothers who had been kept especially to protect Bhishma attacked Arjuna even before he could reach him. In the meantime, Drishtadyumna engaged Drona in a fierce battle which went on for hours. Drona broke his bow a number of times. Bhima intervened and rescued Drishtadyumna. Duryodhana sent the Kalinga forces to forestall Bhima who slaughtered most of them in no time. He killed all their leaders including the king. Bhishma came to relieve the Kalinga forces. Satyaki who was close behind Bhima killed Bhishma's charioteer. The horses bolted carrying the grandsire out of the field.

Abhimanyu sought out Duryodhana's son Lakshmana and fought so fiercely with him that he was forced to flee for his life from the field. He then turned to help Bhima.

At the end of the day the Kauravas had suffered great losses. Bhima had destroyed the entire elephant brigade of the Kalingas as well as most of their leaders. For the rest of the battle, the Kalingas fought as a part of some other army. That evening our camp was filled with music and laughter while the Kaurava camp looked gloomy and dark.

THIRD DAY

On the third day, the Kauravas had the Garuda Vyuha (eagle) and we had the Chandrakala or the crescent moon. Bhima was placed on the right horn of the crescent surrounded by many kings. Next to him was placed Virata, Drupada and Nila. Next came Dhrishtaketu and the Chedis and many others who I couldn't recognise. Drishtadyumna and Shikandin with the Panchala army were stationed in the middle. Yudhishtira was also in the middle of the crescent surrounded by the elephant division. Next to him on this side was Satyaki and Draupadi's sons, Iravan and Ghatotkacha. My Lord with Arjuna formed the left horn of the crescent. As usual my Lord prompted Partha to seek out and fight with Bhishma. He was joined by his son Abhimanyu. Drona, Kripa and Aswatthama immediately came to help the grandfather. Bhima's son Ghatotkacha by his *rakshasi* wife now entered the fray and killed thousands of the Kaurava army.

The Kauravas were well aware of Bhishma's worth so they took care to see that he was guarded all the time from all sides. Duryodhana and his brothers rushed to stop Bhima, but Ghatotkacha used his bow known as Navachandra and wounded many of the brothers and broke

Duryodhana's armour and sent him tumbling down from his horse in a deep faint.

My Lord kept driving the chariot towards the grand-father, urging Arjuna to do his best with him. He had been doing this for the past three days, but Arjuna was still fighting in a half-hearted fashion and avoiding a serious confrontation with his beloved grandfather.

Bhishma knew that he was not doing his best because always his heart was given to the Pandava side and he was always hoping they would win, but having promised Duryodhana he started to harass Bhima, forcing him and Ghatotkacha to retire from the field.

FOURTH DAY

The Kauravas used the Chakra Vyuha on this day. In fact they used it many times. It was Drona's brilliant formation and very few other than Arjuna and his son Abhimanyu knew the secret of breaking it and coming out. Abhimanyu only knew the method of penetrating it and not of coming out. Totally unconcerned about his own safely, this brave child entered the Vyuha but of course his father closely followed him. They were attacked on all sides by the Kaurava princes. Bhima also followed the path cut out by Abhimanyu and started attacking the Kaurava brothers with his mace. Bhima really came to his own on this day. He was the greatest smiter of the whole army and by now he had practiced to perfection the method of killing elephants. Duryodhana sent a huge force of elephants to stop Bhima who immediately jumped out of the chariot and attacked them with his iron mace. They scattered and trumpeting in terror, they stampeded into the Kaurava forces and killed many of them. He then proceeded to devastate the elephant division of the Magadhas. The Kalingas and Magadhas and Pragjyotishas were all from the north-eastern region of Aryavrata and they had huge woolly elephants resembling mammoths. He had already destroyed the Kalingas on the second day and now he destroyed the Magadhas.

Duryodhana told all the car warriors to attack Bhima who was on foot. Standing on the ground he forestalled all the weapons which were thrown at him by the Maharathis (great car warriors) and pounced on Duryodhana's brothers and killed eight of them who were arrayed against him. He then turned on Duryodhana and felled his cobra banner and wounded him so badly in a duel that his charioteer Shalya had to take him away from the scene.

Soon after, Bhima was struck by an arrow on the chest by one of the brothers and sat down dazed. His two charioteers Ashoka and Vishoka pulled him back into his chariot and drove off.

The death of his eight brothers was the first shock of the battle to the arrogant king of the Kurus. Filled with sorrow at the loss of his dear brothers, he stormed into Bhishma's tent in the evening and accused him of not doing his best.

"How is it that we who have such a superior army and so many distinguished Maharathis on our side, are still being beaten by the Pandavas?"

"The Pandavas have justice on their side, O Bharata. Have you forgotten all the injustices you have done to them over the years? I advise you to stop this war and opt for peace and give them their due. Otherwise you will live to see many more horrifying scenes being enacted before your eyes!"

Duryodhana glared at him and told him to fulfill his promise to kill ten thousand Pandava warriors every day!

FIFTH DAY

That evening I asked my Lord to give me an assessment of the tactics used by each party.

"We are using many new tactics and formations never used before so they don't know the method of breaking our *vyuhas*. Many times Bhishma has been forced to change his own plans and go to the points where he is needed most despite the fact that they have masses of officers and warriors.

The Kauravas seem to be depending only on Bhishma and on their numerical superiority and the grandsire feels helpless since he has too much to do. Due to his hatred of the Pandavas, Duryodhana broke off from his *vyuha* on both the third and fourth days to fight with Bhima and thus disrupted Bhishma's original plan. As soon as they saw Ghatotkacha and Bhima, the Kauravas rushed out to kill them and were themselves killed.

"In our army all our warriors are fighting for the sake of *dharma* whereas the Kauravas have different desires and reasons for fighting. None of our warriors are afraid of getting their hands dirty. Look at Bhima! He has no qualms about jumping out of the chariot and attacking the elephants on foot. His helpers are my own sons (he looked at me piercingly when he said this.) They are the twin sons of the hunchback of Mathura known as Kubja. They are called Ashoka and Vishoka. They are not Yadavas and thus they are not part of the Yadava army, so they were free to come to the Pandava side and become Bhima's charioteer and his back protector.

Of course I immediately asked him, 'Who was Kubja? Did you really marry her? I never knew of this.'

He laughed his usual infectious laugh and said, "I have married only sixteen thousand, one hundred and eight ladies, nothing less and nothing more. Surely you know that!"

I nodded and he continued, "I see your eyes are growing rounder and rounder with curiosity so I will tell you the story of Kubja. When I was twelve years old, my uncle Kamsa sent my other uncle Akrura to Gokula to bring me to Mathura where he planned to have me killed by his huge wrestlers, Mushtika and Chanoora. All the Gopalas were with me as we passed through the streets of Mathura. We had never seen a big city before so we were all highly thrilled! Suddenly in front of me I saw a strange figure approaching. She was well-dressed but she had three humps so she was known as Trivakra. She couldn't walk straight and was hobbling towards us carrying a silver bowl filled with sandal paste for Kamsa. I went straight up to her and stood right in front of her. She did her best to straighten herself and look at me but couldn't manage it."

'But she saw your lotus feet,' I said. I have no idea why I said such a thing.

He smiled, "Yes, she saw my feet. I asked her, 'O Sundari! For whom are you taking this sandal paste?' She answered, 'Only for you my Lord!'

'Nobody had ever called her Sundari (beautiful one) before,' I said. 'She had always been called Trivakra (with three humps) or Kubja (hunchbacked).'

"You are right. She looked so awkward that no one had seen her beauty."

'But you had seen it,' I said.

"Yes," he answered. "She had been following me for many lives so I decided to bless her. Placing my forefinger under her chin, I pressed her foot with my big toe and lifted her up so that she could look straight into my eyes. 'Let the world see the beauty of your soul in your face,' I said.

"She gazed and gazed at me as if she would devour me with her eyes, overflowing with love. I could sense her confusion and asked her, 'For whom are you taking this sandal paste?'

'Whom else but for you my Lord,' she stammered.

"Scooping up that sandal paste meant for the king of the land, she anointed me. I thanked her and was about to move on but I could sense her panic. What if she never saw me again? She must have found that thought unbearable. Shamelessly she caught hold of my *uttareeyam* and pulled me back. 'Come to my house,' she whispered. 'I cannot leave you.'

"My elder brother Balarama was with me as well as the rest of the *gopalas*. He was looking disapprovingly at me telling me not to encourage the advances of this shameless woman, who had the temerity to hang round my neck in broad daylight before the interested gaze of so many spectators! He walked ahead without a word. I looked at the girl and

Kubja catching hold of the Lord's *uttareyam* on the streets of Mathura.

said, 'After completing the task for which I have come, I shall surely come to your house.'

'She was quite bereft and ran after you for a while, but since you walked on without a backward glance she stopped and slowly went to the king's palace carrying the empty bowl and her empty heart.'

"How do you know all this?" he asked.

'I don't know anything, Lord. But you know everything so you should know.'

He tilted my chin with his forefinger and asked, "Is this how I tilted your chin so long ago?"

My eyes brimming with tears I said, 'So I was Kubja. Why did you go to the house of such a lowly person?'

"You should know by now that pure love attracts me as nothing else. Poor girl, what did she have to offer me but her body filled with love. What right did I have to refuse that?"

'I waited and waited for you. I could not believe that you would keep your promise. You – the enchanter of the world! Why should you visit a woman like me? In this city of Mathura filled with beauties why should you have chosen me, the hunchback of Mathura? My heart beat fast and my eyes filled with tears of joy every time I thought of you. I could neither sleep nor eat. I came to the arena and watched you kill Mushtika and then Kamsa. Now he will come to me, I thought and went back and prepared everything for your visit. One evening after I had lit the lamp I heard your footsteps outside the door. I opened the door and there you were shining as if a blue lamp had been lit inside you, wearing a garland of wild flowers. The perfume of *tulsi* preceded you. I took your hand and brought you inside my humble abode which was suddenly transformed by your divine presence. I offered you *arghya* and *tambulam* and made another garland for you and placed it round your deep blue neck. Then I twined my arms round your neck like another garland and drowned in your blue-black eyes which bored into me and discovered all my secrets – discovered how I was longing for you to make love to me. How I was longing to have something of you which I could always keep, for I knew that I could never have you for myself. I knew that you belonged to the whole world but I also knew that in some strange way you belonged to me – poor and helpless and scorned as I was by the world. Just as you were everything to me, so I was everything to you for that one magical night. I lost myself in you as the wave loses itself in the ocean, as the cloud loses itself in the sky, as the river loses itself in the sea. I was the first woman to bear your sons. It is said that a man always remembers his first love. Is that why you came to me when I was sitting all alone on that beach in the purple twilight and took my hand and brought me to Dwaraka?

'My beloved Dwarakanatha, my one and only Vanamali. How long have I searched for you? How many nights and days have I cried and wept, not knowing for whom or what I was weeping? How many men have I spurned, for I found none who could ever compare with you? And now I have found you, I will never let you go. Now I have no desire for your body but only for your Self which I know to be the same as my Self and can never ever be parted from me. Now I know that through the ages you have been with me. How many lives have I taken, how many forms but you have never deserted me. Wherever I walked I would look back because I could hear your footsteps behind me, smell the perfume of *tulsi* and hear the call of the flute. All my senses were flooded with you and you alone. My beloved Lord, I have found you again or you have found me again or perhaps you have just revealed yourself to me again. Now I can never leave you. You and I are one, we can never be two.' I fell at his feet and kissed them again and again.

'Tell me did you return to my hut after that first night? I can't remember anything of that.'

"As long as I was in Mathura I used to come to you. I was with you when you had your sons. Then I left for Dwaraka and never saw you again. Another chapter of my life had finished. It is not my way to look at the past. The past is always part of the present and makes up the future so why should I cry over it. I have no regrets about the past and no hopes for the future. My concern is only with the present. But I knew it would not be the same for you and that you would not be able to survive the physical parting from me. I returned and brought the boys back with me to Dwaraka when they were five years old."

'Did I ever take another birth?'

"You have taken many births my child but the one which people will always remember you by is that of Kubja. But there is another one which you might recall. You remember the statue of Vishnu in Dwaraka which was worshipped by my parents? When I leave this human body, Dwaraka will be submerged in the ocean and that statue will be floating on it. At that time Brihaspati, our *guru* will take the help of Vayu, the wind god and will carry that idol and consecrate it in a place far down to the south of Aryavrata. That place will become a very sacred place for my worship. Your name was Manjula and you were born there in a very poor and outcaste family and you were my great devotee. You used to make exquisite garlands for me but you were not allowed to give them to me since you were an outcaste. So you used to hang the garlands on the peepul tree, which was a few yards away from the temple and worship me from afar. I used to give you *darshana* from there. In fact you were given a vision of me which was denied even to the priest. This went on for some years and then one day the priest of the temple found a strange garland on the neck of the idol in the temple, which was not made according to the usual standards. It was a very beautiful garland so he tried to find out from where it came. Every morning he would find a garland and he was desperate to find out the source. Eventually it was traced to you and they realised that you were my great devotee and that I preferred your garlands to any made by the temple personnel. From that day on you were allowed to make garlands for me as you used to do in Mathura. In the end you merged into me – your Vanamali. Actually you have been making garlands for me in every one of your births."

'Ah! So I was Manjula. I have heard of her and felt a great bond with her. Did I take any more births?'

"Your next famous birth was as Mira, the unfortunate princess of Mewar. You fell in love with me when you were only a child. You had a statue of me lifting up the mountain to save the *gopalas* and *gopis* of Vrindavana. This you used to worship all the time and refused to marry anyone else since you insisted that you were married to me. But you were forced into a marriage with a prince. You took the statue with you and worshipped me and sang and danced for me and made garlands for me and composed many songs for me. Your husband did not like this and even tried to kill you but of course I saved you from everything. At last one day you decided to leave him. Taking nothing from the palace, you wandered out to the wide world, singing and dancing your way from place to place until you reached Vrindavana. There you merged into me at the temple."

'No wonder I feel so drawn to her. Did I take any more births?'

"You took many births my dear and your last one was in a village near the place called Badarikashrama to which I had taken you. That is why you were so attracted to that place. You used to roam about the whole mountain side plucking flowers and mountain *tulsi* to make garlands for me. You always had an image of me in your heart and no one ever came to that standard, so you died disappointed since you were always searching for me in every person. Your heart's desire was only to find me and merge in me and that has never been fulfilled."

'Will it be fulfilled in this life?'

"Yes. This life was given to you to make the world realise my divinity in a way in which the modern mind can understand and accept. My way is the way of God and God can never be understood by the human mind. We can love him, we can hate him, we can accept him and we can reject him but we can never understand him or his ways. He will always be a mystery to the human mind so how can anyone hope to understand me? I don't expect to be understood but only to be loved and for such a person I'm always available. It is easy to understand someone who says 'hate violence' but very difficult to understand someone who says 'accept violence as you accept non-violence'. As I told you, we can never have a non-violent world unless we understand and accept violence. We can never have happiness if we cannot accept unhappiness. *Dharma* and *adharma* go hand in hand. When does *dharma* cease to be *dharma* and become *adharma*? If *dharma* accepts *adharma* and refuses to fight it due to cowardice masking itself as courage, then does *dharma* lose its charm and beauty and become *adharma*. This is what I have told Arjuna. He seeks to escape from his duty using the cloak of mercy and tolerance. This in turn will result in his accepting *adharma* and meekly living under the rule of the tyrant, again under the cloak of fidelity to one's family! I have come to destroy *adharma* but I will fail. I might succeed for some time but *adharma* has to rear its head once again for it can't stay away from *dharma*. It is attracted by it. Our path to liberation lies in accepting both. We have a left and a right hand and we need both to clap. So also we need both *dharma* and *adharma* if we want to live in this world. But that does not mean that we should stop fighting *adharma* when we see it. That is also part of our duty. We will succeed for some time and fail for some time. That also has to be accepted as a part of life. Strength and perfection only lie in my supreme abode. If you surrender your ego to me, I will take you above both these opposites. Only I can dare to do so because only I am above the law and am prepared to accept the consequences whatever they might be."

'Help me to understand you, my Lord. I know you need no defence, yet I would like to defend you and present you to the world as the perfection that you are. If we think God is perfect then we should see you as perfect. Why does God kill small children? Why does God exalt the criminal and punish the good? These are the type of foolish questions that are asked about God. And these are the type of foolish people who question your actions in this war. So allow me to be your advocate, my

Lord. Reveal yourself to me so that I can portray the real you to a world which is hungry for you.'

"I promise that you will be able to write a full account of my life as it is which even Vyasa was not able to write. This is my boon to you."

'Tell me, when you brought me from the shore to Dwaraka long ago, two boys were there holding your chariot. Were those my sons?' He nodded. 'Ah! I remember that I thought I had recognised them. Why didn't you tell me then?'

"I told you my dear that everything has a time and place and this is it."

'Did you know my real name?'

"Yes it was Malini."

'Will you ever leave me again?'

"Everything that has a beginning must have an end."

'Does that mean that you will leave me? I cannot bear to think that.'

"My child, I have never left you even for a second of all your many lives. But our bodies are perishable and will have to part some time or other."

'Then promise me that your memory will never fade – that I will always be able to recall you like this, as we are now – you sitting on this rock and I sitting at your feet looking up at your beloved face.'

"So be it," he said. "I also promise you that one of your sons will become a great scholar and will write a commentary on the Satvata Tantra. Now come, we have another busy day tomorrow." So saying he took my hand and pulled me up and we went into the tent.

Aum Namo Bhagavate Vaasudevaaya

Radha laid the snare with her eyes,
And caught the beautiful parrot, Shyam.
She held him, adoring in the cage of her ribs,
Tying him with the chain of her heart.
Taming him, she tended him,

And fed him on the nectar of her love.
She taught him how to speak,
"Radha! Radha! Radha!"
But the faithless bird cut the link of her chain,
To fly away to Mathura,
And Kubja, the hunch-back, held him there!"

Keshava Das. "Rasikapriya"

ॐ

Yamalarjuna bhajanaaya Namaha!

CHAPTER THIRTY-ONE

Bhishma

On the fifth day Bhishma arranged the Makara Vyuha or crocodile formation with a tail like a peacock. We chose the vulture formation. The vulture has a defensive posture. It waits for a body to die and then feeds on it. The beak of this vulture was Bhima, the eyes Shikandin and Drishtadyumna, Satyaki the head, Arjuna the neck, Drupada the left wing and Kekaya the right wing. The Upa Pandavas were at the back. The twins and Yudhishtira made up the tail.

Bhima went straight for Bhishma and Arjuna moved up and took his place. The Kaurava army didn't stand a chance under the joint attack of the two strongest Pandavas fighting side by side. Drona now came and attacked Satyaki. Bhima killed another eight Kaurava brothers. He had decided that he would not kill Duryodhana till the end, until he had seen all his brothers dead due to his own folly, but he wounded him again while Abhimanyu defeated Duryodhana's son once again. He could easily have killed many of the Kaurava brothers but desisted since he knew that his uncle Bhima wanted to kill them himself.

SIXTH DAY

Drona was taunted by Duryodhana for protecting the Pandavas so he rushed forth like a fury and destroyed more of our forces than had been killed on the preceding days.

Seeing the Kaurava brothers standing before him, Bhima jumped out of his chariot and gave chase to them and killed thirteen of them and made Duryodhana unconscious so that he had to be carried away by his brother-in-law, Jayadratha.

The twang of Arjuna's bow and the blast of the Panchajanya sent spirals of fear down the spines of the Kaurava troops. Arjuna was incessantly pouring arrows like showers on all sides making the sky dark so that people thought the sun had set. The Kaurava warriors were totally depressed, many of their their steeds slain and elephants killed. They huddled close to Bhishma hoping he would be able to protect them.

SEVENTH AND EIGHTH DAYS

The seventh day saw Bhima's tally of the total number of Kauravas killed come up to twenty-six and Duryodhana actually wept when he saw this and again complained to the grandsire who was most unsympathetic and told him, "It is too late to grieve. Warriors go to battle expecting to die."

On the eighth day Bhima killed another eight of Dritarashtra's sons and wounded Duryodhana again. Our spies came and told us that he went to Bhishma's tent in the night and begged him to do something about the terrible slaughter of his armies. Bhishma gave him a potion to relieve his pain caused by Bhima's arrows and told him that the only way was to stop the war and beg for mercy. Of course he refused to do this. Apparently later on he asked his brother Dusshasana to go to the grandsire and ask him to retire so that Karna could take over! Bhishma promised to do his best the next day. I have no doubt that all that happened here in our camp was also faithfully reported to Duryodhana.

I think the sons of Dritarashtra had been pampered and spoilt so much that they fully expected Bhishma to do their dirty work for them. When they found that this was not going to be as easy as they expected, they became frightened and decided that perhaps Karna would be a better bet!

That day nature decided to take a hand and a huge dust storm arose out of nowhere which made the confusion worse. The Kauravas were not a disciplined force in the first place and due to the dust storm they could hardly see their opponents. The Maharathis were whirled around by the storm and ended up fighting different people. Bhishma killed Satyaki's charioteer and his horses ran amok. For the first time Aswatthama came into the picture and engaged Arjuna in battle. Of course Arjuna refused to come to grips with him since he was his Guru's son and asked my Lord to steer clear of him.

In the meantime, Satyaki returned with his ten sons and started fighting with the Kaurava forces away from the main battlefield. For the first time in the battle, *divyastras* (divine weapons) were used when Satyaki's sons invoked them and killed a whole bunch of the Kaurava host. The old warrior Bhurisravas saw this and was so furious that he attacked Satyaki and rained arrows at him and his sons. He then proceeded to kill all the ten sons of Satyaki. Satyaki destroyed the chariot and jumped out of his own chariot and the two of them fought with swords. Seeing this, both Bhima and Duryodhana went to their aid. Bhima picked up Satyaki and Duryodhana took up Bhurisravas and took him to safety.

The Kauravas had lost thirty-five thousand chariots and the Pandavas had lost the ten precious sons of Satyaki who were all great warriors.

My Lord had given Iravan the boon that he could live to participate in the battle for another eight days. Though he was considerably maimed, hardly a skeleton, he was still an invincible warrior. In fact between him and Bhima's son Ghatotkacha, they could easily have wiped out the whole of the Kaurava forces. The eighth day saw Iravan at his best. He was Arjuna's son by Ulupi, the Naga princess so he took on the form of numerous vicious cobras spitting out venom and struck terror in the hearts of the Kaurava soldiers. He was challenged by Alambusha, the son of Duryodhana's *rakshasa* friend but Iravan defeated him easily. Alambusha now waited till Iravan had exhausted all his venom then he swooped down from the sky in the form of an eagle. He then resumed his *rakshasa* form and cut off Iravan's head with a sword. When he heard this Arjuna was filled with sorrow for his wonderful son who despite his handicap had continued to fight for them so bravely for eight days. My Lord comforted him and ordered Iravan's head to be stuck on a pole so that he could see the battle till the end. This was something he had promised him.

NINTH DAY

That night my Lord called Arjuna and said, "Partha, I want you to go to Duryodhana and ask him for the five potentiated golden arrows that Bhishma has given him."

"What are these arrows and why should he give them to me?" asked the bewildered Arjuna.

"You remember that day in the forest when you rescued Duryodhana from the attack of the Gandharva prince, Chitrasena, he asked you to choose some boon which you refused and said that you would ask him when the time arose. Well, this is the time. Go and ask him for the arrows immediately."

Arjuna left without another question. He always obeyed my Lord implicitly.

'What are these arrows?' I asked my Lord.

"Yesterday night when the Kauravas were losing, Duryodhana approached the grandfather and accused him of not fighting the battle using his full strength because of his affection for the Pandavas. Bhishma was infuriated by the constant accusations and he took up five golden arrows and muttered some *mantras* and gave them to Duryodhana and said that they had been potentiated to kill the Pandavas. Duryodhana has them with him and will not hesitate to use them tomorrow." Of course I did not ask the obvious question as to how my Lord knew about this. I knew that he knew everything.

Very soon Arjuna returned with the arrows and said, "Vaasudeva, I went and asked him for the arrows and he was stunned and asked me how I came to know of their existence. Of course I told him that you were the one who told me about them. He was shocked to hear of your omniscience and I could see that he was cogitating in his mind as to whether to believe in your divinity."

"So what did he do then?" asked my all-knowing Lord, pretending to know nothing.

"I think he has gone back to Bhishma to try and persuade him to give him another five potentiated arrows," Arjuna said.

After Arjuna left I asked, 'Will Bhishma give it to him?'

My Lord replied with a smile, "Of course not. Bhishma told him that he had already spent the merits of his lifetime of celibacy on those arrows which were potent enough to kill all the five Pandavas. The will of God is irrefutable."

'I suppose he must have told him that you know everything past, present and future and that was why he was unable to use those arrows against the Pandavas who were under your protection!' I looked at my Lord and he smiled back.

On the ninth day Bhishma was fighting like a maniac since he felt that he had not been doing his best till now due to his love for the Pandavas, as Duryodhana kept reiterating and taunting. His fiery arrows burnt up the Pandava army and all of us felt that as long as he was alive we had no hope of victory. Again and again my Lord drove the chariot towards Bhishma but Arjuna balked at killing his beloved grandsire. His arrows seemed to have no effect on him.

At last my Lord lost his patience and jumped out of the chariot and went flying towards Bhishma's chariot carrying a broken chariot wheel in his hands since he was not supposed to carry any weapons.

"If you are so squeamish about killing him, I will do it myself," he shouted. My Lord's show of anger had two reasons. He was able to fulfil Bhishma's desire to see him take up arms even at the cost of transgressing his own word, and he was able to whip up the desired wrath in Arjuna. He also indirectly reprimanded Bhishma for his *adharmic* act in killing Sweta on the very first day.

Bhishma smiled and welcomed him with folded palms, "Hail, O lotus-eyed one! I am indeed fortunate if I can meet death at your hands. I see that you are prepared to overthrow your own word not to take up any weapon in order to uphold my word that I would force you take up arms!"

Arjuna jumped out of the chariot and dashed after my Lord and grabbed his feet and begged him not to break his vow and promised to do his best the next day.

Bhishma continued to wreak havoc on our army. He appeared to be the incarnation of the God of Death himself. Arjuna's brave son Abhimanyu fought with Alambusha whom he had been chasing ever since he had killed his brother Iravan. At last Alambusha retired defeated.

Our spies told us that Duryodhana had again taunted and derided the grandfather for his half-hearted attempts against the Pandavas, even though he was keeping up his promise of killing ten thousand Pandava soldiers daily. Drona also had been similarly insulted by the haughty prince to the point of desperation. Drona would have quit had it not been for his son Aswatthama who was Duryodhana's boon companion and who kept urging his father to do his best for his friend.

That night Drishtadyumna called a council of war and declared that unless we killed Bhishma, we had no hope of winning the war. My Lord now suggested, "Let us go and meet the grandsire and ask him how we can kill him. Nobody can kill him without his consent."

I was really struck by this strange war in which son fought against father and father against grandfather, yet none hated the other and each one was happy to sacrifice his life for the sake of the other. Indeed in this aspect it was a *dharma yuddha* on the part of the Pandavas. Of course it was totally a different picture in the Kaurava camp where there was only hatred, jealousy and rivalry and the *gurus* and grandfathers were being used for their own nefarious purposes.

When darkness fell and the soldiers on both sides were chanting round the fires, the five brothers along with my Lord slipped into the tent of their beloved grandsire. There was a look of great joy on the old man's face at the sight of these men whom he loved so dearly. Tenderly he asked them why they had come and Yudhishtira answered.

"Grandfather! It is impossible for us to attain victory so long as you lead the Kuru host. We have come to ask you to tell us how we can kill you, for Vaasudeva has told us that you cannot be killed without your volition!"

It was a strange question for a grandchild to put and stranger still was the answer which was given without the slightest hesitation. Bhishma knew that his time for release had come. He had the power to depart from this life as and when he pleased. That fidelity which had for such a long time bid him stay to ensure the safety of the Kuru dynasty, was now beckoning him to leave. He was tired of life, tired of carrying a burden which was not his to bear, tired of the indiscriminate slaughter of the past nine days, tired of listening to Duryodhana's incessant taunts! All these years he had done his best to keep aloft the banner of the Kurus, even at the cost of his personal happiness. Now he realised that the only way to make his life's mission a success was for the Pandavas to rule. For the accomplishment of this purpose, he would have to make the last and final sacrifice of his own life, for as long as he lived they would never win and for this he was totally prepared.

"It is true my child," he said, "that your hope of victory while I live is in vain. Nobody except Vaasudeva can kill me while I am armed. But mark this carefully. I will not fight against those who are afraid, or those who are weak from wounds or illness or those who have surrendered to me. Nor will I take up arms against a woman or one who had been a woman before. Arjuna, if you attack me from behind one like this, you will accomplish your purpose and give me release from this life which has become a burden to me."

I was surprised to hear the tone of his voice. He spoke calmly as if he was discussing the weather rather than the method of his end, abiding to the last by the high code of chivalry which he had always followed.

"Is there such a one in our army who was a woman before?" asked Arjuna.

My Lord answered, "Yes Shikandin, brother of Panchali is such a one. She was Amba, the princess of Kasi in a previous birth and had a grudge against Bhishma. She gave up her life and took this birth in order to slay him. She was born as a girl called Shikandini but changed her sex and is here with us and determined to kill him. The grandsire is referring to her."

He looked at Bhishma who nodded his head and said, "Keeping Shikandin in front of you, shoot as many arrows as you like at me and I will not retaliate."

A wave of love and remorse swept over Arjuna as the plans were completed. He remembered the days of his childhood when he used to be dandled and fondled on the old man's knees, for he had always been his favourite. How could he, who had been so loved, aim the fatal arrow at the heart of this beloved warrior? Arjuna wept unashamedly and it was Bhishma himself who had to remind him of his duty as a Kshatriya and nerve him to a stern performance of it! My Lord's compassionate glance swept over Bhishma and blessed him.

"You will never be born again and will always be remembered as the greatest man that graced the Kuru dynasty." Bhishma smiled in gratitude.

The brothers departed as silently as they had come, leaving Bhishma with a vast sense of relief that at last the long and weary journey was coming to an end and he could return to his celestial abode. He had been one of the eight Vasus, who were the attendants of Indra, king of the gods.

I was always astonished by the devious methods chosen by my Lord to bring his devotees into the limelight and declare their greatness to others. He knew everything and could easily have told the Pandavas the method of killing Bhishma, but as usual he preferred to allow the true nature of each character to unfold itself so that the world would come to realise the greatness of his devotees! I gave him a meaningful look and he smiled.

TENTH DAY

The tenth day dawned and Bhishma knew it was to be his last day of fighting in the battlefield of life. Happily he propitiated the gods before proceeding to the battle field. Many bad omens were seen by the Kauravas. However as he rode out on his silver chariot with the palm banner waving merrily in the wind, the sun rose bright behind him and cast a halo over him. He blew his conch shell and plunged into the fray. Duryodhana had placed Dusshasana and several others to guard him. He remembered what the grandsire had told him about Shikandin and always took care to intercept him whenever he came near the grandsire. That morning I heard my Lord reminding Shikandin of his previous birth as Amba, whose life had been ruined by the celibate Bhishma who had stopped her from marrying the man of her choice and then had refused to marry her himself even though she had begged him to forget his vow of celibacy and save her from disgrace. My Lord had already told me this story the previous night.

Wherever Bhishma went Arjuna's chariot pursued him with Shikandin beside him. Shikandin stood in front beside my divine charioteer and Arjuna from behind the maiden-knight shot arrow after arrow at his beloved grandsire. Scorning to shoot at one who had once been a woman, Bhishma would laughingly aim an arrow at Arjuna whenever a sudden turn of the wheels gave him a chance. He showed no leniency to Arjuna that day. Shikandin was only a cloak. The actual battle was between him and Arjuna.

With a smile Bhishma told Dusshasana who was supposed to be protecting him, "These arrows coursing towards me in a continuous flow like flashes of lightning are all Arjuna's."

Even though Bhishma had told him to use Shikandin as a shield, the fact was that Arjuna did not actually do so except in the beginning when they entered the battlefield together. After that initial entrance, Arjuna removed Shikandin to a side and started raining arrows at Bhishma. It was a full and fair combat between the two. Not even the Kauravas could doubt that. So to say that Bhishma was killed through my Lord's manipulations is totally unfair and untrue. Duryodhana sent all his best *rathis* to protect Bhishma, but my Lord manoeuvred the chariot so brilliantly that he dodged all of them and brought Arjuna's chariot right up to the grandsire's. Bhishma laughed with joy for he knew the end was approaching and was determined to terminate his earthly career in a blaze of glory, doing his duty to the last! He let fly showers of arrows at Arjuna's chariot, carefully avoiding Shikandin.

Tears ran down from my eyes when I saw my Lord bleeding in many places from Bhishma's arrows which he accepted as flowers from his devotee as he had accepted the blows of Jambavan, the bear. In between the fierce battle he looked down at me and smiled and I was in a state of ecstasy for he made me see him in a new light – looking resplendent with droplets of blood all over his face and long, dusty eyelashes. He turned and flashed the same enchanting smile at Bhishma who rejoiced and felt refreshed at the sight of his wondrous form brandishing a whip and manoeuvring the frisky horses right in front of him. Arjuna's and Shikandin's arrows which were clustering thicker and thicker on his body seemed like mere darts to him for all he could see was my Lord's bewitching smile. Suddenly with a swoop my Lord closed in on him preventing anyone else from coming in between. Arjuna fought as one possessed for he had shut his mind to everything but the stern call of duty. Rising above the dualities of love and hate, pain and pleasure as advised by my Lord during his discourse, he sent arrow after arrow at his beloved grandsire piercing him all over. At last the time for the mortal wound had come, the end of the day and the end of his life and Arjuna sent the arrow straight at his heart.

All the Kaurava heroes were yapping around us like a pack of wolves but none could go near Bhishma nor prevent Arjuna and Krishna - Nara and Narayana from putting an end to the drama of his life.

My Lord knew the time had come for the fatal arrow, so out of his infinite compassion he diverted the old knight's thoughts away from the battle and fixed it on the sound of Aum. He threw back his head and lifting his conch shell, the Panchajanya to his lips, he blew long and loud. It was the primeval sound of Aum. It filled Bhishma's ears and his mind became fixed on that Absolute which the sound represented. His eyes were pinned on the physical form of that Absolute which he was fortunate enough to perceive before his dying eyes, holding the reins of his destroyer's chariot! That formless one who had taken on a form in order to enchant the whole world now seemed to be calling him to stop the game and return to him!

Slowly he fell from the chariot, while the gods clustered with folded palms in the skies, but his body did not touch the ground for he was entirely covered with arrows and he lay as it were, on a couch of arrows – a fitting bed for a wonderful warrior. Even now death dared not approach him for as he fell the thought flashed across his mind that the time was Dakshinayana, the six months of the year when the sun is moving towards the south which is an inauspicious time for passing from this world. He wanted to wait for the beginning of the summer solstice – Uttarayana when the sun would start its northward journey.

A huge wail rose from both sides as the mighty warrior fell down. Fighting stopped and everyone crowded round to pay their last respects to this greatest of all warriors who had shed his last drop of blood for such an unworthy cause, out of mistaken loyalty.

Duryodhana shouted at Arjuna, "You traitor! You have killed your own grandfather to get the kingdom for yourself. How could you have ever done such a dreadful thing? Sin alone shall accrue to you from this."

My Lord spoke in his deep authoritative voice, "O Duryodhana! Did the thought of sin ever pass your mind when you dragged the princess of Panchala into the open assembly and tried to disrobe her? Bhishma is a warrior and has had a warrior's death in the battlefield. What is the great sin that Arjuna has done by killing him? What sort of treachery was it to invite the Pandavas to a palace in Varanavata and set fire to it? And yet you talk of treachery in killing a warrior face to face in the middle of a battlefield! It is better for you not to mention the words sin and treachery. Every act of yours against the Pandavas has been filled with treachery from the time they came to the Kuru court from the forest. Our Pitamaha (grandfather) died a glorious death, fighting to the last and Arjuna was only an instrument for his death. No sin shall accrue to him for this!"

The Kuru prince was silenced by my Lord's apt accusations. He turned to his brothers and ordered them to carry Bhishma away to a place of safety but he refused to move from the spot where he fell, impaled on arrows.

"This is a fitting bed for a warrior," he said "but I'm uncomfortable. My head is hanging down since it's the only part of my body which is free from arrows."

Duryodhana hurriedly asked for soft pillows to be brought for him but he would have none of those. "Arjuna, my child!" he said, looking at the one who had provided him with his arrow bed, "get me something to rest my head upon as you have given me a bed. Only your arrows have stuck to my body. Shikandin's have dropped off."

Arjuna was standing dumb with grief, hardly able to look at that beloved face but he understood his request and shot three arrows down to the earth with such accuracy that they formed a correct support for the hoary head of the mighty warrior.

Bhishma looked gratefully at Arjuna and said, "My child! I have a raging thirst. My tongue clings to my palate. Give me some water."

Duryodhana sent for a jar of water but he turned his head away from it and looked again at Arjuna with an unmistakable message. He immediately shot an arrow deep into the bowels of the earth and a gush of water sprang forth straight into Bhishma's mouth. Ganga, his mother had heard his plea and had come to quench the thirst of her beloved son! Bhishma gave a sigh of relief and looked gratefully at Arjuna. Like the cooling waters of the Ganga, that look helped to assuage in some small measure the burning pain in Partha's heart.

Once again Bhishma tried to talk sense to Duryodhana, "Even now it is not too late to make peace with the Pandavas." But of course though Duryodhana wept, no doubt for his own sake, he was deaf to all reason. It was as if he had mounted on a chariot with horses totally out of control, hurtling down a slope to inevitable destruction.

A trench was dug round Bhishma to keep out wild animals and Yudhishtira ordered a canopy to be erected over him.

Bhishma said, "Those of you who are alive after the war may come and see me at the beginning of Uttarayana. Until then I would like to be left alone to spend my remaining days in solitude and worship."

News was brought to us that in the night Karna went to meet the old warrior to pay his last respects. "Radheya, the *Suta Putra* salutes you my Lord," he said.

Bhishma opened his weary eyes and said, "You are not the son of Radha but the son of Kunti! I recognised your valour but downgraded you in order to keep you alive for serving Duryodhana till the last day."

Tears streamed down Karna's eyes when he thought of all that had happened between them and he begged the grandsire to forgive him. Bhishma simply smiled and placed his bleeding hand on Karna's head when he bent it over him. He refused all offers of food or water and waved him away with his hand.

'Why did Bhishma have to punish himself and live on for some more days on a bed of arrows?' I asked my Lord.

"It is true that Bhishma never did any selfish action. He is a mighty warrior and learned and respected. But remember he too chose to fight on the side of *adharma*. Actually if he and Drona and Karna had refused to fight, Duryodhana would never have decided on war. He depended entirely on them, so really speaking these three are responsible for the war! Bhishma again was obsessed by the oaths he had given his father. One, that he would remain a celibate and the other that he would unquestioningly comply with the bidding of the King of Hastinapura whoever it might be. This vow he refused to break even when it involved fighting with his beloved grandnephews who he knew well had never done anything wrong."

'Is it wrong to stick to one's vows?' I asked.

"Of course one should always stick to one's vows but if it ends up by making you serve evil, the vow should be discarded. Bhishma put his vow above everything else even though the vow had become an instrument of evil. Even his first vow of total chastity should have been renounced when he saw that the kingdom was being jeopardised. Had he broken his vow and married Amba, all this misfortune would never have overtaken the house of the Kurus! So you see that even a good thing if stretched too far turns bad!! I have told you before that good and bad are two sides of the coin of life and we can never say when one will turn into the other."

Aum Namo Bhagavate Vaasudevaaya

ॐ

Tamalashyamalakritaye Namaha!

CHAPTER THIRTY-TWO

Abhimanyu

All of us expected that Karna would be chosen as commander-in-chief since he had been waiting for Bhishma's fall to take charge. However, we heard that Karna refused to take charge since he said that he had not been fighting for the past ten days and the great warriors of their army would not be happy if he took over. He believed that his presence would cause dissension amongst the leaders. He advised Duryodhana to make Drona the commander-in-chief in which case nobody would object. He was their preceptor and much revered by all. Of course Karna was promoted to the highest rank of Athiratha. The Acharya warned Duryodhana that he was a Brahmin and he lacked the courage and prowess which characterised the Kshatriya. However he promised to do his best. Duryodhana again warned his *guru* in no uncertain terms that if he didn't fight with all his heart, he would be replaced by Karna. He could be sure of Karna's loyalty but he could never be quite sure of Drona's! Duryodhana now made a tactical error and told Drona that his first duty was to capture Yudhishtira alive. Of course as my Lord told me, it's much more difficult to capture than kill someone.

ELEVENTH DAY

On the eleventh day as if to prove his mettle, Drona laid out the Kaurava warriors in the Shakata Vyuha or cart wheel formation. In response to this Drishtadyumna made the Krouncha (stork) formation. Yudhishtira was placed in the centre and Arjuna and my Lord stood at the point of the beak with Drishtadyumna at our side. Drona fought with unabated fury especially against Drishtadyumna who he knew had been born to kill him.

Abhimanyu was determined to capture Duryodhana's son Lakshmana who had been avoiding him like a coward, and after a brief duel he captured and tied him to his chariot. Drona, Shakuni and Dusshasana tried to rescue him, but the young lad routed them all and drove off in his chariot dragging Lakshmana behind him. Jayadratha and Karna now came to rescue him but were again chased off by this brilliant son of Arjuna. Shalya rushed at him and would have overpowered him, but Bhima came and gave a blow which made him fall unconscious. Abhimanyu remonstrated with his uncle for having done this and while the argument was going on, Lakshmana managed to free himself and taking the unconscious Shalya into a chariot he fled from the scene. Shalya came back again and the brilliant Abhimanyu fought all of them single-handed, including Jayadratha, Kritavarma and Paurava.

Duryodhana was mad when he heard of his son's humiliation and told his *guru* that the only way he could compensate for this was by capturing Yudhishtira alive, in which case the war would have to stop and he could get the Pandavas to return to the forest for another period of exile. In the meantime the Kaurava forces tried their best to get past Arjuna so as to get to Yudhishtira. However the Cart wheel could not even touch the beak of the Stork!

When Duryodhana heard of Drona's failure to capture Yudhishtira, he poured all his bottled up venom on him and told him to be ashamed that he was beaten by his disciple!

Drona retaliated and said, "As long as Bhima with his mighty mace and Arjuna guided by Krishna are protecting Yudhishtira, we have no hope of capturing him either alive or dead!"

Seeing Abhimanyu's expertise and courage I asked my Lord to tell me about him. He said, "Abhimanyu learnt many things even when he was in his mother's womb. At one time Arjuna was describing to Subhadra the method of getting into the *padma vyuha* or *chakra vyuha*, which is a very complicated battle formation. Very few people know the art of getting in and out of it. The baby listened with rapt attention and learnt it while still in the womb. Before Arjuna could finish the method of exiting from the *vyuha*, Subhadra had fallen asleep. I burst upon the scene just at that time so the boy never knew the method of coming out. Of course his father could easily have taught him the method of egress after he was old enough to learn but for some reason he never did so."

Suddenly I was struck with a thought and asked him, 'Did you do this deliberately to stop the baby from learning it all?'

He replied, "Everything is ordained by the law of *karma*. I only carry out instructions."

'Why was it ordained?' I asked.

"Abhimanyu is the incarnation of Varchas, the son of the moon god, Chandra. The gods asked Chandra to allow his son to incarnate on earth to help the Pandavas. He agreed on the condition that his son would be allowed to remain on earth only for sixteen years, as he could not bear to be parted from him. I knew all this and that is why I did not let him hear the whole of the explanation which Arjuna was giving Subhadra. Moreover Subhadra fell asleep and the boy is now sixteen years old."

'Is he going to die now?'

"Maybe."

'Why can't you stop it?' I cried.

"I told you that I don't meddle in the working out of the law. I only play my part when called upon to do so."

For the first time I wished I was a solid person who could stop Abhimanyu from whatever danger was threatening him. I felt quite desperate at my helplessness. I felt like a bird that had wings yet could not fly.

He looked sympathetically at me and said. "My child, life has to be allowed to run its course. You cannot put impediments in its way."

'But you will put impediments when it's a question of saving the Pandavas.'

"That is also according to the plan! But I will let you into a secret. His wife Uttara is carrying his son in her womb and he will be the heir to the throne of the Kurus."

And with that I had to be content but I was always looking out for the danger which was approaching Abhimanyu. I knew it would have something to do with the formation of the *padma vyuha*.

12TH DAY

On the 11th evening we got the news that the Trigarta brothers had volunteered to lure Arjuna away from the field of battle since Drona had said that if Arjuna was removed he could manage to control Bhima and capture Yudhishtira alive since Duryodhana's plan was to hold him hostage and thus force the other brothers to give up. Drishtadyumna immediately made plans to protect Yudhishtira from all sides. Arjuna and Abhimanyu were to be in the front, Bhima just behind and Nakula and Sahadeva on the sides. However the Trigartas as promised, challenged Arjuna to a battle a couple of miles away and he was forced to leave, but he gave strict instructions to his son and brothers not to leave the Eldest unprotected at any time. My Lord extracted a promise from Yudhishtira that he was to retreat if cornered by Drona since his capture would prove fatal to the Pandava cause.

On the 12th day, the Kauravas made the Garuda Vyuha (eagle formation) and the Pandavas kept to their previous day's Krouncha (stork formation) since it had proved to be very strong.

Drona managed to break through Yudhistira's strong bodyguard made up of some of the best men in our army and rushed at the Eldest. He moved purposefully towards Yudhishtira while the Kaurava brothers tried to scatter his body guard made up of Drupada's sons, Shikandin and

Drishtadyumna along with Bhima and Satyaki. Drona was intercepted by Drupada's brother Vrika and some other warriors, but he was in a really terrible mood that day and indiscriminately killed anyone who stood in his way. Drona almost had his hands on Yudhishtira when the latter remembered the promise given to Krishna and rode away on the fastest horse, leaving Shikandin and Satyaki to thwart Drona from giving chase. Under the onslaught of Satyaki's brilliant archery, Drona was forced to retreat from the field only to be received by Duryodhana's caustic remarks. Had Drona managed to capture the Eldest as he had promised, the battle would have ended on that day.

After giving the Trigarta brothers a good thrashing and killing the eldest, my Lord told Arjuna to leave them and return to the main scene of battle. Of course he knew what was going on and that is why he made Arjuna return instead of pursuing the Trigartas. Narakasura's son, Bhagadatta with his gigantic tusker called Supritika, which was a veritable war machine, was creating havoc in our army. Bhagadatta was considered to be the greatest warrior in Aryavrata in elephant warfare. Even Bhima, who was the greatest smiter of elephants, found it impossible to kill Supritika despite the fact that he used all the tricks he knew about subduing elephants. Bhima used to kill elephants by cutting off their trunks and smiting their foreheads, but this mammoth caught him in his trunk and would have dashed him to the ground but somehow by smiting his forehead he managed to get out of its hold. Bhagadatta forged ahead destroying countless numbers of our army. As soon as we arrived on the scene, Arjuna started to harass Bhagadatta with numerous arrows shot in a steady stream. The elephant, Supritika was a most well-trained war elephant, the equivalent of a thousand foot soldiers, and it tried its best to strike Arjuna and my Lord with its trunk and bring us down to the ground. It was a huge elephant which towered above the chariot so it could easily have done so but for the brilliant way in which my Lord evaded and dodged the charges of this dreadful pachyderm.

Bhagadatta also had the Vaishnavastra which had been given to him by his father. The incantation for the *astra* which in this case was the Narayana *mantra* could be used on any weapon to potentiate it. Like all *astras* it was invincible and could not be used twice in one day. Bhagadatta's weapon was the elephant goad so now he decided that it was time he used it against his adversary. He charged his goad with the *mantra* and flung it at Arjuna. It streaked like lightning towards him cleaving through the steady flow of arrows which Arjuna was discharging in defence. Had it reached its mark it would have meant the end of Arjuna. Seeing the flaming missile coming towards them, my Lord cast off his whip and reins and stood up in the chariot, blocking Arjuna from its path, ready to receive the fatal weapon on his own chest. I shrieked but of course no one heard me. Arjuna could not move due to shock. To the amazement of all who were watching, the *astra* changed into a garland of wild flowers – *vanamala*, the emblem of Lord Vishnu and adorned the neck of my divine charioteer who was none other than the incarnation of Vishnu!

With his usual disarming smile my Lord told Arjuna how this *astra* had been given by him in another incarnation to the Earth Goddess who in turn had given it to her son Narakasura who gave it to his son, Bhagadatta. It was a benign *astra* which would never kill an unarmed person and that was why my Lord had stood up without any arms. Unfortunately Bhagadatta did not realise that he had used the Vaishnavastra against the incarnation of Vishnu himself. Of course it would not kill him but had changed into the *vanamala* round his neck!

I clapped my hands in joy. It was such a display of divine power and all done in the most unobtrusive fashion which was ever his way. I kissed his feet again and again.

"Without his goad, Bhagadatta and the elephant are both vulnerable, so kill the elephant first and then kill him," said my Lord.

Arjuna immediately discharged a sharp arrow which sank into the elephant's forehead and killed him instantly. Then he discharged another arrow which killed the brave veteran Bhagadatta.

Arjuna turned round to face Shakuni's two sons, Vrisha and Achala and killed them easily. He then spent his full fury on their wicked father who was following close behind but coward that he was, he turned tail and ran.

The sun was almost setting when the two adversaries Karna and Arjuna met and had a glorious duel which everyone watched, but just at that time Yudhishtira must have mentally called to my Lord because he did not give Arjuna time to finish the duel but quickly drove the chariot towards the Eldest who was being threatened by Drona. We managed to rescue him and drive away since the conch shell denoting the end of the battle had been blown.

Thus the twelfth day ended with defeat for Drona who was again berated by the scornful Duryodhana. Apparently he taunted him with his inability to capture Yudhishtira. Unable to bear this any longer, Drona swore, "Tomorrow I will make the *padma vyuha* (lotus formation) or *chakra vyuha* (wheel formation) in which I will capture Yudhishtira, failing which I promise that I will certainly kill one of the greatest of the Pandava warriors!"

Duryodhana muttered, "I have no belief in the promises made by a Brahmin! They never keep their word!"

I thought to myself that Duryodhana's barbed words must be more painful to the *guru* than all the arrows discharged by Arjuna!

THIRTEENTH DAY

On the thirteenth day Drona arranged the Kaurava army in the *chakra vyuha*, which was a labyrinthine formation in the shape of a lotus. It was made up of circles and circles of soldiers revolving and rotating with rage to capture the Pandava army. He stayed in the centre and kept all the great warriors of their army in each of the concentric circles. This was a ploy to capture Yudhishtira. On our side only my Lord and his son Pradyumna and Arjuna were aware of the secret technique to break this seven-tiered spiral formation. Abhimanyu knew only the method of entering the formation but did not know how to come out of it as I had been told.

Drishtadyumna arranged our army in the Makara Vyuha or the crocodile formation.

That morning I was still filled with fear and ran to the women's tent where Abhimanyu was being decorated as befitting a great warrior. His arms were red with the sandal paste which was spread on them. His wife put garlands of yellow and red *champaka* flowers over his armour. Subhadra placed silver chains with golden capsules containing protective herbs round his neck. He bid a fond farewell to his mother and wife. Draupadi took a talisman which she had made potent with many *mantras* and tied it on his arm and told him to wear it always as it would protect him from all harm. He fell at her feet and got her blessings as well as those of his mother and hugged his wife before going out in a fanfare of bugles and conch shells.

Duryodhana again gave the Trigarta brothers the task of luring Arjuna away from the main battle. The five brothers, Susarma, Satyavarta, Satyavarma, Satyaasu and Satyadharma formed a suicide squad known as the samsaptakas. They swore to Duryodhana that they would fight to the last man and keep Arjuna at bay till Yudhishtira was captured in the *chakra vyuha*. Arjuna asked my Lord to give chase to the Trigartas who had challenged him. Before leaving he gave strict orders that Bhima, Satyaki, Drishtadyumna and Abhimanyu were to protect Yudhishtira at all cost. My Lord told me to stay back in Bhima's chariot with my sons of a previous incarnation.

I felt that some calamity was approaching Abhimanyu. 'Why you are taking Arjuna away from the battle!'

"I'm only his charioteer. I obey his orders!"

Before I could question him further he had driven away and I got into Bhima's chariot as he wanted me to do.

Very soon it became obvious that unless the *chakra vyuha* was broken, our army would be totally wiped out. Yudhishtira and Drishtadyumna were at their wits end. At last the Eldest approached Abhimanyu and asked, "It is absolutely necessary for us to break this *vyuha*. Only your father and you know the method. As Arjuna is not here I request you to take the initiative."

My heart leapt in terror when I heard this. I knew this was the final call for Arjuna's son.

Abhimanyu replied, "I will most certainly do this but I know only how to enter the *vyuha* and not the method of breaking it and coming out so that it is open for everyone to enter. Moreover my father has specially asked me to guard you."

"Don't worry about me," said Yudhishtira. "All the great car warriors are inside the *vyuha* so I can easily manage to guard myself. Your uncle Bhima will follow on your heels and keep the path open to enable you to return. Nakula and Sahadeva will be my guards today."

I jumped out of Bhima's chariot and ran towards Abhimanyu to try and stop him even though I knew it was futile. My eyes were drawn to something glittering on the ground as he rode off. I picked it up. It was the talisman given to him by Draupadi. I clutched it and tried to run after him but of course I could do nothing. I hugged the talisman and sobbed.

Abhimanyu was only too happy to obey his uncle. He was just dying to get into the *vyuha*. He set off at a spanking pace with his charioteer Sumitra. Invoking the *mantra* taught to him by my Lord, he multiplied each of his arrows into hundreds and soon drove a wedge into the impenetrable *padma vyuha*. Fully expecting his uncle to follow hot on his heels, this boy hero drove right through, cutting down the opposing hordes on all sides with deadly arrows which never missed their mark! The spectacular speed with which this brilliant lad of sixteen whizzed through the formation left Bhima breathless.

Bhima was close on his heels and I kept urging him to go faster since Abhimanyu was going like a flash of lightning, but Duryodhana's brother-in-law Jayadratha, who had been waiting for an opportunity to use the power given to him by Shiva to be able to thwart four of the Pandavas, now jumped through the gap formed by Abhimanyu and stood in Bhima's path determined to stop him from following his nephew. He had his elephant brigade with him. He had also received a garland of unfading flowers from Shiva and this he threw in Bhima's path. Bhima was rooted to the spot when he saw Shiva's garland.

"Not even for the sake of saving the life of my nephew will I cross over and desecrate the garland of my Lord," he said. He fought against the elephants which came charging up at him and killed a number of them.

I always felt very sad when elephants were killed but I suppose there was no way out of this.

Suddenly I felt myself floating over the air into the *vyuha*. I guessed that my Lord had heard my wish and was giving me the chance. Without turning back, the brave young lad was pushing deep into the Kaurava ranks. Of course Jayadratha allowed him to pass through with a wicked grin.

Determined to exit the *chakra vyuha* by shattering it from within, Abhimanyu went on rampage. He forged ahead fighting with all the *maharathis* who were stationed at every spiral and reached the heart of the trap. Drona and Duryodhana were waiting like spiders in the middle of a web. I was filled with admiration at the way this boy fought as one possessed. He was fighting with such daring and lack of fear that none from the Kaurava side could beat him in a duel (*dwanda yudha*). He defeated all the *maharathis* one by one. He injured Shalya so badly that he fainted and then he killed his younger brother who came to help him and then pierced Drona and Kripa with his lance. He then turned on Dusshasana and trounced him. He even cut off Karna's bow and hurt his arm. He killed Karna's brother who came to help him and Brihadbala, the king of Kosala of the Ikshwaku dynasty. Though the *chakra vyuha* was meant to capture Yudhishtira and kill countless Pandava soldiers, thanks to Abhimanyu's amazing courage, the tables were turned and the Kauravas lost three quarters of an *akshauni* through his ability alone.

Incensed at the admiration expressed by Kripa and Drona for the boy's expertise, Duryodhana attacked him himself. Abhimanyu spared him for he knew, he was reserved for his uncle or else he could easily have killed him then and there and forced the war to come to an end. But he brought him down from his chariot and left him weaponless.

Lakshmana had been nursing a grudge against Abhimanyu from the time that Balarama's daughter, Vatsala had chosen Abhimanyu in preference to himself. He flew at Abhimanyu with upraised sword but with a single arrow Abhimanyu killed Lakshmana and dispersed his army. Filled with sorrow and rage, Duryodhana ordered all the Maharathis to attack the boy. I could see the disgust on Abhimanyu's face at this terrible breach of battle etiquette as he countered all their attacks with ease. He then attempted to capture Duryodhana who ran off crying to Drona, berating him about his inability to conquer one small boy! He was further incensed when he heard both Drona and Kripa expressing their admiration for the boy. Actually everyone except the Kauravas was filled with admiration for this remarkable boy who was able to fend off all the great warriors who were yapping around him like mongrels!

"This lad must be killed at all cost," shouted Duryodhana. "If not I don't want my kingdom or my life. Let there be no more talk of fair play!" He shouted to Drona, "Do something about this boy who is like a blazing meteor and bring him down before he kills everyone in the army." Stung by Duryodhana's doubts about his abilities, Drona suggested that the only way that Abhimanyu could be killed was by multiple and simultaneous attacks. It was as if the great *acharya* who should have known better, was determined to save his pride and reputation even if he had to use *adharmic* means to achieve this end.

Duryodhana was all for using *adharmic* means and ordered all the Kaurava *maharathis* to attack Abhimanyu, who countered all their attacks with the greatest of disdain for attempting such an unrighteous fight. As if there was ever a talk of righteous means, I thought to myself. From the time he had entered this hideous trap he had been exposed to the most unfair and treacherous treatment one could ever imagine anyone indulging in, least of all these great souls who called themselves Brahmanas and Kshatriyas!

"Do anything you like but kill this boy before he kills us," shouted the irate Duryodhana.

"The only way you can kill him is by cutting off his bow, bow-string, the reins of his steeds, the steeds themselves and his two charioteers." Turning to Karna he said, "O mighty bowman! Son of Radha, if you think you are competent then you can do this. With his bow in hand he is incapable of being vanquished even by the *asuras* and *devas* together. If you wish you can deprive him of his chariot and divest him of his bow!"

Following the orders of the commander Karna cut off his bow and then these two great Brahmanas, Drona and Kripa killed his horses and charioteers aided by Kritavarma. Though he was deprived of both his bow and his chariot, this brave son of Arjuna was still undaunted and drew out his sword and shield and continued to wreak havoc on anyone who dared to come near him.

The Kauravas now closed in on him and attacked him from all sides as he stood in the centre of the lotus. He really looked like the stamen of the lotus, so beautiful was he to look at, even though dripping blood from all over. In fact he shone with an unnatural lustre like the moon.

I wondered if his father, the moon was actually shedding his glow on him.

Drona crept up from behind and destroyed the hilt of his sword and Karna his shield. I cried when I saw this amazing warrior lift up a chariot wheel lying on the ground and start whirling it around his head and fending off his attackers, looking like my Lord holding the *chakra*. Still they harassed him. Unarmed and defenceless as he was, those dreadful beasts continued to make him more defenceless by shattering his wheel. He was now surrounded by Drona, Karna, Kripa, Aswatthama, Kritavarma, Dusshasana and Duryodhana. He immediately picked up a fallen mace and pounced on Aswatthama who took to his heels.

Like a proud lion facing a pack of jackals, he faced his opponents, undaunted, daring son of a daring father. With amazing brilliance he kept his attackers at bay, probably hoping against hope that that his uncle would soon come to his rescue. With lightning movements of the mace he managed to prevent even a single arrow from scratching him. Suddenly he sprang onto Drona's chariot and smashed it to pieces and laughed at him. This enraged Drona to such an extent that he totally disregarded all codes of decent warfare and cut off the lad's right arm which was brandishing the mace. Undaunted Abhimanyu took up the mace in his left hand and continued to terrorise his opponents. But Drona cruelly sent another arrow which smashed the mace. At Duryodhana's instigation Karna crept up from behind and smashed the weak, bleeding boy's skull with his mace while Dusshasana's son closed in on him and hacked him to death as he lay fallen on the ground. All the Kaurava soldiers wept unashamedly when they saw this fair flower of Aryan manhood felled so shamefully by his murderers who were all old enough to be his fathers and grandfathers! Only Duryodhana, Dusshasana, Shakuni and Jayadratha rejoiced at the sight! His death was a murder rather than a death on the battlefield. The Kauravas committed the biggest breach of ethics and code of warfare on this day. The massacre of Abhimanyu was such a dastardly act that it is supposed to have marked the end of the Dwapara Yuga and ushered in the fourth Yuga of Kali – the Iron Age.

My tears were falling in a steady stream and when I looked up I saw the vultures that flew round the battlefield shrieking and saying, "Not thus! Not thus! We don't want any share of this body!!"

I returned to Bhima's chariot. The news had just been brought to Yudhishtira who fell from his chariot in a faint. When he recovered he wailed, "I'm his real killer for having sent him to his doom." Bhima who loved him more than his own sons cried, "I know he could never have been slain in a fair fight."

I returned to my Lord's side as he and Arjuna were returning after annihilating the *samsaptakas*. Arjuna was feeling very uneasy, he knew not for what. My Lord who knew everything thought that Arjuna might try something desperate if he heard of his son's death. He invoked Indra's aid. Indra came in the form of an old man and made a huge fire and was just preparing to jump into it as my Lord and Arjuna passed by. Arjuna jumped out and tried to stop the old man who said, "I'm sure you would do the same if you lost your only son as I have."

In order to comfort him Arjuna replied, "Please refrain from this ignoble act. I swear to you by my Lord Krishna and my Gandiva that were I to lose my son, I would never stoop to such an act!"

The old man seemed appeased by this announcement and went on his way. Arjuna returned to the chariot but my Lord took the extra precaution of hiding his weapons.

On reaching the camp Arjuna was met by a foreboding silence. Everyone seemed to be avoiding his eyes and he asked my Lord, "What calamity has befallen us? Have they captured the Eldest?" He looked at my Lord's face and saw a glimmer of tears in those lotus eyes.

"Tell me what has happened?"

My Lord answered sadly, "My nephew has been murdered."

Unable to bear the shock, Arjuna fainted and had to be revived. On recovering he took the mangled remains of his son in his arms and lamented, "O mighty hero! You were able to discharge your arrows even before your enemies could string their bow, so how could they have killed you? Have you really gone to the realm of the dead? Why did I leave you and go? What will I say to your poor mother?"

Turning to his brothers he continued, "O brothers! Knowing how much I loved him, how could you have sent him alone to his doom? Sahadeva light a fire. I want to join my son!"

Sahadeva obeyed without protesting for he knew my Lord would save him. Yudhishtira was too scared to interfere and could only look imploringly at my Lord. Arjuna refused to look at my Vanamali for he knew that he could have saved Abhimanyu's life if he had wished to do so.

The pyre was lit and Abhimanyu's body placed on it. Arjuna circumambulated it three times before jumping into it. My Lord must have summoned Indra for suddenly he appeared in the form of the old man and reminded Arjuna of his oath not to take his own life. Arjuna stopped short and turned to my Lord at last for comfort.

My Lord said with deep compassion in his voice, "My friend! I have told you at the beginning of the battle that birth and death are only two sides of the coin of life. You cannot have one without the other. Abhimanyu's time was up. He passed like a comet through the battlefield creating terror in the hearts of our enemies. He lived a glorious life and died a glorious death. What is there to grieve in this? Shake off your unmanliness therefore and set about destroying the man who was the only cause for his death. Though all the Kauravas had a dastardly hand in his actual killing, the fact is that it is only because of Jayadratha that Bhima was unable to follow him as he had promised to do. Remember Jayadratha had got a boon from Shiva that he would be able to keep four of the Pandavas at bay for one day and this was his opportunity to do so. Had it not been for him, Bhima would have followed Abhimanyu and opened a path for the rest of the army to follow. So your duty now is not to sit and mourn for your son but to find out Jayadratha and kill him! This is the only thing you can do for your son now. This is what he will expect you to do."

My Lord knew Arjuna's fiery nature and knew also that the only way to shake him out of his despondency was to direct his anger against Jayadratha even though he was only a cog in the whole machine. Yet it broke Arjuna's spell of sorrow which seemed to have enfolded him, and forced him into some action. I marvelled at my Lord's ability to gauge every situation and make the best decision.

When he heard of Jayadratha's perfidy Arjuna shook off his sorrow and swore, "I swear by Krishna and my Gandiva that if I do not kill Jayadratha by sunset tomorrow, I shall immolate myself in the fire!"

The other brothers were vastly relieved by this temporary respite and looked gratefully at my Lord. Krishna said, "Jayadratha has practiced severe austerities to Lord Shiva as you all know in order to kill all of you. Though Shiva had granted him many boons, he had warned him that his evil machinations would have no effect on all of you since you are protected by me. His father also wrested a boon from Shiva that the one who made his son's head fall on the ground would have his own head shattered into smithereens. So Arjuna! Remember when you kill him, you should be careful not to drop his head on the ground!"

"What should I do with it?" asked the bewildered Arjuna.

"Using the Pasupatastra given by Shiva you should transport the head and let it fall into the lap of Jayadratha's father who is meditating on the other side of the lake."

After this, all of us retired for the night but Yudhishtira in his obsession to adhere strictly to *dharma* ordered Ghatotkacha to inform Duryodhana of Arjuna's oath. Ghatotkacha obeyed reluctantly and was rudely received by Duryodhana who was far from being grateful for the message and proceeded to abuse the messenger as being a *rakshasa* who ate human flesh!

Ghatotkacha retorted, "I may be a *rakshasa* but I will never stoop to poisoning my enemies, secretly setting fire to their homes, stripping women in public and murdering a defenceless boy by surrounding him with all the heroes at your command! Need I go on? You know the list of your inequities better than I!"

When Jayadratha heard of his death sentence he was terrified and all set to flee to Sindhu, his own country but Duryodhana assured him that he would be given every protection. Next morning he was sent to a cave twelve miles away from the Pandava camp.

That night my Lord took Arjuna to another cave and invoked Lord Shiva. He said, "We have come to you so that you can bless Arjuna and allow him to kill Jayadratha who has received boons from you."

Shiva said, "Jayadratha is my devotee but has resorted to *adharma* so you are free to kill him. I will show you how the Pasupatastra can be used since that is the only weapon that can kill him. It has to be discharged with the proper *mantra* and recalled also with another *mantra*."

I think Arjuna was slowly beginning to realise the power of this Being who had taken the role of his charioteer, whom he still considered to be just a friend despite the fact that he had seen his cosmic form. But the human mind is so fickle that it takes for granted someone who is always with us and who acts the part of a friend and never displays his greatness. My Lord always underplayed his act so that even those who were closest to him failed to recognise his divinity. He showed this only to a limited few and Arjuna was one of the lucky ones. So was I. But then I was always overawed by his actions and never overstepped my limits even though he was so close to me.

That night I cried myself to sleep. I'm sure Subhadra, Uttara and Draupadi must have done the same.

Aum Namo Bhagavate Vaasudevaaya

ॐ

Gopagopeeswaraaya Namaha!

CHAPTER THIRTY-THREE

Drona

FOURTEENTH DAY

Even though Abhimanyu's death was a brutal murder, Drona felt that his reputation had been saved and he had justified himself in Duryodhana's eyes. However the repercussions were drastic for the Kauravas. The Pandavas were seething with anger over the heinous manner in which Abhimanyu had been killed and spent all their fury on the Kauravas. Drona was irritated and unable to make any firm decisions since Duryodhana kept changing his orders. The focus had shifted from Yudhishtira to Jayadratha and he was told to protect Jayadratha at all cost since Duryodhana thought that this was his golden opportunity to see Arjuna dead! I laughed when I heard this. Surely this prince wasn't so stupid as to think that my Lord would allow Arjuna to die!

Arjuna urged my Lord to push forward and find Jayadratha before the sun set. The remnants of the *samsaptakas* now tried to block him, but he despatched them to their heavenly abode and drove on. By now I felt that Drona had totally lost his wits. On the fourteenth day morning, he made a strange combination of three *vyuhas*- Shakata, Padma and Soochi (cart, lotus and needle). Drona stood at the head of the *vyuhas* and intercepted Arjuna who was desperate to get through the formations and reach Jayadratha before sunset. He bowed to his *guru* and said, "Though you played an active role in my son's death, you are my preceptor and I will not kill you so let me pass for I must get to Jayadratha soon."

Drona was already bitterly regretting the part he had played in the brutal murder of the Pandava prince, so he allowed him to pass. Arjuna fought his way through the ranks of the Kauravas, all of whom had been sent to detain him at all cost. Next he was accosted by Srutayudha, son of Varuna who had a mace which could kill anyone in a face to face fight, but if sent against an unarmed person it would ricochet back and destroy the person who sent it. After a fierce exchange with arrows, Srutayudha flung his mace with deadly accuracy at Arjuna's chest but once more my beloved Lord, saviour of his devotees, protected him by changing the direction of the chariot so that the mace fell squarely on his own chest! As foretold the mace bounced back on Srutayudha and ended his life. Arjuna turned and bowed to my Lord. I think slowly he was beginning to realise that he owed every moment of his life, to the grace of my Lord and not to his own skill. He then killed Srutayudha's two brothers as well as the king of Kamboja.

Drona then gave a thick suit of armour to Duryodhana and told him to go and halt Arjuna's progress. He himself turned on Drishtadyumna and would have killed him, but Satyaki came just in time and carried our commander away from the scene. Bhima encountered Dusshasana and his brothers and killed another seven of them. He was doing his best to reach Arjuna but Drona stopped him. Bhima spoke bitterly to his preceptor. "This entire massacre could have been avoided if people like you had adhered to their own *swadharma*! Abandoning your duty as a Brahmana and a *guru,* you have not only taken on the duty of a Kshatriya but have also sided with the wicked!"

Drona was shocked at this bit of truth and allowed Bhima to pass. Before he could reach Arjuna, Karna challenged him and they had a fierce fight. Karna tried to keep him away with a shower of arrows but Bhima was determined to come to grips with him. At last Karna had him at his mercy, but he remembered the promise he had made to his mother that he would only kill Arjuna and thus spared him. Bhima killed another twenty-five of the Kaurava brothers. In all the Pandavas destroyed eight of the eleven *akshauhinies* of the Kaurava army on that day.

The tired and exhausted Satyaki was now challenged by Bhurishravas who had a grudge against Satyaki's grandfather. He defeated the worn out Satyaki and dragged him out of his chariot. He placed his foot on his head and was about to behead him when my Lord saw this and urged Arjuna to shoot him. He sent an arrow which cut off his right arm, which had been upraised to cut off Satyaki's head. He looked around and said to Arjuna, "How could you do this? While I was fighting with another man you shot me and severed my hand. Anyone with Kshatriya blood in him wouldn't do such a dastardly act. The cow-herd must have influenced you."

Arjuna flared up and he said, "Where was your Kshatriya *dharma* yesterday when you joined the others to surround my son – a sixteen year old boy and stab him from behind? Do you dare to tell me this when all I did was to save the life of my loyal friend?"

Bhurishravas was over seventy and when he heard this just accusation he decided to end his life and sat down next to his chariot and closed his eyes. Satyaki recovered consciousness and saw his hand still clutching the sword on the ground. He picked up the sword and cut off the old man's head before fully realising what he was doing since he had still not entirely recovered from his faint. Both my Lord and Arjuna shouted at him to stop but he did not seem to hear. Karna now came galloping up to stop Arjuna from proceeding further, but my Lord hurriedly steered clear of him and left him to battle with the tired Satyaki.

The day was wearing on and still we had not reached Jayadratha. My Lord drove like the whirlwind weaving in and out of the phalanxes of the Kaurava army who were determined to thwart him. Despite his best efforts we were making very little progress. As the sun was sinking down, Arjuna fought with the fury of a man determined to avenge the death of his beloved son, but still they had not discovered their quarry. The red disc of the son began to slip fast into the arms of the western horizon and once more the Lord intervened to save the life of his beloved devotee. He flung his discus at the sun and thus caused an eclipse so that everyone thought the sun had set. Arjuna was totally dejected. Jayadratha crept out of his lair. The gleeful Duryodhana ordered a pyre to be made so as to make it easy for Arjuna to keep his vow of self-immolation. He got out of the chariot and told my Lord, "Vaasudeva! You know everything. If you want me to die in this fashion I shall do so." My Lord remained silent and Arjuna walked towards the fire. Just before he reached it my Lord said, "I would like to hear the twang of your Gandiva once again."

Arjuna had left his bow behind but he returned and took it up and at that moment my Lord withdrew the Sudarshana *chakra* so that it appeared as if the eclipse had passed and the sun came out in a blaze of glory just before it set. My Lord galvanised Arjuna to action and shouted, "There is the sun and there is the slayer of your son creeping out of his lair like a jackal. Use the Pasupatastra immediately."

Swift as lightning Arjuna strung his bow and used the Pasupatastra with deadly effect and cut off Jayadratha's head, but my Lord knew that the danger to Arjuna's life was not yet over. Jayadratha's father had obtained another boon from Shiva that anyone who made his son's head fall on the ground would perish. This fact had already been told to Arjuna but he was not sure if he remembered it so he shouted to him. "Don't let the head fall on the ground. Send a relay of arrows to carry the head to the banks of the Syamanta Panchaka Lake and let it fall into the lap of Brihadkshatra, Jayadratha's father who is sitting on the banks of the lake in meditation."

Arjuna shot a relay of arrows which one after the other supported and took the head to the lake.

I could imagine the scene when the gruesome object dropped into the old man's lap with a thud. He would have jumped up and of course the head would have dropped to the ground and his own head would have broken into fragments as per his own wish.

Duryodhana was in despair when he saw his brother-in-law's death and as usual vented his anger on his *guru*. My Lord returned with Arjuna whose life had been spared again due to his intervention. All the brothers fell at his feet and thanked him. As usual he disclaimed all credit. "A noble man's anger is a most potent weapon. The gods will not sit idle and watch the good suffer even though they may give boons to the wicked!"

This was the most terrible day of the war. The ten days of Bhishma's commandership had been truly a *dharmic* war, but the five days of Drona's leadership were surely the worst. All pretexts at *dharmic* warfare were completely thrown overboard, maybe due to the negative vibrations which had been unleashed by Abhimanyu's slaughter. Shakuni obviously whispered to Duryodhana that they should not wait for the morning. Drona seconded this and ordered the soldiers to continue fighting even after the sun had set and the conch shell blown to end the fighting for the day. They lit huge fire brands. In this flickering light they fought as if they were all possessed. In the darkness and confusion men slew their own kinsmen. Yudhishtira sent men with huge oil torches to light up the blood-red plain and the battle raged for many hours. The night was filled with horrors since the men were tired and maddened with the thirst for blood.

At last Arjuna called for a truce and the men were made to sleep on the bloody field, the charioteer in his chariot, the rider on his horse and the elephant owner on his elephant. We heard later that Duryodhana had secretly approached Drona and told him to go and kill the Pandavas as they slept on the field. When Drona refused he derided him and told him to step down and let Karna take charge. Again and again he accused him of deliberately avoiding coming to grips with Arjuna due to his partiality for him. Drona retorted, "You will reap the consequences of your misdeeds and your taunts. However I promise that tomorrow either I or Arjuna will die!"

The warriors had only a couple of hours' rest. When the bright moon rose the conflict was renewed. Countless numbers on both sides were killed on that awful night. This was the moment for Bhima's son Ghatotkacha to come into his own. For the first four days of Drona's leadership, we never heard about the *rakshasa* prince but my Lord with his acute foresight realised the potential we had. The strength of the *rakshasas* doubled during the night so my Lord invited Ghatotkacha to enter the fray and use all his illusionary skills since Drona had already invited Alayudha and other *rakshasas* to come to their aid.

For the first time I saw Aswatthama enter the fray and make a desperate bid to kill Drishtadyumna since he knew that he had been born to kill his father, Drona. Karna was in full form and defeated Nakula and Sahadeva but refrained from killing them, remembering his promise to Kunti. He then turned on Satyaki and fought furiously, but Satyaki escaped and Karna again came towards Arjuna. Once more my Lord steered the chariot away from him.

Ghatotkacha could not be stopped. He gleefully cut off the head of Jatasura's son and presented it to Duryodhana. He killed hordes of soldiers and cut off Alayudha's head. He rent the air with his weird war cries which struck terror into the hearts of the opposing army. He could have managed to finish the whole army all by himself had he been given permission. As it was, he stalked about with his huge hob-nailed footwear killing countless men in the process. Duryodhana was desperate and begged Karna to stop him before he decimated his whole army. He towered above the chariots and even Karna appeared like a midget in front of him. All Karna's arrows simply bounced off the giant without creating even a dent! He laughed loud and long when the puny arrows were shot at him. The air was filled with blazing arrows but nothing made an impression on this colossus. Duryodhana was frantic and looked around for Drona to ask him to kill the giant with his Brahmadanda but the *guru* was nowhere to be seen. He was still trying to capture the Pandava king as he had promised to do. Turning to Karna, he begged him to use all his *astras* if necessary and kill the monster before his whole army was exterminated. Karna was in a dilemma since only two of his weapons, the '*Shakti*' given by Indra and the '*Nagastra*' were capable of killing this *rakshasa*. He had been carefully nurturing these two for his momentous meeting with Arjuna since he could use them only once. In view of the destruction caused by Bhima's son, even the warriors started to beg Karna to try and kill him. "Why are you not using the divine *Shakti* given by Indra? This is the time to use it". In the meantime, Ghatotkacha killed Karna's horses and was moving towards him for the final kill when Karna leapt to the ground and discharged Indra's famous dart, the *Shakti*. The missile whizzed towards the giant with lightning speed and pierced the veil of *Maya* woven by him and plunged into his chest. I could see the look of surprise and pain on Ghatotkacha's face as the dart gored into his vitals. But even in death, Bhima's son thought only of helping his father's side and expanded his size and flew into the air so that when he fell he crushed thousands of Kaurava soldiers.

The Pandavas were steeped in grief but my Lord appeared to be very joyful and consoled them by saying that Ghatotkacha had sacrificed his life to save the life of his uncle, Arjuna.

'Is this why you refused to let Arjuna come to grips with Karna all along?' I asked.

"Of course," said my Lord. "That dart is invincible. If it had been used on Arjuna he would have died on the spot."

"Do you care only for Arjuna?'

"My dear I've told you again and again that every creature has to come to an end of its earthly existence at some time and place. Ghatotkacha's time had come. He had played his role in this life and even in death he was a hero like Abhimanyu. They both sacrificed their lives for a noble cause. Aryavrata has to be ruled by righteous people if you want the common people to live a good and honourable life. For this purpose the Pandavas are indispensable. Therefore I am bound to protect them. Moreover as you know they have surrendered totally to me. They are willing to do whatever I tell them. Don't you think I owe a duty to such persons?"

'Don't you think Arjuna can beat Karna without any help?'

"Of course he can but Arjuna has only the Brahmastra now, since he used the Pasupatastra against Jayadratha. He will never use the Brahmastra against Karna or anyone in this war since it will cause serious harm to many generations of human beings. Karna on the other hand has one more *astra*, the Nagastra which is a very potent weapon. Arjuna will be helpless against it."

'So how will you protect him against that?' I asked.

"Let's see when the time comes," he said and thus finished the session.

I realised that my Lord never pre-planned anything. He just took advantage of every situation as and when it came and arrived at the best solution.

The armies clashed again and Drona, inflamed by Duryodhana's constant insinuations, resorted to most cruel tactics and destroyed the Pandava army without any compunction, throwing overboard every code of war agreed upon earlier.

My Lord told me that at night the sage Bharadwaja, Drona's father and other sages had gone to him and told him to stop his indiscriminate slaughter. They told him of all the great crimes he had committed as a Brahmana. Drona felt miserable and wished he would die the next day so that there would be an end to all the killing.

FIFTEENTH DAY

The fifteenth day dawned and once more Duryodhana accused Drona of partiality for the Pandavas. Drona had been destroying the enemy troops with no consideration of fair play. This unjust accusation as well as his own indiscriminate slaughter of innocents which was quite against his *swadharma* as a Brahmana, as Bhima and his father had told him, made him feel thoroughly disgusted with life. Yet he fought on furiously, determined to kill or be killed. He defeated and killed three of the grandsons of Drupada. Drona now chased his childhood friend and later enemy, Drupada, Panchali's father and slew him, then turned on king Virata and slew him also. This victory brought no joy to him. All the scenes of his boyhood spent with his friend flooded his mind and he felt a bitter disgust at the strange role that fate had forced upon him. His hostility with Drupada had only been for the sake of his son Aswatthama and now he was committing moral suicide with his indiscriminate slaughter. Suddenly a feeling of utter revulsion overcame him and a strong wish to end it all.

Drishtadyumna rushed to avenge his father's death but the old Brahmin routed him easily. Arjuna now proceeded to engage the aged preceptor, but he proved to be invincible for on that day he was fighting with utter disregard for his own life and none dared approach him.

As he drove Arjuna's chariot towards him, my Lord's eyes locked with Drona's and he saw the despair and the disgust for life which was mirrored there. He also knew that Drona could never be killed unless he laid down his weapons, since he was using the Brahmadanda. Therefore my Lord went to Yudhishtira and told him that the only way to kill him would be to say that his son Aswatthama was dead in which case he would lay down his weapons and Drishtadyumna would be able to kill him.

My Lord said, "He is using the divine missile known as Brahmadanda, against ordinary soldiers. This missile contains the powers of the seven sages who had come to meet him yesterday night and they had warned him never to use it. No one knows how to foil the Brahmadanda since this is the one *astra*, the secret of which Drona never divulged, even to his favourite disciple Arjuna or to his beloved son. Thus he is doubly guilty. This has made him invincible. Actually the Brahmadanda is purely a defensive weapon and should never be used in offensive warfare as Drona is doing now. It is capable of nullifying the effects of every other weapon. It can even nullify the Brahmastra. So the only way to stop him from his massacre of the Pandava forces is to use *adharmic* methods. There is nobody present here who can defeat him while he uses the Brahmadanda. He knows he is committing a crime but doesn't care about anything anymore. He will slaughter the whole of our army today if he is not stopped. The only way we can save our army is for you to tell a small lie. Taking into consideration the fact that he is prepared to go totally against all rules of *dharmic* warfare for the sake of Duryodhana, surely you can say a small lie for the sake of your people. What are you going to lose by this? For the preservation of *dharma* you will have to do a small *adharmic* act as to tell the preceptor that Aswatthama is dead. This is nothing compared to the colossal destruction he is engaged in today. If you insist, Bhima will kill an elephant called Aswatthama and when Drona asks you, as he is sure to ask, if his son is dead, you have to tell him that, Aswatthama is dead and add the fact that it is the elephant Aswatthama which is dead. You will have to be prepared to do this otherwise everything will be lost. The *acharya* by himself is capable of totally annihilating our army, since he is using the Brahmadanda which he knows has been totally prohibited by the *rishis,* even though they are the ones who made it."

Yudhishtira was very unhappy about this. All his life he had held up his adherence to truth as a banner that shielded him from the real facts of his own character. He knew that he was indeed a coward who could never face the consequences of a war. Fate had cast him into the role of a Kshatriya but had denied him the characteristics of a Kshatriya. The very thought of fighting was anathema to him. He had come to his own during the twelve years in the forest and would have gladly gone back for another term had Duryodhana ordered it. But he was forced into this war even though he had lost all pride and begged for even five houses for himself and his brothers. But even this, Duryodhana was not willing to give so there was no option for him but to fight. He knew that without Arjuna and Bhima they would not stand a chance against the mighty machinery of the Kauravas led by Bhishma and Drona. For these fifteen days he had put up a poor show on the battlefield and now he was asked to tell a lie. This meant that he would have to forego even this defence. I could see all these things passing through his mind. I wished he had listened to my Lord's talk to Arjuna. How could someone who had never known falsehood ever know truth? Life is made up of dualities as my Lord said, and unless we accept both we can never go above both which is the only way we can get out of the wheel of *samsara* (transmigratory existence). All of us opt for only the positive side of duality yet we cannot deny the fact that bad cannot exist without good and vice versa. There is a point when even good can become bad and bad, good. Yudhishtira had reached that point now. His adherence to truth had become an obsession with him. It was not as if he had never said an untruth. The whole time that they spent in the court of Virata he had to be constantly telling lies – about his name and the names of his brothers and pretending that he did not know any of them and so on. But it was something which was required of him if they wanted to get out of their predicament. This problem was not very different. If he did not agree he would have to forfeit his own life and the lives of his brothers. Yet he was not prepared to agree to my Lord's most reasonable request. Thus poor Bhima had to go and kill an innocent elephant just to protect Yudhistira's obsession with truth. I looked at my Lord and I knew he had read my mind and agreed with it.

Drona was the very opposite of Yudhishtira. He had a Brahmana body and a Kshatriya mind. He had never performed the six duties of a Brahmana, like learning the Vedas, teaching the Vedas, performing *yagas* and having others perform *yagas*, giving *dana* (charity) and accepting *dana*. He had also lived a life of delusion like Yudhishtira, thinking himself to be very great since he had great knowledge of weapons which was something a Brahmana was not supposed to have!

Bhima killed the elephant and shouted loudly so that Drona could hear, "Aswatthama has been killed." Drona however did not trust Bhima and turned to Yudhishtira for confirmation. Yudhishtira mumbled, "*Ashwathama Hataha, naro va Kunjaro va*," – (Aswatthama is dead but I'm not sure if it is the man or the elephant.) Drona heard only the first half of the sentence since my Lord blew his conch shell loudly at this point so that the rest of the sentence was drowned.

Drona had been waiting for an opportunity to end this senseless slaughter into which he had been projected by Duryodhana's constant taunts. He had taken on this job of teaching the Kuru princes only for the sake of his son and it was only because of him that he had to fight this unjust war. He had lost count of the atrocities he had committed. In fact after he took over from Bhishma, everything the Kauravas did was *adharmic*. He had promised to capture Yudhishtira instead of killing him. He was the one who had made the *chakra vyuha* into which they had lured Abhimanyu. All the great *maharathis* had joined together and murdered the boy. He had allowed them to continue the battle well after the sun had set. He had used the Brahmadanda on innocent people. He could not bear to think of his inequities. His son was the only person he had ever loved and now that he was no longer here there seemed to be no point in living this sinful life. Leaving his bow in the chariot he got out and sat in a meditative pose in the middle of the battlefield. He looked up to see my Lord standing in front of him.

"*Acharya*!" he said, "I see that you are thinking of all the *adharmic* acts which you have committed. At the end of your life you became the commander of the Kaurava forces and committed every type of atrocity, as you know only too well. You put your obligation to Duryodhana over your adherence to *dharma* so that no one could question your honour. You remained a mute spectator when Draupadi was humiliated by Dusshasana. You, who have such love for your son joined in the massacre of Arjuna's son! Did you not think that Arjuna would have the same love for his son as you have for yours? Yet Arjuna was prepared to do his duty to his brothers and to his country by continuing the fight, but you who are a Vedic scholar and the son of the sage Bharadwaja have such attachment to your son that you are prepared to forego your life and your duty to Hastinapura, which you have been flaunting all your life. You are ready to die because you think your son has died. What if I tell you that it is an elephant called Aswatthama which has died and not your son! Will you jump back into the chariot and continue your ceaseless carnage?"

Drona answered, "Everyone hopes for a son who will save him from going to the seven types of hell. I have lived my whole life for the sake of my son, so why should I live after his death?"

My Lord said, "O *Acharya*! Know me to be the *karmaphaladata* (the giver of the fruits of action). I am telling you now that neither son nor wealth nor power can carry you to the celestial abode. The only thing which will support you after the death of your body is your adherence to *dharma*. The charities you have given, the good words you have spoken, the lack of attachment to the things of this world and constant contemplation on the divine – these are the things that will support you at the end of your life and not your son! Therefore detach yourself from thoughts of your son and fix your mind on that Supreme and you will reach the heavenly abode."

Hearing this, the great Dronacharya bowed to my Lord for he knew that what he spoke was but the truth. He realised that the one small contribution he could make to help in the victory of *dharma* over *adharma* was to give up his life, for if he lived the Pandavas would never be able to get victory. He had practised some *yogic kriyas* and knew the method of drawing up his *prana* and releasing it through one of the higher *chakras*. He sat in contemplation of the divine and drew up all his vital energies from the *muladhara chakra* to the *swathishtana* and then to the *manipura* and to the *anahata* and to the *vishudhi chakra*. But try as he might he was not able to raise it higher to the *sahasrara chakra* and let it pass through the *Brahmarandra* as a true *yogi* would have done. So finally he allowed his *prana* to come out of his mouth. My Lord and I were the only ones to see it coming out of his mouth and spiralling its way to the heavens. Just then Drishtadyumna came upon the scene and cut off the head from the shell of his body from which life had already flown. He took the head and threw it at Duryodhana and said, "Here is the head of your mighty *guru*. I will cut off the heads of each Kaurava prince in the same manner!"

Fighting came to a halt as everybody gathered round to lament over their fallen preceptor. The furious Aswatthama now rushed to the scene like a comet and swore to slay Drishtadyumna and all his kindred. He blamed him for his unrighteous act, forgetting the dastardly way he and his father had joined in the killing of Abhimanyu and the fact that his father was guilty of using the Brahmadanda.

He turned on Yudhishtira and taunted him about his *adharmic* act in having told a lie.

For once Yudhishtira retaliated. "Indeed it is true that he was our preceptor who professed to cherish friendly feelings for us, so let me enumerate all his loving deeds towards us. He was the one who caused the son of Subhadra to be slain by a multitude of wicked warriors. He was the one who sat beside Bhishma and watched unmoved while Panchali was dragged into the assembly and begged him to say the truth of whether she had been staked before or after I had staked myself. He was the one who gave Duryodhana invulnerable armour when he wanted to kill Arjuna and appointed him to protect Jayadratha who was the one who had prevented Bhima from following Abhimanyu and helping him. He was the one who kindly told us to go into the forest when our friends begged him to withhold his permission, as we were being cruelly exiled and cheated out of our kingdom. The final treachery he committed today was to use the Brahmadanda against our innocent troops when he knew that there was no one here who knew the *mantra* to forestall this celestial *astra*. He had taken care to see that he did not impart this knowledge to any of his disciples, so today he was the sole possessor of this *astra* and therefore today he was invincible and he took full advantage of that and killed indiscriminately. Alas that great friend of ours has been slain by the son of one whom he beheaded so cruelly! And now you dare to taunt me with my telling a lie! If my one falsehood is weighed against the infinite number of lies and treacheries you and your bosom friends have committed, I assure you my small lie will be totally crushed under the weight of your mountainous villainous acts. Anyway you are a fitting son to a fitting father. Go and accomplish your task of killing our entire clan but don't think you will go scot free. There is a law which is above all of us and that law will see to it that you get your just deserts! Moreover Narayana himself in the humble guise of Partha's charioteer is protecting us. So you will never succeed in your fiendish attempts!"

Aswatthama was not interested in listening to his or his father's inequities and swore to annihilate Drishtadyumna and the whole army of the Panchalas before the sun set.

I asked my Lord where Drona had gone wrong.

"I have already told you about all his inequities. The first wrong step he took was to put his loyalty to his employer before his dedication to his principles. This he did due to over attachment to his son who was committed to helping his friend Duryodhana. This was similar to Bhishma who put his dedication to the throne of Hastinapura before his dedication to *dharma*."

'Surely he must have known that his son had been given a boon by which he was placed amongst the *chiranjivis* (those who live for the whole of this age). Then why should he have believed the rumour about his son's death?'

"Indeed it is true. He did know that his son could never be killed but he took the opportunity to end his own life which had become a burden to him!"

I asked my Lord, 'What is the story of Aswatthama?

My Lord said, "Aswatthama, also known as Drauni, is the son of Dronacharya as you know. The great sage Bharadwaja was his grandfather. Drona did severe *tapasya* to Lord Shiva to get a son who would have all the characteristics of Mahadeva himself. Hence it is said that he is an incarnation of one of the eleven Rudras who are all filled with ferocity. Shiva was the one who blessed him that he would be a *chiranjeevi* (one who would remain alive through the whole of this *Yuga*). He was born with a jewel on his forehead which gives him power over all living beings lower than humans. It also protects him from attacks by ghosts, demons, snakes and poisonous animals. He is a master of the science of weapons, but as you know his father did not teach him everything since he knew that he lacked discrimination. He has studied with Parasurama who taught him Dhanurveda (martial arts) and Brahmavidya. Once when I was sitting on the sea shore, Aswatthama approached me and asked me for my weapon, the *chakra.* I told him he could have it if he was able to lift it out of the sand where I had fixed it. Try as he could, he failed to budge it even an inch from the sand. At last he gave up. I asked him why he wanted it and he said it was to kill me and make Duryodhana the ruler of the world! He has a brilliant intellect but no heart. Compassion and love are not to be found in him. Whatever love he is capable of giving was misplaced in Duryodhana who merely fostered his ego and led him to the most reckless actions."

Aum Namo Bhagavate Vaasudevaaya

ॐ

Gopagpeeswaraaya Namaha!

CHAPTER THIRTY-FOUR

Aswatthama

As the Kauravas raced back to battle intent on avenging Drona's death, the sun started to sink towards the west. There was no way they could kill Drishtadyumna by using standard weapons. Aswatthama then thought about the Narayana *astra*.

'What is the Narayana *astra*?' I asked my Lord.

"It is Lord Narayana's personal weapon just like the Pasupatastra is Lord Shiva's personal weapon. The Narayana *astra* can rain millions of deadly missiles simultaneously. The intensity of its power will increase with resistance. It can be used only once in a war and if someone tries to use it twice it will turn round and devour the user's own army."

'Is there no defense against it?' I queried.

"Yes," said my Lord. "The only way is to show total submission before it hits us. This will cause it to stop and spare the target."

'My Lord! You are Narayana alone and that is why it has all your qualities of infinite compassion to those who surrender to you and depend only on you,' I said looking at him with tears in my eyes.

Our army was still standing beside the decapitated body of the *guru*. When Aswatthama came within half a mile of us, he bent down and touched some water and whispered the celestial incantations to invoke the missile, as he placed his arrow on his bow. He then sent the deadly arrow flaring into the air. A deep roar came from the sky and everyone looked up in terror. Tens of thousands of fiery arrows appeared on the battlefield and flew towards the Pandava army like the scorching rays of a gigantic sun. Countless red hot iron balls fell from the sky like meteors. Razor edged discuses, flaming spears, spiked maces and sharp axes filled the air and covered our army so that the Kauravas could not even perceive us. All of us were terrified. Blazing weapons seemed to be springing into existence in every part of the battlefield where we were standing. Our troops fell by the thousands, cut to pieces by the relentless assault. All our great warriors tried to resist the attack but the more they tried, the worse it became. As my Lord had told me resistance lent extra force to it. Seeing his army being scorched like this Yudhishtira gave the order to retreat. His panic-stricken voice rose above the din of the falling weapons.

"Flee for your lives," he shouted, "Do not look back. This *astra* cannot be repelled. This is the price we have to pay for killing our *guru*. O warriors return to your homes. I and my brothers will enter the fire and sacrifice ourselves."

I really felt sorry for this poor man who in his terror forgot the fact that he was being protected by Narayana himself. All he had to do was to ask my Lord to shield them as he had been doing all along, but in his panic he forgot everything.

In fact everyone was in a panic. The Panchalas, the Srinjayas and the Pandava brothers except for Arjuna were all frantic. Wherever it was contended by the *maharathis*, the missile became very powerful and showered more and more weapons. The troops were being killed all over the place. Seeing his army running about in a frenzy and his brothers indifferent, Yudhishtira again shouted, "O Drishtadyumna, fly away with your Panchala troops. Satyaki, take the Vrishni clan with you and run for your lives! I think Duryodhana's wishes will be fulfilled today."

All this transpired while my Lord had been sitting in the chariot and watching Yudhishtira's fear-stricken antics. At last he decided to take a hand even though Yudhishtira had not approached him. Standing up in the chariot he called out to the soldiers, "O Kshatriyas! This is the weapon of Narayana. Throw aside your weapons and come down from your chariots and elephants. Lie flat on the ground without any weapons and prostrate to that mighty power of Lord Narayana. Whatever you do, I advise you not to attempt to fight this missile for that will only increase its power. Even if you think of combating this weapon you will be slain." He pulled Arjuna out of the chariot and told him to prostrate himself on the ground.

The warriors had total faith in my Lord's words and they all jumped out of their chariots and off their horses and elephants and threw themselves on the ground with their hands stretched forward in supplication. At this, the countless weapons generated by the *astra* passed harmlessly over their heads. All over the field the Pandava warriors threw down their weapons and prostrated before the oncoming weapons. For some reason, Bhima who normally had infinite faith in my Lord's words decided to display his Kshatriya heroism and shouted, "Don't lay aside your arms. Don't fear this *astra*. I will personally check it with my swift arrows. I will strike Drona's son and send him on the path to his father. O Arjuna! How can you lay aside your Gandiva and lose your fame and name? Stand up and fight. I will bear the brunt of this weapon on my broad chest. Today everyone will see my power!"

Arjuna shouted back, "Bhima! My vow is never to use the Gandiva against Brahmins, cows and any weapon of the Lord Narayana. You should do the same. This all-devouring weapon cannot be checked by the force of arms."

Bhima paid no attention to Arjuna and rushed at the Kauravas. Undeterred by the shower of missiles falling on him, he stood in his chariot sending fierce arrows at Aswatthama who simply smiled for he knew it was just a matter of minutes before Bhima succumbed. Now that the whole Pandava army was lying on the ground, the *astra* concentrated its fury on Bhima. He started to look like a sacrificial fire. Seeing this Arjuna invoked the Varuna weapon which covered Bhima with water, but he knew that before long he would be overpowered. He looked pleadingly at my Lord who ran towards Bhima calling Arjuna to come with him. The two of them seized hold of Bhima and dragged him down from his chariot. Bhima roared with rage as Arjuna tore his mace away from him.

My Lord whispered angrily, "What do you think you are doing? If it was possible to check this weapon by fighting we would all have fought. Lie down and don't act so foolishly."

Reluctantly Bhima followed my Lord's instructions and put his weapons aside and threw himself on the ground. The *astra* receded and its numerous missiles went up to the sky and vanished. When the battlefield was clear, the Pandavas and their troops got up and took up their weapons. Jumping on to their various vehicles, they roared their battle cries.

Duryodhana was mad when he saw this and shouted to Aswatthama, "Send that weapon again for the Pandavas seem to have rallied and will start to attack us again."

Aswatthama shook his head. "The Narayana *astra* can only be used once by any person. If invoked again, it will slay the person who invoked it. Krishna seems to have known the secret of foiling it and it has retreated."

Duryodhana cursed aloud and said, "O son of Drona! Then use whatever weapons you possess and slay the murderers of your father immediately!"

Hearing this Aswatthama rushed into the battle to seek out Drishtadyumna. He slew his charioteer and four horses and smashed his chariot. Drishtadyumna was on the ground and resisted with his sword and shield. Satyaki saw his predicament and came quickly to his assistance. He enveloped Aswatthama in a network of arrows and killed his horses and charioteer. His uncle, Kripa came to his aid and took him away as many others came to join the fray. Aswatthama returned with a fresh chariot towards Drishtadyumna and again Satyaki came to his aid.

Aswatthama shouted to him, "If you try to protect him I will kill you without any compunction."

He showered his arrows on him so that he was forced to retreat. Aswatthama was in a frenzy and he attacked Drishtadyumna again and again. No one had seen him fight so ferociously before. All the Pandavas now came to rescue Draupadi's brother, but Aswatthama fought as one possessed and released the Agneya *astra*. A thick gloom enveloped the battlefield and fiery meteors started dropping down. Fierce winds blew in every direction lashing at the soldiers with stones. Terrifying cries of ghosts and ghouls resounded from the darkness and jackals howled from all sides. The Pandava forces shrieked in fear and pain. Horses, men and elephants were burnt to cinders but Agni remembered the help given to him at Khandavaprastha by Arjuna and my Lord and passed harmlessly over them.

Seeing the fire god's irresistible energy summoned for their destruction, Arjuna looked enquiringly at my Lord who nodded his head and told him to go ahead and use the Brahmastra. Arjuna closed his eyes and invoked this most powerful weapon and dispatched it. At once it dissipated the fiery blasts which were constantly being thrown indiscriminately. It neutralised the effect of the Agneyastra and very soon the sky cleared and a cool breeze began to blow. My Lord told Arjuna to immediately recall the power of the Brahmastra which could cause immense damage and could only be used in dire circumstances. As it was, thousands of warriors lay on the battlefield, their bodies burned beyond recognition.

'Why can't Aswatthama realise that his father had reached the end of his tether and wanted to die rather than keep adding to the great store of bad *karma* he had already accumulated? In fact thanks to you my Lord, I feel that he will get a better fate than if he had continued this insane slaughter,' I said.

My Lord answered, "My dear, Aswatthama has a lot of very bad *karma* to his credit due to which he can't see or think clearly. Power given in the hands of those who are morally unfit for it will always lead to disaster. His father should never have given him the knowledge of these *astras*. In fact this is not the end of his misdoings. He is steeped in *tamas* and the only way to save him is to make his body undergo immense suffering. This is bound to happen."

Aswatthama was shocked to see that Arjuna had remained unscathed by the missile which had killed thousands of other warriors. My Lord and Arjuna had been right in the path of the missile and neither of them was even scratched! I could see Aswatthama's look of defeat on his face. First the Narayana *astra* and now the Agneya – both had been foiled by Krishna and Arjuna. They seemed to be invincible. He threw his weapons down and ran from the battlefield.

'What will happen to him now?' I asked my Lord.

"He will meet sage Vyasa and will ask him why his weapons are ineffective against Arjuna and Krishna"

'What will the sage say?'

"He will tell him that I am the Supreme Lord – Narayana clothed in the form of humanity. He tried to use the Narayana *astra* against Narayana himself, so how could he succeed? No living being can overpower me and those who are protected by me. Even Shiva bows before me."

When he heard this I think Aswatthama felt a bit comforted, since obviously there was no one who could defy my Lord and those who were protected by him. As long as my Lord and Arjuna stood united in the same chariot, there seemed to be no point in fighting them.

My Lord said, "I think Aswatthama now realises that human beings can only do their duty and leave the rest to God. But he is returning to the battlefield for he feels his duty is to remain with Duryodhana and to punish the one who killed his father."

The sun started to set on that fateful day. The armies were totally exhausted after fighting for almost two days and a night. The Kauravas were despondent and Duryodhana now felt that only Karna could rescue their drowning boat. In our camp however there was the sound of trumpets, drums and music.

Sage Vyasa was waiting for us to return. Arjuna jumped out of the chariot and bowed at his feet. He said, "O all-knowing one! I have a question to ask from you. As I was shooting my arrows, I saw before me the huge figure of a person shining like fire. He held a blazing trident in his hand and whichever way he turned, my enemies were destroyed. He never used his trident or any other weapon yet his energy appeared to be able to annihilate my foes. Pray tell me who this personality is."

The sage placed his hand on Arjuna's head who was kneeling with bowed head before him and said, "O son of Kunti! You have seen Shankara, the great destroyer. Out of his love for Vaasudeva he walks before your chariot, scorching your enemies with his irresistible energy. He also guards your camp. Go and fight with full confidence. As long as Janardana is beside you, there can be no defeat for you. Fear not, the war will be over very soon."

Aum Namo Bhagavate Vaasudevaaya

As water is to sea creatures,
Nectar of the moon to the chakora birds,
Companiable darkness to the stars.
So is my love for Krishna.
My body hungers for his as a mirror image hungers for twin of flesh.
His life cuts into my life as the stain of the moon's rabbit engraves the moon.
And if a day comes when no sun comes up,
And no colour comes to the earth,
That is how it is in my heart when he goes away.

Poems of Vidyapati

ॐ

Yogine Namaha!

CHAPTER THIRTY-FIVE

Karna

News was brought to us that both Aswatthama and Kripa now advised Duryodhana to stop the war, but hope brims ever in the human heart and after having appointed his dear friend Karna as the commander of his forces, he was sure that the tide would change in his favour despite the fact that almost all his dear brothers had been killed by Bhima.

He told Karna, "You can do one thing for me and that is to kill at least one Pandava. They have killed ninety-eight of my brothers, but if I can see at least one dead Pandava I can forget my misfortunes and I know that only you can do it. Arjuna was always spared by both Bhishma and Drona since they loved him, but I know you hate him and will stop at nothing to kill him!"

Karna told Duryodhana, "I shall not fail you at this hour even though everyone else has either deserted you or been killed. I can never forget your many acts of kindness. I can only repay you by killing Arjuna. Kill him I shall, provided you give me a charioteer who is the equal of Vaasudeva. You have such a man in your army. He is Shalya, king of Madra, uncle of Nakula and Sahadeva. Please try and persuade him to come as my charioteer."

Shalya was not at all happy to be degraded to a charioteer's position. "I will never be the charioteer of that low-born *suta putra*! I should cut off your tongue for asking such a thing."

Duryodhana brought out very persuasive arguments, "Isn't Krishna the charioteer of Arjuna? What is the shame in your being Karna's charioteer?"

At last Shalya relented but insisted that Karna should be warned to hold his tongue and not reprimand him, whatever he did. Duryodhana promised that he would insist on this.

SIXTEENTH DAY

The sixteenth day of battle dawned over a grim and mutilated battlefield and Karna came to his own. Water, made fragrant with herbs and flowers was poured over his head from vessels of gold and elephant tusks and bull horns in order to install him as commander of what remained of the Kaurava army. It was a bit of a farce and Karna knew it but he was determined to make a bid to kill Arjuna as he had promised. Duryodhana presented him with a gold necklace with a breast ornament and ten thousand cows. Fair and handsome with dark, curly hair wet from the holy water, Karna rode out with the sun making a halo round him. He strung his bow Vijaya which had been given to him by Parasurama, which was his height and which only he could bend. His arms were red with sandal paste. A garland of fragrant *champa* flowers had been placed round his neck. Another chariot followed him carrying sixty million arrows of iron and steel bearing arrowheads with different heads.

Before we set out, Arjuna also put flowers over his armour and fastened talismans and herbs sealed in golden capsules strung on silver chains on his arm.

The sky became overcast hiding us in fog and mist. Thunder rolled over the heavens and the rain fell in torrents over our heads. Indra's rainbow made an arch over us as if to protect his son from all harm. Then the sun god Surya angrily pushed away all the clouds and bathed his son, Karna in sunlight which glinted off his armour and necklaces.

Duryodhana had ordered the Yadava army known as the Narayana Sena to fight with Arjuna. Many of my Lord's own sons were in the army and Duryodhana knew that Arjuna would not be happy to fight with them. However he did not know my Lord. All people were equal in his eyes. He made no differentiation between his sons and other people's sons, as he had told Arjuna in the discourse on the first day of battle. In fact he urged Arjuna to kill them since they had ranged themselves on the opposite side.

In the meantime, Shalya seemed to be doing his best to provoke Karna and kept baiting him about his low birth and his inferiority to Arjuna. They seemed to be having heated arguments all the time. At last they seemed to have got over their differences and Shalya drove straight towards Arjuna. My Lord was doing the same thing as Shalya and kept praising Karna to Partha.

"O son of Pandu! I think the mighty Karna is your equal. His arms are long, his chest is broad, and he resembles a lion in the formation of his body. He is invincible and is the foremost of heroes. I don't think anyone can kill him."

My Lord's provocative words only strengthened Arjuna's resolve to kill Karna whereas Shalya's words seemed to inflame Karna so that he retaliated word for word!

'Why do you provoke Arjuna like this?' I asked. 'Moreover this is not quite true. Remember he defeated Karna and the Kauravas on the day when they came to raid Virata's cattle.'

"I have to goad Arjuna to strive his best, only then will he be able to defeat Karna. Remember that Arjuna has been fighting incessantly for sixteen days whereas Karna has only come to the battlefield for six days, so he has an added advantage over Arjuna who is already tired of the war and embittered over the loss of his beloved son. It will be a very close shave between them since they are both equally matched. However I am committed to help Arjuna who has put his life into my hands."

'What about Karna? Since you are God should you not help him also?'

"My child, I told you that the same divine energy fills Karna and Arjuna as well as all the Kauravas and everyone in all places. Without that divine energy no one would be able to do anything. Didn't you listen to my discourse on the five factors which go up to make any action? These factors are the body, the agent (or person doing the action), the sense organs, the different types of effort made by the organs of action and the fifth is something called '*daivam*' or divine providence. The first four depend on the agent who is doing the action and are in his control, but the last one is something beyond his ability to control. This is the sum total of his *karmas* which will decide what sort of result he will get from the action. This is something which he has no idea of and which obviously he can't control. He may be physically very strong and mentally sharp and all his organs may be intact and he might be using the best type of instruments available, yet no one can say whether he will be successful or unsuccessful. This is because the final decision is made by the Law of Karma which is a natural law which cannot be bypassed by anyone. However this law can be mitigated by God if the devotee asks for help. I always wait for the moment when my devotee asks me to help him. If he does so I will certainly step in. If he is happy to depend only on his own ability then I leave him to it and let him do what he wants, but if the person asks me to help him, then of course I am bound to go to him. You pity Karna because of the conditions in which he has been placed, but you must remember that he chose to follow the path he was given and is immensely proud of his abilities. This strength comes from his father, the sun god. He has never asked for my help and has refused to follow my advice (that is the *asura* in him), whereas Arjuna who has equal ability, has surrendered to me completely and depends on me to help him, which is why I have been helping him all the time and will help him in the battle with Karna which is going to come tomorrow."

Nakula was the first to meet Karna. He was defeated but Karna refused to kill him. He humiliated him by touching his shoulder with the tip of his bow. However he killed his son, Niramitra.Then he encountered Yudhishtira in a fierce duel in which Yudhishtira fought with great fury but of course he was no match for Karna. At last he was forced to retire to his tent after having been badly wounded by Karna who kept his promise to Kunti and refused to kill him.

Karna now turned his fury on Bhima who hurt him so badly that he fainted. Bhima desisted from killing him since he was reserved for Arjuna. He turned away and concentrated on some of the Kaurava brothers.

Karna recovered fast and was accosted by Sahadeva. He defeated him very soon and touched him with his bow tip and said, "Go away my child, one day you will feel proud to have battled with me."However he killed Sahadeva's son Suhotra.

I saw him turn his face away to hide his tears and I really felt so sorry for him. My Lord looked at me lovingly and said, "I know how you feel. But remember the Law of Karma makes no distinctions. Everyone gets what he deserves. Never forget that."

Karna now forced himself to meet Arjuna again. It was a long and fierce battle in which Karna seemed to be getting the better of Arjuna. He surrounded Arjuna with a network of arrows so that the chariot could hardly move. My Lord did his best to instigate Arjuna but he appeared strangely reluctant to come to grips with his opponent.

"What is the matter, O Partha?" he asked. He was surprised to hear his reply.

"Govinda! I see only my brother Yudhishtira's face in front of me and not Karna's. Please forgive me and take me away from here. I can't fight with him."

With a mighty effort my Lord broke through the network of arrows and took Arjuna to Yudhishtira's tent. The Eldest was in severe pain due to Karna's arrows and was being treated by the camp physician. He immediately asked, "Have you killed Karna?"

Arjuna bowed his head and remained silent and my Lord jokingly said, "I tried my best to encourage Partha to fight, but he refused because he said he saw you in him and so he couldn't fight with him!"

Due to his pain Yudhishtira said in an irritated tone, "Is your Gandiva a bow or just a blade of grass?"

To everyone's surprise Arjuna became furious and aimed an arrow at the Eldest. He had taken an oath to kill anyone who insulted the Gandiva!

Yudhishtira did not know how to react so my Lord as usual saved the situation. "Partha, abusing an elder is equivalent to killing him so go ahead and abuse him." Arjuna let flow a string of violent expletives which pained Yudhishtira so much that he threatened to give up everything and go back to the forest. My Lord as usual undertook the role of pacifier and somehow the brothers were reconciled. Actually the strain of the war was taking its toll on everyone's temper. It was only my Lord who remained calm throughout.

The carnage of the sixteenth day ended at sunset as usual. Our spies reported that Duryodhana had summoned a council of war and declared, "This is the sixteenth day of war and most of our greatest heroes have been killed. Many of my brothers have been brutally murdered by that wicked Bhima. I have no one but you, O friend," he said, turning to Karna.

Karna assured him, "Fear not comrade, tomorrow I shall slay Arjuna or be slain by him."

That night he could not sleep due to the memories which came crowding into his mind. The whole talk with my Lord and all his comments now came to haunt him. A refreshing breeze laden with the perfume of roses assailed his nostrils and he felt some sense of relief. The insanity of the last sixteen days weighed heavily on his mind. It looked like the beginning of the end for his army. Thousands of warriors had fallen. The carrion birds were filling the air with their raucous cries. After the sun had set on the sixteenth day, he had taken a cold plunge in the cool waters of the lake and consumed many cups of wine hoping to erase the pain of both his body and mind. He knew that the next day would bring about the battle that he had waited for his whole life and possibly release him from the wretched contradictions of his existence. His heart was heavy and he felt as if a huge weight had been kept on his shoulders. The meeting with my Lord and with his mother had removed the hatred he had harboured all these years for the Pandavas. How could he hope to fight without hate?

His son Vrishatsena walked into his tent at that moment; his son was a splitting image of himself. "My son!" he exclaimed, "Why are you not sleeping? You have a heavy day tomorrow."

"Father, I cannot sleep today. I am excited about tomorrow when you will meet the Pandavas and destroy them single-handed."

What youth lacks in experience, it makes up with passion, Karna thought to himself. This was the first time that his son was in a major battle and Karna could see the same eagerness, fire and passion within him that he himself had had, many years ago.

"Yes, my dear son, we will win the war for our king tomorrow but that will happen only tomorrow. Time does not stop for anyone; not even the Gods. Even Lord Indra cannot command Time. Go to sleep now, you will need all your energy for the battle tomorrow."

After a warm embrace, his son left him alone. Karna could not bear to think of what would happen to him in the coming days. He still could not sleep as his memories kept tormenting him. He knew that he would have to face Arjuna the next day. He had promised his mother that he would spare the lives of Yudhishtira, Bhima, Sahadeva and Nakula but not Arjuna. The world would see the battle between the two great warriors. It was a fight, which they both had waited for. There was space for only one of them in the world; only one could command the title of the greatest warrior!

He closed his eyes, desperate to get some sleep but again memories kept flashing before his eyes!

SEVENTEENTH DAY

The seventeenth day dawned. I think both Karna and Arjuna knew that it would be a battle to the finish on this day. Arjuna worshipped his weapons with utmost care. I'm sure Karna did the same.

As Karna came to the battlefield the sun cast a halo round his head as if to honour his son. He held his head proudly, even though he knew that it would probably be his last day on earth. His standard was of pure gold and bore the device of an elephant's rope adorned with gold, pearls and diamonds, forged by the foremost of artists. The Kaurava warriors cheered as he came onto the field.

First of all he killed one of the sons of Drishtadyumna, but as he turned round he was forced to watch his own son Sushena being killed by Satyaki. The Panchala warriors now closed in on him and there was a fierce fight.

Just then Bhima happened to see Dusshasana in front of him. The dreadful scene which took place thirteen years ago flashed across his mind. This demon in front of him was the one who had dragged his beloved wife by her hair into the assembly. His vile hands had desecrated her modesty and her purity. He lunged forward at him brandishing his mace. Then suddenly he remembered the oaths he had taken that day – that he would tear out Dusshasana's heart and tie up Draupadi's hair with his bloody hands and that he would drink his blood. With a blood-curdling roar Bhima threw away his mace and pounced on him and pulled his hair and brought him out of the chariot as he had done to Draupadi thirteen years ago. Using his adamantine fists he broke the bones in Dusshasana's right arm and feet and finally wrenched his right arm away shouting in frenzy, "This was the arm that peeled away my Draupadi's clothes. This was the arm that dragged her hither and thither." With these words he dragged the wicked Dusshasana up and down the battlefield by his long hair. He howled and begged for mercy but Bhima said, "The wheel of *karma* turns very slowly but it grinds to dust everything in its path. It will catch up with everyone sooner or later. It has caught up with you now and you will have to reap the consequences of your brutal actions. At that time all you Kauravas exulted and watched in glee while a noble woman was insulted and tormented beyond all consideration. I can still see her desperate look of appeal to me since she knew that I was the only one who might be able to help her. My hands were tied at that time but now they are free and I will make you pay tenfold for all you did to my beloved wife!" With these words he threw him onto the ground and pounded his chest and ripped it open and drew out his heart and scooped some blood in his palms to drink it as he had vowed to do.

My Lord shouted to him, "Don't drink the blood. Keep it in your mouth and spit it out. Your oath has been fulfilled."

Karna was totally demoralised by this macabre scene for he also recalled that shameful incident when Draupadi was disrobed. He remembered with shame his own comments and the dreadful oaths taken on that day by the helpless Pandavas. He had joined in Duryodhana's loud laughter and enjoyed the lewd remarks of the other Kauravas. In fact he had even told Panchali to choose one of the Kauravas as her husband since her own could not help her. He had laughed when Duryodhana slapped his thighs and told her to sit on them! The desperate look on her face was to haunt him for many months.

I must admit that all of us who were watching this terrible scene were shaken to the core. I could hardly bear to look at Bhima who was covered all over with blood and had blood dripping from his mouth and looked as if he had turned into some sort of *rakshasa*. He had totally lost all sense of proportion and shouted to Duryodhana to come and see the end of his dear brother. At last he put an end to Dusshasana's misery by lifting him above his head and whirling him round and round and flinging him far off like a sack of flour.

Aswatthama made a last minute appeal to Duryodhana to stop the war, but after having witnessed the brutal scene of his brother's death, he was in no mood to listen. He shouted to Karna to make good his oath of killing Arjuna.

At last the two great protagonists came face to face for they knew that this was the moment of truth from which only one of them would survive. At first it was just a display of skill and the charioteers also were displaying their skill in manouvering the chariots skillfully to avoid the flying arrows. War on all fronts was stopped as all the warriors from both sides came to watch the deadly combat between these mighty heroes. Arjuna's arrows fell on Karna like summer rain for they didn't seem to hurt him at all. However Karna's arrows were like stinging snakes and they drank Arjuna's blood. At last one arrow cut the string of Partha's bow and Arjuna said, "Wait till I string my bow. It is against all rules of warfare to shoot at someone who has no weapons."

However Karna paid no heed and showered arrows which wounded Arjuna on his chest despite my Lord's manouvering of the chariot. Despite his injuries, Arjuna managed to re-string his bow and cast a volley of arrows at his foe. But Karna was more than a match for him.

Finally Karna decided that the Nagastra was the only one which could finish off Arjuna. He placed that golden arrow on his bow which he had been worshipping and keeping only to be used against Arjuna. During the time of the burning of the forest of Khandava, Arjuna had inadvertently killed a snake that had been carrying a baby. This snake had vowed vengeance on Partha and had quietly entered the arrow that Karna fixed on his bow. Karna pulled the arrow towards his ear aiming at Arjuna's neck. The sky became overcast and meteors started to fall. Shalya now said, "Aim at his chest and not his throat!"

Karna proudly said, "Concentrate on your driving and don't tell me what to do. A brave warrior never shifts his aim after fixing it!"

My Lord saw that arrow speeding towards them with the open mouth of a vicious cobra. He was not at all perturbed but simply pressed down that chariot into the ground which had become soft due to the previous night's rain. The horses bent their knees and knelt on the ground. Indra with his host appeared in the sky to applaud my Lord's act which would save his son. The arrow which had been aimed at Arjuna's neck now simply ripped off the diadem on his head which had been given to him by his father Indra. Arjuna was a bit shaken by this close shave with death. In the meantime the snake which had missed its mark darted back to Karna and told him to aim him once again since he was determined to kill Arjuna who was equally his foe. Karna who was always filled with pride over his prowess now told the snake, "I don't desire victory if I have to rely on another's might. Moreover I would never shoot the same shaft twice."

The snake was furious to hear this and decided to go by himself and bite Arjuna to death. My Lord told Arjuna to immediately slay the snake which was winging his way to him with deathly intent. "Who is this snake who is so opposed to me?" asked Partha.

Then my Lord told him the story of the snake whose mother had been killed by him during the burning of the forest of Khandava. His name was Ashwasena and it was the second most poisonous serpent in the world. My Lord told Arjuna to have a look at his diadem which had been given to him by his father. It had turned black when the snake had spilt its poison on it, thinking it to be Arjuna's head. My Lord told him to cut off the snake in mid-air with six keen shafts.

While Arjuna was killing the vicious snake, my Lord got out of the chariot and started to raise up the chariot from the soft mud. Then Karna pierced my Lord with ten arrows having peacock feathers. My Lord seemed totally unperturbed and continued with his work of freeing the wheel. The attack on my Lord inflamed Arjuna who shot a huge shaft at Karna which penetrated his armour and came out the other side and entered the earth. Karna retaliated by showering arrows at Arjuna. This incensed Arjuna who cut off Karna's diadem adorned with gems and smashed his armour. Both of them were bleeding badly.

Having pierced Krishna and felled Partha's standard, Karna killed many of the Somakas that followed Partha. These warriors retaliated and shrouded Karna with showers of straight shafts like masses of clouds hiding the light of the sun. Highly accomplished as he was in the use of weapons, Karna stupefied those advancing warriors with his shafts and baffled all the weapons shot by them and destroyed their cars and steeds and elephants. The Kauravas thought victory was theirs and that Karna had defeated the team composed of my Lord and Arjuna. However Partha recovered and shot an *astra* which made darkness fall over the whole field. He then shot both Karna and Shalya and all the Kuru warriors surrounding them. I was surprised to find that a soft wind carrying the fragrance of many flowers blew over all of us. He then pierced Karna in all his vital parts so that Karna trembled in pain, and slew all the Kuru warriors with their cars and steeds who formed his protective bodyguard surrounding him from all sides. I was sorry to see that all of them abandoned Karna at that point and fled. However the two heroes were bent on killing each other and continued their fight using the most fearful weapons. It is said that both Indra and Surya came and wiped away the blood and sweat on the faces of their beloved sons.

This was the time for Karna to have used the great *astras* given to him by his *guru* Parasurama but when he tried to recollect them, he found that he just couldn't remember the invocatory *mantras.* Then he recalled that he had been cursed by Parasurama that he would forget the *mantras* when he needed them most! However he had relented and had given him the Bhargavastra and his bow, Vijaya and told him that he would achieve immortal fame and everlasting glory.

I remembered this story which I had heard from my Lord and I could see the torture on Karna's face as he tried to remember the *mantra* for the Bhargavastra. I never felt as sorry for him as I did then, even though I was quite angry with him for having shot my Lord when he was trying to free the wheel. As if to avenge this, the earth began to devour Karna's chariot wheel. It slowly started sinking into the soft mud. Shalya refused to get out of the chariot to dislodge the wheel. "I am not your servant to get out of the chariot and lift your wheel," said Shalya.

Karna rebuked him and retorted, "I am a *Suta Putra*, son of a charioteer. I have no problem in doing this work. I have been used to chariot wheels all my life. I will get down and pull the wheel out myself." At this Shalya angrily flung down his whip and threw the reins into his face and left him to his fate. Karna must have remembered the curse of the Brahmin at that time. After leaving Parasurama he had gone to the forest to practice the method of killing an opponent by directing an arrow towards the sound rather than the sight of the enemy. Unfortunately he killed a Brahmin's cow and the Brahmin cursed him that he would meet his end when he was helpless and without any weapon!

Karna started ranting and raving at the dreadful way that fate had treated him. "Surely have I been singled out by fate for her choicest boons, and now everyone seems to have deserted me including my charioteer!"

However he pierced my Lord with three terrible arrows and Partha with seven. Arjuna retaliated and pierced Karna with potent arrows which pierced him and came out of his body and fell on the ground.

Karna shouted to Arjuna, "O Partha! You know the rules of warfare well. Give me time to extricate my wheel and then I will deal with you. You know that it is unfair to shoot at a fallen foe."

Then my Lord spoke, "When all the great *maharathis* surrounded Arjuna's son and slew him, why did you not talk about *dharma* to them instead of to Partha at this moment? How dare you talk of fair play when you applauded Dusshasana when he brought Draupadi into the court dragging her by the hair? Didn't you tell her to choose another husband from among the Kauravas since her own husbands were incapable of protecting her virtue? You were a witness to the way the Kauravas treated the Pandavas by trying to poison Bhima and attempting to burn them all in a house of lac."

Karna remembered everything and hung his head but he recovered and started to fight again. He cut off the string of Partha's Gandiva again and again until at last Arjuna was forced to sit down in the chariot to recover. Karna availed himself of this respite to extricate the chariot wheel.

'Why does he have to extricate the wheel now?' I asked my Lord. 'He can continue to fight from the stationary car since you are also keeping your chariot in one place and not moving it around. This is a good time for him to use his divine weapons. He has only used the Nagastra. I'm sure he has others.'

"Don't you remember that he has been cursed that he won't be able to remember the *mantras* for any of them? But of course he can fight with his other weapons since even Arjuna is not using his *astras*. But you are right and I don't see any reason for him to try to lift his wheel at this precise moment and jeopardise his life."

Then Arjuna true to his nature wanted to give him time to recover but the Lord told him to do his duty and to attack him fiercely since Karna would do the same if he could. Thus another fight began since Karna had recovered and started to retaliate with extraordinary shafts even though he could not remember the *mantras* for the *astras*. He surrounded Arjuna with crackling flames which set fire to the clothes of many of the warriors. Arjuna then quickly muttered some *mantras* and let fly his arrows which shed waters as if they were rain clouds and put out all the fires. Karna retaliated and from his bow a hot desert wind swept over the field and dried all the waters. As suddenly as all this phenomenon had occurred, the sun returned and wind died down and we were where we started. With arrows sticking all over him, Karna shot and cut the Gandiva's string with a snap which made my ears ring. Arjuna had to pause while he restrung his bow but Karna kept shooting arrows at Partha.

My Lord now spoke, "Kill him now Partha! What mercy did he show to your son when he was helpless and without weapons? This is the precise moment when his *karma* has to be fulfilled."

Karna remembered his own part in that dreadful episode and knew that the Lord spoke but the truth. With a sigh he remounted and continued to fight from his stationary chariot. My Lord also kept our chariot stationary so that both had equal chances. Again there was a flurry of arrows but though Arjuna wounded him severely he was unable to kill him. My Lord said that Karna could not be killed until his entire stock of merit had been exhausted.

Suddenly I saw my Lord jumping out of the chariot and taking on the form of a beggar. He approached Karna and begged for alms. Sadly Karna said, "I have nothing to give you."

The beggar said, "I have come to ask you for your *punya* (spiritual merit). I shall be content with that."

Karna knew that it was another test for him so he unhesitatingly replied, "Gladly will I give you all the merit I have accumulated, am accumulating and might accumulate in the future if that will satisfy you!"

Thus by surrendering even his spiritual merits to my Lord who is the giver of all merits, Karna achieved immortality. But my Lord had not done with him yet. He was determined to let the world know his greatness. So he said, "A gift to a Brahmana has to be solemnised with water."

Karna said, "I am not able to find some water even to quench my thirst but this I can do." So saying he drew out an arrow which was embedded in his body and solemnised the gift with a spurt of blood. As he collapsed from loss of blood, the beggar gently supported him against the chariot wheel. Feeling drops of water falling on his face, Karna wearily opened his eyes and was thrilled to behold the glorious vision of the Lord upholding him with one arm and gazing at him with lotus eyes overflowing with love, from which a few drops of compassion had splashed!

"O Karna!" said my Lord, "Your name and fame will live forever. You have amply atoned for all your sins. You may ask for any boon and I will grant it."

Karna whispered, "What terrible sins have I committed against my own brothers and sister-in-law! My only comfort is that I feel I have paid my debt of gratitude in full to Duryodhana and that I have never failed to give to anyone whatever has been asked of me. If I have to take another birth, grant me the boon that once again I will never be able to deny anything to anyone!"

The Lord smiled gently and said, "Your sins are insignificant when compared to the merit accrued by your charity and magnanimity. Your present physical suffering is due to those sins but fear not O hero, by your final act of surrendering even your merit to me, I shall take on the burden of your sins and relieve you from your present pain!" So saying he gently released himself and went back to Arjuna and told him to shoot the fatal arrow.

Arjuna was reluctant to shoot a fallen enemy but my Lord said, "His time for death has come. I have given him the final benediction so you can shoot your arrow without any qualms."

My Lord spoke in the same non-committal tone of voice that he had used when he asked Arjuna to shoot arrows at his own sons who were in the Narayana Sena which he had given to Duryodhana. The latter had ordered the Sena to go and fight with Arjuna for he knew that he would be reluctant to fight with them and he wanted to test how my Lord was going to handle this difficult situation. He handled it in the same way he handled the situation with Karna. He knew that Karna's time was up, just as he knew that many of his sons were going to get killed in the war by Arjuna's arrows. He took it as part of their *karma*.

Arjuna took this as the command of God and discharged the Anjalika missile which was Indra's second most powerful weapon. The *Shakti* was the first and that he had given to Karna. The shaft was endued with the energy of the sun and caused all the points of the compass to blaze with light.

Thus fell the mighty hero of the Mahabharata war. The sun was at its zenith and Surya, the son god, turned Karna's body crimson as his decapitated head fell from its trunk and rolled on the ground. Everyone saw a light come out of his body and wind its way to the midday sun. The Kaurava warriors did not want to fight any more. Everyone from both sides crowded round Karna. He still looked handsome and calm.

Yudhishtira said, "For thirteen years I have lived in dread of Karna and imagined the fight between the two of you and now here he lies dead. I cannot believe it."

Kunti came rushing to the scene as she had promised Karna. She took his head on her lap and lamented loud and long and announced to that entire crowd that he was her first born. The Pandavas could not believe what she was saying. "What are you saying?" shouted Yudhishtira. "If this is true why did you not reveal it before?" All the brothers were really angry and started shouting at her.

"Who was his father?" demanded Yudhishtira.

"Karna was the son of the Sun God. He is Surya *Putra* and not *Suta Putra*. I bore him when I was still a maid and floated him down the river. He was found by the Suta, Adhiratha and his wife Radha who brought him up as their own son."

Yudhishtira was too stunned to speak. At last he whispered, "Karna was my elder brother!"

Arjuna was shocked and bitterly regretted that he was the killer of his own brother.

My Lord rebuked him and said, "Karna was killed by his own *karmas* and the curses he had received from so many people. You were just an instrument."

All the brothers were prostrated with grief. Turning to Kunti, Yudhishtira asked, "Did Karna know this?"

Krishna answered for her and said, "Yes, he knew."

All of them hung their heads in shame when they thought of the number of times they had taunted him with the appellation '*Suta Putra*' and he had remained silent.

"Mother how could you do this to us?" asked Yudhishtira and walked away, refusing to talk to her, leaving her to her grief.

Duryodhana rushed to the scene. If there was anyone in the world that he was genuinely fond of, it was Karna. When he heard Kunti's lament, he realised that Karna had already known of his parentage and had still fought against his brothers only out of love for him. He couldn't believe that anyone could be so noble and he cried bitter tears over his dear friend's body. "Had he lived I would have shared the kingdom with him," he said.

Arjuna now understood why he had found a striking resemblance between Karna and Yudhishtira. Karna's wife Kanchanamala now came on the scene and threw herself on his body and mourned for him. All the Pandavas now turned on my Lord and protested that he must have known this fact and blamed him for keeping it away from them.

My Lord said, "Karna himself made me promise not to reveal his secret until he had died. On two occasions I had given you hints about his identity, but you were not prepared to understand. None of you cared to enquire when Panchali confessed to having a sixth person in her mind, nor did Arjuna enquire why he saw his brother in Karna."

I asked my Lord later that night why he had to do this to Karna. He said, "If you have heard the Ramayana story you will know that in my incarnation as Rama, I helped Sugriva, the son of Surya to fight and kill Vaali, the son of Indra from the back. The debt had to be repaid in this incarnation, so I helped Arjuna, the son of Indra to kill Karna, the son of Surya from the back. *Karma* is the great law of unerring, never-failing justice; the mysterious workings of which stretch from the innermost atom to the outermost cosmic space; from the birth of a thought to the birth of the universe. When the gods take on a human form, even they have to come under this law."

I thought to myself that actually the Kauravas had had all the cards stacked in their favour. They had eleven *akshauhinies* to the seven of the Pandavas. They had the three greatest warriors – Bhishma, Drona and

Karna on their side not to mention a host of others, while really speaking the Pandavas had only two great warriors – Bhima and Arjuna since my Lord was not fighting. Yet the Pandavas were surely winning. As Bhishma had told Duryodhana and Vyasa had told Aswatthama, the battle was between *dharma* and *adharma* and the gods would always side with *dharma*. Unfortunately even now Duryodhana was not capable of seeing this. Kripa's suggestion to make peace was scorned by the arrogant prince.

He said, "After the wrongs I have done against the Pandavas, how can I ask or expect mercy at their hands? Let the war go on till the bitter end."

Aum Namo Bhagavate Vaasudevaaya

Honey bee, Krishna's flute is honey-sweet.
We hear and our very breath is immersed in love,
Like a wick immersed in oil, shining hot and bright.
And the moths that see the flame,
And destroy their greedy bodies,
Like a fish that yearns for a sliver of meat,
And seizes a bamboo hook or a crooked thorn.
Which twists the heart and will not come out.
As a hunter sounds a horn and draws a herd of deer.
Shoots an arrow and threads their hearts upon the shaft.
As a dacoit lures a pilgrim with balls covered with wine.
Making him drunk and trusting,
Taking his money and his life.
Just so O honey bee, Hari takes our love by deceit,
Sur's Lord tore up the sweet sugar-cane,
And planted a garden of longing.

Chandi Das

ॐ

Kodisuryasamaprabhaaya Namaha!

CHAPTER THIRTY-SIX

Suyodhana

The eighteenth day dawned dark and gloomy as if the sun god was withholding his rays to mourn for the death of his son. The end was a foregone conclusion but Duryodhana still hoped for a miracle. After some consultation with Aswatthama, Shalya was chosen as the new commander. He promised to kill both Arjuna and Krishna! The army had dwindled to almost nothing. Hardly any heroes were left so it was decided to avoid all duels.

Gandhari was desperate when she heard that one by one all her sons had been killed by Bhima. She hoped to save at least Duryodhana. Vyasa had told her that by the power of her chastity she could make his body as hard as a diamond if she took off the bandage round her eyes and gazed at him with uncovered eyes. So she asked him to take a bath and come to her naked. As he was coming out of the lake my Lord and I were taking a stroll along the banks as we did every evening and my Lord laughed to see the great Duryodhana in this state of total nudity. Duryodhana also felt shy and quickly wrapped a cloth round his loins. So when his mother took off the bandage over her eyes, her piercing gaze fell over his whole body except his thighs which were covered. So his weak point was his thighs which in any case were the part which Bhima had sworn to break.

Shalya rode out on his chariot on which his flag with a silver elephant and four golden peacocks was waving merrily on his flagstaff tied with sheaves of wheat. He fought with the inspiration born out of despair but the Pandavas were irresistible. Our army was arranged in three divisions led by Drishtadyumna, Satyaki and Shikandin. Shalya proved to be invincible on this day. He routed Bhima and even Arjuna! My Lord now suggested that the person who was meant to kill him was the Eldest who was quite an expert with the javelin. I was amazed at Yudhistira's expertise with the javelin. I had never seen the Eldest look like this. His eyes were trembling with rage and he broke Shalya's bow and cut off his chariot wheels. Shalya picked up his sword and jumped on the ground holding his dark blue shield with a thousand diamond stars in front of him. I had never seen Yudhishtira use a javelin before. He challenged Shalya and there was an incredible battle between the two. At last Yudhishtira invoked my Lord's name and hurled his javelin made of coral and steel tinkling with little bells at Shalya who tried to catch it. But the spear went through his shield and pierced his chest and fell to the earth. Shalya also fell, bathed in blood and died immediately, no doubt happy that he had served Duryodhana well. Everyone exclaimed at Yudhistira's skill with the javelin and my Lord said, "It is not the lance but the accumulated effects of his *dharma* that has killed Shalya."

I thought to myself that what he meant was that it was not his prowess but the effects of his *dharma*! I could well believe it since I had never seen him fight so well before. In fact he hardly ever fought. The Kaurava army was thoroughly demoralised by the death of all their leaders. The soldiers broke up and started retreating in terror. Duryodhana tried to rally them but to no avail. Shakuni's son Uluka was singled out by Nakula who fulfilled his oath and killed him under the very eyes of his father. Now it was Sahadeva's turn to make good his oath to kill the arch villain of the Mahabharata – Shakuni, Prince of Gandhara! Shakuni jumped on his mountain horse holding aloft his long shining lance and tried desperately to flee from Sahadeva's wrath. He made a detour behind the

Pandavas and sped through the carcasses through which no chariot could go. Nakula and Sahadeva got out of their chariots and chased him on two horses having dark and white manes and tails. Sahadeva wore one black glove on his right hand which held his sword. At last the twins caught up with him and felled him from his horse and slashed him into three pieces and left him to die in mortal agony!

I looked round in horror and observed the field of death. Kurukshetra was covered with hammers and darts, yokes and chains, broken spears and elephant bells, wheels, swords and bloody arrows and fallen heads bright with golden earrings, iron tiger-claws held in severed hands and open mouths filled with blood! Arrows whistled through the air and heads and bodies fell incessantly on all sides. Vultures and carrion birds were slowly circling down, waiting for us to leave before swooping down on their prey. They had never had such a feast before. Bhima's thirst for blood had not abated and he pressed the men onwards through the sticky mud. Many of the men in the Kuru army died out of sheer fright just seeing Bhima's diabolic glare. All rules of warfare had been broken. Horses ran down foot soldiers and chariots were crushed by elephants. Men fought with anyone, not knowing if they were friend or foe! Like a broom sweeping up debris, Drishtadyumna went around and killed the last of the Kurus.

EIGHTEENTH DAY

At the end of the eighteenth day only fourteen warriors remained. My Lord, the five Pandava brothers, Satyaki, Drishtadyumna and Yuyutsu on our side and Duryodhana, Aswatthama, Kripa, Vrishaketu (son of Karna) and Kritavarma on the Kaurava side. My Lord told me later on that Arjuna had developed a great affection for Vrishaketu and regarded him as his son and took him on all his expeditions.

Now the Pandavas set out to exterminate everyone in the opposite camp. By noon only four men were left in their camp – Duryodhana, Aswatthama, Kripa and Kritavarma who was actually part of the Yadava army. Seeing the immense expanse of the bloody remains of his vast army, Duryodhana wept bitter tears. He thought he was the only survivor and fought like one possessed. His arrows pierced every Pandava soldier who was left. He kept hurling lances from his elephant at everyone, quite oblivious of the rules. None dared to approach him. When his bow was broken he cut down arrows with his sword but then the elephant died under him and the last I saw of him was when he leapt like a panther to the ground holding only his mace bound in hemp. He loped off into the forest.

On our side I noticed that Yuyutsu who was standing under his plain gold banner was the only surviving Kaurava other than Duryodhana. He survived because he had deflected to the Pandava camp on the very first day of battle. Yudhistira's flag was a golden moon with all the planets around it. I could see the lion with the golden mane on a white background which was Satyaki's flag and the silver swan of Sahadeva's and the Sarabha with eight legs and four eyes with a golden back which belonged to Nakula.

Dritarashtra had sent Sanjaya to the battlefield to search for the Prince. Drishtadyumna and Satyaki drew up their chariots in front of him and Drishtadyumna said, "What is the use of keeping Sanjaya alive? He is a puppet of the Kauravas." Drawing his sword he jumped out of his chariot. Sanjaya kept a tight hold on his ivory-handled sword and prepared for death. At that precise moment my Lord and Arjuna thundered on the scene and my Lord shouted at Drishtadyumna, "Don't kill him. He is protected by Vyasa."

Satyaki got out of his chariot and folded his palms before Sanjaya and said, "Give me your sword which has never been wet with blood." He took his sword but Drishtadyumna was still angry. My Lord looked at Sanjaya and smiled and said to the Panchala prince, "Here is a spear into which I have put all the anger that god has with this man. Let us see how it will kill him." With these words he threw the spear high into the sky and it came hurtling down towards Sanjaya's head like a bright orange flame. It was so bright that everybody had to close their eyes. Sanjaya stood there fearless with closed eyes and folded palms and when we opened our eyes we were astonished to find that the spear had changed into a garland of flowers round his neck!

Sanjaya bowed to my Lord and walked through the field to the road leading to Hastinapura. Wounded men, women and sentries were all running to the city. Yuyutsu came to Yudhishtira and asked for permission to herd them together and escort them back to the city. Permission was granted and he sped away on his chariot. Sanjaya refused to go with him and we could see him walking down the road. All of us now started a hunt to find the Kuru prince who seemed to have disappeared. Unless he was found and killed there would be no rest that night. At last some hunters came to us. They were the ones who always brought venison for Bhima and they told us their story.

"My Lords," they said, "we were walking in the forest trying to catch a deer for prince Bhima when we suddenly saw the glint of armour and crept up to see the Yuvaraja, Duryodhana badly wounded and holding his mace and steadying himself against a tree near the lake. His eyes were blinded by tears so he did not even notice us. Then we saw Sanjaya going to him and trying to persuade him to return with him to Hastinapura. He refused and said, 'You are the only friend I have seen so far. All the others must be dead. Why should I return to Hastinapura to face my parents? Lead me to the Dwaipayana Lake nearby. The demons taught me the trick of charming the water so I can stay hidden in the water and no one will find me.' So saying we saw Sanjaya taking him to the water. The Yuvaraja slipped into the cool waters and stayed there using a reed to breathe."

"Is he still there?" asked Bhima.

The hunters replied, "We were just coming here to give you this news when we saw a chariot with Kripa, Kritavarma and Aswatthama. They jumped out when they saw Sanjaya and asked him, what had happened to the Yuvaraja? Sanjaya replied that he was hiding in the lake.

They went close to the waters and said, 'O Duryodhana! The three of us have escaped. Come out and we will return and fight with the Pandavas.' But the Yuvaraja replied that he was too tired and told them to return the next day. At this we left and came hurrying here to give you the news so that you can go and catch him."

Bhima gave a lavish gift to the hunters for their information and all of us including Satyaki left in three chariots to the lake.

We traced him by the bubbles which were coming out of the water. When Bhima tried to beat the water of the pool with his mace he found that Duryodhana had charmed the water and made it solid.

Bhima shouted, "Come out you coward and face your end. Aren't you ashamed to hide yourself after all your brothers have been killed?"

Like an elephant rising from the water Duryodhana rose out of the lake drenched and covered with blood. He magnanimously offered the kingdom to Yudhishtira! All of us laughed to hear this generous offer from the defeated prince and told him as he had once told Yudhishtira at the start of the war that if he wanted his kingdom he would have to fight for it. Then the Eldest in his usual quixotic fashion which often bordered on foolhardiness, offered to give over the entire kingdom to the winner of a duel between him and one of his brothers, quite forgetting that Bhima had sworn to kill him. His brothers gasped at this stupid offer but kept quiet, even though they knew that this might well result in the collapse of all their hopes.

My Lord said, "It seems that Kunti's sons are born to spend their lives like beggars in the forest and never enjoy their kingdom!"

Luckily for the Pandavas, the cold war between Duryodhana and Bhima had gone on too long for the former to even contemplate fighting with any of the others. He looked scornfully at Yudhishtira as if he despised him for making such a weak offer. His blood boiled when he thought of Karna, and how Bhima had killed all his brothers. Then he turned and glared at Bhima. They had many scores to settle with each other and they both knew that the moment of reckoning had come. Even at this moment

Duryodhana was confident of victory since he had been practicing on an iron effigy of Bhima for many years, striking at all his weak points so he thought it would be a walk-over. Moreover Gandhari's blessing of the night before had made his entire upper body hard as iron.

Just as they were about to start the fight Balarama appeared, clad in blue, flaunting his one earring, with a garland round his neck and a wine jar in his hand.

"I see that the Pandavas have won and I am in time for the last fight but this is no place for a fight. Follow me and I will take you to the edge of the lake where there is no sand."

Without a word all of us followed him single file until we came to the place he had chosen.

The two mighty protagonists faced each other and slowly started to circle round each other warily looking for a place to strike. Suddenly they jumped at each other like maddened bulls with wounds oozing blood. The sound made by their maces was like claps of thunder and set off burning sparks like lightning. At first they circled cautiously around each other looking for a loophole and then pounced on each other. At times they stood still and sometimes jumped high into the air to avoid a blow and sometimes backwards, dodging and bending and striking whenever the opportunity arose. Their faces were reddened with blood. Suddenly Duryodhana asked Bhima for his vulnerable spot and he truthfully pointed at his head. Of course Duryodhana immediately smote him on the head and Bhima fell and all of us thought he had died, but he recovered himself and was mad with Duryodhana and asked him to show his weak spot, but of course the Kaurava prince as usual told a lie and pointed to his own adamantine head! When Bhima smote him on his head, he laughed for his head was hard as iron and the blow had absolutely no effect on him. In fact his whole body was like adamantine due to his mother's blessings so Bhima's mace made not even a dent on his body. Duryodhana laughed a diabolic laugh for he felt sure that Bhima would never be able to defeat him. In fact all the maces which Bhima hurled at him broke into smithereens! Still they circled around each other warily looking for a weak spot.

What a coincidence that my Lord and I were taking a walk the previous evening and saw Duryodhana running naked after his dip in the lake to keep his tryst with his mother. Obviously his thighs which he covered out of shame were his only vulnerable points and he could never be killed by any opponent except by hitting the thighs. I thought to myself *adharma* has to perish and there is nothing called coincidence in life. Everything comes under the master plan and that is why we were taking a walk at that precise time. I looked at my Lord and he looked back at me. Of course he knew what I was thinking. Was he not the *antaryami* (inner dweller)? How fortunate I was to be with him, talking to him, learning from him and trying to understand him. We humans are hemmed in with petty notions of a middle-class morality beyond which we dare not tread. Unless we learn to go beyond human ethics to divine ethics, we will never understand the intricate workings of the divine mind.

'Has Bhima forgotten his oath to kill him by striking his thighs? Obviously he can never be killed by striking at any other part of his body,' I whispered to my Lord.

"It looks as if he had forgotten it," my Lord replied. "I will remind him."

He turned and looked piercingly at Arjuna's thighs and Arjuna turned and looked at his own thighs to see what the matter was. Obviously Bhima saw the look and remembered his oath. He swung his mace high up in the air as if to hit Duryodhana's head and the latter jumped high into the air to avoid the blow and the mace hit his thighs instead. Of course that was Duryodhana's weak point which had not been pierced by Ghandari's look and he fell like a broken log cut down in its prime with a roar of surprise. Bhima bellowed his roar of triumph. Filled with the lust of the kill, he rushed forward to press his foot on Duryodhana's head as one would do to a poisonous snake but Yudhishtira stopped him.

There was a moment of silence before the Pandava soldiers realised what had happened and then all of them cheered wildly and cymbals and drums boomed in exultation. Bhima bowed at the feet of his eldest brother and offered him the throne of Hastinapura.

Balarama now rushed at Bhima with upraised plough and shouted, "You have violated the code of mace fighting by hitting below the waist! I should kill you for this!"

My Lord intervened and said, "Why didn't you kill Duryodhana when he committed the heinous crime of disrobing Panchali? Why didn't you kill him when he killed Arjuna's son by surrounding him with all the *maharathis*? Why didn't you protest when they were cheated at dice and sent to the forest? Why didn't you rebuke him when he slapped his thighs in the court of the Kurus and made an obscene remark to Panchali, asking her to sit on his thighs? At that time Bhima had sworn to kill Duryodhana by smashing his thighs so why should you stop him from fulfilling his vow now? The sage Maitreya had cursed Duryodhana at that time, 'The mighty Bhima will smash your thighs with a stroke of his mace.' None of those who heard him thought that it was an unfair curse since Duryodhana deserved it for insulting the princess of Panchala. You know full well that Duryodhana had resorted to the feat called *Avasthana* which you yourself had taught him which involves jumping as high as you can in order to avoid a blow. Bhima had aimed at his head but when Duryodhana jumped the blow fell on his thighs. Moreover you know that the smashing of thighs is quite common in mace fighting. Bhima killed many Yakshas by smashing their thighs when he went to get the flower from Kubera's garden. Duryodhana was well aware of Bhima's oath to smash his thighs and should have taken precautions against this. But the fact is that however calculating a man may be, he can never take full precautions against the back lash of his own wicked *karmas*. One day or other they will catch up with him. How is it that you who are so quick to point out flaws in the Pandavas are totally blind to the crimes of the Kauravas?"

Without a word the angry giant walked away flourishing his ploughshare over his shoulder. He had never expected to be rebuked by Krishna but he knew that his brother spoke only the truth.

Despite his agony, the fallen prince embarked on a tirade against my Lord, "I don't blame Bhima! You are the conniving wretch who helped the Pandavas time and time again. Without your machinations they would never have won!"

My Lord spoke severely, "O Suyodhana! Think of all the evil and suffering you have caused to so many people. All this bloodshed could have been avoided had you cared to listen to Yudhishtira's most reasonable request for a fair share of his patrimony. I myself came to the court and begged you to consider his most noble request and so did all the elders, but you chose to disregard everyone and listen only to the evil Shakuni and your friend Karna! Why do you blame me or anyone else now for getting your just deserts? Everyone reaps the consequences of his own actions. Nobody can avoid this, however powerful or great they might be. You boast about how you have lived a full life like a king and not like slaves as the Pandavas lived for thirteen years. You boast about all the great things you have accomplished and that you have never bowed your head to any man, but remember a person may live as he likes but he will not be able to die as he likes! The results of his actions are not decided by him but by another force against which he is helpless! And those results have now caught up with you and despite your great prowess you are powerless to fight against it. You blame me for helping the Pandavas and even resorting to stratagems to ensure their safety and victory. Why should I not do that? I am bound to help those who have surrendered themselves to me and depend solely on me to help them. Both you and Arjuna came to me at the same time to enlist my aid in the battle. You had an equal chance to get my support but you preferred to choose my army whereas Arjuna chose me alone, unarmed and unresisting. From that moment onwards I was bound to support them. Even now at the point of death you are plotting some scheme by which you can still kill your noble cousins who have never done you any injury. But remember I always side with the righteous and I will never forsake my devotees!"

Aum Namo Bhagavate Vaasudevaaya

Obeisance to Lord Krishna, who is both the abode and the indweller of all beings! Though reputed as born or Devaki, he is really the eternal and ancient one. Surrounded by the attendants of the Yadu clan, he destroyed the forces of adharma by the prowess of his arms. He redeemed all beings, animate and inanimate, from their sins. By his benign and smiling countenance, he inspired divine love in the hearts of the gopis and gopas of Vraja and Mathura.

Srimad Bhagavatam Skanda 10. Chapter 90. Verse 48.

ॐ

Yadavendraaya Namaha!

CHAPTER THIRTY-SEVEN

Drauni

'Don't you think it's dangerous to leave Duryodhana while he is still alive?' I asked my Lord. 'I feel that he will continue his machinations against the Pandavas till he draws his last breath.' My Lord didn't say a word. He seemed to be in a bit of a hurry to hustle them off and took Yuyutsu and Satyaki with us and stopped just outside the Kaurava camp.

"Why have you brought us here?" asked Arjuna. "Let us return to our camp. There is not even a fire in this camp." My Lord didn't say a word.

He stopped the chariot in front of the camp and told Arjuna, "Please take your Gandiva and arrows and get out of the chariot fast. I shall dismount after you." He gave me a nudge told me also to jump out. He then dropped the reins and jumped out of the chariot. As he jumped he shouted to Arjuna, "Stand back!" At the same time I noticed that Hanuman who had been sitting for eighteen days on the pennant had also vanished.

In front of my bewildered eyes I saw the chariot along with the horses slowly turning into ashes even though there was no fire. An angry wind came along and swept up the ashes and whirled them round and round the battlefield.

The Pandavas watched aghast and Arjuna asked, "Why did the chariot turn to ashes?"

Krishna replied, "Everything in the world is created for a certain purpose and when that is over it will come to an end. This is true even for me. This chariot had already been burned to ashes by Drona's Brahmadanda. You were protected by your *mantras* but the chariot was not. It has served its purpose and has to be returned to the elements from which it was made. All these days it was held up by my power alone!"

Drishtadyumna told Yudhishtira of his decision to spend the night in the Pandava camp. He went to the Panchala camp and brought all his people and musicians etc. to the Pandava camp and no doubt they had a rollicking time with wine, food and women.

My Lord now congratulated Yudhishtira formally. "My Lord," said Yudhishtira, "Nothing would have been possible without your grace."

Krishna said, "There is a custom that the victors should never spend the night in either camp. Come, let us go to the river banks where there will be a cool breeze to refresh our fevered bodies and take some rest."

Thus the Pandavas, Satyaki and Yuyutsu went to the river banks and slept as they had never slept before. They begged my Lord to go to Hastinapura and comfort the bereaved parents of the Kauravas while they slept. My Lord went without a demur. Sanjaya had apparently lost his power of tele-vision as soon as Duryodhana fell. He had gone ahead and had already prepared them for the worst. Vidura was also there but all of them were dumb before the fire which seemed to blaze from Dritarashtra's blind eyes and the sparks which were being emitted through the folds of Gandhari's scarf which bound her eyes. Before she could speak a word, my Lord went and knelt at her feet and took her hand in his and said, "Mother, do you remember what you told Duryodhana when he came and asked you to bless him with victory?" She remembered only too well for she had told him, "Victory will go where there is *dharma*!" Tears started to roll down her face and appeared to put out some of the sparks as she realised that the whole holocaust had been brought about through her son's arrogance. She clung to my Lord's hand as if she drew some strength from it. My Lord sat by her side for a while then asked her permission to leave and assured her that he would be back soon with the Pandava brothers. Reluctantly she agreed to let him go. I felt an urgency in him to return but he refused to answer my queries. Dawn was just breaking on the other side of the river as we returned. It was a pale and wintry sun which rose reluctantly over the river. The brothers and Satyaki were just waking up.

Just then Drishtadyumna's charioteer came on the scene and hobbled towards us with great difficulty. He appeared to be mortally wounded.

"What is the matter? Where is your master?" asked Yudhishtira.

With the greatest of difficulty the charioteer gasped out a dreadful tale of vengeance and cruelty.

"O King!" he exclaimed, "All is lost. My master as well as your sons are all dead!"

"What!" gasped the distraught king. "What are you babbling about?"

I looked at my Lord's face. He wore his enigmatic gaze and would not look at me. I realised that this was the reason why he was in such a hurry to get back to the camp from Hastinapura. I also realised that had it not been for him the five Pandava brothers would also be dead. Time and again he had saved them. I wondered if they realised the depth of his love and concern for them. I wished that I could also evoke such love for me. Hardly had the thought passed through my mind than his eyes locked with mine and he nodded. Again I was in bliss.

With difficulty the charioteer continued. "Soon after you left the Yuvaraja to bleed to death, I noticed that the only three survivors of the Kauravas were creeping back to see him. I followed them for I suspected that they were up to some mischief. The Yuvaraja was writhing on the ground covered with blood and dirt, weltering in agony. Carnivorous animals were growling and slowly circling nearer and nearer.

"Aswatthama ran to him and bowed low, 'O Duryodhana! You were not born to die like this groveling in the mud without anyone by your side. You are our king! Command us and we will do anything you want,' he cried.

'Then come here,' said the dying prince. He raised himself up with the greatest of difficulty on his elbow. Taking some blood from his shattered thigh he applied it to his Guru's son's forehead and said, "I appoint you as the general of our forces.'"

'Consisting of three', I thought to myself.

"'What can I do for you, my king?' asked Aswatthama.

'Kill at least one Pandava for me,' Duryodhana said with bitterness, spitting blood as he spoke. 'I will be happy to depart from this world if I can see at least one Pandava's head! After I am dead my friend, you should marry my wife and beget sons on her who will rule this land for which I lived and died!'"

I had always suspected that it was unwise to leave him without killing him, but I suppose my Lord who knew everything had his own reasons.

"'So be it', said Aswatthama, filled with a burning desire to please his friend. All three of them crept away into the forest and lay down under a huge banyan tree on which many crows were roosting. I returned to the camp feeling very uneasy and sure that they were plotting something. I was not able to sleep and returned to the forest in time to hear their discussion. 'Wake up Kritavarma! I have found the exact method of killing the Pandavas without them knowing anything about it. See that tawny owl! He swoops down on the flock of sleeping crows and picks up one and disappears without the rest of the flock knowing. We will do the same. We will go now to the Pandava camp and kill them as they are sleeping and quickly take the heads to our king so that he can die in peace.'

'Have you gone out of your mind?' asked Kritavarma. 'Can you commit such a dastardly deed and remain at peace with yourself for the rest of your life? I will have none of this.'

'There is no other way by which we can fulfill Duryodhana's desire,' Aswatthama said and persuaded the other two to accompany him."

The charioteer continued. "I returned as fast as I could and stood at the gate knowing that the great Lord Shiva was protecting your camp.

Sure enough the three of them were stopped from entering by a huge figure with three eyes and blue throat, wearing a tiger skin and a snake round his neck. Aswatthama fought furiously with him but suddenly he realised that this was indeed Shankara and threw himself at his feet. He heard the voice of the destroyer coming from above, 'All these days I have protected the sons of Draupadi but now their time is up. You may enter.'"

"Then what happened?" asked Arjuna.

"Aswatthama told Kripa and Kritavarma to guard the two gates and ensure that nobody escaped while he entered my master, Drishtadyumna's tent thinking it to be the Pandavas'. I saw him kick his body not knowing who it was. I rushed to obstruct him but he turned on me with a snarl and hacked me with his sword. His face was the face of a devil and I fell back and watched in horror as he unstrung his bow and strangled my master to death, even though he begged to be killed by a sword or arrow. My arm which had been hacked was so painful that I could not move to go to his aid. Shikandin was sleeping next to my master and he brutally kicked him to death even before he could wake up fully. He then looked around for all of you and saw five people sleeping in a row. He was exultant that at last he had found the Pandavas and chopped off all the five heads. He then killed Yudhamanyu, Uttamaujas, and Janamejaya. He then brutally killed Chekitana, and the kings of Chedi, Panchala, Karoosha and Kashi. I was the only one who knew that he had murdered your sons. Somehow I managed to escape from the camp, even as Kripa and Kritavarma were running around with blazing torches setting fire to all the tents!" With these words the poor charioteer collapsed.

The Pandavas gasped in horror and ran to their chariots and flew to the camp. I shuddered at the ghastly scene which awaited us. The whole camp was in shambles with charred bodies and bloody entrails. While Aswatthama was doing his diabolic deed, Kripa and Kritavarma had set fire to all the tents so that none could escape. We ran to Drishtadyumna's tent and found everything as described by his charioteer. He had been strangled to death and only the headless bodies of the Upa Pandavas were left to tell the gory tale.

My Lord murmured, "I suppose Aswatthama thought he was killing the Pandavas. He would not have recognised the boys in the dark. He must have taken the heads to present to his dear friend."

'I would have liked to see Duryodhana's face as he saw the heads of the Upa Pandavas and realised that fate had played him another trick.'

All the Pandavas except Bhima fainted for a moment when they saw the headless bodies of their innocent sons! My Lord had to revive them.

"O Vaasudeva!" Yudhishtira wailed, "Is this a victory? What is the use of our kingdom if we have no sons to inherit the kingdom? What am I to tell their mother?"

Luckily that night, Draupadi had gone to the Panchala tent to be with her brothers. When she heard that they had come to the Pandava tent, she stayed on with the other ladies and did not bother to return. Hearing the wails and cries of the people outside the camp she rushed in.

"What has happened? Where are my brothers? Where are my children?" she cried.

"They have all been murdered while they were sleeping," Yudhishtira replied in an expressionless voice controlling the sobs which were threatening to overwhelm him. There was a stunned silence. For a moment she could not say anything, perhaps she could not even believe that such a thing had happened. She ran to each of the bodies and hugged the poor headless corpses and lamented aloud. "O Krishna! Why am I being punished like this? What wrong have I ever done?" Piteously she held out her hands to my Lord and cried, "I thought my heart had broken that day when the wicked Dusshasana pulled my hair and dragged me into the open court and tried to disrobe me, but I see now that it was nothing compared to what I feel now. How can a mother ever reconcile herself to the death of her five sons at the same time, all killed in this hideous fashion, and my dearest brothers? I would have felt better had they been killed on the battlefield. Who is the devil who was responsible for this diabolic deed?" she demanded. "I must have vengeance."

"Aswatthama, the *guru*'s son, aided and abetted by Kripa and Kritavarma, is the one who is guilty of this ghastly deed," said Bhima.

Suddenly her whole face changed. Her face took on the resemblance of Kali. She controlled her sobs and cried out loud, "My heart is bursting with sorrow at the fate of my beloved children. I must have revenge. Bhima please catch him and tear off his head from his shoulders as you did to Dusshasana." As usual she always knew that she could rely on Bhima to do her bidding.

Without a word Bhima jumped into his chariot with Nakula as his charioteer. My Lord and Arjuna followed for he knew the power of Aswatthama's fatal *astra.*

We found him in Vyasa's *ashrama.* My Lord said, "Obviously he must have taken the heads to Duryodhana who must have realised that these were not the heads of the Pandavas and now he has come to Vyasa's *ashrama* to ask for atonement."

Aswatthama was terrified when he saw Bhima approaching looking like the picture of Yama, thirsting for his blood, with Arjuna and Krishna following close behind. He jumped onto his horse and took to his heels with Bhima in hot pursuit. He was forced to jump off when he reached the river. He turned round with a snarl. Bhima fitted an arrow on his bow and took careful aim. It was only now that I realised how tall he was – much taller than even Bhima with black, flashing eyes and long black hair flowing to his shoulders. The jewel on his forehead glowed with a red fire which appeared to wax and wane with his breath.

The *guru's* son was desperate. He remembered that he had the most formidable weapon of all – the Brahmastra. He forgot or chose to forget that he had been strictly told by his father not to use it under any provocation against human beings. Since he had no weapons with him, he plucked a blade of grass and invoked the divinity in the *astra* totally regardless of the consequences of his action. Immediately my Lord guessed what he was doing and told Arjuna to invoke the same *astra*. Aswatthama threw the potentiated blade of grass into the sky and said, “Go and destroy all the Pandavas along with Vaasudeva!”

Arjuna sent his potentiated arrow into the air with the words, “For the peace of the world and all creatures.”

The two divine weapons rushed towards each other. For a while they hung like golden globes in the sky shimmering and sizzling and emitting tongues of fire. The heat generated by them made the river steam and the earth crack. Had they met, it would have resulted in a cataclysmic collision that would have totally annihilated the whole surface of the earth.

Vyasa now shouted to my Lord, “I'm holding Aswatthama's missile with my power, ask Arjuna to withdraw his missile.”

My Lord said in a soft whisper to Arjuna, “O Bharata! Withdraw your missile. I know it's much harder to withdraw than to release. If you make the slightest mistake, you as well as the whole earth around you will perish and become barren for many years.”

Arjuna obeyed without a question. But the strain was too much for him and he collapsed to the bottom of the chariot fighting for his breath. My Lord stroked his head lovingly and slowly he started to recover.

Vyasa was holding back Aswatthama's missile and asked him to withdraw it and promised to protect him as it came down. But try as he might, the *guru's* son was unable to bring it down. He cursed his father for not teaching him everything as he had taught his favourite pupil Arjuna.

‘Why did Dronacharya give it to him in the first place?’ I asked my Lord.

“Aswatthama overheard his father giving instructions to Arjuna and begged him to let him have the secret *mantra.* Drona could not refuse his son anything, but he gave him only a partial instruction and deliberately did not teach him the method of withdrawing it since he would have been tempted to use it again and again. A warrior who can invoke and withdraw an *astra* can use it many times. Drona did not trust his son to use the weapon with discrimination."

Seeing his inability to withdraw the *astra*, Vyasa told him to direct it towards a single, isolated object far away from the habitation of men. Instead of doing this, the sinful Aswatthama directed it towards Uttara's womb since he knew that she was carrying Abhimanyu's son!

I gasped in horror when I heard his dreadful words and Bhima pounced on him and tied him and dragged him back to Draupadi and told her to pronounce the method by which he should be killed.

By this time Draupadi had calmed down and said, "He is the cold-blooded murderer of my sons and brothers and deserves the worst form of death, but he is our *guru's* only son and I don't want his mother to suffer what I am suffering now. By killing him I will not be able to revive my sons!"

Arjuna looked frustrated."Panchali! Have you forgotten that he is the one who has killed our sons?"

"Let him go," she said again and went forward to unbind Aswatthama herself.

"Why are you doing this?" shouted Bhima.

Draupadi said, "He is the only son of your *guru*. The scriptures say that the son of a *guru* should be treated as a *guru*. If you kill him you will be guilty of killing a Brahmin as well as a *guru* and will have to suffer for it. His mother, Kripi is all alone in the world. Her husband is dead. Aswatthama is all she has. I cannot take on the sin of depriving her of her son."

Draupadi started weeping but continued, "Kripi has committed no crime. I don't want her to feel my pain."

"We cannot leave him unpunished!" Bhima declared.

"I forbid you to kill him," Draupadi said, "We don't want any more killing!"

I realised that this was another play of my Lord who wanted the world to recognise the greatness of his devotee, Draupadi. Her answer was a surprise to everyone and showed her greatness. But of course the wrong-doer could not go unpunished so my beloved Vanamali, the all merciful one, took on the task of chastising him and thus saved Draupadi from ill fame.

My Lord spoke, "O Bhima, Panchali has shown great mercy. However this villain cannot be allowed to go scot free. Shame him by shaving his hair in four places and pluck off the precious jewel he wears on his head which is protecting him against disease and all weapons."

Bhima jumped to do his bidding and caught hold of the sullen brute and shaved off his hair in four places and plucked out his crest jewel leaving a hole in his head. He then presented the jewel to Draupadi who in turn gave it to Yudhishtira.

Just then Subhadra came running and begged my Lord to save her daughter-in-law, Uttara who was carrying Abhimanyu's child in her womb. He would be the last of the progeny of the Pandavas. "Brother!" she cried, "There is a dreadful fiery *astra* pursuing Uttara and trying to kill her. Only you can save this remaining seed of the Pandavas."

My Lord immediately invoked and sent his *chakra* against the *astra.* He then chased Aswatthama who had taken to his heels after Bhima plucked out his jewel. He caught up with him and pronounced a dreadful curse on him. "You are the son of a Brahmin and yet you have stooped to a crime which even a Chandala would not indulge in. Instant death is too good a retribution for you. You will be forced to wander alone till the end of the Kali Yuga, shunned by all, with the festering wound still on your head. But rest assured that your dreadful desire to see the end of the Pandava lineage will not work. I will protect the foetus and see that it is born alive."

Much later when Bhima asked Draupadi what hurt her most about losing her children, she replied that what made her really sad was the fact that they died in their asleep because of which they could not even think of the Lord or call him to come to their aid.

'You knew what was going to happen, didn't you? That was why you refused to let the Pandavas sleep in their own tent! Why didn't you remove their sons also?'

"Didn't you hear the charioteer say that he heard Shankara say that their time was up and that is why he didn't stop Aswatthama from entering? I am not authorised to prolong the life of someone who is already fated to die at that moment."

He looked at me questioningly as if he suspected that I was going to ask something else but I kept quiet. He had an answer for anything.

I had another question. 'Will the Pandavas have no progeny at all?'

"Actually Bhima has one son called, Sarvatrada by Jalandhara, the princess of Kasi, who will become the ruler of Kasi. He had gone somewhere and did not participate in the war."

'What about the foetus in Uttara's womb, Arjuna's grandson?' I asked anxiously.

"Even though he will be still-born, fear not, I will revive him as soon as he is born and he will be the heir to the throne and will rule for sixty years."

It was a sad and sorrow-stricken party which turned towards the battlefield. The sun had already risen, but it was a pale and sickly looking sun as if loathe to light up a prospect of such desolation and despair. My Lord stood with the Pandavas surveying the dismal sight. Though they were uninjured and victorious, around them lay the death of all their hopes. They had won an empire at the cost of their sons. The throne of the Kurus was theirs but their hearts and homes were empty. Scattered on the bloody field of Kurukshetra lay the flower of Aryan knighthood, silent forever. Those who had marched to battle with flying flags, prancing steeds, gaily bedecked chariots and blaring conch shells and trumpets just eighteen days ago now lay on the cold, cold, earth, a prey to kites, vultures, jackals and wolves. Screaming eagles and carrion birds fanned the dead with their wings as they circled ever closer and closer to the ground. At other places wolves and hyenas stealthily came and dragged away arms and legs still adorned with bracelets.

All along the road to the capital we could see the wailing women, wives of the Kauravas, with their hair hanging like mantles behind them, beating their breasts and trudging to the field of death. Their faces were smudged with collyrium due to the tears which were streaming incessantly from their eyes. The Pandavas trembled when they gazed at these faces that had never been seen beyond the four walls of their palaces. Now they walked on the street with utter disregard of the public eye, as once Draupadi had walked, nay had been dragged through the streets of Hastinapura. They wailed and mourned for their husbands and sons as once Draupadi had wept when their husbands had so callously dragged her, the greatest of them all, into the court of the Kurus, fourteen years ago in the full bloom of her youth and beauty. There had been no one to shed a tear for her at that time, but today her husbands wept when they saw this pathetic procession, for the milk of human kindness still flowed in their hearts and they mourned as deeply as the women for the deaths of their husbands for which they had been instrumental. I remembered my Lord's words to Panchali, "Don't worry, O Panchali, one day you will see the women of the Kauravas with their hair trailing loose over their shoulders as your tresses are hanging now!"

What prophetic words they were. I realised now the extent of his omniscience.

Bhanumathy, Duryodhana's wife cried out in despair, "You won Yudhistira's kingdom with the dice but now Bhima has won your life!"

Karna's wives Subhangi and Kanchanamala wept over his body and over the bodies of their sons.

Yuyutsu had returned to the battlefield, sent by Dritarashtra to make pyres of fragrant wood for his hundred sons.

Yuyutsu and Satyaki went over the field lighting pyres with their torches and burning the bodies of all the heroes coming from far off places and kingdoms like Panchala, Matsya, Sindhu, Madra, Gandhara, Trigarta and many others.

My Lord knew that the Pandavas were unable to face this sight any longer so he said, "The war is over. Come, it's your duty to go and offer what comfort is possible to the bereaved parents of the Kauravas." It was not a task that anyone of them relished but it had to be done.

Aum Namo Bhagavate Vaasudevaaya

> Krishna, that centre of holiness and spiritual excellences, has eclipsed the sanctifying efficacy of the Ganga, the holy water flowing from his feet, through his sportive actions as the Divine Incarnate, the accounts of which are easily available for us to hear and are most efficacious in purifying the mind. He absorbed into himself all who came to him with intensity of feeling, whether it was through love or antagonism. His invincible majesty received the humble attention and services of Sri Devi whose favour all the devas seek. His name effaces the sins of all who chant it or hear it chanted. He propagated the Vedic Dharma through the gotras of the various rishis. All these achievements are not to be wondered at since Krishna wields the mighty wheel of Time as his weapon.
>
> *Srimad Bhagavatam. Skanda 10. Chapter 90.*

ॐ

Vanamaline Namaha!

CHAPTER THIRTY-EIGHT

The Dowager Queens

We did not wait to see what happened, but drove our chariots to Hastinapura where the blind king was waiting for us with his blindfolded queen. Thinking over the death of their hundred sons, both of them burned with feelings of revenge. All they could remember was the inequities committed by the Pandavas. They had completely forgotten the terrible acts committed by their own sons. Though outwardly they pretended to have got over the sorrow, inwardly they were burning with thoughts of revenge. The blind king was terribly strong. The anger he felt against Bhima who had killed all his sons was so great that he wanted to kill him with his own bare arms. Vidura knew his brother only too well and he warned the Pandavas to be careful. Dritarashtra opened his arms wide as Yudhishtira announced himself. "Come to me," he said, "Now you are my sons." He clasped Yudhishtira to his chest and then asked for Bhima. The iron effigy of Bhima, on which Duryodhana had been practicing wrestling for many years, was kept at the side of the hall. Quick as a thought, my Lord thrust this effigy into the arms of the vengeful king who hugged the effigy so hard that it cracked and hurt his own chest so that it began to bleed. "Have I killed him?" he asked anxiously.

Sanjaya comforted him and said, “Knowing your wrath, Krishna gave you an iron effigy of Bhima.” Turning to Bhima he said, “Now you may go to him and you will be safe.”

GANDHARI

Bhima, Arjuna and the twins now came forward and were embraced by the king. Yudhishtira now turned to the queen whose heart was burning with a sorrow that was never to come to an end. He knelt before her and she turned her head away so that her look would not harm him. From the beginning she had a premonition that the war would see the end of her household. She also realised that it was her husband’s weakness coupled with his greed that had led to this disaster. She had blindfolded herself of her own free will from the day she had been brought to this palace as a beautiful young bride, denying herself the light of day so as not to enjoy a world that was denied to her lord. Such was her fidelity and such the power of her wrath that she feared to even look at the faces of the Pandavas in case the fire of her anger should burn them, even though a thick scarf was wound over her eyes. However as she turned, her glance from beneath the bandage caught the tip of Yudhistira’s toes and I saw to my horror that his toes turned black. Such was the power of her chastity. Arjuna quickly took refuge behind my Lord who smiled and winked at me.

Her glance passed over all of them and she told them to go and meet their mother Kunti. They were meeting her after fourteen years. She caressed them and ran her fingers over their wounds. Taking Draupadi in her arms she did her best to comfort her. At last all of them followed the king and Gandhari to the battlefield which they insisted on seeing even though neither could actually see. Gandhari turned to Draupadi and said, “My child! I have lost all my sons as you have. Who is to comfort whom? Look at me my daughter and comfort yourself. I have lost hundred to your five. Both of us can mourn for our dead sons. Vidura prophesied this a long time ago and Krishna gave due warning when he came as the ambassador of the Pandavas.” She looked at the battlefield which she could see in her mind's eye. She beheld all the horrific scenes and slowly her gaze turned to my Lord. She looked fearlessly at him, knowing full well that even her direct gaze had no power to harm him. She pointed out the dead forms and the women who were mourning for them. She could see all the scenes in her mind's eye. She could see Uttara weeping over her dead husband, Abhimanyu. They had been married but six months. Her daughters-in-law were all keening and wailing over their husbands. Seeing all this in her mind, her anger which she had been trying to control flared up once again. She realised that all of them were like pieces in a game of Chaturanga (chess). All of them were being manipulated by a master hand. Her piercing look bored through the folds of the scarf which was covering her eyes and she spoke directly to my Lord. "Behold, O lotus-eyed one! Behold the daughters of my house, widowed and bereft with locks unbound and eyes swollen with tears. Can't you hear their piteous laments, brooding over the dead bodies of their heroes? Behold them seeking for the faces of their loved ones on this field. The whole ground is covered with these childless mothers and widowed wives. Where are they now, my splendid sons who were like burning meteors? The battlefield is scattered with their costly gems and golden armour, their splendid ornaments and diadems. Their weapons lie in confusion on the field, never to be dispatched again upon their dreadful errands. Beholding these pitiful images in my mind, O Vaasudeva, my whole body is afire with anguish. I feel as if the elements themselves have been destroyed. Like the darkened coals of a dead fire lie the powerful heroes who took part in this mighty battle. They, who had slept cradled on the soft bosoms of their wives, now sleep on the cold, hard breast of the earth. Jackals alone chant their glory in lieu of bards. The wailing of the women mingles with the howling of the hungry beasts. What was that destiny, O Madhusudana that pursued my sons from the time they were born? Whence came this curse on the house of the Kurus? Why does not my heart break into a thousand fragments at these dreadful happenings? What sin have I and these weeping daughters of mine committed that such a disaster should have befallen us?"

My Lord remained silent as he wanted her to pour out all her woes which would bring some solace to her sorrowing heart.

Suddenly it flashed upon her that the whole battle was like a game in which the two armies had been skillfully manoeuvred until they destroyed each other. She also realised that both the director and the producer of the drama was standing beside her, ready to catch her if she fell. Unable to control her anger and fear, she turned to my Lord and cursed him.

"O Janardana! Two huge armies have perished on this field. Where were you while they put an end to each other's lives? Were you blind like my husband or had you deliberately blindfolded yourself like me? O slayer of Kamsa! I know you could have prevented this had you so wished. Why did you withhold your hand? By the power of my chastity I pronounce a curse on you and your race. Thirty-six years from now, you shall become the slayer of your own kinsmen. Having brought about the destruction of your own sons and relations, you will perish alone in the wilderness as my son Duryodhana did, unaided and helpless beside the lake even though he was the king of the Kurus. The women of your race, deprived of their sons, husbands and friends shall weep and wail in their bereavement as the wives of my sons are wailing today!"

I shuddered and crept close to my Lord's side as she uttered these dreadful curses. He said nothing but pressed me to his side. As her voice died down in sobs, my Vanamali looked tenderly at her and said, "Blessed are you, O Mother for you have aided me in the completion of my task. My people, the Yadavas are incapable of defeat, and therefore they have to die by my own hands. Behold, O Mother, with folded palms I gladly accept your curse!"

Then that Divine Being bent down to the aged queen who had sunk to the ground in sorrow and lifted her up gently, "Arise, O Gandhari!" he said. "Have you forgotten the wrongs inflicted on the virtuous Pandavas by your sons over the years which they bore so patiently? At that time it was you who was indifferent, not I and now you blame me for indifference! The law of *karma,* though inexorable is also just. He who sows the wind has perforce to reap the whirlwind. Your sons brought about their fate by their own actions as did the Pandavas. Every person whether good or bad must inevitably be mown down by Time, the wielder of the scythe. It is the Lord's power as Time that has contrived the end of your sons as well as the sons of the Pandavas. Set not your heart on grief, O Queen! By indulging in sorrow one increases it double-fold. The cow brings forth male offspring for the bearing of burdens, the Brahmin woman bears sons for the practice of austerities, the serving woman adds to the ranks of the workers, but the Kshatriya woman bears sons who are destined to die on the battlefield. Why then do you grieve?"

Gandhari listened in silence to his words. Only too well did she realise the truth of what he spoke. With her inner vision clarified by her great sorrow, she understood the unreality of the world. There was nothing more to be said. She fell at his feet and begged him to pardon her. He raised her up gently and wiped the tears which were streaming down from below her scarf. All of us now followed the women to the banks of the Ganga to perform the last rites for the heroes. The fires over the burning bodies were slowly dying down when we went to the river to take our purifying baths. Vyasa was already there standing knee deep in the water muttering incantations for the departed.

That night I asked my Vanamali, 'My Lord! Is it true what Gandhari said? Is there a Master Plan for all of us and did you manipulate everything?'

"Yes, there is a Master Plan which is entirely dictated by the Law of Karma. As you sow, so you shall reap. Every conscious action of the human being produces a cause which has to end in an effect. The effect is decided by the cause, and the person whose action produced the cause has to bear the consequences of his own action and accept the result, whatever it might be. There is no point in trying to blame another person and trying to reduce the effect of your own actions. As for your second question – no, I did not manipulate anything. I only carried out the orders of that law which is beyond all reprieve. Now are you satisfied?" he asked with a questioning look.

'Then she did you a grievous wrong by cursing you.' I said.

"Actually she did me a favour and that was also according to the *karmic* plan. My clan has to perish at some time or other. They have enjoyed more than most people could have enjoyed and there has to be an end to that also!"

KUNTI

When Kunti saw Karna's wives lamenting over his body, she burst into sobs and spoke her agony aloud. "The same river that had taken my baby so many years ago is now carrying away his ashes. How unjust I have been to you, my beloved son! Will I ever be forgiven for what I did to you?"

I looked at the river. It was flowing on placidly, indifferent to the cares and worries of humankind.

For one full month we stayed in tents by the river banks in order to complete the obsequies for all the dead. Karna had only one son left, Vrishaketu who performed his obsequies along with the Pandavas.

My Lord was always conscious of the needs of his devotees. Sometimes he sent others to help them, sometimes he went himself. He knew the state of Yudhistira's mind. He was inconsolable. Of all of them, he had been the only one who had been able to foresee the miseries caused by a fratricidal war, but he had been unable to stop it and now he felt himself to be a murderer. My all-knowing Lord sent Vyasa and Narada to comfort him.

'Why don't you comfort him yourself?' I asked

"I have to go and comfort Kunti," he said.

'Why don't you send someone else as you sent to Yudhishtira?' I asked.

"No. I have to go myself. She is feeling quite desolate. All her life she listened only to her own heart's dictates. She was far stronger than her husband, Pandu and decided to use the *mantra* given to her by the sage Durvasa when she realised that her beloved husband was incapable of giving her children. She had never told him about her first born and had carried her secret like a fiery torch in her own heart. After the death of her husband, her whole life was wrapped around her five sons. She lived for them, suffered with them, followed them to the palace of lac and then to the forest, all the while nurturing the desire that one day they would get their rightful place in the world. Now at last it appears that this dream had come true but as with all human dreams, it has turned to ashes in her mouth. I know that she is bitterly regretting the injustice she has done to her first born. She sacrificed him twice, once to save her own reputation and once to save her other five sons. And now they are sitting in judgment over her and shunning her. They turn their heads away whenever she appears. I know what she must be going through and must go to comfort her."

She rose up from her seat when he approached and looked at him with grief-stricken eyes. "Salutations to you, O thou divine being! Just as an ignorant person cannot recognise an actor when he is on the stage, so also we have failed to recognise you, who have chosen to mask your divinity under the guise of an ordinary human being. Due to your grace, I have been able to penetrate the mask and perceive your divinity. Salutations to you, O noble one! Just as you released your parents from the tyranny of Kamsa so you have saved me and my sons from countless murderous attempts by the Kauravas. And now you have saved our line from extinction by saving the foetus in Uttara's womb."

My Lord held her as she was going to fall at his feet and said, "Mother, ask for any boon and I shall grant it."

To my amazement Kunti said, "O noble One! I pray to you to give me misfortunes all the time. Let dangers surround me always for it is only when peril threatens us that we are able to feel your divine presence. Our minds become single-pointed only in extreme sorrow and then we are able to call you with intensity. At that time you come running to rescue your devotees from all harm. Therefore I do not pray for comfort. When we are surrounded by ease on all sides, the treacherous mind fails to focus on you, who alone are responsible for both joy and sorrow. Therefore I thank you for having given me a load of sorrow to bear all my life. I thank you for not having given me wealth because of which I have realised that you are my only treasure. You alone are the wealth of those who have no wealth. I care not for kingdom or glory, but only wish to have your blessed vision all my life. I deem you to be the eternal time spirit, endless and irresistible, which makes no distinction between good and evil, small and great. This is what brings about feuds among people leading to their death and destruction. The apparent birth and activities of the unborn and unchanging spirit, the soul of the universe is indeed a mystery. O Lord of Lords! Pray do not abandon us who are totally dependent on you. I have no refuge except your lotus feet. Like the Ganga flowing towards the ocean, let my mind constantly flow towards you for you are the infinite ocean of compassion, the never-ending stream of love and delight. O Krishna! Friend of Arjuna! Protector of the weak and holy! Master of *yoga!* I salute you again and again!"

So saying she fell like a log at my Lord's feet, overpowered with ecstasy at having the vision of this glorious Being who stood before her in flesh and blood. I too fell like a log at his feet for she was only uttering my words, my love and my feelings. My Lord cast his compassionate gaze on her and on me and said, "O Mother! You will always have total and undying devotion to me and I will always protect you under all circumstances as I have always done." So saying he placed his lotus hands on her head and blessed her and helped her to rise.

'Why do you love her so much?' I asked. I suspected that I was always a little jealous of anyone he loved.

"*Bhakti* is something which draws me to people. It is the invisible rope which is capable of tying the Infinite to the finite. My mother, Yashoda was even able to tie me with a grass rope to a mortar! This was because I was already tied to her with the rope of love, so I allowed her to tie me with the rope of hemp."

'Were the *gopis* the same? Did they also tie you with this invisible rope?'

"Their *bhakti* was something beyond worldly pleasures and beyond the liberation of oneness with God. It was an eternal dance, an endless night of love. It was the intoxication of their very soul so that they saw nothing but me, their eternal lover in everything."

'But isn't that the same as *jnana*?'

"It's only a difference of phraseology. Their bliss lay in ignorance and the jnani's bliss in wisdom."

'Which is the better of the two?' I persisted.

"My child, I have told you once that both are the same from the point of view of the goal, but the difference lies in the path. Both reach the goal of union with me, but the *jnani* has to make the climb all by himself. He asks for no help and no help is given. The *bhakta* on the other hand is always asking me to hold her hand and thus I am with her at every step holding her and carrying her if necessary. I give *jnana* easily but I am stingy about giving *bhakti.* Only a few chosen ones can attain the state of the true *bhakta.*"

'But isn't the *bhakta* always troubling you in one way or the other? So why don't you prefer the *jnani*!'

"I have no favourites but let me tell you a secret, the *jnani* who is also *a bhakta* is the greatest of all."

'Why is that?' I queried.

"Because the *jnani* does not love me for any gain he can get from me. He loves me as the universal self which is also present in his own self and thus loves me as his own self. The love of the self is the greatest of all loves. There is no love greater than that and that is why the very thought of death is so abhorrent to the ordinary man who superimposes the divinity of his self onto his body and thus fears the death of the body. The *jnani* however has no such fears since he knows his own Self to be deathless and immortal and also knows that the body is only an appendage which will drop off when the Self decides to leave that body." My Lord looked at me lovingly and asked. "Have you understood?"

I looked yearningly at him and whispered, 'Can I ask one more question?'

He nodded smilingly knowing full well what was going to come.

'Which of these am I?'

"Which do you think you are?" he asked teasingly.

'I want to be a *jnana bhakta*.' I whispered.

"Come!" he said, holding out his hand. "Let us away. We have a lot of work to do."

I knew that it was the end of the discourse and trotted happily after him.

After the month of mourning was over, Yudhishtira reluctantly agreed to hold the coronation at my Lord's insistence. All preparations were made for the coronation. The auspicious date was chosen by Vyasa. In the huge assembly of great *rishis* and kings, my Lord led Yudhishtira to the golden throne of the Kurus. It was a unique moment when the Lord himself placed the jeweled crown on Yudhistira's head.

I remembered the story of the Ramayana. In it Rama (god incarnate) was crowned by Vasishta, a mortal, whereas here it was just the opposite. Yudhishtira, the mortal was being crowned by God incarnate! This was a unique event and never to be repeated in history. All the bards and Brahmins were there chanting the Vedas. Musicians and dancers and artistes of various types flooded the city of Hastinapura which was slowly looking brighter. Draupadi was looking more beautiful than ever and she was crowned along with her husband as Empress. Next Bhima was crowned as *yuvraja* (heir apparent). Arjuna was made foreign minister as well as commander-in-chief of the army. Nakula was made the head of the army and Sahadeva, the king's personal protector. Vidura was made into Yudhistira's personal counsellor and Chief Minister. Sanjaya was in charge of finance and Dhaumya was the high priest. Yuyutsu, the only surviving son of Dritarashtra was made personal assistant to his blind father and Gandhari and manager of the outlying districts.

At last my Lord's great work for Bharatavarsha was being realised. He wanted to make a land in which kings were also spiritual leaders. In fact this was his great contribution to the world - that governance should go hand in hand with spirituality. For this reason the Pandavas were his chosen instruments for they were both rulers as well as followers of the eternal dictates of the cosmic *dharma*.

It was a month-long celebration. At the end of it Yudhishtira approached my Lord and said, "My Lord! You have given me back my kingdom. In your affection for us you have played the role of a human being – you who are worthy of being worshipped as the Supreme Person (Purushottama). You have wept with us and laughed with us and fought with us. You are our guiding star. What can I give you in return to whom we owe our very lives? The only thing I can do is to fall at your feet and wash them with my tears." So saying he fell at my Lord's feet. All the Pandavas followed suit and Krishna hugged them and blessed them in his usual jovial fashion, brushing aside all their praises as nothing.

Aum Namo Bhagavate Vaasudevaaya

The process of offering is Brahman,
What is offered is Brahman,
The fire is nothing but Brahman,
Thus Brahman offers himself into the fire of Brahman,
Thus seeing everything as the action of Brahman,
The person attains Brahman.

Srimad Bhagavat Gita. Chapter 4.

ॐ

Peetavaasase Namaha!

CHAPTER THIRTY-NINE

Devavrata

Despite being advised and comforted by sages and by my Lord, Yudhishtira could not control the great sorrow which overpowered him whenever he thought of the part he had played in this holocaust. He was always looking sorrowful and even made the rest of us feel sad.

"I will leave Kurujangala!" he said. "I will wander through the forests and beg for my food from the trees. I will injure no creature. I shall fear no creature and oppress no one."

I asked my Lord, 'Why is it that he does not realise that everything happens due to the divine will and our own *karma?* Surely he is wise enough to know this?'

My Lord answered, "My child, it is easy to preach but difficult to practice. The thought that I am the doer of my action is so deeply rooted in us that we find it almost impossible to believe that it is the Lord's will to action which prompts us. Do you remember my advice to Arjuna that day on the battlefield? I told him to be an instrument in my hands. The instrument is never held responsible for its actions. The hand that holds it is responsible. If a person acts with this belief, he will never have to suffer for his actions. As long as we think that we are the doers, we have to bear both the pleasant and unpleasant effects of the action. Now

Yudhishtira is sunk in gloom since he thinks he is responsible for bringing about the destruction of his race. What can one do?"

'Can't you comfort him?' I asked.

"I am not the one to do it," he said. "Bhishma is waiting for us. We will go to see him and he will give him a discourse on *dharma.*"

'Ah! He wants to bless Bhishma before he passes and also wants him to get all the credit,' I thought to myself.

Satyaki drove all of us across the devastated field of the Kurus, past the piles of dead animals and skulls and carrion animals too full even to move. We could see the palm tree banner flying ahead as we reached the place where Bhishma was lying. Two horsemen rode up to us. One was from the Pandava army and the other from the Kaurava. Yudhishtira jumped out of the chariot and bowed to them. "Who are you?" they asked.

"I am Yudhishtira, the Pandava king," he said. The horsemen immediately jumped from their horses and bowed to him and allowed us to go. Obviously they had been kept there to guard the old knight. Bhishma was still lying impaled on his bed of arrows. My Lord passed his healing hands over the pain-wracked body of the old knight and immediately he must have felt calm for he opened his eyes and looked straight at my Lord and started to speak in a strong voice.

With great effort he lifted his hands and brought his palms together and said with tears streaming from his eyes, "Your ways are indeed inscrutable. You are God incarnate and you have been the constant companion of the Pandavas and still they have been beset with troubles. You are the storehouse of *dharma* yet you have brought them to me to impart this lesson to them. This is part of your game to bring glory to your devotees."

My Lord said, "What you speak will be like another Veda and will bring undying fame to you so speak on." He gently propelled Yudhishtira in front of the old man's gaze so that he did not have to turn his head to see him.

With tears in his eyes Bhishma said, "My son, strange indeed are the ways of God. Your family has the son of Dharma as its head, is protected by Bhima, the son of the all-powerful Vayu and Arjuna, the greatest archer on earth and above all you have been guided by Lord Krishna, the Supreme Being! Yet you have been stalked by misfortune. None can know the will of that Being. Even the *rishis* have tried their best to fathom the divine mind and have failed. Therefore, O Bharata! Know that all that has happened has been wrought by divine providence alone. Try to understand and follow that will. It is the duty of the king to protect his people who are like unclaimed orphans now. To follow the dictates of *dharma* is to follow the evolutionary path. Therefore do your *swadharma* without coming under the sway of the opposites. Your duty is to act as befitting a king and not sit and lament over what has passed. The Lord alone is the doer and the instigator. Neither the credit nor the discredit is yours. Action done with attachment leads to bondage and the same action done with detachment leads to liberation. Strange it is that you, who have the Lord Narayana himself as your companion, have approached me for advice."

He paused a while and then continued, "The problem is that you have been looking on him as your uncle's son, as your dear friend, as your ally and well-wisher. You have taken advantage of his love for you and have used his services as a messenger, as an ambassador and even as a charioteer. He in turn has played all these various roles, feeling neither elation nor humiliation. In his infinite mercy he has now brought you here for he knows that the time for my departure has come. I pray to you my Lord to stand before me and fix your radiant eyes on me when I leave this mortal plane."

Yudhistira's eyes filled with tears when he heard this. In fact all the Pandavas were weeping when they thought of the infinite love which my Vanamali had poured over them and was still pouring and how ungrateful they had been not to have recognised his greatness. I saw my Lord turning his compassionate gaze on him for he must have known what was passing through his mind.

"This is your opportunity to question the grandsire about all aspects of *dharma,* for you will never get this chance again. I shall give him the strength to answer your questions," said my Lord.

Yudhishtira questioned him and the old man replied without even a tremor in his voice.

"Destiny is no doubt powerful but the one who adheres to truth can never fail. *Satyameva jayati (*Truth alone will triumph). A king should be neither too soft nor too stern. Compassion should be combined with discipline. *Adharma* should not be tolerated under any pretext. It will lead to downfall. Love is the most constructive force and can overcome all obstacles. *Dharma* is our only friend for it follows the body when it has been abandoned by all in death."

Then Yudhishtira asked, "In what form and manner should I worship the Supreme?"

Bhishma smiled and looked at my Lord's resplendent figure standing before him. I'm not sure in what form he gave him *darshana.* It must have been splendid for the aged knight's voice became strong and firm and he said. "The Supreme God, the sole refuge of humankind is standing before me. By meditating on him and chanting his manifold names, one can transcend all sorrow. Surrender your heart and soul to him for his is indeed the Supreme Purushottama."

With these words, Bhishma fixed his failing gaze on the shining form of my Lord and chanted the Vishnu Sahasranama (thousand and one names of Lord Vishnu.) He then lay back exhausted, yet exalted. This seemed to have exhausted him and in a weakening voice he told them to go and return when Uttarayanam (the summer solstice) commenced. Sahadeva looked at the sky and saw that the sun had not yet started its northward journey. So we returned but came back on the very first day of Uttarayanam when the sun started to move towards the north.

My Lord went and stood at Bhishma's feet so that he would have no difficulty in seeing him. Bhishma fixed his gaze on him and said, "You are the Lord of the universe, the Uttama Purusha, the universal soul. Grant me leave to cast off this body and permit me to reach the highest state. Please reveal your cosmic form to me."

None of us were able to see his Viswaroopa so I don't know which he showed, whether it was the one he showed in the Kuru Assembly or the one he showed Arjuna. However it must have pleased the old man very much for he folded his palms and asked for flowers to worship him. With great effort he cast them and by my Lord's magic they fell at his feet,

My Lord spoke, "O Devavrata! I grant you permission to return to your divine abode. You will never be born again in this world of mortals. Death is waiting at your doorstep like a humble servant, and you have my permission to summon him."

Bhishma bowed to him and once more exhorted the Pandavas, "Remember that wherever Vaasudeva, the eternal self dwells, there will be *dharma*. Where *dharma* is, victory will follow."

He then closed his eyes. As he gently willed himself to die, we were able to see how he gathered his vital forces up to the Sahasrara Chakra at the top of his head and then passed out in the form of a great light. All of us watched fascinated at the wonderful glow coming out of his head and spiraling its way to the heavens. A gentle breeze blew and sounds of celestial music filled the air. I felt exalted at being able to witness this wonderful scene. What a difference there was in his death and Drona's, I thought. Nobody cried since we did not feel as if we had participated in a death scene but a glorious return to the divinity from which he had come. My Lord passed his hands over his mutilated body and the arrows dropped off and the scars were gone. He lifted him and laid him gently on the earth. Then the Pandavas wrapped him in a golden cloth and laid him on a pyre made of sandal and aloes. They covered him with garlands and sprinkled sandal wood oil and burnt incense and over this was placed a seven-tiered white umbrella and a palm leaf, a yak tail fan and his white helmet and bow. Vyasa gave a flaming brand into Yudhistira's hand and told him to light the pyre.

The funeral rites were done and his body cremated according to the prescribed rules.

The next day the Pandavas accompanied by my Lord took his ashes to the Ganga. As the ashes were being immersed I noted that the river stopped her flow and I saw the form of a beautiful woman come out of the waters and bow before my Lord. I saw him bless her and she returned comforted and opened her waters wide to receive her marvelous son.

'How old was Bhishma?' I asked my Lord.

"One hundred and thirty-five years. He is the eldest living ancestor of the Pandavas. He has passed through five generations. As you know the Pandavas themselves are grandparents. He has looked after the fortunes of the Kurus from the time he was twenty-one, denying himself all the pleasures of the senses in order to be true to the promise he gave his father. He has worked incessantly for the welfare of the dynasty, uncaring of the problems he faced. It is time for him to return."

Yudhishtira seemed a bit more peaceful after having spoken with Bhishma. We returned to Hastinapura. My Lord was anxious to return to his city of Dwaraka. But the Pandavas begged him to continue for a few more months and help them with the affairs of the state and my Lord agreed and postponed his departure.

Before we left, my Lord went to pay his respects to the blind king and queen.

Dritarashtra asked, "Vaasudeva you are the knower of all things, past, present and future. Tell me, what have I done in my previous birth to have been born blind?"

My Lord answered, "O King! In your previous birth you were a tyrant king. One day while walking on the lakeside you saw a swan surrounded by a hundred cygnets. Just for the fun of it you ordered your men to scoop out the mother bird's eyes and kill the cygnets. You then walked on pleased with your day's deed. Now you can understand the event which led to your blindness and the death of all your hundred sons!"

At last the departure could no longer be postponed. Bidding a fond farewell to the Pandavas, we got into our chariot. Though they had seen their kith and kin slaughtered in front of their eyes, the Pandavas had not felt such a sense of bereavement as when my Lord left. They were all unashamedly weeping. Even in the midst of their many crises, they had thought themselves to be invincible, sheltered as they were by his presence in their midst. Arjuna especially could not bear to be parted from him and accompanied us right to the gates of the city. My Lord had to force him to return since he knew how important he was to Yudhishtira. I turned round in the chariot and watched him. He was standing there with brimming eyes and probably waited till our Garuda flag could no longer be seen. Hundreds of citizens had also followed us to the gate and they also returned filled with sorrow. I could well imagine how they felt. The very thought of being parted from my Lord filled me with terror and I felt a great weight on my chest. He looked at me reassuringly and I pressed close to his side.

When we reached close to the desert we were stopped by an old Brahmin who had been a friend of my Lord's. His name was Uttanga. My Lord jumped out of the chariot and caught his hands and said, "Where have you been all these years? Why is it that you never come and visit me?"

Uttanga was a desert dweller and hardly ever went to the cities. He now asked my Lord, "How are your people? I see that you are coming from Hastinapura. Do tell me of the state of affairs of the Pandavas and the Kauravas."

My Lord replied, "Haven't you heard of the Great War which took place between them? All the Kauravas are dead and Yudhishtira rules in Hastinapura"

"I never leave the periphery of this desert and I know nothing of the happenings of the world. Where were you my friend when all this happened? Surely you could have stopped them?"

"I tried my best to stop the war but the Kauravas had tortured the Pandavas for too long. They refused to give them their share of the kingdom and hence they were forced to fight."

The old man got really angry when he heard this, "I know you could have stopped them had you willed it. Why didn't you do it?"

My Lord said, "In every age I incarnate in the world to uplift the ancient *dharma* (Sanatana Dharma) which decays now and again. Sometimes this can only be accomplished by the destruction of the unrighteous and then I appear in the form of Kaala (Time) which is the only killer. Unrestricted freedom granted to an individual can only lead to downfall as was seen in the case of Duryodhana. I tried my best to bring him to the path of righteousness, but steeped as he was in arrogance he would not listen to me. Thus a battle became inevitable. Calm down my friend and I will show you my form in which you can see exactly what happened before the war which led to it." So saying he showed him another of his Viswaroopas. I realised that each was different from the other.

This seemed to pacify the old man and he begged leave to continue his journey. My Lord said, "You may choose a boon and I will be happy to oblige you."

"I have no desires my Lord, but if you insist you may grant me the boon that I will get water whenever I need it. As you know I live in the desert and sometimes it is very difficult to get water so this boon will be of great help to me."

Krishna smiled and said, "You will never run short of water but remember it may not always come to you in the way you expect it to come!"

So saying we parted and I asked my Lord to tell me the story of Uttanga.

"He has a very interesting story. He is the disciple of the sage called Veda. After he had served his time at the Gurukula he asked his *guru* to tell him what he wanted and he would get it for him as *dakshina.* The *guru* being a sage had no desires but he told him to ask his wife and he would accept that as *guru dakshina.* She told Uttanga that the only thing she wanted was the pair of earrings of the wife of King Pausha. On his way to Pausha he was accosted by a huge man on a bull. When he heard his errand he advised him to eat the bull's faeces. Naturally Uttanga recoiled from this, but the man insisted that without eating this he would never be able to get the earrings. At last the Brahmin complied. When he reached Pausha he told the king the reason for his visit. The king told him to go to the queen who would surely accede to his wishes. She gladly gave him the earrings but told him to be careful of the serpent king, Takshaka who had been eyeing her earrings for a long time and would lose no opportunity to grab them. On his way back, he noticed that he was being followed by a naked mendicant who was actually the serpent Takshaka in disguise. When Uttanga kept the earrings on the ground to perform his ablutions, the mendicant grabbed the earrings and ran off. Uttanga chased him and was just about to catch him when he changed into his original form of a snake and dived into a hole. At that time Indra took pity on him and sent him his weapon, the *vajra* (thunderbolt) which dug a hole so that Uttanga could follow. There he saw two women weaving. One wove with white thread and one with black. The machine had a wheel which had twelve spokes, run by six young men. He was wondering how to get the earrings back when he saw a man on a horse who told him to blow into the horse's anus to bring the snakes out. As soon as he blew, fire came out of all the horse's orifices. Soon the whole place was filled with smoke and Takshaka came out reluctantly and gave the earrings back to him. The guru's wife had only given him four days to get the earrings and return and the time was almost over and Uttanga wondered how he was going to get back. The man on the horse offered his horse and Uttanga was able to reach the hermitage in time and get the blessings of the *guru* and his wife. Naturally Uttanga was quite bewildered by all the strange things that had happened to him and narrated the whole story to his *Guru*. The *guru* told him that the two women were known as Dhata and Vidhata and they were weavers of night and day with their black and white threads. The wheel represented one year and the six young men were the six seasons. The bull he had seen earlier was Airavata, Lord Indra's elephant. The horse itself was Indra and the man riding it was Agni, Lord of fire. The bull dung he had consumed was *amri*t, the nectar of immortality and that was why he hadn't died in the land of the snakes. Indra had helped Uttanga because he was the *guru's* friend."

'This is really a most interesting story,' I said. 'Now what is going to happen to him? I feel sure there is more to his story.'

"You are right," said my Lord. "Just this very moment he is crossing the desert and is desperate for some water. I have asked Indra to go to him in the form of an outcaste and offer him water out of his leather bag. Of course this caste Brahmin will refuse. We will meet him again I assure you and you can hear the rest of the story."

We carried on and then came to the edge of the desert where we met Uttanga again. The angry Brahmin scolded my Lord for having sent him an unclean outcaste to offer him some water. My Lord laughed and said, "My friend! What is the use of being a Brahmin when you are still bound in ignorance? You cannot see that the same Lord resides in the outcaste and in you. That outcaste was actually Indra whom I had persuaded to offer you the nectar of immortality. By your pride of birth you lost the opportunity to be an immortal."

Uttanga realised his mistake and begged the Lord to forgive him.

We returned to Dwaraka but did not stay for too long since once again my Lord said that there was some devotee of his in the famous city of Mithila, the birthplace of Sita, the wife Rama, who was anxious to see him.

"The kings of Videha are famous for their devotion and their wisdom," he said, "and the present king Bahulasva has invited me to come there. Actually I have accepted the invitation in order to bless a poor Brahmin called Srutideva who is something like my friend Kuchela and has no desires and no wants. He gets enough for his upkeep and is totally satisfied with that."

I was reminded of his words to Arjuna on the battlefield that the hallmark of a noble soul is that he should be satisfied with whatever comes unasked, since he is secure in the knowledge that the Lord would look after all his material wants.

We set out accompanied by Uddhava and Satyaki. As we came closer to the city of Mithila, I was thrilled to see that the streets were thronged with the populace who had heard of my Lord's visit. The whole city seemed to be in a festive mood and was gaily festooned with palm fronds and flowers. The king arrived at the gate with a full entourage to invite my Lord to his palace. My Lord agreed and accompanied him. Just then he looked down from his chariot and saw the poor Brahmin running after him. He stopped the chariot and jumped down and hugged the old man much to the amazement of all.

"What can I do for you?" He asked in his mellifluous voice.

"I beg of you to come to my house tomorrow. It is a most auspicious day and time and it is my great good fortune that I was able to see you," said Srutideva.

I felt a bit sad since I had just heard the king Bahulasva inviting him to the palace on the same day and at the same time. It was stupid of me to have doubted even for a minute as to what he would say. "Of course I will come," he replied without a moment's hesitation.

The next day we set out for the palace where we were given a royal welcome as can be imagined. The king himself washed my Master's feet and sprinkled the water on everyone and attended to all his wants. We were entertained and fed in a fabulous way on golden plates. Bahulasva begged my Lord to stay on in their city for some more time and thus bless everyone. My Lord agreed in his usual charming fashion.

The auspicious time was nearly over. 'Don't you want to go to Srutadeva's house?' I enquired, surprised to see that he had chosen affluence to poverty. Of course he knew what was passing through my mind and told me to go and check for myself what was happening at the Brahmin's house. By his magic he wafted me there and I was stunned to see him sitting on a wooden plank in the old Brahmin's house, obviously delighting in the arrangements which had been made for him. I didn't know what to say. I looked around for Uddhava and Satyaki but they were not to be seen. Obviously they fitted into the royal background. Here he had brought only the sages. The mud floor had been swept clean and covered with straw mats and sprinkled with tender shoots and some other auspicious articles. Shrutideva had just finished washing my Lord's feet and was drinking the water with relish and sprinkling a little on the heads of the others. He was so overwhelmed by his presence that he started dancing and singing. He offered the Lord some herbal water in mud bowls and some gooseberries. When water is drunk after eating gooseberries it always tastes sweet. Out of the many bowls that were presented to him, my Lord picked out one which was a little crooked and had not been baked perfectly. Srutideva exclaimed, "O Divinity, clothed in human form! It is fitting that out of all these cups you should have chosen the faulty one. This is how you shower your blessings on frail people like me!"

My eyes filled with tears when I remembered how he had picked me, the hunchback of Mathura to shower his blessings! I realised the extent of my great good fortune as to have been the first to bear his seed! He who could have had the greatest beauties of Aryavrata had chosen me, poor and miserable as I was, to bless for all eternity. My gaze met his and he smiled for of course he knew what was passing through my mind. I seemed to be drowning in his eyes. My head was whirling and my life before I met him on the seashore seemed to have faded away into the distance. My life during his *avatara* was becoming clearer and clearer. Suddenly I remembered the day we had met. I remembered the perfume of sandal mixed with saffron that I was taking to King Kamsa. I came from a family of *devadasis* who were brought up to be dancers in temples. If the priest or any of the Lords who came to the temple fancied us, we had to go with them. My name was Malini and I was hardly twelve years old when I was married to a man called Angaraka, the son of Kamsa's chief royal mahout. My mother used to work in Kamsa's household preparing the perfumes which were needed for the king and his consorts. Soon after marriage I had a serious disease which crippled me and made me into a deformed hunch-back and my husband threw me out of his house. My sisters used to be dancers at the temple, but of course due to my deformity I was never a dancer and thus never exposed to the lust of men. I was happy to be let off from this particular profession, but my sisters used to despise me and tell me tales of the extravagances they were used to having. They were both very beautiful like my mother. I was the only ugly one. I had never seen my face in the polished metal which reflected their faces so I never knew what I looked like. In our house there was never a place for someone who had no work. At last my mother appointed me as her assistant and I helped to prepare the sandal paste to anoint the king and queen. This was something I knew since it meant I had to bend over the grinding stone and grind the block of sandalwood for hours to make the paste. Many wonderful unguents had to be added to this to make it fit for anointing royalty. I was already so bent that I had no difficulty in doing this. On that fateful day which was to change my life forever, I had taken hours to get the preparation correct, not that I cared for the king but because I felt that this was going to be a great day for me. Rumours were rife about the king and the curse he had incurred. People said that his slayer had already arrived in Mathura. His slayer was none other than his nephew, son of his sister, Devaki. Kamsa had put her and her husband Vasudeva in jail as soon as a heavenly voice declared that her eighth son would be his killer! But apparently the child was divine and had been smuggled out of the dungeon by his father and had been brought up in the cow-herd settlement of Gokula. Now it appeared that his nephew, known as Krishna had come to Mathura. Kamsa had prepared many death traps for him and no one knew if he would escape and be able to kill his uncle as prophesied by the heavenly voice at the time of their marriage.

I had heard all this and I longed with all my heart to be able to see this divinity for I knew that he would be divine, but who was I to be able to see such a great person? I hobbled along the dusty road for I was already late with my perfumes and had to reach the palace before the king finished his bath. Suddenly I was stopped by a pair of lotus petal feet with pink-tipped nails which stopped right in front of me and stopped me from taking another step.

"O Sundari! Who are you?" asked the most mellifluous voice I had ever heard.

'People call me Kubja, the hunchback" I answered, 'and I am a maker of sandal paste.' I tried my best to lift my head and see this wonderful being who had called me "Sundari" (beautiful one). Never in all my born days had anyone called me that. I had almost forgotten my original name. I had always been called Kubja, the hunchback. I had three bends in my body not just one, because of which I was also called Trivakra. Whose was this strange voice calling me "Sundari?" Who could it be? I strained and bent backwards in my efforts to look at him and would surely have fallen back had he not caught me. I could feel the pain on my toes as he pressed his feet on mine. I could feel his strong hand cupping my chin. And then I felt him lifting me up higher and higher until I was standing tall and straight up to his chin. I could tilt my head back and look at him. I can't describe the ecstasy which washed over me at that time. Waves of bliss passed over me and I drowned in the deep pool of his eyes which bored into me.

"Let the world see the beauty of your mind in your face, O Sundari," he said. He still had his forefinger under my chin so that I was so close to him that I could see every detail of his youthful face. His upper and lower lips were like twin rainbows, his eyes were like dark mysterious pools in a forest, his nose was straight and slightly curved at the tip and his brows looked like bows from under which he was shooting arrows of compassion at me. I drowned and clutched his upper garment for I felt myself to be falling. To an onlooker it might appear that we were in a close embrace. His voice broke through my haze of delight.

"For whom have you made this sandal paste?" he asked.

'Who else but for you, my Lord,' I stammered.

"Then apply it on me," he commanded and there in broad daylight in the middle of the busy street of Mathura, he allowed me to smooth the paste on his arms and chest. I suppose people on the road and women hanging over the balconies in order to see his advent into their city must have found the scene to be most enticing but I knew nothing but the joy of touching his limbs and adorning them with my paste. At last he said, "I have to go. My brother is frowning at me and the Gopalas are calling me to go and see the sights of this city."

He thanked me for my trouble and turned away. A wave of fear and sorrow overwhelmed me when I thought that I would never see him again. It was not possible. He was my saviour. How could I not see him again? As he turned his *uttareeyam* swung round and I caught it and hung on to it like a drowning man catching hold of a rope. I would not let him go.

"Krishna!" shouted the voice of his brother, I suppose, "What are you doing? Let us go!"

Krishna turned round and looked at me and said in a gentle voice, "Please let me go."

'No never!" I panted, 'I will never let you go until you tell me when I can see you again.'

He smiled his charming smile and said, "I will come to you when I have finished the work I have come to do."

Reluctantly I relinquished my tight hold on his shawl and let him go out of my sight but he was lodged forever in my heart. He had called me beautiful! He had called me beautiful! My heart sang this song over and over again.

I was dragged back to the present by Srutideva who prostrated before my Lord and begged him to bless him.

My Lord replied, "Fall at the feet of the sages for they are my very self. Those who worship my idols in temples and disregard the sages are guilty of a great crime. They have come here now to bless you. Bow to them therefore and offer your worship to them."

I was always struck aback by his humility and how he always strove to place his devotees before himself. I had observed so many such incidents like this when he would push his devotees forward so that they would get the praise.

On the way back I questioned him about the different aspects of riches and poverty. 'My Lord, I have heard it said that it is easier for a poor man to get liberation than a rich man. Is this true?'

"I have just showed you the personalities of two such men – one a king and the other a pauper. I have also showed you that I do not discriminate between them. It is true that it is easier for a poor man to approach me because he has no one to turn to except God - no gold hidden away in chests to depend upon. Hence he is constantly calling on me. But look at the king, Bahulasva. He thinks that he is only a custodian of the wealth given to him by the grace of God. He spends a good portion of his wealth in helping the poor and needy and attending to the wants of the sages. Thus both poor and rich have equal chances of reaching me. I place the highest value only on the heart which should be humble and devoted."

I knew this only too well. Once again I was wafted to Mathura where I waited impatiently for his coming. 'Would he come? Would he forget his promise? Was I chasing a dream which had no chance of coming true?' I was beset by doubts which came into my fickle mind but deep inside I knew that he would never break his promise. I knew that the love he gave me was totally unconditional and did not depend on what I had to offer him. In any case what did I have to offer? My bruised heart and body, both of which he had made whole. Whom else could I offer both but to the one who had made them complete?

I was not allowed to live with my mother and sisters in the grand house they kept for suitors who fell for their charms after seeing them dance in the temple and came to visit them. They came in chariots, carrying rich presents and flowers. I would have been an inauspicious sight for them, so I had been given a small hut at the bottom of the garden where I cooked my own food and went about my own business which was to make sandal paste and unguents for the royal household.

I went out to find out the latest news and was told that my Lord had strung the mighty bow of Shiva which no one could even lift and had broken it. He had killed the elephant that had been kept to kill him and he was now proceeding to the arena where the mightiest and meanest of the court wrestlers were waiting to wrestle with him and kill him at the earliest opportunity. I was in a panic and rushed to the arena which was thronging with people eager to see this match. The amphitheatre was adorned with wreaths and garlands. Trumpets and drums heralded the arrival of the king, Kamsa. With trembling heart and a bold front he sat on the golden throne of the Bhojas surrounded by his ministers and sycophants. He was clutching and de-clutching the sword hanging by his side and wore a worried look on his face. The *gopalas* from Gokula who had accompanied Krishna were seated in the places reserved for them. The wrestlers were already there, looking like gigantic mountains with bulging muscles and cruel faces and moustaches which they kept twirling. They kept slapping their arms and thighs and making loud noises and grunting like wild animals. They had secret orders to show no mercy and to dispatch the boys to the abode of Yama (God of Death) at the earliest opportunity.

Just then my Lord and his brother came in. He was just the opposite of the wrestlers. Young and slim with a charming face and delicate features, he was looking so beautiful that I could not take my eyes off him. In fact he was the cynosure of all eyes. The brothers were each armed with a tusk of the elephant they had killed at the entrance. In my eyes he was the very incarnation of Manmatha, the god of love and I think all women must have felt the same. In and through the human mask which he always wore I could see the divinity shining through him and flowing towards all people including the wrestlers and Kamsa who must have seen him as the emissary of death!

The mighty wrestler Chanoora approached them and scornfully said, "O sons of Nanda! You are famous as heroic young men who are experts in wrestling. Are you ready to wrestle with us?"

Krishna replied, "We are poor nomadic forest dwellers who have only engaged ourselves in bouts with our friends who are comparable to us in strength and age. We have never wrestled with experts like you."

"You have just killed the mighty elephant, Kuvalayapeeda and can in no way be counted as mere boys. You may show your prowess against me and Balarama can challenge Mushtika."

With these words he led them to the centre of the arena opposite the king's throne so that he could get a good view. I was totally charmed by the way in which my Lord threw himself into this unequal fight with the same enthusiasm which he brought into everything he did. I did not think I could watch this unequal fight. Many of the spectators got up and left the arena since they said that it would be a sin even to witness such an *adharmic* fight. I wanted to leave but was unable to tear myself away from his divine presence. I just kept my eyes closed and muttered *mantras* for his protection. When I opened my eyes I saw the slender boy lifting the mountainous Chanoora and whirling him round and round and dashing him to the ground. Mushtika was felled by Balarama with a careless blow of his left hand. The rest of the wrestlers fled in terror.

By now Kamsa was in a panic and giving the most absurd orders to his body guards, "Catch him, kill him etc." My Lord slipped through their grasp and jumped onto the platform where Kamsa stood shouting orders. There was a hush as uncle and nephew faced each other. All of us were well aware of the prophecy and waited with bated breath for the grand finale. Though shaken to the core, Kamsa ran forward brandishing his sword to kill the defenceless boy. Krishna laughed and caught hold of the tuft of hair on his head from which the crown had fallen off and threw him on to the dust and dirt of the arena. There lay the mighty king of the Yadavas, terror of the Bhojas and Andhakas. My Lord jumped down lightly from the dais on to his chest. At the touch of his feet, Kamsa's soul which had been thirsting for release rose up in a shining spiral of light and melted into the aura surrounding my Lord! I couldn't believe it. Pandemonium broke loose but I didn't wait to see anything else and ran back to my hut waiting for him to keep his promise. Every day I would wash myself and keep aside some sandal paste for him and apply a little on my own body. I would trim my little earthen lamp and keep it ready for lighting and still he hadn't come. My sisters mocked at me and said, "How foolish you are to think that such a great personage will come to you! You'd better learn to dance and come with us to the temple. Who knows, someone might fancy you. Now that you no longer have a hump, you look quite pretty."

The very thought was abhorrent to me. My body was a temple into which I had invited my Lord to come. Only he could dwell in it. No one else. I knew he would come and waited, keeping my lighted lamp at the window so that he would have no difficulty in finding the place. And one night.... my whole frame shuddered when I thought of that night. I heard a knock at my door and when I opened it there he was - the most beautiful person in the whole world. He came in and shut the door behind him and I ran into his arms which were thrown open to receive me. I felt no sense of shame or modesty as he took off my clothes. Shame comes only with duality. When only unity exists, where is the place for shame? He was my very self, my heart beat in tune with his, my limbs twined and melted into his, my face was cradled close to his, my eyes were drowning in the twin pools of his eyes, my lips were melting into his, the perfume of the sandal penetrated into my nostrils as he penetrated into my body which had been kept only for him and which would never again know the touch of any human being. Was this ecstasy? I did not know. Was this the meaning of Samadhi? If Samadhi means the loss of one's ordinary consciousness and the merging into a super-consciousness then surely I was in a state of Samadhi for I knew nothing, felt nothing and was in a state of bliss of the highest order. I did not even know when he left me. It must have been in the wee hours of the morning. When I came out of my Samadhi, for indeed I had been in Samadhi, I was alone but not alone. I would never be alone again. He was always with me. For the next few days I walked about in a state of super-consciousness, hardly aware of my surroundings, doing my daily chores by force of habit, not able to respond to the talk of the others who moved in and out of my life like clouds in the sky. Slowly, slowly I came back to normal consciousness and I knew that I was carrying his seed in me. The whole of those ten months I walked like a zombie bathed in a sea of bliss, uncaring of what my sisters and mother said to me and what people talked about me. My whole heart and mind were fixed on him alone and in some miraculous fashion I found that all my needs were totally cared for. I always had enough to eat and clothes to wear. For myself I cared not but I did care for the precious burden I was carrying. Every day and every minute was both agony and ecstasy – agony of not knowing whether I would ever see him and ecstasy of knowing that I was carrying him in my womb and then the miracle when I discovered that there were two of him, not just one......I was jolted out of my reverie when the chariot came to a stop in Dwaraka. He looked at me and smiled. Now I recognised that smile. It was reserved for me alone. I had seen it in all my births.

Aum Namo Bhagavate Vaasudevaaya

ॐ

Gopalaaya Namaha!

CHAPTER FORTY

Parikshit

My Lord was unable to stay for long in Dwaraka. It seemed as if the life of the Pandavas was inextricably bound with his. He had been their saviour throughout their storm-tossed lives and it looked as if they were always looking for a loophole to ask him to return to Hastinapura. The loophole was provided by Vyasa. Apparently he advised Yudhishtira to perform the Ashwamedha Yaga and of course couriers were immediately posted to Dwaraka begging my Lord to come. Krishna laughed when the news was brought by the messenger urging him to come to Hastinapura as soon as possible. He looked at me as if asking my opinion!! Of course I knew he was teasing me.

"In any case my presence is urgently needed in Hastinapura," said my Lord.

'Why?' I glanced at him.

"Uttara's confinement is approaching and I have to be there to save the baby."

'How is it that it was not killed when Aswatthama sent the Brahmasiras *astra* with the dreadful curse?' I asked.

"Yes," he looked at me and smiled. "You have guessed right. I was guarding it."

'Can you not guard it now without going there?'

"Sometimes I have to be there in person," was his enigmatic reply.

On our way I pestered him as usual with more questions. 'What is an Ashwamedha Yaga? What are the things that have to be done for it?'

"The king has to let loose the sacrificial horse to wander all over the countryside followed by his army. If anyone stops the horse, the army will fight to prove the superiority of their master. The royal horse has already been released and Arjuna is following it with his army. He has conquered almost all the lands to the north of Kurujangala – Trigarta, Pragjyotisha and Sindhu. Karna's only remaining son Vrishaketu, has been sort of adopted by Arjuna and is with him. Vrishaketu looks on Arjuna as his own father and adores him. Arjuna also sees his own son Abhimanyu in him so it's a perfect relationship and would have made Karna very happy."

'Please tell me what they are doing,' I begged my Lord.

"All right. They are approaching Manaloorapura. Their king Babruvahana is Arjuna's son by the princess Chitrangada. You remember he had a lot of affairs during his period of wandering alone."

'Wasn't that the time when he came to Dwaraka and fell in love with Subhadra?' I asked.

My Lord smiled and nodded his head. 'Does Babruvahana know that he is Arjuna's son?'

"Yes indeed he does. He did not tie up the horse and wage war with him, but bowed politely to him and invited him to stay there. For some reason this did not please Arjuna, 'Had I come unarmed, your conduct would have been correct but now that I have come prepared for war it is your duty as a Kshatriya to fight with me!' said Arjuna."

My Lord continued, "At this time Ulupi, princess of the Nagas, who is another of Arjuna's wives, approached Babruvahana and exhorted him to fight with his father. Arjuna was pleased at his son's dexterity but Babruvahana aimed an arrow straight at Arjuna's heart which made him faint. Vrishaketu rushed to his help. Babruvahana also fainted when he saw what he had done. His mother, Chitrangada now hurried to the scene and blamed Ulupi for all that had happened. Babruvahana came out of his stupor and became very sad to see his mother sitting beside his father and weeping. Ulupi, being a Naga princess, knows many mystical arts and she gave a stone to Babruvahana and told him to place it on Arjuna's heart. The stone is very potent and Arjuna slowly revived. He felt a bit ashamed of having fainted from his son's arrow but Ulupi comforted him and said, 'You have now atoned for the sin of having killed Bhishma. Otherwise you would have had to face a greater misfortune.'"

'Then what happened?' I asked breathlessly.

"Well Arjuna is now proceeding with Vrishaketu to Hastinapura where he is acclaimed with joy by Yudhishtira. The other brothers have gone to the Himalayas to collect more wealth."

By the time we reached Hastinapura, Arjuna had returned after his triumphant journey behind the sacrificial horse. The other brothers also returned with lots of wealth so everything was ready for the Yaga.

Just as we reached the city, Subhadra ran to my Lord and said, "O Brother! Uttara is in labour. I'm frightened for her. She has been in pain ever since that wretched Aswatthama sent his missile against her, but somehow the foetus seems to have been protected but now the time for delivery has come. I am so happy to see you for I fear something dreadful is going to happen."

Without even waiting to greet Yudhishtira, my Lord rushed to the labour room. It was filled with all sorts of talismans to ward off evil spirits and black magic. There were bright weapons kept at special places, mustard seeds scattered everywhere and flickering fires in urns which gave off certain odours meant to keep off spirits. Potentiated water was kept in jars at special points. Old women who were really midwives were there as well as doctors. Poor Uttara was writhing with pain and moaning. "Vaasudeva! Help me! Help me!"

I knew that my Lord had been preserving the foetus intact through these six months from the time that Aswatthama had discharged the dreaded Brahmasiras. But now it appeared that the infant did not have the strength to cope with the agonising pain of birth and seemed to be still-born. There was a wail of distress from all the women. My Lord took the tiny baby in his lotus palms and kept him there for some time. I felt a tremendous current passing from him to the baby and suddenly to everyone's surprise the baby cried out loud and long. Draupadi ran to give the good news to Yudhishtira. I was standing next to my Lord and saw the infant look long at my Lord's radiant face so close to his own. I know that normal newborn babies don't open their eyes and stare like this, but it seemed as if the infant recognised the face which had been guarding him for six months in the womb.

The whole town went mad with joy. This infant was the only one left to carry on the line of their king. I looked at my Lord and asked, 'It appears that the Yadava line is going to rule Hastinapura!'

"How do you make that out?" he asked as if he knew nothing.

'Well, Kunti's father was a Yadava so Arjuna has Yadava blood in him and he is Abhimanyu's father so Abhimanyu has Yadava blood in him and Parikshit is Abbhimanyu's son!!'

"How clever of you to figure that out!" he said teasingly.

Yudhishtira proclaimed a month long festival. The child was named Parikshit (one who is always searching) since from the time he was born he was always searching for the Supreme Lord in all beings, whom he had been constantly seeing during his months in the uterine womb. He was also called Vishnurata (one who is protected by the Lord). Dhoumya their Guru wrote his horoscope and predicted that he would be ever devoted to *dharma*, to Krishna and to religious principles. He would always adhere to truth and would be a wise monarch like Rama. He would be an exemplary warrior like his grandfather Arjuna and would bring fame and glory to his family.

The Ashwamedha was a double festival. Not only was it a *Yaga* but it was also a celebration of the birth of the last of the line of the Pandavas. The king ploughed the land chosen by Bhima with a golden furrow.

Learned Brahmins and kings from all over Aryavrata came for the occasion. Charity was given lavishly. Gold-hoofed cows with calves were gifted to worthy Brahmins. Gold and pearls were piled into earthen jars and guests could dip their hands in it and take what they wanted. Along the roads Yudhishtira set up rest houses to give food and water to travellers. Bhima was in charge of food and he had made mounds of cooked foods and sweets and grains with rivers of wine and lakes of milk and pools of water. No one had heard of such bounty before and surely none would ever hear such things again.

At the end of it at the insistence of the Pandavas we stayed on until Parikshit began to crawl. The moment he started to crawl he made his way to whatever part of the palace my Lord was sitting in and looked adoringly at him. The child recognised the face which had been so familiar to him during the last six months of pregnancy. My Lord would lift him up and place him on his lap and whisper many things to him which even though I strained to hear, I couldn't follow. Over the baby's head, my Lord's eyes brimming with suppressed laughter looked at me! I pouted and pretended to be annoyed.

'Tell me more about this child,' I said.

"As you know he is the last in the Pandava lineage and he will be one of their best rulers – wise and noble and respected by everyone."

'How long will he reign?' I asked.

"Sixty years," he answered. "In fact the Pandava line will rule for another hundred and twenty-four generations, that is a period of four thousand, one hundred and fifty-seven years nine months and fourteen days to be exact."

'Who will come after that?' I enquired.

"Mlecchas will come after that and *dharma* will go down once again and I will have to take on another incarnation."

'So your plan to put *dharma* back on the throne has succeeded.' I said.

"Did you doubt it?" he asked laughingly.

'But why should this ancient *dharma* perish now and again and have to be revived?'

"There is a rise and fall in everything. What goes up has to come down. The waves rise ever so high and then come crashing down. So also with this Sanatana Dharma. I will keep sending *vibhutis* (special manifestations like the sages) all the time, but a time will come when even they will not be able to cope with the *adharma* and then I will appear in another form."

'Will I be there and will I be able to recognise you?' I asked holding my breath.

"You will always be there and you will always be able to recognise me. Anyway you have nothing to fear for even if you don't recognise me, I will know you and take you under my wing."

I snuggled up closer to him in gratitude.

"Now we have to return to Dwaraka," he said and reluctantly the Pandavas allowed him to depart. Arjuna could never bear to be parted from his beloved friend for long and he arrived in Dwaraka soon after. I think my Lord noticed that Partha was feeling rather proud of himself and his abilities. He also was proud of the fact that my Lord loved him most and that he was the greatest of all *bhaktas*! Krishna knew that it was time that he brought down his friend's ego a little.

"Come let's go and visit a friend of mine," he told Arjuna.

Arjuna was always ready for a ride, so we set off in the morning on horseback to the *ashrama* of his devotee, Mayurasanma. The latter was overwhelmed by the fact that the Lord had condescended to come to his humble abode and invited him to partake of his simple meal. My Lord agreed but said, "I want only one dish. Are you prepared to give it?"

"Everything I have is yours, my Lord. You have only to ask."

"I want a dish made of the right half of your son's body. But remember that neither you nor your wife or son should shed a tear!"

Without blinking an eyelid the Brahmin slaughtered his only son. Unfortunately a tear dropped from the left eye of the dying boy.

I was of course a witness to this gory scene and didn't know what to say.

Seeing the tear my Lord said in mock anger, "Now that the boy is crying I don't want any part of him."

The boy immediately said, "Only my left eye is shedding tears because it feels sad that you have discarded the left side and have asked only for the right!"

Krishna looked at Arjuna to see whether he recognised the pinnacle of *bhakti* which was ready to sacrifice anything for the sake of the divine beloved. Arjuna did not say a word and hung his head. Of course before we left my Lord touched the poor mangled remains of the boy and brought him to life. The couple bowed to him. They were truly *sthitha prajnas* (enlightened beings). They were neither drowned in sorrow at the death of their son nor filled with elation when he was brought back to life. In fact they knew that my Lord was testing them and they were truly happy to be able to pass the test with flying colours.

On another occasion the friends disguised themselves as ordinary wayfarers and went roaming about near the edge of the desert. Suddenly we were struck by the strange sight of a Brahmin sharpening his huge knife on a stone and muttering imprecations under his breath. We went closer and Arjuna asked, "Why are you, a Brahmin resorting to violence?"

The old man replied, "There is no sin in killing for the sake of the Lord. I have been wanting to kill four people who have tormented my Lord in all sorts of ways. I keep this knife always sharpened so that I will not be lacking in a weapon if I happen to meet any of them!"

"Who might they be?" questioned Arjuna.

"The first is the *asura* boy, Prahlada who forced my Lord to take form of a lion in order to kill Hiranyakashipu, the second is the sage Narada who never gives a moment's peace to my Lord by constantly repeating the *mantra* 'Narayana'! The third is that wretch Sudama,

(Kuchela) who forced my Lord to wash his filthy feet and to eat his unclean rice flakes."

"And who may be the last?" asked my Lord with a lilt in his voice.

"The last is Arjuna, the middle Pandava who forced my Lord to drive his chariot!!"

"This is a most creditable desire," said my Lord, "but how are you going to accomplish your task? Prahlada died long ago, Narada is never to be found in one place for long but I suppose you could manage to trace Sudama to his house and as for Arjuna I passed him a while ago. If you hurry you might just manage to catch him and slit his throat!" He turned and looked roguishly at his friend. Arjuna covered his head very firmly with the dirty shawl they were both wearing in order to hide their identities. He was in a great hurry to get away even though my mischievous Lord urged him to stay a while!!

We returned to Dwaraka with a chastened Arjuna but even then my Vanamali felt that he had not completely lost his ego and had certainly forgotten the discourse given by him on the battlefield.

Once when the two of them were sitting on the balcony of the palace, a Brahmin came and placed the corpse of his dead child in front of my Lord and said, "How is it that in a place ruled by you and Balarama, both incarnations of Vishnu, such terrible things happen? This is my ninth child and all of them were born lifeless. I have heard that you revived the still-born grandson of your friend here so how is it that you cannot revive my child!"

My Lord pretended to be very sad and told the Brahmin, "I'm helpless against the dictates of *karma.*"

Muttering imprecations the Brahmin returned home. Arjuna could not believe this and questioned his friend as soon as the Brahmin left. "Why can't you do something about this? Why are you remaining silent?"

My Vanamali said solemnly, "My dear Partha! What can I do? That Brahmin is not fated to have any children. It is his *karma* and that of his sons. There is nothing that I can do about it."

I could see that Arjuna was not at all happy with this glib explanation. Soon after, I saw him stealthily going to visit the Brahmin's house. Of course my Lord knew everything and when I looked enquiringly at him, he said, "All right. You have my permission to go and see what's happening."

Nothing loathe, I ran after Partha and found that he had made a bee-line for the Brahmin's house. He found the couple in a state of deep distress.

"What is the problem?" he asked.

"You heard what I told Vaasudeva. Nine sons have died at childbirth and now my wife is expecting her tenth and we are both terrified that it will also die. For some reason Lord Krishna seems to be quite indifferent to my sorrow." The wife was sitting and softly weeping to herself. She looked as if she was full-term pregnant.

Thinking himself to be the hero of the Mahabharata war, and forgetting totally to whom he owed his victory, Arjuna drew himself to his full height and said proudly, "O noble One! Never fear when I am here. Don't you know me? I'm Partha the son of Pandu. There is none to beat me in archery. I am quite sure I can save your last child for you."

The Brahmin was not impressed by Arjuna's claims to be an expert in midwifery, but he was ready to clutch at any straw and said, "I will let you know as soon as she goes into labour."

The day before the woman was due, Arjuna was creeping out armed with his bow and arrows when suddenly my Lord accosted him. "Ah Arjuna! Where are you sneaking off to at this time of the morning?"

Arjuna stammered a bit and said, "I thought I would go for a walk."

"Going for a walk carrying your Gandiva?" exclaimed my Vanamali, "are you expecting to be attacked by wild animals in the city of Dwaraka?"

Arjuna had no proper answer to this one and muttered, "I may go hunting after that, so don't expect me to return for lunch!!"

"My dear friend! I hope you will not get into any problem. You know that you have only to ask me if you want help and I'll come rushing to you."

Arjuna nodded and didn't answer. My Lord winked at me and signalled that I should follow him. I was very happy and ran after him. He went straight to the Brahmin's house and was updated with the latest bulletin. He made a cage of arrows outside the house and made the wife who was already in labour, sit inside this cage. He sat at the entrance so that no one could go in or out without his knowledge.

He was patrolling the cage with great vigilance. Very soon there was a big cry and the Brahmin came rushing out shouting at the top of his voice. "Vile wretch! What have you done with my child? Nine times this has happened but at least I was able to see the corpse of the baby but now thanks to your meddling even the body has vanished!" He ranted and raved in this fashion for a while. Arjuna became pale and as soon as he could get a word in he swore to the Brahmin that he would get his son back. "Please don't panic and please don't shout. I swear on my honour that I will get your child back alive. If not I shall immolate myself in the fire!!"

The Brahmin was not one to mince his words. His temper was always precariously balanced and this was the last straw. Pointing scornfully at the woodshed, he continued, "There lies the woodshed. Help yourself to what you need. At least let me have the satisfaction of seeing you roast alive. I should never have listened to your bragging. What can you do when the Lord himself said he could do nothing?"

Arjuna had gone so pale I was afraid he might faint. "Give me a little time," he begged. "I'll search the whole world. If your baby is anywhere in all the three worlds, I'll surely discover him and bring him back to you!"

The Brahmin gave him a sceptical look and reluctantly allowed him to go for a period of three days. I was surprised that even at this juncture Arjuna stubbornly refused to ask my Lord for help.

I returned to my Lord and gave him the news which he knew in any case.

'Now what's he going to do?' I asked.

"Come we will go to the Brahmin's abode and see what's happening," my Lord said with a wink.

When we reached there we saw that the Brahmin had thoughtfully arranged the firewood in a pyre to make it easier for Arjuna to light it and jump in. Obviously he had no faith in his self-given praise and oath to bring back his child. Of course my Lord was invisible to his eyes so we could see everything without being seen.

'Where has Arjuna gone?' I asked.

"He has appealed to Shiva to help him and has gone to Yama's abode as well as Indra's heaven and will soon return empty handed."

Sure enough Arjuna returned looking very crestfallen. Without a word to the Brahmin he prepared himself to jump. For once the Brahmin was looking rather pleased and kept another piece of wood on the pile and kindly lighted the fire which soon started to blaze. Arjuna went back three steps in order to give an impetus to jump. As he took the third step my Lord who was standing just behind him became visible and held him firmly in his loving arms. Even at this moment Arjuna never thought of invoking his dearest friend and tried to shake him off. But it is a fact that even if the devotee forgets to call him, the Lord never fails to go to the devotee's aid.

"Leave me, I'm determined to end my life!" he said.

"What temper!" my Lord said, turning the distraught Arjuna around. "Why couldn't you have approached me? Don't you know that there is nothing I wouldn't do for you? You are my friend and devotee. You are in me, and I in you. How can I desert you? Even if you forget me, I can never forget you. Come with me and I'll show you something." So saying he left the gaping Brahmin who was mad at being deprived of his prey and took off in his chariot, driven by Garuda. It rose into the air and it appeared as if we passed many different types of worlds and eventually reached Vaikunta, the abode of Vishnu. It was breathtakingly beautiful. There was an expanse of billowing white waves which I guessed must be milk since Vishnu is supposed to be sleeping on the milky ocean. Above was a brilliant blue sky. He seemed to be sleeping on some sort of carved wooden bed which on closer inspection proved to be the wound up coils of the great snake, Adishesha who represents Time. Vishnu, the sustainer of the universe was sleeping on a bed of Time. The snake's eyes gleamed ruby red above Vishnu's head, shedding a rosy glow over the Lord's face. Lying on this strange bed, we saw the Supreme Lord Mahavishnu, blue as the infinite, wearing yellow garments like my Lord and was adorned with all his normal ornaments. His face was indescribable. I could hardly look at it for long. It was incredibly beautiful with eyes over-flowing with compassion. He had the *Sreevatsa* mark on his chest like my Vanamali and wore the huge ruby pendent known as Kaustubha and of course he had the inevitable *vanamala* round his neck. But this *vanamala* was made of celestial flowers and was luminous. The flowers glowed and retreated and then glowed again in rhythm with our heart beats. He was surrounded by the sages, his attendants and his accoutrements which had assumed forms.

My Lord made obeisance to him as part of his celestial drama and Arjuna prostrated with great excitement. The Supreme One spoke in a voice which I heard within my heart and not as an external sound. "I brought the sons of the Brahmin here so that I could meet you both at the same time. As you know, you are both the incarnations of the great sages, Nara and Narayana who are my own selves."

He turned to Arjuna and pointed to the children who were happily playing around him.

"Your time in heaven is over," he told them, "and now you must return to your earthly parents who are anxiously awaiting you."

"We don't want to go," they said altogether, but the Holy One made them close their eyes for a moment so that they forgot where they were and came back with us to the earthly plane. When we returned, we found that the Brahmin and his wife were sadly sitting on the front step of their house and crying bitterly over their lost babes. They couldn't believe their eyes when they saw ten sons in lieu of the one which Arjuna had promised them. They ranged in years from ten to the newly born who was being carried by the eldest. The Brahmin fell at my Lord's feet and begged his pardon for having doubted him. Arjuna followed suit and begged for his forgiveness. He realised I think, as I did, that all the enterprises of a human being which we believe to have been achieved by our own efforts are really the operation of the Lord's grace.

My Lord smiled tenderly at him and said, "Remember, O friend! That we are both linked together as the Supreme Lord has just said. The moment a person surrenders to me I will set his steps in the right direction. In fact my dear I am prepared to carry him safely through the jungle of this earthly existence as a mother cat carries her kittens!"

On hearing these wonderful words of my Lord, I too fell at his feet and kissed them with my tears. I knew that he had been carrying me through the turbulent waves of my life and had sheltered me with his love all the time.

We returned to Dwaraka where Arjuna spent a while with all the friends he loved so much and then returned reluctantly to Hastinapura.

Aum Namo Bhagavate Vaasudevaaya

How can I describe his relentless flute,
Which drags virtuous women from their homes,
Drags them by their hair to Shyam. (Krishna).
As thirst and hunger pulls the deer to the snare.
Chaste ladies forget their lords.
Wise men forget their wisdom.
Clinging vines shake loose from their trees,
Then how shall a simple dairy maid withstand its call?
Kaala (Time), the puppet master,
Leads the dance.

Poems by Chandidas.

ॐ

Sarvapaalakaaya Namaha!

CHAPTER FORTY-ONE

Vidura

The years seemed to pass so quickly. I hardly knew the passage of time sheltered as I was in my divine Vanamali's shade. I never knew the heat of summer or the cold of winter. I was always basking in the mild warmth of his love. Fifteen years had passed since the Great War and my Lord said, "We have to go to Hastinapura."

Yudhistira's rule was an exemplary one and peace reigned in the whole of Aryavrata. However peace did not reign in the heart of the old king Dritarashtra and his wife. I think my Lord knew this and that is why he decided to make a trip to Hastinapura. We heard that the Elders had decided to retire to the forest. Vidura told my Lord that Dritarashtra had heard Bhima boasting of his prowess in having killed all the hundred Kauravas and this made him feel really miserable. He also remembered his role in the carnage and that he could have stopped it if he had so wanted. Vidura urged him to give up the comfort of the palace and take to the forest. My Lord gave his consent. Of course Gandhari, Kunti, Sanjaya and Vidura decided to accompany him. Vidura said, "A Kshatriya should die on the battlefield or in the forest as a recluse."

Yudhishtira was desperate when he heard this. He feared that Dritarashtra's decision was due to some negligence on his part. The old man assured him that this was not the case. When he heard that his mother was also going to accompany them, his sorrow was doubled. He begged her to reconsider her decision but she was adamant. Her parting words to the brothers were, "Take care of Sahadeva, my youngest. Never swerve from *dharma.* As for me, I have to go with the old king and queen. It is my duty to look after them till they die. This is the only compensation I can make to them for my sons having killed their sons."

What a wonderful woman she was, I thought to myself. Obviously my Lord thought the same and he blessed all of them. Before they set out for the forest, Dritarashtra asked Vidura to ask Yudhishtira for money from the treasury to distribute to the poor in memory of Bhishma, Drona and his hundred sons. Even though Bhima opposed this, Yudhishtira opened his treasury to his beloved uncle and told him to take as much as he wanted. Dritarashtra then distributed the money and apologised to the citizens and asked them to forgive him for all his follies.

Accompanied by Gandhari, Kunti, Vidura, Sanjaya and a host of Brahmins, Dritarashtra reached the banks of the Bhagirathi River. Vidura told him that they should go to the hermitage of Shatayapu where they would be instructed on the type of routine which should be followed by an ascetic.

Time flowed and a year later we returned to Hastinapura and my Lord found that Yudhishtira was getting desperate to see the Elders again. So we decided to go and check on their whereabouts. When we reached the Kamyaka forest where the Pandavas had spent a great part of their exile, we found that the recluses were living in small wattle huts. They had none of the comforts of the palace. Yudhishtira urged them again and again to return to Hastinapura but all of them were adamant that they would not go back. Vidura was not to be seen so Yudhishtira asked, "Where is my uncle?"

Dritarashtra answered, "My son, Vidura is performing *ghora tapasya* (terrible austerities). He has given up all food and lives only on air. He goes about naked looking like a lunatic but he is filled with an inner fire. Some Brahmins say that they saw him in a most emaciated state roaming round a desolate place, deep in the forest."

Just as he said this, in the distance there suddenly appeared a naked *yogi* with matted locks, and limbs smeared with mud and pollen. As soon as he saw everyone, the *yogi* disappeared back into the forest. Yudhishtira ran after him and cried out, "Please stop. I must see you."

My Lord and I followed him without anyone noticing us.

At last we saw him and could hardly recognise him. He was so emaciated that he had only the external form of a human being. Yudhishtira went and stood before him and said, "O Uncle! It's I, Yudhishtira, your favourite nephew."

Vidura was leaning on a tree for support. He fixed his unblinking gaze on him and then I saw a strange thing. Limb by limb he seemed to be merging into Yudhistira's body. Using the power of his austerities he allowed his life breath and senses to merge with Yudhistira's. The light had totally passed out of him and entered Yudhishtira. I saw the King hold himself up high as if he felt some strange strength pass into him and his face took on the aspect of an enlightened being. He stretched out his arms and caught Vidura's body as it fell from the trunk of the tree which was supporting him.

He carried the body which was as light as a bunch of twigs back to the *ashrama* and placed it before Dritarashtra. Dritarashtra broke down and wept when he envisioned the skeleton of his dear brother. He realised how much he had always depended on Vidura's advice. He was much younger than he and he had gone first.

Yudhishtira wanted to cremate the body but my Lord said, "His subtle body and powers have already entered into you. As for him, he has attained the eternal world of no return due to his great austerities. What you carried is only a shell. Therefore, O King! You should not grieve. Leave the shell of his body where you found it and let it return to the elements from which it came."

But Yudhishtira looked back on all the wonderful things that Vidura had done for him. He had been more to him than his own father or Dritarashtra. He had saved him and his brothers from death many times. My Lord comforted the remaining three and Yudhishtira again urged them to return with him to the city but they refused.

The sage Narada came to them and told Dritarashtra, "The gods are pleased with your severe austerities. You have three more years left after which you will leave this world along with Gandhari."

Sadly the Pandavas returned to Hastinapura. My Lord and I returned to Dwaraka. Three years later, Narada came to us and gave us the news of the Elders. He had gone first to Hastinapura to give the news to Yudhishtira before he came to us.

Narada said, "After Vidura passed, both Dritarashtra and Gandhari undertook severe penance. Kunti looked upon them as her own parents and cared for them while they did *tapas.* One day Dritarashtra decided to go to the source of the Ganga along with the others. He was carrying the pot containing fire for *yajnas* and while walking, the pot overturned and started a huge conflagration in the forest. Sanjaya tried to persuade him to go to a safer place but he refused and allowed his body to be consumed by the fire. Gandhari and Kunti followed suit and all were scorched by the flames. Sanjaya alone did not stay but went to the Himalayas to continue his *tapasya.*"

"What did Yudhishtira say?" asked my Lord.

"The King was stricken with grief. He proceeded to do all the obsequies for the departed souls in the River Ganga."

Strumming his lute Narada proceeded on his way to the heavenly regions.

After he left I asked my Lord to tell me the story of Vidura's life. I knew only little bits of his story and wished to hear it all.

'What is the reason for such a strong bond between Yudhishtira and Vidura which appears much stronger than the bond he had with the other Pandavas?'

My Vanamali with his usual patience told me his story. "You know that Yudhishtira is said to be the son of Dharma Raja, the Lord of Death and Righteousness. Well, Vidura is also an incarnation of the same deity. Let me take you back to the time of Vidura's birth. Vichitravirya was Bhishma's nephew. As you might have heard, Bhishma went to the *swayamvara* held in Kasi and brought back all three princesses - Amba, Ambika and Ambalika as brides for his nephew. Amba had already given her heart to Shalya and refused to marry anyone else, but the other sisters married him. However Vichitravirya died before he had any children and his mother Satyavati feared that there would be no successor to the throne of the Kurus. The custom in those days was that if a king died childless, a holy man could beget progeny on his wife. So Satyavati invited Vyasa to bless Ambika and Ambalika. Vyasa was a sage and his appearance was not one to excite passion in any woman so apparently Ambika shut her eyes when he approached her and that is why her son Dritarashtra was born blind. Ambalika turned pale with fright when she saw the fearsome form of the sage and her son, Pandu had a pale and strange look. When Vyasa informed Satyavati about these happenings, she begged him to approach Ambika once again and give her a perfect child. However Ambika was too frightened to go to the sage for a second time and sent her maid Parishrami to Vyasa. The maid was most honoured to be asked to bear the son of such an eminent sage so she went to him with all humility and worshipped him and begged him to give her a worthy son. Vyasa realised that this was all the play of the divine for he knew that she would be the mother of a great soul. He blessed her and Vidura was the fruit of their union. He is said to be a partial incarnation of the Lord of righteousness and has all the qualities of that Lord."

'How did he become a partial incarnation of Dharma Raja?' I asked.

"For that I will have to tell you the story of his previous birth. Once there was a great sage called Mandavya. He was sitting on the banks of the river in deep Samadhi when some robbers who were being chased by soldiers of the king's army came that way. They threw their loot at his feet and escaped. When the soldiers saw the jewels they suspected the sage to be the thief and brought him before the king who ordered him to be impaled on a stake. This is a very painful type of punishment and was common in those times. A long stake is thrust through the anus of the person and made to go out through the neck. When the sage came out of his Samadhi he found himself impaled on the stake. Just then the soldiers caught the real thieves and brought the news to the king who was abjectly sorry for what he had done to the sage. He fell at his feet and begged him to forgive him for his unpardonable offense. The sage however was not angry with the king. Due to his great austerities he was able to talk with Yama, the Lord of death and demanded to know what crime he had committed in order to be given such a terrible penalty. Yama told him that in his childhood his favourite pastime was to impale dragonflies on sticks and watch them flutter and die. That was why he had to experience this terrible punishment. Mandavya *rishi* now declared that he had done such a thing when he was not old enough to differentiate between right and wrong and the punishment was far in excess of the crime. Therefore he cursed Yama that he would be born as a Shudra and bear up with all the insults which would be hurled at him. Thus Yama Dharma Raja was born as Vidura."

My Lord continued, "Vidura was brought up and educated by Bhishma along with his half- brothers, Dritarashtra and Pandu. However since neither of his parents were of royal blood, he was not eligible for kingship even though he was far more qualified for it than either of his brothers. Instead he was made prime minister to the kings, Pandu and Dritarashtra. When Pandu went to the forest, Vidura took over the reins of government for all practical purposes since Dritarashtra was not capable of it. He married a girl from my community, called Sulabha.

"At the time when Draupadi was insulted in the open court, Vidura was the only one who protested vehemently against it. He was viciously rebuked by Duryodhana who called him an ungrateful wretch. When the war was decided upon, again Vidura was the only one who had the courage to protest and as a sign of his disapproval he resigned his post as the king's Prime Minister and broke his famous bow in front of the Assembly. He left the palace and took up his residence in a small hut outside the gates of the city. Unlike Bhishma, Drona, Kripa and Karna, Vidura did not have any obligation to Duryodhana. He chose to side with the Pandavas and uphold *dharma*.

"When I came to Hastinapura as the ambassador of the Pandavas, Duryodhana offered me a palace and a banquet which as you know I declined and went and stayed with Vidura and his wife in his hut, much to Duryodhana's disgust. I knew that Duryodhana's intentions were dishonourable and that Vidura's invitation was made out of pure love.

"I loved him very much. He was indeed Dharma Raja, the Lord of Truth and righteousness. He was the epitome of wisdom, always steadfast in upholding *dharma* and always impartial in his judgements. His advice to Dritarashtra on statecraft which was noted down by Sanjaya will become the basis for all issues pertaining to good governance in future. I can truthfully say that he was the embodiment of the inner consciousness of this great land of Aryavrata.

"As you perhaps know, when Yudhishtira became king he appointed Vidura as the prime minister with complete control over the government. However due to his age and his disgust with the way things had got out of control in the war, he did not have the heart to govern. Moreover he knew that unless he urged him, his elder brother would stay on in the palace addicted as he was to an easy life. He persuaded him to leave his life in the Palace and accompany him to the forest. Gandhari and Kunti followed him. He was the first of the royal ascetics to die."

'My Lord, why is it that the naked ascetic is considered superior to the clothed ones?'

Krishna answered, "Clothes, my dear are necessary only for the person who is steeped in body consciousness. One who thinks he is the body alone can never go without clothes. They are a necessary part of his body. Therefore the ascetic who discards his clothes and goes about naked is one who no longer thinks of himself as the body. He knows that this body is not his essential part and therefore there is no need for him to spend time adorning it. This is the reason I stole the *gopis'* clothes when they were bathing in the Kalindi and made them come out naked one by one with their hands above their heads. I wanted to take them above the attachment to the body. Moreover I wanted them to realise that shame is something which comes only when there is 'another'. When one is by oneself there is no shame. I wanted them to accept the fact that I was not 'another'. I was their real Self and thus they did not have to feel shame in front of me. These are the many ways in which I raised them to the level of the *avadhutas* or the naked *yogis,* like Vidura became at the end."

Aum Namo Bhagavate Vaasudevaaya

Ajaaya Namaha!

CHAPTER FORTY-TWO

Yadava

Thirty five years had passed since the end of the Kurukshetra War. I did not even realise it till one day my Vanamali said, "This era is coming to a close. The time stipulated by Gandhari for the destruction of the Yadavas was thirty-six years."

'What will happen now?' I cried clutching his arm.

"Wait and see," was all he said.

'Surely you can do something to avert whatever it is that is going to happen?'

"Perhaps I don't want to avert it as I didn't want to avert the battle of Kurukshetra!"

'Why? Why? Why?' I cried in despair.

"My child everything in this world that has come into being at a certain time and place has to come to an end at another time and place. I've told you this before. Therefore the wise will always try to discover that entity which is beyond time and space and hang on to it."

'Like I hang on to you?'

"If you are hanging on to my body, then you will be disappointed but if you have discovered my true identity which is beyond time and space and which is eternal, then you will not be disappointed."

'I'm attached to both,' I said looking expectantly at him as if hoping a miracle would occur and he would say that he would live forever.

He just looked at me with great compassion and my eyes overflowed for I felt that our parting was imminent. How many years had I been living with him? I had no idea. He had not aged. He looked as fresh and young as when I met him on the seashore so very long ago. Had I aged? I did not know. I saw no reflection when I tried to look at myself in the highly polished brass mirrors which hung in every room. Who was I? I had no idea.

"You are Vanamali," he said. "A devotee grows into the likeness of her Lord. After some years of pure, unadulterated devotion all the differences which existed between them is wiped out. Only the surface personality looks different. Inside they are the same. Are you satisfied?" Of course he knew what was passing through my mind and had answered my question without being asked.

"Come with me," he said. "Let us go for a walk through the town."

Arm in arm we set out. The city was peaceful and prosperous. Everywhere there were signs of affluence and along with this affluence came a decline in morals. This could be seen not only in the citizens but also in his children. As usual he never gave advice without being asked.

His parents had seen his divine form at birth but as is usual with the human mind, familiarity breeds contempt and increasing intimacy had made them forget that glorious vision. But now when they were reaching the end of their lives they remembered the advice of the sages at Syamanta-panchaka and approached him for advice.

"Considering this perishable body as the self, I have been thinking of you, the Supreme Self as my son alone. Human birth with all the faculties of the mind intact is very difficult to get. Having got it I have wasted it without thinking about its real purpose which is to seek union with you, the Supreme Self. You have bound this whole world with the cord of attachment. At your very birth you had declared to me the reason for your incarnation, yet bound as I am to this body I had forgotten that message. Pray instruct me how I can get rid of the ego and my feelings of being the doer which is what blocks the path to liberation. My son, you have given liberation to so many, will you not tell me, your father how best I can attain it?"

My Lord bowed to his father and said, "Sire! You and I and everything moving and unmoving should be regarded as a manifestation of the Divine, not just me, your son. There is nothing wrong in thinking 'this is mine'. The problem comes when you limit this outlook to your family alone. Now you are able to see the divinity in me alone – your son. Expand your vision so that it embraces the whole world. Look upon all men and women as your sons and daughters and thus recognise the divinity in them also. I am Visvatma – the soul of all. Therefore you should consider the whole world as your own and every creature in it as myself. The entire universe is only an extension of your own self. The spark of divinity that glows at the core of your being blazes in the heart of all creation. Do not limit your ego to the narrow confines of your own body and family but let it expand to embrace the whole creation. Therein lies your path to liberation."

How simple was his message and so suited to the personality of his father. I always marvelled at the way he gave advice. Each one was given that which suited their particular temperament.

The next person to approach him was his mother Devaki. "Krishna! My beloved son! I know you to be that Supreme Being who for some mysterious purpose of his own has taken birth in my womb. Though I have been glorified by that contact, I am still weak and cannot get over my maternal instincts. I long to be able to have a glimpse of my six sons who were born before your advent. I have heard it said that you brought back your Guru's son from the dead. Will you not accede to my request and show me my other sons who were murdered by my brother Kamsa?"

My Vanamali smiled his assent and immediately it seemed to Devaki that her six children were dancing about before her eyes. She picked them up and satisfied the unfulfilled longing of her heart to nurse them. Deluded by the illusory power of the Lord's Maya, she seated them in her lap and embraced and kissed them. They in turn prostrated to her and to my Lord and vanished to the divine spheres. Devaki was filled with wonder at these strange happenings and asked my Lord, "O Son! I know you to be a master *yogi*. Tell me did you conjure up these infants by magic? Were they real or were they only an illusion?"

Krishna laughed and said, "Mother the whole world is only an illusion. It has no permanence. Everything we experience with the five senses is transitory. Some things last for a few seconds, some for a few hours, some for a few years and others for a few centuries. But they all have to come to an end, sometime or other. Everything is subject to change – birth, growth, decay and death. These are the inherent qualities of all things. The only true, everlasting and immutable entity is God himself. So put not your desire on these ephemeral things like husband, house and children which can at best yield only a passing joy, but place it at the lotus feet of him who is full of unending bliss and who is the only true reality. Surrender to him wholeheartedly and he will guide you to the life eternal. Attach yourself to him and he will take you to the shore of infinite bliss."

So seldom had I heard him give advice to anyone but when he did, it was always so simple yet so pertinent. I considered myself truly fortunate at having got so much from him during these glorious years that I had spent at his side.

I was sad to see that none of his sons or grandsons thought of approaching him and as I knew only too well, my Lord never thrust his advice on those who were not receptive.

I asked him about this. 'Don't you think you have a duty to your sons? Should you not advise them to mend their ways?'

"I have already fulfilled my duty to them when they were small. Now they are adults and it would be wrong on my part to force my opinions on them. If they want to listen I'm always here for them, but I will not thrust my ideas on them. Knowledge is not to be bartered in the market place or shouted from the roof tops. One who seeks wisdom should approach a teacher in all humility and only then will he be able to benefit from it."

Thus he never thrust unwanted advice on his sons, neither did he criticize them or try to dissuade them from their chosen path. It was ever his way to be the witness, detached and uncritical, unless called upon to exert his will.

Thirty-six years had passed since the battle and people had almost forgotten it. This was the time stipulated by Gandhari for her curse to be fulfilled. I trembled whenever I thought of it and tried to put it out of my mind, but it was like a sword of Damocles hanging over my head as it was hanging over the heads of all the Yadavas.

I asked my Lord in a vain attempt to avert the events which had been prophesied, 'My Lord, Aryavrata has been at peace for thirty-five years. Yudhishtira has proved to be a just and wise ruler and has brought peace and contentment to all. The wicked rulers have been wiped out and no one will dare to challenge the might of the Kuru dynasty. Why should Gandhari's curse come to pass?'

My Vanamali looked tenderly at me, "My child, you are right. No one will dare to challenge the might of the Kuru dynasty, but you have forgotten the Yadavas. They can and will challenge it. Our country stretches from Mathura on the Yamuna to Dwaraka on the western coast. We are invincible warriors and none will dare attack us. However the citizens have become habituated to a life of luxury. They enjoy every type of prosperity and luxury. As you know our cities are fantastic. Our mode of living is unimaginably luxurious, our men are healthy and strong, our women beautiful and attractive. What more can we want? But it's always the perfect rose that is eaten by the worm and affluence is like a canker taking its toll. The principles of physical fitness and spiritual brilliance that characterised my generation has given way to moral and physical decadence. My sons are no exception to this and I will certainly not show any leniency to them just because they happen to be my sons. The Yadavas cannot be checked by any other power and soon they will become a curse to this country. Before that happens, I will have to put an end to their existence. Hence Gandhari's curse is a blessing in disguise."

'What will you do?' I asked tremulously.

"Wait and see," was his answer.

There was a place of pilgrimage known as Pindaraka and all the Yadava youths went there to have some fun. Unknown to his sons, my Lord and I followed them. At that time some great sages like Kanva, Vishvamitra and Narada happened to come. The boys nudged each other and decided to have some fun at the expense of the sages. They had totally forgotten their father's advice to be respectful to sages. They dressed my Lord's son, Samba as a pregnant woman and approached the sages in mock humility and said, "O sages of unerring insight, here is a young and beautiful woman who is expecting to be a mother soon. She is anxious to know the sex of the child and is too bashful to question you directly and wants us to do so. Perhaps with your great powers you could satisfy her curiosity."

I squirmed inwardly at the sarcastic tone of voice in which all this was said. How could they ever talk like this to such great saints, I wondered and looked at my Lord. His face was impassive. In fact we were behind a pillar of the temple and though we could see them, they could not see us.

The holy ones turned a scornful gaze at them and pronounced a dire curse. "O fools! It will be neither a girl nor a boy but an iron pestle which will cause the destruction of your entire clan!" With this decree they passed on their way to the city.

The boys burst into loud guffaws at this seemingly impossible pronouncement of these foolish greybeards but their mirth was short-lived. Hardly had the sages left than Samba started writhing in mortal agony and very soon an iron pestle came out of his stomach. My Lord did not stay to see any more and we left for the city. The boys were terrified and ran back to the city and confessed everything to King Ugrasena and gave him the pestle. I think they were frightened to approach their father. The king was in a panic when he heard this and even at that point I wondered why neither the king nor the boys ever thought of asking for my Lord's help. Ugrasena consulted Satyaki and Kritavarma and they decided to give the pestle to a blacksmith to be ground to fine dust. However one small bit defied all attempts to pulverise it. The iron filings and the bit were thrown into the sea. My Lord watched all this with unconcern.

'What will happen to the filings?' I asked.

"They are being carried to the farther shore of Prabhasa where they will grow into a kind of grass called *erakka*, which will be strong and sharp like swords."

'What about the small bit of iron which could not be filed?' I asked somehow sensing that this was going to have a great impact on us.

"It will be eaten by a fish which will be caught by a fisherman. He will take the piece of iron from its stomach and give it to a hunter's son called Jara."

Nobody said a word of any of these doings to my Lord but of course he knew everything and did nothing to counteract the evil effects of the curse. I knew him to be the spirit of all consuming Time, which mows down all creatures. I knew that all these things came to pass with his full approval.

Rumours of all these strange happenings and of the curse of the *rishis* began to circulate amongst the people and a nameless terror held them in thrall. I could see the fear in their eyes as I wandered around the city. At the moment when their pride was at its height, a shadow seemed to be looming over them. Ugrasena knew that they had no external enemies that might prove a danger to them. Their enemies were all within them. The king took strong measures and forbade the sale of intoxicating liquor within the city.

One night I witnessed the strange spectacle of many gods approaching my Lord and extolling him. Brahma said, "O gracious Lord, you have achieved the purpose of your incarnation and have established the rule of *dharma* in this land. One hundred and twenty-five years have elapsed since you incarnated yourself in the line of the Yadus. It is now time for you to return to your transcendental abode."

My Lord gave his gracious consent and the gods disappeared as suddenly as they had arrived.

Aum Namo Bhagavate Vaasudevaaya

At the end of all pujas, the devotee who offers himself to me enters into me.

Bhagavata Mahapurana

This is part of the advice given to Uddhava and has to be said at the end of a puja.

ॐ

Mathuranaathaaya Namaha!

CHAPTER FORTY-THREE

Uddhava

One day when we were both in a pensive mood and sitting in the garden, Uddhava came rushing up and flung himself at my Lord's feet. He had gone on a pilgrimage to some far-off place and got to know all the news only when he returned.

"O Master! I'm filled with dread for I have heard of the curse of the *rishis* and I fear you are planning to leave this mortal plane after bringing about the destruction of your own clan. Had you wished you could have warded off the curse, but the fact that you kept silent makes me believe that it is your wish. O Master Yogi! By taking an incarnation in this clan you have purified us and the earth on which your holy feet have trod. O Master! My friend! My Lord! I cannot think of a life without you. I cannot remain on this earth even for a second without seeing your beloved form. Even those who have only heard of you cannot envisage a return to their mundane life. How then can I, who have been serving you for the whole of my life, bear to be parted from you? We have eaten together, slept together, walked and talked and played together. I have always worn your cast-off clothes and garlands and adorned myself with the remains of the sandal paste which you had used and eaten the remnants of your food. Thus I have lived in your shadow O Master for over a hundred years. How can I bear to be parted from you? O Lord of Lords!

Friend of the friendless! Don't leave me behind. Take me with you when you go to your divine abode."

I looked at my Lord with adoration and then at Uddhava in gratitude for he had simply taken the words out of my mouth and told him whatever I wished to tell him. He looked at me with compassion over-flowing from his lotus eyes and then turned to Uddhava and smiled tenderly at him for he was very dear to him, having known him from the time he came to Mathura from Gokula. He gently lifted him up from the ground where he had thrown himself like a log at his feet and said, "O my dear friend! Your guess is correct and I am indeed going to leave this world since my work here is over, but for you there is still much to be done. You shall be the bearer of my last message to the world. Having surrendered your ego at my feet from the time you met me, your life has always been easy, my friend. I have carried you through the tempestuous storms of this earthly existence. But now you will have to be the bearer of a message meant for all posterity which I will give you. Come let us sit comfortably and I will give you my blessings."

Uddhava and I now settled ourselves at the feet of my Lord and listened to his glorious discourse. I had heard his discourse to Arjuna and though some parts were similar, in some ways this was totally different. To Arjuna, the man of action, his advice was to fight regardless of whether the result was success or defeat. To Uddhava, the man of contemplation, his advice was to renounce the world and go to the Himalayas and meditate.

"Go, O Uddhava! Abandon all attachments to your relations and surrender yourself to me. Know that this world as it is understood by the mind and senses, is but a passing show. It is transitory. The perception of multiplicity is only a trick of the senses to bind the immortal *atman* to the mortal world. So train your mind to accept all dualities with equanimity. One who recognises the world to be nothing but the Supreme Lord is filled with joy and sees no differences and thus meets with no opposition. Such a person neither avoids the bad due to compulsion nor promotes the good because it is advantageous. His responses are spontaneous and unmotivated, like those of a child. Ever established in the truth of the Self he roams about freely, seeing the Lord as the sole essence of this passing show of the world."

Uddhava replied with all humility, "O Lord! This state of equanimity is indeed difficult for people like me to achieve. Pray instruct me for you are the Supreme Teacher."

I thanked Uddhava again for he was echoing my sentiments exactly.

"My Friend! Everyone is endowed with the capacity to investigate the nature of truth and lift themselves from this mire of confusion. They don't need a teacher for this. The faculty called the intellect (*buddhi*) has been given for this purpose. The world is filled with illustrations pointing out the nature of the Spirit. I will tell you a story about this. Once, our ancestor King Yadu happened to see a naked *yogi* lying on the sands of the river, in a state of bliss, oblivious of everything. The king approached him and asked him with all humility. 'O Holy one! Pray tell me what it is that fills you with joy even though you possess none of the objects of enjoyment?'

"The sage was none other than the great *yogi,* Dattatreya and he replied. 'Hear from me, O King of my twenty-four *gurus* from whom I have learnt everything.

'My first *guru* is the earth itself from which I learned patience and non-retaliation. From the element of air which is not affected by the different odours that pass through it, I concluded that the sage could remain unpolluted by the good and bad effects of contacts with sense objects. The sky remains unaffected by the clouds that pass over it and this made me realise that the *atman* is unaffected by the disabilities of the body it inhabits. The sage should be pure and sweet like water. Like fire he should be unpolluted by anything, and have the ability to purify everything that comes in contact with it. The moon appears to be waxing and waning but it's only an appearance and not a reality, so also the changes of the body do not affect the *atman.* The sun is one but it can be reflected in all bodies of water, big and small so also is the one spirit reflected in all things.'

"The sage continued, 'once during my wanderings I came upon a family of doves and realised that intense attachment to the family will end in death for oneself. The father dove saw his wife and children caught and struggling in the fowler's net and wilfully threw himself into the net and the whole family perished together. The sage should be like the ocean whose boundaries are unaffected by the amount of water which comes into it. Sense objects are there to attract us but if we fall a prey to them we will perish like the moth in the flame which beguiles it. The honeybee taught me a double lesson. It takes only a drop of nectar from one flower at one time so also the mendicant sage should only accept a small amount of food from each house. It also taught me the dangers of hoarding for the bee will perish when the hive is burnt by the one who collects the honey. The python taught me not to be attached to the sense of taste. It eats everything that enters its mouth. The elephant taught me the dangers of the sense of touch. It is enticed into the pit by the touch of the she-elephant. The weak point of the deer however is its sense of hearing. It is trapped by the hunter who imitates the call of its mate. The fish of course perishes due to its attachment to the sense of taste so the sage should be abstemious in his eating habits. Animals have only one weak sense organ, but all the five sense organs are extra sharp in the human being and all strive to bring us down so we should be on guard on all fronts. My observation of the antics of an osprey taught me that one should never covet something which is attractive to others. Once it found a piece of meat and flew off with it but was followed and attacked by all the other carrion birds. The moment it dropped the piece of meat, the others stopped chasing it. Children playing on the beach taught me that the sage who is ever immersed in the bliss of the *atman* should be free from all worries.

'I learned dispassion from the famous courtesan Pingala. She was hanging over the gate of her house waiting for a good client, but the evening wore on and still no one came to her door. At last she was tired of waiting for men and realised that desire is the source of all sorrows and only the one without desire will know the meaning of true joy. She went into her house and started contemplating on God who is the only true source of joy. Another time as I walked along, I noticed a maiden who was pounding corn. She wore a number of bangles on her wrists which made tinkling noises when she pounded. In the front room some people had come with a proposal of marriage for her. She must have thought that if the people heard the sound of her bangles they would realise that her family was very poor and had no servants to do the work and the daughter of the house had to do all the work. This would be a blot on the name of her family, so one by one she removed her bangles so that eventually only one was left and then she could pound away without being afraid of the noise she was making. From this I learnt that a sage should always walk alone if he did not want to be caught up in unnecessary matters.

'My next teacher was an arrow-smith who had such concentration on sharpening the tip of an arrow that he actually did not even notice the royal procession which was passing along the road beside his shop. I was most impressed by him and decided to concentrate my mind fully on whatever I was doing. My second lesson on concentration was from the wasp which lays its eggs and closes the hole and stays outside and concentrates on the eggs until they hatch out. Thus I realised that whatever object a person concentrates upon, whether out of love, fear or hate, he will attain the state of that object.

'Observation of a snake which always lived in holes prepared by other creatures, made me understand that a sage is far better off not to have an abode of his own, to which he will become attached, but to make use of whatever accommodation is made available for him wherever he wanders. The spider taught me that the Supreme Being creates, manifests and withdraws the universe from himself and into himself just as the spider does with its web. Finally my own body has been my best teacher for I learnt both dispassion and discrimination from it. Looking at other people dying and being cremated or being eaten by dogs and vultures, I learnt never to be attached to this body, which has been given for a specific purpose which is to strive for the attainment of the ultimate good.'

"With these words the sage went on his way totally fearless and totally detached."

Unlike most doctrines that stress the importance of a life of *sannyasa*, my Lord always extolled the way of action. Everyone should follow their *swadharma* was his advice regardless of whether it was lowly or exalted.

"The *jiva's* entanglement with the world arises from its identification with its body which is only a product of the *gunas* of Prakriti. Only the knowledge of its real nature will put an end to this false identification. Until then the *jiva* will continue to be terrorised by the Lord's power as Time."

Uddhava asked, "How can the *atman* be bound and free at the same time?"

My Lord replied, "Bondage and liberation apply only to the body and mind equipment which are products of the *gunas.* They do not apply to the *atman*. The *jiva* and the *atman* are like two birds sitting on the same tree. One pecks at the fruits, enjoying the sweet ones and discarding the sour and bitter ones, continuously swayed by its likes and dislikes. It is bound by its strong desire for the objects of the senses and the fruits of its actions. It equates itself with the body and has to suffer the pangs and pleasures of it. The other bird, the *atman* sits on the same tree and thrives, even though it eats nothing. The enlightened sage has a body but is free from the domination of its urges. He is only a witness of the cavorting of his body and mind."

"My Lord!" asked Uddhava, "What are the signs of a true devotee?"

"One who is kind, forbearing, truthful, who is vigilant and courageous, calm and helpful to all is a true *sadhu* as well as a true devotee. Above all, the devotee is one who concentrates his entire energies on worshipping me. He may not be learned or have any knowledge of my infinity but he feels that I am his only support. Such a person is the greatest of all devotees. The *gopalas* and *gopis* of Vrindavana were like this. They lost awareness of their relations and even of their bodies and thus attained me through the force of their single-pointed love. As rivers lose their individuality when their waters mingle with the ocean, so the inhabitants of Vraja lost their sense of separateness and attained union with me. Therefore, O Uddhava! Abandon all reliance on the injunctions and prohibitions given by the scriptures and surrender your entire being - body, mind and intellect to me, the All-comprehensive Being. You shall attain liberation by that alone. My true devotees long for nothing, O Uddhava! Not for power, wealth, *siddhis*, or even liberation. Their only desire is to attain me. Such people are dearer to me that my own self. I personally follow the footsteps of such people to ensure that they come to no harm. The dust of their feet is capable of purifying all the worlds! Just as a flaming fire reduces even faecal matter to ashes, so devotion to me has the ability to destroy every type of sin. Neither intelligence nor power nor Vedic study nor austerity has the power to attract me as much as intense *bhakti.*"

"How can one attain this exalted state, O Madhava?"

"The mind of a person which always dwells on some sense object becomes attached to it so the mind of one who constantly thinks of me will dissolve in me. Therefore think of me at all times, even when you are engaged in work that is mundane, like the lover whose mind is always with his beloved. This is the supreme secret and the easiest path to attain me. I'm letting you into this secret because you are supremely dear to me."

The greatest teaching of my Lord to the world through Uddhava is the Bhagavata Dharma which is the doctrine of absolute surrender.

"Tell me the difference between *jnana* and *bhakti,*" said Uddhava.

"*Jnana* is that knowledge which sees the one Supreme Consciousness alone, in all creatures from Brahma, the creator, to the smallest of his creations. When a person recognises that permanent substance in the midst of all changing modes, he can be called a *jnani.* I have already told you about *bhakti* but I will make it clearer. The senses, O Uddhava have been given in order to worship the divine in all things. The hands are to be used to offer worship to me in the form of service to all creatures, the eyes to discover my beauty in creation, the nose to smell my perfume everywhere, the ears to hear the sanctifying accounts of my glories and the tongue to taste the divinity in all food and to extol me through speech, song and hymn. The whole of creation provides both the method and the means for my glorification, leading to self-fulfillment. By constantly practicing such disciplines a person can reach the state of complete self-surrender and unmotivated devotion."

"My Lord! Please tell me the true meaning of the different virtues like charity, truth, valour and so on."

My Lord replied, "Uddhava, the highest charity is to refrain from thinking ill of others and to refrain from harming them. Truth is to see God in everything. Valour lies in the control of one's own mind and lower nature and not in killing enemies. The greatest profit is the attainment of devotion and not mere wealth. Beauty comes through desirelessness and austerity and not the mere decoration of the body. Hell is not a region but the dominance of the *guna* called *tamas.* The greatest relation is the Guru and he is none other than God. The wealthy person is the one who is rich in virtue and the pauper is the greedy one who is never satisfied with what he has. The house is the human body and its master is the one who is free from attachment to it. The slave is the opposite. But remember Uddhava that virtue lies in transcending these opposites. What we call good and bad can apply only in certain situations, dictated by time and place. What is right in one context can be wrong in another. Not to care for the home and family is wrong for the householder but right for the *sannyasi.* An act which is a sin for an evolved person need not be so for one who is ignorant of the rules. The one who is already on the ground cannot fall any further but the higher you are, the greater the fall. Thus we see that those who are already evolved have a greater responsibility and need to set an example to others.

"The tree of life is ever being chopped down by that master chopper – Time. Before it is completely felled, those with wisdom will take their seat at my feet which is firm and unshakeable. Attach yourself to me therefore and I shall take you across to the farther shore."

Uddhava then asked, "Master please tell me about the phenomenon called death. What is it that transmigrates from body to body? I know that the *atman* can never die and the body will certainly disintegrate and return to the elements from which it has come, so what is it that takes another body?"

My Lord replied, "Death is the complete forgetfulness of the old body and birth is the complete identification with the new body. I will tell you how that happens. The mind along with the five senses and the *vasanas* (tendencies) derived from our *karmas*, constitute what is known as the *linga sarira* or causal body. This is what transmigrates from body to body. The dying man is always obsessed by those thoughts that have attracted him most in this life. This last thought is what will propel him into a new body in order to fulfill his unfulfilled desires. Thus he enters into a new body by the very intensity of his thoughts. With the emergence of the new body there is complete oblivion of the old one and its history. This is similar to the experience of the dreamer who is completely oblivious of the waking body and gets identified with the dream alone. Time subjects the bodies of all creatures to the aging process. The *atman* is only the witness of these changes which happen between birth and death but it is not subject to these changes. The *atman* is the knower of the body and its transformations but is not a partner to them. One who does not know this identifies himself with the changes of the body and is swept into the cycle of births and deaths.

"The mind alone is the sole cause of turning this mighty wheel of *samsara*. The one who conquers it is the true hero. The *atman* is the sole reality and the appearance of 'another' is merely a figment of the mind's imagination. People blame the planets for their misfortunes but how can the planets affect the *atman*? Only the body can be affected by the planets. The *atman* is beyond all dualities. With whom then can one be angry or afraid? Does one knock out one's teeth because they happen to bite one's tongue? It is only the one who has not awakened to this truth that lives in fear of others."

"How should I act, Lord, without getting involved in the wheel of Karma?"

My Lord replied, "The essence of the Bhagavata Dharma which I have taught you is to do all actions as a dedication to me without expectation of reward. Even mundane actions like crying or running away if done as a dedication to me, come to have spiritual potency. Why then speak of those highly spiritual actions which one practices consciously? To reach me, the immortal, with the help of this mortal body is the wisdom of the wise and the skill of the skilful. Thus, O Uddhava, do your work after having dedicated the fruits to me, regardless of success or failure. It is my duty to see that you get your just results. The greatest advocate should not really care whether his case will be successful or not. His duty is only to place the facts before the judge. It is for the judge to pass judgment. Therefore let me be the judge of your actions."

Uddhava then asked. "There are many rituals which have been advocated in the scriptures. Please tell me which are the ones I should follow?"

My Lord replied. His infinite patience always astounded me.

"Many ritualistic practices have been given in scriptural texts which you can practice if you like, but let me reiterate that the safest rule is to offer everything to me as I have already told you. But if you still yearn to make some gross offering to me, than remember that whatever you offer with love, be it a fruit, a flower, a leaf or even a drop of water, I will be satisfied. The best "*puja*" is that which is done by my devotee without any desire for fruits. Then I myself will decide what is best for my devotee.

At the end of the *puja* you should renounce the sense of doership and offer your very self to me and then the ritual will purify you."

"Marthyo yada tyakta samastha karma, Nivedidatma vichikeershitome
Tadamritatwam pradipadyamano, mayatma bhuyayata kalpathe vai"

Uddhava again questioned, "What should I do if I'm in a desert and cannot get even a drop of water for my *puja*?"

My Lord gave the sweetest reply I had ever heard. "As long as the water in your eyes has not dried up, my dear friend, do not fear. One drop from my devotee's eyes is more precious to me than the costliest diamond!"

Both Uddhava and I were overwhelmed when we heard this. I threw myself at his feet and bathed them with my tears. Uddhava's eyes brimmed over and he could not speak for some moments. At last he rallied himself and asked another question which I felt was for posterity and not for himself.

"My worshipful Lord, the Age of Kali will set in as soon as you leave this planet when people have short lives and short memories and no time to accomplish anything. Give me a short cut which will lead me to you."

My Vanamali smiled tenderly at him and replied, "Till my advent, O Uddhava, a dip in the holy waters of the Ganga was supposed to eradicate all the sins of a lifetime, but now a dip in the holy stories of my life is enough to cleanse the sins of a thousand lifetimes. He who listens to my stories, he who narrates them or explains them to others will sanctify himself as well as his listeners. If you find even this to be too difficult, then chant my names for that alone is capable of granting liberation. My names are not difficult like the Vedic *mantras* and they can be repeated by anyone, regardless of birth or sex. Like a calf following its mother, I will follow the one who calls my name and see to it that that no harm ever comes to him. Sweeter than honey is my name and those who chant it will cross over the river of mortality with ease."

Both Uddhava and I stood speechless after hearing my Lord's nectarine words. He then controlled himself and asked another question mainly for the sake of those who would come after him.

"After shedding these mortal coils, where will we find you? Where should people seek you?"

"Go to my temples, O Uddhava! I shall be residing in them. And remember my temples are not made of mud and stones but my temples are in the hearts of my devotees. Go to where my devotees live for I will ever reside in their hearts."

Uddhava remained speechless with grief at the thought of the imminent parting. My Lord looked at him with infinite compassion and said, "My dear one, have your doubts been cleared? Have I satisfied you? Have you heard enough?"

With his voice choking with sobs, Uddhava replied, "Just as a burning fire dispels not just darkness but also cold and fear from those who sit around it, so too, I, who have lived in the glowing light of your presence, have never felt any fear. Now that you have lit the ever burning flame of your name in my heart, whatever remaining doubt that I might have, has also vanished. You have permeated my entire being so that nothing else exists for me anymore. What can I give you in return, who has given me my all? I have only myself to give. Therefore I place myself as an offering at your lotus feet, O Lord! I have nothing else to give you."

So saying he threw himself like a log in front of that soul of compassion and catching hold of his lotus feet he cried out, "Prostrations to you! O Master Yogi! I have surrendered at your lotus feet. I have no other refuge. Bless me with undying devotion to you. Wherever I may wander, whatever I may do, let my mind be fixed on you every minute, every second with unswerving devotion."

"Namostute Mahayogin, prapannamanushatimaam,

Yada twat charanaambhoje, ratisyad anapaayini." Bhagavat Purana. Skanda 10. Chapter 12

Uddhava was only repeating my words, my sentiments and I also fell at my Lord's lotus feet and bathed them with my tears. Seconds passed - eons passed - time stood still. At last I felt my Lord's hand on my head and no doubt on Uddhava's head also.

He helped him to his feet gently and said, "O Uddhava! Proceed immediately to the famous place in the Himalayas known as Badarikashrama which is sanctified by my presence. Wearing clothes made out of bark, subsisting on roots and fruits, free from all desire for worldly enjoyments, live without caring for the extremes of climate. Ponder deeply on the Bhagavata Dharma that I have taught you and live according to it and you will quickly pass through this material realm and attain to my abode."

Though his intellect had grasped the Lord's message yet his heart grieved at the thought of leaving his divine Master and going so far away to the Himalayas. He circumambulated the Holy One and prepared to leave but his feet refused to turn and walk away from him. He stood rooted to the spot gazing in agony at the beloved face as if he could not bear to tear his gaze from it.

My Lord understood what was passing through his mind and said, "Dearer to me than my sons, dearer to me than my wives, are you O Uddhava! You have fettered me with the bonds of your intense love yet the time has come for our bodies to part for they are made of the five elements and must return to them. So go, my faithful friend and do as I have instructed you."

Still Uddhava lingered. Seeing his reluctance my Vanamali said, "In my previous incarnation as Rama, when I had to part with my beloved brother, Bharata, I gave him my sandals. Today I shall give them to you, for you have been attached to my feet which are the ultimate goal of all devotees. Take them therefore and proceed to Badarikashrama for I have no further use for them."

Reverently Uddhava accepted the precious gift and addressed the sandals, "O divine sandals, do not curse me for being the cause for your having to part from his lotus feet. Taste the ambrosia of his feet once again before we depart."

So saying he placed the divine footwear once again on the Holy One's feet and then kept them reverently on his head and circumambulated that Holy presence once more. With eyes blinded by tears he tore himself away and moved forward with many a backward glance. When he reached the bend in the road, he turned round once more and saw my Vanamali's eyes following him and for the first time he saw a glimmer of tears in those lustrous orbs. Turning round he ran back and fell at his feet once again. The Lord said nothing but gently placed his right foot on his head and granted him the supreme vision. He lifted him up and kissed him on the forehead and turned him in the direction he had to go. Having got this final unction, Uddhava was filled with peace and proceeded on his way. Suddenly I felt the presence of divine beings and heard celestial music. I turned to look at my Lord and found him gazing lovingly at me. I caught his hand and pressed it to my cheek.

Aum Namo Bhagavate Vaasudevaaya

Kayena vacha manasendriyaiva, bhuddyatmanavat, prakrite swabhavat,
Karomi yad yat sakalam parasmai, Sri Narayanayeti samarpayami.
Whatever I may do, or think through the intellect or by force of nature,
All this do I surrender to thee O Narayana!

This is the essence of the Bhagavata Dharma which Lord Krishna taught.
Bhagavat Purana. Skanda 10. Chapter 12.

ॐ

Dwarakanaathaaya Namaha!

CHAPTER FORTY-FOUR

Purushottama

Dwaraka seemed to be in the throes of some deadly cancer which seemed to be gnawing at its very vitals and depleting its strength surely and rapidly. Day after day, dry strong winds blew from the ocean, shriveling everything in their way. The streets which had once been strewn with jasmine and rose petals now swarmed with rats and mice. Mud pots started cracking for no reason and cranes were heard to hoot like owls and goats to howl like wolves. Asses were born from cows and donkeys from elephants. Kittens were fathered by dogs and mice from mongooses. The sun as it rose and set over the doomed city seemed to be encircled with headless bodies. Several foreboding omens were perceived. My Lord's accoutrements, the discus – the Sudarshana Chakra, his conch shell – the Panchajanya, his mace – the Kaumodaki, his bow – the Sarnga, and his sword – the Nandaki, which used to be seen rounding the city now and again, now disappeared. Along with this, Balarama's ploughshare also vanished. All these accoutrements were responsible for guarding the city so when they started to disappear one by one, the citizens trembled with fear since the sages had been insulted. A nameless dread held them in thrall. However the *adharmic* acts continued. Husbands and wives kept on deceiving each other and liars and murderers flourished.

I asked my Lord the reason for the disappearance of the weapons. He replied, "These weapons have been given to me to use on this earthly plane but since I am about to depart, they have been commanded to return to their celestial abode."

I trembled with fear and again questioned my Lord. 'I thought the Yadavas would be immortal. So many of the devas are supposed to have come and incarnated themselves in this clan to help you. Why do they have to perish now? I know you can stop it if you want. What is stopping you?'

He looked at me with a glance of infinite tenderness and said, "My child I have told you that good and bad are opposite sides of the same pole. They can meet and they can mingle with each other and they can destroy each other and turn into each other!"

'What do you mean?'

"I mean that in certain cases, too much of goodness can turn into bad, too much of sweetness can become nauseating, and there comes a time when even bad can turn into good. They are counter-correlatives and cannot remain separate. If one is there, the other also has to be somewhere in the vicinity. The Yadavas have become too strong, too rich, too powerful and too haughty. This is the point when good turns into bad. I have eradicated most of the haughty kings of this country; can I hesitate to expel the Yadavas just because they are my people?

"I have nothing or no one to call my own. I belong to all. I love all equally, both the saint and apparent sinner. But my duty in this birth is to eradicate *adharma* and if that *adharma* stems from my own people I have no option but to remove them from this drama. I made them what they are and I have to see that they will not start to defile this noble land after I depart."

Then the Yadavas came to my Lord in dread of the destiny which seemed to be looming over them. My Lord had been waiting for them. The time had come for the words of Gandhari, burning with grief at the death of her hundred sons, to be fulfilled. He did not attempt to turn aside the course of destiny but set himself calmly and cheerfully to make the path of events smooth.

A meeting was held at the assembly hall called Sudharma and my Lord spoke in his calm and cheerful voice, "It is true that terrifying omens are being seen here. My sons have incurred the curse of the *rishis*. The only way to mitigate the curse is to counterbalance it with good. Let us all go to the holy spot called Prabhasa where the River Saraswati flows west into the sea. There we will take our purifying baths in the sea and offer *yajnas* and *pujas* to the gods and worship the sages. We must all abstain from malicious talk and liquor and eat only *sattvic* foods. No one should carry any weapons. In this way we will be able to avert the disaster which is threatening us."

Before leaving he asked the king Ugrasena to take the women and old people to the island of Shankachuda while the rest of them went to Prabhasa.

"It will be wise to remove everyone from Dwaraka," he said. No one questioned his decisions.

'Why would it be wise to remove everyone from Dwaraka?' I asked.

"Dwaraka will be inundated by the sea soon after my departure from this realm."

I realised that there were times when even my tongue was struck dumb while my heart filled with unshed tears.

Everyone agreed to my Lord's proposal. They rowed down in boats along the shore until they reached the holy site called Prabhasa. They took all their provisions with them as well as a large store of wine and spirits despite the fact that my Lord had explicitly forbidden the taking of liquor. This had been illicitly brewed since Ugrasena had placed a ban on the making and drinking of intoxicants. They pitched their tents and settled down to a prolonged stay.

I noticed that the site they had chosen was very close to a vast clump of erakka grass which flourished like swords on the shore. For a couple of weeks they followed my Lord's advice and engaged themselves in worship of the gods and sages. But soon they stopped their fasting and worship and started feasting and carousing. Surreptitiously at first and then with abandon, wine started to make its appearance at the feasts and soon flowed like a river in flood. The reason for their pilgrimage was totally forgotten and the shores echoed and re-echoed with the strains of music, revelry and raucous laughter. Plays, tournaments and feasts took the place of Vedic chants and hymns. Deprived of discrimination they started to imbibe heavier and heavier doses of the heady, sweet wine called 'Maireya'.

'Can't you stop them?' I begged.

My Lord was sitting on a rock on the seashore watching the waves. Pointing to the sea he said, "Can I stop those waves from crashing against each other and destroying themselves on the beach?"

I felt so helpless watching this degeneration of the Yadavas. Satyaki who was normally very friendly with Kritavarma went across to where he was sitting and started to shout at him.

"You are the cruel killer of innocent children! How could you have schemed with that wretch Aswatthama and killed the Upa Pandavas when they were sleeping?"

Kritavarma was also filled with liquor. He jumped up and shouted, "What about you? Who will cut off the head of a man who has laid down his arms and is meditating? The Pandavas have done more wrong than the Kauravas. Drishtadyumna cut off the Guru's head after he laid down his weapons!"

Satyaki was furious and jumped on Kritavarma with these words, "Here's an end to the coward who kills sleeping children," and stabbed him with a short dagger which he had secretly hidden in the folds of his clothes. A spark will cause a conflagration if the timber is dry. Kritavarma's supporters immediately fell upon Satyaki. Pradyumna rushed to his defence and both were killed in the ensuing fray. Under the influence of drink and my Lord's will, the Yadavas seemed to be intent on killing each other. My Lord went to the edge where the erakka grass was growing tall and strong. He plucked one and it turned into a sharp sword in his hands.

He started to slay those who had killed Satyaki. The others followed suit and all of them picked up the erakka grass which turned into swords in their hands and started attacking and killing everyone indiscriminately. The scene which had been of a carousal now changed into that of a slaughter-house. The Yadavas having reached their hour of doom rushed upon death like moths to the flame. Not one of them thought of flight. Preys to delusion, the great Yadava heroes fought with each other, totally oblivious of their kinship. Sons killed fathers and fathers' sons, brothers fought with brothers, uncles with nephews, friends with friends and relatives with relatives all intent on self-destruction. My Lord alone stood calmly in the midst of this fray and watched in silence as his deluded kinsmen destroyed one another. At last the only ones who were left were my Lord and his charioteer Daruka. Balarama was not on the scene so he was not killed with the others. The entire race was destroyed like a fire generated by the mutual friction of bamboos which consumes the entire grove!

My Lord stood silently and looked at the carnage with calm eyes. Without a word he turned and went to the forest and found Balarama seated under a tree in deep meditation. Just then a huge snake came out of his head and disappeared into the sea. The *avatara* of Sesha had come to an end.

I was frightened that he would also give up his breath in *yogic* trance as his brother had done. I clung to his hand and he looked at me tenderly and shook his head. I don't know whether he actually spoke out loud but I felt his voice, "I have taken on the role of a human being and I have to act in accordance to the rules of the game."

Forlornly I followed him as he made his way through the forest beyond Prabhasa. Reaching the hidden depths of that dense jungle, he sat silently beneath an *asvattha* (peepul) tree and established himself on a super-conscious plane. I clung to his feet and cried out in agony, 'My Lord please do not forsake me.'

"Who are you my child? Are you not part of me? Do you have a life apart from me? How can I forsake something which is a part of me? What life will the shadow have after the body has gone?"

Yet foolish as I was I felt all the pangs which Uddhava had gone through. 'My Lord! My beloved!' I murmured. 'Take me with you.'

He sat down on a stone beneath a tree. Leaning back on the tree trunk with his left foot crossed over his right thigh, he said, "Sit down beside me and watch what happens to this body which has fulfilled its destiny. Do you remember the iron pestle which the *rishis* foretold would be the cause of the destruction of the Yadavas? Well, the dust into which it had been ground was washed ashore at Prabhasa and out of that sprang the erakka grass. A tiny piece could not be ground and that was swallowed by a fish that was caught by a fisherman. He found the metallic piece inside the fish and gave it to a hunter boy called Jara who made it into an arrowhead. That boy is now approaching this place. In the gloom he will mistake my foot for the face of a deer and he will shoot the arrow at it. The death of this mortal body will be caused by that, thus fulfilling the words of the sages. As you might remember the sage Durvasa told me that my foot was my vulnerable point since I hadn't smeared the *payasam* (milk pudding) on it. So be it. Let all prophecies and curses be fulfilled. Stay close to me and be a witness to my departure. Always remember that you are a part of me and can never leave me even if you want to." He cupped my face in his lotus palms and placed his lips on my forehead. I felt as if I was raised to some exalted place in which I seemed to float and yet it appeared as if I could still witness the scene which he was enacting below.

He closed his lotus eyes and went into his own lofty state. A brilliant purple light seemed to be emanating from him, illumining all the surroundings with its lustre, like a fire without heat or smoke. Strangely I was part of that enfolding purple aura. His form seemed to have changed into that of Vishnu and had the mark called the Sreevatsa on his chest and the fish-marked earrings, girdle, diadem, bracelets, anklets and necklaces. A *vanamala* made from all the five flowers he loved seemed to be glowing on his neck. Somehow I felt that I was part of that *vanamala* – a small *tulsi* leaf nestling on his chest. Suddenly I felt a piercing pain shoot through me as the hunter shot the fatal arrow at my Lord's foot which was peeping through the folds of his clothing. The boy ran to collect his prize and was stunned to behold that divine personage. He threw himself at my Master's feet and begged to be forgiven.

My Lord opened his lotus petal eyes and smiled at his slayer and blessed him. I was reminded that the first liberation he had given in his incarnation as Krishna was to Putana, the wicked woman who had come to kill him with her poisoned-tipped breasts and the last one was now being given to the poor hunter boy who had shot him with a poison-tipped arrow.

Jara cried, "O Dwarakanatha! Lord of Vaikunta! Deign to pardon this miserable wretch who has committed this heinous crime in ignorance. Kill me soon, hunter of wild animals that I am so that I may never commit such atrocious crimes again. Even the gods fail to understand the mystery of your creation. How can I, a most ignorant and humble hunter like me understand the purpose of your divine *lila*?"

My Lord smiled and said, "Arise O Jara! It is due to my own resolve that you acted in this cruel way so you have my blessings. You shall precede me to my divine abode of Vaikunta. You may have forgotten your previous life but I will tell you a secret. You were the monkey chief called Vali in my incarnation as Rama and circumstances forced me to shoot you from behind a tree. Divine though I am, having taken on the form of humanity, I must pay my debt. My *karma* is being played out through you. Today I am the victim and you are the one to shoot me from behind a tree! So fear not. Everything comes to pass according to the divine will."

Just then I noticed an aerial vehicle which had been hovering in the air. It came down and rested next to my Lord. He told Jara to climb into it and it took off into the air once again. Just then his charioteer, Daruka

The Lord blessing the hunter boy who shot the fatal arrow at the sole of his foot.

came rushing up. He saw his master beneath the *asvattha* (peepul) tree glowing with a divine radiance. Daruka prostrated before him and said, "I lost track of you, my Lord and have been wandering in the wilderness like a lost soul enmeshed in darkness after the sun has set. Suddenly the divine fragrance of your *vanamala* reached my nostrils and I followed it and found you. Please don't desert me, Master. I have served you faithfully for a hundred years and I cannot bear the thought of being parted from you."

"Daruka! I have work for you my faithful friend. Proceed to Dwaraka and inform all those that remain there that I have abandoned my earthly body. Tell everyone to evacuate the city immediately. Those who have taken refuge on the island should also return. Seven days from now the city will be swallowed by the ocean. My parents, wives and all others with their families should proceed to Hastinapura. After giving them this message you should speed immediately to Hastinapura and give the news of my departure to the Pandavas. Ask Arjuna to accompany you and take the women and others back to Hastinapura. Tell Yudhishtira that my grandson, Vajra should be made king of the Yadavas.

"As for you, O Charioteer! Remember that I am the Divine Charioteer seated in the heart of every human being. Follow the Bhagavata Dharma that I have expounded to both my friends, Arjuna and Uddhava. Know that the whole universe is but an expression of my *Maya*. Leave the reins of your life in my hands and remain at peace."

Daruka circumambulated his master thrice, with copious tears flowing from his eyes and prostrated before him and reluctantly traced his way back to Dwaraka.

I watched fascinated as the sky turned a soft lavender shade in which were thronging many celestials who had come to watch the final act of the drama of his life in this world. The divine death is as mysterious as the divine birth. Inexplicable is his *Maya* which brings into apparent existence that which is ever existent and once again gives an appearance of having ceased to exist. I felt as if I could hear him say, "Birth and death are the two sides of the coin of creation and have no meaning when applied to the Creator himself."

Beholding these divine beings, my Lord's wondrous eyes, filled with the knowledge of eternity, glowing with a love that was boundless, overflowing with compassion for all creation, gently closed, like a lotus closing its petals for the night. I don't know how I saw all this but I did see it because he wished me to see it. His world-enthralling form which is the most auspicious object for meditation glowed with an unearthly light and slowly started to melt into the elements. As it was melting I jumped back to my place on his breast - a *tulsi* leaf in his *vanamala*.....

I opened my eyes and found that I had slept on the beach outside the temple of Dwarakanatha. I was not sure of where I was. I saw the beach on which I was lying, the *shikara* (turret) of the temple in the distance turning to gold in the rays of the setting sun. The flag which was hoisted daily was waving merrily in the wind. The golden orb of the sun was already half way into the sea and rapidly disappearing into the waters. In the purple, velvet darkness which followed, the perfume of my Lord's *vanamala* seeped into my nostrils filling me with delight. I knew he was right beside me, my Master, my Lord, my Vanamali......

Aum Namo Bhagavate Vaasudevaaya

You took this broken reed my Lord,
And lo a flute was born.
You put it to your lips my Lord,
And lo a symphony flowed,
Like the flutters of a butterfly's wings,
Like water over liquid pearls,
Like dancing rays of sunlight gold,
Like the flow of fluid honey,
Thy lips slid over the reed and made it whole,
At thy feet I place this hollow reed.
Thine to do as you will.
Vanamali! My only Love!
Vanamali! My Lord! My God!

THE CITY OF DWARAKA
(Including Underwater Remains Excavated Recently)

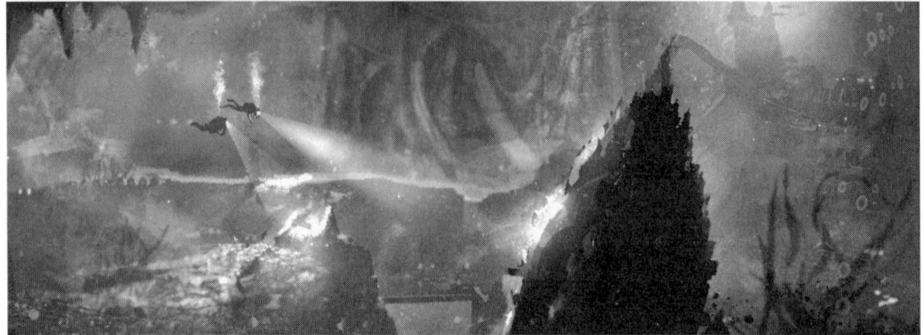

Artist's view of Dwaraka going under the water.

Jagannathaya Namaha!

List of Characters

SAGES

Agastya	great sage of the south who was short in stature
Asita	great sage
Bharadwaja	Drona's father
Brihaspati	guru of the gods
Chyavana	sage who made the famous Ayurvedic medicine called Chyavanaprasha
Dattatreya	avadhuta sage who is a partial incarnation of Vishnu
Dhoumya	guru of the Pandavas
Durvasa	Krishna's guru. Noted for his short temper
Garga Muni	guru of the Yadavas who performed naming ceremony for Krishna
Gautama	great sage who lived during the Ramavatara
Jaimini	sage who is the founder of the Mimasa philosophy
Kalamamuni	sorcerer
Kanva	rishi who was the foster father of Shakuntala
Kashyapa	one of the patriarchs
Kratu	great sage
Lomasa	great sage who accompanied the Pandavas in their travels in the forest

Maitreya	sage who gave spiritual instructions to Vidura
Mandavya	sage who was hoisted on a pole for an offence he had committed in childhood
Markandeya	sage who was given a boon that he would live for the whole of this eon
Nara-Narayana	sages who are living in the Himalayas. Arjuna and Krishna are said to be their incarnations
Narada	celestial sage known as the greatest devotee of Lord Krishna
Paila	great sage
Parashara	father of Vyasa
Raibya rishi	sage who did tapas in Rishikesh and his hair spread all over
Sukracharya	guru of the asuras
Sumantu	great sage
Vaisampayana	sage who was narrating the whole Mahabharata
Vamadeva	great sage who became enlightened at birth
Vasishta	guru of the kings of the solar dynasty
Vishwamitra	great sage who was the one who heard the sound of Aum
Vyasa	Author of the Mahabharata and all the Puranas; divided the Vedas into 4.

RIVERS

NAMES OF GANGA

Ganga, Bhagirathi, Alakananda

Pushpabhadra	name of Ganga on the banks of which Markandeya had his ashram

DWARAKADISH KRISHNA, LORD OF DWARAKA.

Krishna's family. The Yadavas

Krishna's names, Vaasudeva, Govinda, Damodara, Madhava, Shyamasundara, Vanamali, Hrishikesha, Janardana, Madhusudana, Aravindaksha

Vasudeva (father), Devaki (mother), Balarama (brother), Kamsa (uncle)
Nanda/Nandagopa, Yashoda (foster father and mother)
Subhadra (sister) Arjuna's wife, Abhimanyu (their son), Uttara (his wife)
Rukmini, Satyabhama, Jambavati, Kalindi, Mitravinda, Madra, Bhadra, Satya (Krishna's chief wives)
Pradyumna, Samba, Charudeshna, Gada (Krishna's sons), Aniruddha, Vajra/Vajranabha (grandsons), Charumati (Krishna's daughter by Rukmini)
Aniruddha's wives (Usha, Rochana)
Uddhava, Satyaki (his cousins and friends)
Daruka (charioteer), Kritavarma (general of the Yadava army)
Kuchela/Sudama (old Brahmin friend), Sandipany (guru)
Revathi (Balarama's wife), Nishastha, Ulumukha, Vatsala (Balarama's children)
Kakudmi (Revathi's father; King of Anarta)
Ugrasena (Kamsa's father; King of the Yadavas)
Shoora (ancestor of the Yadvas)

PANDAVAS

Yudhishtira, Bhima, Arjuna, Nakula, Sahadeva
Pandu (father), Kunti/Pritha (mother of the first three), Madri (mother of the last two)
Draupadi/Panchali (wife of the Pandavas)
Drupada (father of Draupadi), Drishtadyumna, Shikandin (Draupadi's brothers)
Prativindhya, Srutasena, Srutakirti, Satanika, Srutakarma (Draupadi's sons)
Hidimbi (Bhima's rakshasi wife), Gatotkacha (their son)
Iravan (Arjuna's son by Ulupi, the naga princess)
Babruvahana (Arjuna's son by Chitrangada, Princess of Manaloorapura)
Subhadra (Krishna's sister; Arjuna's wife), Abhimanyu (their son), Uttara (his wife)
Parikshit/Vishnurata (Abhimanyu's son by Uttara)
Karunamati (Nakula's wife)
Kanka (Yudhishtira), Brihannala (Arjina), Granthika (Nakula), Tantripala (Sahadeva), Kanakabhatta (Bhima), Sairandri (Draupadi) (names taken by Pandavas during their stay in the country of Matsya incognito)

FAMILY OF THE KURUS

Bhishma/Devavrata (grandfather), son of Santanu
Satyavati (stepmother of Bhishma)
Chitrangada, Vichitravirya (Satyavati's children)
Ambika, Ambalika (Vichitravirya's wives), Amba, their sister who took birth as Draupadi's brother, Shikandin
Dritrashtra, Pandu (sons of Ambika and Ambalika), Vidura (step brother, noted for his wisdom)
Gandhari (wife of Dritarashtra), Shakuni (her brother)
Sanjaya (Dritarashtra's minister)
Kunti and Madri (wives of Pandu, mothers of the Pandavas)
Kauravas (100 sons of Dritarashtra and Gandhari)
Duryodhana/Suyodhana (eldest Kaurava), Dusshasana (2nd), Dusshala (only sister), Jayadratha (her husband), Vikarna (another brother)
Lakshmana (Duryodhana's son)
Yuyutsu (Duryodhana's half brother)
Karna (actually Kunti's son who was floated on the river and brought up by the charioteer Athiratha and his wife, Radha, and was thus known as Radheya/Sutaputra)
Karna's wives, Subhangi and Kanchanamala
Sahasrakavacha. Karna was this asura in a previous life
Drona (Brahmin Guru of the Kauravas and Pandavas), Aswatthama (his son), Kripa (his brother-in-law), Kripi (his wife)

NAME OF WEAPONS

Sudarshana chakra (Lord Krishna's discus)
Sarngi (Lord Krishna's bow)
Nandaki (Lord Krishna's sword)
Kaumodaki (Lord Krishna's mace)
Panchajanya (Lord Krishna's conch shell)
Gandiva (Arjuna's bow)
Devadatta (Arjuna's conch shell)
Poundra (Bhima's conch shell)
Anantavijaya (Yudhistira's conch shell)
Vijaya (Karna's bow)

Aditi	mother of the gods
Agni	God of Fire
Akrura	Yadava chief
Alambhusha	rakshasa warrior; Duryodhana's friend
Alayudha	rakshasa warrior
Amba	princess of Kashi who took another birth as Shikandin
Ambika; Ambalika	sisters of Amba who married Vichitravirya, king of the Kurus
Ankaraga	Malini's husband; Kamsa's chief royal mahout
Arundhati	wife of Vasishta
Ashoka and Vishoka	Bhima's chariot boys
Ashwini Kumaras	divine physicians
Airavata	Indra's elephant
Bahulasva	king of Videha
Bakasura	demon in the form of a stork
Banasura	father of Usha, wife of Aniruddha
Bhagadatta	Narakasura's son
Bhagiratha	King who was responsible for bringing Ganga to earth
Bhanumati	Duryodhana's wife
Bharata	any of the kings belonging to the Kuru dynasty can be called Bharata
Bhishmaka	Rukmini's father
Bhu Devi	earth goddess
Bhurishravas	king of Vahlika.
Brihadbala	king of Kosala
Brihadkshatra	Jayadratha's father
Brihatsena	king of Madra
Chandra	moon god
Chandrakaushika	sorceror
Chitralekha	Usha's friend who was a great artist
Chitrasena; Chitragupta	leader of the Gandharvas

Damaghosha	king of Chedi; father of Shisupala
Dandavaktra	Shisupala's friend; King of Karusha
Dhamaraja	Yama, God of Death
Drishtaketu	Ruler of Chedi
Durga	maiden goddess
Dusshala	Duryodhana's sister
Dyuman	Salva's general
Hanuman	monkey god
Hayagriva	horse-necked incarnation of Vishnu
Hiranyaksha	demon to kill whom Vishnu took the incarnation of the boar
Indra	king of the gods
Indrajit	Ravana's son
Indrani	Indra's wife
Jambavan	bear who was living during the time of Rama; Jambavati's father
Janaka	King of Mithila; Sita's father
Jara	hunter's boy who accidentally shot an arrow at Lord Krishna
Jarasandha	King of Magadha
Jaya; Vijaya,	guards of Lord Vishnu
Jayadratha	king of Sindh
Jimutan	wrestler in the court of Virata
Kaikeyi	another name of Krishna's wife Bhadra
Kalayavana	barbarian king
Kali	fierce aspect of the goddess
Kama	god of love
Kamsa	king of the Bhojas; Krishna's uncle
Kapidwaja	Arjuna (one with a monkey on his flag)
Kapila	founder of the Nyaya philosophy
Karthyayini	name of the goddess; the cosmic mother

Kartikeya	son of Shiva; General of the gods
Kichaka	general of King Virata and his brother-in-law
Kubera	king of the Yakshas; keeper of wealth
Kubja/Malini/Trivakra	hunch back of Mathura; Krishna's first love
Kumbakarna	brother of Ravana noted for the way he slept for 6 months
Kuntibhoja	father of Kunti (mother of the Pandavas)
Lakshmanaa	Duryodhana's daughter
Lakshmi Devi	Wife of Vishnu; goddess of wealth;
Lalitambika	most beautiful aspect of the goddess
Mahabali	great asura king
Mahadeva/Shiva	third in the Hindu trinity; god of destruction
Mahavishnu/Vishnu	second in the Hindu trinity; god of preservation
Mahishasuramardini	goddess who killed the buffalo demon – Mahisha
Manjula	garland maker in Krishna temple of Guruvayoor
Manmada/Kama	Cupid; god of love
Matali	Indra's charioteer
Matsyavatara	incarnation as fish
Mayan	celestial architect
Meera	princess of Mewar; great devotee of Krishna
Mushtika and Chanoora	wrestlers kept by Kamsa to kill Krishna
Nagnajit	king of Kosala; father of Satya
Nagnajiti	another name of Satya, wife of Krishna, daughter of Nagnajit
Nahusha	king who was cursed to become a snake
Nalakubera and Manikooda	sons of Kubera who were cursed to become twin trees
Narakasura/Bhauma	asura king of Pragjyotisha

Narayana	Vishnu; one who sleeps on the waters
Nriga	king who was cursed to become a garden lizard
Padmanabha	Vishnu; one who has the lotus in his navel
Padmavati	Poundraka's wife
Parasurama	6th incarnation of Vishnu
Parishrami	Vidura's mother
Partha	Arjuna; son of Pritha or Kunti
Parvati	consort of Shiva
Poundraka	king who professed to be Krishna Vaasudeva
Prahlada	son of asura Hiranyakashipu; great devotee of Vishnu
Prasena	brother of Satrajit, father of Sathyabhama
Punardatta	son of Krishna's guru, Sandipany
Putana	killer of infants; tried to kill baby Krishna
Radha	most famous of the gopis
Rama	7th incarnation of Vishnu
Rati	wife of Kama
Ravana	demon king of Sri Lanka
Rochana	grand-daughter of Rukmi
Rohini	Balarama's mother
Rukmavati	daughter of Rukmi, Rukmini's brother
Rukmi	Rukmini's brother
Sahadeva	son of Jarasandha; also the name of the youngest Pandava
Salva	king of Matrikavarta who had a nuclear missile
Sambara; Sambarasura,	asura who stole Pradyumna when he was a baby
Santardana	crown prince of Kekaya
Sarvatrada	Bhima's son by Jalandara
Satrajit	Sathyabhama's father

Satyavrata	king to whom Vishnu appeared in his 1st incarnation as fish
Shakradeva	name of Poundraka's son
Shalya	king of Madra; Nakula and Sahadeva's uncle
Shatadanwa	man who had been engaged to Sathyabhama
Shesha	the serpent bed on which Lord Vishnu lies
Shikandini /Shikandin	Draupadi's sister who changed her sex and became Shikandin
Shishupala	prince of Chedi; Krishna's cousin
Shiva/Shankara/Mahadeva	Names of Shiva
Shridhara	name of Vishnu; Krishna
Shrutakirti	Bhadra's mother, queen of the Kekaya kingdom
Srutideva	old Brahmin devotee of Krishna in Videha
Soora	ancestor of the Yadavas
Sringalavala	another name for Poundraka
Sudeshna	son of king of Kasi; Duryodana's brother-in-law,
Surya	sun god
Susharma	leader of the Trigartas
Sushena	Karna's son
Sweta	Virata's eldest son
Takshaka	king of snakes; most poisonous of all snakes
Trigarta brothers	Susharma, Satyavarta, Satyavarma, Satyaasu, Satyadharma
Trivikrama/Vamana	name of Vishnu in his 5th incarnation as the dwarf
Uluka	Brahmin sent as ambassador to Kuru court by the Pandavas
Uluka	Shakuni's son, different from the above
Ulupi	Arjuna's wife; Naga princess
Urvasi	celestial dancer in Indra's court

Usha	daughter of Banasura who married Aniruddha
Uttanga	Brahmin friend of Krishna
Vaali	monkey warrior in the Ramayana
Vamana	5th incarnation of Vishnu as the dwarf
Varaha	3rd incarnation of Vishnu as the boar
Varchas	son of moon god incarnated as Abhimanyu
Varuna	Lord of the Waters
Vasishta; Arundhati	great sage and his wife Arundhati
Vatsala	daughter of Balarama; 1st wife of Abhimanyu
Vayu	god of the wind
Vibhishana	Ravana's brother who befriended Rama
Viduratha	king who was a friend of Jarasandha and Shisupala
Vinda, Anuvinda	Princes of Avanti; Mitravinda's brothers
Virata	King of Matsya, Sudheshna, his wife,Uttara Kumara, Sweta, his sons and Uttara his daughter who married Abhimanyu
Vishnu	the maintainer of the word order in the trinity
Vishnurata	another name of Parikshit, the sole survivor of the Pandavas
Vishwakarma	architect of the gods
Vrika	Drupada's brother
Vrisha and Achala	Shakuni's two sons
Vrishatsena	Karna's son
Vyala; Dhama; Kata	3 demons
Yama	god of death
Yogamaya	name of goddess who was born to Yashoda

Madhavaya Namaha!

Glossary of Sanskrit Terms

abhaya	without fear
abhicharya	black magic rites
abhisheka	ceremonial bath; coronation or consecration ceremony in which water or milk is poured over the head.
acharya	teacher or guru
adharma	unrighteousness
advaita	basic Hindu precept that all creation is the projection of the one Brahman or supreme force
Agneyaastra	missile which invokes the fire god and rains fire on the opponents
agrapuja	worship of the foremost or noblest person
ahamkara	ego
akshara	non-perishable
akshaunis	battalion in an army
akshaya patra	the bowl from which food is never exhausted
amavasya	night of the new moon
amrita	the nectar of immortality
amsa	fraction; portion
anaadi	without a beginning

anahata	soundless sound
ananta	without an end
Anjalika	the missile that Arjuna used to kill Karna
anjana	black stone
antaryami	inner dweller
apsaras	celestial dancers
arghya	water given in the hand for cleansing
artha	wealth; worldly prosperity
artharatha(s)	chariot warrior who needs to be helped by foot soldiers
arya	noble
Aryavrata	ancient name of India
ashrama	retreat for spiritual aspirants
Ashwamedha Yaga	Vedic horse sacrifice conducted by a king in order to proclaim himself as emperor
astra	missile
asura	a demonic being; opposite of deva
Asvattha	peepul tree; sacred to Hindus
athirathas	same as artharathas
atma(n)	individualised expression of the Brahman or supreme force
Aum	mystic sound denoting the Supreme
avabhritha snana	ceremonial bath taken in a river after the conclusion of a yaga
avadhutas	enlightened ascetic who wanders about naked; expressive of total freedom
avasthana	a type of tactic used in mace fighting
avatara	incarnation of God
ayudhapuja	worship of weapons before commencement of war
badari	a type of berry
Badarikashrama	very holy place in the Himalayas
bethua	a type of edible greens loved by Krishna
Bhagavata Dharma	spiritual gospel taught by Krishna

bhakta	devotee
bhakti	devotion; love of god
bharas	measurement of weight roughly eighty kilograms
Bharatavarsha	ancient name of India
bhava	mood or attitude pertaining to God
bhavana	subjective state of feeling
Brahma	the creator in the Hindu trinity
Brahmadanda	a type of nuclear weapon
Brahman	the supreme transcendent force which is immanent in all creation
brahmana(s); brahmin	the priest caste in the Hindu caste system
brahmarandra	the fontanelle or soft part on top of the head
Brahmasiras	nuclear weapon capable of annihilating whole countries.
Brahmastra	nuclear weapon like Brahmasiras
buddhi	intellect
chakora	a bird which is supposed to drink the nectar from the moon
chakra	wheel; often used for the weapon used by Krishna
chakra vyuha	wheel like formation used in battle
champaka; champa	a type of sweet smelling flower
chandrakala	crescent moon; spark of the moon
chathurdasi	14th day of the lunar month
chaturanga	ancient game played by kings.(the forerunner of chess)
chaturmasya	four months; normally referring to the four monsoon months
chiranjeevi(s)	one who would remain alive for the whole of this yuga or age
daivam	divinity existing in everything
daivic	pertaining to deva or god

dakshina	monetary gift to a holy person or teacher
Dakshinayanam	six months of the year from July to December when the sun goes towards the south
dana	charity
darbha	kind of grass used in pujas
darshana	divine vision
dasyu	misconduct; person from a lower order
desha	space; place
deva	a god
devadasis	women who used to dance in temples and were considered to be of a low order
Devadatta	name of Arjuna's conch shell
devataru	tree of the gods; a type of cypress found in the Himalayas
dharma	righteousness; duty; cosmic law; religion
dharma yuddha	a righteous war
Dharmakshetra	field of righteousness
dhoti	an unstitched cloth worn by men
digvijaya	conquest of enemy territories by a king who wants to proclaim his suzerainty over them
divyastra	divine weapons; usually given by some god
durva	type of grass like dharbha
dwadasi	12th day of the lunar fortnight
dwanda yuddha	duel
Dwapara Yuga	the 3rd of the 4 ages through which the world goes through; Krishna lived in this yuga which ended with his death.
ekadasi	11th day of the lunar fortnight; a day of fast for devotees of Vishnu
erakka	type of grass with sharp ends like swords
gada	mace
ganas	Lord Shiva's attendants
Gandhara	old name for Afghanistan

gandharvas	celestial musicians
Gandiva	name of Arjuna's bow
Garga muni	sage who was called for the naming ceremony of Krishna and Rama
garuda vyuha	battle formation like an eagle
Garuda	eagle vehicle of Vishnu
ghatika	an ancient type of water clock
ghats	steps made on river banks for easy bathing
ghora	terrible; very strict
gopala(s)	cow-herd boy
gopis	girls belonging to the cow-herd community of Vraja
gotra	brahminical clan into which one is born
gunas	three qualities or modes of nature: sattva (harmony), rajas (kinesis or action), tamas (inertia, dullness)
gunateeta	one who is above the gunas; a realised sage
guñjâ	type of grass
guru dakshina	fee given to guru at the end of the course of study
guru	spiritual preceptor
gurukula	hermitage of the guru
hala	ploughshare
homa	yajna; yaga; fire ceremony
howdah	a kind of decorated hood kept on top of elephants
Indraloka	the world of Indra, king of the gods
Janapadas	kings who owned a lot of land
japa	continuous repetition of the Lord's name
jiva; jivatma	the individual embodied soul
jivan mukta	a liberated sage
jnana	wisdom; spiritual insight

jnana-bhakta	a devotee who has spiritual knowledge
jnani	a wise sage with spiritual insight
kaala	Time
Kaalaswarupa	the fierce form of the Lord as all-consuming Time
kadamba	a type of tree with sweet smelling flowers
Kali Yuga	The 4th of the cosmic ages in which we are living now
kama	lust; desire; passion
kamandalu	water pot made of a double coconut shell carried by sages
Kapidwaja	name of Arjuna; (one with a monkey on his flag)
karma	action; also refers to the cosmic law of moral cause and effect
karma- sannyasi	one who has given up all action
karma yoga	the yoga of action without expectation of personal benefits
karmaphaladata	the giver of the fruits of action that is God alone
Kaumodaki	name of Krishna's mace
Kauravas	100 sons of Dritarashtra
Kaustubha	ruby worn by Vishnu and his incarnations
kavacha	armour
kaya kalpa	that which gives immortality to the body
krauncha	crane
krtya	an evil spirit
kriyas	spiritual and religious rituals
kshara	perishable; changeable; impermanent
kshatriya	2nd caste in the Hindu social hierarchy
kshetra	field; temple; manifest universe
kshetrajna	knower of the field; the Lord himself
kula guru	the preceptor of the clan
kundala	earrings

Kurukshetra	battlefield of the Kurus
kusa	a type of grass used in rituals
lac	an inflammable material used in seals
lagna	the moon sign under which you are born
lakh	one hundred thousand
laya	dissolution
lila	play or game of God
lilavatara	sporting incarnation of god
linga sarira	causal body; subtle body
linga(m)	rounded stone symbol of Lord Siva
madhuparka	a concoction of honey and milk offered to special guests on arrival
madhurya	sweet as honey
madhyama	middle
Magadhas	those who live in the country of Magadha
mahajanapadas	the great kings who carved out huge countries for themselves
mahakalpa	the lifetime of Brahma the creator
maharathis	1st category of car warriors who needed no help from foot soldiers
mahatma	great soul
mahayugas	the four great yugas taken collectively
makara vyuha	battle formation in the shape of a crocodile
mala	a necklace
manas	mind
mandala	mystic symbol; 41 days
mandara	the mythical mountain which was used for churning the ocean
manipura	the psychic centre in the navel
mantra	sacred formula to be used in uplifting consciousness
margashirsha	name of month nov/dec

Matsya Purana	the purana given by the Lord in his incarnation as the cosmic fish
Maya Sabha	hall of illusions built in Indraprastha
maya	delusory power of the Lord which conceals the Reality
mlecchas	barbarians; those who did not believe in the Vedas
mohanastra	a missile which causes confusion in the enemy ranks
moksha; mukti	liberation from the chain of births and deaths
mridangam	a type of percussion instrument
mudra	seal; chop
muhurta	name for a period of time little over an hour
muladhara chakra	psychic centre at the bottom of the spine
muni	sage
munja	a type of grass used in rituals
murajas	a type of drum
nagas	snakes
nagastra	powerful missile of the cobra
Nandaki	name of Lord Krishna's sword
Narayana sena	Yadava battalion given to the Kauravas
nau	boat; English word navy comes from this
Navachandra	name of Ghatotkacha's bow
nimitta	cause; instrument
niranjana	purificatory rites
padma	lotus
padma vyuha	battle formation in the shape of a lotus
padukas	wooden footwear
pala	measurement of weight
pana	measurement of weight
pancha	five
Panchajanya	name of Lord Krishna's conch

Pandavas	the five sons of Pandu who were Lord Krishna's chosen instruments in the cause of the establishment of dharma
parakiya dharma	the duty of a lover
paramahamsa(s)	enlightened soul
Paramatma(n)	the Supreme soul
parijata	celestial tree from Indra's garden
Pasupatastra	Lord Shiva's missile
Paundra	name of Bhima's conch
payasam	milk pudding with rice
peepul tree	sacred tree; fiscus
pitambaram	yellow cloth which Krishna always wore
pournami	full moon
prajna; sthitha prajna	intellect; man of steady intellect
Prakriti	nature
pralaya	deluge; flood
prana	vital breath which is the same in all beings
prapti	total surrender to god
prarabdha karma	the karma which we bring from another life
prasada(m)	remains of food offerings to God
pravara	lineage
Prayaga	the confluence of the three rivers, Ganga, Yamuna and Saraswati at modern Allahabad
prema	highest form of love; unconditional love
puja	ritualistic worship
pundit	learned person
punya	spiritual merit
Puranas	sacred treatises, 18 in number written by Vyasa
purnavatara	supreme incarnation; Krishna
Purusha	the unmanifested, actionless aspect of the world as opposed to Prakriti which is the active aspect
Purushottama	Supreme person; also called Uttama Purusha

raga	melody
raja	king
rajas	one of the three modes of nature which instigates action
rajasic	full of action and passion, motion, desire
Rajasuya yajna	Vedic ceremony conducted by kings to prove their supremacy
raja vidhi	dictates of the king
rakshasa	a cannibalistic tribe which existed in ancient India
rakshasi	female of rakshasa
rathis	charioteers
rishis	sages
rudraksha	a type of berry sacred to Shiva
sabha	hall; assembly
sadhana	spiritual practice
sadhu	holy man; renunciate
sahasrara chakra	psychic centre on the top of the head
samadhi	super conscious state of bliss achieved in meditation
samarathi	lesser type of chariot warrior
Samkhya Yoga	one of the systems of Indian philosophy
samsaptakas	the seven brothers who had sworn to kill Arjuna
samsara	this world; transmigratory existence
samsara chakra	wheel of life which keeps us rotating from life to life
samsara sagara	ocean of existence
Sanatana Dharma	real name of Hinduism; the eternal law or religion
sanatana	ancient
sandal	sandalwood tree or paste
sannyasa	the 4th stage in Hinduism in which we renounce the world

sannyasi(n)	one who has renounced
saptarishis	the seven sages
sarathi	charioteer
Sarnga	name of Lord Krishna's bow
sarpa	snake; (verb means faster)
sat	pure existence; goodness; truth
sataghni	fire at the end of creation
satsang	company of noble people
sattva	one of the modes of nature; harmony, intelligence; clarity
sattvic	pertaining to sattva; pure;
Satvata Tantra	one of the books on Tantra
satya	truth
Satya Yuga	the 1st age in Hinduism in which all people follow truth
Satyameva Jayati	one of the statements from the Upanishads Truth alone will win
sena	army
shakata vyuha	battle formation in the form of a cart
shakata	cart
shakti	energy; power; usually thought of as cosmic energy which is feminine; name of weapon given by Indra to Karna
shastras	spiritual texts
Shaturagdini	name of Bhima's mace
shikara	turret; peak
shrivatsa	imprint on chest of Vishnu and his avataras
shudras	4th class in the Hindu caste system
siddha	one who has siddhis
siddhi(s)	supernormal power got through spiritual disciplines
sindoor	red powder applied on the forehead of women
soma	herb with medicinal and spiritual properties used in Vedic yagas

Sreevatsa	sign in the shape of a footprint found on the chest of Vishnu and his avataras
srimad	auspicious
Sri Yantra; Sri Chakra	most famous of all yantras pertaining to the divine mother
stambha	pillar
sthita prajna	enlightened soul; one of firmly established intellect
Sudarshana (chakra)	name of Lord Krishna's discus
Sudharma	name of assembly hall in Dwaraka
sumangali(s)	married woman
sundari	beautiful woman
Surya	sun god
Surya putra	name of Karna; son of the sun god, Surya
suta	charioteer
sutaputra	son of a charioteer; name given to Karna
swadharma	law of action pertaining to one's own station in life
swathisthana	psychic centre just above the base of the spine
swayamprakasha	self-effulgent
swayamvara	marriage by choice of the bride
Syamanta-panchaka	name of a place with a lake
tadastu	so be it
tamas	one of the modes of nature; inertia; laziness; darkness; ignorance
tambulam	mixture of betel leaves and other ingredients given after food
tandava	cosmic dance of shiva
tantric	pertaining to a type of discipline known as tantra
tapas; tapasya	spiritual discipline like meditation, austerity
tilaka	auspicious mark on the forehead made with sandal paste
Treta Yuga	the second of the yugas

trigunatita	enlightened soul who has gone above the three gunas
tripuras	3 asuras possessing three flying cities
Trivakra	another name of Kubja; the three-humped one
truti	time taken for half a blink
tula	a measurement of weight
tulsi	the holy basil; essential for pujas for Vishnu and his avataras
tyagi	a renunciate
Upanishad(s)	the last portion of each Veda which deals with Advaita or monism
uttama	supreme; highest
Uttarayanam	the summer solstice from January 14th to July 14th
uttareeyam	upper garment worn by men
vaidya	Ayurvedic physician
vaikunt ekadasi	the 11th day of the lunar month which comes at the end of the year
vaishnava	devotee of Lord Vishnu or his avatars
Vaishnavastra	the missile given by Lord Vishnu
Vaishyas	the 3rd or economic class in the Hindu hierachy
vajra	weapon of Indra; thunderbolt
valampiri	conch shell which is turned to the right
vanamala	garland made of 5 wild flowers of which tulsi is the main, worn by Vishnu and his avatars
varnas	colours; different castes
varnashrama dharma	duties pertaining to one's caste and state in life
vasanas	desires carried along with the genes which give rise to our present life; inherent tendencies

vatsalya bhava	love for children; devotees of Krishna often have this attitude towards him as if he is a child
Vedanta	end of the Vedas; refers to the Upanishads
Vedas	the most ancient scriptures of the world found in Hinduism
veena	a stringed instrument like a lute always carried by the sage Narada
vibhuti(s)	sacred ash; extraordinary manifestations of god
Vijayadasami –	the 10th day of the yearly worship of goddess Durga
vijnana	scientific knowledge
vimana	aeroplane
viraha	separation
vishada	sorrow
Vishnu Sahasranama	thousand and one names of LordVishnu
Vishudhi chakra	psychic wheel at the base of the throat
Vishvarupa	Krishna's cosmic form which he showed Arjuna and at the court of the Kurus in Hastinapura
Vrishni	one of the tribes of the Yadavas
vyuha	formation; generally in battle
Yadavas	Lord Krishna's clan
yaga; yajna	sacrificial ceremony using fire
yajamana	master; one conducting the yajna
yajna purusha	presiding deity of the yajna
yajnashala	hall where the yajna is conducted
yaksha	a type of celestial being
yamas	moral virtues like non-violence, truthfulness, continence
yantra	instrument; mystic design
yoga	spiritual disciplines which will enable you to attain union with God

yogashastra	books which deal with attaining union with God like the Bhagavad Gita
yogi	one who practices yoga
yogic kriyas	yogic practices
yojana	measurement of distance (about ten miles)
yuddha	war
yuga	epoch
yuvaraja	heir apparent; crown prince

Yogashastra — Books which deal with ... God ... the Bhagavad Gita